Lecture Notes in Computer Science 8142

Commenced Publication in 1973
Founding and Former Series Editors:
Gerhard Goos, Juris Hartmanis, and Jan van Leeuwen

Joachim Weickert   Matthias Hein
Bernt Schiele (Eds.)

Pattern Recognition

35th German Conference, GCPR 2013
Saarbrücken, Germany, September 3-6, 2013
Proceedings

 Springer

Volume Editors

Joachim Weickert
Saarland University
Faculty of Mathematics and Computer Science, Campus E1.7
66041 Saarbrücken, Germany
E-mail: weickert@mia.uni-saarland.de

Matthias Hein
Saarland University
Faculty of Mathematics and Computer Science, Campus E1.3
66041 Saarbrücken, Germany
E-mail: hein@cs.uni-saarland.de

Bernt Schiele
Max-Planck-Institute for Informatics
Computer Vision and Multimodal Computing, Campus E 1.4
66123 Saarbrücken, Germany
E-mail: schiele@mpi-inf.mpg.de

ISSN 0302-9743   e-ISSN 1611-3349
ISBN 978-3-642-40601-0   e-ISBN 978-3-642-40602-7
DOI 10.1007/978-3-642-40602-7
Springer Heidelberg New York Dordrecht London

Library of Congress Control Number: 2013946305

CR Subject Classification (1998): I.5, I.4.6, I.4.8, I.4, I.2.10, I.2.6, I.3.5, H.4

LNCS Sublibrary: SL 6 – Image Processing, Computer Vision,
Pattern Recognition, and Graphics

Typesetting: Camera-ready by author, data conversion by Scientific Publishing Services, Chennai, India

Printed on acid-free paper

Springer is part of Springer Science+Business Media (www.springer.com)

Preface

Welcome to the proceedings of the 35th German Conference on Pattern Recognition (GCPR) which was held in Saarbrücken during September 3rd and 6th, 2013.

This year's conference differed in several aspects from the previous ones: Perhaps the most evident difference was the transition to an English name. Previous conferences were named *DAGM Symposium Mustererkennung*, which translates to *Symposium of the German Association for Pattern Recognition*. To reflect the stronger internationalization that had taken place in the last decade, it was felt appropriate to switch to an English name. Furthermore, we extended the Program Committee (PC) by a larger number of experts from outside Germany than previous DAGM conferences. In total we have been supported by 54 PC members from 11 countries.

In spite of the fact that this year there were extraordinarily many related conference deadlines in the submission month, our call for papers resulted in 79 submissions from institutions from 15 countries. Each paper underwent a rigorous double-blind reviewing procedure by three PC members, sometimes with support from additional experts. Afterwards one of the three PC members was asked to moderate a discussion among the reviewers and to write a synthesis report with a recommendation. During the PC meeting that took place in Saarbrücken on June 7, 2013, these reviews and synthesis reports were discussed in detail. On this basis, 40 out of 79 submissions were accepted, 10 of which after some compulsory amendments that were checked again by a PC member. From the 40 accepted papers, the organisers selected 22 for oral presentation and 18 for poster presentation. All accepted submissions are published in these proceedings and have been given the same number of pages. The program covers the entire spectrum of pattern recognition, machine learning, image processing, and computer vision. We thank all reviewers for their valuable service to our scientific community and all authors for their GCPR submissions.

As in previous years, GCPR 2013 also featured a Young Researchers' Forum (YRF), where bachelor or master students had the opportunity to present their work as a poster and as a six-page article in the proceedings. The reader can find three contributions from this year's YRF, along with three from last year that were erroneously not included in the DAGM 2012 proceedings.

We are happy that three world leaders in their field have accepted our invitation to give a keynote lecture at GCPR 2013: Jitendra Malik (UC Berkeley, USA), Jean-Michel Morel (ENS Cachan, France), and Gene Myers (MPI of Molecular Cell Biology and Genetics, Dresden, Germany).

The program of GCPR 2013 has been enriched by a number of additional events, such as a *Special Session on Robust Optical Flow* and a *Recent Related Research (R³) Poster Session*. Moreover, three satellite workshops took place:

one on *Unsolved Problems in Pattern Recognition and Computer Vision,* one on *Imaging New Modalities,* and one on *New Challenges in Neural Computation and Machine Learning.* Last but not least, we had half-day tutorials on *Computational Plenoptic Imaging* and on *Shape from Shading in Theory and Algorithms.*

It is our pleasure to thank Bosch, Fraunhofer ITWM, Google, the Intel Visual Computing Institute, MVTec, Toyota, and Ersatzteile-24 for their generous sponsorship of GCPR 2013. We are also grateful to the town of Saarbrücken for sponsoring the welcome reception in the town hall, and to the KWT for their organizatorial support. Last but not least, a big thanks goes to our administrative assistants Cornelia Balzert, Irmtraud Stein, and Ellen Wintringer for their great support, and to Nico Persch for his help in assembling the proceedings volume and the program booklet.

We wish you an exciting journey through the proceedings of GCPR 2013.

September 2013   Joachim Weickert
                                                             Matthias Hein
                                                             Bernt Schiele

Organization

Conference Committee

General Chair

Joachim Weickert   Saarland University, Saarbrücken, Germany

Program Co-chairs

Matthias Hein   Saarland University, Saarbrücken, Germany
Bernt Schiele   MPI for Informatics, Saarbrücken, Germany

Program Committee

Luis Alvarez	Universidad de Las Palmas de Gran Canaria, Spain
Horst Bischof	Technical University of Graz, Austria
Thomas Brox	University of Freiburg, Germany
Andres Bruhn	University of Stuttgart, Germany
Joachim Buhmann	ETH Zurich, Switzerland
Daniel Cremers	Technical University of Munich, Germany
Andreas Dengel	Technical University of Kaiserslautern, Germany
Joachim Denzler	University of Jena, Germany
Michael Felsberg	Linköping University, Sweden
Gernot Fink	Technical University of Dortmund, Germany
Boris Flach	Czech Technical University, Prague, Czech Republic
Jan-Michael Frahm	University of North Carolina, USA
Uwe Franke	Daimler AG, Germany
Juergen Gall	MPI for Intelligent Systems, Tübingen, Germany
Peter Gehler	MPI for Intelligent Systems, Tübingen, Germany
Michael Goesele	Technical University of Darmstadt, Germany
Fred Hamprecht	University of Heidelberg, Germany
Olaf Hellwich	Technical University of Berlin, Germany
Vaclav Hlavac	Czech Technical University, Prague, Czech Republic
Joachim Hornegger	University of Erlangen-Nuremberg, Germany
Xiaoyi Jiang	University of Münster, Germany

Reinhard Koch	University of Kiel, Germany
Walter Kropatsch	Vienna University of Technology, Austria
Christoph Lampert	IST Austria, Klosterneuburg, Austria
Bastian Leibe	RWTH Aachen, Germany
Ales Leonardis	University of Birmingham, UK
Marco Loog	Delft University of Technology, The Netherlands
Diana Mateus	Technical University of Munich, Germany
Helmut Mayer	Bundeswehr University Munich, Germany
Rudolf Mester	University of Frankfurt, Germany
Fernand Meyer	Mines Paris Tech, France
Krystian Mikolajczyk	University of Surrey, UK
Klaus-Robert Müller	Technical University of Berlin, Germany
Mads Nielsen	University of Copenhagen, Denmark
Sebastian Nowozin	Microsoft Research, Cambridge, UK
Thomas Pock	Technical University of Graz, Austria
Gerhard Rigoll	Technical University of Munich, Germany
Olaf Ronneberger	University of Freiburg, Germany
Bodo Rosenhahn	University of Hannover, Germany
Stefan Roth	Technical University of Darmstadt, Germany
Volker Roth	University of Basel, Switzerland
Carsten Rother	Microsoft Research, Cambridge, UK
Hanno Scharr	Forschungszentrum Jülich, Germany
Daniel Scharstein	Middlebury College, USA
Christoph Schnörr	University of Heidelberg, Germany
Rainer Stiefelhagen	Karlsruhe Institute of Technology, Germany
Peter Sturm	INRIA Grenoble - Rhone-Alpes, France
Christian Theobalt	MPI for Informatics, Saarbrücken, Germany
Klaus-Dieter Tönnies	University of Magdeburg, Germany
Joost van de Weijer	Autonomous University of Barcelona, Spain
Thomas Vetter	University of Basel, Switzerland
Friedrich Wahl	University of Braunschweig, Germany
Martin Welk	UMIT Hall, Austria

Additional Reviewers

Ahmed Abdulkadir	University of Freiburg, Germany
David Adametz	University of Basel, Switzerland
Ziad Al-Halah	Karlsruhe Institute of Technology, Germany
Jesus Angulo	Mines Paris Tech, France
Freddie Åström	Linköping University, Sweden
Mathieu Aubry	Technical University of Munich, Germany
Florian Baumann	University of Hannover, Germany
Robert Bensch	University of Freiburg, Germany
Mahapatra Dwarikanath	ETH Zurich, Switzerland

Sandro Esquivel   University of Kiel, Germany
Michele Fenzi   University of Hannover, Germany
Philipp Fischer   University of Freiburg, Germany
Oliver Fleischmann   University of Kiel, Germany
Georgios Floros   RWTH Aachen, Germany
Simon Fojtu   Czech Technical University, Prague,
                                  Czech Republic
Markus Franke   University of Kiel, Germany
Simon Fuhrmann   Technical University of Darmstadt, Germany
Hua Gao   Karlsruhe Institute of Technology, Germany
Stefan Heber   Technical University of Graz, Austria
Andreas Jordt   University of Kiel, Germany
Anne Jordt   University of Kiel, Germany
Margret Keuper   University of Freiburg, Germany
Fabian Langguth   Technical University of Darmstadt, Germany
Dmitry Laptev   ETH Zurich, Switzerland
Laura Leal-Taixé   University of Hannover, Germany
Kun Liu   University of Freiburg, Germany
Dominic Mai   University of Freiburg, Germany
Muhammad I. Malik   DFKI Kaiserslautern, Germany
Dennis Mitzel   RWTH Aachen, Germany
Naveen S. Nagaraja   University of Freiburg, Germany
Peter Ochs   University of Freiburg, Germany
Tommaso Piccini   Linköping University, Sweden
Gerard Pons   University of Hannover, Germany
René Ranftl   Technical University of Graz, Austria
Lukas Rybok   Karlsruhe Institute of Technology, Germany
Thorsten Schmidt   University of Freiburg, Germany
Uwe Schmidt   Technical University of Darmstadt, Germany
Christian Schulze   Technical University of Clausthal, Germany
Viktoriia Sharmanska   IST Austria, Klosterneuburg, Austria
Erik Soltow   University of Hannover, Germany
Mohamed Souiai   Technical University of Munich, Germany
Frank Steinbrücker   Technical University of Munich, Germany
Michael Stoll   University of Stuttgart, Germany
Jan Stühmer   Technical University of Munich, Germany
Juergen Sturm   Technical University of Munich, Germany
Patrick Sudowe   RWTH Aachen, Germany
Levi Valgaerts   MPI for Informatics, Saarbrücken, Germany
Sebastian Volz   University of Stuttgart, Germany
Tobias Weyand   RWTH Aachen, Germany
Lilian Zhang   University of Kiel, Germany
Vasileios Zografos   Linköping University, Sweden

Sponsoring Institutions

Robert Bosch GmbH	Hildesheim, Germany
Fraunhofer ITWM	Kaiserslautern, Germany
Google Research	London, Great Britain
Intel GmbH	Feldkirchen, Munich, Germany
MVTec Software GmbH	Munich, Germany
Toyota Motor Europe	Zaventem, Belgium
Ersatzteile-24.com	Merchweiler, Germany

Table of Contents

Young Researchers' Forum

Statistical Methods and Learning

Applications

Optical Flow

Pattern Recognition

Shape Recognition and Scene Understanding

Reconstructing Reflective and Transparent Surfaces from Epipolar Plane Images

Sven Wanner and Bastian Goldluecke

Heidelberg Collaboratory for Image Processing

Abstract. While multi-view stereo reconstruction of Lambertian surfaces is nowadays highly robust, reconstruction methods based on correspondence search usually fail in the presence of ambiguous information, like in the case of partially reflecting and transparent surfaces. On the epipolar plane images of a 4D light field, however, surfaces like these give rise to overlaid patterns of oriented lines. We show that these can be identified and analyzed quickly and accurately with higher order structure tensors. The resulting method can reconstruct with high precision both the geometry of the surface as well as the geometry of the reflected or transmitted object. Accuracy and feasibility are shown on both ray-traced synthetic scenes and real-world data recorded by our gantry.

1 Introduction

Multi-view stereo methods have made tremendous progress in the past years and offer ever higher accuracy on standard benchmarks like the Middlebury data sets [1]. However, at its core, multi-view stereo and structure from motion rely on the detection of corresponding regions between images, based on the assumption that a scene point looks the same in all views where it is observed - the scene surfaces need to be diffuse reflectors, i.e. Lambertian. While this assumption is completely unrealistic, as a quick look into any natural scene will immediately make obvious, using priors and optimization one can usually obtain robust results at least for surfaces which exhibit only small amounts of specular reflections.

In the presence of partially reflecting surfaces, however, the Lambertian assumption and thus correspondence matching based on comparison of image color completely breaks down. The overlay of information from surface and reflection causes ambiguous information, which leads to a failure0 of matching based methods, see Figure 1. Furthermore, it seems unlikely that a traditional stereo pair offers enough information to reliably reconstruct the scene structure in such a setting, although there has been some success in restricted scenarios [2].

We therefore propose to analyze reflecting surfaces in a 4D light field, which can be understood as a collection of views with a special structure. What sets a light field apart from standard multi-view imagery is that the views are densely sampled, and thus we can assume the light field to be defined on a continuous space of rays. In particular, it is possible to compute derivatives of tensor fields on this ray space in view point direction.

J. Weickert, M. Hein, and B. Schiele (Eds.): GCPR 2013, LNCS 8142, pp. 1–10, 2013.

Center view and stereo reconstruction   Proposed double orientation analysis

Epipolar plane image and two recovered orientations at the center location

Fig. 1. Reconstructing a mirror. An algorithm based on the Lambertian assumption cannot distinguish the two signals from mirror plane and reflection and reconstructs erroneous depth for the mirror plane. In contrast, the proposed light field analysis framework correctly separates the data for the mirror plane from the reflection.

In the present work, we contribute a method to leverage this differential structure to simply and reliably reconstruct the geometry of partially reflective or transparent surfaces, which is a quite hard challenge to achieve from unstructured multi-view data [3,4,5]. To this end, we employ an image formation model for which reflections or transparencies manifest as overlaid line structures in epipolar plane image space, whose orientation is related to disparity. We then show how to separate these structures into the two different layers (for e.g. mirror and reflection component) using straight-forward pattern analysis methods, see Figure 1. In particular, we use higher order structure tensors for multiple oriented patterns as developed in [6] in order to analyze the directional structure. That way, we derive local estimates for the disparity of both layers, which can be further processed in global optimization schemes. In experiments, we demonstrate the feasibility and accuracy of our method on both ray-traced synthetic as well as real world data sets from a gantry.

2   Related Work

While there has been progress in the field of non-Lambertian reconstruction under controlled lighting conditions [7,8,9,10], it remains quite hard to generalize the standard matching models to more general reflectance functions if only a set of images under unknown illumination is available. Previous attempts employ a rank constraint on the radiance tensor [3] to derive a discrepancy measure for non-Lambertian scenes. While this improves upon the standard Lambertian matching models and allows to reconstruct surface reflection parameters, the results still somewhat lack in robustness. An interesting alternative approach is Helmholtz stereopsis [11], which makes use of the symmetry of reflectance or Helmholtz reciprocity principle in order to eliminate the view dependency of specular reflections in restricted imaging setups. By alternating light source and camera at two different locations, one can obtain a stereo pair where specularities are exactly identical and thus classical matching techniques can be employed for

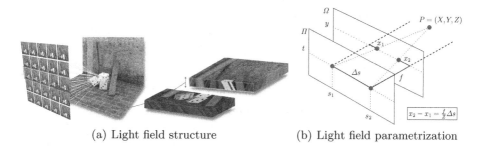

(a) Light field structure   (b) Light field parametrization

Fig. 2. (a) A 4D light field is essentially a collection of images of a scene, where the focal points of the cameras lie in a 2D plane. Additional structure becomes visible when one stacks all images along a line of view points on top of each other and considers a cut through this stack (green border above). The 2D image in the plane of the cut is called an *epipolar plane image (EPI)*. (b) Each camera location (s, t) in the view point plane Π yields a different pinhole view of the scene. The two thick dashed black lines are orthogonal to both planes, and their intersection with the plane Ω marks the origins of the (x, y)-coordinate systems for the views (s_1, t) and (s_2, t), respectively.

non-Lambertian scenes. Other works try to remove reflection data from images using prior assumptions or user input . However, none of the approaches above allow to infer anything about the geometry of the reflected objects.

The method in [2] conveys similar ideas than ours, but it does not make use of structure tensors and tries to recover the information from only a stereo pair. Consequently, the problem is much more ill-posed and only very restricted settings are analyzed.

Two other works which are closely related to ours are [4,5]. They both separate a scene which can partially consist of two different layers by considering an epipolar volume constructed from camera motion. At their heart, these works still rely on classical correspondence matching, since they optimize for two overlaid matching models in a nested plane sweep algorithm using graph cuts or semi-global matching, respectively.

In contrast, in our proposed method we do not try to optimize for correspondence. Instead, we build upon early ideas in camera motion analysis [14] and investigate directional patterns in epipolar space. The two layers manifest as overlaid structures, which we investigate with higher order structure tensors [6] as a consequent generalization of [15]. As a result, we obtain a direct continuous method which requires no discretization into depth labels, and which is highly parallelizable and quite fast: a center view disparity map for both layers can be obtained in less than two seconds for a reasonably sized light field, around a hundred times faster than the shortest run-times reported in [5].

3   The Structure of Epipolar Plane Images

Light Fields and Epipolar Plane Images. A 4D light field or Lumigraph can be imagined as a collection of pinhole views with the same image plane Ω

and focal points lying in a second parallel plane Π. see Figure 2(a). We choose the parametrization detailed in [15]. Coordinates $(s, t) \in \Pi$ define view point locations, and for each such pair, a local (x, y) coordinate system gives the pinhole projection through (s, t) with image plane in Ω, such that a ray $R[s, t, 0, 0]$ passes through the focal point (s, t) and the center of projection in the image plane, as detailed in Figure 2(b). This parametrization for ray space is slightly different from the standard one for a Lumigraph [16], and inspired by [14].

A light field L is a map which assigns an intensity value (grayscale or color) to each ray. Of particular interest are the images which emerge when the space of rays is restricted to a 2D plane. If we fix for example the two coordinates (y^*, t^*), the restriction L_{y^*, t^*} is the map

$$L_{y^*, t^*} : (x, s) \mapsto L(x, y^*, s, t^*), \tag{1}$$

other restrictions are defined in a similar way. Note that L_{s^*, t^*} is the image of the pinhole view with center of projection (s^*, t^*). The images L_{y^*, t^*} and L_{x^*, s^*} are called *epipolar plane images*. They can be interpreted as horizontal or vertical cuts through a horizontal or vertical stack of the views in the light field, see Figure 2(a), and have a rich structure which resembles patterns of overlaid straight lines. Their slope yields information about the scene structure.

EPI Structure for Opaque Lambertian Surfaces. Let $P \in \mathbb{R}^3$ be a scene point. It is easy to show, see e.g. [15], that the projection of P on each epipolar plane image is a straight line with slope $\frac{f}{Z}$, where Z is the *depth of P*, i.e. distance of P to the plane Π, and f the focal length, i.e. distance between the planes Π and Ω. The quantity $\frac{f}{Z}$ is called the *disparity* of P. In particular, the above means that if P is a point on an opaque Lambertian surface, then for all points on the epipolar plane image where the point P is visible, the light field L must have the same constant intensity. This is the reason for the single pattern of solid lines which we can observe in the EPIs of a Lambertian scene.

In [15], this well-known observation was the foundation for a novel approach to depth estimation, which leveraged the structure tensors of the epipolar plane images in order to estimate the local orientation and thus the disparity of the observed point visible in the corresponding ray. While in conjunction with visibility constraints this leads to a certain robustness against specular reflexes, the image formation model implicitly underlying this method is still the Lambertian one, thus the method cannot deal correctly with reflecting surfaces.

EPI Structure in the Presence of Planar Reflectors. We now introduce an idealized appearance model for the epipolar plane images in the presence of a planar mirror - a translucent surface is an obvious specialization where a real object takes the place of the virtual one behind the mirror. It is kept simple in order to arrive at a computationally easily tractable model, but we will see that it captures the characteristics of reflective and translucent surfaces reasonably well to be able to cope with real-world data. A similar appearance model was successfully employed in [5].

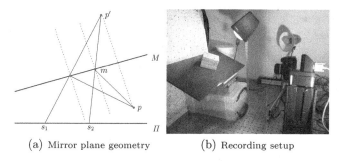

(a) Mirror plane geometry   (b) Recording setup

Fig. 3. (a) Geometry of reflection on a planar mirror. All cameras view the reflections of a scene point p at a planar mirror M as the image of a virtual point p' which lies *behind* the mirror plane. (b) Our gantry construction we employed to record the real-world light fields.

Let $M \subset \mathbb{R}^3$ be the surface of a planar mirror. We fix coordinates (y^*, t^*) and consider the corresponding epipolar plane image L_{y^*, t^*}. The idea of the appearance model is to define the observed color for a ray at location (x, s) which intersects the mirror at $m \in M$. Our simplified assumption is that the observed color is a linear combination of two contributions. The first is the base color $c(m)$ of the mirror, which describes the appearance of the mirror without the presence of any reflection. The second is the color $c(p)$ of the reflection, where p is the first scene point where the reflected ray intersects the scene geometry, see Figure 3(a). We do not consider higher order reflections, and assume the surface at p to be Lambertian. We also assume the reflectivity $\alpha > 0$ is a constant independent of viewing direction and location. The epipolar plane image itself will then be a linear combination

$$L_{y^*, t^*} = L^M_{y^*, t^*} + \alpha L^V_{y^*, t^*} \tag{2}$$

of a pattern $L^M_{y^*, t^*}$ from the mirror surface itself as well as a pattern $L^V_{y^*, t^*}$ from the virtual scene behind the mirror. In each point (x, s) as above, both constituent patterns have a dominant direction corresponding to the disparities of m and p. The next section shows how to extract these two dominant directions.

4   Double-Orientation Detection on an EPI

Structure Tensors for Multi-Orientation Models. We briefly summarize the theory for the analysis of superimposed patterns described in [6]. A region $R \subset \Omega$ of an image $f : \Omega \to \mathbb{R}$ has orientation $\boldsymbol{v} \in \mathbb{R}^2$ if and only if $f(x) = f(x + \alpha \boldsymbol{v})$ for all $x, x + \alpha \boldsymbol{v} \in R$. Analysis shows that the orientation $\boldsymbol{v}$ is given by the Eigenvector corresponding to the smaller Eigenvalue of the structure tensor [17] of f. However, the model fails if the image f is a superposition of two oriented images, $f = f_1 + f_2$, where f_1 has orientation $\boldsymbol{u}$ and f_2 has orientation $\boldsymbol{v}$. In this case, the two orientations $\boldsymbol{u}, \boldsymbol{v}$ need to satisfy the conditions

$$\boldsymbol{u}^T \nabla f_1 = 0 \text{ and } \boldsymbol{v}^T \nabla f_2 = 0 \tag{3}$$

individually on R.

Center view	Single orientation	Double orientation model	
		(front layer)	(back layer)

Fig. 4. Reconstructing a transparent surface. The single orientation model cannot distinguish the two signals from the dirty glass surface and the objects behind it. In contrast, multi-orientation analysis correctly separates both layers.

Analogous to the single orientation case, the two orientations in a region R can be found by performing an Eigensystem analysis of the second order structure tensor, see [6],

$$\mathcal{T} = \int_R \sigma \begin{bmatrix} f_{xx}^2 & f_{xx}f_{xy} & f_{xx}f_{yy} \\ f_{xx}f_{xy} & f_{xy}^2 & f_{xy}f_{yy} \\ f_{xx}f_{yy} & f_{xy}f_{yy} & f_{yy}^2 \end{bmatrix} \mathrm{d}(x,y), \tag{4}$$

where σ is a (usually Gaussian) weighting kernel on R which essentially determines the size of the sampling window. Since $\mathcal{T}$ is symmetric, we can compute Eigenvalues and Eigenvectors in a straight-forward manner using the explicit formulas in [18]. Analogous to the Eigenvalue decomposition of the 2D structure tensor, the Eigenvector $\boldsymbol{a} \in \mathbb{R}^3$ corresponding to the smallest Eigenvalue of $\mathcal{T}$, the so-called *MOP vector*, encodes the orientations. Indeed, the two disparities are equal to the Eigenvalues λ_+, λ_- of the 2×2 matrix

$$\begin{bmatrix} a_2/a_1 & -a_3/a_1 \\ 1 & 0 \end{bmatrix}, \tag{5}$$

from which one can compute the orientations $\boldsymbol{u} = [\lambda_+ \; 1]^T$ and $\boldsymbol{v} = [\lambda_- \; 1]^T$. The additional material contains source code fragments for the above key steps for easy reimplementation of our method.

Merging the Results into a Single Disparity Map. From the steps sketched above, we obtain three different disparity estimates for both the horizontal as well as vertical epipolar images: one from the single orientation model, and two from the double orientation model. It is clear that the closer estimate in the double orientation model will always correspond to the primary surface, regardless of whether it is a mirror or translucent object. Unfortunately, we do not know yet of a reliable mathematical measure which tells us whether the two-layer model is valid or not. We therefore impose a simple heuristic: if at a given point, the disparity values of horizontal and vertical EPIs agree up to a small error for both the primary and secondary orientation, we flag the double orientation model as valid, and choose its contribution in the disparity maps. Otherwise, we choose the estimate from the single orientation model.

Center view   Single orientation   Front layer   Back layer

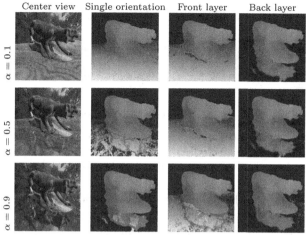

Reflection coefficient	Point-wise result				Result after TV-L^2 denoising			
	Single orientation		Double orientation		Single orientation		Double orientation	
	front	back	front	back	front	back	front	back
$\alpha = 0.1$	0.0034	0.7409	0.0078	0.1191	0.0025	0.7392	0.0036	0.09924
$\alpha = 0.3$	0.0236	0.5994	0.0061	0.0349	0.0086	0.6273	0.0032	0.02371
$\alpha = 0.5$	0.0869	0.3735	0.0066	0.0236	0.0252	0.5111	0.0036	0.01377
$\alpha = 0.7$	0.1807	0.1547	0.0101	0.0239	0.1434	0.1821	0.0060	0.01053
$\alpha = 0.9$	0.2579	0.0365	0.0389	0.0473	0.2557	0.0312	0.0249	0.00980

Fig. 5. Influence of reflectivity on accuracy. The table shows mean squared disparity error in pixels of the single and double orientation model for both the mirror plane as well as the reflection. While the single orientation model shifts from reconstruction of mirror to reflection with growing reflectivity α, the double orientation model can still reconstruct both when even a human observer has difficulties separating them. The images show the point-wise results.

5   Results

We compare our method primarily to the single orientation method [15] based on the first order structure tensor, which is similar in spirit and an initial step in our algorithm in any case. However, it is clear that any multi-view stereo method will have similar problems than the single orientation method if the underlying model is also the Lambertian world. More results and full-resolution images which would exceed the allowed space of the paper can be found in the additional material. The light fields as well as the complete source code for the method to reproduce the results will be available online.

Synthetic Data Sets. Figure 5 shows reconstruction accuracy on a synthetic light field with varying amounts of reflectivity α. The scene was ray-traced in a way which exactly fits the image formation model. As expected, the disparity reconstructed with the single orientation model is close to the disparity of the mirror surface if α is small, and close to the disparity of the reflection if α is large. In between, the result is a mixture between the two, depending on whose texture

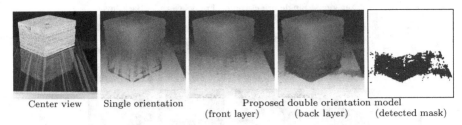

Center view   Single orientation   Proposed double orientation model
                    (front layer)   (back layer)   (detected mask)

Fig. 6. In the absence of a structured background, the reflecting surface can of course only reliably be detected where a reflection of a foreground object is visible. The blue region indicates where the double orientation model returns valid results.

is stronger. In contrast, the double orientation model can reliably reconstruct both reflection as well as mirror surface for the full range of reflectivities α, even when it is already difficult for a human to still observe both.

While the point-wise results are already very accurate, they are still quite noisy and can be greatly improved by adding a small amount of TV-L^2 denoising [19]. We deliberately do not employ more sophisticated global optimization in this step to showcase only the raw output from the model and what is possible at interactive performance levels. For all of the light fields shown, at image resolutions upwards of 512×512 with 9×9 views, the point-wise disparity computation for the whole center view takes less than 1.5 seconds on an nVidia GTX 680 GPU.

Real-World Data Sets. In Figures 4, 6, and 7, we show reconstruction results for light fields recorded with our gantry, see Figure 3(b). Each one has 9×9 views at resolutions between 0.5 and 1 megapixels. For both reflective and transparent surfaces, a reconstruction of a single disparity based on the Lambertian assumption produces major artifacts and is unusable in the region of the surface. In contrast, the proposed method always produces a very reliable estimate for the primary surface, as well as a reasonably accurate one for the reflected or transmitted objects, respectively. For the results in the figures, we employed a global optimization scheme [20,15] to reach maximum possible quality, which takes about 3 minutes per disparity map. The same scheme and parameters were used for both methods and all data sets. To show what is possible in near real-time, we also provide the raw point-wise results in the additional material.

The results show that certain appearant limitations of the model are not practically relevant. In particular, different to our simplified model, the reflectivity α is certainly not constant everywhere due to influences of e.g. the Fresnel term, but since all estimates are strictly local and the angular range small, the variations do not seem to impact the final result by much. A stronger limitation, however, is the planarity of the reflecting or transparent surface. We predict that it can be considerably weakened, since the main assumption of the existence of an object "behind" the primary surface (which is of course only virtual in case of a mirror) also holds for more general geometries. However, exploring this direction is left for future work.

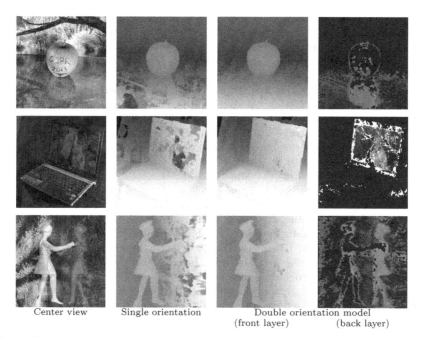

Center view   Single orientation   Double orientation model
                                        (front layer)   (back layer)

Fig. 7. Reconstructing a mirror. Like multi-view stereo algorithms, the single orientation model cannot distinguish the two signals from mirror plane and reflection and reconstructs erroneous disparity for the mirror plane. In contrast, the proposed double orientation analysis correctly separates the data for the mirror plane from the reflection. The reflection layer is masked out where the double orientation model does not return valid results as specified in section 4, and the results for this layer have been increased in brightness and contrast for better visibility (raw results and many more data sets can be observed in the additional material).

6   Conclusion

We have described a method to simultaneously compute disparity maps for both a planar reflective or transparent surface as well as the reflected or transmitted object in a 4D light field structure. In this scenarios, two different oriented structures are overlaid on the epipolar plane images, which we propose to analyze using second order structure tensors. We have demonstrated that this approach leads to reliable disparity estimates which can be computed at interactive speeds. Since the problem of reconstructing reflective or semi-transparent surfaces is hard to solve efficiently with conventional methods based on stereo matching techniques, we believe that the proposed method could turn out to become a foundation for unique applications of 4D light fields and their acquisition technologies.

References

1. Seitz, S., Curless, B., Diebel, J., Scharstein, D., Szeliski, R.: A comparison and evaluation of multi-view stereo reconstruction algorithms. In: Proc. International Conference on Computer Vision and Pattern Recognition, pp. 519–528 (2006)

2. Borga, K.: Estimating multiple depths in semi-transparent stereo images. In: SCIA (1999)
3. Jin, H., Soatto, S., Yezzi, A.: Multi-view stereo reconstruction of dense shape and complex appearance. International Journal of Computer Vision 63(3), 175–189 (2005)
4. Tsin, Y., Kang, S., Szeliski, R.: Stereo matching with linear superposition of layers. IEEE Transactions on Pattern Analysis and Machine Intelligence 28(2), 290–301 (2006)
5. Sinha, S., Kopf, J., Goesele, M., Scharstein, D., Szeliski, R.: Image-based rendering for scenes with reflections. ACM Transactions on Graphics (Proc. SIGGRAPH) 31(4), 100:1–100:10 (2012)
6. Aach, T., Mota, C., Stuke, I., Muehlich, M., Barth, E.: Analysis of superimposed oriented patterns. IEEE Transactions on Image Processing 15(12), 3690–3700 (2006)
7. Davis, J., Yang, R., Wang, L.: BRDF invariant stereo using light transport constancy. In: Proc. International Conference on Computer Vision (2005)
8. Alldrin, N., Zickler, T., Kriegman, D.: Photometric stereo with non-parametric and spatially-varying reflectance. In: Proc. International Conference on Computer Vision and Pattern Recognition (2008)
9. Ruiters, R., Klein, R.: Heightfield and spatially varying BRDF reconstruction for materials with interreflections. Computer Graphics Forum (Proc. Eurographics) 28(2), 513–522 (2009)
10. Goldman, D., Curless, B., Hertzmann, A., Seitz, S.: Shape and spatially-varying BRDFs from photometric stereo. IEEE Transactions on Pattern Analysis and Machine Intelligence 32(6), 1060–1071 (2010)
11. Zickler, T., Belhumeur, P., Kriegman, D.: Helmholtz stereopsis: Exploiting reciprocity for surface reconstruction. International Journal of Computer Vision 49(2–3), 215–227 (2002)
12. Levin, A., Zomet, A., Weiss, Y.: Separating reflections from a single image using local features. In: Proc. International Conference on Computer Vision and Pattern Recognition (2004)
13. Levin, A., Weiss, Y.: User assisted separation of reflections from a single image using a sparsity prior. IEEE Transactions on Pattern Analysis and Machine Intelligence (2007)
14. Bolles, R., Baker, H., Marimont, D.: Epipolar-plane image analysis: An approach to determining structure from motion. International Journal of Computer Vision 1(1), 7–55 (1987)
15. Wanner, S., Goldluecke, B.: Globally consistent depth labeling of 4D light fields. In: Proc. International Conference on Computer Vision and Pattern Recognition, pp. 41–48 (2012)
16. Gortler, S., Grzeszczuk, R., Szeliski, R., Cohen, M.: The Lumigraph. In: Proc. SIGGRAPH, pp. 43–54 (1996)
17. Bigün, J., Granlund, G.H.: Optimal orientation detection of linear symmetry. In: Proc. International Conference on Computer Vision, pp. 433–438 (1987)
18. Smith, O.: Eigenvalues of a symmetric 3x3 matrix. Communications of the ACM 4(4), 168 (1961)
19. Chambolle, A.: An algorithm for total variation minimization and applications. Journal of Mathematical Imaging and Vision 20(1-2), 89–97 (2004)
20. Pock, T., Cremers, D., Bischof, H., Chambolle, A.: Global solutions of variational models with convex regularization. SIAM Journal on Imaging Sciences (2010)

Structure from Motion Using Rigidly Coupled Cameras without Overlapping Views

Sandro Esquivel and Reinhard Koch

Christian-Albrechts-University, Kiel, Germany

Abstract. Structure from Motion can be improved by using multi-camera systems without overlapping views to provide a large combined field of view. The extrinsic calibration of such camera systems can be computed from local reconstructions using *hand-eye calibration* techniques. Nevertheless these approaches demand that motion constraints resulting from the rigid coupling of the cameras are satisfied which is in general not the case for decoupled pose estimation. This paper presents an extension to Structure from Motion using multiple rigidly coupled cameras that integrates rigid motion constraints already into the local pose estimation step, based on dual quaternions for pose representation. It is shown in experiments with synthetic and real data that the overall quality of the reconstruction process is improved and pose error accumulation is counteracted, leading to more accurate extrinsic calibration.

1 Introduction

Multi-camera systems play an important role in computer vision and are used in various tasks such as object tracking, 3d reconstruction, and Augmented Reality. Combining cameras with minimal or no shared viewing areas is especially helpful for *Structure from Motion* (SfM) applications, i.e. 3d reconstruction of *a priori* unknown scenes from video sequences, due to their large combined field of view. Existing approaches [18,8,7] need an accurate intrinsic and extrinsic calibration of the cameras. While extrinsic calibration is solved in general by matching features between camera images or using calibration objects that are visible in all cameras [12,19], calibration without overlapping views is far less treated in literature, starting with Caspi & Irani for colocated cameras [1].

It is convenient to reduce this problem to *hand-eye calibration* [4,5,11]. These approaches – dubbed *eye-to-eye calibration* in the context of this work – compute the pose transformation between the cameras from the rigidity constraints on relative motions of the cameras. Typically, relative poses are computed first for each camera individually from synchronously captured images using monocular SfM. Afterwards the relative pose of cameras to each other are recovered from the rigidi motion constraints by solving the equation $\mathbf{AX} = \mathbf{XB}$ known from robotic hand-eye calibration, where $\mathbf{A}$, $\mathbf{B}$ are relative pose transformations of the "hand" – a mobile gripper – and the "eye" – a visual sensor mounted on the gripper – at the same instant of time and $\mathbf{X}$ is the Euclidean transformation from the "eye" to the "hand" coordinate frame. However, due to noise resp. estimation errors,

J. Weickert, M. Hein, and B. Schiele (Eds.): GCPR 2013, LNCS 8142, pp. 11–20, 2013.

the rigidity constraint between $\mathbf{A}$ and $\mathbf{B}$ is not satisfied in practice, especially when the poses are computed by SfM. This constraint violation induces errors in the calibration step. Lébraly et al. [11] propose to use a bundle adjustment with minimal parametrization for local camera poses – using the local poses of a designated *master* camera for each frame and the time-independent relative poses between the other cameras and the master camera – as a post-processing step while computing the initial extrinsic calibration from deficient local poses.

Our Approach. In this work we will integrate the enforcement of rigidity constraints into the pose estimation step of multi-camera Structure from Motion, in contrast to existing approaches which ignore it or try to remedy it after extrinsic calibration, e.g. using global optimization techniques. This is done by parametrizing motions properly to model the constraints explicitly.

First, we will address the motion constraints on rigidly coupled cameras explicitly and interpret them geometrically. Since the formulation of these constraints depends on the parametrization of the camera poses, we will consider different suitable parametrizations based on *screw motions*.

In the main part we will present a multi-camera SfM framework that considers rigid motion constraints already during intialization and local pose estimation while the eye-to-eye transformation is yet unknown.

We evaluate the initialization and pose estimation steps of rigidly coupled multi-camera SfM with synthetic data, rendered and real video sequences using an implementation of our approach, as well as afterward eye-to-eye calibration.

2   Motion Constraints of Rigidly Coupled Cameras

In the following we will consider N rigidly coupled cameras with local coordinate frames $\mathcal{C}_k$, $k = 1, \ldots, N$, captured at M local poses $\mathbf{T}_k^\ell$ with respect to the reference coordinate frames $\mathcal{C}_k$. The transformation $\Delta\mathbf{T}_k$ between the local coordinate frames of the k-th camera and the first camera (*master* camera) – denoted as *eye-to-eye transformation* in the context of this work – satisfies the *rigid motion equation* illustrated in fig. 1:

$$\mathbf{T}_1^\ell \Delta\mathbf{T}_k = \Delta\mathbf{T}_k \mathbf{T}_k^\ell \tag{1}$$

Each $\mathbf{T}$ describes a Euclidean transformation consisting of rotation $\mathbf{R}$ and translation t. Hence the rigid motion constraint (1) can be decomposed into a rotation constraint $\mathbf{R}_1^\ell \Delta\mathbf{R}_k = \Delta\mathbf{R}_k \mathbf{R}_k^\ell$ and a translation constraint $\mathbf{R}_1^\ell \Delta t_k + t_1^\ell = \Delta\mathbf{R}_k t_k^\ell + \Delta t_k$ for rigidly coupled motion pairs $(\mathbf{T}_1^\ell, \mathbf{T}_k^\ell)$.

Solving (1) for $\Delta\mathbf{T}_k$ is called *eye-to-eye calibration*. Approaches differ mainly by the motion parametrization. Tsai & Lenz [17] showed that at least two general motions with different rotation axes are needed to solve this problem inambiguously, independent of the chosen pose parametrization.

The rigidity constraints on local motions of rigidly coupled sensors were described within the context of hand-eye calibration by Chen [2] as the *congruence theorem*. The constraints include a *rotation angle constraint* and a constraint on the rotation axis and the translation parallel to the rotation axis, referred to as the *pitch constraint* in this work. They become obvious when motions are considered as *screw motions*: A general motion of a camera with translation t can be decomposed into a rotation by angle α around a rotation axis r, a translation pr with $p = t^\top r$ parallel to the rotation axis r, and a translation $u = t - pr$ orthogonal to the rotation axis r. This can equally be described by a rotation by α around a line in space with direction r followed by a slide of length p along the line (*Chasles' theorem*), formulated algebraically either as a screw motion [2] or equivalently by means of dual quaternions [3].

Rotation Angle Constraint. Given N rigidly coupled local rotations $\mathbf{R}_k$ with rotation angles $\alpha_k \in [0, \pi]$ around rotation axes r_k, all rotation angles α_k must be equal. It can be easily proved from eq. (1) that the following equivalence is valid:

$$\mathbf{R}_1 = \Delta\mathbf{R}_k \mathbf{R}_k \Delta\mathbf{R}_k^\top \quad \Leftrightarrow \quad r_1 = \Delta\mathbf{R}_k r_k \text{ and } \alpha_1 = \alpha_k \quad \text{for all } 2 \leq k \leq N \quad (2)$$

Hence the local rotation estimation problem for N rigidly coupled cameras can be reduced to the estimation of N rotation axes r_k and a single angle $\alpha \in [0, \pi]$.

Pitch Constraint. Given N rigidly coupled local motions $(\mathbf{R}_k, t_k)$, the amount of translation parallel to the rotation axes, the so called *pitch* $p_k = t_k^\top r_k$, must be equal for all motions. This also follows directly from eq. (1):

$$t_k^\top r_k = \underbrace{\Delta t_k^\top (\mathbf{R}_1^\top - \mathbf{I}) r_1}_{=0} + t_1^\top r_1 \quad \text{for all } 2 \leq k \leq N \quad (3)$$

Hence the local translation estimation problem for N rigidly coupled cameras can be reduced by $N - 1$ parameters when the local rotation axes are known.

The pitch constraint holds when the local translations of all cameras have the same scale. Otherwise, it yields the scalar factor between the coordinate frames of the cameras, given that the motion is not planar. Assume that all translations are only known up to scale, i.e $\hat{t}_k$ with $s_k \hat{t}_k = t_k$ are given. Then the relative scale $\lambda_k = \frac{s_k}{s_1}$ from the k-th to the master coordinate frame is given by:

$$\lambda_k = \frac{\hat{t}_1^\top r_1}{\hat{t}_k^\top r_k} \text{ and } s_k = s_1 \lambda_k \quad \text{for all } 2 \leq k \leq N \quad (4)$$

2.1   Rigidly Coupled Pose Parametrization

To enforce the rotation angle constraint and pitch constraint by using a common parameter for rotation angle and pitch respectively, a pose parametrization is needed that is computationally simple, has minimal redundancy, and explicitly decouples angle and pitch from the remaining pose parameters. Hence, *dual quaternions* provide a natural choice for rigidly coupled pose parametrization.

Quaternions of unit length (see e.g. [10]), represented as 3d-vector/scalar pairs $\mathbf{q} = (q, q)$, are commonly used for rotation estimation in computer vision and computer graphics since they provide an efficient and only slightly overparameterized representation, do not suffer from singularities, and are still computationally easy to apply. Related to the angle/axis representation, they also explicitly state the rotation angle. *Dual quaternions* $\check{q} = (q, q')$ (see e.g. [3]) provide an equally elegant way to describe rigid motions in 3d space, closely related to the screw axis, angle, and pitch of screw motions. The dual quaternion describing a rotation by angle α around axis r and translation by t is given by the pair:

$$q = \left(\sin(\frac{\alpha}{2})r, \cos(\frac{\alpha}{2})\right) \quad q' = \frac{1}{2}\left(\cos(\frac{\alpha}{2})t + \sin(\frac{\alpha}{2})(t \times r), -\sin(\frac{\alpha}{2})t^\top r\right) \quad (5)$$

where q is referred to as the *real* and q' as the *dual* part of the dual quaternion. The rigid motion of a 3d point X is described by $R(q)X + t(q, q')$ with:

$$R(q) = I + 2q[q]_\times + 2[q]_\times^2 \quad t(q, q') = 2(qq' - q'q + q \times q') \quad (6)$$

where $[q]_\times$ is the skew-symmetric matrix describing the cross product with q. The space of such dual quaternions is constrained by $\|q\| = 1$ and $q^\top q' = 0$, i.e. $\|\check{q}\| = 1$. Since q and $-q$ describe the same rotation, we will restrict the real quaternion part to $q \geq 0$. Under this limitation, we conclude from eq. (2) and (3) that all dual quaternions representing rigidly coupled motions have equal scalar parts (q, q'), since these only depend on the rotation angle and motion pitch.

Minimal Parametrization. Using unit dual quaternions to represent rigidly coupled motion, the rigid motion constraint can be simply enforced via parameter reduction, i.e. using a single parameter pair (q, q') for the scalar quaternion part. Nonetheless, the parametrization is not minimal, so we will need additional constraints, i.e. unit length constraints $\|q\| = 1$ and orthogonality constraints $q^\top q' = 0$, which is not recommended for nonlinear optimization. We consider a minimal parametrization for nonlinear optimization instead. Assuming w.l.o.g. that r_z is the largest absolute element of the rotation axis r with sign σ_z, we can enforce the unit quaternion constraint by replacing q with $(q_x, q_y, \sigma_z\sqrt{1 - q_x^2 - q_y^2 - q^2})$. This yields a valid parametrization as long as the rotation is not too small. The orthogonality constraint is enforced by replacing q' with $(q_x', q_y', -\frac{q_x q_x' + q_y q_y' + qq'}{\sigma_z\sqrt{1 - q_x^2 - q_y^2 - q^2}})$. A second strategy is to renormalize the non-minimal parameters prior to pose evaluation. This is equivalent to using $\sqrt{1 - q^2}\frac{q}{\|q\|}$ and $q' - \frac{q^\top q' + qq'}{q^\top q}q$ instead of q and q'. For an extensive review of minimal rotation parametrization for nonlinear optimization see e.g. [14].

3   Rigidly Coupled Multi-camera Structure from Motion

In the following we will describe how to enforce rigid motion constraints into the two main stages of SfM for multiple coupled cameras prior to eye-to-eye calibration. We will show that the resulting reconstruction yields more consistent results which will improve the global registration of all cameras.

3.1   Relative Pose Estimation

Relative pose estimation from two views evaluating the epipolar geometry is commonly used as the first step in SfM applications (see [6]). Given n corresponding normalized image points $\boldsymbol{x}_i$, $\boldsymbol{x}_i'$ of 3d points $\boldsymbol{X}_i$ in two camera images $\mathcal{I}$ and $\mathcal{I}'$ with relative pose $(\mathbf{R}, \boldsymbol{t})$, i.e. $\boldsymbol{x} \sim \boldsymbol{X}$, $\boldsymbol{x}' \sim \boldsymbol{X}' = \mathbf{R}\boldsymbol{X} + \boldsymbol{t}$, the essential matrix $\mathbf{E}$ can be written as $\mathbf{E} = \mathbf{R}^\top [\boldsymbol{t}]_\times$. $\mathbf{E}$ is a non-zero 3×3 matrix of rank 2 that satisfies the *epipolar constraint* (a.k.a. *Longuet-Higgins equation* [6]):

$$\boldsymbol{x}_i^\top \mathbf{E}\boldsymbol{x}_i' = 0 \quad \text{for all } i = 1, \ldots, n \tag{7}$$

An illustration for rigidly coupled cameras is shown in fig. 1.

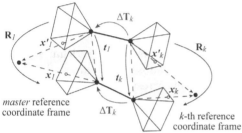
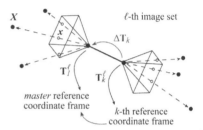

Fig. 1. Local relative pose estimation from 2d-2d correspondences $\boldsymbol{x} \leftrightarrow \boldsymbol{x}'$ for rigidly coupled cameras

Fig. 2. Local pose estimation from 2d-3d correspondences $\boldsymbol{x} \leftrightarrow \boldsymbol{X}$ for rigidly coupled cameras

Enforcing the Rotation Angle Constraint. As a first step, the essential matrices $\mathbf{E}_1, \ldots, \mathbf{E}_N$ of all cameras are computed individually from their respective image pairs using traditional algorithms. They are then decomposed into rotations $\mathbf{R}_1, \ldots, \mathbf{R}_N$ resp. unit quaternions $\mathbf{q}_1, \ldots, \mathbf{q}_N$ and translation vectors $\hat{\boldsymbol{t}}_1, \ldots, \hat{\boldsymbol{t}}_N$ up to individual scales (see e.g. [6]). W.l.o.g. we assume that all $\|\hat{\boldsymbol{t}}_i\| = 1$.

The next step is to re-estimate the relative rotations subject to the rotation angle constraint. A straight-forward approach is to average the scalar parts q_k of all unit quaternions $\mathbf{q}_k$ resulting in the constrained rotation parametrization $(q, \boldsymbol{q}_1, \ldots, \boldsymbol{q}_N)$ with $q = \frac{1}{N} \sum_{k=1}^N |q_i|$ and re-normalized vector parts $\boldsymbol{q}_k$. This averaging however does not take the epipolar constraints into account. This can be done by reformulating eq. (7) in terms of unit quaternions and minimizing the joint epipolar error function for all cameras at the same time.

Parametrizing rotations by unit quaternions $\mathbf{q}_k = (\boldsymbol{q}_k, q)$ and translations by unit vectors $\hat{\boldsymbol{t}}_k$, we obtain from eq. (7) for each point correspondence $(\boldsymbol{x}_{k,i}, \boldsymbol{x}_{k,i}')$ one constraint $f_{k,i}^{\text{epi}}(q, \boldsymbol{q}_k, \hat{\boldsymbol{t}}_k) = 0$ which can be formulated as a cubic equation of the parameter vector:

$$f_{k,i}^{\text{epi}}(q, \boldsymbol{q}_k, \hat{\boldsymbol{t}}_k) = \boldsymbol{x}_{k,i}^\top \mathbf{R}((\boldsymbol{q}_k, -q))[\hat{\boldsymbol{t}}_k]_\times \boldsymbol{x}_{k,i}' = 0 \tag{8}$$

Enforcing all $(\boldsymbol{q}_k, q)$ and $\hat{\boldsymbol{t}}_k$ to have unit length in nonlinear optimization of (8) can be achieved by using one of the methods described in 2.1, i.e. minimal parametrization of unit quaternions and unit translation vectors, or renormalizing quaternions and translations. In this work we minimize the joint error function $\sum_{k=1}^{N} \sum_{i=1}^{n_k} f_{k,i}^{\text{epi}}(q, \boldsymbol{q}_k, \hat{\boldsymbol{t}}_k)^2$ using the Levenberg-Marquardt algorithm [13]. The starting point is given by the averaged unit quaternions.

Enforcing the Pitch Constraint. Given that the motion is non-planar, we can rescale all estimated translations $\hat{\boldsymbol{t}}_k$ with respect to the master coordinate frame as described by eq. (4), yielding absolute translations $\boldsymbol{t}_k$ that satisfy the pitch constraint, i.e. $p = \boldsymbol{t}_1^\top \boldsymbol{r}_1 = \cdots = \boldsymbol{t}_1^\top \boldsymbol{r}_N$ where $\boldsymbol{r}_k = \frac{\boldsymbol{q}_k}{\|\boldsymbol{q}_k\|}$ is the rotation axis of the k-th resulting unit quaternion. The final parameters of the initial camera poses are then given by $(q, q', \boldsymbol{q}_1, \boldsymbol{q}_1', \ldots, \boldsymbol{q}_N, \boldsymbol{q}_N')$ where the dual quaternion parts are $q' = -\frac{1}{2}(\sqrt{1 - q^2})p$ and $\boldsymbol{q}_k' = \frac{1}{2}(q\boldsymbol{t} + \boldsymbol{t} \times \boldsymbol{q}_k)$ derived from eq. (5).

3.2   Pose Estimation

After initialization, the local reconstruction part of the SfM algorithm starts, i.e. local 2d-3d correspondences are tracked within subsequent camera images, the local camera poses are re-estimated from 2d-3d correspondences, and new 3d points are computed from 2d-2d correspondences using the current pose. While any approach could be used for local SfM, we recommend to use an approach based on dual quaternions for motion representation such as [15] in order to prevent frequent conversions between different parametrizations. Given n 2d-3d correspondences $(\boldsymbol{x}_i, \boldsymbol{X}_i)$ for an image $\mathcal{I}$ such that $\mathbf{R}^\top(\boldsymbol{X}_i - \boldsymbol{t}) \sim \boldsymbol{x}_i$, the local camera pose $(\mathbf{R}, \boldsymbol{t})$, should minimize the normalized *reprojection error*:

$$f(\mathbf{R}, \boldsymbol{t}) = \sum_{i=1}^{n} \|\mathbf{P}(\mathbf{R}^\top(\boldsymbol{X}_i - \boldsymbol{t})) - \mathbf{P}(\boldsymbol{x}_i)\|^2 \tag{9}$$

where $\mathbf{P}: \mathbb{R}^3 \to \mathbb{R}^2, \boldsymbol{X} \mapsto (X_x/X_z, X_y/X_z)$ denotes the perspective projection. Pose estimation from local 2d-3d correspondences is illustrated in fig. 2.

Enforcing the Rigid Motion Constraint. Given N rigidly coupled cameras and n_k local 2d-3d correspondences $(\boldsymbol{x}_{k,i}, \boldsymbol{X}_{k,i})_{i=1,\ldots,n_k}$ for the k-th camera, the local poses are first computed from individual monocular SfM, and then converted to the dual quaternion representation $(q_k, q_k', \boldsymbol{q}_k, \boldsymbol{q}_k')_{k=1,\ldots,N}$ as described in sec. 2.1. Similar to the relative pose problem, the rigid motion constraint can be enforced by simply averaging the scalar parts in the constrained parametrization $(q, q', \boldsymbol{q}_1, \boldsymbol{q}_1', \ldots, \boldsymbol{q}_N, \boldsymbol{q}_N')$. This parametrization is again not optimal with respect to the reprojection error, but is instead used as an initial solution for minimization of the joint error function $\sum_{k=1}^{N} \sum_{i=1}^{n_k} f_{k,i}^{\text{reproj}}(q, q', \boldsymbol{q}_k, \boldsymbol{q}_k')$ where

$$f_{k,i}^{\text{reproj}}(q, q', \boldsymbol{q}_k, \boldsymbol{q}_k') = \|\mathbf{P}(\mathbf{R}(\boldsymbol{q}_k, -q)[\boldsymbol{X}_{k,i} - \boldsymbol{t}((\boldsymbol{q}_k, q), (\boldsymbol{q}_k', q'))]) - \mathbf{P}(\boldsymbol{x}_{k,i})\|^2 \tag{10}$$

Enforcing the unit length constraint for all dual quaternions in nonlinear optimization of (10) using the Levenberg-Marquardt algorithm is again achieved by the minimal parametrization discussed in 2.1, or renormalizing the parameters.

3.3 Registration and Global Reconstruction

As soon as we have computed local poses that are suitable for eye-to-eye calibration – i.e. the angle between the rotation axes of the first and current motion is above a threshold θ for each camera [17] – the eye-to-eye transformations $\Delta \mathbf{T}_k$ between k-th camera and master camera can be estimated. It is convenient to use a dual quaternion based approach [3] but any approach could be used.

After eye-to-eye calibration the local 3d reconstructions can be merged into a global reconstruction, and optimized by a multi-camera bundle adjustment as described in [11]. This approach refines the reprojection error with respect to 3d points, master camera poses, and eye-to-eye transformations – ensuring that the resulting camera poses satisfy the rigid motion constraint.

Afterwards, SfM can proceed using an approach with known eye-to-eye transformations such as [8] to enhance the stability of the pose tracking. The eye-to-eye transformations can be further refined over time.

4 Tests and Evaluation

4.1 Relative and Absolute Pose Estimation

First we evaluated relative and absolute pose estimation with and without rigid motion constraint enforcement (RMCE) for a large number of random configurations (1000/test) for $N = 2$ cameras with 1 cm distance and $30 - 120°$ rotation difference. Gaussian noise with $\sigma \approx 0.2\%$ image size was added to all points. The *Gold Standard* methods were used for decoupled pose estimation [6]. Relative poses were scaled using the pitch constraint while the master translation length was fixed to 1 m. Fig. 3 shows that the average estimation error improves for absolute rotation estimation, and in general when the number of correspondences is < 15. We also conducted tests with increasing number of cameras and minimal parameters vs. renormalization but the results did not change significantly.

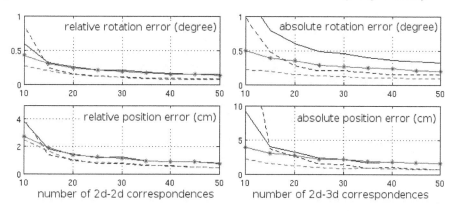

Fig. 3. Average relative/absolute pose error per camera and test, w/o RMCE (upper black line) and with RMCE (lower red line, dashed lines show standard deviation)

To evaluate the impact on eye-to-eye calibration, we further estimated $M = 3, \ldots, 8$ poses with and w/o RMCE and computed the eye-to-eye transformation between $N = 2$ cameras using the method from [3]. The average results for 1000 random datasets per number of poses are improved as shown in fig. 4.

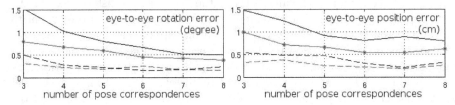

Fig. 4. Average eye-to-eye calibration error from increasing number of random poses estimated w/o RMCE (upper black line) and with RMCE (lower red line)

4.2   Structure from Motion with Rendered Video

The full SfM approach from 4.1 (i.e. without bundle adjustment) with and without RMCE is tested first with a rendered image sequence of a scene consisting of textured boxes. The camera system contains $N = 2$ cameras that are set 25 cm and 15° apart. The motion trajectory covers ca. 1.5 m and 60° rotation. Note that we use a very similar setup as the real scenario in sec. 4.3. Feature points are detected and tracked in subsequent images using a KLT tracker [16]. Relative pose estimation is performed between the 1 and 21st image, followed by absolute pose estimation every 20 images. The relative poses are scaled as in the previous test. Fig. 5 shows that the accuracy of pose estimation is improved by RMCE, especially pose drift over time is counteracted. Eye-to-eye calibration is performed afterwards using every 20-th image. The calibration error is improved from 1.21° and 1.9 cm w/o RMCE to 0.49° and 1.27 cm for this setup.

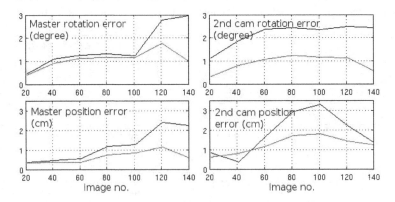

Fig. 5. Pose error during SfM w/o RMCE (upper black line) and with RMCE (lower red line) for a rendered video sequence (total motion covers ca. 1.5m, 60°)

4.3   Structure from Motion with Real Video

A real video sequence was captured with a stereo camera setup consisting of $N = 2$ cameras mounted onto a rig with ca. 24.5 cm $\pm$ 0.8 horizontal offset and $17.2 \pm 0.62°$ rotation difference, viewing a box scene similar to the virtual test case in sec. 4.2 (see example image in fig. 7). Note that we use a setup with partly overlapping views to recover extrinsics for comparison using a default stereo calibration approach. The proposed SfM procedure was applied for every 10-th image and eye-to-eye calibration was computed afterwards from every 20-th estimated local pose pair. The difference between stereo calibration and eye-to-eye calibration is $0.71°$, 4.1 cm w/o RMCE, and $0.54°$, 2.5 cm with RMCE. Fig. 6 shows how much the rigid motion constraint between master and 2nd camera is violated during unconstrained SfM, especially over time.

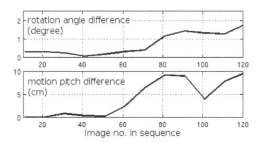 

Fig. 6. Rigid motion constraint violation during SfM w/o RMCE for a real video sequence (total motion covers ca. 1m, 50°)

Fig. 7. Example image from real video sequence

5   Conclusions

In this work we have revisited rigid motion constraints for local pose estimation of rigidly coupled cameras, and described how to incorporate these constraints into existing SfM algorithms. The resulting constrained local poses have been shown to be more robust against drift and improve extrinsic calibration of the multi-camera setup using calibration methods that depend on the rigid motion constraints. Especially SfM resp. extrinsic calibration with few input poses benefits from the constraint enforcement. The results presented here are very useful for systems consisting of few cameras covering the full 360° field of view.

Future Work. The results presented in this work are designed for general motions of the camera system. Further inspection of common degenerate motion classes such as planar motion could be done to modify the multi-camera SfM so that these cases can also be handled by integrating additional knowledge about the scene and motion. Although we have presented a very basic SfM approach here for the sake of clarity, we should also be able to integrate our method easily into more sophisticated and efficient SfM approaches such as e.g. PTAM [9].

References

1. Caspi, Y., Irani, M.: Alignment of non-overlapping sequences. International Journal of Computer Vision 48(1), 39–51 (2002)
2. Chen, H.H.: A screw motion approach to uniqueness analysis of head-eye geometry. In: Computer Vision and Pattern Recognition, CVPR 1991, pp. 145–151 (1991)
3. Daniilidis, K.: Hand-eye calibration using dual quaternions. International Journal of Robotics Research 18, 286–298 (1999)
4. Dornaika, F., Chung, C.K.R.: Stereo geometry from 3d ego-motion streams. IEEE Transactions on Systems, Man, and Cybernetics, Part B: Cybernetics 33(2), 308–323 (2003)
5. Esquivel, S., Woelk, F., Koch, R.: Calibration of a multi-camera rig from non-overlapping views. In: Hamprecht, F.A., Schnörr, C., Jähne, B. (eds.) DAGM 2007. LNCS, vol. 4713, pp. 82–91. Springer, Heidelberg (2007)
6. Hartley, R.I., Zisserman, A.: Multiple View Geometry in Computer Vision, 2nd edn. Cambridge University Press (2004)
7. Kim, J.H., Li, H., Hartley, R.I.: Motion estimation for nonoverlapping multicamera rigs: Linear algebraic and l_∞ geometric solutions. IEEE Transactions on Pattern Analysis and Machine Intelligence 32(6), 1044–1059 (2010)
8. Kim, J.H., Chung, M.J.: Absolute motion and structure from stereo image sequences without stereo correspondence and analysis of degenerate cases. Pattern Recognition 39(9), 1649–1661 (2006)
9. Klein, G., Murray, D.: Parallel tracking and mapping for small AR workspaces. In: 6th IEEE and ACM International Symposium on Mixed and Augmented Reality, ISMAR 2007 (2007)
10. Kuipers, J.B.: Quaternions and rotation sequences. In: International Conference on Geometry. In: International Conference on Geometry, Integrability and Quantization, GEOM 1999, pp. 127–143 (1999)
11. Lébraly, P., Royer, E., Ait-Aider, O., Deymier, C., Dhome, M.: Fast calibration of embedded non-overlapping cameras. In: IEEE International Conference on Robotics and Automation, Shanghai, China, pp. 221–227 (May 2011)
12. Luong, Q.T., Faugeras, O.: Self-calibration of a stereo rig from unknown camera motions and point correspondences (1993)
13. Moré, J.J.: The Levenberg-Marquardt algorithm: Implementation and theory. Numerical Analysis 630, 105–116 (1978)
14. Schmidt, J., Niemann, H.: Using quaternions for parametrizing 3-d rotations in unconstrained nonlinear optimization. In: Vision, Modeling, and Visualization, VMV 2001, Stuttgart, Germany, pp. 399–406 (2001)
15. Shao, L., Walker, M.W.: Estimating 3-d location parameters using dual number quaternions. In: Computer Vision, Graphics, and Image Processing (CVGIP): Image Understanding, vol. 54 (3), pp. 358–367 (1991)
16. Tomasi, C., Kanade, T.: Detection and tracking of point features. Tech. Rep. CMU-CS-91-132, Carnegie Mellon University (1991)
17. Tsai, R.Y., Lenz, R.K.: A new technique for fully autonomous and efficient 3d robotics hand/eye calibration. IEEE Transactions on Robotics and Automation 5(3), 345–358 (1989)
18. Weng, J., Huang, T.S.: Complete structure and motion from two monocular sequences without stereo correspondence. In: International Conference on Pattern Recognition, ICPR 1992, pp. 651–654 (1992)
19. Zisserman, A., Beardsley, P.A., Reid, I.D.: Metric calibration of a stereo rig. In: IEEE Workshop on Representations of Visual Scenes, pp. 16–23 (1995)

Highly Accurate Depth Estimation for Objects at Large Distances

Peter Pinggera[1,2], Uwe Franke[1], and Rudolf Mester[2,3]

[1] Environment Perception, Daimler R&D, Sindelfingen, Germany
[2] VSI Lab, Computer Science Dept., Goethe University Frankfurt, Germany
[3] Computer Vision Laboratory, Dept. EE, Linköping University, Sweden

Abstract. Precise stereo-based depth estimation at large distances is challenging: objects become very small, often exhibit low contrast in the image, and can hardly be separated from the background based on disparity due to measurement noise. In this paper we present an approach that overcomes these problems by combining robust object segmentation and highly accurate depth and motion estimation. The segmentation criterion is formulated as a probabilistic combination of disparity, optical flow and image intensity that is optimized using graph cuts. Segmentation and segment parameter models for the different cues are iteratively refined in an Expectation-Maximization scheme. Experiments on real-world traffic scenes demonstrate the accuracy of segmentation and disparity results for vehicles at distances of up to 180 meters. The proposed approach outperforms state-of-the-art stereo methods, achieving an average object disparity RMS error below 0.1 pixel, at typical object sizes of less than 15x15 pixels.

1 Introduction

In safety-relevant driver assistance applications it is crucial to detect traffic participants at maximum distances and to estimate their depth and motion as accurately as possible. Stereo vision has become a key sensor in intelligent vehicles, and typical sensor configurations (with baselines of 30 cm and resolutions of 20 px/°) allow reliable object distance measurements up to approximately 100 m.

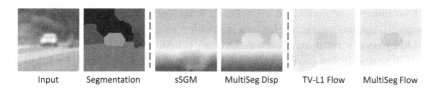

Input   Segmentation   sSGM   MultiSeg Disp   TV-L1 Flow   MultiSeg Flow

Fig. 1. Example of a car at approx. 150 m distance with a width of 15 px. Our multi-cue approach yields a correct segmentation of object and background as well as an accurate local disparity map ('MultiSeg Disp') and flow field ('MultiSeg Flow') compared to subpixel smoothed SGM ('sSGM') [12] and TV-L1 Flow [20]. (Best viewed in color)

J. Weickert, M. Hein, and B. Schiele (Eds.): GCPR 2013, LNCS 8142, pp. 21–30, 2013.
© Springer-Verlag Berlin Heidelberg 2013

While this is sufficient for traffic at moderate speeds, a range of up to 200 m is required for high speed scenarios, e.g. on highways. Fig. 1 illustrates an example: a car at a distance of 150 m has a size of 15x12 pixels and a stereo disparity of roughly 2.5 pixels, which differs from the background disparity by less than one pixel. Here the smoothness constraints of modern dense disparity estimation schemes such as Semi-Global Matching [14] hinder the clear distinction of separate objects. Extensions have been proposed to reduce this effect, for example by discontinuity-preserving disparity smoothing [12]. However, in this work we argue that measuring depth and motion at such distances requires a combination of precise object segmentation and disparity estimation. The estimation of parametric displacement models inside of image segments helps to prevent oversmoothing of small objects, sharpens object boundaries and increases sub-pixel accuracy through optimized local support regions and strong regularization.

Image segmentation has widely been applied as a method to improve the accuracy of dense disparity as well as optical flow estimation. In the area of stereo computation, recent work includes [9], where high sub-pixel accuracy by iterative segmentation and parameter estimation based on a given global disparity map and color segmentation is demonstrated. In [3], a joint stereo matching and object segmentation approach is proposed, describing each object by a plane in disparity space and a color model by fusing various segmentation and model parameter proposals. In optical flow estimation, recent work demonstrates improvements in accuracy by using motion segmentation, especially in the case of rigidly moving objects [19,21].

While such approaches achieve good results in their respective setting, most depend on the availability of a single reliable segmentation cue (color, motion), or a high quality initialization of disparity map or flow field. These conditions are not fulfilled for traffic scenes at large distances, which are the focus of this work. One method to reduce such dependencies in segmentation tasks is the combination of multiple cues. Early work combining both motion and disparity for segmentation showed promising results on synthetic stereo images [1]. Several authors have since demonstrated the benefit of combining multiple cues in video segmentation, however not with a focus on high accuracy disparity or flow estimation [4,8,16].

In this work, we present an approach for the combination of robust multi-cue object segmentation and highly accurate disparity and optical flow estimation. We formulate disparity, optical flow and image intensity as random fields and state a combined segmentation criterion in a Bayesian framework. The need for heuristically chosen weighting factors is avoided as each of the cues is implicitly weighted by its discriminative power. To simultaneously solve for both image segmentation and segment parameter models of disparity, optical flow and intensity, we employ an iterative Expectation-Maximization (EM) algorithm. We further show how priors from global disparity and flow algorithms can be integrated to additionally increase robustness. The proposed method yields high quality segmentation results and highly accurate disparity estimates, as we demonstrate on challenging real-world data.

2   Probabilistic Iterative Multi-cue Segmentation

Given two rectified image pairs of a stereo video sequence at times t and $t-1$, we consider a rectangular image patch around a selected object of interest as input to our algorithm. An object of interest can be determined by either using an appearance-based object detector, or by complementary sensors such as radar. Our goal is to find a precise binary segmentation of the image patch, separating the object from the background, and at the same time to perform an accurate estimation of the disparity of the object. However, in the considered scenes the background cannot be described accurately by a single disparity, optical flow or intensity model — it requires a representation using several separate segments. An example can be seen in Fig. 1, where road plane, background vegetation and road infrastructure have to be distinguished for a correct representation of the scene. Each segment k is described by its pixel support Ω_k, parametric models for disparity d_k and optical flow $\boldsymbol{v}_k$, as well as a non-parametric intensity model i_k.

We consider the different segmentation cues as realizations of independent random fields with the respective probability densities $p(\boldsymbol{v}|\ell)$, $p(d|\ell)$ and $p(i|\ell)$, dependent on the segmentation or image labeling ℓ. While the assumption of independence between disparity and optical flow will not hold in general scenes, we assume it to be approximately fulfilled in our case of very small disparity ranges, where flow magnitudes are dominated by rotational camera motion and independent object motion. The posterior probability distribution of all possible labelings can then be described in a Bayesian manner:

$$p(\ell|\boldsymbol{v},d,i) = \frac{p(\boldsymbol{v},d,i|\ell)\cdot p(\ell)}{p(\boldsymbol{v},d,i)} \cong \frac{p(\boldsymbol{v}|\ell)\cdot p(d|\ell)\cdot p(i|\ell)\cdot p(\ell)}{p(\boldsymbol{v})\cdot p(d)\cdot p(i)} . \qquad (1)$$

The sought-for segmentation corresponds to the MAP estimate of ℓ. We employ an EM scheme to iteratively refine both the segmentation and the respective segment parameters.

Disparity and Optical Flow as Random Fields
To formulate optical flow $\boldsymbol{v}$ and disparity d directly as random fields with parametric probability distributions, we apply the approach used by [10] and [18] for pure motion segmentation. Based on the brightness constancy assumption between corresponding pixels and the well-known linearized flow error [15], the deviation of the observed flow $\tilde{\boldsymbol{v}}_k(\boldsymbol{x})$ from its unknown true value $\boldsymbol{v}_k(\boldsymbol{x})$ at pixel $\boldsymbol{x} = [x\ y]$ of segment k is modeled as a normally distributed random variable: $\tilde{\boldsymbol{v}}_k(\boldsymbol{x}) = \boldsymbol{v}_k(\boldsymbol{x}) + \mathcal{N}(0,\boldsymbol{\sigma}_{v_k}^2)$. Plugging this formulation into the linearized flow and the corresponding disparity error equations [15] yields the probability densities $p(\boldsymbol{v}_k|\ell)$ and $p(d_k|\ell)$ for flow and disparity, with variances $\sigma_{v_k}^2$ and $\sigma_{d_k}^2$, given the image segmentation ℓ. Denoting the image gradient as $\boldsymbol{g} = [g_x\ g_y]^T$ and intensity differences between video frames and stereo images at each pixel as I_t and I_s, respectively, yields

$$p(\boldsymbol{v}_k|\ell) = \frac{1}{\sqrt{2\pi\sigma_{v_k}^2}} \cdot \exp\left(-\frac{(\boldsymbol{g}^T\boldsymbol{v}_k + I_t)^2}{2 \cdot |\boldsymbol{g}_v|^2 \cdot \sigma_{v_k}^2}\right), \quad \sigma_{v_k}^2 = \frac{1}{|\Omega_k|} \cdot \sum_{\Omega_k} \frac{(\boldsymbol{g}^T\boldsymbol{v}_k + I_t)^2}{|\boldsymbol{g}_v|^2}, \quad (2)$$

$$p(d_k|\ell) = \frac{1}{\sqrt{2\pi\sigma_{d_k}^2}} \cdot \exp\left(-\frac{(g_x d_k + I_s)^2}{2 \cdot |g_x|^2 \cdot \sigma_{v_k}^2}\right), \quad \sigma_{d_k}^2 = \frac{1}{|\Omega_k|} \cdot \sum_{\Omega_k} \frac{(g_x d_k + I_s)^2}{|g_x|^2}. \quad (3)$$

The terms $|\boldsymbol{g}_v|$ and $|g_x|$ represent the image gradient magnitudes in the direction of the estimated optical flow and disparity, respectively.

Intensity Distribution

We describe the intensity model of each segment by a non-parametric probability distribution $p(i_k|\ell)$, which can in general have multiple modes. A kernel density estimation is used to approximate the intensity distributions from the segment support regions Ω_k.

2.1   Segmentation

The MAP estimate labeling $\ell^* = \arg\max_\ell(p(\ell|\boldsymbol{v}, d, i))$ is determined by minimizing the respective negative log-likelihood, i.e. the negative logarithm of $p(\ell|\boldsymbol{v}, d, i)$ as defined in Eq. (1). The constant denominator has no influence on the location of the minimum and can be dropped. This negative log-likelihood can be written as an energy of the common form $E = E_{data} + \gamma \cdot E_{prior}$, where the parameter γ is used to balance data and prior terms.

Within the data term E_{data}, the variances of the disparity and flow model of each segment serve as implicit inverse weighting factors. Considering Eq. (2) and (3), the displacement estimates of homogeneous image segments will in general tend to have higher variances and therefore less influence on the location of the energy minimum. Conversely, such segments will show more discriminative peaks in their intensity distributions, and vice versa.

Using a Markov Random Field model, we choose a common contrast-sensitive cost function for the prior energy E_{prior} as in [7]. This encourages smoothness in homogeneous regions and label discontinuities at high image gradients.

To efficiently compute a high quality approximate solution to the energy minimization problem we use the graph cut approach of [5,6].

2.2   Parameter Update

Given the result of the segmentation step, the parameters of each segment are updated. To parametrize flow and disparity, either a translational or an affine parameter model is assigned to each segment. We use affine parameter models to approximate slanted surfaces in the world which cannot be reduced to fronto-parallel planes even at large distances.

In the following we describe the estimation procedure for the optical flow parameters ϑ_k. All results can be simply transferred to the case of one-dimensional displacement for the disparity parameters.

The optical flow vector at each pixel is given as $v_k(x) = C(x)\vartheta_k$ with

$$C_{affine}(x) = \begin{bmatrix} x & y & 1 & 0 & 0 & 0 \\ 0 & 0 & 0 & x & y & 1 \end{bmatrix} \qquad C_{transl} = \begin{bmatrix} 1 & 0 \\ 0 & 1 \end{bmatrix} \qquad (4)$$

$$\vartheta_{affine,k} = \begin{bmatrix} \vartheta_{1,k} & \cdots & \vartheta_{6,k} \end{bmatrix}^T \qquad \vartheta_{transl,k} = \begin{bmatrix} v_{x,k} & v_{y,k} \end{bmatrix}^T . \qquad (5)$$

Plugging this formulation into the energy formulation described in Section 2.1, setting the respective partial derivative to zero and solving for ϑ_k yields the closed form solution $\vartheta_k = A^{-1}b$ with

$$A = \sum_{\Omega_k} \frac{C^T gg^T C}{|g_v|^2} \qquad b = -\sum_{\Omega_k} \frac{C^T g \cdot I_t}{|g_v|^2} . \qquad (6)$$

For higher accuracy we follow [17] and perform several iterations of the parameter estimation step by successively warping one image with the current parameter estimates ϑ_k and computing the additive parameter updates $\vartheta_k \leftarrow \vartheta_k^- + \Delta\vartheta_k$. Convergence is attained when $\Delta\vartheta_k$ falls below a specified threshold.

Finally, the variances of the parameter models of each segment are estimated according to Eq. (2) and (3).

The updates of the non-parametric intensity models $p(i_k|\ell)$ are simply computed from the intensity values of the pixel support of each segment.

3   Improved Robustness and Accuracy

3.1   Global Priors

Computing local displacement parameter estimates can yield erroneous results in homogeneous image areas. Fig. 2 shows an example where the segment parameter solution diverges in the featureless regions of the road plane. Here global correspondence algorithms benefit from strong regularization, propagating values from more reliable image areas outside the local image patch.

Hence, we describe how prior flow, provided by dense global algorithms such as [20], can be included into our approach to constrain the local parameter solution (analogous for disparity). To integrate the prior flow results $\hat{v}$ into our probabilistic model, $p(v|\ell)$ in Eq. (1) is replaced by $p(v|\hat{v}, \ell)$:

$$p(v|\hat{v}, \ell) = \frac{p(\hat{v}|v, \ell) \cdot p(v|\ell)}{p(\hat{v}|\ell)} . \qquad (7)$$

The term $p(\hat{v}|v, \ell)$ represents the likelihood of the prior flow $\hat{v}$ being in accordance with the locally computed values v. Since the prior flow is independent of the segmentation, the constant factor $p(\hat{v}|\ell)$ can be dropped in the optimization. Formulating $p(\hat{v}|v, \ell)$ as a Gaussian distribution with mean v allows to use its variance $\sigma_{\hat{v}}^2(x) = \begin{bmatrix} \sigma_{\hat{v}_x}^2(x) & \sigma_{\hat{v}_y}^2(x) \end{bmatrix}^T$ to define the desired influence of the prior,

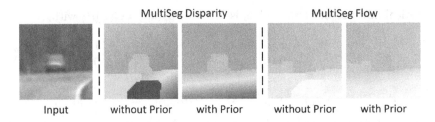

Fig. 2. Integrating priors from global algorithms prevents diverging local disparity and flow estimates in featureless regions such as the road plane

depending on the image gradient magnitude $|g|$ at each pixel, normalized by its local mean $|\widetilde{g}|$:

$$\sigma_{\hat{v}_x}^2(\boldsymbol{x}) = \alpha_{prior} \cdot \left(\frac{|g_x|}{|\widetilde{g}_x|} + 1\right)^2, \qquad \sigma_{\hat{v}_y}^2(\boldsymbol{x}) = \alpha_{prior} \cdot \left(\frac{|g_y|}{|\widetilde{g}_y|} + 1\right)^2. \qquad (8)$$

This rather heuristic choice is motivated by the desire that in homogeneous regions with low image gradients the confidence in the global prior should be higher than in the locally computed parameters while at object edges and in structured regions the local solution should be allowed to deviate from the prior. Performing a first order Taylor expansion on the prior terms and solving for the flow parameters as in Section 2.2 then yields

$$A = \sum_{\Omega_k} \left(\frac{C^T g g^T C}{|g_v|^2 \cdot \sigma_{v_k}^2} + \frac{C^T f_x f_x^T C}{\sigma_{\hat{v}_x}^2} + \frac{C^T f_y f_y^T C}{\sigma_{\hat{v}_y}^2} \right) \qquad (9)$$

$$b = -\sum_{\Omega_k} \left(\frac{C^T g \cdot I_t}{|g_v|^2 \cdot \sigma_{v_k}^2} + \frac{C^T f_x \cdot (\hat{v}_x - v_{x,k}^-)}{\sigma_{\hat{v}_x}^2} + \frac{C^T f_y \cdot (\hat{v}_y - v_{y,k}^-)}{\sigma_{\hat{v}_y}^2} \right) \qquad (10)$$

with $f_x = \begin{bmatrix} -1 \\ 0 \end{bmatrix}$, $f_y = \begin{bmatrix} 0 \\ -1 \end{bmatrix}$, and flow results v_k^- of the previous iteration.
This represents a least squares parameter solution with priors similar to the one in [2] but with additional adaptive weighting factors depending on both $\sigma_{v_k}^2$ and the selected $\sigma_{\hat{v}}^2(\boldsymbol{x})$.

3.2   Robust Estimation

A further increase in robustness can be achieved by using Laplacian distributions to model errors in the segment parameter estimates. The resulting L1 error norms are less sensitive to outliers than the L2 error norms related to Gaussian distributions. Integrating this modification into the parameter update yields an iteratively reweighted least squares solution for the displacement parameters with adaptively weighted priors:

$$A = \sum_{\Omega_k} \left(\frac{C^T g g^T C}{|g_v| \cdot b_{v_k} \cdot |I_t|} + \frac{C^T f_x f_x^T C}{b_{\hat{v}_x} \cdot |\hat{v}_x - v_{x,k}^-|} + \frac{C^T f_y f_y^T C}{b_{\hat{v}_y} \cdot |\hat{v}_y - v_{y,k}^-|} \right) \qquad (11)$$

$$b = -\sum_{\Omega_k} \left(\frac{C^T g \cdot I_t}{|g_v| \cdot b_{v_k} \cdot |I_t|} + \frac{C^T f_x \cdot (\hat{v}_x - v_{x,k}^-)}{b_{\hat{v}_x} \cdot |\hat{v}_x - v_{x,k}^-|} + \frac{C^T f_y \cdot (\hat{v}_y - v_{y,k}^-)}{b_{\hat{v}_y} \cdot |\hat{v}_y - v_{y,k}^-|} \right) . \quad (12)$$

For the scale parameter $b_{\hat{v}}(x) = \begin{bmatrix} b_{\hat{v}_x}(x) & b_{\hat{v}_y}(x) \end{bmatrix}^T$ the squares in Eq. (8) are simply replaced by absolute values.

3.3 Parameter Refinement

After the segmentation algorithm has converged, a final parameter refinement step is performed. For highest sensitivity and sub-pixel accuracy in the proximity of the solution, the gradient-based normalization of Eq. (6) and the robust extensions employed during segmentation are removed. The refinement of the final parameters then corresponds to the solution of the original formulation of [17] with optimized support regions and initial values.

4 Experimental Results

To evaluate the performance of our proposed approach, we test it on challenging real-world stereo data of traffic scenes recorded from a moving vehicle. The camera setup has a focal length of 1,253 pixels with a baseline of 33 cm.

In a first step we apply a sliding-window vehicle detector, based on the NN/LRF classifier approach of [11], to select objects of interest and provide image patches as input to our algorithm. As an initialization for the segmentation, the image patches are split into a regular pattern of nine non-overlapping squares with translational displacement models and four larger overlapping regions with affine parameter models. To include priors as described in Section 3.1, global dense disparity maps and flow fields are computed based on [13] and [20], respectively. The initial displacement values of all segments are simply set to zero since the parameters are pulled towards meaningful values by the global priors in the first iteration.

A qualitative assessment shows that our proposed probabilistic multi-cue approach yields good segmentation results even on challenging scenes where single-cue approaches have major difficulties. Fig. 3 depicts two examples where the combination of multiple cues leads to a significant improvement of segmentation quality. Segmentation errors are observable only in rare cases where none of the different cues is sufficiently discriminative.

The computed disparity maps and optical flow fields show valid scene structure and sharp object boundaries, as can be seen in Fig. 1, 2 and 3.

Focusing on the computed disparity results, we perform a quantitative evaluation using a reference radar sensor. Radar measurements of distances of oncoming and leading traffic are very accurate and provide an appropriate quasi-groundtruth for the computed disparity. As a test data set we use 14 stereo sequences with a total of 1,000 frames. In each sequence, the disparity values of one leading vehicle in a distance range between 100 m and 180 m are computed

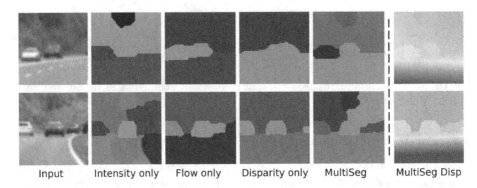

| Input | Intensity only | Flow only | Disparity only | MultiSeg | MultiSeg Disp |

Fig. 3. Combining multiple cues ('MultiSeg') yields good segmentation results on challenging data, in contrast to using separate cues only. The center segment considered as the object of interest is shown in green. The corresponding computed disparity maps are shown on the right.

for every frame. To minimize the influence of errors in the extrinsic camera parameters, a possible disparity bias is estimated on a second data set. This data set consists of 1800 frames of comparatively close range (50 m - 100 m) leading vehicles. We use sub-pixel smoothed SGM ('sSGM') [12] as well as a standard 1D-KLT fixed window disparity computation [17], where KLT window sizes are set appropriately as to not include any background pixels. The bias estimated using both methods differs by only 0.02 pixels, with an average of 0.37 pixels.

In both data sets, only vehicles close to the image center are considered to avoid errors caused by deviations in the estimated intrinsic camera parameters.

Table 1 shows the average RMS disparity error of the proposed algorithm ('MultiSeg') over the test data set. For comparison we show the corresponding results of sSGM [12] and fixed window KLT stereo [17]. The window for KLT computation is set to the location and size returned by the car detector, sSGM object disparity is computed as the median of the dense disparities over this window. The MultiSeg image patch input is set to twice the KLT window size. The results of sSGM and KLT are very similar, with errors of 0.15 and 0.13 pixels, respectively. MultiSeg outperforms both methods with an average RMS error of only 0.08 pixels.

Aside from the absolute error values, another key aspect is the use of disparity measurements to estimate the velocity of moving objects. In this case, the

Table 1. Average disparity RMS errors for 14 sequences with vehicles at distances from 100 m to 180 m, over a total of 1,000 frames. The proposed approach ('MultiSeg') clearly outperforms sub-pixel smoothed SGM ('sSGM') and fixed window KLT stereo.

	sSGM	KLT	MultiSeg
RMS error [px]	0.15	0.13	0.08

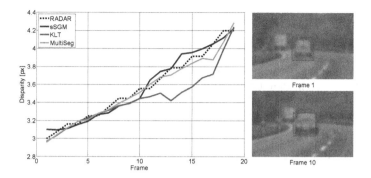

Fig. 4. Estimated disparity over time of an oncoming car compared to reference radar data. The steps visible in the radar signal are caused by asynchronous sensor readout. Structured background in the KLT patch (red) causes a drift beginning at frame 10, while our segmentation-based approach (green) is unaffected. Note that the disparity deviation of the KLT result at frame 13 corresponds to a distance error of over 10 m.

temporal continuity of the disparity values is crucial. Fig. 4 depicts an example of the disparity results of an oncoming car compared to a reference radar signal over time. Our segmentation-based approach closely follows the radar signal throughout the sequence, whereas interfering background features cause a significant drift in the standard fixed window KLT results.

5   Conclusion

In this paper we presented a probabilistic multi-cue segmentation formulation that allows for a highly accurate estimation of depth and motion in large-distance stereo sequences. We combined parametric disparity, optical flow and non-parametric intensity distributions to robustly and accurately segment objects using graph cuts. The formulation of the segmentation criterion does not require additional weighting factors since the individual cues are implicitly scaled by their discriminative power. Segmentation and segment parameter estimates are iteratively refined in an EM scheme. We further proposed extensions to improve robustness by adding priors from globally computed disparity maps and flow fields as well as by the use of robust distributions. Combining the segmentation results with a parameter refinement step yields highly accurate disparity and optical flow estimates. Tests on real-world traffic scenes show that the proposed multi-cue segmentation performs well where single-cue methods have major difficulties. In a quantitative evaluation using reference radar data, an average object disparity RMS error of less than 0.1 pixels is achieved.

Future work includes the temporal coupling of segmentation and parameter estimation over several video frames as well as an extension to object tracking.

Acknowledgements. Author R. Mester is currently with Linköping University, funded by the ELLIIT programme of the Swedish government.

References

1. Altunbasak, Y., Tekalp, A.M., Bozdagi, G.: Simultaneous Motion-Disparity Estimation and Segmentation from Stereo. In: Proc. ICIP (1994)
2. Baker, S., Gross, R., Matthews, I.: Lucas-Kanade 20 Years On: A Unifying Framework: Part 4. Tech. Rep. CMU-RI-TR-04-14, Carnegie Mellon Univ. (2004)
3. Bleyer, M., Rother, C., Kohli, P., et al.: Object Stereo - Joint Stereo Matching and Object Segmentation. In: Proc. CVPR (2011)
4. Boltz, S., Herbulot, A., Debreuve, E., et al.: Motion and Appearance Nonparametric Joint Entropy for Video Segmentation. IJCV 80(2), 242–259 (2008)
5. Boykov, Y., Kolmogorov, V.: An Experimental Comparison of Min-Cut/Max-Flow Algorithms for Energy Minimization in Vision. TPAMI 26(9), 1124–1137 (2004)
6. Boykov, Y., Veksler, O., Zabih, R.: Fast Approximate Energy Minimization via Graph Cuts. TPAMI 23(11), 1222–1239 (2001)
7. Boykov, Y., Funka-Lea, G.: Graph Cuts and Efficient N-D Image Segmentation. IJCV 70(2), 109–131 (2006)
8. Brox, T., Rousson, M., Deriche, R., et al.: Colour, Texture, and Motion in Level Set Based Segmentation and Tracking. IVC 28(3), 376–390 (2010)
9. Chang, Y.J., Liu, H.H., Chen, T.: Improving Sub-Pixel Stereo Matching with Segment Evolution. In: Proc. ICIP (2010)
10. Cremers, D., Yuille, A.: A Generative Model Based Approach to Motion Segmentation. In: Michaelis, B., Krell, G. (eds.) DAGM 2003. LNCS, vol. 2781, pp. 313–320. Springer, Heidelberg (2003)
11. Enzweiler, M., Gavrila, D.M.: Monocular Pedestrian Detection: Survey and Experiments. TPAMI 31(12), 2179–2195 (2009)
12. Gehrig, S.K., Badino, H., Franke, U.: Improving Stereo Sub-Pixel Accuracy for Long Range Stereo. CVIU 116(1), 16–24 (2012)
13. Gehrig, S.K., Eberli, F., Meyer, T.: A Real-Time Low-Power Stereo Vision Engine Using Semi-Global Matching. In: Fritz, M., Schiele, B., Piater, J.H. (eds.) ICVS 2009. LNCS, vol. 5815, pp. 134–143. Springer, Heidelberg (2009)
14. Hirschmüller, H.: Accurate and Efficient Stereo Processing by Semi-Global Matching and Mutual Information. In: Proc. CVPR (2005)
15. Horn, B.K.P., Schunck, B.G.: Determining Optical Flow. Artificial Intelligence 17(1), 185–203 (1981)
16. Khan, S., Shah, M.: Object Based Segmentation of Video Using Color, Motion and Spatial Information. In: Proc. CVPR (2001)
17. Lucas, B.D., Kanade, T.: An Iterative Image Registration Technique with an Application to Stereo Vision. In: Proc. Int. Joint Conf. on Artificial Intel. (1981)
18. Schoenemann, T., Cremers, D.: Near Real-Time Motion Segmentation Using Graph Cuts. In: Franke, K., Müller, K.-R., Nickolay, B., Schäfer, R. (eds.) DAGM 2006. LNCS, vol. 4174, pp. 455–464. Springer, Heidelberg (2006)
19. Unger, M., Werlberger, M., Pock, T., et al.: Joint Motion Estimation and Segmentation of Complex Scenes with Label Costs and Occlusion Modeling. In: Proc. CVPR (2012)
20. Wedel, A., Pock, T., Zach, C., Bischof, H., Cremers, D.: An Improved Algorithm for TV-$L1$ Optical Flow. In: Cremers, D., Rosenhahn, B., Yuille, A.L., Schmidt, F.R. (eds.) Visual Motion Analysis. LNCS, vol. 5604, pp. 23–45. Springer, Heidelberg (2009)
21. Xu, L., Chen, J., Jia, J.: A Segmentation Based Variational Model for Accurate Optical Flow Estimation. In: Forsyth, D., Torr, P., Zisserman, A. (eds.) ECCV 2008, Part I. LNCS, vol. 5302, pp. 671–684. Springer, Heidelberg (2008)

A Low-Rank Constraint
for Parallel Stereo Cameras

Christian Cordes, Hanno Ackermann, and Bodo Rosenhahn

Leibniz University Hannover, Germany
{ccordes,ackermann,rosenhahn}@tnt.uni-hannover.de

Abstract. Stereo-camera systems enjoy wide popularity since they provide more restrictive constraints for 3d-reconstruction. Given an image sequence taken by parallel stereo cameras, a low-rank constraint is derived on the measurement data. Correspondences between left and right images are not necessary yet reduce the number of optimization parameters. Conversely, traditional algorithms for stereo factorization require *all* feature points in both images to be matched, otherwise left and right image streams need be factorized independently. The performance of the proposed algorithm will be evaluated on synthetic data as well as two real image applications.

1 Introduction

Image sequences taken by a stereo camera system are important input to many problems in computer vision. This article proposes a low-rank constraint on the feature trajectories which can be used in applications such as rigid or non-rigid 3d-reconstruction, motion segmentation or trajectory completion.

Given only two, three or four images taken by cameras in general configuration, 3D-reconstructions can be computed using the *epipolar constraint*. If the single-camera sequence consists of more than four images, a commonly employed heuristic is to estimate reconstructions from each two, three or four consecutive image segments, and use these to initialize a *bundle adjustment* [12].

The so-called *factorization algorithm* [11], conversely, is able to compute a 3d-reconstruction from arbitrary many images taken by *affine* cameras[1]. Its popularity stems from its simplicity: a matrix consisting of the feature points is factorized by means of a single *singular value decomposition*.

Generalizations exist to handle missing data [13,10] and uncalibrated projective cameras [5]. Low-rank constraints were also derived for multi-body [4] and non-rigid [2] 3D-reconstructions. Furthermore, algorithms resting on factorization also exist for other problems such as motion segmentation [7], trajectory completion as well as optical flow estimation [6].

---

[1] This model requires that the distance between camera and object is large as compared with the variation of depth within the scene. The requirement is necessary for any affine camera model, be it orthographic, weak-perspective, paraperspective or the more flexibel one proposed in [9]. For a comprehensive treatment on affine camera models confer to [8].

J. Weickert, M. Hein, and B. Schiele (Eds.): GCPR 2013, LNCS 8142, pp. 31–40, 2013.
© Springer-Verlag Berlin Heidelberg 2013

A factorization algorithm which estimates a 3d-reconstruction from non-rigidly deforming objects taken by a *convergent* stereo camera was proposed in [3]. However, *during the factorization stage*, this method need consider the two cameras separately if not all correspondences are known across left and right image streams. The stereo constraint is imposed only by means of a subsequent optimization. Given arbitrarily many, static camera rigs, a rank-12 constraint was derived in [1].

Both aforementioned works do not consider the case of missing data which naturally occurs due to tracking failure or scene occlusion. In this work, we consider a stereo setup of *parallel* cameras. In contrast to the algorithm proposed in [3] a low-rank constraint is derived which can be imposed *during the factorization stage*. As compared with the algorithm in [1], the low-rank constraint introduced here is significantly smaller leading to more robust estimates particularly in the presence of missing data.

The contributions made in this article can be summarized as follows:

- A *low-rank constraint* is derived assuming a pair of parallely-aligned stereo cameras.
- It can be imposed by means of *matrix factorization*.
- As significantly fewer variables are involved during factorization it is more robust with respect to noise and missing data.
- The proposed solution does not require correspondences between left and right images of the cameras. If available, these can be used to further reduce the degrees of freedom within the model.
- Missing correspondences can be handled.

The proposed solution will be evaluated quantitatively with synthetic data. We demonstrate the versatility of the algorithm by drawing on two real-image sequences. One application draws on rigid 3D-reconstruction while the other achieves trajectory completion given a scene in which several rigid bodies move independently from each other.

In Sec. 2 we will briefly review the factorization algorithm before deriving a low-rank constraint given stereo cameras in Sec. 3. The evaluation on synthetic data is presented in Sec. 4. Results of real-image experiments are demonstrated in Sec. 5. Lastly, we conclude this article with Sec. 6.

2   Rigid Factorization Algorithm

Given N 3D-points X_j, $j = 1, \ldots, N$ observed by M affine cameras P_i, $i = 1, \ldots, M$, the projection x_{ij} of the jth point into the ith image can be modelled by

$$x_{ij} = P_i X_j. \tag{1}$$

The difference to perspective projection is that equality holds in Eq. (1) whereas the latter implies equality up to scale, only.

Each affine projection matrix P_i can be decomposed into an 2×3 affine calibration matrix K_i, a 3×3 rotation matrix R_i indicating the orientation of the camera at image i, and a 3-vector t_i which implies the position of the camera

$$P_i = K_i \begin{bmatrix} R_i^{-1} & -R_i^{-1}t_i \end{bmatrix}. \tag{2}$$

The homogeneous vectors X_j indicate the x, y, and z-coordinates of the jth 3D-point. As model of the affine camera we assume weak-perspective projection. The matrices K_i then are defined by

$$K_i = s_i \begin{bmatrix} 1 & 0 & 0 \\ 0 & 1 & 0 \end{bmatrix} \tag{3}$$

where s_i denotes a scalar.

The projection of all 3D-points into all images can then be formulated as

$$\underbrace{\begin{bmatrix} x_{11} & \cdots & x_{1N} \\ \vdots & \ddots & \vdots \\ x_{M1} & \cdots & x_{MN} \end{bmatrix}}_{W^{2M \times N}} = \underbrace{\begin{bmatrix} P_1 \\ \vdots \\ P_M \end{bmatrix}}_{P^{2M \times 4}} \underbrace{\begin{bmatrix} X_1 & \cdots & X_N \end{bmatrix}}_{X^{4 \times N}} \tag{4}$$

$$\tag{5}$$

Assuming that the cameras are generally oriented and that the 3D-shape is not degenerate, the matrices P and X both have rank 4. This implies that the rank of matrix W cannot be larger than 4.

By means of singular value decomposition, we may therefore factorize W into

$$W = U \Sigma V^\top \tag{6}$$

where all but the largest four singular values on the diagonal of matrix Σ are identically zero. This idea was first proposed in [11] and is known as the factorization algorithm.

Consequently, matrices U and V can be truncated to those four vectors corresponding to the four non-zero singular values. Similarly, we truncate Σ to be of size 4×4. With a slight abuse of notation, denote these truncated matrices by U, Σ, and V in the following.

Affinely distorted estimates of P and X can be taken by U and $\Sigma V^\top$, respectively. To obtain undistorted estimates, a correcting matrix A need be determined by affine self calibration similarly to the self calibration step necessary for projective reconstruction.

3   Affine Stereo Factorization

3.1   A Low Rank Constraint on Parallel Stereo Cameras

Assume that we are given two affine cameras P^1 and P^2 parallelly oriented and with equal distance c to the center in between them. Further assume that this center is located in the origin of the world coordinate system.

If we align the camera orientations with the coordinate axes and take the basis line parallel to the x-axis we obtain

$$P^1 = K \begin{bmatrix} I & v \end{bmatrix} \quad \text{and} \quad P^2 = K \begin{bmatrix} I & -v \end{bmatrix} \tag{7}$$

where I denotes the identity matrix and $v = \begin{bmatrix} c & 0 & 0 \end{bmatrix}^{\top}$.

A rigid transformation of the stereo camera system by an rotation R_i and translation t_i amounts to multiplication with

$$H_i = \begin{bmatrix} R_i^{\top} & -R_i^{\top} t_i \\ \mathbf{0}^{\top} & 1 \end{bmatrix} \tag{8}$$

where $\mathbf{0}$ denotes a 3-vector consisting of zeros. For P_i^1 and P_i^2 we obtain

$$P_i^1 = K_i \begin{bmatrix} R_i^{\top} & -R_i^{\top} t_i + v \end{bmatrix} \quad \text{and} \quad P_i^2 = K_i \begin{bmatrix} R_i^{\top} & -R_i^{\top} t_i - v \end{bmatrix}. \tag{9}$$

By defining $t_i^1 = -R_i^{\top} t_i + v$ and $t_i^2 = -R_i^{\top} t_i - v$ we can simplify Eq. (9) to

$$P_i^1 = K_i \begin{bmatrix} R_i^{\top} & t_i^1 \end{bmatrix} \quad \text{and} \quad P_i^2 = K_i \begin{bmatrix} R_i^{\top} & t_i^2 \end{bmatrix}. \tag{10}$$

Let the *joint projection matrix* be

$$P_i = K_i \begin{bmatrix} R_i^{\top} & t_i^1 & t_i^2 \end{bmatrix}. \tag{11}$$

The projection of the jth 3D-point into the ith images can be expressed by

$$x_{ij}^1 = P_i \begin{bmatrix} X_j^{\top} & 1 & 0 \end{bmatrix}^{\top} \quad \text{and} \quad x_{ij}^2 = P_i \begin{bmatrix} X_j^{\top} & 0 & 1 \end{bmatrix}^{\top}. \tag{12}$$

Denote by W^1 and W^2 the matrices consisting of all feature points of the first and second images, respectively. We now arrive at the affine stereo constraint

$$\begin{bmatrix} W^1 & W^2 \end{bmatrix} = \begin{bmatrix} P_1 \\ \vdots \\ P_M \end{bmatrix} \begin{bmatrix} X_1 & \cdots & X_N & X_1 & \cdots & X_N \\ 1 & \cdots & 1 & 0 & \cdots & 0 \\ 0 & \cdots & 0 & 1 & \cdots & 1 \end{bmatrix}. \tag{13}$$

We immediately see that the *joint measurement matrix* $W = \begin{bmatrix} W^1 & W^2 \end{bmatrix}$ can have rank 5 at most as both matrices on the right side of Eq. (13) have rank 5 assuming general motion and non-degenerate structure.

As for the factorization algorithm for a single moving camera, we can obtain affinely distorted estimates of motion and structure by singular value decomposition of W into U and $\Sigma V^{\top}$, respectively.

The model defined by Eq. (13) assumes that no correspondences between the two images taken at the same time are known. Otherwise, the number of parameters can be reduced even further.

3.2   Affine Stereo Self Calibration

Given affinely distorted estimates of structure and motion, the *affine stereo self calibration* problem is to determine a 5×3 matrix A such that each two rows U_i of U are transformed to

$$K_i R_i = U_i A. \tag{14}$$

Letting $Q = AA^\top$ we can eliminate the unknown rotations by squaring both sides

$$K_i K_i^\top = U_i Q U_i^\top \tag{15}$$

Assuming a weak-perspective camera model, we arrive at

$$0 = \left(u_i^1\right)^\top Q\, u_i^1 - \left(u_i^2\right)^\top Q\, u_i^2 \quad \text{and} \tag{16a}$$

$$0 = \left(u_i^1\right)^\top Q\, u_i^2 \tag{16b}$$

where $\left(u_i^1\right)^\top$ and $\left(u_i^2\right)^\top$ denote the vectors corresponding to the first and second rows of U_i.

As the rank of matrix Q equals 3, the problem defined by the Eqs. (16) and the rank-3 constraint is nonlinear. However, according to our experience, straightforward nonlinear minimization converges fast and reliably to a good optimum. The rotation matrices can then be reconstructed by $R_i = U_i A$. The correcting transformation A can be obtained from the eigendecomposition of $Q = V D V^\top$ by taking $A = V D^{\frac{1}{2}}$ as Q is positive semi-definite. To strictly enforce that each R_i is a rotation matrix we can use polar decomposition.

For a 3D-reconstruction we further need estimates of t_i^1 and t_i^2. We can obtain these by

$$\begin{bmatrix} t_i^1 & t_i^2 \end{bmatrix} = U_i\, Q_\perp \tag{17}$$

with $Q_\perp = I - QQ^+$ where the symbol $(\cdot)^+$ denotes the generalized inverse.

Having estimated the motion parameters K_i, R_i, t_i^1 and t_i^2, the structure can be inferred by triangulation. A linear solution to this problem is given by

$$\begin{bmatrix} X^1 & X^2 \end{bmatrix} = \begin{bmatrix} P_1 \\ \vdots \\ P_m \end{bmatrix}^+ \begin{bmatrix} W^1 & W^2 \end{bmatrix} \tag{18}$$

If not all entries of W^1 or W^2 are known, we can use a nonlinear optimization algorithm for matrix completion, see Sec. 4. An excellent guide on affine 3D-reconstruction can be found in [8].

4   Experiments on Synthetic Data

We created $N = 146$ 3D-points which were projected $M = 80$ times in two images according to the affine stereo camera model. For each camera six of these images are shown in Fig. 1.

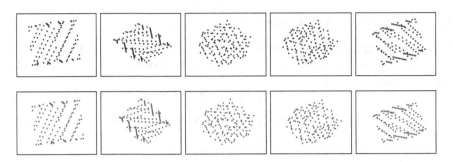

Fig. 1. Five images of 146 simulated 3D-points projected into forty images. The upper row corresponds to the left camera of the stereo system, the bottom row to the right.

We simulated occlusion by making all but the measurements along the main diagonal of both W^1 and W^2 invisible. The amount of unknown data was varied in between 0% and 30% in steps of ten percent. We added normally distributed noise with standard deviations $\sigma = \{0, 1, 2, 3\}$. For each combination of missing data and noise, we performed ten trials, i.e. perturbed the data ten times differently.

For estimating the motion U under missing entries of W, we used alternating-least-squares (ALS). The proposed algorithm was compared with the one introduced in [3].

We computed the root-mean-square-error (RMSE) between the visible, unperturbed matrix entries and the estimates. To assess the accuracy of subspace fitting we measured the sum of the canonical angles between the estimated subspace and the noise-free ground truth (SSP error). Lastly, a 3D-error was computed as the average sum of the Euclidean distances between the estimated 3D-points and the ground truth. This error was further normalized by the Frobenius norm of the matrix consisting of the ground truth 3D-points.

Average results of the ten trials are shown in Fig. 2. The plots from left to right correspond to the RMSE, the subspace error and the 3D-error. The dark grey indicates the algorithm proposed here, the lighter grey line the one in [3]. The solid, dashed, and dash-dotted colored lines correspond to 10%, 20% and 30% unknown data. As can be seen, the proposed algorithm performs superior.

As the algorithm is based upon ALS iterations, its computational complexity is slightly lower than that of the reference algorithm as the latter requires the larger rank-8 factorization.

5   Experiments on Real Images

5.1   Application 1: Rigid 3D-Reconstruction

Figure 3 shows five out of 74 images of a sequence of a rigid scene. The images in the upper row are taken by the left camera, those in the bottom row by the right

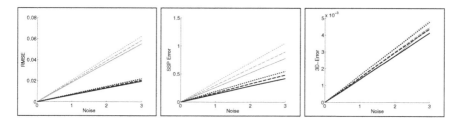

Fig. 2. From left to right: root-mean-square-error (RMSE); subspace error (SSP, sum of canonical angles); normalized 3D-error. The dark grey line indicates the proposed algorithm, the lighter grey the one in [3]. The solid, dashed and dash-dotted lines correlate to 10%, 20% and 30% missing data.

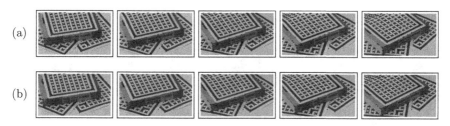

(a)

(b)

Fig. 3. Five out of 74 images of a sequence of a rigid scene. A total of 2112 3D-points were tracked through the images. Starting from the first image, each 15th image is shown. The joint measurement matrix has 32% unknown entries. The upper row shows the images taken by the left camera, the bottom right the images to the right camera.

camera. A total of 2112 feature trajectories was followed through the images. The joint measurement matrix has 32% unknown entries.

The images weren taken by a HDC-Z10000 stereo camera with focal length set to $28mm^2$ The object was about $4m$ apart from the camera and measured approximately $30cm$ in diameter. The optical axes were set such that a 3D-view appeared on the camera screen.

Some feature points are located at lines and do not move rigidly. We thus perform a simple outlier rejection. First, the standard deviation of the image-to-image motion vectors is computed. We then execute the alternating-least-squares method and remove trajectories whose estimated motion vectors differs from the known motion vectors by more than two standard deviations. These two steps are iterated until no more outlying trajectories are detected.

Six views of the 3D-reconstructions of 1658 trajectories are shown in Fig. 4. The different planes are perpendicular, and the repetitive patterns of the 2D-points is well reflected by the 3D-points.

5.2   Application 2: Trajectory Completion

Figure 5 shows five out of 251 images of a sequence in which two rigid bodies move independently. The images in the upper row are taken by the left camera,

---

^{2} This amounts to a focal length of $320mm$ in terms of a $35mm$ sensor).

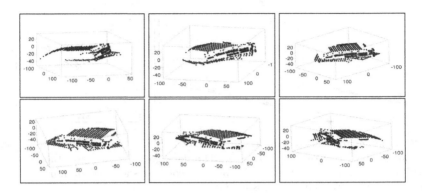

Fig. 4. Six views of the 3D-reconstruction from the data shown in Fig. 3

(a)
(b)

Fig. 5. Five out of 251 images of a sequence with two rigid bodies moving independently. Starting from the first image, each 50th image is shown. A total of 5605 3D-points were tracked. The joint measurement matrix has 34% unknown entries. The upper row shows the images taken by the left camera, the bottom images to the right camera.

those in the bottom row by the right camera. A total of 3967 trajectories was found in the sequence. The joint measurement matrix has 38% unknown entries.

The images were also taken by a HDC-Z1000 stereo camera. The two boxes were approximately $2m$ in front of it. The depth variation within the scene is larger than $0.5m$ hence the assumption required by the affine camera is strongly violated.

As both bodies move independently, each of the two sets of trajectories spans a 5-dimensional subspace. Therefore, we can perform a rank-10 factorization of the joint measurement matrix. Although some outliers were present in the data, we did not perform any filtering.

Using these estimates, we impute missing data and compare the results with a regular factorization. The latter needs to process both image streams independently, as not all 2D-points are matched across the left and right image streams.

As not all correspondences are known *between* the two image streams, a regular matrix factorization needs to process each camera stream independently. Results of the estimated 2D-points using a rank-8 alternating-least-squares on the data to the left camera stream are shown in Fig. 6. The two images correspond to the first and last frames shown in Fig. 5(a). As can be seen, many points are placed randomly. The shown results are representative for the other images since many points move randomly in all images of the sequence.

Figure 7 shows the completed trajectories using the proposed algorithm. The images in the upper row correspond to the left camera stream shown in Fig. 5(a), those in the bottom row to the right stream of Fig. 5(b). The three images in each row of Fig. 7 show the estimates corresponding to the first, third and fifth frame shown in Fig. 5. As can be seen, the proposed algorithm estimates missing feature points correctly throughout the complete sequence.

Fig. 6. Results of a rank-8 matrix factorization (cf. [3]) on the data to the left camera stream. The two images correspond to the first and last image of the sequence shown in Fig. 5(a). As can be seen, many points are erroneously estimated.

(a)

(b)

Fig. 7. Estimated 2D-points for the left (a) and right (b) camera streams shown in Fig. 5. The three images correspond to the first, third and fifth images shown in Fig. 5

6 Summary and Discussion

Given image streams taken by a parallely-aligned affine stereo camera system, this article introduced a low-rank constraint which trajectories across both images of both streams need to satisfy.

Conversely, existing algorithms for stereo cameras need to factorize both streams independently if not all correspondences are known between *the two image streams*. In other words, the stereo constraint cannot be considered.

The viability of the derived low-rank constraint was evaluated using synthetic data. Furthermore, two different applications using real images demonstrated that the algorithm is indeed able to estimate high-quality results. The introduced constraint does not only apply to rigid data but can be readily generalized to multi-body or non-rigidly deforming scenes.

References

1. Angst, R., Pollefeys, M.: Static multi-camera factorization using rigid motion. In: International Conference on Computer Vision (ICCV), pp. 1203–1210 (2009)
2. Bregler, C., Hertzmann, A., Biermann, H.: Recovering non-rigid 3d shape from image streams. In: IEEE Computer Vision and Pattern Recognition (CVPR), Hilton Head, SC, USA, pp. 690–696 (2000)
3. Bue, A.D., de Agapito, L.: Non-rigid stereo factorization. International Journal of Computer Vision (IJCV) 66(2), 193–207 (2006)
4. Costeira, J.P., Kanade, T.: A multibody factorization method for independently moving objects. International Journal of Computer Vision (IJCV) 29(3), 159–179 (1998)
5. Heyden, A., Berthilsson, R., Sparr, G.: An iterative factorization method for projective structure and motion from image sequences. Image Vision Comput. 17(13), 981–991 (1999)
6. Irani, M.: Multi-frame optical flow estimation using subspace constraints. In: International Conference on Computer Vision (ICCV), pp. 626–633 (1999)
7. Kanatani, K.: Motion segmentation by subspace separation: Model selection and reliability evaluation. International Journal of Image and Graphics 2(2), 179–197 (2002)
8. Kanatani, K., Sugaya, Y.: Factorization without factorization: complete recipe. Tech. Rep. 1&2, Okayama University, Japan (March 2004)
9. Kanatani, K., Sugaya, Y., Ackermann, H.: Uncalibrated factorization using a variable symmetric affine camera. In: Leonardis, A., Bischof, H., Pinz, A. (eds.) ECCV 2006. LNCS, vol. 3954, pp. 147–158. Springer, Heidelberg (2006)
10. Ruhe, A., Wedin, P.: Algorithms for separable nonlinear least squares problems. Society for Industrial and Applied Mathematics Review 22(3), 318–337 (1980)
11. Tomasi, C., Kanade, T.: Shape and motion from image streams under orthography: a factorization method. International Journal on Computer Vision (IJCV) 9(2), 137–154 (1992)
12. Triggs, B., McLauchlan, P.F., Hartley, R.I., Fitzgibbon, A.W.: Bundle adjustment – A modern synthesis. In: Triggs, B., Zisserman, A., Szeliski, R. (eds.) ICCV-WS 1999. LNCS, vol. 1883, p. 298. Springer, Heidelberg (2000)
13. Wold, H.: Estimation of principal components and related models by iterative least squares. In: Krishnaiah (ed.) Multivariate Analysis, pp. 391–420 (1966)

Multi-Resolution Range Data Fusion for Multi-View Stereo Reconstruction

Andreas Kuhn[1,2], Heiko Hirschmüller[2], and Helmut Mayer[1]

[1] Institute for Applied Computer Science, Bundeswehr University Munich
[2] Institute of Robotics and Mechatronics, German Aerospace Center

Abstract. In this paper we present a probabilistic algorithm for multi-view reconstruction from calibrated images. The algorithm is based on multi-resolution volumetric range image integration and is highly separable as it only employs local optimization. Dense depth maps are transformed in an octree data structure with variable voxel sizes. This allows for an efficient modeling of point clouds with very variable density. A probability function constructed in discrete space is built locally with a Bayesian approach. Compared to other algorithms we can deal with extremely big scenes and complex camera configurations in a limited amount of time, as the solution can be split in arbitrarily many parts and computed in parallel. The algorithm has been applied to lab and outdoor benchmark data as well as to large image sets of urban regions taken by cameras on Unmanned Aerial Vehicles (UAVs) and from the ground, demonstrating high surface quality and good runtime performance.

1 Introduction

In spite of all impressive progress, 3D reconstruction from sets of calibrated real world images is still a challenging problem. This was recently demonstrated once again by Vu et al. [21]. While modeling of landscapes is often done in 2.5D, there is a need for detailed 3D modeling particularly for urban regions. Unfortunately, algorithms for 2.5D reconstruction cannot be extended easily. 3D reconstruction algorithms using n-Layer heightmaps expand 2.5D reconstruction algorithms and achieve impressive results for urban regions [7] with one dominant direction.

Recently, multi-view-stereo (MVS) algorithms for 3D modeling made considerable progress concerning accuracy and runtime performance. They yield surfaces of impressive quality, e.g., for the Middlebury multi-view benchmark [16]. Nevertheless, only few of the algorithms can deal with real world data sets such as introduced by Strecha et al. [18]. Too the best of our knowledge there are very few methods which are scalable in a way that they can process hundreds or even thousands of high-resolution images, i.e., with tens of Megapixels. Especially, there are almost no methods which can deal well with image configurations with very different distances to the surfaces, which occur, e.g., when combining images from UAVs and from the ground. Thus, this paper focuses on the fusion of an arbitrary number of 2.5D models, which are in our case range images, into one large model including all 3D details.

J. Weickert, M. Hein, and B. Schiele (Eds.): GCPR 2013, LNCS 8142, pp. 41–50, 2013.
© Springer-Verlag Berlin Heidelberg 2013

2   Previous Work

Algorithms for 3D surface reconstruction are often posed as variational problems minimizing an error function. Among them are algorithms based on global optimization that either do not scale well concerning computational and memory requirements, or have a need for additional information such as the visual hull of the object. The visual hull is often impossible to estimate robustly for cluttered scenes. In particular, global volumetric algorithms based on a regular decomposition of the reconstructed volume, i.e., voxels, can become unfeasibly complex if they are using graph cuts [2,15] or total variation [23,24].

There are only a few algorithms which were designed for cluttered outdoor scenes. A current detailed overview is given by Vu et al. [21]. Furukawa et al. [5] presented one of the first algorithm with the potential to handle large scenes without constraints, such as dominant directions [6]. It generates a semi-dense set of patches, which is filtered and optimized based on photometric consistency. Unfortunately, the transformation of the filtered point cloud into triangle meshes does not scale well for big scenes. Arguably the best results for the full 3D reconstruction of large outdoor scenes are obtained at the moment by Vu et al. [21]. Their algorithm starts from semi dense point clouds and derives sets of tetrahedra for visibility checks. After a transformation into triangle meshes these are optimized using graph cuts and variational refinement, restricting the scalability with respect to the runtime efficiency. A scalable algorithm was proposed by Jancosek et al [13]. Filtering on a limited number of images at a time makes their algorithm suitable for large scenes in spite of using global optimization.

Nevertheless, volumetric algorithms using local optimization like level-set methods [8] motivated by Curless and Levoy [3], or EM-based approaches [17] have potential. However, they need several improvements to be scalable for large datasets with challenging geometric configurations.

Local probabilistic optimization is commonly used by algorithms for online processing. To avoid filtering outliers as postprocessing step, these algorithms consider the outlier probability in modelling mixture functions, like the sum of Gaussian and uniform functions [20], or graph-based mixture functions [22,9]. Those algorithms do not reach the quality of offline-processing. Additionally, they do not take varying distances from the camera into account either.

Like most volumetric approaches, our algorithm is based on range image integration, as proposed by Curless and Levoy [3]. In their algorithm an iso-surface is extracted. A high surface quality is obtained because the algorithm is optimal in the least squares sense. A combination of cumulative weighted signed distance functions is the basis for the extraction of the surface minimizing the least squares distance to all depth maps. A simple, but robust algorithm for multi-view reconstruction based on this algorithm was presented by Goessele et al. [8]. Unfortunately, the least-squares minimization is not suitable for varying surface-qualities. It is essential to consider the quality of the surfaces when dealing with surfaces imaged from strongly differing distances.

We extend these algorithms in three aspects: Firstly, using multi-resolution voxels with dynamic sizes. Like introduced by Fuhrmann et al. [4], our algorithm can model surfaces acquired in configurations with variable distances. Secondly, by using the Gaussian Cumulative Distribution Function (CDF), we also a employ a cumulative weighted distance function, even with a sound statistical background. Thirdly, by adding an additional postprocessing step that filters conflicting outliers, we achieve an improved completeness rates. The outlier detection is visibility-based, like presented by Merell et al. [14].

3   Reconstruction Pipeline

The reconstruction pipeline of our algorithm consists of the following steps:

1. Estimation of disparity maps by Semi-Global-Matching (SGM) [11,12].
2. Propagation of discrete 1D probability functions on the lines-of-sight.
3. Optimization of points on the surface based on the probability function.
4. Filtering by visibility checks.
5. Triangulation of the resulting point cloud.

For the estimation of disparity maps we use SGM, as it maintains small details due to pixelwise matching and has low processing time and memory requirements for large images. Expressing the disparities as probabilistic functions needs further discussion of the geometric error model, as described in Section 4.

Step 1 can be performed for all suitable image pairs separately. To allow for parallelization of the next steps, the volumetric space is divided and merged at the end. This allows processing on systems with limited main memory and offers scalability for very large scenes. Furthermore, it makes computing faster, for example on clusters with hundreds or thousands of cores. For dividing space, the algorithm runs in a preprocessing step through all depth maps and divides the total volume in subvolumes with the size depending on model resolution, memory size and number of cameras in a subarea. For merging the subvolumes the overlap of neighboring subvolumes has to be big enough so that meshes are equivalent in the merged volumes. More precisely, the overlap has to be at least twice of the local neighborhood used for meshing. This allows for a very easy fusion process as the meshes are equivalent in the inner half of the overlapping area. Triangles in the outer half are simply not considered. Steps 2 to 4 are complex and thus described in Sections 4.2 to 4.4. For step 5 we use a local triangulation for building the final triangle mesh incrementally [1].

4   Volumetric Modelling

We represent depth as a random variable. Because it comprises the most important part, at the moment we only consider the error in the direction of the line-of-sight. This error depends on four geometric parameters [10]:

$$\Delta P_z = \Delta p \frac{P_z^2}{ft} \sqrt{2} \ , \tag{1}$$

with the length of the baseline t, the focal length of the camera f, the depth P_z and the expected error of the disparity Δp. Besides the last, all other parameters are known for a calibrated image set.

Basically, there is no information about the error of the disparity. Setting it to a constant of half a pixel was empirically found to be a good approximation. We consider a Gaussian $\mathcal{N}(\mu, \sigma)$ with expected value $\mu = d_i^x$, where d_i^x is the depth derived by SGM, and standard deviation $\sigma = \Delta P_z$ with $\Delta p = 0.5$.

In summary, the function for the expected noise of a depth value can be expressed by

$$p(d_i^x) = \mathcal{N}(d_i^x, 0.5\frac{(d_i^x)^2}{ft}\sqrt{2}), \tag{2}$$

4.1 Choice of Voxel Size

An important step to efficiently handle disparity maps of varying density is the choice of the voxel size v_s in the octree. In our case the octree cubes correspond to the voxels. Because the fusion of data is only reasonable for related data, the algorithm chooses the voxelsize for all disparities individually. The idea is that data are fused (cf. Section 4.2) with others having at minimum half and at maximum double the quality. This is due to the fact, that the voxelsize in an octree is rising by a factor of 2. Hence, the voxel is chosen, which has a sidelength of $\sigma < av_s < 2\sigma$, where a is a smoothness term. For practical applications $a \in [2, 3]$ was found to be suitable to maintain the details, but to avoid pitted surfaces. Our algorithm estimates a depending on the number of cameras in the neighborhood. The range is from $a = 2$ for a small number of cameras, like the TempleSparseRing from the Middlebury multi-view benchmark [16], to $a = 3$ for the complete Temple sequence. To avoid quantization artifacts, the probabilistic function is established also in a second, neighboring voxelsize.

4.2 Propagation into Probabilistic Space

We allocate a probability to those voxels in discrete space, which lie on the line-of-sight of our depth value in an area d_a around the estimated depth, whose size corresponds to a couple of voxels. This area can be seen as an $\mathcal{L}^\infty$ norm, which reduces the influence of outliers on the surface quality. For our results, d_a was set to a size of eight voxels.

Along the line-of-sight we estimate the probability, that the voxel v_i lies behind the detected surface (Fig. 1). We use $p(v_i^0)$ and $p(v_i^1)$ for the probability that a voxel lies in front or behind the surface, respectively.

As the probability $p(v_i^1)$ is the integral of the Gaussian from $-\infty$ to the distance a_i of the camera center to the intercept point of the line-of-sight and the voxel v_i, one can take the Gaussian CDF instead of the Probability Density Function (PDF) to estimate it immediately:

$$p(v_i^1) = \int_0^{a_i} \mathcal{N}_{pdf}(x)dx = \mathcal{N}_{cdf}(a_i) \tag{3}$$

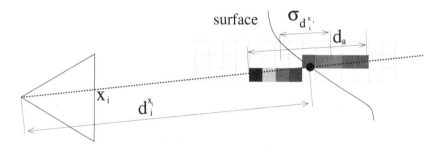

Fig. 1. Discrete probability of surface – Point with pixel coordinate x_i and expected distance $d_i^{x_i}$. $\sigma_{d_i^{x_i}}$ is the standard deviation of the 3D point position along the line-of-sight. The colored voxels represent the probability that a voxel lies behind the surface.

The Gaussian CDF is numerically estimated with the Gauss error function.

Probabilities on different rays from the same image that fall in the same voxel are averaged. Because for several occupancy grid approaches Bayes theorem proved to be appropriate, we employ a statistical framework for fusion of data from different images. We write the Bayesian theorem assuming independent measurements as:

$$p(v_i^1 | D = d) \propto p(v_i^1) \prod_{j \in 1,\ldots,n} p(D_j = d_j | v_i^1). \tag{4}$$

Since the probabilistic state of the surface is binary, i.e., a voxel is either occupied or not, we use the Binary Bayes Filter for probabilistic fusion [19].

$$l_i = log \frac{p(v_i^1)}{p(v_i^0)} = log \frac{p(v_i^1)}{1 - p(v_i^1)} = \sum_j log \frac{p(v_{ij}^1)}{1 - p(v_{ij}^1)} \tag{5}$$

4.3   Optimization of Point Positions on the Surface

The surface is characterized by neighboring voxels for which the probability that one is in front of the surface and the other is behind the surface is maximum. To achieve a better accuracy than the estimated distances d_x^i, we make use of the probabilistic voxel grid described in the last Section. We shift the estimated point along the line-of-sight for twice the standard deviation in both directions. We then consider all voxels I in the area and take the neighboring two, for which the product of probabilities that one is in front of and the other is behind the surface is maximum:

$$\arg\max_{i \in I}(p(v_i^0)p(v_{i+1}^1)) \ . \tag{6}$$

To obtain the position with subvoxel accuracy, we fit a Gaussian to the neighboring voxels of v_i and v_{i+1}. For this we use Maximum Likelihood estimation:

$$d_n = \frac{1}{4} \sum_{j=i-1}^{i+2} d_j \frac{e^{l_j}}{1 + e^{l_j}} \tag{7}$$

4.4   Filtering of Point Space by Visibility Checks

Octrees allow for efficient local consistency-checking based on raytracing. Even though raytracing is a global method, we use it locally because outliers have a detrimental influence on the surface quality particularly if they appear nearby. Solitary outliers are ignored in the later step of mesh generation. The idea of local raytracing is to filter conflicting points having relative lower quality as they occlude others with a better quality. In our case the quality is described by the maximum probability of the voxel surface estimated by function (6).

For all voxels v, which have been classified as occupied above, consistency is checked. Rays are cast to those cameras the voxel has been seen from. If there is another occupied voxel on the ray, a conflict is detected. For all voxels the maximum quality of conflicting voxels i on all rays is saved. Those voxels are filtered, whose qualities are worse than the highest quality for all conflicting voxels. If a conflict occurs for voxels on different octree levels, the voxels on the lower resolutions are filtered immediately.

5   Results

We present results for different data sets ranging from laboratory data to large area outdoor models. The given runtimes relate to parallel processing on a cluster with hundreds of CPU cores. A 32 bit architecture is used, so no more than 4 GB of RAM is used per core. All data sets are processed with the same parameter settings. The multi-resolution capability is demonstrated by Figs. 2 and 4.

Fig. 2. Textured and shaded multi-resolution 3D model from 54 images (left column). The size of the largest voxels is about 200 times larger than the size of the smallest.

5.1   Compact Objects

Our algorithm is designed for big cluttered data sets of outdoor scenes. When evaluating it on the Middlebury data sets [16], the untextured laboratory background causes spurious responses around the silhouettes. As this does not occur

Fig. 3. Evaluation for the EttlingenFountain and Herzjesu8 sequences [18]. In the left and centre images the *absolute error* ranges from 0.002m (white) to 0.06m (black). The right figure shows the cumulated error function of the *absolute error* in meters.

in cluttered scenes, we filter all disparities of the dark background to obtain results which can be compared to other algorithms. With this constraint we get state-of-the art results for all data sets from sparse to full sequences.

Because our algorithm assumes very accurate calibration of the image sets and does not consider texture in the optimization step, our results do not keep up with the best global methods. However, for the full sequences, where the redundancy of the images compensates for the calibration inaccuracy, the probabilistic optimization leads to results comparable to the best in the Dino sequence which is very sparsely textured. Particularly on those data sets with a lack of texture, algorithms using global optimization tend to overfit. In the Middlebury ranking [16] we obtain on average only a place in the middle of all algorithms, but we are able to handle all datasets, from sparse to dense sequences. However, by optimizing locally we are able to process the full sequences in parallel in a couple of minutes, setting our algorithm apart from others. In comparison with Goessele et al. [8] we achieve on average a similar surface quality (0.58mm [8] versus 0.615mm), but much better completeness rates (67% [8] versus 90%). This is a considerable improvement, even considering different densities of the underlying stereo techniques. It should also be noted that in contrast to [8] we do not use additional information like the slant to the surface.

5.2 Large Buildings

A benchmark test set was provided by Strecha et al. [18]. Unfortunately, the evaluation is not provided any more. LIDAR data but without accuracy information is available as ground truth for the EttlingenFountain and the Herzjesu8 sequences. Thus, we could conduct only an evaluation measuring the *absolute* instead of the relative error (Fig. 3) and, therefore, a numerical comparison to other algorithms is not possible. Visually, our results almost reach the quality of the algorithms using global optimization like Furukawa et al. [5]. Particularly, scalable algorithms like Jancosek et al. [13] achieve a much lower quality. Additionally, we obtained results that contain even tiny details of the scene as shown in Fig. 4. Our algorithm is one of the first working on dense depth maps and reaching state of the art quality. I.e., it has no tendency to generate ghost surfaces in empty areas like algorithms working on sparse point clouds.

Fig. 4. Result for Strecha's data sets. The upper image shows a combination of the Ettlingen10, Ettlingen30 and the EttlingenFountain images in one model. The region to the right of the fountain shows shows a transition between very different resolutions (cf. also in detail in the right – top: low versus bottom: high). The lower image shows Herzjesu25 with small details as the metal bar (top) and the stair railings.

We measured the runtime for the largest sequence of Ettlingen30. 3D space was divided in 100 subvolumes which were processed in parallel. The total runtime amounts to one hour, mainly split in depth estimation ($\approx$ 20 min), modeling ($\approx$ 30 min) and meshing ($\approx$ 10 min). The runtime could be further reduced by using more cores and more subvolumes.

5.3   Large Area Models

Our method makes it possible to process a nearly arbitrary number of calibrated high-resolution images. For demonstration we processed a data set acquired with ten Megapixel cameras on different UAVs. It shows a village with a large number of buildings in more then 600 images.

The model, for which one view with details is shown in Fig. 5 was computed, based on over thousand submodels with a total runtime of about five hours.

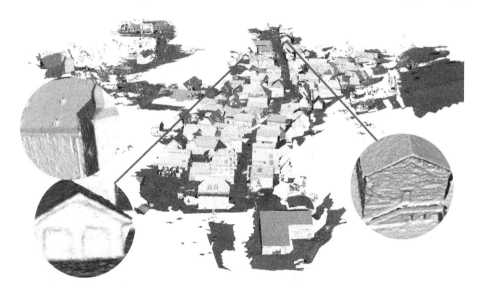

Fig. 5. 3D model of a village from 603 images made with UAVs showing small details

6 Conclusions and Outlook

A flexible multi-resolution approach for multi-view stereo reconstruction has been presented. Because it uses local optimization, it allows for the 3D reconstruction of scenes of nearly unlimited size with complex imaging configurations. Furthermore, the images are processed in parallel at any time. In spite of this, we obtain a quality that is state of the art for ambitious image sequences.

We made three main contributions. First, a local multi-resolution approach for optimization of range images suitable for images taken from very different distances and thus varying detail. Second, a probabilistic function of a 3D point using the Gaussian CDF providing a better statistical background for fusion of different qualities. Third, a postprocessing step for filtering occlusions having a lower quality in terms of the probabilistic function.

Concerning future work, several issues regarding error modeling of points need to be analyzed in more detail. Currently, points are represented as random variables with a Gaussian probability function of the disparity error that is assumed to be constant. Furthermore, also other attributes such as the strength of the texture and the angle with the normal vector of the surface, e.g., derived from nearest neighbors, probably have an influence on the disparity error. At the moment no 3D regularization is considered. There is a potential to get a better completeness using a local regularization term. Finally, the probabilistic representation allows us to take additional information like the covariance of the projection matrices from calibration into account.

References

1. Bodenmüller, T.: Streaming Surface Reconstruction from Real Time 3D Measurements. Ph.D. thesis, Technical University Munich (2009)
2. Campbell, N.D., Vogiatzis, G., Hernández, C., Cipolla, R.: Using multiple hypotheses to improve depth-maps for multi-view stereo. In: CVPR (2008)
3. Curless, B., Levoy, M.: A volumetric method for building complex models from range images. In: SIGGRAPH (1996)
4. Fuhrmann, S., Goesele, M.: Fusion of depth maps with multiple scales. In: Proceedings of the 2011 SIGGRAPH Asia Conference (2011)
5. Furukawa, Y., Ponce, J.: Accurate, dense, and robust multiview stereopsis. PAMI (2010)
6. Gallup, D., Frahm, J.M., Mordohai, P., Yang, Q., Pollefeys, M.: Real-time plane-sweeping stereo with multiple sweeping directions. In: CVPR (2007)
7. Gallup, D., Pollefeys, M., Frahm, J.-M.: 3D reconstruction using an n-layer heightmap. In: Goesele, M., Roth, S., Kuijper, A., Schiele, B., Schindler, K. (eds.) Pattern Recognition. LNCS, vol. 6376, pp. 1–10. Springer, Heidelberg (2010)
8. Goesele, M., Curless, B., Seitz, S.M.: Multi-view stereo revisited. In: CVPR (2006)
9. Guan, L., Franco, J.S., Pollefeys, M.: 3D Object Reconstruction with Heterogeneous Sensor Data. In: 3DPVT (2008)
10. Hirschmüller, H.: Stereo Vision based mapping and immediate virtual walkthroughs. Ph.D. thesis, De Montfort University (2003)
11. Hirschmüller, H.: Stereo processing by semiglobal matching and mutual information. PAMI (2008)
12. Hirschmüller, H., Scharstein, D.: Evaluation of stereo matching costs on images with radiometric differences. PAMI (2009)
13. Jancosek, M., Shekhovtsov, A., Pajdla, T.: Scalable multi-view stereo. In: 3DIM09 (2009)
14. Merrell, P., Akbarzadeh, A., Wang, L., Mordohai, P., Frahm, J.M., Yang, R., Nistér, D., Pollefeys, M.: Real-time visibility-based fusion of depth maps. In: CVPR (2007)
15. Mücke, P., Klowsky, R., Goesele, M.: Surface reconstruction from multi-resolution sample points. In: VMV (2011)
16. Seitz, S.M., Curless, B., Diebel, J., Scharstein, D., Szeliski, R.: A comparison and evaluation of multi-view stereo reconstruction algorithms. In: CVPR (2006)
17. Strecha, C., Fransens, R., Gool, L.J.V.: Combined depth and outlier estimation in multi-view stereo. In: CVPR (2006)
18. Strecha, C., von Hansen, W., Gool, L.J.V., Fua, P., Thoennessen, U.: On benchmarking camera calibration and multi-view stereo for high resolution imagery. In: CVPR (2008)
19. Thrun, S., Burgard, W., Fox, D.: Probabilistic Robotics (Intelligent Robotics and Autonomous Agents). MIT Press (2005)
20. Vogiatzis, G., Hernández, C.: Video-based, real-time multi-view stereo. Image Vision Comput (2011)
21. Vu, H.H., Labatut, P., Pons, J.P., Keriven, R.: High accuracy and visibility-consistent dense multiview stereo. PAMI (2012)
22. Woodford, O.J., Vogiatzis, G.: A generative model for online depth fusion. In: Fitzgibbon, A., Lazebnik, S., Perona, P., Sato, Y., Schmid, C. (eds.) ECCV 2012, Part V. LNCS, vol. 7576, pp. 144–157. Springer, Heidelberg (2012)
23. Zach, C.: Fast and high quality fusion of depth maps. In: 3DPVT (2008)
24. Zach, C., Pock, T., Bischof, H.: A globally optimal algorithm for robust tv-l1 range image integration. In: ICCV (2007)

3D Object Class Geometry Modeling with Spatial Latent Dirichlet Markov Random Fields*

Hanchen Xiong, Sandor Szedmak, and Justus Piater

Institute of Computer Science, University of Innsbruck
{hanchen.xiong,sandor.szedmak,justus.piater}@uibk.ac.at

Abstract. This paper presents a novel part-based geometry model for 3D object classes based on latent Dirichlet allocation (LDA). With all object instances of the same category aligned to a canonical pose, the bounding box is discretized to form a 3D space dictionary for LDA. To enhance the spatial coherence of each part during model learning, we extend LDA by strategically constructing a Markov random field (MRF) on the part labels, and adding an extra spatial parameter for each part. We refer to the improved model as spatial latent Dirichlet Markov random fields (SLDMRF). The experimental results demonstrate that SLDMRF exhibits superior semantic interpretation and discriminative ability in model classification to LDA and other related models.

1 Introduction

During the past decades, computer vision has made remarkable progress in visual object understanding, e.g. classification, pose estimation and segmentation, etc. However, most previous study of object modeling is based on 2D images, in which appearance is the main and only information source for various tasks, so most attention is focused on increasing the robustness of algorithms to lighting changes, intra-class appearance variation and viewpoint variation [4]. Meanwhile, 3D geometry properties of objects have been rarely exploited and used to increase the expressiveness of object models. Recently, pioneering work [7,13] has attempted to add 3D geometric information to object models, demonstrating that the accuracy and robustness of such algorithms can be enhanced with extra 3D geometry clues. However, there still exists an obvious gap between 2D appearance modeling and 3D geometry modeling with respect to their interpretation and representation abilities, and it has been advocated [7,13] that robust 3D geometry modeling is highly desirable. Motived by this gap and desire, this paper puts forward a novel 3D object class geometry model in the light of state-of-the-art techniques developed in machine learning and computer graphics. Part-based models have displayed merits in 2D appearance modeling [4] for handling partial occlusion, our 3D geometry model is likewise part-based and inherits these strengths. The training data of our algorithm are collections of 3D

---

* The research has received funding from the European Community's Seventh Framework Programme (FP7) under grant agreement no. 270273, Xperience.

J. Weickert, M. Hein, and B. Schiele (Eds.): GCPR 2013, LNCS 8142, pp. 51–60, 2013.
© Springer-Verlag Berlin Heidelberg 2013

Fig. 1. Different object instances of the same class should share similar 3D structure of composing parts, although their parts can slightly vary from one instance to another

models of different instances which belong to the same category (Figure 1). The basic underlying principle of our modeling is the concept that different object instances of the same class should share similar 3D structure of composing parts, although their parts can slightly vary from one instance to another. For example, all bicycles are composed of a frame and two wheels, and the geometric relation between these three parts are similar across different instances (Figure 1). In this paper, 3D objects are represented by point cloud data (PCD), which is a general and popular representation of 3D shapes and can easily be converted from other data formats (e.g. meshes). First, for each class, different PCDs of object instances are aligned using point cloud registration methods. Secondly, the main learning step is inspired by latent Dirichlet allocation (LDA) [1] and computer graphics [5]. LDA is a state-of-the-art machine learning tool for discovering latent topics within document collections. Here we apply LDA by considering each object point cloud as a document, and each part as a topic. With the bounding box volume discretized into a 3D grid dictionary, the part can be mined out as a multinomial distribution over the discrete 3D space, and each object is a multinomial distribution over parts. However, standard LDA ignores the spatial coherence, which is of great importance in our task but not generally taken into account in natural language applications. Based on discoveries in computer graphics [5] and other work on LDA [8,11], we develop a spatial latent Dirichlet Markov random field (SLDMRF) model with extra undirected links between topic labels and spatial parameters. The proposed SLDMRF can co-segment all point clouds simultaneously under a prior of coherence of correspondence, spatial continuity and spatial smoothness. According to our empirical results (section 3), compared to standard LDA and other related models, SLDMRF can achieve much more consistent and semantically meaningful segmentations of 3D point clouds, and the learned class geometry models display better discriminative ability in classification.

1.1   Related Work

The starting point of 3D geometry modeling in visual object understanding is the difficulty in dealing with appearance variation due to different viewpoints. There have been several attempts to embed 3D geometric information into object models [2,3,7,13], and all of them have reported improvement in accuracy and robustness, although different 3D geometry information are exploited and modelled in their work. In [2] 3D object shapes are probabilistically modelled as continuous distributions in $\mathbb{R}^3$ with a kernel density estimator (KDE). However, that work explicitly addresses neither category-level tasks nor semantic segmentation. Objects are considered as Gausssaian mixtures and expectation-maximization (EM) is applied to estimate corresponding Gaussian parameters and weights. One observation of Gaussian-mixture-based segmentation is that discovered parts rarely display good semantic interpretability since usually the part geometry is too complex to be modelled as a Gaussian (section 3.1). Other work attempts to improve the expressiveness of object geometry models in different ways. For example, Detry et al. [3] represent objects as hierarchically-organized spatial distributions of distinct feature types, but did not seek to produce semantically-meaningful segmentations. Other models [7,13] extract 3D geometry information at the class level. However, in [7] the segmentation is again based on Gaussian mixtures and EM, and most [13] do not model object classes in a part-based manner to avoid segmentation. Meanwhile, another thread of segmentation-based visual modeling is the application of Latent Dirichlet allocation (LDA) in computer vision [10,11,8]. LDA was originally developed to discover hidden topics in text corpora by clustering words into different topics [1]. Standard LDA, however, ignores spatial coherence, which is problematic in vision applications. Therefore, spatial LDA (SLDA) [11] and Latent Dirichlet Markov random fields (LDMRF) [8] were put forward to produce better, spatially-coherent segmentations. In addition, with higher emphasis of the smoothness of parts and consistent correspondences, 3D segmentation in computer graphics [5] constructs graphs with neighboring intra-links and correspondence inter-links among objects, and min-cut is used on graphs for segmentation.

The main contribution of this paper is an extension of LDA for 3D object class geometry modeling, which we refer to as Spatial Latent Dirichlet Markov Random Fields(SLDMRF). The proposed model is built with inspiration from recent advances in different fields [1,11,8,5], and it yields superior interpretability and representational capability in modeling 3D object class geometry.

2   3D Object Class Geometry Modeling

With the point cloud representations of 3D object shapes, the alignment of different instances of the same class is achieved with point cloud registration algorithms. While any suitable registration procedure can be used, we adopted a novel method [12] since it is very efficient and robust to non-rigid transformation, which suits the case of intra-category shape variation. An example of aligning dogs is displayed in Figure 2.

2.1   Latent Dirichlet Allocation

LDA [1] is a generative model that utilizes the information of co-occurring words to find out hidden topics shared by documents. In LDA, each document is considered as a finite mixture of topics; each topic is a finite mixture of words. The graphical model of LDA is shown in Figure 3(a). The generative process of LDA

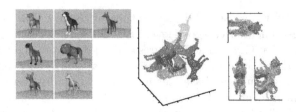

Fig. 2. Alignment of different dog instances by point cloud registration [12]. Left: original 3D shapes of different dog instances; middle: point clouds generated from the shapes on the left; right: three views (top, profile, front) of the point clouds (middle) after alignment.

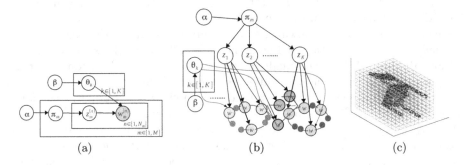

(a)   (b)   (c)

Fig. 3. (a) Graphical model of LDA; (b) Application of LDA to model 3D object categories; (c) Construction of 3D dictionary by discretizing the 3D space of the bounding box.

is as follows: (1) for each topic $k \in [1, K]$, a multinomial parameter $\boldsymbol{\theta}_k$ over words is sampled from Dirichlet prior $\boldsymbol{\beta}$; (2) for each document $m \in [1, M]$, a multinomial parameter $\boldsymbol{\pi}_m$ over K topics is sampled from Dirichlet prior $\boldsymbol{\alpha}$; (3) for each word $w_m^{(n)}$, $n \in [1, N_m]$ in document m, a topic label $z_m^{(n)}$ is first sampled from multinomial distribution $z_m^{(n)} \sim \text{Multinomial}(\boldsymbol{\pi}_m)$, then the word $w_m^{(n)}$ is sampled from the multinomial distribution parametrized with $\boldsymbol{\theta}_{z_m^{(n)}}$, $w_m^{(n)} \sim \text{Multinomial}(\boldsymbol{\theta}_{z_m^{(n)}})$. Hyperparameters $\boldsymbol{\alpha}$ and $\boldsymbol{\beta}$ define the Dirichlet priors governing the parameters of multinomial distributions. Usually $\boldsymbol{\alpha}$ and $\boldsymbol{\beta}$ are set in a symmetric manner and using low values [6]. In [10], LDA is applied on a collection of images. Each image is considered as a document, objects correspond to topics, and visual words are generated using vector quantization on extracted features. In our case, however, LDA is utilized for 3D object class geometry modeling with objects of the same category as documents, and parts shared by different instances correspond to topics (Figure 3(b)).

3D Dictionary. In our task, LDA is expected to work effectively under the assumption that different objects of the same category should share very similar structure. Therefore, when LDA is applied on each collection of categorical object point clouds, the co-occurring patterns are the 3D space occupied by 3D points.

In each collection, all instances can be aligned to a canonical pose, based on which the 3D space of the bounding box is discretized into a grid, where each block represents a 3D word. Therefore, when transferring point clouds to corresponding documents, word w_k will replace 3D point x_i if x_i lies within block w_k. In this way, the discovered part actually is a distribution over 3D space, and a category is a mixture of these distributions. The concept of dictionary discretization is illustrated in Figure 3(c).

For label inference and parameters learning in LDA, a collapsed Gibbs sampling [6] can be formulated as

$$q_{\text{LDA}}(z_m^{(n)} = k) \propto \frac{\mathbf{N}^{(k)}_{-mn,w_m^{(n)}} + \beta_{w_m^{(n)}}}{\sum_w^W (\mathbf{N}^{(k)}_{-mn,w} + \beta_w)} \cdot (\mathbf{N}^{(m)}_{-mn,k} + \alpha_k) \tag{1}$$

where $\mathbf{N}^{(k)}_{-mn,w}$ is the number of words in the corpus with value w assigned to topic k excluding the nth word in document m, and $\mathbf{N}^{(m)}_{-mn,k}$ is the number of words in document m assigned to topic k excluding the nth word in document m. From (1), it can be seen that LDA prefers to cluster together those words that often co-occur in the same document. Therefore, simply applying LDA on the 3D dictionary, unfortunately, is not expected to work because it misses a lot of spatial and correspondence information, which is not meaningful in the text processing case: (1) *Spatial coherence* is an important issue when LDA is applied in vision applications [11,8]. For example, in all point clouds of dogs, 3D words located in the hip and in the head will always co-occur. So by using (1), the hip and head of dogs can be clustered into a part, which is a spatially (of course also semantically) unreasonable segmentation. (2) *Correspondence coherence* is likewise important. LDA can find synonyms by finding their co-occurring patterns in documents. However, the "synonyms" in the 3D dictionary are identified by spatial correspondence. For example, in Figure 2, the legs of different dogs can rarely match exactly due to different species or standing poses. However, since all legs are close and correspond to each other, they should be clustered into the same part.

2.2   Spatial Latent Dirichlet Markov Random Field

To enhance the spatial coherence, in Spatial LDA (SLDA) [11] 2D images are decomposed into small overlapping regions, which are used as documents to ensure that the pixels belonging to one part should be close to each other. Latent Dirichlet Markov random fields (LDMRF) [8], on the other hand, construct Markov random fields on the part label variables to enhance the local spatial coherence. However, both of them ignore the correspondences across the segmentations of different instances. Inspired by these improved versions of LDA and consistent co-segmentation in computer graphics [5], we put forward a novel spatial latent Dirichlet Markov random field (SLDMRF) that inherits virtues from both SLDA and LDMRF. However, rather than being a simple combination of SLDA and LDMRF, the proposed SLDMRF goes beyond them in several ways.

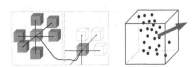

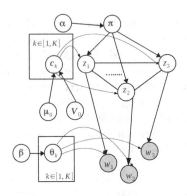

(a) Left: for each word (red block), there are two types of connections in SLDMRF: neighboring spatial connections (blue blocks) and correspondence connections (green block); right: the normal vector of each word in the document is estimated by using the points lying within the word.

(b) Graphical model of SLDMRF: compared to the standard LDA (Figure 3(a)), there are extra directed links between topic labels and spatial Gaussian parameters c_k.

Fig. 4. SLDMRF modeling

First, instead of going through all small overlapping sub-volumes as SLDA does, we explicitly model the positions of all parts by parameters c_k such that 3D words that share the same label k are likely to be close to c_k. Second, similarly to LDMRF, SLDMRF constructs a Markov random field on the neighboring label variables. However, different from LDMRF, we assign different potential functions based on the prior that the segmentation boundaries should be located at the point where abrupt curvature changes take place. The potential function is defined as

$$g(z_i, z_j) = \delta(z_i, z_j) \exp(|\langle o_i, o_j \rangle|) \tag{2}$$

where $\delta(z_i, z_j)$ equals 1 when z_i and z_j are neighbors, and 0 otherwise (Figure 4(a)), and o_i, o_j are the normal vectors estimated by using the points lying within word i and j respectively (Figure 4(a)). Last but not least, SLDMRF enhance the correspondences of segmentation across different instances. Inspired by the co-segmentation used in [5], we construct inter-connections between corresponding parts across different objects, and correspondences are matched by finding the nearest neighbors in other objects after alignment. In this way the segmentation can be more consistent within a category. The potential function $g(z_m^{(i)}, z_n^{(j)})$ for correspondence connections is set in the same way as spatial connections (2); $\delta(z_m^{(i)}, z_n^{(j)})$ is 1 if $z_m^{(i)}$ and $z_n^{(j)}$ are nearest neighbours of each other, and 0 otherwise. Because the part weights are already taken into account by LDA (parameter π), the labels within the Markov random fields are modeled as:

$$p(\mathbf{Z}) \propto \exp\left(\sum_{(i,j)} g(z_i, z_j)\right) \tag{3}$$

The graphical model of SLDMRF is presented in Figure 4(b). Hyperparameters μ_0 and $\mathbf{V}_0$ (similar to α, β) specify the Gaussian prior of part positions $c_k \sim \mathcal{N}(\cdot; \boldsymbol{\mu}_0, \mathbf{V}_0)$. Given the part position $\mathbf{c}_k$, the label is sampled as $z_i \sim \mathcal{N}(\hat{w}_i; \mathbf{c}_k, \boldsymbol{\Lambda})$, where $\hat{w}_i$ denotes the 3D coordinates of word w_i. Since we do not expect the label distribution to be truly Gaussian, $\boldsymbol{\Lambda}$ is set relatively large. The joint probability of 3D words in SLDMRF $p(\{w_m^{(n)}\}_{m=1,n=1}^{M,N_m} | \boldsymbol{\alpha}, \boldsymbol{\beta})$ is:

$$
\frac{1}{\mathbf{Q}} \prod_{m=1}^{M} \prod_{n=1}^{N_m} \left(\int_{\boldsymbol{\pi}_m} \int_{\boldsymbol{\theta}_{z_m^{(n)}}} \int_{\mathbf{c}_{z_m^{(n)}}} p(\boldsymbol{\pi}_m | \boldsymbol{\alpha}) \sum_{z_m^{(n)}=1}^{K} \left(p(z_m^{(n)} | \boldsymbol{\pi}_m) p(w_m^{(n)} | \boldsymbol{\theta}_{z_m^{(n)}}) \right) \right.
$$
$$
\left. \mathcal{N}(w_m^{(n)}; \mathbf{c}_{z_m^{(n)}}, \boldsymbol{\Lambda}) \mathcal{N}(\mathbf{c}_{z_m^{(n)}}; \boldsymbol{\mu}_0, \mathbf{V}_0) \times \prod_{x,y \in \tilde{z}_m^{(n)}} \sqrt{\exp(g(z_m^{(n)}, z_x^{(y)}))} \right)
$$
(4)

where $x, y \in \tilde{z}_m^{(n)}$ denotes the set of all word labels (the yth word in the xth document) connected with $z_m^{(n)}$, i.e. $\delta(z_m^{(n)}, z_x^{(y)}) = 1$, and $\mathbf{Q}$ is the normalization term induced by Markov random fields.

2.3   Inference and Learning

Similar to the inference and learning in LDA, based on (4), we can develop a collapsed Gibbs sampler by integrating out $\boldsymbol{\pi}_m, \boldsymbol{\theta}_{z_m^{(n)}}, \mathbf{c}_{z_m^{(n)}}$ in SLMRF. The sampler can be more easily interpreted as a "combined" sampler by using clues from LDA, MRF and Guassian mixtures:

$$
q^*(z_m^{(n)} = k) \propto q_{LDA}(z_m^{(n)} = k) \cdot q_M(z_m^{(n)} = k) \cdot q_c(z_m^{(n)} = k)
$$
(5)

where $q_{LDA}(z_m^{(n)} = k)$ is the collapsed Gibbs sampler of LDA (1),

$$
q_M(z_m^{(n)} = k) \propto \frac{\exp \left(\sum_{(z_j, z_m^{(n)})} g(z_j, z_m^{(n)} = k) \right)}{\sum_h \exp \left(\sum_{(z_j, z_m^{(n)})} g(z_j, z_m^{(n)} = h) \right)}
$$
(6)

is the Gibbs sampler based on the Markov random field, and

$$
q_c(z_m^{(n)} = k) \propto \frac{\mathcal{N}(\hat{w}_m^{(n)}; \boldsymbol{\mu}_l^{(k)}, \boldsymbol{\Lambda}_l^{(k)})}{\sum_h \mathcal{N}(\hat{w}_m^{(n)}; \boldsymbol{\mu}_l^{(h)}, \boldsymbol{\Lambda}_l^{(h)})}
$$
(7)

is a collapsed Gibbs sampler of Gaussian mixtures, with

$$
\boldsymbol{\Lambda}_l^{(k)-1} = \boldsymbol{\Lambda}_0^{-1} + l\boldsymbol{\Lambda}^{-1} \qquad \boldsymbol{\mu}_l^{(k)} = \boldsymbol{\Lambda}_l^{(k)2} \left(\frac{\boldsymbol{\mu}_0}{\boldsymbol{\Lambda}_0^2} + \frac{l\overline{\hat{w}^{(k)}}}{\boldsymbol{\Lambda}^2} \right)
$$
(8)

where l is the number of words which are labeled with k, and $\overline{\hat{w}^{(k)}}$ is the mean of 3D coordinates of words which are assigned to part k until the current iteration. Similar to [6], parameters $\{\boldsymbol{\pi}_m\}_{m=1}^{M}$, $\{\boldsymbol{\theta}_k\}_{k=1}^{K}$ can be estimated after the convergence of Gibbs sampling:

$$
\boldsymbol{\pi}_m^{(k)} = \frac{\mathbf{N}_k^{(m)} + \alpha_k}{\sum_{k=1}^{K}(\mathbf{N}_k^{(m)} + \alpha_k)} \qquad \boldsymbol{\theta}_k^{(w)} = \frac{\mathbf{N}_w^{(k)} + \beta_w}{\sum_w^{W}(\mathbf{N}_w^k + \beta_w)}
$$
(9)

Since hyperparameter $\boldsymbol{\alpha}$, in our case, is categorical part weight, we estimate it by simply compute the average of $\boldsymbol{\pi}_m$: $\boldsymbol{\alpha} = \frac{1}{M} \sum_{m=1}^{M} \boldsymbol{\pi}_m$. In addition, parameters $\{\mathbf{c}_k\}_{k=1}^{K}$ are read out as $\{\boldsymbol{\mu}_l^k\}_{k=1}^{K}$ (8).

3   Experiments

To evaluate the proposed model, 5 object classes (cars, bikes, dogs, motorcycles, airplanes) from the Princeton shape benchmark (PSB) [9] database are used. Since 3D shapes in the PSB are represented as triangulated meshes, we convert them to point clouds by uniformly sampling points within triangles.

3.1   3D Object Class Geometry Modeling

For comparison, LDA [1], LDMRF [8] and Gaussian Mixtures (GM) models are tested on the same data (aligned point clouds of categorical instances). Since LDMRF requires manual interference (semi-supervision), to avoid human bias during comparison, here we construct the same Markov random fields for both LDMRF and SLDMRF so that LDMRF can also work in an unsupervised manner. All four models are implemented with Gibbs sampling for label inference and learning. To ensure fairness, the same part number and iteration number (200) is applied. A test example of motorcycle modeling is presented in Figure 5. LDA does not find consistent and meaningful parts because of the intra-class variation (each object is labeled as a part since LDA only focuses on co-occurring patterns). LDMRF, on the other hand, discovers some locally continuous and consistent segments on different objects. However, the global spatial coherence of parts is poor; parts are shattered. GM establishes more globally obvious segmentation pattern by finding more consistent and meaningful parts. Nevertheless, GM ignores local spatial coherence, so parts are not well segmented; they tend to be of blob shape and to overlap each other. By contrast, SLDMRF produces best convincing segmentations in terms of consistence, local and global spatial coherence and semantic meaning. The SLDMRF modeling results of other four object classes are illustrated in Figure 6.

3.2   Geometry Model Classification

To illustrate the parts learned by SLDMRF is more accurate, and thus more discriminative, we conduct quantitative comparisons on classification task. Since LDA and LDMRF are far from being qualified for practical part-based modeling, here we are only concerned with the comparison between GM and SLDMRF. 3D shapes of 5 object classes are divided into training (70%) and test sets (30%). The model learning is conducted in the same way as in section 3.1. Although Markov random fields and spatial parameters greatly assists in segmentation and model learning of SLDMRF, they are not used in the final category models. A learned bicycle model is shown in Figure 6(e). It can be seen that the part position information and neighboring correlation are already encoded in the categorical part parameter θ. Therefore, for the sake of simplicity and computation feasibility, we only use learned LDA as our 3D object category models for classification. To test an object M^*, it is first aligned to the canonical poses

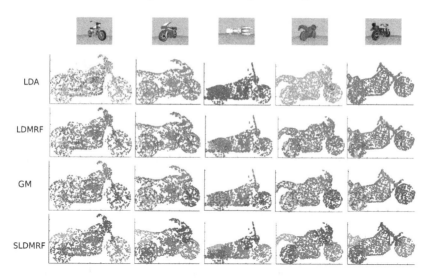

Fig. 5. Comparison of segmentation by using LDA, LDMRF, GM and SLDMRF, SLDMRF qualitatively yields more reasonable segmentations than the others

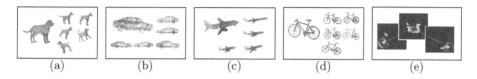

| (a) | (b) | (c) | (d) | (e) |

Fig. 6. SLDMRF modeling of dogs (a), cars (b), airplanes (c) and bikes (d); (e): the learned part parameters $\boldsymbol{\theta}_k$ of bikes

of different class models. In SLDMRF case, the likelihood that M^* belongs to a class $x \in \{$cars, bikes, dogs, motorcycles, airplanes$\}$ is computed as:

$$p(M^*|\mathcal{M}_x) = \prod_{i=1}^{|M^*|} \left\{ \sum_k \int_{\boldsymbol{\pi}} p(w_i|\boldsymbol{\theta}_k)p(k|\boldsymbol{\pi})p(\boldsymbol{\pi}|\boldsymbol{\alpha}) \right\} \tag{10}$$

where $|M^*|$ is the number of points in object M^*. By contrast, in the GM case:

$$p(M^*|\mathcal{M}_x) = \prod_{i=1}^{|M^*|} \left\{ \sum_k \mathcal{N}(w_i; \boldsymbol{\theta}_k)\pi_k \right\} \tag{11}$$

Since no other prior knowledge is given, the classification can be done in a maximum-likelihood fashion. A global model learned with one single multinomial distribution on 3D dictionary is also provided as baseline for comparison. The classification performances of GM, SLDMRF and global model are evaluated using confusion matrices. The comparison in in Figure 7 demonstrates that SLDMRF is superior to GM with respect to discriminative ability in classification.

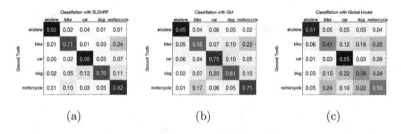

Fig. 7. The classification confusion matrcices of 5 object classes with SLDMRF (a), GM (b) and global model (c)

4 Conclusion and Discussion

We improved LDA model for geometry modeling with better semantic interpretation and promising discriminative capabilities. Meanwhile, learning and application of the model require good initial alignment, which is difficult for noisy and partial occluded 3D point cloud in practice. So a promising future work is to cooperate 3D geometry model with 2D image models to describe both structure and appearance, which thus enhance model's expressiveness and practical value.

References

1. Blei, D., Ng, A., Jordan, M.: Latent Dirichlet Allocation. Journal of Machine Learning Research 3, 993–1022 (2003)
2. Detry, R., Piater, J.: Continuous surface-point distributions for 3D object pose estimation and recognition. In: Kimmel, R., Klette, R., Sugimoto, A. (eds.) ACCV 2010, Part III. LNCS, vol. 6494, pp. 572–585. Springer, Heidelberg (2011)
3. Detry, R., Pugeault, N., Piater, J.: A Probabilistic Framework for 3D Visual Object Representation. PAMI 31(10), 1790–1803 (2009)
4. Felzenszwalb, P.F., Girshick, R.B., McAllester, D., Ramanan, D.: Object Detection with Discriminatively Trained Part-Based Models. PAMI 32(9), 1627–1645 (2010)
5. Golovinskiy, A., Funkhouser, T.A.: Consistent segmentation of 3D models. Computers and Graphics 33, 262–269 (2009)
6. Griffiths, T.L., Steyvers, M.: Finding scientific topics. Proceedings of the National Academy of Sciences 101(suppl. 1), 5228–5235 (2004)
7. Liebelt, J., Schmid, C.: Multi-View Object Class Detection with a 3D Geometric Model. In: CVPR (2010)
8. Mackey, L.: Latent Dirichlet Markov Random Fields for Semi-supervised Image Segmentation and Object Recognition (2007)
9. Shilane, P., Min, P., Kazhdan, M.M., Funkhouser, T.A.: The Princeton Shape Benchmark. In: SMI, pp. 167–178. IEEE Computer Society (2004)
10. Sivic, J., Russell, B.C., Efros, A.A., Zisserman, A., Freeman, W.T.: Discovering object categories in image collections. In: ICCV (2005)
11. Wang, X., Grimson, E.: Spatial Latent Dirichlet Allocation. In: NIPS (2007)
12. Xiong, H., Szedmak, S., Piater, J.: Efficient,General Point Cloud Registration with Kernel Feature Maps. In: Canadian Conf. on Computer and Robot Vision (2013)
13. Yan, P., Khan, S.M., Shah, M.: 3D model based object class detection in an arbitrary view. In: ICCV (2007)

Discriminative Joint Non-negative Matrix Factorization for Human Action Classification

Abdalrahman Eweiwi[1], Muhammad Shahzad Cheema[1], and
Christian Bauckhage[1,2]

[1] Bonn-Aachen International Center for IT, University of Bonn, Germany
[2] Multimedia Pattern Recognition Group, Fraunhofer IAIS, Germany

Abstract. This paper describes a supervised classification approach based on non-negative matrix factorization (NMF). Our classification framework builds on the recent expansions of non-negative matrix factorization to multiview learning, where the primary dataset benefits from auxiliary information for obtaining shared and meaningful spaces. For discrimination, we utilize data categories in a supervised manner as an auxiliary source of information in order to learn co-occurrences through a common set of basis vectors. We demonstrate the efficiency of our algorithm in integrating various image modalities for enhancing the overall classification accuracy over different benchmark datasets. Our evaluation considers two challenging image datasets of human action recognition. We show that our algorithm achieves superior results over state-of-the-art in terms of efficiency and overall classification accuracy.

1 Introduction

Non-negative matrix factorization has been widely used in image analysis and pattern extraction during the last few years. This can be attributed to the convenient interpretation of the factorized components and its direct relation to other probabilistic frameworks. Recent research has spanned the applications of NMF from retrieval and clustering to various domains including multiview learning. Multiview learning, in the context of retrieval systems for example, aims at profitting from auxiliary sources of information in improving retrieval performance on the primary dataset. Such performance gain becomes plausible by estimating meaningful latent structures that explicitly models the co-occurrences between primary and auxiliary data sources. In this sense, one can interpret any supervised classification task as a multiview problem that benefits from the auxiliary category information in extracting discriminative latent structures between different classes.

Although multiview learning has venerable tradition, there is a renewed interest of it in computer vision and image analysis. *Canonical correlation analysis* (CCA) [14] and *partial least squares* (PLS) [15] aim at revealing latent components from different modalities that maximally explain the correlation (CCA) or covariance (PLS) distributions of different views. Donner et al.[10] harness CCA for fast model searching of active appearance models(AAM). Kim et al.

J. Weickert, M. Hein, and B. Schiele (Eds.): GCPR 2013, LNCS 8142, pp. 61–70, 2013.
© Springer-Verlag Berlin Heidelberg 2013

[17] extend CCA for tensor analysis of human actions, where similarities among action's videos are measured through joint shared spaces. PLS on the other hand has been recently used for modeling the appearance and pose variations in different views [9,13], achieving state-of-the-art over multiple benchmark datasets. In this study, we emphasize on discriminative learning using NMF through multiview learning in a supervised setting, where feature categories play the role of auxiliary view of the datasets, and classification results simply approximate the posterior probabilities of target classes.

Multiview learning through NMF is receiving increasing interest owing to the convenient and the semantic interpretation of parts for the extracted bases. Akata et al. [1] suggest learning shared spaces from different views of image datasets through joint non-negative matrix factorization (JNMF) for the applications of segmentation and indexing. Caicedo et al. [4] present asymmetric algorithm for the construction of shared latent spaces that first derives a semantic representation from the reliable view of the dataset, and then follows by an adaptation over other views. While on the other hand, Gubta et al. [12] argue for limiting the number of shared spaces learned from JNMF to cope with the diversity among various data sources. Liu et al. [21] propose a NMF-based multiview clustering algorithm by searching for a factorization that gives compatible clustering solutions while maintaining meaningful and comparable results across multiple views.

In the domain of human action recognition, it is often the case that the outcome is not associated with any single view, but rather the synergy of multiple measurements like body pose, appearance, motion, and scene representation. Earlier works on action recognition have generally considered a single view approach for defining the human action [11,16,23,26]. However, recent studies pointed out for the significance of combining multiple views for an accurate modeling of human actions [28]. Yao and Fei-Fei [29] propose coupled features of pose and appearance by learning body part appearance models. In a similar fashion, [22,27] capture local appearances of multiple body parts using *poselets* [3]. Others follow a kernelized approach in a support vector machine (SVM) setup to fuse the various feature sets obtained from scene and person appearances [6], or motion and scene appearance models [24] to reach to a common consensus of the identity of an action. Despite their good performance on multiple datasets, these approaches have to deal with heterogeneous features of different modalities which are sometimes difficult to combine.

Our contribution in this paper presents an effective approach for adapting JNMF for multi-class human action classification. Also, we demonstrate the efficiency of our algorithm in integrating various image modalities for enhancing the overall classification accuracy over different benchmark datasets. The rest of this paper is organized as follows: Section 2 reviews the basics of NMF, its multiview adaptation presented in [1], and our proposed extension for discriminative analysis. Section 3 elaborates on the extracted features used for capturing different action modalities. Finally, Section 4 presents our evaluation on two benchmark datasets, and compare our approach with other state-of-the-art approaches.

2   Non-negative Shared Spaces Learning via JNMF

Our discriminative joint space learning method is formulated under the framework of nonnegative matrix factorization (NMF). This section will first review NMF and its expansion for multiview learning using JNMF, then introduce our adaptation of this algorithm for the extraction of discriminative shared spaces for classification.

2.1   Data Factorization Using NMF

NMF has been used recently in various image analysis and computer vision fields. It became widely known after Lee and Seung [20] investigated its proprieties and presented simple algorithms for the factorization. Formally, NMF aims to factorize a non-negative data matrix $X \in \mathbb{R}^{N \times M}$ into a product of a basis matrix $W \in \mathbb{R}^{N \times K}$ and its coefficient matrix $H \in \mathbb{R}^{K \times M}$. This factorization can be viewed as a least squares optimization problem, and read as:

$$\min_{W, H} \|X - WH\|_F^2$$
$$s.t. W, H \succcurlyeq 0. \tag{1}$$

Both factorized matrices W, H are constrained to be non-negative. In contrast to other factorization techniques such as singular value decomposition (SVD) and principal component analysis (PCA), the extracted bases W presents an intuitive part-based representation for applications where the analyzed matrices consist exclusively of non-negative measurements like color histograms or bag-of-words data representations. These bases also achieve some level of sparsity due to the nonnegativity of matrix H as the basis vectors (parts) can only be added and hence participate in a sparse manner to reconstruct the data matrix X.

2.2   JNMF for Multiview Learning

Recent attempts [1,4,12,21] presented several adaptation techniques of NMF to the problem of multiview learning. Our work is directly motivated by their efforts along with the study of [2] that explains the statistical discrimination capabilities of traditional multiview learning algorithms like canonical correlation analysis (CCA) and partial least squares (PLS). We follow the adaptation of [1] in learning fully shared spaces among primary and auxiliary representations of the dataset. Formally, they assume different modalities of a given dataset of M samples captured by matrices $X \in \mathbb{R}^{N \times M}$ and $Y \in \mathbb{R}^{L \times M}$. The basic idea of this algorithm is to find K suitable basis vectors $W \in \mathbb{R}^{N \times K}$ and $V \in \mathbb{R}^{L \times K}$ for both modalities that are coupled implicitly via a common coefficient matrix H. In other words, the algorithm aims at finding two low rank approximations such that:

$$X = WH \quad \text{and} \quad Y = VH \tag{2}$$

The proposed solution can be formulated as a convex combination of two constrained least squares problems

$$\min_{W,H}(1-\alpha)\|X-WH\|_F^2+(\alpha)\|Y-VH\|_F^2$$

$$(3)$$

$$s.t \quad V,W,H \succcurlyeq 0.$$

where $\alpha \in [0,1]$ controls the residual error penalty on each factorized view. This optimization objective can be solved using a similar multiplicative update rules as presented in [20], with a small modification to fit the multiview setup. The multiplicative updates rules for bases of both views W, V are

$$W = W \odot \frac{XH^T}{WHH^T} \quad \text{and}$$

$$V = V \odot \frac{YH^T}{VHH^T}$$

$$(4)$$

while the update rule for the shared coefficients matrix H among different views factorizations is

$$H = H \odot \frac{(1-\alpha)W^TX + (\alpha)V^TY}{((1-\alpha)W^TW + \alpha V^TV)H}$$

$$(5)$$

2.3   Discriminative Analysis Using JNMF (DA-JNMF)

Direct adaptation of JNMF for statistical discrimination has been investigated in this study, and compared with the proposed approach. In this setup, we assume an annotated feature set for M samples of G different categories, we encode the auxiliary information of group membership of feature matrix $X \in \mathbb{R}^{N \times M}$ using the indicator matrix $Y \in \mathbb{R}^{G \times M}$ as in [2] as

$$\begin{bmatrix} 1_{m_1} & 0_{m_1} & \cdots & 0_{m_1} \\ 0_{m_2} & 1_{m_2} & \cdots & 0_{m_2} \\ \vdots & \vdots & \ddots & \vdots \\ 0_{m_g} & 0_{m_g} & \cdots & 1_{m_g} \end{bmatrix}$$

where m_g denotes the number of features of class g. One major drawback of such adaptation is related to the optimization problem itself of (Eq. 3), which aims at minimizing the weighted difference of the Frobenius norm simultaneously for all categories. This adaptation often leads to a quick descend into local minima for both W and V, therefore, the extracted bases fail to capture the discriminative latent space of the training dataset. To remedy this limitation, we suggest proceeding in an incremental fashion where the joint factorization is performed individually to obtain seperate bases W_g, V_g for each class, and afterwards combine them together to form W, V. We hypothesize that such a

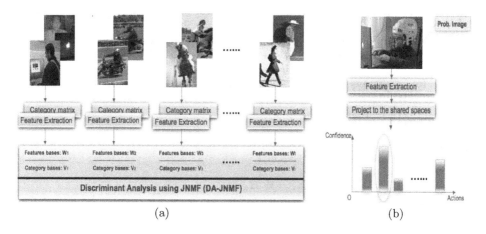

Fig. 1. General diagram of DA-JNMF classification for (a) training phase: learn the bases vectors W, V by combining the extracted bases vectors of each class (b) testing phase: estimation of posterior class memberships for test query

technique results with more discriminative latent structures, and consequently, provides better models for classification. In the test phase, we classify a test sample X_t by solving for the coefficent matrix H_t instead of H in (Eq. 3) using the learned bases W, V. Finally, we estimate the posterior probabilities of class membership for X_t as $Y_t = V H_t$ (see Fig. 1). Our empirical results, detailed in section 4, validate this observation over multiple benchmark datasets.

Earlier studies [8] revealed that by estimating $W D^{-1}$ or alternatively DH where $D \in \mathbb{R}^{K,K}$ is diagonal matrix defined as $D_{k,k} = \sum_i W_{i,k}$ promotes all formal properties of a conditional probability matrix where each column of H define to which degree feature i is associated for the basis k. Given this fact, we normalize all extracted bases from both views using the diagonal matrix D. Empirically, we observed that normalizing the extracted bases led to a slight enhancement on the performance of our algorithm, results are further detailed in Section 4.

3   Action Representation in Still Images

Human action recognition in still images has recently received considerable interest in computer vision. We evaluate our proposed algorithm on this problem as human actions, in general, can be naturally characterized by different views such as human pose, appearance and context. Observing that these multiple views often provide compatible and complementary information, it appears natural to integrate them for better performance rather than relying on a single view. As our algorithm provides an approximation of the posterior probability for an action given its view features, it would be interesting to integrate those multiple approximations from different views to gain a better performance over what each individual view might achieve.

Algorithm 1. DA-JNMF algorithm

1: **procedure** DA-JNMF(X, Y, X_t, K, G)   ▷ K: number of bases for NMF, G: number of classes, X: train features, Y: ground truth, X_t: test features
2:     Initialize W, V to empty matrices.
3:     **for** $g = 1$ to G **do**
4:         $W_g, V_g \leftarrow$ solve optimization of (eq. 3) using (eq. 4) and (eq. 5)
5:         $W_g \leftarrow W_g D_g^{-1}$
6:         $V_g \leftarrow V_g D_g^{-1}$
7:         aggregate class bases W_g in W
8:         aggregate class bases V_g in V
9:     **end for**
10:     $H_t \leftarrow$ solve for H_t in $X_t = W H_t$
11:     $Y_t \leftarrow V H_t$
12:     return Y_t
13: **end procedure**

In this paper, we follow the conventional approach to capture scene and pose appearances. To capture scene information, we densely sample local features every 6 pixels at multiple scales and compute SIFT features [7]. Then we construct a codebook using Kmeans and encode the image features using Locality Linear Coding (LLC) [25]. Maximum pooling is carried out afterwards over three levels of the spatial pyramid of the image plane [19]. Finally, we concatenate all features from different levels and obtain our appearance view of the action. To capture human pose appearance in scenarios where most of the human body parts are visible, we use the Histogram of Oriented Gradients (HOG) [5]. We follow the standard construction of this descriptor with 8×8 cell size and an overlapping blocks of size 2×2. Our motivation for using this descriptor is that certain activities such as "walk" or "play golf" show only limited variations of pose and appearance. In such situations, we observed that global templates can still provide accurate representations of the action and therefore enhance the precision of our classifier. Both descriptors were used with our DA-JNMF algorithm 1,the results were later fused by using the sum rule [18] for different views and selecting the class that had the maximum confidence as the action of the queried image.

4   Evaluation

We evaluate our classification scheme on two benchmark datasets for human action recognition. This section elaborates on our experimental evaluation, and compares our technique with current state-of-the-art techniques used for action recognition for still images.

4.1   Datasets

For experimental evaluation, we selected two diverse and challenging datasets of human action images. Our goal was not only to show the competitive perfor-

Fig. 2. Example human action images from Willow action dataset (first row), and Ikizler action dataset (second row)

mance of our classification scheme in terms of accuracy and performance, but also to investigate the merits of integrating multiple views of action images for the purpose of action recognition. The first dataset is the Willow dataset[1] of [6]. This dataset consists of seven different actions (interacting with computer, taking photo, playing music, riding bike, riding horse, walking, and running). The total number of images is 968 and split into training, testing and validation sets. The dataset contains normal consumers photos obtained from Flickr, and captures a wide variation of poses, views, and scenes. The second dataset[2] is presented by [16]. It contains a total of 2458 images downloaded from the Internet. We operated on the processed version of the dataset with cropped and aligned human body with respect to head position. The dataset consists of five different actions (dancing, playing golf, sitting, running and walking). It was randomly split into $\frac{1}{3}$ for training and the rest for testing. Pictures in this dataset are characterized by a better visibility of human body parts, but still represent a challenge as they show wide pose variations. Examples from both datasets are shown in Fig. 2

4.2 Results

We followed the experimental procedure proposed by [6] for the Willow dataset. We considered pose appearance captured in terms of human bounding boxes using a three level spatial pyramid with LLC encoding (F.SPM), and the scene view using the original images with the same feature (B.SPM). In both cases, images were re-sized to a maximum size of 300 pixels before extracting the features. For the Ikizlier dataset [16], we captured human pose appearance using the HOG descriptor while the scene is represented using a three level spatial pyramid. Finally both results were integrated as we have already mentioned in Section 3. Figure 3 depicts the classification accuracy of each action view on both datasets using the proposed approach.

---

[1] `www.di.ens.fr/willow/research/stillactions`

[2] `http://cs-people.bu.edu/ncinbis/actionsweb/dataset_release`

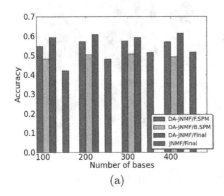
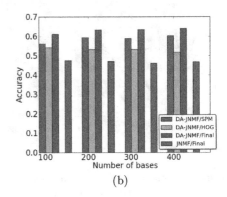

(a)   (b)

Fig. 3. Classification accuracy for different numbers of bases K using JNMF and our proposed approach DA-JNMF (a) Willow dataset, (b) Ikizler dataset

Table 1. Results on Willow and Ikizler datasets

methods on Willow ds.	overall acc.	mean per-class
BOF+LSVM [6]	-	62.14
Our approach	61.04	61.57
methods on Ikizler ds.		
Baseline [16]	56.45	52.46
Latent Poses[27]	61.07	62.09
Our approach	**64.05**	**64.44**

As discussed above, our classification model needs only to specify the number of latent bases K used in the DA-JNMF algorithm. We observed a small variation in classification accuracy as we select K between 100 and 400. Selecting the parameter K beyond these values results in a worse performance in terms of overall accuracy (if $K < 100$), or in terms of training time (if $K > 400$). Figure 3 (a) and (b) show the effect of varying this parameter on over all classification results obtained from both views on both dataset using both JNMF and DA-JNMF.

Table 1 compares our results with other state-of-the-art results on both datasets. Note that our results on the Ikizlier dataset significantly outperform the baseline result [16] and state-of-the-art [27] as both our features capture complementary action properities of pose using HOG and scene using the spatial pyramid. While on the Willow dataset, our results still compare with state-of-the-art. One major advantage of our algorithm compared to other state-of-the-art methods is in our classification model, which can be very efficient in real time applications as it requires only simple matrix multiplications, and summations. Finally, the confusion matrices of both datasets are depicted in Fig. 5. Note that the major confusion within the Ikizler dataset occurs in the case of *dance* action with *sit*, as both stands for different body pose articulations. Similarly, a noticeable

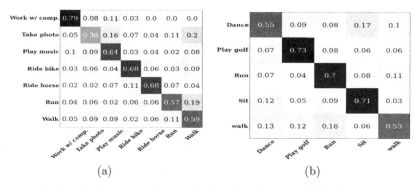

Fig. 4. Confusion matrices of (a) Willow dataset (b) Ikizlier dataset

confusion occurs between actions of *walk* and *run* as both have close pose and appearance views. While for the Willow dataset, the action of *taking photo* is highly confused with other actions due to the limited visual clue of the presence of a camera for this action.

5   Conclusion

We presented a novel classification algorithm based on recent advances in multiview NMF. The evaluations of this algorithm took over challenging action recognition datasets and demonstrated not only its significance for multiclass classification, but also its capability in benefiting from heterogeneous action modalities in a late fusion process. We showed also that the resulting classification model rely only on matrix multiplications in estimating classes posteriors, therefore, it represent a good candidate for real time applications where interest in classification confidence goes beyond one class to all other classes.

Acknowledgements. This work was carried out in the project "automatic activity recognition in large image databases " which is funded by the German Research Foundation (DFG).

References

1. Akata, Z., Thurau, C., Bauckhage, C.: Non-negative matrix factorization in multimodality data for segmentation and label prediction. In: CVWW (2011)
2. Barker, M., Rayens, W.: Partial least squares for discrimination. J. Chemometrics 173, 166–173 (2003)
3. Bourdev, L., Malik, J.: Poselets: body part detectors trained using 3d human pose annotations. In: ICCV (2009)
4. Caicedo, J., BenAbdallah, J., González, F., Nasraoui, O.: Multimodal representation, indexing, automated annotation and retrieval of image collections via non-negative matrix factorization. Neurocomputing 76, 50–60 (2012)

5. Dalal, N., Triggs, B.: Histograms of oriented gradients for human detection. In: CVPR (2005)
6. Deltaire, V., Laptev, I., Sivic, J.: Recognizing human actions in still images: A study of bag-of-features and part-based representations. In: BMVC (2010)
7. Lowe, D.G.: Distinctive image features from scale-invariant keypoints. IJCV 60(2), 91–110 (2004)
8. Ding, C., Li, T., Peng, W.: On the equivalence between non-negative matrix factorization and probabilistic latent semantic indexing. Comput. Stat. Data Anal. 52, 3913–3927 (2008)
9. Dondera, R., Davis, L.: Kernel pls regression for robust monocular pose estimation. In: CVPR-Workshops (2011)
10. Donner, R., Reiter, M., Langs, G., Peloschek, P., Bischof, H.: Fast active appearance model search using canonical correlation analysis. TPAMI 28, 1690–1694 (2006)
11. Eweiwi, A., Cheema, S., Thurau, C., Bauckhage, C.: Temporal key poses for human action recognition. In: ICCV-Workshops (2011)
12. Gupta, S., Phung, D., Adams, B., Tran, T., Venkatesh, S.: Nonnegative shared subspace learning and its application to social media retrieval. In: KDD 2010 (2010)
13. Haj, M., Conzaíez, J., Davis, L.: On partial least squares in head pose estimation: How to simultaneously deal with misalignment. In: CVPR (2012)
14. Hotelling, H.: Relations between two sets of variates. Biometrika 28, 321–377 (1936)
15. Hskuldsson, A.: Pls regression methods. J. Chemometrics, 211–228 (1988)
16. Ikizler-Cinbis, N., Cinbis, R., Sclaroff, S.: Learning actions from the web. In: ICCV (2009)
17. Kim, T., Wong, K.K., Cipolla, R.: Tensor canonical correlation analysis for action classification. In: CVPR (J)
18. Kittler, J., Hatef, M., Duin, R.P.W., Matas, J.: On combining classifiers. TPAMI 20, 226–239 (1998)
19. Lazebnik, S., Schmid, C., Ponce, J.: Beyond bags of features: Spatial pyramid matching for recognizing natural scene categories. In: CVPR (2006)
20. Lee, D.D., Seung, H.S.: Learning the parts of objects by non-negative matrix factorization. Nature 401(6755), 788–791 (1999)
21. Liu, J., Wang, C., Gao, J., Han, J.: Multi-view clustering via joint nonnegative matrix factorization. In: SDM (2013)
22. Maji, S., Bourdev, L., Malik, J.: Action recognition from a distributed representation of pose and appearance. In: CVPR (2011)
23. Thurau, C., Hlavac, V.: Pose primitive based human action recognition in videos or still images. In: CVPR (2008)
24. Wang, H., Klaeser, A., Schmid, C., Cheng-Lin, L.: Action recognition by dense trajectories. In: CVPR (2011)
25. Wang, J., Yang, J., Yu, K., Lv, F., Huang, T., Gong, Y.: Locality-constrained linear coding for image classification. In: CVPR (2010)
26. Willems, G., Becker, J.H., Tuytelaars, T., Van Gool, L.: Exemplar-based action recognition in video. In: BMVC (2009)
27. Yang, W., Wang, Y., Mori, G.: Recognizing human actions from still images with latent poses. In: CVPR (2010)
28. Yao, A., Gall, J., Fanelli, G., Gool, L.V.: Does human action recognition benefit from pose estimation? In: BMVC (2011)
29. Yao, B., Fei-Fei, L.: Action recognition with exemplar based 2.5D graph matching. In: Fitzgibbon, A., Lazebnik, S., Perona, P., Sato, Y., Schmid, C. (eds.) ECCV 2012, Part IV. LNCS, vol. 7575, pp. 173–186. Springer, Heidelberg (2012)

Joint Shape Classification and Labeling of 3-D Objects Using the Energy Minimization Framework

Alexander Zouhar, Dmitrij Schlesinger, and Siegfried Fuchs

Dresden University of Technology

Abstract. We propose a combination of multiple Conditional Random Field (CRF) models with a linear classifier. The model is used for the semantic labeling of 3-D surface meshes with large variability in shape. The model employs multiple CRFs of low complexity for surface labeling each of which models the distribution of labelings for a group of surfaces with a similar shape. Given a test surface the classifier exploits the MAP energies of the inferred CRF labelings to determine the shape class. We discuss the associated recognition and learning tasks and demonstrate the capability of the joint shape classification and labeling model on the object category of human outer ears.

This paper addresses the problem of labeling 3-D objects with large variability in shape. A 3-D object is represented by a 2-D surface mesh embedded in $\mathbb{R}^3$, defining its boundary. The labeling densely covers the surface capturing the part structure of the underlying object.

Organic shapes such as categories of human teeth (e.g., the canine), categories of human bones (e.g., the femur), the outer ear anatomy of humans, and many others are typical examples of object categories with large variability in shape across individuals. It is extremely challenging to label surfaces of such object categories consistently.

To achieve this, our approach employs multiple CRFs [14] each of which models the label distribution for a group of surfaces with a similar shape. The partitioning of a category of objects into sets of similar shapes is performed prior to learning the CRFs for example via manual selection by domain experts. A linear classifier takes the MAP energies of the CRF labelings of a surface as an input and determines the shape class. The labeling model associated with this shape class produces the best quality labeling of the surface.

The use of multiple, shape specific labeling models has several advantages. First, each model may be kept simple. No additional shape prior is needed to ensure consistency of labeling across all objects. Second, no model assumption about the nature of the shape variation is required. The shape information is captured in terms of classes of similar shapes for which the CRFs are learned. Third, the MAP energy of the inferred labelings may be used for classification. This is a key aspect of our work, since the energy value associated with the optimal labeling can normally not be regarded as a readily useful quantity.

J. Weickert, M. Hein, and B. Schiele (Eds.): GCPR 2013, LNCS 8142, pp. 71–80, 2013.

Related Work and Contribution

Numerous tasks in geometric modeling and manufacturing of 3-D meshes rely on their segmentation into parts. CRF based approaches exploit local spatial interactions between the parts and allow the use of rich overlapping descriptors without the need to model the possibly complex dependencies between them. Superior labeling performance compared to previous mesh segmentation methods [16,8,9] has recently been reported in [11] for the Princeton Segmentation Benchmark (PSB) [4]. However, the proposed model is complex and lacks interpretability. Specifically, the choice of the features and their geometric relationship are not well founded. For example, the distinctiveness of the difference of the neighboring feature vectors tends to be sensitive to variations of the mesh resolution and to variations of the mesh tessellation. The latter drawback also holds for the model in [20].

In this work we employ CRFs with pairwise Potts interactions between the neighboring labels together with 3-D shape contexts [12] as local observations of the mesh vertices. 3-D shape contexts yield distinct local representations of regional or global shape except for symmetries. Other distribution based descriptor schemas, such as spin images [10], intrinsic shape contexts [17] and multi-scale surface descriptors [5] form histograms of ambiguous surface attributes and are therefore less discriminative on our data.

Model-based object recognition methods of 2-D images often combine object specific segmentation models with shape priors in order to cope with visual variability and other non-ideal conditions. See for example [13,6,19] and the references therein. However, models which describe the desired form of the segmentation usually tend to be complex resulting in high computational costs of learning and recognition. Moreover, the nature of the underlying shape variation of an object category may be unknown or difficult to model. Instead of using a single labeling model we employ a linear classifier that sits on top of multiple, shape specific labeling models of low complexity.

The shape specific labeling problem may also be formulated within the framework of Structured Support Vector Machines (SSVM). See, for example [15] and the references therein. However, from a practical point of view this may be inconvenient especially when larger data sets are involved. For example, relearning of an SSVM classifier involves all training instances each time a novel observation is added to the training data. Our approach requires a single shape specific labeling model to be relearned together with a few additional classifier parameters. This only involves data members of the shape class to which a novel observation is assigned.

The capability of our model is demonstrated on the object category of human outer ears. Mesh labeling is highly significant in digital hearing aid manufacturing. It serves as a pre-requisite for automated surface manipulation in order to reduce the amount of human intervention in the manufacturing process [18].

In the next section we derive the joint shape classification and labeling model. Section 2 covers the resulting learning and recognition tasks. Experimental results are presented in section 3. A brief discussion concludes the paper.

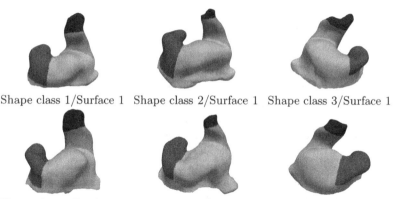

Shape class 1/Surface 1   Shape class 2/Surface 1   Shape class 3/Surface 1

Shape class 1/Surface 2   Shape class 2/Surface 2   Shape class 3/Surface 2

Fig. 1. Example shape classes of the ear population each of which is arranged column by column. The ear geometry is composed of 6 non-overlapping parts whose anatomical interpretation is color-coded.

1   Joint Shape Classification and Labeling Model

We consider the following model. A surface mesh $X = (V, E, F)$ consists of vertices V, edges E and faces F. A labeling $Y : V \rightarrow H$ of X assigns a part label $Y_v \in H$ to each vertex $v \in V$. For example, figure 1 shows 6 surfaces capturing the left or right ear geometry of different individuals. The human outer ear is composed of $|H| = 6$ parts whose anatomical interpretation is denoted by the colors (see [20] for details). Moreover, there exist K distinct subsets of surfaces with a similar shape which we refer to as shape classes. The partitioning of the data was performed using a known clustering algorithm (see section 3 for details). This resulted in a pre-labeled and pre-classified set of surfaces with reduced variability inside the shape classes compared to the variability in the set of all meshes. Each column in figure 1 depicts two representative examples of three shape classes of the ear population.

We continue with a model for the joint probability over elementary events (X, Y, k), i.e.,

$$p(X, Y, k) \propto p(k|X)p(Y|X, k). \tag{1}$$

The labeling model associated with class k is the conditional probability

$$p(Y|X, k) = \frac{\exp\{-U(X, Y, k)\}}{Z(X, k)}, \tag{2}$$

where $U(Y, X, k)$ denotes the energy of a labeling Y of X using the k-th model and $Z(X, k)$ denotes the observation specific partition function of the k-th model. The distribution $p(k|X)$ on the right hand side of equation (1) indicates the confidence for a surface X being a member of class k based on its shape. The energy term $U(X, Y, k)$ is given by

$$U(X,Y,k) = \sum_{v \in V} \phi_v(Y_v, X) + \sum_{\{v,w\} \in E} \psi_{v,w}(Y_v, Y_w), \qquad (3)$$

where the unary potentials $\phi_v(\cdot, \cdot)$ use descriptors of regional or global surface geometry characterizing the shape of the neighborhood around each vertex $v \in V$. Surface descriptors, including 3-D shape contexts [12], normally reside in a high dimensional space. This is why we use randomized decision trees for the unary potentials similar to [19]. For each vertex $v \in V$ a decision tree returns a distribution over the part labels in H. The pairwise potentials $\psi_{v,w}(\cdot, \cdot)$ incur a constant positive cost for neighboring labels being different and zero otherwise.

We define the classification of a surface X as the problem of maximizing equation (1) jointly with respect to the variables k and Y, i.e.,

$$f(X) = \arg\max_k \max_Y p(k|X)p(Y|X,k), \qquad (4)$$

or equivalently

$$f(X) = \arg\max_k \max_Y [\log p(k|X) + \log p(Y|X,k)] \qquad (5)$$

$$= \arg\max_k \max_Y [\beta(X,k) - U(Y,X,k)], \qquad (6)$$

where

$$\beta(X,k) = \log p(k|X) - \log Z(X,k). \qquad (7)$$

The two terms in equation (7) have similar qualitative properties. When the shape classes form compact clusters the posterior probability $p(k|X)$ is peaked, that is, if X belongs to class k then the first term assumes a large value and a small value otherwise. Likewise, for a given X the quantity $Z(X,k)$ assumes a large value when X belongs to class k and a small value otherwise because, in the former case, there should exist labelings with both high and low energies. It is therefore reasonable to assume that equation (7) may be approximated by a sum of two univariate functions, say,

$$\beta(X,k) \approx \beta(X) + \epsilon_k \qquad (8)$$

where $\beta(X)$ depends on X and ϵ_k depends on k. In general this may not be true. Note, that this assumption is weaker than, e.g., to assume the decomposability of $Z(X,k)$. We provide empirical evidence in section 3.

Equation (6) then simplifies to

$$f(X) = \arg\max_k \left[\epsilon_k - \min_Y U(X,Y,k)\right]. \qquad (9)$$

To further simplify the notation we set

$$q_k(X) = -\min_Y U(Y,X,k) \qquad (10)$$

and obtain

$$f(X) = \arg\max_k [q_k(X) + \epsilon_k]. \qquad (11)$$

The set of free parameters of the resulting classifier $f(X)$ comprises the unary and pairwise potential parameters of the K energy functions given in equation (3) along with the class specific constants $\epsilon = (\epsilon_1, ..., \epsilon_K)$.

2   Learning and Inference

Given a pre-classified and pre-labeled set of training surfaces $\mathcal{T}$ we learn the unary and pairwise potential parameters for each of the K labeling models in equation (3) using a supervised algorithm similar to [19,20]. Learning involves growing decision trees for the unary potentials and learning of the pairwise potential parameters via cross-validation. Alternatively the maximum-likelihood method may be applied for parameter learning as well as the techniques described in [15].

Approximate MAP inference of the part labels may be carried out efficiently using the alpha expansion algorithm [3] after which the quantities $q_k(X)$ in equation (10) are computed. In the remainder of this section we describe the procedure for learning the class specific constants ϵ.

For a training surface $X \in \mathcal{T}$ with known class association k the classifier $f(X)$ correctly decides for k if

$$q_k(X) + \epsilon_k > q_{k'}(X) + \epsilon_{k'}, \; \forall k' \neq k. \tag{12}$$

Thus, for each $X \in \mathcal{T}$ there are $K - 1$ constraints of the form (12) yielding a total of $(K - 1)|\mathcal{T}|$ constraints for the training set $\mathcal{T}$.

We follow the Support Vector Machine (SVM) approach and minimize the upper bound of the empirical risk, i.e.,

$$L(\epsilon) = \sum_X \sum_{k' \neq k} \max\{0, 1 - q_k(X) - \epsilon_k + q_{k'}(X) + \epsilon_{k'}\} \to \min_\epsilon, \tag{13}$$

where $k \leq K$ denotes the true class of a surface X. Equation (13) is sometimes referred to as the hinge loss function. Since $L(\epsilon)$ is convex a minimizer $\epsilon^* = \min_\epsilon L(\epsilon)$ can be obtained globally. Moreover, $L(\epsilon)$ is subdifferentiable [2] and can be minimized iteratively by a subgradient method. A typical subgradient method iterates

$$\epsilon^{(l+1)} = \epsilon^{(l)} - \alpha_l g^{(l)} \tag{14}$$

where $g^{(l)}$ denotes the subgradient of $L(\epsilon^{(l)})$ at $\epsilon^{(l)}$, α_l denotes the step-size and $l \geq 0$ denotes the iteration index. The subdifferential of equation (13) is given by

$$\partial L(\epsilon) = \sum_i \partial L_i(\epsilon), \tag{15}$$

where the sum is over all inequalities in equation (12) and all X.

If for the current $\epsilon^{(l)}$ and for the i-th example X we have $q_k(X) + \epsilon_k^{(l)} - q_{k'}(X) - \epsilon_{k'}^{(l)} \leq 1$ then $g_k^{(l)} = -1$ and $g_{k'}^{(l)} = 1$ with $g_k^{(l)}$ and $g_{k'}^{(l)}$ denoting the k-th

Input   : Training set $\mathcal{T}$, Class alphabet $\{1, ..., K\}$, Iterations $n \geq 1$
Output: A minimizer ϵ^* of $\min_\epsilon L(\epsilon)$

$\epsilon^{(0)} \leftarrow 0$;
for $l \leftarrow 0$ **to** $n - 1$ **do**
    $g^{(l)} = 0$; // Initialize subgradient of $L(\epsilon^{(l)})$ with zero
    for $i \leftarrow 1$ **to** $|\mathcal{T}|$ **do** // $\mathcal{T} = \{X_1, ..., X_i, ..., X_{|\mathcal{T}|}\}$
        for $k' \leftarrow 1$ **to** K *and* $k' \neq k$ **do** // k is true class of $X_i \in \mathcal{T}$
            if $q_k(X_i) + \epsilon_k - q_{k'}(X_i) - \epsilon_{k'} \leq 1$ **then**
                $g_k^{(l)} \leftarrow g_k^{(l)} - 1$; // Update k-th component of g
                $g_{k'}^{(l)} \leftarrow g_{k'}^{(l)} + 1$; // Update k'-th component of g
            end
        end
    end
    $\epsilon^{(l+1)} \leftarrow \epsilon^{(l)} - g^{(l)}/(l+1)$;
end
$\epsilon^* = \epsilon^n$;

Algorithm 1. Subgradient method for solving the problem $\epsilon^* = \min_\epsilon L(\epsilon)$.

and k'-th component of the subgradient of $L_i(\epsilon^{(l)})$. Otherwise the subgradient of $L_i(\epsilon^{(l)})$ is equal to zero.

The step-size α_l in equation (14) is determined prior to running the iteration. A classical step-size rule is given by

$$\alpha_l \geq 0, \sum_{l=0}^{\infty} \alpha_l^2 < \infty, \sum_{l=0}^{\infty} \alpha_l = \infty, \tag{16}$$

for example $\alpha_l = 1/l$ where $l > 0$. Algorithm 1 summarizes the proposed subgradient method for solving the problem $\epsilon^* = \min_\epsilon L(\epsilon)$.

Given a test surface X recognition is conducted by first running the α-expansion algorithm for each of the K labeling models. The energy values returned by the algorithm are then used to compute the quantities $q_k(X)$ after which equation (11) can be solved. In the next section we show some experimental results.

3   Experiments

We have experimented with our model using a data set of 200 human outer ear impressions which in turn were laser scanned to reconstruct 3-D triangular mesh representations. The resulting meshes were composed of roughly 20000 vertices. Each surface was labeled by an expert along anatomical lines using a CAD software system. In this way 6 compact, non-overlapping regions are obtained as illustrated in figure 1. These regions play a significant role in the design of personalized hearing aid devices [18].

We randomly picked 90% of the surfaces for training while setting the other 10% of the surfaces aside for testing. The whole data set was then partitioned

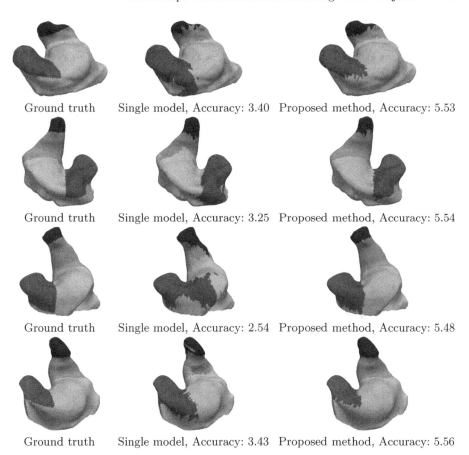

Ground truth   Single model, Accuracy: 3.40 Proposed method, Accuracy: 5.53

Ground truth   Single model, Accuracy: 3.25 Proposed method, Accuracy: 5.54

Ground truth   Single model, Accuracy: 2.54 Proposed method, Accuracy: 5.48

Ground truth   Single model, Accuracy: 3.43 Proposed method, Accuracy: 5.56

Fig. 2. Example segmentations using a single labeling model (middle) and the joint shape classification and labeling model (right)

into $K = 5$ shape classes via clustering using the algorithm in [7]. As a measure of pair-wise shape distance we chose the 3-D shape context matching score under a bipartite matching model similar to [1]. This resulted in a pre-classified and pre-labeled set of training examples with reduced anatomical variability inside the clusters (the shape classes). Three example classes are depicted in figure 1.

Next, each of the K labeling models was learned as described in section 2 using the class members as an input. Prior to learning the class specific constants ϵ the quantities $q_k(X)$ were computed using equation (10). The class specific constants ϵ were then learned using algorithm 1. The latter converged quickly after a few iterations.

For a test surface the solver returns the estimated class and the labeling. If ϵ is set to zero, i.e., when ϵ_k is removed from equation (11) then 70% of the training data and 30% of the test data were assigned to the correct class, i.e., the learned class while at the same time the labeling model of this class generated the best

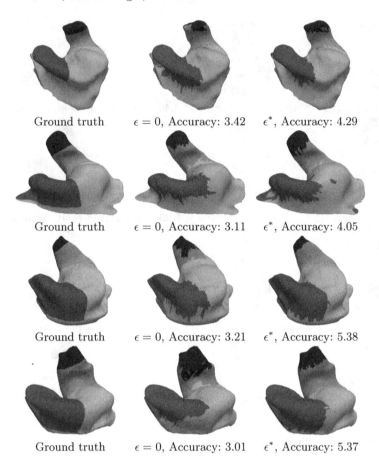

Ground truth $\epsilon = 0$, Accuracy: 3.42 ϵ^*, Accuracy: 4.29

Ground truth $\epsilon = 0$, Accuracy: 3.11 ϵ^*, Accuracy: 4.05

Ground truth $\epsilon = 0$, Accuracy: 3.21 ϵ^*, Accuracy: 5.38

Ground truth $\epsilon = 0$, Accuracy: 3.01 ϵ^*, Accuracy: 5.37

Fig. 3. Labeling result using the joint shape classification and labeling model with $\epsilon = 0$ (middle) and with the learned $\epsilon^* \neq 0$ (right). The labeling model associated with the learned shape class of a test candidate performs best (right).

quality labeling. On the other hand, for the learned vector $\epsilon^* \neq 0$ a correct class assignment was achieved for 92% of the training data and for 78% of the test data while at the same time the labeling models of these classes performed best.

Figure 2 illustrates the result of four test candidates. The first column shows the ground truth labeling of the surfaces. The second column depicts the labeling result achieved as the MAP estimate using a single model given in equation (3). Note, how various regions are over- and under-segmented. The third column shows the labeling result using the learned joint classification and labeling model for which we observe the best agreement with the ground truth. The quality of labeling is indicated by the quantity below the surfaces. For a label, first the Dice coefficient of the estimated region and the corresponding ground truth was computed as a measure of labeling accuracy per part. The labeling accuracy of a test candidate is defined as the sum of the part scores with 6 being the maximum score. The result suggests that the joint model copes better with the shape variability versus using a single labeling model of comparable complexity.

Figure 3 depicts the labeling result of four test surfaces when the estimated shape classes differ from the learned classes (middle) and when the surfaces are assigned to their learned classes (right). The result shows that the labeling model of the learned class achieves the best agreement with the ground truth.

The outcome of the experiment provides empirical evidence for the assumption in equation (8).

4 Discussion and Future Work

We introduced a joint shape classification and labeling model using the energy minimization framework. The model integrates shape information in terms of multiple shape specific labeling models each of which is learned using a training set of surfaces with a similar shape. As demonstrated in the experiments the labeling accuracy greatly improves over using a single labeling model of comparable complexity. Moreover, the best performance was achieved when the labeling model of the estimated shape class was used. The preliminary experiments are promising given the simplicity of the labeling model. In the future we plan to investigate the capability of the method when the labeling model includes more complex constraints about the object structure.

References

1. Belongie, S., Malik, J., Puzicha, J.: Shape matching and object recognition using shape contexts. IEEE PAMI 24(24) (2002)
2. Boyd, S., Vandenberghe, L.: Convex Optimization. Cambridge University Press (2004)
3. Boykov, Y., et al.: Efficient approximate energy minimization via graph cuts. PAMI (2001)
4. Chen, X., Golovinskiy, A., Funkhouser, T.: A benchmark for 3D mesh segmentation. ACM Transactions on Graphics (Proc. SIGGRAPH) 28(3) (August 2009)
5. Cipriano, G., Phillips Jr., G.N., Gleicher, M.: Multiscale surface descriptors. IEEE Transactions on Visualization and Computer Graphics (Proceedings Visualization 2009) (October 2009)
6. Flach, B., Schlesinger, D.: Combining shape priors and MRF-segmentation. In: da Vitoria Lobo, N., Kasparis, T., Roli, F., Kwok, J.T., Georgiopoulos, M., Anagnostopoulos, G.C., Loog, M. (eds.) S+SSPR 2008. LNCS, vol. 5342, pp. 177–186. Springer, Heidelberg (2008)
7. Frey, B.J., Dueck, D.: Clustering by passing messages between data points. Science 315, 972–976 (2007)
8. Golovinskiy, A., Funkhouser, T.: Randomized cuts for 3D mesh analysis. ACM Transactions on Graphics (Proceedings SIGGRAPH Asia) 27 (2008)
9. Golovinskiy, A., Funkhouser, T.: Consistent segmentation of 3D models. Computers and Graphics (Shape Modeling International 09) 33(3), 262–269 (2009)
10. Johnson, A.E., Hebert, M.: Using spin-images for efficient multiple model recognition in cluttered 3-D scenes. IEEE PAMI 21(5), 433–449 (1999)

11. Kalogerakis, E., Hertzmann, A., Singh, K.: Learning 3D mesh segmentation and labeling. SIGGRAPH 2010 (2010)
12. Koertgen, M., Park, G.J., Novotni, M., Klein, R.: 3D shape matching with 3d shape contexts. In: Proceedings of The 7th Central European Seminar on Computer Graphics (2003)
13. Kumar, M.P., Torr, P.H.S., Zisserman, A.: Obj cut. In: Proceedings of the IEEE Conference on Computer Vision and Pattern Recognition, San Diego, vol. 1, pp. 18–25 (2005)
14. Lafferty, J.D., McCallum, A., Pereira, F.: Conditional random fields: probabilistic models for segmenting and labeling sequence data. ICML (2001)
15. Nowozin, S., Lampert, C.H.: Structured learning and prediction in computer vision. Foundations and Trends in Computer Graphics and Vision 6(3-4), 185–365 (2011)
16. Shapira, L., Shamir, A., Cohen-Or, D.: Consistent mesh partitioning and skeletonisation using the shape diameter function. Visual Computing 24, 249–259 (2008)
17. Shi, Y., et al.: Direct mapping of hippocampal surfaces with intrinsic shape context. Neuroimage (2007)
18. Slabaugh, G., Fang, T., McBagonluri, F., Zouhar, A., Melkisetoglu, R., Xie, H., Unal, G.: 3-D Shape Modeling for Hearing Aid Design. IEEE Signal Processing Magazine (2008)
19. Winn, J., Shotton, J.: The layout consistent random field for recognizing and segmenting partially occluded objects. In: CVPR (2006)
20. Zouhar, A., Baloch, S., Tsin, Y., Fang, T., Fuchs, S.: Layout Consistent Segmentation of 3-D meshes via Conditional Random Fields and Spatial Ordering Constraints. In: Jiang, T., Navab, N., Pluim, J.P.W., Viergever, M.A. (eds.) MICCAI 2010, Part III. LNCS, vol. 6363, pp. 113–120. Springer, Heidelberg (2010)

A Coded 3d Calibration Method
for Line-Scan Cameras

Erik Lilienblum, Ayoub Al-Hamadi, and Bernd Michaelis

Institute for Information Technology and Communications
Otto von Guericke University Magdeburg, Germany
{erik.lilienblum,ayoub.al-hamadi}@ovgu.de

Abstract. This paper presents a novel 3d calibration method for line-scan cameras using coded straight line patterns. We describe an algorithm to calculate the 3d-points of intersection between the straight lines of the pattern and the viewing plane of the camera. By a simple encoding we can identify the intersections of multiple patterns unambiguously. For the actual 3d calibration we reduce the dimensionality of the camera model and solve the calibration problem within the viewing plane. After that 2d calibration we transfer the camera model back into 3d. Some real test results are shown to confirm the functionality of the proposed calibration method.

1 Introduction

The precise acquisition of the 3d surface shape of workpieces is an important tool for automated quality control in industrial production. In most cases, acquisition systems based on matrix cameras can be used. But under certain conditions there is a need to apply line-scan cameras instead of matrix cameras. An example of a 3d application with a stereo line-scan system is given in [4]. In [1] some basic aspects are discussed about using line scan cameras in machine vision systems.

However, to use line-scan cameras in 3d acquisition systems, they need to be calibrated. The well-known calibration methods for matrix cameras, as described in [5], can not be used here. Either, there is only the information on a single line available, or the cameras have to be moved relative to the measuring object. There are different approaches to solve the calibration problem for line-scan cameras. These approaches differ considerably in their handling, robustness, and accuracy. It depends on the requirements of an application, whether a particular approach is suitable.

There are two main strategies for the calibration of line-scan cameras, those with and those without movement. The captured images we call scanned and static images, respectively. The scanned images are 2d images, where we can detect 2d-markers as in common matrix camera images. If the movement is reproducible one can apply adapted methods with space resection, linearizing and least squares adjustment. Examples of calibration methods with linear movement are described in [7] and [3]. But in some applications those calibration methods are not suitable.

J. Weickert, M. Hein, and B. Schiele (Eds.): GCPR 2013, LNCS 8142, pp. 81–90, 2013.
© Springer-Verlag Berlin Heidelberg 2013

Possible reasons could be that there is not enough place to scan a calibration field or that there is no reproducible movement due to vibrations.

Therefore, it is advantageous to use a static image acquisition, which makes the camera calibration independent of the movement. In [6] a calibration method has been proposed which utilizes a pattern with straight lines on two parallel planes. By considering the ratio of segments one can obtain the intersection points of the straight lines of the pattern with the viewing line of the camera. With these intersection points and their corresponding pixel values in the captured image line the intrinsic and extrinsic camera parameters were calculated by classical calibration methods of matrix cameras.

In our paper we propose an alternative straight line pattern and present a novel algorithm to obtain the intersection points. The new pattern allows us to increase the number of lines which generally leads to an increase in accuracy. Also we can unambiguously encode distinct patterns to make the calibration method robust for non-specialist users and for an automatic operation. The new algorithm allows us to abandon both the exact parallelism of planes as well as the exact parallelism of lines. This facilitates the preparation of the calibration field considerably. After obtaining the intersection points we will show a way of simplifying the classical calibration by reducing the dimensionality of the camera model. In the result section we present real measurements that are based on image acquisition with and without movement.

2   Design of the Calibration Field

The basic concept is to use vertical and diagonal lines which are combined to coded targets. The line targets are placed side by side on planes with different height. Each line target consists of a fixed number of vertical lines placed right and left of a block of diagonal lines. Figure 1 shows a calibration field with a total of 4 × 3 line targets on two levels. Width, spacing and alignment of lines are depending on the camera to be calibrated.

The spacings between the diagonal lines of a block are divided into three classes: wide, medium and narrow. The wide and the narrow spacing serve the actual coding. The medium spacing is for classification and orientation. The viewing line has not to be horizontal aligned but should intersect all lines of a

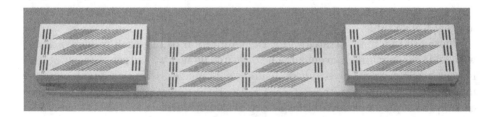

Fig. 1. Calibration field with 12 line targets on two levels

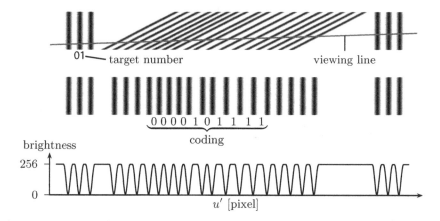

Fig. 2. Design of target 01 (above), a static image of the target on the viewing line (center) and the brightness profile on a single line of the static image (below)

target for proper identification. Figure 2 schematically illustrates the viewing line within target 01 and the coding on the corresponding static image.

For both encoding and calibration the pixel values of intersection points between the target lines and the viewing line are needed. They can be detected by one-dimensional search of the extremes in the brightness profile. A target design with soft edges generally enables the detection of intersection points with sub-pixel accuracy.

To calculate the intersection points in 3d the target lines have to be known in the reference coordinate system. Thus each line on the calibration field has to be measured. It can be done by every calibrated 3d measurement system with the appropriate resolution and accuracy. It should be noted that through geometric changes of the calibration field, such as temperature variations, the measured basis changes and systematic calibration errors are caused.

3 Getting the Viewing Plane

The viewing plane can be calculated by fitting a plane into the 3d intersection points of targets on different levels. Thus, how to get the 3d intersection points is the actual problem. As already proposed in [2], we can solve the problem by using the cross-ratio of collinear points which is invariant under central projection. Neglecting distortion and other sources of systematic errors, the pinhole model of a line-scan camera corresponds exactly to a central projection. Figure 3 shows the geometric relations of a central projection of four points on the viewing line to four points on the sensor line.

Because of the invariance under central projection, the value of cross-ratio

$$\lambda = \frac{\overline{AD} \cdot \overline{BC}}{\overline{BD} \cdot \overline{AC}} = \frac{\overline{A'D'} \cdot \overline{B'C'}}{\overline{B'D'} \cdot \overline{A'C'}} \tag{1}$$

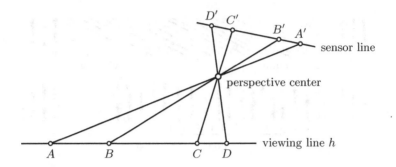

Fig. 3. Central projection of points from the viewing line to the sensor line

is independent from the spacial position of the line-scan camera. Because the positions of A', B', C', D' can be measured at the line-scan image λ can be calculated directly. So the cross-ratio of arbitrary groups of intersection points on the viewing line is also known.

With the precondition from section 2 that the targets on the calibration field have already been measured, each straight line on the target can be described in the reference coordinate system by a linear equation. Since all lines of a target are located on the same plane, we can transform these spatial linear equations by parallel projection into the xy-level without changing the distance relationship between points on these lines. The transformed lines are noted in Cartesian normal form with

$$x = g(y) = a + by \qquad (2)$$

where due to the vertical alignment of the lines, y is mapped on x. Together with the measured plane equation we yield back for each known 2d-point on a target a 3d-point in the reference coordinate system.

Now we take from a measured target three vertical lines noted by

$$
\begin{aligned}
g^A(y) &= a^A + b^A y \,, \\
g^B(y) &= a^B + b^B y \,, \\
g^D(y) &= a^D + b^D y \,,
\end{aligned}
\qquad (3)
$$

and one diagonal line noted by

$$g^C(y) = a^C + b^C y \,. \qquad (4)$$

The four lines pass through the associated points A, B, C, D on the viewing line h from figure 3. Because the measured vertical lines are only approximately in parallel we have to define additionally virtual vertical lines by

$$
\begin{aligned}
g_*^A(y) &= a_*^A + \bar{b}y \quad \text{with} \quad a_*^A = x - y\bar{b} \quad \text{and} \quad A = (x, y) \,, \\
g_*^B(y) &= a_*^B + \bar{b}y \quad \text{with} \quad a_*^B = x - y\bar{b} \quad \text{and} \quad B = (x, y) \,, \\
g_*^D(y) &= a_*^D + \bar{b}y \quad \text{with} \quad a_*^D = x - y\bar{b} \quad \text{and} \quad D = (x, y) \,,
\end{aligned}
\qquad (5)
$$

having a mutual slope of

$$\bar{b} = \frac{b^A + b^B + b^D}{3} . \tag{6}$$

Obviously they also pass through the points A, B, D, respectively.

Because the lines g_*^A, g_*^B, g_*^D are in parallel the cross-ratio of the intersection points with a virtual viewing line h' is invariant relative to an arbitrary rotation in point C. Figure 4 shows a rotation in particular where h' runs parallel to the x-axes. From equation 1 it follows

$$\lambda = \frac{\overline{A''D''} \cdot \overline{B''C}}{\overline{B''D''} \cdot \overline{A''C}}. \tag{7}$$

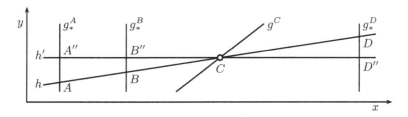

Fig. 4. Rotation of the virtual viewing line h' in point C

The line segments in equation 7 can be calculated by putting in equations 4 and 5. It holds

$$\begin{aligned}
\overline{A''D''} &= g_*^D(y) - g_*^A(y) = a_*^D - a_*^A , \\
\overline{B''C} &= g^C(y) - g_*^B(y) = a^C - a_*^B + (b^C - \bar{b})y , \\
\overline{B''D''} &= g_*^D(y) - g_*^B(y) = a_*^D - a_*^B , \\
\overline{A''C} &= g^C(y) - g_*^A(y) = a^C - a_*^A + (b^C - \bar{b})y ,
\end{aligned} \tag{8}$$

whereby the alignment in parallel with the x-axis leads to a mutual y parameter. Thus we have only one unknown in equation 7, which we can rearrange to

$$y = \frac{(a_*^D - a_*^A)(a^C - a_*^B) - \lambda(a_*^D - a_*^B)(a^C - a_*^A)}{(\lambda a_*^D - \lambda a_*^B - a_*^D + a_*^A)(b^C - \bar{b})} \tag{9}$$

getting the y-coordinate of C directly. Together with equation 4 and the known plane of the calibration field we obtain the complete intersection point C.

But the points A, B, D for defining the virtual vertical lines in equation 5 are initially unknown. Thus we have to start the calculation here with approximate values. This obviously creates an error, since the actual points A, B, D are not exactly on the virtual vertical lines and thus equation 7 is not true. For minimizing the error we define an iteration scheme.

At first we assume a viewing line h_0 in parallel to the x-axis and in center of the target. The intersection points of h_0 with the measured vertical lines g^A, g^B, g^D we note by A_0, B_0, D_0, respectively. They are the approximate values initializing the iteration which is defined according to equation 5 for all steps $i \geq 1$ by

$$
\begin{aligned}
g_i^A(y) &= a_i^A + \bar{b}y \quad \text{with} \quad a_i^A(y) = x - y\bar{b} \quad \text{and} \quad A_{i-1} = (x, y), \\
g_i^B(y) &= a_i^B + \bar{b}y \quad \text{with} \quad a_i^B(y) = x - y\bar{b} \quad \text{and} \quad B_{i-1} = (x, y), \\
g_i^D(y) &= a_i^D + \bar{b}y \quad \text{with} \quad a_i^D(y) = x - y\bar{b} \quad \text{and} \quad D_{i-1} = (x, y).
\end{aligned}
\tag{10}
$$

Based on these virtual vertical lines the point C is calculated according to equation 9 by

$$
y = \frac{(a_i^D - a_i^A)(a^C - a_i^B) - \lambda(a_i^D - a_i^B)(a^C - a_i^A)}{(\lambda a_i^D - \lambda a_i^B - a_i^D + a_i^A)(b^C - \bar{b})} .
\tag{11}
$$

A regression over all C-points yields a new h_i which is an improved approximation of the viewing line. It leads to improved intersection points A_i, B_i, D_i. The iteration already converges with $A_i \to A$, $B_i \to B$ and $D_i \to D$ in a few steps, if the measured vertical lines are approximately in parallel. It follows $h_i \to h$, which makes equation 7 and therefore the whole approach correct.

After finishing the iteration all C-points of a target can be calculated in 3d by using the associated plane equation. The C-points of all targets totally seen by the line-scan camera should be approximately located on the viewing plane. If at least two captured targets are located on different levels we can get the viewing plane by fitting a plane into the C points.

It remains to be clarified the postulation of neglecting distortion at the beginning of this section. In general, if the target size is much smaller then the image radius the distortion has no considerable influence on the accuracy of our approach. The reason is that we use as inputs only differences of image coordinates, thus relative values. This statement can be confirmed by investigating the deviation of C-points from the calculated viewing plane. An example is shown in section 5 on figure 6.

In general three vertical lines would be sufficient to realize our approach. But we use six instead. If the lines g^A, g^B, g^D from equation 3 are combined in various over all vertical lines of a target we can calculate each C-point 18 times. Thus measurement errors on the detection of single vertical lines can be compensated. The method gains significant stability and accuracy.

4   Calibration Approach

With the calculation of the viewing plane the conditions for a classical 3d camera calibration method using a distortion corected pinhole model are met. The line-scan camera is treated as a special variant of a matrix camera, where the vertical image coordinates and the vertical principal point is defined with 0. With the 3d intersection points on the calibration field and the corresponding 1d image points on the line sensor we can perform a space resection in order to calibrate the camera. In practical tests with our own calibration software for matrix cameras we obtain adequate results.

However, the calibration method can be optimized by taking advantage of special characteristics of the line camera. Because all control points, the projective center and the sensor line are located in the same viewing plane we can reduce the dimensionality of the calibration problem.

At first, we apply a rotation matrix R_s transforming the viewing plane in parallel with the xz-level of the reference coordinate system. Thus, the y coordinates can be reduced without any loss. For the 3d control points $\mathbf{x}_1, \mathbf{x}_2, \ldots, \mathbf{x}_n$ with $\mathbf{x}_j = (x_j, y_j, z_j)^T$ and the perspective center $\mathbf{O} = (O_x, O_y, O_z)^T$ we obtain

$$\mathbf{R}_s \cdot \mathbf{x}_j = \begin{bmatrix} x'_j \\ y_s \\ z'_j \end{bmatrix} \quad \text{and} \quad \mathbf{R}_s \cdot \mathbf{O} = \begin{bmatrix} O'_x \\ y_s \\ O'_z \end{bmatrix}. \tag{12}$$

For the exterior camera parameter concerning the angles ω, φ, κ and the rotation matrix $\mathbf{R} = \mathbf{R}_\omega \cdot \mathbf{R}_\varphi \cdot \mathbf{R}_\kappa$ we obtain

$$\mathbf{R}_s \cdot \mathbf{R} = \mathbf{R}_{\varphi'}. \tag{13}$$

Together with the horizontal principal point H_u, the camera constant c and the radial symmetric distortion parameters A_1 and A_2 we yield a parameter vector

$$\mathbf{p} = \left(c, H_u, A_1, A_2, O'_x, O'_z, \varphi'\right)^T \tag{14}$$

with 7 unknowns instead of 11 unknowns related to an ordinary matrix camera model. The geometric relationships in the viewing plane with the interior and exterior camera parameters and the 2d control points are illustrated in figure 5.

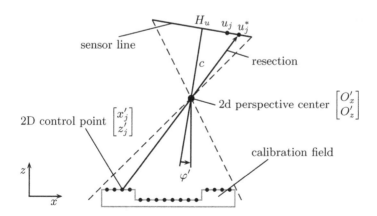

Fig. 5. Geometric relationships regarding 2d resection in the viewing plane

Figure 5 also shows the 2d resection from a control point $(x'_j, z'_j)^T$ to a sensor point u^*_j and the corresponding detected sensor point u_j. The differences between the resection points based on camera parameters and the observation points based on a captured 1d image are registered in a residual vector

$$q = \begin{bmatrix} u_1 - u_1^* \\ u_2 - u_2^* \\ \vdots \\ u_n - u_n^* \end{bmatrix} . \tag{15}$$

Implementing an objective function

$$F(\mathbf{p}) = \mathbf{q} \tag{16}$$

we can iteratively optimize the parameter vector $\mathbf{p}$ by linearizing and least-squares adjustment. Approximate values, which are needed for linearizing the objective function can be obtained by a direct linear transformation being adapted for 2d cases.

After calculating the camera model in the viewing plane we have to transform the exterior camera parameter back into the reference coordinate system. According to equations 12 and 13 we get the 3d perspective center with

$$\mathbf{O} = \mathbf{R}_s^T \cdot \begin{bmatrix} O_x' \\ y_s \\ O_z' \end{bmatrix} \tag{17}$$

and the rotation matrix with

$$\mathbf{R} = \mathbf{R}_s^T \cdot \mathbf{R}_{\varphi'} . \tag{18}$$

5   Results

First, we briefly look at the calibration field design. In many tests we could verify a robust detection of all targets at various geometrical positions. Since the coding is located between the diagonal lines, we can distinguish between a large number of different targets without loosing measurements for the actual calibration. By customizing the width of lines even blurry images are not a problem. That is important because on the one hand line-scan cameras usually have a very small depth of field and on the other hand the calibration field needs sufficient height distances to achieve a high accuracy of 3d measurement. However, the design of the proposed calibration field can be easily adapted for various 3d measurement setups and requirements.

Now we examine the accuracy in determining the viewing plane. In figure 6 we observe the y-deviation between the fitted viewing plane and the calculated C-points. It is depicted the y-deviations of an example captured by a single line over the targets 01, 04, 07 and 10 of the calibration field shown in figure 1. The maximum deviation is 20.6 μm and the mean deviation is 5.3 μm. At our setup with a 4k line sensor, an image ratio of 1:10 and a pixel size of 10 μm the mean

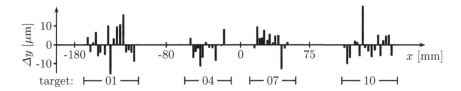

Fig. 6. Viewing plane deviations of C-points

deviation correspond to $1/20$ pixel what is a good value for the underlying 1d detection of the lines. It also shows that the method for calculating the viewing plane works at different targets of the 3d calibration field without significant errors. Considering that we get the viewing plane through fitting over four targets with a total of 62 diagonal lines with C-points, we obtain quite accurate results.

To check the calibration method we consider the precision (or repeatability) of calculated camera parameters and the mean residues of resection. In table 1 the results are listed. In the first three rows we consider single lines of a static image leading to mean residues below 0.1 pixel. This value is comparable to results in matrix cameras. Within the viewing plane there are typical calibration dependencies between interior and exterior parameters, particularly between c and O_z. The parameters O_y and ω are mainly dependent on the viewing plane position and are evidence of the robustness.

In the second three rows we consider single lines of an image captured by scanning the calibration field with a linear stage. Here we hold the interior camera parameters over all lines constant, which generally leads to some larger residues. But that gives us the ability to avoid local errors and at the same time to reconstruct the linear movement by regression. In the underlying case we obtain a linear movement of $(0.0, 0.099, 0.0)^T$ in mm per line.

Table 1. Calibration results of single lines in static and scanned images

line number		static image			scanned image		
		50	100	150	100	250	400
O_x	[mm]	-45.075	-45.085	-44.936	-45.481	-45.558	-45.465
O_y	[mm]	4.910	4.959	4.970	20.430	5.468	-9.226
O_z	[mm]	1017.4	1016.9	1017.3	1020.0	1020.0	1020.1
ω	[rad]	-0.0020	-0.0020	-0.0020	-0.0014	-0.0015	-0.0018
φ	[rad]	-0.0013	-0.0014	-0.0011	-0.0019	-0.0019	-0.0017
κ	[rad]	-0.0006	-0.0006	-0.0007	-0.0006	-0.0005	-0.0005
c	[pix]	-9545.3	-9540.6	-9543.9	-9567.3	-9567.3	-9567.3
H_u	[pix]	1969.4	1970.9	1969.5	1970.8	1970.8	1970.8
A_1	$[10^{-10}]$	2.1290	1.7321	2.3523	3.7021	3.7021	3.7021
A_2	$[10^{-17}]$	-2.5801	-1.7470	-3.0133	-4.0134	-4.0134	-4.0134
res.	[pix]	0.0946	0.0928	0.1048	0.0942	0.1061	0.1244

6   Conclusion and Further Work

The proposed method is well suited for a 3d calibration of line-scan cameras. It is based on a calibration field with vertical and diagonal straight lines taken together in several coded targets on different levels. By using the cross-ratio of collinear points we calculate 3d intersection points between the straight lines of the targets and the viewing line of the camera. From the intersection points we obtain the viewing plane of the camera with a plane fitting. The viewing plane is used to apply a 2d calibration method by reducing the dimensionality of the actual calibration problem. On example it was shown that the calibration leads to good results both on static images and on scanned images.

The main application for the proposed calibration method is the measurement of 3d surfaces with line-scan camera systems. Thus it should be investigated how the 2d calibration can be applied in a system of two or more cameras being collinearly adjusted. Using well known test objects it should be validated that the calibration method leads to accurate 3d measurements. However, it would indirectly prove the accuracy of the calibration method. Another idea to exploit the proposed method is to apply it for matrix cameras by the benefit of getting much more control points than using ordinary circular targets.

Acknowledgment. This work was supported by AiF/Germany grants (FKZ: KF2188303SS1).

References

1. Godber, S.X., Robinson, M.: Machine vision using line-scan sensors. In: Society of Photo-Optical Instrumentation Engineers (SPIE) Conference Series, vol. 1823, pp. 114–130 (1992)
2. Horaud, R., Mohr, R., Lorecki, B.: On single-scanline camera calibration. IEEE Transactions on Robotics and Automation 9(1), 71–75 (1993)
3. Hui, B., Wen, G., Zhao, Z., Li, D.: Line-scan camera calibration in close-range photogrammetry. Optical Engineering 51(5), 053602-1–053602-12 (2012)
4. Ilchev, T., Lilienblum, E., Joedicke, B., Michaelis, B., Schnitzlein, M.: A stereo line sensor system to high speed capturing of surfaces in color and 3d shape. In: Proceedings of the International Conference on Computer Graphics Theory, pp. 809–812 (2012)
5. Luhmann, T., Robson, S., Kyle, S., Harley, I.: Close range photogrammetry: Principles, methods and applications. Whittles Scotland, UK (2006)
6. Luna, C.A., Mazo, M., Lazaro, J.L., Vazquez, J.F.: Calibration of line-scan cameras. IEEE Transactions on Instrumentation and Measurement 59(8), 2185–2190 (2010)
7. Spinnler, Y.C.K., Wolfsmantel, A.: Calibration of 1d cameras. In: Vision, Modeling, and Visualization 2004: Proceedings, November 16-18, p. 55. PressInc., Standford (2004)

Confidence-Based Surface Prior
for Energy-Minimization Stereo Matching

Ke Zhu[1], Daniel Neilson[2], and Pablo d'Angelo[3]

[1] Chair of Remote Sensing Technology, Technische Universität München, Germany
[2] Department of Computer Science , University of Saskatchewan, Canada
[3] The Remote Sensing Technology Institute, German Aerospace Center, Germany

Abstract. This paper presents a novel confidence-based surface prior for energy minimization formulations of dense stereo matching. Given a dense disparity estimation we fit planes, in disparity space, to regions of the image. For each pixel, the probability of its depth lying on an object plane is modeled as a Gaussian distribution, whose variance is determined using the confidence from a previous matching. We then recalculate a new disparity estimation with the addition of our novel confidence-based surface prior. The process is then repeated. Unlike many region-based methods, our method defines an energy formulation over pixels, instead of regions in a segmentation; this results in a decreased sensitivity to the quality of the initial segmentation. Our confidence-based surface prior differs from existing surface constraints in that it varies the per-pixel strength of the constraint to be proportional to the confidence in our given disparity estimation. The addition of our surface prior has three main benefits: sharp object-boundary edges in areas of depth discontinuity; accurate disparity in surface regions; and low sensitivity to segmentation. We evaluate our method using Middlebury stereo sets and more challenging remote sensing data. Our experimental results demonstrate that our approach has superior performance on these data sets.

1   Introduction

Dense stereo matching has been an active area of research in computer vision for over two decades. The goal is to estimate the distance, or depth, to an imaged object in every pixel of an input image; at its core, this is achieved by finding pixel correspondences between the source image and one or more matching images.

Many of the best stereo matching algorithms are framed as global energy minimizations, but these algorithms tend to have problems when applied to real-world data due to radiometric changes, large baseline and complicated scenarios. Global energy minimization algorithms that are defined over image regions, rather than pixels, achieve the top few ranks in the de-facto standard Middlebury online benchmark when sorted according to depth discontinuities (disc) [1,2,6,8,11,12]. Our own experience, and the Middlebury benchmark, indicate that these region-based methods are preferable around object boundaries and in large homogeneous areas; the use of regions helps propagate strong matches into sub-regions with poor matches. However, defining an energy minimization over regions, rather than pixels, imposes a hard constraint that forces depths to lie on the smooth surface associated with a region; removing fine-level details from the depth map in the process. The results are very sensitive to the given segmentations.

J. Weickert, M. Hein, and B. Schiele (Eds.): GCPR 2013, LNCS 8142, pp. 91–100, 2013.

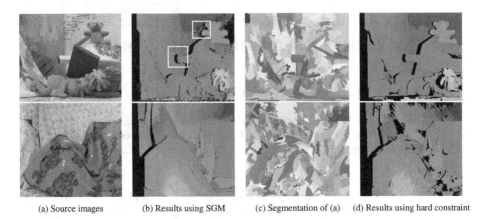

(a) Source images   (b) Results using SGM   (c) Segmentation of (a)   (d) Results using hard constraint

Fig. 1. Segmentation-based stereo matching methods perform sharp edges on the Middlebury online benchmark. However the results are very sensitive to a given segmentation. As the hard plane constraint works well on **Teddy**, segmentation artifacts are observed on the result of **Cloth3**.

In this paper, we propose the addition of a confidence-based surface prior over pixels to an energy minimization formulation of dense stereo matching that addresses these problems:

- *Foreground/background fattening*: Often observed in the occlusion areas of disparity maps, objects are dilated into weakly matching areas as demonstrated in Figure 1: the pink teddy bear and the chimney highlighted within the white windows. The matching costs are ambiguous, causing the energy minimization to dilate the objects beyond their borders.
- *Incorrect matching in large homogeneous areas*: In a large low-texture or homogeneous area, parametric match costs can be unreliable; even when using a global energy minimization algorithm. This is demonstrated in the church roof in Figure 6. Non-parametric, window-based, matching costs like census [14] can overcome this problem, but can lead to dilated edges.
- *Sensitivity to image segmentation*: As shown in Figure 1, segmentation-based methods can perform very well, if the given segments are correlated with the object boundaries [1,6,11,12]. However, the results are very sensitive to the given segmentations. Oft over-segmentation is required. In texture-rich regions, artifacts from segmentation can be appeared.

In our method, we relax the hard region-surface constraint imposed by these methods and continue to gain the benefits of region-based methods by defining an energy minimization over pixels that incorporates a soft constraint that depths lie near, rather than on, a pre-calculated smooth surface. We adjust the strength of our constraint using a measure of the confidence we have that the smooth surface is correct; relaxing the constraint when we believe that it will not benefit the disparity calculation.

The rest of this paper is organized as follows. In Section 2 we outline the general energy minimization framework, and discuss related work. Section 3 describes the novel confidence-based surface prior. We introduce a modified semi-global matching method to use the proposed surface prior in energy space in Section 4. In Section 5 we discuss the performance of our algorithm on both the Middlebury benchmark and airborne data. We conclude in Section 6, and provide some directions for future work.

2   Stereo through Global Energy Minimization

Given a stereo image pair, $\{\mathcal{I}_s, \mathcal{I}_m\}$, a disparity map, $\Delta : \mathcal{I}_s \to \mathbb{Z}^{>0}$, for $\mathcal{I}_s$ can be expressed as the function that minimizes the energy equation:

$$\mathrm{E}(\Delta) = \sum_{p \in \mathcal{I}_s} C(p, \Delta(p)) + \lambda \sum_{\{p,q\} \in \mathcal{N}} V_{p,q}(\Delta(p), \Delta(q)) \qquad (1)$$

where p and q denote pixels in $\mathcal{I}_s$, $\mathcal{N}$ is the set of neighbouring pixel pairs in $\mathcal{I}_s$, $C : \mathcal{I}_s \times \mathbb{Z}^{>0} \to \mathbb{R}$ is a match cost function that provides a measure of fitness for assigning disparity values to pixels, and $V_{p,q}(\delta_1, \delta_2) : (\mathbb{Z}^{>0})^2 \to \mathbb{R}$ is a smoothing term that encodes a smoothness constraint on the resulting disparity map.

Many [6,11,12] of the best ranked methods in the Middlebury online benchmark use a region-based, rather than pixel-based, approach. These approaches define Equation 1 in a way that assigns a smooth surface (usually a plane) to image regions, rather than depth to pixels. The performance of this hard constraint, that all depths in a region be on the same smooth surface, is highly influenced by the quality of the subdivision of the image into regions. If depth discontinuities are not coincident with the border between regions, then they will be lost in the resulting disparity map. Thus, these methods rely on over-segmentation of the image into small regions to maintain good accuracy. By incorporating a probabilistic, rather than a hard, constraint our method is very robust to the segmentation of the image into regions.

Sun et al. [9], Bleyer et al. [1], and Woodford et al. [13] have all proposed different soft constraints for region-based stereo methods that are different from our proposed prior. The soft constraint proposed by Sun et al. is most similar to our approach in that they propose the addition of a single soft constraint term to the energy minimization formulation in Equation 1 that encourages the disparity of a pixel to lie near a plane calculated from a given disparity estimation. However, their soft region constraint does not incorporate confidence; they assume that the provided planes are trustworthy. The algorithm proposed by Bleyer et al. subdivide a given segmentation into overlapping subsegments, and adds a term to their formulation that softly constrains overlapping segments to contain a single contiguous surface. Unlike our proposed method, Woodford et al. utilize an over-segmentation of the image into many small regions, and propose a weighting of their smoothness term that discourages disparity edges from cutting through regions.

Common methods for deriving an approximate minima of Equation 1 include belief propagation [10], graph cuts [3]. The semi-global matching method (SGM) proposed by Hirschmüller [5] is widely used in the photogrammetry, remote sensing, and intelligent vehicle application areas due to being orders of magnitude faster than the other methods of optimization while still producing high quality results.

3   Confidence-Based Surface Prior

We calculate a disparity map Δ for $\mathcal{I}_s$ and denote the probability of $\Delta(p) = \delta_p$ being correct as $P(\delta_p)$ where $P(\delta_p) = \max\{P(\delta) : \forall \delta\}$. Then we segment $\mathcal{I}_s$ into contiguous regions using the well-known mean-shift segmentation algorithm [4] [1]. Using the disparity map Δ and the segmentation Seg_s, we fit a slanted plane, in disparity space, to each region in the segmentation. The plane fitting results in a dense disparity plane map for $\mathcal{I}_s$ that we will denote $\Delta^{pl} : \mathcal{I}_s \to \mathbb{Z}^{>0}$. Each pixel $p \in Seg_s^m$ has to belong to a disparity plane Π^m with $m \in [0, ..., |Seg_s|)$. The disparity of pixel p after plane fitting is denoted as d_p, which can differ from the δ_p calculated from the initial pixel based matching process.

The plane fitting provides an unique assignment for each pixel. The goal of our work is to use this result as an additional surface prior for global frameworks in a probabilistic way. Thus we assume:

Assumption 31. $\forall p \in \mathcal{I}_s$: $P(\Delta^{pl}(p)) \sim N(\mu = d_p, \sigma^2)$

Assumption 32. $P(\Delta(p) = d_p) \ll P(\Delta(p) = \delta_p) \Rightarrow \Delta(p) \notin \Pi^m$

Assumption 31 indicates that the probability of $\Delta^{pl}(p)$ is normally distributed at mean $\mu = d_p$ calculated by plane fitting. Assuming a normal distribution allows us to take advantage of its properties and make inferences from a hard planar constraint to a probabilistic surface prior. Assumption 32 builds the probability of $\Delta(p) \in \Pi^m$ according to a confidence observed from the initial pixel based matching. The confidence is obtained by comparison of $P(\delta_p)$ and $P(d_p)$. The standard deviation is then defined as:

$$\sigma = t(P(d_p), P(\delta_p)) \tag{2}$$

where t is a function such that $\sigma^2 \propto \log(P(\delta_p)/P(d_p))$. Recall that a high value for $P(d_p)$ indicates that d_p is a good candidate match for p. Thus, since σ^2 is the variance, it will cause a sharply peaked Gaussian distribution with its maximum at $\mu = d_p$ when we are confident that $P(d_p)$ is a good candidate for the disparity of p, and a spread out distribution when we are less confident.

Through the probabilistic interpretation of Δ^{pl}, we relax the hard planar constraint as a surface prior according to confidence obtained from previous matching. We describe our surface prior more formally in energy space in the next section.

4   Energy Minimization via iSGM3

In this work, the initial disparity maps for source and match images are calculated using SGM [5] respectively. After consistency checking, the plane-fit disparity map Δ^{pl} is generated by the voting-based plane-fitting algorithm proposed by Wang and Zheng [12]. The comparison of [12] shows the voting-based plane-fitting algorithm is better than the RANSAC method for fitting disparity maps.

---

[1] Note that we do not require that this segmentation be an over-segmentation.

In our proposed iterative algorithm we introduce the addition of a confidence-based surface prior as a new term, $S : \mathcal{I}_s \times \mathbb{Z}^{>0} \to \mathbb{R}$, to Equation 1:

$$E_i(\Delta) = \sum_{p \in \mathcal{I}_s} C(p, \Delta(p)) + \lambda \sum_{\{p,q\} \in \mathcal{N}} V_{p,q}(\Delta(p), \Delta(q)) + \kappa \sum_{p \in \mathcal{I}_s} S(p, \Delta(p)) \quad (3)$$

where λ and κ are two user-defined constants to control their term strengths, respectively. i denotes the iterative step with $i \geq 1$. The energy at $i = 0$ is initialized by Equation 1. The additional surface prior S favors disparities close to object planes. Our method is iterative that the confidence used for the surface prior can be updated.

The SGM minimization introduced by Hirschmüller approximates a global, 3D smoothness constraint by combining many 1D constraints from different aggregation directions for pixel-wise matching. To solve Equation 3, we introduce a modified semi-global matching method, called iSGM3. Compared to SGM [5], our iterative iSGM3 aggregates the path-wise costs in direction r with three terms including data cost, smoothness penalty the additional surface cost function $S(p, \delta)$ as:

$$L_r(p, \delta) = C(p, \delta) + V_{p,p-r}(\delta, \delta') + S(p, \delta). \quad (4)$$

where $V_{p,q}$ is a truncated linear smoothing term with $V_{p,q}(\delta, \delta') = \min\{|\delta - \delta'|, \tau\}$. δ' denotes the disparity at q. The aggregated match costs in different directions are then summed in $E_i(p, \delta)$:

$$E_i(p, \delta) = \sum_r L_r(p, \delta) \quad (5)$$

where i denotes the energy calculated at the i-th step. The initial energy at $i = 0$ can be calculated by Equation 1.

According to assumption 31, we denote the function $f(\delta) = N(\delta, \sigma(\delta))$. Using the confidence introduced in Equation 2, we define σ in energy space as:

$$\sigma(\delta) = (E_{i-1}(p, \delta) - E_{i-1}(p, \delta_p) + \epsilon)^2 \quad (6)$$

where ϵ is a user-defined parameter to avoid a sharply peaked penalty. In our implementation, ϵ is chosen to be equal to 1.5. We select a quadratic function over the confidence to smooth the penalties if $E_{i-1}(p, d_p)$ is very close to $E_{i-1}(p, \delta_p)$. The surface cost function is then defined as:

$$S(p, \delta) = (f(d_p) - f(\delta)) \cdot \frac{E_{i-1}(p, \delta_p)}{f(d_p)} \quad (7)$$

$S(p, \delta)$ penalizes the cost of a pixel belonging to an estimated plane according to its confidence. Choosing $\delta_p = \arg\min_\delta \{E_{i-1}(p, \delta) : \forall \delta\}$ causes the strength of our surface constraint similar as the data cost and smoothness penalty. Therefore, the further the variable δ is away from d_p, the higher cost will be penalized. The ratio of the penalty of δ at different disparity levels is decided by the shape of $f(\delta)$, whose σ is derived from the confidence.

Figure 2 demonstrates the influence of the confidence by fusing the previous calculated $E_{i-1}(p, \delta)$ and the surface penalty, $S(p, \delta)$. We define δ'_p as the new calculated disparity at pixel p for the step i with $\delta'_p = \arg\min_{\delta'}\{E_i(p, \delta') : \forall\delta'\}$. A small difference between $E_{i-1}(p, \delta_p)$ and $E_{i-1}(p, d_p)$ indicates a good confidence for disparity of p lying on the plane shifting δ'_p near to d_p. Conversely, a bad confidence causes a small penalty that δ'_p remains at the same position.

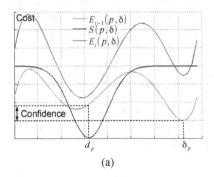
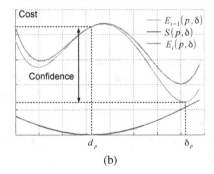

(a)   (b)

Fig. 2. Cost fusion: The green line denotes the previous computed cost. The blue line is the surface penalty S from plane fitting. The fused cost is shown in red line. **(a)** Good confidence: The disparity is shifted near to the plane-fit result. **(b)** Bad confidence: Surface penalties are overall similar. The disparity remains on the early position.

Our proposed algorithm to employ this confidence-based surface prior is outlined in Figure 3. This algorithm employs an iterative feedback loop to incrementally improve the produced disparity estimates; in practice we observe convergence of the depth estimation in one to three iterations.

5   Experimental Results

We use both the Middlebury Benchmark [8] as well as more challenging airborne datasets to evaluate the robustness and accuracy of our confidence-based soft surface prior. The airborne images were acquired using DLR's 3K camera system with 15 cm/pixel ground resolution [7]. Due to space limitations we only demonstrate our algorithm with the truncated absolute difference [2]. We have also tested our algorithm with census and mutual information match cost functions, and determined that it improves accuracy with those cost functions as well. To demonstrate the benefits of our proposed confidence-based surface prior, we compare the results with and without our proposed prior; disparity maps are coloured with a heat scale such that hotter (red) colours are closer to the camera than colder (green/blue/violet) colours. We run our algorithm with identical parameter settings throughout these results.

Figure 4 demonstrates improved accuracy when utilizing our surface prior on some images from the Middlebury benchmark. The proposed confidence-based surface prior

---

[2] Truncated L1 norm in RGB space.

```
1:  procedure CALCDISPARITY($\mathcal{I}_L, \mathcal{I}_R$ )
2:      $\text{Seg}_L \leftarrow$ Segmentation($\mathcal{I}_L$)
3:      $\text{Seg}_R \leftarrow$ Segmentation($\mathcal{I}_R$)
4:      $C_L, C_R \leftarrow$ CalculateMatchCosts($\mathcal{I}_L, \mathcal{I}_R$)
5:      $(\Delta_L, E'_L) \leftarrow$ SGM($C_L, \mathcal{I}_L$ as $\mathcal{I}_s$)                    ▷ Eq. 1
6:      $(\Delta_R, E'_R) \leftarrow$ SGM($C_R, \mathcal{I}_R$ as $\mathcal{I}_s$)                    ▷ Eq. 1
7:      repeat
8:          $\Delta'_L, \Delta'_R \leftarrow$ LeftRightConsistency($\Delta_L, \Delta_R$)
9:          $\Delta^{pl}_L \leftarrow$ RegionBasedPlaneFitting($\text{Seg}_L, \Delta'_L$)
10:         $\Delta^{pl}_R \leftarrow$ RegionBasedPlaneFitting($\text{Seg}_R, \Delta'_R$)
11:         $S_L \leftarrow$ CalculateConfidenceConstraint($\Delta^{pl}_L, E'_L$)
12:         $S_R \leftarrow$ CalculateConfidenceConstraint($\Delta^{pl}_R, E'_R$)
13:         $(\Delta_L, E'_L) \leftarrow$ iSGM3($C_L + S_L, \mathcal{I}_L$ as $\mathcal{I}_s$)         ▷ Eq. 3
14:         $(\Delta_R, E'_R) \leftarrow$ iSGM3($C_R + S_R, \mathcal{I}_R$ as $\mathcal{I}_s$)         ▷ Eq. 3
15:     until $N$ iterations completed
16:     $\Delta'_L, \Delta'_R \leftarrow$ LeftRightConsistency($\Delta_L, \Delta_R$)
17:     return $\{\Delta'_L, \Delta'_R\}$
18: end procedure
```

Fig. 3. Proposed iterative algorithm. Given a stereo image pair, $\{\mathcal{I}_L, \mathcal{I}_R\}$, our algorithm calculates a disparity map for each image.

converts the hard constraint of the plane-fit disparity into a soft prior that is not as reliant on the plane-fit disparity. Sharp edges and sloped surfaces can be generated naturally via a global energy minimization without the hard constraint imposed by plane-fit disparity. Furthermore Table 1 demonstrates quantitative improvement when applying our surface prior on the Middlebury online benchmark. Compared with our SGM implementation, improvement is obtained under all criteria for all four datasets. Our results perform similar as [13] expected on **Venus**, because our segmentation is not tuned for the online benchmark. It seems, color segmentation works well on these four data, thus the methods using segmentation-based hard constraint perform superiorly [12,9]. However, as shown in Figure 1, methods using hard plane constraint are extremely sensitive to the given segmentation.

In contrast to many methods using soft surface priors [13,1], the proposed confidence measure for our surface prior is calculated from an energy minimization without reference to planar surfaces or regions. Thus it is independent of the plane fitting process. Using this confidence, the Gaussian interpretation of the plane-fit result in energy space makes our surface prior more robust to the quality of the segmentation. To demonstrate the effectiveness of our confidence measure we compare disparity maps produced by our proposed confidence-based Gaussian surface prior and the soft surface prior defined using disparity distance between δ_p and d_p in Figure 5. Absent scaling by our confidence measure, the soft surface prior causes the reconstruction of the bowling ball to be relatively planar in vertical stripes. The round shape of the bowling ball is correctly reconstructed when using the confidence-based surface prior.

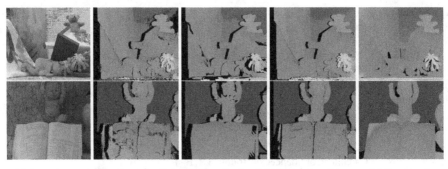

(a) Source images.   (b) Results without (c) Plane-fit disparity (d) Results with our   (e) Ground truth.
                     our surface prior.   from (b).   surface prior.

Fig. 4. Comparison on Middlebury data sets. We compare the disparity results, after left-right consistency checking, with and without the proposed confidence-based surface prior. The plane-fit disparity maps that are calculated from (b) are shown for reference. **Top**: The dilation of the chimney and Teddy bear are reduced in (d). **Bottom**: Discrete disparity levels in the low-texture curved book surface in (c) is partially smoothed out in (d). The baby doll is also better reconstructed in (d).

Table 1. Evaluation on Middlebury online benchmark with Error Threshold > 1. Our SGM results differ from [5] due to different match cost function and post processing for filling occlusion holes used in our implementation. The iSGM3 performs similar as [13] expected on **Venus**, probably due to the color segmentation used.

Algorithm	Tsukuba			Venus			Teddy			Cones		
	nonocc	all	disc	nonocc	all	disc	nonocc	all	disc	nonocc	all	disc
iSGM3	2.40	3.16	10.1	1.47	2.49	14.2	10.2	16.3	21.4	4.2	11.4	12.7
SGM	2.73	3.60	11.4	2.0	3.32	15.9	12.1	18.0	23.2	5.41	13.5	13.8
2OP+occ [13]	2.91	3.56	7.33	0.24	0.49	2.76	10.9	15.4	20.6	5.42	10.8	12.5

Non-lambertian reflectance, and scene complexity all combine to make dense stereo matching on real-word data challenging in contrast to Middlebury benchmark. Figure 6 demonstrates a result of our algorithm on an airborne stereo pair in urban area that includes high buildings, large homogeneous roof areas and shadowed streets. Obvious improvements in accuracy are obtained by our proposed algorithm: sharp building edges, complete roof regions, and less noise on the streets. Along the indicated white arrow through the large homogeneous church roof area, we demonstrate the improvement obtained by our confidence-based surface prior in Figure 6 (d). In contrast to a lot of unreliable disparities after consistency checking on the disparity map without applying our soft surface prior [3], a smooth and gradual changing roof is reconstructed when incorporating our confidence-based surface prior. Additionally, the church edges are perfectly generated without any dilation into the shadowed streets below.

---

[3] Indicated by solid black regions.

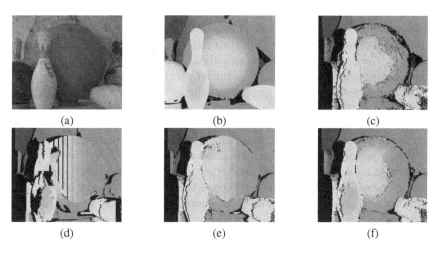

Fig. 5. Results comparison on **Bowling2**: (**a**) Reference image. (**b**) Ground truth. (**c**) Result without soft prior: matching on the boundary areas of objects failed a bit. But the shape of the ball remains well. (**d**) Plane-fit disparity from (c): The ball is reconstructed as a set of vertical stripes, and the pin has become poorly defined. (**e**) Result using soft prior without confidence: Edges are well defined, and vertical striping that is influenced by the plane-fit disparity is visible. (**f**) Result using our surface prior: The rounded shape of the ball is better reconstructed than in (e) and the edges are shaper than in (c).

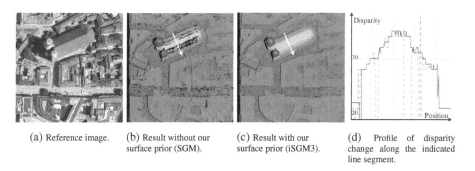

(a) Reference image. (b) Result without our surface prior (SGM). (c) Result with our surface prior (iSGM3). (d) Profile of disparity change along the indicated line segment.

Fig. 6. Comparison of results on the airborne images. (**b**) Without our surface prior there is a lot of false matching on the street level and homogeneous roof regions. The reconstructed building edges are dilated into the shadow areas. (**c**) With our surface prior, accuracy is improved in all surface areas, building edges, and roof areas when compared with (b). (**d**) Profile on the homogeneous church roof area. The profile shows the disparity change along the indicated white arrow both with (green line) and without (blue line) our surface prior. The use of our surface prior reconstructs a closer approximation to the roof surface, absent the extreme outliers observed in (b). Additionally, the building edges are sharper when our surface prior is utilized.

6   Conclusions

In this work, we have introduced a confidence-based surface prior for energy minimization stereo matching that is easy to integrate into existing energy optimization stereo frameworks. The proposed prior constrains disparities to lie near the fit planes during the energy minimization and varies the per-pixel strength of the constraint proportionally to the confidence in our given disparity estimation.

We have demonstrated that our surface prior: prevents inappropriate dilation of objects into weekly matched image regions; can smooth-out and correct incorrect matches in large homogeneous regions even when using match cost functions that are known to result in poor performance in these regions; and prevents the over-smoothing into surrounding object surfaces. Furthermore, our proposed confidence-based surface prior exhibits low sensitivity to parameter selection, and is robust on a variety of data sets.

In further work, we are investigating segmenting a disparity map to refine a colour-based image segmentation by splitting or merging regions based on the disparity segmentation. Our goal is to derive an alternative confidence measure for regions to further improve results in occluded regions and large homogeneous areas.

References

1. Bleyer, M., Rother, C., Kohli, P.: Surface stereo with soft segmentation. In: CVPR, pp. 1570–1577 (2010)
2. Bleyer, M., Rother, C., Kohli, P., Scharstein, D., Sinha, S.: Object stereo — joint stereo matching and object segmentation. In: CVPR, pp. 3081–3088 (2011)
3. Boykov, Y., Kolmogorov, V.: An experimental comparison of min-cut/max-flow algorithms for energy minimization in vision. PAMI 26(9), 1124–1137 (2004)
4. Comaniciu, D., Meer, P.: Mean shift: A robust approach toward feature space analysis. PAMI 24(5), 603–619 (2002)
5. Hirschmüller, H.: Stereo processing by semiglobal matching and mutual information. PAMI 30(2), 328–341 (2008)
6. Klaus, A., Sormann, M., Karner, K.: Segment-based stereo matching using belief propagation and a self-adapting dissimilarity measure. In: ICPR, vol. 3, pp. 15–18 (2006)
7. Kurz, F., Türmer, S., Meynberg, O., Rosenbaum, D., Runge, H., Reinartz, P., Leitloff, J.: Low-cost optical camera systems for real-time mapping applications. PFG 2, 159–176 (2012)
8. Scharstein, D., Szeliski, R.: A taxonomy and evaluation of dense two-frame stereo correspondence algorithms. IJCV 47(1-3), 7–42 (2002),
   http://vision.middlebury.edu/stereo/
9. Sun, J., Li, Y., Kang, S.B., Shum, H.Y.: Symmetric stereo matching for occlusion handling. In: CVPR, vol. 2, pp. 399–406 (2005)
10. Sun, J., Zheng, N.N., Shum, H.Y.: Stereo matching using belief propagation. PAMI 25(7), 787–800 (2003)
11. Taguchi, Y., Wilburn, B., Zitnick, L.: Stereo reconstruction with mixed pixels using adaptive over-segmentation. In: CVPR (2008)
12. Wang, Z.F., Zheng, Z.G.: A region based stereo matching algorithm using cooperative optimization. In: CVPR (2008)
13. Woodford, O.J., Torr, P.H.S., Reid, I.D., Fitzgibbon, A.W.: Global stereo reconstruction under second-order smoothness priors. PAMI 31-12, 2115–2128 (2009)
14. Zabih, R., Woodfill, J.: Non-parametric local transforms for computing visual correspondence. In: Sandini, G. (ed.) ECCV 1992. LNCS, vol. 588, Springer, Heidelberg (1992)

A Monte Carlo Strategy to Integrate Detection and Model-Based Face Analysis

Sandro Schönborn, Andreas Forster, Bernhard Egger, and Thomas Vetter

Department for Mathematics and Computer Science
University of Basel, Switzerland
{sandro.schoenborn,andreas.forster,bernhard.egger,thomas.vetter}@unibas.ch

Abstract. We present a novel probabilistic approach for fitting a statistical model to an image. A 3D Morphable Model (3DMM) of faces is interpreted as a generative (Top-Down) Bayesian model. Random Forests are used as noisy detectors (Bottom-Up) for the face and facial landmark positions. The Top-Down and Bottom-Up parts are then combined using a Data-Driven Markov Chain Monte Carlo Method (DDMCMC). As core of the integration, we use the Metropolis-Hastings algorithm which has two main advantages. First, the algorithm can handle unreliable detections and therefore does not need the detectors to take an early and possible wrong hard decision before fitting. Second, it is open for integration of various cues to guide the fitting process. Based on the proposed approach, we implemented a completely automatic, pose and illumination invariant face recognition application. We are able to train and test the building blocks of our application on different databases. The system is evaluated on the Multi-PIE database and reaches state of the art performance.

1 Introduction

Face image understanding is a very important problem in computer vision. We propose a method to extend the model-based image explanation concept combining Top-Down and Bottom-Up knowledge. Generative models are a wide-spread Top-Down method to interpret images. An image is explained by model parameters obtained with an Analysis-by-Synthesis approach [11]. Given a target image, the model's parameters are adapted (fitting) until the generated image is most similar to the input image and the corresponding parameter values (fit) are taken as image description.

We apply a 3DMM [16] to explain images of human faces. Traditionally, the fitting of a 3DMM to an image requires a good initialization of the applied optimization algorithm to find the best set of parameters. As automatic detection (Bottom-Up) of facial feature points is unreliable regarding strong pose and illumination variation, a new concept is needed to properly integrate such information.

We present a method to reinterpret the model fitting process, which opens doors to the integration of various sources of information. As a concrete example, we show how to integrate unreliable face and facial feature point detectors

J. Weickert, M. Hein, and B. Schiele (Eds.): GCPR 2013, LNCS 8142, pp. 101–110, 2013.

without forcing an early detection decision, which might be based on too little information. Not only the single best detection but the detector response over an area is fused with the prior knowledge of the 3DMM in the fitting process.

We formulate the 3DMM as a probabilistic model and the fitting problem as an inference problem. The fitting process is generalized to a sampling process, drawing samples from the posterior distribution over the model's parameters given an input image. The Metropolis-Hastings algorithm, which is the core of the integration, allows us to include different sources of information as proposal distributions. The used method is an example of a DDMCMC method, as proposed by Tu [21] for image parsing. Combined with Random Forests for feature point detection, this leads to a fully automatically initialized fitter which can deal with unreliable information of different origins in the form of proposal distributions.

To successfully integrate the detection into the model fitting of a 3DMM, we first need to detect face candidates. For each possible face box, the detection maps of facial features need then to be interpreted using model knowledge, this is stated as a sampling process. The samples from all the face boxes need to be combined into a single distribution ("detection posterior") which is then, in the last step, conditioned on the image to obtain the posterior distribution ("image posterior"). The samples from this final distribution represent the model-based image explanation.

To demonstrate the use of the proposed approach, we solve a face recognition task on the Multi-PIE database [12] with state of the art results. The recognition system is built as a direct application on-top of this general purpose face image understanding method. The result is a database-independent recognition system. As a big advantage, the concept of our approach would remain valid and applicable, if the model will be extended to incorporate additional information, such as expressions, ethnic variability or masks to cope with outliers like hair, glasses or beards.

2   Prior Work

2.1   Morphable Model

A 3DMM has been proposed by Blanz and Vetter [3,4] to generatively explain and analyze images of faces. The 3DMM consists of a parametric statistical model of the 3D shapes and textures of faces obtained from a 3D scanner. The faces are brought into dense correspondence before building the statistical model. The model [16] has been successfully used to solve a wide range of problems.

An image is generatively explained or interpreted by the 3DMM by adapting the set of parameters to the image. In a Analysis-by-Synthesis setting, a cost function, measuring the degree of fit of a rendered image, is optimized by standard procedures, such as LBFGS or conjugate gradient methods leading to a fit, often ending in a local optimum. The optimization process needs to be initialized since an exhaustive search is not feasible. This initialization is usually provided by manually annotated landmarks.

2.2   Detection

A good overview of approaches for face detection is given by [23]. The most influential work during the last decade was by Viola and Jones [13]. We use similar features but combine these with a derived Random Forest algorithm based on [5]. Many elaborate approaches tackle facial landmark localization, such as [2] or [6]. We use the same Random Forest algorithm as for face detection.

The idea of local detection is limited by principle, the different local parts have no global consistency. The global consistency additionally needs a model coupling the individual responses. We use the 3DMM to provide the prior knowledge needed. Other important approaches include the pictorial structures models operating in the image plane [9,1].

2.3   Markov Chain Monte Carlo

Markov Chain Monte Carlo methods proved to be a useful tool to handle probability distributions which are more complicated than the most simple analytically tractable ones. In our case, we apply the Metropolis-Hastings algorithm [20]. As the algorithm is very general in nature, it is applied to a variety of different computer vision problems [10,21,22,19].

In computer vision, a useful parametric model consists of many parameters of different scale and meaning to the image forming process. It is not straightforward to design a sampler which can efficiently deal with this.

Most MCMC methods rely completely on designed and fixed proposal distributions, mostly random walks in parameter space. A newer development in the sampling literature are data-driven proposal distributions which make use of the input data to form probably useful proposals (heuristics). DDMCMC methods have been used to segment images [21], do inference about a complex 3D scene using only monocular input [22], to infer the pose of a human body model [19] or to localize faces [15].

Compared to other approaches, our model is not of a composite form. We need to adapt a complex parametric model having many continuous parameters with different interactions and will not use detection to propose additional object hypotheses. We will focus not on model selection but on the adaption step of models with continuous parameters, the fitting. The model we use parameterizes the geometry and appearance of a surface rendered to a 2D view and has thus more parameters with very different roles in the image formation process.

3   Methods

3.1   Bayesian Face Model

The generative 3DMM is a parametric face model which is able to render an image $I_M(\theta)$ given some parameter values θ. The parameters include camera settings, the illumination and the PCA face description split into a shape and a texture part. Using an additional noisy observation model of the generated image $P(I|I_{\mathrm M}(\theta))$, this model can be interpreted in a probabilistic framework and used in a Bayesian setting. The Bayesian posterior distribution then consists of the image formation part and the prior on the model parameters $P(\theta)$:

$$P(\theta|I) \propto P(I|\theta)P(\theta). \tag{1}$$

The traditional fitting approach then corresponds to a maximum-a-posteriori (MAP) inference, finding the parameters with the highest posterior probability. In practice, this yields only local optima of the cost function.

As a noise model, we use the probabilistic interpretation of the traditional least squares cost function which is the isotropic Gaussian distribution, treating each pixel independently

$$P(I|\theta) = \prod_{p\in \mathrm{FG}} \mathcal{N}(I(p)|I_{\mathrm M}(p;\theta), \Sigma) \prod_{p\in \mathrm{BG}} \mathcal{N}(I(p)|\mu_{\mathrm{BG}}, \Sigma_{\mathrm{BG}}), \tag{2}$$

where $\Sigma = \sigma^2 I_3$ is the covariance matrix. The pixels lying outside the generated face are considered background (BG) and their likelihood is evaluated using a multivariate Gaussian $\mathcal{N}(\mu_{\mathrm{BG}}, \Sigma_{\mathrm{BG}})$ trained on all pixels in the observed image. A background model is needed to fully explain the observed image preventing partial explanation effects, such as "shrinking" of the face in the image. We evaluate all values related to pixels in the RGB color space.

We adopted the rendering process of the original 3DMM (see [3]) but changed the illumination model from a Phong model to a spherical harmonics-based global illumination model with two bands [18]. Such an illumination model allows us to obtain the optimal illumination coefficients by solving a linear system, for a fixed geometric setting.

For the 3DMM, we use a slightly modified Basel Face Model (BFM) [16] without ears and throat. The model comes with a statistical prior on the face shape and face texture. We use a broad multivariate Gaussian prior for the camera and illumination models, obtained by analyzing 20k face images in the AFLW database [14].

The 3DMM can also render the position of the facial feature points in the image plane $\hat{\boldsymbol{x}}_i(\theta)$. The observation model of these points is again an independent isotropic Gaussian distribution with standard deviation σ_{LM}. It provides the likelihood of F observed landmark positions $\{\boldsymbol{x}_i\}_{i=1}^{F}$

$$P(\boldsymbol{x}_1, \boldsymbol{x}_2, \ldots, \boldsymbol{x}_F|\theta) = \prod_{i=1}^{F} \mathcal{N}(\boldsymbol{x}_i|\hat{\boldsymbol{x}}_i(\theta), \sigma_{\mathrm{LM}}^2). \tag{3}$$

3.2 Fitting by Sampling from Posterior

The probabilistic interpretation of the 3DMM allows us to deal with uncertainty and thus also to integrate unreliable hints properly. The fitting process changes from an optimization problem to a process inferring the posterior distribution (1).

The rather complicated image generation setting leads to a posterior distribution without a simple representation. We resort to the Metropolis-Hastings algorithm to simulate samples from the posterior. The algorithm transforms samples θ' from a proposal distribution $Q(\theta'|\theta)$ into samples distributed according to the target posterior distribution $P(\theta|I)$ by stochastically accepting or rejecting samples. The specific choice of this algorithm additionally allows us to work with an unnormalized posterior distribution.

Using the simple Propose-and-Verify architecture of the algorithm, we combine many different proposal distributions in a mixture distribution and thus integrate information from many sources, including our detections, directly into the posterior inference process. As only point-wise evaluation of (1) is necessary, we can also include proposals without a simple analytic representation. Traditional gradient moves and optimization steps can be integrated by restating them as additional proposals.

As basic proposals, we make use of Gaussian diffusion moves which lead to a random walk in parameter space. A random walk is not very efficient but can prevent the method from being stuck in local optima. Since the nature and scaling of the different parameters in the model (light, shape, texture and camera) varies drastically, we designed the random walk to be a mixture of block-wise alternating form, with different model parts as blocks. For each block we mix three different parameter scales, leading to a mixture of Gaussians distribution for the random walk stepping. Where appropriate, we included prior world knowledge to decorrelate the proposal distributions, such as compensating for scaling in distance modification proposals thus separating scaling and perspective effects. From time to time, the illumination is explicitly optimized, as the strongest part of mismatch between the rendered and the observed image is usually due to non-adapted light and dominates all other sources of misfit.

3.3   Detections

To include the face and landmarks detection results into the inference process we need a probabilistic output from the detectors in the form of a detection map, assigning each point in the image a likelihood of seeing a specific facial feature at that location.

The face detector and 9 facial feature point detectors (see Figure 1b) were trained using a standard Random Forest algorithm closely related to [5]. For each Random Forest detector we trained 256 trees. Each of these trees is learned using 30% of the training data, randomly selected. A node is split if it is not at a maximal depth of 30 and the data reaching that node is not pure. For a node to learn a random candidate set of 500 features is generated. Based on the information gain criterion the best threshold for each feature is calculated and the best split is selected. A leaf stores the percentage of positives in the data reaching that leaf. This is the certainty of a classification given the patch reaches the leaf. The response of the forest is then the mean of all responses of the trees

The training patches were gathered in a manner proposed in [7]. From the AFLW database [14], we selected for each detector approximately 25k positives and 100k negatives. For the face detector, we selected additional 400k negative patches randomly sampled from the PASCAL-VOC 2012 [8] marked as not containing any person. To have more positive face samples we mirrored the face patches horizontally. As features we used Haar-like features also used in [13].

To detect faces we use a standard sliding window approach over all possible scales. The image is scaled by a factor of 0.9 between subsequent scales. We select the 10 best candidates not having a higher overlap than 60%. The feature response maps are then computed in a 40% enlarged area around each selected face box. The maps are averaged from three neighboring scales around the one the face is detected in.

The detection map $D_i(x)$ of landmark i needs to be combined with the observation noise model for landmarks (3). This is accomplished by performing a maximum convolution with the distance term on the response map as proposed in [9]. At each location x we then get

$$\log P(x|D_i) = \max_t \left\{ -\frac{\|x - t\|^2}{2\sigma_{\text{LM}}^2} + \frac{1}{2}\log P(D_i(t)) \right\}. \tag{4}$$

3.4   Data-Driven Proposals

To properly integrate the information provided by the feature point detectors, this information must be stated as a proposal distribution which is used to generate samples in the parameter space of the model. As we have no explicit parameters encoding directly the position of the feature points, we resort to a generative type of inclusion.

The proposal distribution is created in an iterative Bayesian manner. For each possible face box, we build a proposal distribution by filtering unbiased proposals from the prior through a Metropolis acceptance-step, thus biasing the proposals with the ith face box's position and size and all the landmarks detection likelihoods $\mathcal{D}_i$ of the respective face box:

$$P(\theta) \to P(\theta|\text{box}_i, \mathcal{D}_i). \tag{5}$$

The proposals from all the possible face boxes are combined in a mixture proposal and put through a Metropolis filter step which evaluates a proposed sample using the likelihood of the best face box available for each proposal, corresponding to an OR/union of the different boxes. This step thus mixes the different face box-conditionals (5) according to their consistency with the model:

$$\frac{1}{10}\sum_i^{10} P(\theta|\text{box}_i, \mathcal{D}_i) \to P(\theta|\text{allboxes}, \mathcal{D}). \tag{6}$$

The distribution $P(\theta|\text{allboxes}, \mathcal{D})$ includes knowledge about all the possible detections but never forces us to take an explicit decision on the detection results.

Samples from the distribution (6) prefer other face boxes than the strongest detection in roughly one third of the cases. This implements an implicit model-based verification step without an explicit choice of a face box. A few samples from (6) for a single image are visualized as a video and available as supplementary material.

3.5   Integration

The samples of the landmarks posterior (6) can now be used in the next step. By conditioning additionally on the actual image using the observation model (2) leads to the desired posterior distribution, summarizing all information:

$$P(\theta | \text{allboxes}, \mathcal{D}) \rightarrow P(\theta | I, \text{allboxes}, \mathcal{D}). \tag{7}$$

This rather wasteful generative approach to generate samples is feasible, as the evaluation of the landmark distribution is precomputed in (4) and is very cheap compared to the rendering needed to evaluate the image likelihood (2) at the end. The landmarks detection maps and the pinhole camera model used do not allow for a fast analytical calculation of the landmarks detection posterior anyway.

The system as a whole is able to integrate knowledge from different parts and allows uncertainty by its probabilistic nature. To gain full benefit of this integrative system, one is encouraged to include many different Bottom-Up heuristics increasing the probability that at least one makes a good guess.

4   Experiments and Results

We evaluated our method on an unconstrained face recognition task on the Multi-PIE database [12]. Multi-PIE consists of 755k images including pose, illumination, expression and time (sessions). For our experiments we used the neutral photographs of 249 individuals in the first session in 3 poses ($0°$, $30°$, $45°$) cut to 512 x 512 pixels (see Figure 1). The exact setting can be easily reproduced by the pose and illumination indication in Table 1.

Contrary to most other approaches, we do not adapt any part of our recognition system to the Multi-PIE database.

The standard deviation $\sigma = 0.05$ of the image color[1] noise model has been obtained empirically by analyzing roughly 200 acceptably explained face images of an internal database. The standard deviation of the landmarks position is in the range of a few pixels. We use a value of $\sigma_{LM} = 4$ pixels. Our system does not use any given knowledge about landmarks, pose or illumination present in the image. The only assumption we take, is that there is exactly one face in every image.

We use the detection maps of 9 fiducial points (mouth corners, eye corners, nose tip, nose wingtips). By drawing 5000 samples from the Markov chain, we adapt the pose, the illumination, 50 texture and 50 shape parameters. For the recognition experiment, we use the best sample (maximum posterior probability) given the image and detection maps obtained during the sampling run. The overall runtime per image is under 10 minutes on current consumer hardware.

---

[1] Color values are ranged $c \in [0, 1]$.

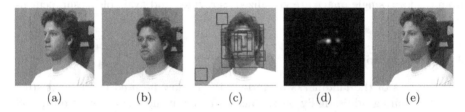

(a)   (b)   (c)   (d)   (e)

Fig. 1. Sample images for the ID 1 in the Multi-PIE database. The poses used for our recognition experiment are a) 45°, b) 30° and c) 0°. Feature points we detect are shown in b). In c), the ten best face candidates are drawn. For the best face box (brightest red) we show the detection map for the right inner eye corner in d). Our fully automatic fitting result is shown in e).

Table 1. Rank-1 Identification rates (percent) and Rank-3 Identification rates (percent, in brackets) across pose, obtained by frontal 0° (051_16) images of all 249 first session individuals as gallery and the respective pose views as probes.

	30° (130_16)	45° (080_16)
our method	90.36 (96.39)	74.70 (86.75)
manual landmarks	93.57 (97.99)	81.93 (90.76)
3DGEM [17]	86.70	65.00

To measure the similarity between two faces f_1 and f_2, the cosine angle between the concatenation of our shape and color model coefficients is used, as suggested by Blanz and Vetter [4]: $d = \langle f_1, f_2 \rangle / (\| f_1 \| \cdot \| f_2 \|)$.

The Rank-1 identification rate refers to the proportion of probe images where the closest face in the gallery is of the same individual as the probe image. The Rank-3 allows the correct face to appear within the 3 closest faces.

Fig. 2. Original image with unreliable face detections (boxes), on the right: face region selected by the algorithm as original (top) and final face reconstruction result (lower) (Image: Keystone/epa/Jason Szenes)

Although our method is much more general (see Figure 2), we outperform state of the art methods for face recognition. Prabhu et al. reached the results closest to ours across pose variation using 3D Generic Elastic Models [17].

Previous approaches to fit a 3DMM [4,16] relied on manually annotated landmarks. If we use our system with these user-provided landmarks, implementing a perfectly reliable feature detection, we can slightly improve the recognition performance.

5   Conclusion

We presented a novel general concept to integrate unreliable information of various sources into the fitting process of a Morphable Model. In contrast to other fitting methods our proposed stochastic approach is not susceptible to local minima. Additionally, the DDMCMC integration concept, based on the Metropolis algorithm, is open to integrate further sources of information like an outlier model for glasses or segmentation of the face into different classes, such as skin, hair and eyes. Regression on the facial pose or expression would add further hints. More information can be used to explore probable hypotheses directly and should therefore improve the final result. All these noisy proposals can be integrated in the proposed approach in contrast to traditional fitters.

Using this concept, we demonstrated a straightforward application integrating unreliable face and landmark detection into model fitting without commitment to a single detection hypothesis. The developed method solves a face recognition task with state of the art performance, without any user input or database adaption.

References

1. Andriluka, M., Roth, S., Schiele, B.: Pictorial structures revisited: People detection and articulated pose estimation. In: IEEE Conference on Computer Vision and Pattern Recognition, pp. 1014–1021. IEEE (2009)
2. Belhumeur, P.N., Jacobs, D.W., Kriegman, D.J., Kumar, N.: Localizing parts of faces using a consensus of exemplars. In: IEEE Conference on Computer Vision and Pattern Recognition (CVPR 2011), pp. 545–552. IEEE (2011)
3. Blanz, V., Vetter, T.: A morphable model for the synthesis of 3d faces. In: SIGGRAPH 1999 Proceedings of the 26th Annual Conference on Computer Graphics and Interactive Techniques, pp. 187–194. ACM Press (1999)
4. Blanz, V., Vetter, T.: Face recognition based on fitting a 3d morphable model. IEEE Transactions on Pattern Analysis and Machine Intelligence 25(9), 1063–1074 (2003)
5. Breiman, L.: Random forests. Machine Learning 45(1), 5–32 (2001)
6. Dantone, M., Gall, J., Fanelli, G., Van Gool, L.: Real-time facial feature detection using conditional regression forests. In: IEEE Conference on Computer Vision and Pattern Recognition (CVPR 2012), pp. 2578–2585. IEEE (2012)
7. Eckhardt, M., Fasel, I., Movellan, J.: Towards practical facial feature detection. International Journal of Pattern Recognition and Artificial Intelligence 23(03), 379–400 (2009)

8. Everingham, M., Van Gool, L., Williams, C.K.I., Winn, J., Zisserman, A.: The pascal visual object classes (voc) challenge. International Journal of Computer Vision 88(2), 303–338 (2010)

9. Felzenszwalb, P.F., Huttenlocher, D.P.: Pictorial structures for object recognition. International Journal of Computer Vision 61(1), 55–79 (2005)

10. Forsyth, D.A., Haddon, J., Ioffe, S.: The joy of sampling. International Journal of Computer Vision 41(1-2), 109–134 (2001)

11. Grenander, U.: Lectures in pattern theory. Applied Mathematical Sciences (1976)

12. Gross, R., Matthews, I., Cohn, J., Kanade, T., Baker, S.: Multi-pie. Image and Vision Computing 28(5), 807–813 (2010)

13. Jones, M., Viola, P.: Fast multi-view face detection. Mitsubishi Electric Research Lab TR-20003-96 3 (2003)

14. Köstinger, M., Wohlhart, P., Roth, P.M., Bischof, H.: Annotated facial landmarks in the wild: A large-scale, real-world database for facial landmark localization. In: IEEE International Conference on Computer Vision Workshops (ICCV Workshops 2011), pp. 2144–2151. IEEE (2011)

15. Liu, C., Shum, H.-Y., Zhang, C.: Hierarchical shape modeling for automatic face localization. In: Heyden, A., Sparr, G., Nielsen, M., Johansen, P. (eds.) ECCV 2002, Part II. LNCS, vol. 2351, pp. 687–703. Springer, Heidelberg (2002)

16. Paysan, P., Knothe, R., Amberg, B., Romdhani, S., Vetter, T.: A 3d face model for pose and illumination invariant face recognition. In: Proceedings of the 6th IEEE International Conference on Advanced Video and Signal based Surveillance (AVSS), pp. 296–301. IEEE (2009)

17. Prabhu, U., Heo, J., Savvides, M.: Unconstrained pose-invariant face recognition using 3d generic elastic models. IEEE Transactions on Pattern Analysis and Machine Intelligence 33(10), 1952–1961 (2011)

18. Ramamoorthi, R., Hanrahan, P.: An efficient representation for irradiance environment maps. In: Proceedings of the 28th Annual Conference on Computer Graphics and Interactive Techniques, pp. 497–500. ACM Press (2001)

19. Rauschert, I., Collins, R.T.: A generative model for simultaneous estimation of human body shape and pixel-level segmentation. In: Fitzgibbon, A., Lazebnik, S., Perona, P., Sato, Y., Schmid, C. (eds.) ECCV 2012, Part V. LNCS, vol. 7576, pp. 704–717. Springer, Heidelberg (2012)

20. Robert, C.P., Casella, G.: Monte Carlo statistical methods, vol. 319. Citeseer (2004)

21. Tu, Z., Chen, X., Yuille, A.L., Zhu, S.C.: Image parsing: Unifying segmentation, detection, and recognition. International Journal of Computer Vision 63(2), 113–140 (2005)

22. Wojek, C., Roth, S., Schindler, K., Schiele, B.: Monocular 3D scene modeling and inference: Understanding multi-object traffic scenes. In: Daniilidis, K., Maragos, P., Paragios, N. (eds.) ECCV 2010, Part IV. LNCS, vol. 6314, pp. 467–481. Springer, Heidelberg (2010)

23. Zhang, C., Zhang, Z.: A survey of recent advances in face detection. Tech. rep., Microsoft Research (2010)

Scale-Aware Object Tracking with Convex Shape Constraints on RGB-D Images

Maria Klodt, Jürgen Sturm, and Daniel Cremers

TU München, Germany

Abstract. Convex relaxation techniques have become a popular approach to a variety of image segmentation problems as they allow to compute solutions independent of the initialization. In this paper, we propose a novel technique for the segmentation of RGB-D images using convex function optimization. The function that we propose to minimize considers both the color image and the depth map for finding the optimal segmentation. We extend the objective function by moment constraints, which allow to include prior knowledge on the 3D center, surface area or volume of the object in a principled way. As we show in this paper, the relaxed optimization problem is convex, and thus can be minimized in a globally optimal way leading to high-quality solutions independent of the initialization. We validated our approach experimentally on four different datasets, and show that using both color and depth substantially improves segmentation compared to color or depth only. Further, 3D moment constraints significantly robustify segmentation which proves in particular useful for object tracking.

1 Introduction

Image segmentation and tracking are of central importance in image analysis. Many successful approaches to image segmentation from monochrome or color images have been proposed in the past [1,18]. Unfortunately, in many real-world applications object and background share similar colors such that purely 2D color-based segmentation methods invariably fail – see Figure 1.

With the rise of novel RGB-D cameras like the Microsoft Kinect, inexpensive sensors became available that provide both color images and depth maps synchronized and at high resolution. While depth alone is usually not sufficient to achieve good segmentation results (different objects may share the same depth), it is well-known that the combination of depth and color information outperforms purely color-based segmentation [10] and allows for significant speed-ups of the segmentation process [17]. Moreover, as we will see in this paper, when prior knowledge about the object is available – like for example, its surface area, centroid, or shape covariance matrix – this knowledge can be exploited during object segmentation.

In this paper, we show how a recently introduced convex framework for color image segmentation [13] can be extended to RGB-D image data. In particular, the contributions of this work are three-fold:

- We show that the data term of respective segmentation energies can be extended to incorporate the local depth information. As a consequence, the respective algorithm favors a separation of object and background based on both color and depth

J. Weickert, M. Hein, and B. Schiele (Eds.): GCPR 2013, LNCS 8142, pp. 111–120, 2013.
© Springer-Verlag Berlin Heidelberg 2013

Fig. 1. Tracking with area constraints: RGB area constraints (first row) cannot deal with camera motion, whereas the RGB-D area constraints (second row) are scale-invariant.

information: It will therefore distinguish structures of the same color but different depth. As a consequence we can segment objects that would be difficult to separate by color or depth alone – see Figure 1.

– We show that the moment constraints introduced in [13] can be made invariant using the depth information to the object's distance from the camera. More specifically, the depth maps enable us to impose constraints on the object's *absolute* shape in 3D, whereas purely color based tracking methods can only impose constraints on the object's *projected* shape. These constraints can either be specified manually by user input, or automatically extracted from an initial segmentation for example for object tracking. In several experiments, we demonstrate that our approach allows us to reliably segment and track humans and plants in RGB-D images. Further, we show that respective moment constraints can be generalized to the RGB-D setting thereby assuring that – for example – the surface area in 3D space is preserved. In tracking experiments beyond constraining the object's sideways motion we can thus also constrain the motion of the object along the camera axis.

2   Related Work

Image segmentation is among the most studied problems in image analysis. Popular algorithms to solve the arising shape optimization problems include level set methods [15], graph cuts [11] or convex relaxation [5], with respective extensions to the multi-region case [6,2,20,14,3].

While it was shown that segmentation results can be substantially improved by imposing shape priors [12,7,9], existing approaches have several limitations: Firstly, apart from a few exceptions such as [19,16], computable solutions are only *locally* optimal thus requiring appropriate initializations and leading to often suboptimal solutions. Secondly, many shape priors require an entire training set of familiar shapes [7,8], making them unpractical for generic interactive image segmentation where the user may have a good idea of what he/she wants but will be hard pressed to construct an entire training set of shapes.

As a remedy it was recently proposed [13] to interactively impose constraints on the lower-order moments of the shape in a convex relaxation framework for image segmentation. The aim of this paper is to generalize these concepts to the problem of RGB-D image segmentation.

3   Tracking in RGB-D Sequences with Shape Constraints

We structured the description of our approach into three parts. First, we introduce in Sec. 3.1 how image segmentation can be formulated as a convex relaxation problem. Second, we describe in Sec. 3.2 how moment constraints can be incorporated during image segmentation. Third, we show in Sec. 3.4 how a user can intuitively provide these constraints with a minimum of effort.

3.1   Segmentation with Convex Relaxation

We formulate the problem of image segmentation as a minimization of functionals of the following form:

$$E(u) = \int_\Omega f(x)\, u(x)\, dx \; + \; \int_\Omega |Du(x)|, \tag{1}$$

Here, $u \in BV(\mathbb{R}^d; \{0, 1\})$ is an indicator function on the space of binary functions of bounded variation, where $u = 1$ and $u = 0$ denote the interior and exterior of a hyper surface in $\mathbb{R}^d$, i.e. a set of closed boundaries in the case of 2D image segmentation or a set of closed surfaces in the case of 3D segmentation.

The second term in (1) is the total variation. Here Du denotes the distributional derivative which for differentiable functions u boils down to $Du(x) = \nabla u(x)dx$. By relaxing the binary constraint and allowing the function u to take on values in the interval between 0 and 1, the optimization problem becomes that of minimizing the convex functional (1) over the convex set $BV(\mathbb{R}^d; [0, 1])$.

Functionals of this form can be globally optimized in a spatially continuous setting by means of convex relaxation and thresholding. The thresholding theorem [4] assures that thresholding the solution u^* of the relaxed problem preserves global optimality for the original binary labeling problem. We can therefore compute global minimizers for functional (1) in a spatially continuous setting as follows: Compute a global minimizer u^* of (1) on the convex set $BV(\mathbb{R}^d; [0, 1])$ and threshold the minimizer u^* at any value $\theta \in (0, 1)$.

With additional depth information from RGB-D images, the boundary length can be measured in absolute values instead of the image domain. Functional (1) can be generalized to

$$E(u) = \int_\Omega f(x)\, u(x)\, dx \; + \; \int_\Omega d(x)|Du(x)|, \tag{2}$$

with depth values $d : \Omega \to \mathbb{R}$. This formulation compensates the fact that objects that are far away to the camera appear smaller in the image due to perspective projection. Weighting with $d(x)$ allows regularization on the absolute size of the boundary – in contrast to assuming a uniform pixel size as in (1).

3.2 Moment Constraints for RGB-D Images

In the following, we will successively constrain the moments of the segmentation with depth information and show how all of these constraints give rise to nested convex sets. We will denote by $\mathcal{B} = BV(\Omega; [0, 1])$ the convex hull of the set of binary indicator functions $u \in BV(\Omega; \{0, 1\})$ of bounded variation on the domain $\Omega \subset \mathbb{R}^d$.

Area Constraint. The 0-th order moment corresponds to the area of the shape u and can be computed by

$$\text{Area}(u) := \int_\Omega d^2(x) u(x) \, dx, \tag{3}$$

where $d(x)$ gives the depth of pixel x. Here, we assume that $d(x) = KD(x)$, with K being the focal length of the camera and $D(x)$ being the depth of the pixel measured in meters. Note that $d^2(x)$ corresponds to the size of a back-projected pixel in 3D space, and thus the integral measures the absolute surface area (scaled by K^2) instead of the projected area in the image. This is in contrast to [13], where all pixels are treated equally.

We can impose that the absolute area of the shape u to be bounded by constants $c_1 \leq c_2$ by constraining u to lie in the set:

$$\mathcal{C}_0 = \left\{ u \in \mathcal{B} \mid c_1 \leq \text{Area}(u) \leq c_2 \right\}. \tag{4}$$

The set $\mathcal{C}_0$ is linearly dependent on u and therefore convex for any constants $c_2 \geq c_1 \geq 0$.

In practice, we can either impose an exact area by setting $c_1 = c_2$, or we can impose upper and lower bounds on the area. Alternatively, we can impose a soft area constraint by enhancing the functional (1) as follows:

$$E_{total}(u) = E(u) + \lambda \left(\int d^2 u \, dx - c \right)^2, \tag{5}$$

which imposes a soft constraint with a weight $\lambda > 0$ favoring the area of the estimated shape to be near $c \geq 0$. Note that the functional (5) is also convex.

Centroid Constraint. The 1-st order moment corresponds to the center of gravity (or *centroid*) of the shape. It can be computed by integrating over all 3D positions of the shape, i.e.,

$$\mu(u) := \begin{pmatrix} \overline{x} \\ \overline{d} \end{pmatrix} = \frac{\int_\Omega \left(\frac{x}{d} \right) u \, dx}{\int_\Omega d^2 u \, dx}, \tag{6}$$

where $\overline{x} \in \mathbb{R}^2$ is the centroid in pixel coordinates and $\overline{d} \in \mathbb{R}$ is the centroid in depth. Together, $\mu \in \mathbb{R}^3$ corresponds to the centroid of the shape in 3D.

We can now impose bounds on the centroid for the object we want to segment by constraining the solution u to the set $\mathcal{C}_1$:

$$\mathcal{C}_1 = \left\{ u \in \mathcal{B} \mid \mu_1 \leq \mu(u) \leq \mu_2 \right\}, \tag{7}$$

where all inequalities are to be taken point-wise and $\mu_1, \mu_2 \in \mathbb{R}^3$. This imposes the centroid to lie between the two constants $\mu_1 \leq \mu_2$. In particular, for $\mu_1 = \mu_2$, the centroid is fixed.

Proposition 1. *For any constants $\mu_2 \geq \mu_1 \geq 0$, the set C_1 is convex. (The proof is analogous to proof 2 in [13].)*

Alternatively, we can impose the centroid as a soft constraint by minimizing the energy:

$$E_{total}(u) = E(u) + \lambda \left| \int_\Omega \left(\mu d^2 - \left(\begin{smallmatrix} x \\ d \end{smallmatrix} \right) \right) u \, \mathrm{d}x \right|^2 ,$$

which is also convex in u.

Covariance Constraint. The proposed concept can be generalized to moments of second order. In the following, we focus on central moments (i.e. moments with respect to a specified centroid μ). The 3D covariance of a shape u is given by

$$\mathrm{Cov}(u) := \frac{\int_\Omega \left(\left(\begin{smallmatrix} x \\ d \end{smallmatrix} \right) - \mu \right) \left(\left(\begin{smallmatrix} x \\ d \end{smallmatrix} \right) - \mu \right)^\top u \, \mathrm{d}x}{\int_\Omega d^2 u \, \mathrm{d}x} . \tag{8}$$

The covariance structure can be considered by the following convex set:

$$C_2 = \left\{ u \in \mathcal{B} \mid A_1 \leq \mathrm{Cov}(u) \leq A_2 \right\} \tag{9}$$

where the inequality constraint should be taken element wise. Here $\mu \in \mathbb{R}^3$ denotes the centroid and $A_1, A_2 \in \mathbb{R}^{3\times3}$ denote symmetric matrices such that $A_1 \leq A_2$ element wise. This constraint is particularly meaningful if one additionally constrains the centroid to be μ, i.e. considers the intersection of the set (9) with a set of the form (7).

Optimization with Moment Constraints. Shape optimization and image segmentation with respective moment constraints can now be done by minimizing convex energies under respective convex constraints. The optimization was implemented using the projection approach as described in [13].

3.3 Tracking with 3D Constraints

The 3D moments of a shape can be used for tracking objects in a sequence of images. Given the moments of the shape in the first frame, constraints can be imposed on segmentations in all subsequent frames. Here, the moments of a shape are computed directly in the 3D space, not in the projection to the image plane. This makes the method independent of the projected size of the object in the image. Without the need of defining a window in which subsequent shapes should be found, the proposed method simply applies the moment constraints of the current frame to the subsequent. We allow the centroid to change inside a small range to handle motion of the camera and/or the object. The area and covariance are supposed to stay constant in the 3D space over all time frames.

Fig. 2. Comparison of tracking an object with and without area constraint. **Top row:** Color-only tracking. **Bottom row:** RGB-D tracking: The surface area is constrained on the absolute dimension via additional information from the depth images.

3.4   Segmentation Priors from User Input

The data term used throughout our experiments has the following form:

$$f(x) = \log \frac{p_{\text{bg}}(I(x))}{p_{\text{obj}}(I(x))}. \tag{10}$$

Here, $I : \Omega \rightarrow \mathbb{R}^n$ refers to an image with n channels. For example, $n = 1$ for depth or gray-scale images, $n = 3$ for color images and $n = 4$ for RGB-D images. The data priors p_{obj} and p_{bg} assign probabilities to each pixel belonging to the object or the background, respectively, and satisfy $p_{\text{obj}} + p_{\text{bg}} = 1$. We compute them from histograms for foreground and background. The moment constraints that we consider in our experiments include the centroid, area and covariance of the shape.

Both the data prior as well as the moment constraints can be specified by the user. We found that an intuitive interface is to ask the user to mark the object of interest with an ellipse (see Fig. 1). From the pixels within and outside the ellipse, we train the n-dimensional color/depth/RGB-D histograms corresponding to the probability distributions p_{obj} and p_{bg}, respectively. Further, we extract the surface area, 3D centroid and 3D covariance matrix that we use as moment constraints during segmentation from the projection of the ellipse into 3D space, with the information of the depth image.

4   Experimental Results

In this section we present an evaluation of our approach for RGB-D image segmentation with moment constraints. The goal of our experiments was to verify that (1) segmentation on RGB-D data is more reliable than segmentation of color or depth images alone, and that (2) object tracking with 3D moment constraints is more robust than 2D moment constraints.

All images and videos shown in this paper were captured using the Microsoft Kinect sensor. Run-times on a GPU implementation are less than 1 second per image, making the method useful for interactive applications.

4.1   Tracking with Moment Constraints

Figure 1 shows results on moment-consistent tracking in 2D and 3D with large camera motion. In the top row we see the results for color-only tracking: The area constraint is imposed on the projected shape of the object. The method cannot cope with increasing and decreasing appearance in the image domain, although the absolute size of the object stays the same. The bottom row shows RGB-D tracking: The area constraint is imposed on the absolute dimension via additional information from the depth images. The method enables area-consistent tracking with arbitrary camera motion. In the Figure, we took images of a plant in an office scene with a hand-held Kinect sensor from different view points. Of course, the basic properties of the 3D shape – and thus the surface area and covariance structure – of the selected object remains the same during the sequence. However, the projection of the object's shape in 2D changes its size due to object and/or camera motion. As a result, simple 2D moment tracking fails, as it tries to keep the area in image space constant. In contrast, 3D moment constraints are scale-invariant and are thus more robust against camera and/or object motion. From these examples, we conclude that in the case of arbitrary camera motion 3D moment constraints are better suited for object tracking than 2D moment constraints.

The image sequence in Fig. 2 was captured by a flying quadrocopter with a Kinect camera mounted on top of it. The towel's shape and color distribution vary over time due to camera motion and wind caused by the quadrocopter's rotors. The figure shows that color-only segmentation (first row) is not sufficient to track the object, whereas additional information from the depth images allow 3D moment constraints to track the exact surface area (second row).

4.2   Segmentation with Color, Depth, and RGB-D

We tested our segmentation method with moment constraints in several scenes to demonstrate that RGB-D segmentation can outperform segmentation based on color or depth alone. To demonstrate this, we segmented different objects in the color, depth, and the (combined) RGB-D image.

Our first example is shown in Fig. 3 where we aimed at segmenting individual persons from the crowd. We found that neither color nor depth information are sufficient to uniquely separate a single person in the image, see Fig. 3(b+c). In more detail, the person in the first row is hard to segment in the color image because of the blue jeans in front of the blue door. The person in the second row wears a black shirt and is partially occluded by the wardrobe, and the person in the third row overlaps with the person in the background, having similar histograms which makes the segmentation task hard. Depth segmentation alone has shortcomings in other regions of the image. We found that there are often pixels in an image with similar depth values as the foreground object – with the exception of the person sitting on the chair, where no other pixels had the same depth values. In the first two rows of Fig. 3, the segmentation problems are resolved when RGB and depth information is jointly considered. To conclude, all persons could be separated well in the RGB-D case.

Another interesting example is depicted in Fig. 4 where we found that even the absence of information in the depth image can be exploited to successfully segment an

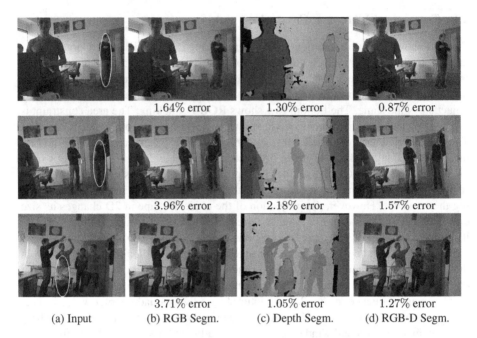

1.64% error	1.30% error	0.87% error
3.96% error	2.18% error	1.57% error
3.71% error	1.05% error	1.27% error
(a) Input	(b) RGB Segm.	(c) Depth Segm.	(d) RGB-D Segm.

Fig. 3. Segmentation of images with ambiguous color and depth information. Moment constraint parameters are derived from user input (a). Purely color (b) and depth (c) images alone do not provide enough information to uniquely segment one person. The combination (d) allows for segmentation of one single person in all three examples. Segmentation errors can be reduced by combining depth and color information.

image. Here, we consider a water glass located on a table. In the color image, the glass is difficult to see because of its transparency. Moreover, the depth of the glass pixels cannot be estimated due to the material's reflective property. By considering both the color and the depth image, we found that the glass is well separable.

4.3 Quantitative Analysis

For a quantitative analysis of the presented method, we measured the amount of pixels that differ from a manually segmented ground truth for segmentation with and without constraints, as well as segmentations using color, depth, and their combination. Segmentation errors were computed for the images in Fig. 3.

Table 1 shows average segmentation errors compared to the ground truth. Here we also compared to segmentations without moment constraints, where segmentations were computed using only the color information of the histograms inside and outside the ellipse drawn by the user. The table clearly shows that the amount of misclassified pixels can be reduced by combining depth and color information for segmentation with moment constraints. Interestingly, segmentation with depth only yields significantly better results than color only.

Table 1. Average segmentation errors with and without moment constraints, compared to ground truth. The combination of color and depth leads to better results, even more improvement is achieved by additionally constraining the moments of the segmentation.

		Average Segmentation Error
Without Constraints:	Color only	29.25%
	Depth only	16.99%
	RGB-D	17.93%
With Constraints:	Color only	3.10%
	Depth only	1.51%
	RGB-D	1.24%

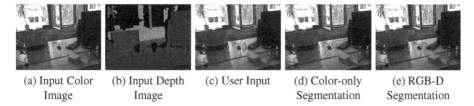

| (a) Input Color Image | (b) Input Depth Image | (c) User Input | (d) Color-only Segmentation | (e) RGB-D Segmentation |

Fig. 4. Segmentation of reflective material. (a+b) Input image and (c) user input. (d) When only the color image is considered, the glass is indistinguishable from the background due to its transparency. (e) When the depth image is taken into account, the glass becomes separable.

5   Conclusion

We introduced a convex framework for interactive RGB-D image segmentation and tracking. Building up on state-of-the-art approaches for color segmentation, we showed that depth information can be integrated in the data terms for image segmentation so as to favor segmentations of coherent depth. In particular objects of similar color but different depth can be discriminated. Moreover, we show that the availability of depth allow to impose constraints on the *absolute* shape rather than the *projected* shape. And lastly we show that one can impose moment constraints in 3D space – thereby we exploit the fact that the 3D motion of a tracked object is constrained over time. Our studies demonstrate that combining color and depth drastically enhances the possibilities of variational segmentation methods. In particular, it allows to generalize respective constraints from the image plane to the physical 3D space. Experiments show that with a minimal amount of user input we can obtain fast interactive segmentations of good quality in a variety of challenging real-world scenarios.

References

1. Boykov, Y., Jolly, M.-P.: Interactive organ segmentation using graph cuts. In: Delp, S.L., DiGoia, A.M., Jaramaz, B. (eds.) MICCAI 2000. LNCS, vol. 1935, pp. 276–286. Springer, Heidelberg (2000)
2. Boykov, Y., Veksler, O., Zabih, R.: Fast approximate energy minimization via graph cuts. IEEE Trans. on Patt. Anal. and Mach. Intell. 23(11), 1222–1239 (2001)

3. Chambolle, A., Cremers, D., Pock, T.: A convex approach for computing minimal partitions. Communications on Pure and Applied Mathematics (2008)
4. Chan, T., Esedoglu, S., Nikolova, M.: Algorithms for finding global minimizers of denoising and segmentation models. SIAM Journal on Applied Mathematics 66(5), 1632–1648 (2006)
5. Chan, T., Esedoğlu, S., Nikolova, M.: Algorithms for finding global minimizers of image segmentation and denoising models. SIAM Journal on Applied Mathematics 66(5), 1632–1648 (2006)
6. Chan, T., Vese, L.: A level set algorithm for minimizing the Mumford–Shah functional in image processing. In: IEEE Workshop on Variational and Level Set Methods, Vancouver, CA, pp. 161–168 (2001)
7. Cremers, D., Osher, S.J., Soatto, S.: Kernel density estimation and intrinsic alignment for shape priors in level set segmentation. Int. J. of Computer Vision 69(3), 335–351 (2006)
8. Etyngier, P., Segonne, F., Keriven, R.: Shape priors using manifold learning techniques. In: IEEE Int. Conf. on Computer Vision. Rio de Janeiro (October 2007)
9. Foulonneau, A., Charbonnier, P., Heitz, F.: Affine-invariant geometric shape priors for region-based active contours. IEEE Trans. on Patt. Anal. and Mach. Intell. 28(8), 1352–1357 (2006)
10. Gordon, G., Darrell, T., Harville, M., Woodfill, J.: Background estimation and removal based on range and color. In: Int. Conf. on Computer Vision and Pattern Recognition, pp. 459–464 (1999)
11. Greig, D.M., Porteous, B.T., Seheult, A.H.: Exact maximum *a posteriori* estimation for binary images. J. Roy. Statist. Soc., Ser. B. 51(2), 271–279 (1989)
12. Grenander, U., Chow, Y., Keenan, D.M.: Hands: A Pattern Theoretic Study of Biological Shapes. Springer, New York (1991)
13. Klodt, M., Cremers, D.: A convex framework for image segmentation with moment constraints. In: IEEE Int. Conf. on Computer Vision (2011)
14. Lellmann, J., Kappes, J., Yuan, J., Becker, F., Schnörr, C.: Convex multi-class image labeling by simplex-constrained total variation. In: Tai, X.-C., Mørken, K., Lysaker, M., Lie, K.-A. (eds.) SSVM 2009. LNCS, vol. 5567, pp. 150–162. Springer, Heidelberg (2009)
15. Osher, S.J., Sethian, J.A.: Fronts propagation with curvature dependent speed: Algorithms based on Hamilton–Jacobi formulations. J. of Comp. Phys. 79, 12–49 (1988)
16. Schoenemann, T., Cremers, D.: A combinatorial solution for model-based image segmentation and real-time tracking. IEEE Transactions on Pattern Analysis and Machine Intelligence (2009)
17. Taylor, C., Cowley, A.: Fast scene analysis using image and range data. In: Proc. of the Intl. Conf. on Robotics and Automation, ICRA (2011)
18. Unger, M., Pock, T., Cremers, D., Bischof, H.: TVSeg - interactive total variation based image segmentation. In: British Machine Vision Conference (BMVC), Leeds, UK (September 2008)
19. Veksler, O.: Star shape prior for graph-cut image segmentation. In: Europ. Conf. on Computer Vision., pp. 454–467 (2008)
20. Zach, C., Gallup, D., Frahm, J.M., Niethammer, M.: Fast global labeling for real-time stereo using multiple plane sweeps. In: Vision, Modeling and Visualization Workshop VMV 2008(October 2008)

Learning How to Combine
Internal and External Denoising Methods

Harold Christopher Burger, Christian Schuler, and Stefan Harmeling

Max Planck Institute for Intelligent Systems, Tübingen, Germany

Abstract. Different methods for image denoising have complementary strengths and can be combined to improve image denoising performance, as has been noted by several authors [11,7]. Mosseri et al. [11] distinguish between internal and external methods depending whether they exploit internal or external statistics [13]. They also propose a rule-based scheme (PatchSNR) to combine these two classes of algorithms. In this paper, we test the underlying assumptions and show that many images might not be easily split into regions where internal methods or external methods are preferable. Instead we propose a learning based approach using a neural network, that automatically combines denoising results from an internal and from an external method. This approach outperforms both other combination methods and state-of-the-art stand-alone image denoising methods, hereby further closing the gap to the theoretically achievable performance limits of denoising [9]. Our denoising results can be replicated with a publicly available toolbox[1].

1 Introduction

Image denoising is the long-standing problem of finding a clean image, given a noisy one. Usually, one seeks to denoise images corrupted with additive white Gaussian (AWG) noise, where it is often assumed that the variance of the noise is known. Most often, the images one wishes to denoise are so-called natural images (i.e. every-day scenes). The quality measure of interest is the peak signal-to-noise ratio (PSNR), which is monotonically related to the mean squared error.

Denoising methods can be divided into *internal* and *external* methods [11]: (i) internal methods denoise image patches using only other noisy image patches from the same image. In contrast, (ii) external methods denoise image patches using external clean image patches (i.e. patches coming from a database of clean images). For instance:

Internal Denoising Methods

- NLM (non-local means) [2] denoises a noisy image using only patches from the same image: No explicit assumptions are made regarding all natural images.
- BM3D [6] is conceptually similar to NLM, but uses a more effective noise-reduction strategy than NLM, which averages similar-looking patches.

---

[1] `http://webdav.is.mpg.de/pixel/prj/neural_denoising/gcpr2013.html`

J. Weickert, M. Hein, and B. Schiele (Eds.): GCPR 2013, LNCS 8142, pp. 121–130, 2013.

External Denoising Methods

- EPLL [14] denoises image patches using a probabilistic prior for the image patches learned on a database of clean image patches.
- MLP is the currently best performing method, see [4,3]. It uses a multi-layer perceptron to automatically learn a denoising method.

Other denoising methods can be less clearly classified, e.g. LSSC [10] learns a dictionary on the noisy image at hand and exploits this dictionary in a manner reminiscent of BM3D (speaking for an internal method), but the initialization of the dictionary is also important. Therefore it seems that external information also plays a role in LSSC, similarly for KSVD [1].

Recent denoising methods (such as BM3D [6], LSSC [10], EPLL [14]) perform on average equally well. This is surprising, considering that the methods rely on fundamentally different approaches. This has naturally led to the question if there are inherent limits to how well it is possible to denoise, and if so, whether current methods are approaching these limits. Even though the approaches taken are different [5,9], the consensus is that current methods are indeed not far away from theoretical limits, especially at lower noise levels.

Contributions: In this paper, we will study the performance of internal and external methods across an image database and patch-wise across single images. Furthermore, we propose a method that automatically combines the advantages of external and internal approaches using learning. In particular our contributions are:

1. We show that internal denoising methods tend to be better for images depicting artificial objects, whereas external denoising methods are better for images of natural scenes.
2. We show that there is no trivial rule to decide whether to use external or internal denoising on a patch-by-patch basis.
3. We show that a combining strategy can be learned by an MLP that outperforms both internal and external approaches across a wide range of images.
4. We show that the new combined approach gets close to theoretical bounds.

2   Related Work

Work on image denoising is extensive and we already mentioned some of the best performing methods in the introduction. In the following we limit our discussion on publications that also try to combine different denoising methods:

RTF. Jancsary et al. [7] observe that there is no single best denoising method, but that even in a single image depending on the image content one method might be preferable over others (see Fig. 5 in [7]). For that reason, they not only consider regression tree fields (RTFs) based on some filterbank (RTF$_{plain}$), but they also study a version that additionally exploits the output of BM3D (RTF$_{BM3D}$) and a version that additionally uses the output of four denoising methods simultaneously (RTF$_{all}$). Their finding is that the approach combining several methods is the best. In general their approach is based on learning RTFs on a large dataset of images, thus automatically determining how image features and different denoising methods can be combined. However, they do not discuss the distinction between internal and external methods.

PatchSNR. Zontak and Irani [13] study the merits of internal vs. external statistics for the task of super-resolution and also for denoising, where they observe that NLM works better with internal noisy patches (internal-NLM) than with noise-free patches from external images (external-NLM). Following up on this work, Mosseri et al. [11] introduce the corresponding distinction between internal and external denoising algorithms. To combine the advantages of these two paradigms, they propose a patch-wise signal-to-noise-ratio called PatchSNR, which as they claim indicates whether an internal (low PatchSNR) or an external (high PatchSNR) denoising method should be applied. The resulting denoised patches are blended together to form a single image, and they show that their results are slightly better than the stand-alone methods.

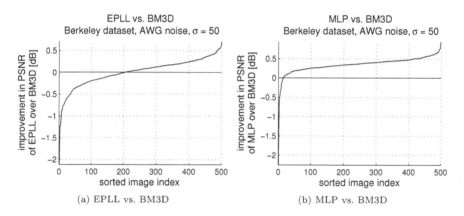

(a) EPLL vs. BM3D   (b) MLP vs. BM3D

Fig. 1. No method is *always* the best. (a) Performance profile of EPLL vs. BM3D. (b) Performance profile of MLP vs. BM3D.

3   Internal vs. External Denoising

3.1   Comparison on a Large Dataset of Images

To compare the performance of two denoising algorithms, we plot the sorted differences between PSNRs achieved on a large set of noisy images. We call such a plot a *performance profile*. Fig. 1 (a) shows such a performance profile for EPLL [14], an external method, against BM3D [6], an internal method. We see that EPLL is worse than BM3D on 40% of the image images (blue line below zero) and better than BM3D on 60% of the images (blue line above zero). On some images EPLL is much better (about 0.5dB), while on other images BM3D is much better (more than 1dB in the extreme case).

Fig. 1 (b) shows a similar comparison for MLP [4,3] (also an external method) vs. BM3D. We see that MLP is the clear winner, being superior on almost all images (blue line above zero). However, there are also some images where BM3D wins (close to image index zero). Even though Fig. 1 (b) shows that MLP is good over a large range of images, we can *not* conclude that one algorithm is the best on *all* images.

MLP vs. BM3D: +0.84dB   MLP vs. BM3D: +0.82dB   MLP vs. BM3D: +0.82dB

MLP vs. BM3D: -1.09dB   MLP vs. BM3D: -0.66dB   MLP vs. BM3D: -0.54dB

Fig. 2. MLP vs. BM3D for $\sigma = 25$: MLP wins (top row), BM3D wins (bottom row)

Is there some underlying principle that would allow us to predict whether an internal (such as BM3D) or an external algorithm (such as MLP) is better on a given image? To answer this question, we show in the first row of Fig. 2 images where MLP excels and in the second row images where BM3D is better. We notice that MLP tends to outperform BM3D on images containing smooth areas or irregular textures, whereas BM3D outperforms MLP mainly on images with regular, repeating textures (many more images supporting this in the supplementary material). Put differently, MLP is better for images of nature, while BM3D is better for images of man-made objects. This also makes sense intuitively, since an internal method like BM3D exploits the self-similarity of images which is much higher in images showing highly regular structures, while common images of nature show many irregular patterns, which are not easily matched to each other by an internal method.

Conclusion. We hypothesize that current internal methods are good at repetitive image structure, while external methods are good at irregular image content. In order to combine the strength of both paradigms, can we easily decide on a patch-by-patch level whether to apply internal or external denoising? To answer this question we compare internal and external denoising methods pixel-wise on single images.

3.2   Pixel-Wise Comparison on Single Images

Having denoised a given image with two methods, we can create a so-called *preference image* that shows a white pixel if the first method is closer to the truth or a black pixel if the second method is better. Such a visualization to compare methods pixel-wise has been previously used in [7] to compare four methods simultaneously (with four colors, Fig. 5 in [7]) and in [11].

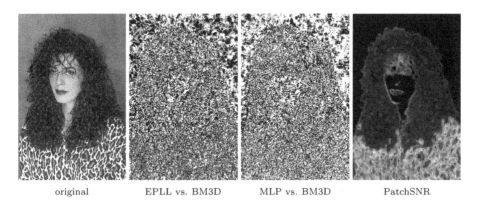

original   EPLL vs. BM3D   MLP vs. BM3D   PatchSNR

Fig. 3. Preference images and PatchSNR for image "woman" ($\sigma = 25$) where external methods (EPLL, MLP) perform better than internal methods (BM3D). EPLL: 24.86dB, MLP: **25.43**dB, BM3D 24.52dB.

Fig. 3 shows the image "woman" used by Mosseri et al. [11], who compare the performance of internal-NLM against external-NLM on that image. They conclude that smooth image patches should preferentially be denoised with an internal denoising method, whereas patches with details should rather be denoised with an external denoising method. Furthermore, they conclude that the higher the noise, the higher the preference for internal denoising. To exploit these insights, they apply the PatchSNR (briefly introduced in Sec. 2). The higher the PatchSNR, the higher the preference for external denoising, and vice-versa for internal denoising. [11] shows that this approach is effective for combining internal-NLM and external-NLM. Their approach also yields better results when combining BM3D and EPLL. However, the two preference images (two middle images in Fig. 3) show that the preference of EPLL or MLP over BM3D is much less clear-cut. This is somewhat surprising since the image "woman" is an example where the external methods EPLL and MLP outperform the internal method BM3D. Also, we used the ground truth to decide which method is better and still do not see a clear pattern for which pixels should use which method.

As a second example, we consider image "Barbara" (see Fig. 4) which is an example of an image where internal methods such as BM3D are better than external methods like EPLL and MLP. The reason for this is that there is a repetitive pattern on the table cloth and the trousers which are hard to recover for external methods. This is supported by the two preference images in the

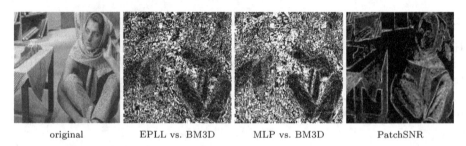

original   EPLL vs. BM3D   MLP vs. BM3D   PatchSNR

Fig. 4. Preference images and PatchSNR for image "Barbara" ($\sigma = 50$), where external methods (EPLL, MLP) perform worse than internal methods (BM3D). EPLL: 24.83dB, MLP: 25.28dB, BM3D: **27.22**dB.

middle of Fig. 4. We clearly see dark areas for the trousers and the table cloth, indicating that BM3D is preferred for those regions. However, across large areas of the image, there is not a clearly preferred approach. On the other hand, PatchSNR gives a strong preference to BM3D on the smooth regions of the image and low preference for the trousers and the table cloth. This is opposite to our findings.

Conclusion. For the analysis of these two images we draw the following conclusions (there are more images in the supplementary material supporting our findings):

1. External denoising is usually better on irregular and smooth regions.
2. Internal denoising is usually better on regular, repeating structures.
3. Overall there is no easy way to determine which is better. In particular, our findings contradict those of the PatchSNR criterion [11].

Further Notes on PatchSNR: Why are our conclusions different from Mosseri et al.'s [11]? The reason lies in the patch size of the methods: [11] compares external- vs. internal-NLM, both of which use small (7×7) patches. External methods using small patch sizes tend to overfit the noise, especially for smooth patches, which has been also noted by Mosseri et al. [11], as well as by Zontak and Irani [13]. In contrast, we consider MLP and EPLL. MLP uses 39×39 patches. Even though EPLL uses small (8×8) patches, it requires several iterations, which spreads out image information and therefore effectively increases the patch size. On the other hand, internal methods (like BM3D) using small patches are less prone to this effect due to the fact that similar patches are likely to be found in the vicinity of a given patch [13].

4   Learning to Combine Internal and External Methods

Since we have seen that there is no trivial criterion to decide whether an internal or an external method should be applied to a given patch, we propose to use a learning approach based on neural networks to combine the complementary strengths of internal and external denoising methods (see Sec. 3.1).

Technically, we could combine any number of denoising methods with a neural network (similar to the learning-based approach proposed by [7], who combine the results of four denoising algorithms). However, we will show that it is sufficient to combine one internal method (BM3D) with one external method (MLP). Our method uses the original noisy image patch together with the denoised patches of MLP and BM3D as input. We choose do so because applying a denoising algorithm inevitably removes information contained in the noisy image. However, exactly that information might be missing in the denoised patches by BM3D or MLP.

Multi-layer Perceptrons. The neural network we employ is a multi-layer perceptron that non-linearly transforms a vector-valued input into a vector-valued output. It is composed of a sequence of differentiable functions whose parameters can be trained efficiently given labeled training data with a combination of the back-propagation algorithm and stochastic gradient descent [8]. Usually, layers performing an affine transformation and layers performing an element-wise non-linearity (such as tanh) are applied in sequence. For example, $f(x) = W_2 \tanh(W_1 x + b_1) + b_2$ is a multi-layer perceptron with a single hidden layer whose parameters $\theta = \{W_1, W_2, b_1, b_2\}$ can be learned.

Training. Our neural network takes as input x the concatenation of three input patches, one from the noisy image, and one from each of the denoising results (BM3D and MLP), extracted from the same image location. The output of the neural network is a clean image patch. As a pre-processing step, we approximately de-correlate the three input patches using a pre-learned 3×3 matrix (one for each noise level). De-correlating the inputs of a neural network is considered good practice [8]. In our case the use of a 3×3 whitening matrix can be intuitively justified by the fact that two of the inputs (BM3D and MLP) look very similar (see supplementary material).

To generate training data, we add noise to images from a large image data set, and apply both BM3D and MLP. This provides us the input/output pairs required for training. Note that BM3D and MLP are computationally relatively inexpensive, allowing us to generate plentiful training data (we denoised approximately 9×10^4 images).

Hyper-parameters. We use four hidden layers with 2047 hidden units each. The input patches are each of size 25×25, the output patch are of size 17×17. We also experimented with smaller architectures, leading to worse results, see supplementary material. We used a constant learning rate of 0.1, as suggested in [4].

Training and Running Times. We train six neural networks, one for each of the noise levels $\sigma = \{10, 25, 35, 50, 75, 170\}$. Training each neural network is computationally intensive: About 4×10^8 training samples are needed before the results converge. This requires roughly one month of training time on a GPU. However, the running time of applying a trained neural network to a noisy image is relatively short: Approximately one minute on a CPU for an image of size 512×512 (such as "Lena"). Running times on GPU are less than six seconds. This compares favorably to other denoising methods such as EPLL (approximately five minutes on CPU) or KSVD [1] and LSSC [10] (approximately one hour on CPU), but unfavorably to BM3D (about five seconds on CPU). The total computation time of our method on an image of size 512×512 is therefore about two minutes on CPU: One minute for MLP, a few seconds for BM3D and one minute for our neural network combining MLP and BM3D.

5   Results

In the following, we show that combining MLP and BM3D with a neural network (as explained in the previous section) outperforms the current state-of-the-art stand-alone methods as well as previous attempts to combine denoising methods. We can also show that the proposed approach further closes the gap to the theoretical limits of denoising.

Comparison against Competing Methods. Tab. 1 compares our method to the combination approach of [11] as well as to stand-alone denoising methods on a (held-out) test set of 100 images, for six different noise levels. In all tested settings, our approach outperforms the existing methods.

Table 1. Average PSNR values [dB] on 100 test images from the BSDS300 dataset. Note that MLP [3] is better than the blend of BM3D and EPLL proposed by Mosseri et al [11] at every noise level.

σ	Mosseri et al. [11] BM3D and EPLL	our results BM3D and MLP	BM3D [14]	EPLL [6]	MLP [3]
170	20.14	**21.96**	19.85	21.21	21.87
75	24.16	**24.53**	23.96	24.16	24.42
50	25.64	**25.95**	25.45	25.50	25.83
35	27.07	**27.36**	26.89	26.98	27.29
25	28.54	**28.79**	28.35	28.47	28.75
10	33.17	**33.34**	33.11	33.17	33.31

Table 2 compares our method to RTF-based methods [7] and to [11] on the dataset used in [7]. Our method achieves the highest PSNR also on these images. Note that it outperforms also RTF$_{all}$ even though RTF$_{all}$ combines four denoising methods, whereas we combine only two.

Table 2. Results obtained with our approach and other methods on the dataset of images used in [7], with $\sigma = 50$. Top: Stand-alone methods, bottom: methods combining the results of other methods. Note that MLP outperforms both RTF$_{BM3D}$ [7] and Mosseri et al. [11]. Our approach outperforms all competitors.

single methods	FoE [12]	BM3D [6]	EPLL [14]	LSSC [10]	RTF$_{Plain}$ [7]	MLP
PSNR	24.47dB	25.09dB	25.18dB	25.09dB	24.76dB	25.45dB

combining m.	RTF$_{BM3D}$ [7]	RTF$_{All}$ [7]	Mosseri [11]	our result	
PSNR	25.38dB	25.51dB	25.30dB	**25.58dB**	

Performance Profiles against the Best Input Method. We now compare the results achieved with our method against the input methods (BM3D and MLP). For each image in a dataset of 2500 test images (that have not been used for training), we compare our method against the best of the two input methods (BM3D and MLP) for that image. Our method outperforms both BM3D and MLP on 76.92%, 89.12%, 96.92%, 99.12%, 98.8% and 93.48% of the images on the noise levels $\sigma = 10, 25, 35, 50, 75$, and 170, respectively. Figure 5 plots these results as performance profiles for four noise levels (more results in the supplementary material). Our method usually achieves results that are better than the best of the two inputs methods.

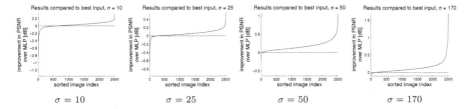

$\sigma = 10$ $\sigma = 25$ $\sigma = 50$ $\sigma = 170$

Fig. 5. Our results are better than the best of the two inputs in almost all cases

Comparison against Bounds. Tab. 3 compares our results against recently estimated bounds for image denoising [9]. Our proposed method that combines BM3D and MLP gets much closer to the bounds (last row). For $\sigma = 50$, half of the remaining possible gain over MLP is achieved. Note, that for noise levels $\sigma = 10$ and $\sigma = 25$, the bounds are difficult to estimate (the lower the noise, the more difficult). On these noise levels, our method achieves still better results than MLP, proving by examples that the limits are not yet reached.

Table 3. Improvements in dB over BM3D on 2500 test images

	$\sigma = 10$	$\sigma = 25$	$\sigma = 35$	$\sigma = 50$	$\sigma = 75$	$\sigma = 170$
gain over BM3D by MLP [3]	0.07	0.3	0.33	0.34	0.38	2.19
gain over BM3D by our results	0.15	0.38	0.45	0.52	0.53	2.32
possible gain over BM3D [9]	–	–	0.6	0.7	1	–

6   Conclusion

Internal and external denoising approaches have complementary strengths and weaknesses. It has been previously claimed that external methods are preferred for patches with details, whereas internal methods are better for smooth patches. Our conclusions contradict previous findings: Internal methods are better on regions with regular, repeating structures. For irregular patterns, external methods are better. We have presented a simple patch-based method using neural networks that effectively combines the results of two denoising algorithms. The results surpass those of any previously published method. Bayesian patch-based bounds on

image denoising have been estimated for medium to high noise levels, but are difficult to estimate at low noise levels. It was therefore not known if further improvements over BM3D at low noise levels were possible, but we have shown by example
that improvements over BM3D were indeed possible at low noise levels.

References

1. Aharon, M., Elad, M., Bruckstein, A.: K-svd: An algorithm for designing overcom-
   plete dictionaries for sparse representation. IEEE Transactions on Signal Processing (TIP) 54(11), 4311–4322 (2006)
2. Buades, A., Coll, B., Morel, J.: A non-local algorithm for image denoising. In:
   International Conference on Computer Vision and Pattern Recognition (CVPR),
   vol. 2, pp. 60–65. IEEE (2005)
3. Burger, H.C., Schuler, C.J., Harmeling, S.: Image denoising with multi-layer perceptrons, part 1: comparison with existing algorithms and with bounds. arXiv:1211,
   1544 (2012)
4. Burger, H., Schuler, C., Harmeling, S.: Image denoising: Can plain neural networks
   compete with BM3D? In: Conference on Computer Vision and Pattern Recognition
   (CVPR), pp. 2392–2399 (2012)
5. Chatterjee, P., Milanfar, P.: Is denoising dead? IEEE Transactions on Image Processing (TIP) 19(4), 895–911 (2010)
6. Dabov, K., Foi, A., Katkovnik, V., Egiazarian, K.: Image denoising by sparse 3-D
   transform-domain collaborative filtering. IEEE Transactions on Image Processing
   (TIP) 16(8), 2080–2095 (2007)
7. Jancsary, J., Nowozin, S., Rother, C.: Loss-specific training of non-parametric image restoration models: A new state of the art. In: Fitzgibbon, A., Lazebnik, S.,
   Perona, P., Sato, Y., Schmid, C. (eds.) ECCV 2012, Part VII. LNCS, vol. 7578,
   pp. 112–125. Springer, Heidelberg (2012)
8. LeCun, Y., Bottou, L., Orr, G., Müller, K.: Efficient backprop. Neural networks:
   Tricks of the trade, pp. 546–546 (1998)
9. Levin, A., Nadler, B., Durand, F., Freeman, W.T.: Patch complexity, finite pixel
   correlations and optimal denoising. In: Fitzgibbon, A., Lazebnik, S., Perona, P.,
   Sato, Y., Schmid, C. (eds.) ECCV 2012, Part V. LNCS, vol. 7576, pp. 73–86.
   Springer, Heidelberg (2012)
10. Mairal, J., Bach, F., Ponce, J., Sapiro, G., Zisserman, A.: Non-local sparse models
    for image restoration. In: IEEE 12th International Conference on Computer Vision
    (ICCV), pp. 2272–2279 (2010)
11. Mosseri, I., Zontak, M., Irani, M.: Combining the power of internal and external
    denoising. In: International Conference on Computational Photography (ICCP),
    pp. 1–9. IEEE (2013)
12. Schmidt, U., Gao, Q., Roth, S.: A generative perspective on mrfs in low-level vision.
    In: IEEE Conference on Computer Vision and Pattern Recognition (CVPR), pp.
    1751–1758. IEEE (2010)
13. Zontak, M., Irani, M.: Internal statistics of a single natural image. In: International
    Conference on Computer Vision and Pattern Recognition (CVPR), pp. 977–984.
    IEEE (2011)
14. Zoran, D., Weiss, Y.: From learning models of natural image patches to whole
    image restoration. In: International Conference on Computer Vision (ICCV),
    pp. 479–486. IEEE (2011)

A Comparison of Directional Distances for Hand Pose Estimation

Dimitrios Tzionas[1,2] and Juergen Gall[2]

[1] Perceiving Systems Department, MPI for Intelligent Systems, Germany
dimitris.tzionas@tuebingen.mpg.de
[2] Computer Vision Group, University of Bonn, Germany
gall@informatik.uni-bonn.de

Abstract. Benchmarking methods for 3d hand tracking is still an open problem due to the difficulty of acquiring ground truth data. We introduce a new dataset and benchmarking protocol that is insensitive to the accumulative error of other protocols. To this end, we create testing frame pairs of increasing difficulty and measure the pose estimation error separately for each of them. This approach gives new insights and allows to accurately study the performance of each feature or method without employing a full tracking pipeline. Following this protocol, we evaluate various directional distances in the context of silhouette-based 3d hand tracking, expressed as special cases of a generalized Chamfer distance form. An appropriate parameter setup is proposed for each of them, and a comparative study reveals the best performing method in this context.

1 Introduction

Benchmarking methods for 3d hand tracking has been identified in the review [7] as an open problem due to the difficulty of acquiring ground truth data. As in one of the earliest works on markerless 3d hand tracking [19], quantitative evaluations are still mostly performed on synthetic data, e.g., [26,2,34,4,21]. The vast majority of the related literature, however, is limited to visual, qualitative performance evaluation, where the estimated model is overlaid on the images.

While there are several datasets and evaluation protocols for benchmarking human pose estimation methods publicly available, where markers [28,1], inertial sensors [3], or a semi-automatic annotation approach [32] have been used to acquire ground truth data, there are no datasets available for benchmarking articulated hand pose estimation. We propose thus a benchmark dataset consisting of 4 sequences of two interacting hands captured by 8 cameras, where the ground truth position of the 3d joints has been manually annotated.

Tracking approaches are usually evaluated by providing the pose for the first frame and measuring the accumulative pose estimation error for all consecutive frames of the sequence, e.g., [28]. While this protocol is optimal for comparing full tracking systems, it makes it difficult to analyze the impact of individual components of a system. For instance, a method that estimates the joint positions with a high accuracy, but fails in a few cases and is unable to recover from errors,

J. Weickert, M. Hein, and B. Schiele (Eds.): GCPR 2013, LNCS 8142, pp. 131–141, 2013.

(a) initial pose   (b) target silh. (synthetic)   (c) target silh. (realistic)

Fig. 1. *Initial pose* (a) and synthetic (b) and realistic (b) *target silhouettes* of one camera view. The benchmark measures the pose estimation error of the joints of both hands. In the synthetic experiments all joints (*all* dots in (a)) are taken into account, while in the realistic only a subset (*black* dots in (a)) is evaluated.

will have a high tracking error if an error occurs very early in a test sequence. However, the tracking error will be very low if the error occurs at the end of the sequence. The accumulation of tracking errors makes it difficult to analyze in-depth situations where an approach works or fails. We therefore propose a benchmark that analyzes the error not over a full sequence, but over a set of pairs consisting of a starting pose and a test frame. Based on the start pose and the test frame, the pairs have different grades of difficulty.

In this work, we use the proposed benchmark to analyze various silhouette-based distance measures for hand pose estimation. Distance measures that are based on a closest point distance, like the Chamfer distance, are commonly used due to its efficiency [19] and often extended by including directional information [9,33]. Recently, a fast method that computes a directional Chamfer distance using a 3d distance tensor has been proposed [16] for shape matching. In this work, we introduce a general form of the Chamfer distance for hand pose estimation and quantitatively compare several special cases.

2   Related Work

Since the earliest days of vision-based hand pose estimation [24,7], low-level features like silhouettes [19], edges [13], depth [6], optical flow [19], shading [14] or a combination of them [17] have been used for hand pose estimation. Although Chamfer distances combined with an edge orientation term have been used in [33,2,31,29], the different distances have not been thoroughly evaluated for hand pose estimation. While a KD-tree is used in [31] to compute a directional Chamfer distance, Liu et al. [16] recently proposed a distance transform approach to efficiently use a directional Chamfer distance for shape matching. Different methods of shape matching for pose estimation have been compared in the context of rigid objects [12] or articulated objects [22]. While previous work mainly considered to estimate the pose of a hand in isolation, recent works consider more complicated scenarios where two hands interact with each other [21,4] or with objects [11,25,10,20,4].

3   Hand Pose Estimation

For evaluation, we use a publicly available hand model [4], consisting of a set of vertices, an underlying kinematic skeleton with 35 degrees of freedom (DOF) per hand, and skinning weights. The vertices and the joints of the skeleton are shown in Fig. 1. Each 3d vertex $\mathbf{v}$ is associated to a bone j by the skinning weights $\alpha_{\mathbf{v},j}$, where $\sum_j \alpha_{\mathbf{v},j} = 1$. The articulated deformations of a skeleton are encoded by the vector θ that represents the rigid bone transformations $T_j(\theta)$, i.e., rotation and translation, by twists $\hat{\xi} \in se(3)$ [18,5]. Each twist-encoded rigid body transformation $\theta_j \hat{\xi}_j$ for a bone j can be converted into a homogeneous transformation matrix by the exponential map operator, i.e., $T_j(\theta) = \exp(\theta_j \hat{\xi}_j) \in SE(3)$. The mesh deformations based on the pose parameters θ are obtained by the linear blend skinning operator [15] using homogeneous coordinates:

$$\mathbf{v}(\theta) = \sum_j \alpha_{\mathbf{v},j} T_j(\theta)\mathbf{v} . \tag{1}$$

In order to estimate the hand pose for a given frame, correspondences between the mesh and the image of each camera c are established. Each correspondence $(\mathbf{v}_i, \mathbf{q}_i, c_i)$ associates a vertex $\mathbf{v}_i$ to a 2d point $\mathbf{q}_i$ in camera view c_i. Assuming that the cameras are calibrated, the point $\mathbf{q}_i$ can be converted into a projection ray that is represented by the direction $\mathbf{d}_i$ and moment $\mathbf{m}_i$ of the line [30,27]. The hand pose can then be determined by the pose parameters that minimize the shortest distance between the 3d vertices $\mathbf{v}_i$ and 3d projection rays $(\mathbf{d}_i, \mathbf{m}_i)$:

$$\underset{\theta}{\mathrm{argmin}} \frac{1}{2N} \sum_{i=1}^{N} \|\mathbf{v}_i(\theta) \times \mathbf{d}_i - \mathbf{m}_i\|^2 . \tag{2}$$

This non-linear least-squares problem can be iteratively solved [27]:

- Extract correspondences for all cameras $(\mathbf{v}_i, \mathbf{q}_i, c_i)$,
- Solve (2) using the linearization $T_j(\theta) = \exp(\theta_j \hat{\xi}_j) \approx I + \theta_j \hat{\xi}_j$,
- Update vertex positions by (1).

In this work, we reformulate (2) as a Chamfer distance minimization problem.

4   Generalized Chamfer Distance

As discussed in Section 2, the Chamfer distance is commonly used for shape matching and has been also used for pose estimation by shape matching. In our context, the Chamfer distance between pixels of a contour $\mathcal{C}$ for a given camera view and the set of projected rim vertices $\mathcal{P}(\theta)$, which depend on the pose parameters θ and project onto the contour of the projected surface, is

$$d_{Chamfer}(\theta, \mathcal{C}) = \frac{1}{|\mathcal{P}(\theta)|} \sum_{\mathbf{p} \in \mathcal{P}(\theta)} \min_{\mathbf{q} \in \mathcal{C}} \|\mathbf{p} - \mathbf{q}\| . \tag{3}$$

This expression can be efficiently computed using a 2d distance transform [8].

The Chamfer distance (3) can be generalized by

$$d_{Chamfer}^{Z,f,d}(\theta,\mathcal{C}) = \frac{1}{Z} \sum_{\mathbf{p}\in\mathcal{P}(\theta)} f\left(\mathbf{p}, \underset{\mathbf{q}\in\mathcal{C}}{\arg\min}\, d(\mathbf{p},\mathbf{q})\right) , \qquad (4)$$

where $d(\mathbf{p},\mathbf{q})$ is a 2d distance function to compute the distance between two points, $f(\mathbf{p},\mathbf{q})$ is a penalty function for two closest points, and Z is a normalization factor. If we use

$$d(\mathbf{p},\mathbf{q}) = \|\mathbf{p}-\mathbf{q}\| , \quad f(\mathbf{p},\mathbf{q}) = d(\mathbf{p},\mathbf{q}) , \quad Z = |\mathcal{P}(\theta)| , \qquad (5)$$

$d_{Chamfer}^{Z,f,d}(\theta,\mathcal{C})$ is the standard Chamfer distance (3). In order to increase the robustness to outliers, $f(\mathbf{p},\mathbf{q}) = \min\left(d(\mathbf{p},\mathbf{q})^2, K\right)$ is used in [29], where K is a threshold on the maximum squared distance.

Orientation can be integrated by penalizing correspondences with inconsistent orientations:

$$d(\mathbf{p},\mathbf{q}) = \|\mathbf{p}-\mathbf{q}\| , \quad f(\mathbf{p},\mathbf{q}) = \begin{cases} d(\mathbf{p},\mathbf{q}) & \text{if } |\phi(\mathbf{p})-\phi(\mathbf{q})|_\phi < \tau \\ K & \text{otherwise} \end{cases} , \quad Z = |\mathcal{P}(\theta)| , \tag{6}$$

or by computing the closest distance to points of similar orientation based on a circular distance threshold τ [9]:

$$d(\mathbf{p},\mathbf{q}) = \begin{cases} \|\mathbf{p}-\mathbf{q}\| & \text{if } |\phi(\mathbf{p})-\phi(\mathbf{q})|_\phi < \tau \\ \infty & \text{otherwise} \end{cases} , \quad f(\mathbf{p},\mathbf{q}) = d(\mathbf{p},\mathbf{q}) , \quad Z = |\mathcal{P}(\theta)| , \tag{7}$$

where $|\phi(\mathbf{p})-\phi(\mathbf{q})|_\phi$ is the circular distance between two angles, which can be signed, i.e., in the range of $[0,\pi]$, or unsigned, i.e., in the range of $[0,\frac{\pi}{2}]$.

The directional Chamfer distance [16] can be written as

$$d(\mathbf{p},\mathbf{q}) = \|\mathbf{p}-\mathbf{q}\| + \lambda|\phi(\mathbf{p})-\phi(\mathbf{q})|_\phi , \quad f(\mathbf{p},\mathbf{q}) = d(\mathbf{p},\mathbf{q}) , \quad Z = |\mathcal{P}(\theta)| . \quad (8)$$

To compute $d_{Chamfer}^{Z,f,d}(\theta,\mathcal{C})$ with (8) efficiently, ϕ can be quantized to compute a 3d distance transform [16]. As in [16], we compute $\phi(\mathbf{q})$ by converting $\mathcal{C}$ into a line representation [23]. $\phi(\mathbf{p})$ is obtained by projecting the normals of the corresponding vertices in $\mathcal{P}(\theta)$.

In order to use the generalized Chamfer distance $d_{Chamfer}^{Z,f,d}(\theta,\mathcal{C})$ for pose estimation from multiple views (2), only f and Z need to be adapted. Let $\mathcal{C}(c)$ denote the contour of camera view c and $\mathcal{P}(\theta,c)$ the set of projected vertices for pose parameters θ and camera c. (2) can be rewritten as

$$\underset{\theta}{\arg\min} \frac{1}{2\sum_c |\mathcal{P}(\theta,c)|} \sum_c d_{Chamfer}^{Z,f,d}(\theta,\mathcal{C}(c)) \qquad (9)$$

$$\text{with} \quad f(\mathbf{p},\mathbf{q}) = \|\mathbf{v}(\theta)\times\mathbf{d} - \mathbf{m}\|^2 , Z = 1 , \qquad (10)$$

where $\mathbf{v}(\theta)$ is the 3d vertex corresponding to $\mathbf{p}\in\mathcal{P}(\theta)$ and $(\mathbf{d},\mathbf{m})$ is the 3d projection ray corresponding to $\mathbf{q}$. $d(\mathbf{p},\mathbf{q})$ can be any of the functions (5)-(8).

In case of (6), instead of adding a fixed penalty term K, correspondences with inconsistent orientation can be simply removed and $\mathcal{P}(\theta,c)$ becomes the set of correspondences with $|\phi(\mathbf{p})-\phi(\mathbf{q})|_\phi < \tau$.

5   Benchmark

We propose a benchmarking protocol that analyzes the error not over full sequences, but over a sampled *set of testing pairs*. Each pair consists of a *starting pose* and a *test frame*, ignoring the intermediate frames to simulate various difficulties. This approach gives new insights and provides means to analyze in-depth the contributions of various features or methods to the overall tracking pipeline under varying difficulty and to thoroughly study failure cases.

In this respect, 4 publicly available sequences[1] are used, containing realistic scenarios of two strongly interacting hands [4]. 10% of the total frames are randomly selected, forming the set of *test frames* of the final pairs. This is the basis to create 4 different sets of image pairs, having 1,5,10,15 frames difference respectively between the *starting pose* and the *test frame*, presenting thus increasing difficulty for tracking systems. These 4 sets and the overall combination constitute a challenging dataset, representing realistic scenarios the occur due to low frame rates, fast motion or estimation errors in the previous frame.

The created testing sets are used in two experimental setups: a purely *synthetic* and a *realistic*. In both cases, the *starting pose* is given by the publicly available motion data outputed by the tracker of [4]. In the *synthetic* experimental setup the *test frame* is synthesized by the hand model and the aforementioned motion data, while the required ground truth exists inherently in them. In the *realistic* setup the *test frame* is given by the camera images, for which no ground-truth data are available, thus the frames have been manually annotated[2]. As error measure, we use the average of the Euclidean distances between the estimated and the ground-truth 3d positions of the joints. For the realistic setup we use only the joints of the model that could be annotated, which are depicted with black color in Fig. 1. For the synthetic setup all joints of the model (black and red) are taken into account.

6   Experiments

6.1   Implementation Details

The aforementioned benchmark is used to evaluate four special cases of the generalized Chamfer distance (Section 4) for hand pose estimation.

CH denotes the Chamfer distance without any orientation information (5).

DCH-Thres rejects correspondences if the orientations are inconsistent, depending on the circular distance threshold τ (6).

DCH-Quant computes a 2d distance field for all quantizations of ϕ and assigns a vertex to one bin based on the orientation of its normal (7). Instead of

---

[1] Model, videos, and motion data are provided at `http://cvg.ethz.ch/research/ih-mocap` . Sequences: *Finger tips touching and praying, Fingers crossing and twisting, Fingers folding, Fingers walking*. Video: 1080×1920 px, 50 fps, 8 camera-views.

[2] The ground-truth annotated dataset, along with a viewer-application, is available at `http://files.is.tue.mpg.de/dtzionas/GCPR_2013.html`.

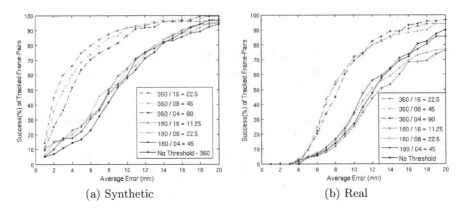

(a) Synthetic   (b) Real

Fig. 2. Performance evaluation of **DCH-Thres** with different values of τ and both signed (360) and unsigned (180) distance $|\cdot|_\phi$. The plots show the percentage of frame pairs (*y-axis*) below a given average error (*x-axis*). The *signed* distance (360) significantly outperforms the *unsigned* distance (180), and the best performing circular distance threshold value is $\tau = 22.5$.

hard binning, soft binning can also be performed, denoted by **DCH-Quant2**. In this case, the two closest bins are used, yielding two correspondences per vertex.

DCH-DT3 denotes the approximation of the directional Chamfer distance (8) proposed by Liu et al. [16]. The approach computes a 3d distance field $DT3$ and depends on two parameters. While λ steers the impact of the orientation term in (8), ϕ is quantized by a fixed number of bins.

As mentioned in Section 4, the *target silhouette* is approximated with linear line segments for all the directional distances DCH, using [23]. We also investigate two versions of the circular distance $|\cdot|_\phi$, namely the unsigned version, denoted by *180*, and the signed version, denoted by *360*.

6.2   Results

We have evaluated all Chamfer distances both on the synthetic and the realistic dataset in order to compare the distances for 3d hand pose estimation, but also in order to investigate the performance predicting abilities of synthetic test data. As measure, we use the average joint error per test frame and compute the percentage of frames with an error below a given threshold. We first evaluated the differences between the signed and unsigned circular distance for DCH-*Thres* and varied the threshold parameter τ. The results are plotted in Fig. 2. The plot shows that the signed distance outperforms the unsigned distance. Since we observed the same result for DCH-*DT3*, we only report results for the signed distance (360) in the remaining experiments.

For DCH-*DT3*, we evaluated the impact of the two parameters λ and the number of quantization bins for ϕ. The results are plotted in Fig. 3. Figs. 3a and 3b show the importance of directional information for hand pose estimation, and reveal that there is a large range of λ that works well. With a finer quantization of ϕ, the original

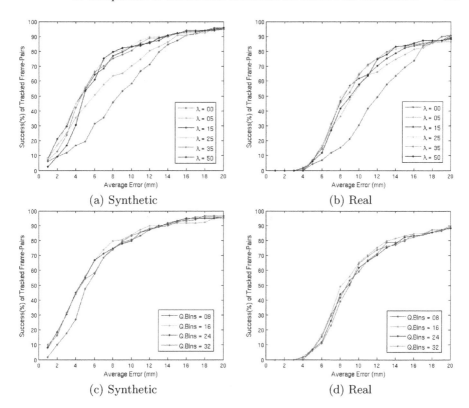

Fig. 3. (a-b) Performance evaluation of **DCH-DT3** with different values of λ, using 16 quantization bins. While the orientation term significantly improves the performance, the performance gets saturated for values in the range [15,35]. **(c-d)** Performance evaluation of **DCH-DT3** with different quantizations of ϕ, using $\lambda = 25$. The synthetic data shows that more than 8 bins are required, though the differences are rather small on the real dataset. This is in accordance with Fig. 2 since a threshold of 22.5 corresponds to 16 quantization bins.

directional Chamfer distance (8) is better approximated. Figs. 3c and 3d show that 16 bins are sufficient for this task.

We finally evaluated the number of bins for *DCH-Quant* and *DCH-Quant2*. Fig. 4 shows that *DCH-Quant2* performs better than *DCH-Quant*. In this case, a large number of bins results in a very orientation sensitive measure, and the performance decreases with a finer quantization, in contrast to *DCH-DT3*.

Fig. 5 summarizes the results for each distance with the best parameter setting. As expected, the results show that directional information improves the estimation accuracy. However, it is not *DCH-DT3* that performs best for hand pose estimation, but *DCH-Thres*, which is also more efficient to compute. While for *DCH-DT3* the full hand model converges smoothly to the final pose, the thresholding

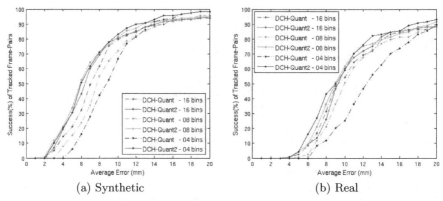

Fig. 4. Performance evaluation of **DCH-Quant** and **DCH-Quant2** with different quantizations of ϕ. Soft-binning outperforms hard assignments and in this case fewer bins perform better than many bins.

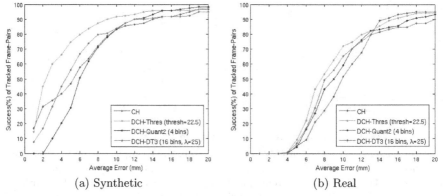

Fig. 5. Comparison of all distances with best settings. Although *DCH-DT3* provides a smoother distance measure, *DCH-Thres* performs best on both datasets.

yields a better fit to the silhouette after convergence (*see supplementary video*[3]). Comparing the performances between synthetic and real data, we conclude that synthetic data is a good performance indicator, but might be misleading some-times. For instance, *CH* performs well on the synthetic data but worst on the real data. This is also reflected by the mean error for the various frame differences provided in Table 1, that introduce an increasing difficulty in the benchmark. De-noted with the term *initial* is the average 3d distance of the joints before running the pose estimation algorithm. The result of a full tracking system [4] is provided for comparison, which expectedly performs better due to the number of features combined. Finally, runtime is provided for the synthetic experiments, giving some intuition about the time efficiency of each method.

---

[3] http://youtu.be/Cbu3eEcl1qk

Table 1. Mean error±std.dev.(mm), av.time (sec) for 1,5,10,15 frame differences. Time measurements regard single-threaded code on a 6-core 3GHz Xeon PC.

		1	5	10	15	All	Time
Synthetic	CH	1.0±1.0	2.5±2.5	4.3±4.6	6.4±6.1	3.5±4.5	103
	DCH-DT3	2.0±1.3	2.3±1.3	3.8±2.9	6.2±5.8	3.6±3.8	115
	DCH-Quant	4.0±1.6	4.2±1.7	5.4±2.5	7.0±4.0	5.1±2.9	161
	DCH-Thres	1.1±0.8	1.3±1.1	2.5±2.4	4.1±4.5	2.2±2.9	077
Realistic	Initial	6.4±2.0	10.5±5.6	16.5±11.5	22.6±16.9	14.0±12.3	-
	Ballan et al. [4]	5.9±1.9	-	-	-	-	-
	CH	7.1±1.9	7.8±2.4	9.3±4.3	10.9±5.9	8.8±4.2	-
	DCH-DT3	6.3±1.5	6.7±2.0	8.7±5.1	11.1±7.9	8.3±5.4	-
	DCH-Quant	6.8±1.6	7.2±2.1	9.0±4.4	10.7±7.3	8.4±4.7	-
	DCH-Thres	6.1±1.3	6.4±1.8	7.6±3.3	9.4±5.3	7.4±3.6	-

7   Conclusion

In this work, we propose a new benchmark dataset for hand pose estimation that allows to evaluate single components of a hand tracker without running a full system. As an example, we discuss a generalized Chamfer distance and evaluate four special cases. The experiments reveal that directional information is important and a signed circular distance performs better than an unsigned distance in the case of silhouettes. Interestingly, a distance using a circular threshold outperforms a smooth directional Chamfer distance both in terms of accuracy and runtime. We finally conclude that synthetic data can be a good indicator for the performance, but might be misleading when comparing different methods. Future plans include adding frame pairs of other sequences with more background clutter and segmentation noise.

Acknowledgments. The authors acknowledge financial support from the DFG Emmy Noether program (GA 1927/1-1) and the Max Planck Society.

References

1. van der Aa, N.P., Luo, X., Giezeman, G.-J., Tan, R.T., Veltkamp, R.C.: Umpm benchmark: A multi-person dataset with synchronized video and motion capture data for evaluation of articulated human motion and interaction. In: Workshop on Human Interaction in Computer Vision, pp. 1264–1269 (2011)
2. Athitsos, V., Sclaroff, S.: Estimating 3d hand pose from a cluttered image. In: CVPR, pp. 432–439 (2003)
3. Baak, A., Helten, T., Müller, M., Pons-Moll, G., Rosenhahn, B., Seidel, H.-P.: Analyzing and evaluating markerless motion tracking using inertial sensors. In: Workshop on Human Motion, pp. 137–150 (2010)

4. Ballan, L., Taneja, A., Gall, J., Van Gool, L., Pollefeys, M.: Motion capture of hands in action using discriminative salient points. In: Fitzgibbon, A., Lazebnik, S., Perona, P., Sato, Y., Schmid, C. (eds.) ECCV 2012, Part VI. LNCS, vol. 7577, pp. 640–653. Springer, Heidelberg (2012)
5. Bregler, C., Malik, J., Pullen, K.: Twist based acquisition and tracking of animal and human kinematics. IJCV 56(3), 179–194 (2004)
6. Delamarre, Q., Faugeras, O.D.: 3d articulated models and multiview tracking with physical forces. CVIU 81(3), 328–357 (2001)
7. Erol, A., Bebis, G., Nicolescu, M., Boyle, R.D., Twombly, X.: Vision-based hand pose estimation: A review. CVIU 108(1-2), 52–73 (2007)
8. Felzenszwalb, P.F., Huttenlocher, D.P.: Distance transforms of sampled functions. Theory of Computing 8(19), 415–428 (2012)
9. Gavrila, D.M.: Multi-feature hierarchical template matching using distance transforms. In: ICPR, pp. 439–444 (1998)
10. Hamer, H., Gall, J., Weise, T., Van Gool, L.: An object-dependent hand pose prior from sparse training data. In: CVPR, pp. 671–678 (2010)
11. Hamer, H., Schindler, K., Koller-Meier, E., Van Gool, L.: Tracking a hand manipulating an object. In: ICCV, pp. 1475–1482 (2009)
12. Han, D., Rosenhahn, B., Weickert, J., Seidel, H.-P.: Combined registration methods for pose estimation. In: Bebis, G., Boyle, R., Parvin, B., Koracin, D., Remagnino, P., Porikli, F., Peters, J., Klosowski, J., Arns, L., Chun, Y.K., Rhyne, T.-M., Monroe, L. (eds.) ISVC 2008, Part I. LNCS, vol. 5358, pp. 913–924. Springer, Heidelberg (2008)
13. Heap, T., Hogg, D.: Towards 3d hand tracking using a deformable model. In: FG, pp. 140–145 (1996)
14. de La Gorce, M., Fleet, D.J., Paragios, N.: Model-based 3d hand pose estimation from monocular video. PAMI 33(9), 1793–1805 (2011)
15. Lewis, J.P., Cordner, M., Fong, N.: Pose space deformation: a unified approach to shape interpolation and skeleton-driven deformation. In: SIGGRAPH (2000)
16. Liu, M.-Y., Tuzel, O., Veeraraghavan, A., Chellappa, R.: Fast directional chamfer matching. In: CVPR, pp. 1696–1703 (2010)
17. Lu, S., Metaxas, D., Samaras, D., Oliensis, J.: Using multiple cues for hand tracking and model refinement. In: CVPR, pp. 443–450 (2003)
18. Murray, R.M., Sastry, S.S., Zexiang, L.: A Mathematical Introduction to Robotic Manipulation. CRC Press, Inc., Boca Raton (1994)
19. Nirei, K., Saito, H., Mochimaru, M., Ozawa, S.: Human hand tracking from binocular image sequences. In: IECON, pp. 297–302 (1996)
20. Oikonomidis, I., Kyriazis, N., Argyros, A.A.: Full dof tracking of a hand interacting with an object by modeling occlusions and physical constraints. In: ICCV (2011)
21. Oikonomidis, I., Kyriazis, N., Argyros, A.A.: Tracking the articulated motion of two strongly interacting hands. In: CVPR, pp. 1862–1869 (2012)
22. Pons-Moll, G., Leal-Taixé, L., Truong, T., Rosenhahn, B.: Efficient and robust shape matching for model based human motion capture. In: Mester, R., Felsberg, M. (eds.) DAGM 2011. LNCS, vol. 6835, pp. 416–425. Springer, Heidelberg (2011)
23. Ramer, U.: An iterative procedure for the polygonal approximation of plane curves. Computer Graphics and Image Processing 1(3), 244 (1972)
24. Rehg, J.M., Kanade, T.: Visual tracking of high dof articulated structures: an application to human hand tracking. In: Eklundh, J.-O. (ed.) ECCV 1994. LNCS, vol. 801, pp. 35–46. Springer, Heidelberg (1994)
25. Romero, J., Kjellström, H., Kragic, D.: Hands in action: real-time 3d reconstruction of hands in interaction with objects. In: ICRA, pp. 458–463 (2010)

26. Rosales, R., Athitsos, V., Sigal, L., Sclaroff, S.: 3d hand pose reconstruction using specialized mappings. In: ICCV, pp. 378–387 (2001)
27. Rosenhahn, B., Brox, T., Weickert, J.: Three-dimensional shape knowledge for joint image segmentation and pose tracking. IJCV 73, 243–262 (2007)
28. Sigal, L., Balan, A., Black, M.: Humaneva: Synchronized video and motion capture dataset and baseline algorithm for evaluation of articulated human motion. IJCV 87, 4–27 (2010)
29. Stenger, B., Thayananthan, A., Torr, P.: Model-based hand tracking using a hierarchical bayesian filter. PAMI 28(9), 1372–1384 (2006)
30. Stolfi, J.: Oriented Proj. Geometry: A Framework for Geom. Computation. Academic Press, Boston (1991)
31. Sudderth, E., Mandel, M., Freeman, W., Willsky, A.: Visual Hand Tracking Using Nonparametric Belief Propagation. In: Workshop on Generative Model Based Vision, pp. 189–189 (2004)
32. Tenorth, M., Bandouch, J., Beetz, M.: The TUM Kitchen Data Set of Everyday Manipulation Activities for Motion Tracking and Action Recognition. In: Int.Work. on Tracking Humans for the Eval. of their Motion in Im.Seq., pp. 1089–1096 (2009)
33. Thayananthan, A., Stenger, B., Torr, P.H.S., Cipolla, R.: Shape context and chamfer matching in cluttered scenes. In: CVPR, pp. 127–133 (2003)
34. Zhou, H., Huang, T.: Okapi-chamfer matching for articulate object recognition. In: ICCV, pp. 1026–1033 (2005)

Approximate Sorting

Ludwig Busse*, Morteza Haghir Chehreghani, and Joachim M. Buhmann

Department of Computer Science, ETH Zurich
8092 Zurich, Switzerland

Abstract. Keeping items *in order* is at the essence of organizing information. This paper derives an information-theoretic method for **approximate sorting**. It is optimal in the sense that it extracts as much reliable order information as possible from possibly noisy comparison input data.

The information-theoretic method for approximate sorting is based on approximation sets for a sorting cost function. It optimizes the tradeoff between localizing a set of solutions in a solution space and "robustifying" solution sets against noise in the comparisons. The method is founded on the maximum approximation capacity principle [3,4]. The validity of the new method and its superior rank prediction capability are demonstrated by sorting experiments on real world data.

1 Introduction

Sorting items into ascending or descending order defines a fundamental topic studied in the context of order information and algorithm design. General-purpose sorting routines that are frequently employed in many real-world problems have been well studied over the past 100 years. An excellent and in-depth overview of concepts for *sorting information* is provided by [9], starting with an elementary discussion on permutations. In fact, sorting algorithms can be understood as methods that operate on the symmetric group $\mathbb{S}_n$ (the space of all permutations over n items = rankings/orderings). At the beginning of a sorting procedure, every element of $\mathbb{S}_n$ (each ordering) is equally likely. With increasing run-time, the sorting algorithm gathers more and more information, i.e. paired comparisons are sequentially queried and provided by an oracle. Thereby, the set of possible orderings is reduced. Finally the algorithm returns one ordering that is (maximally) compatible with the observed pairwise comparisons (see Fig. 1(a)).

Whereas sorting itself is a well studied topic, ordering items when comparisons between objects can suffer from noise is a rarely addressed question. Orderings represent relative importances ("rankings") that should be reliably computed despite the fact that individual, elementary pairwise comparisons may fail.

---

* A preliminary version of this work has been presented as an abstract at the NIPS 2011 workshop on *Choice Models and Preference Learning*.

J. Weickert, M. Hein, and B. Schiele (Eds.): GCPR 2013, LNCS 8142, pp. 142–152, 2013.

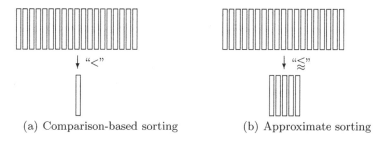

(a) Comparison-based sorting   (b) Approximate sorting

Fig. 1. A paired comparison-based sorting algorithm reduces the number possible orderings until the final output order is obtained (Fig. 1(a)). As it is illustrated in Fig. 1(b), when noise is involved in the pairwise comparisons, sorting from a data source accounts for computing an approximation set of orders (where applicable, the orders are weighted). The more noise in the data, the larger the approximation set will be.

We propose a new method to *optimally sort data in noisy conditions*. In this setting, a pairwise comparison provided by an oracle might be contaminated by noise, i.e. the algorithm might receive an inverted result for its queries "<" between two items. No specific assumptions on the noise are made. Several generative scenarios are imaginable: (i.) The items are very similar to each other and the information about their relative order is confused. (ii.) When eliciting preferences of users or customers, people state wrong comparisons because they are unsure or indifferent. (iii.) In sports games (tournaments), it is natural to observe no absolute order of the teams' performances.

Our approach takes such noise into account by not committing to a single final order, but rather determining a *set* of orderings that exhibit statistically equivalent (or weighted) approximate sortings of the items (see Fig. 1(b)). The output of our algorithm hence is a set of orderings, called the *approximation set*. Its cardinality is a function of the noise level in the data. In the limit of vanishing noise, the approximation set shrinks down to a single ordering which constitutes the special case of standard sorting. Our approach automatically adjusts the cardinality of the approximation set based on the noise type in the data in an effort to extract as much reliable partial order information as possible without being adversely affected by noise. Thereby, there is a tradeoff between informativeness (favors a small approximation set) and stability (advocates a large approximation set).

In order to optimally balance this tradeoff, we rely on an **information theoretic model validation principle** called *Approximation Set Coding* (ASC) [3,4]. The principle benefits from a generic set-based coding and communication scenario. There exists a conceptual analogy between communication and learning: For communication, one demands a high rate (a large amount of information transferred per channel use) together with a decoding rule that is stable under the perturbations of the messages by the noise in the channel [5]. In this paper, we formulate sorting as a conceptual communication problem by setting up a protocol that uses sorting solutions as codewords. Optimal communication then prefers total orders which imply maximal partial order information but still are stable under the noise. We demonstrate how to compute the *capacity* of sorting solutions.

Related Work: Sorting in noisy environments, despite its fundamental importance, is rarely discussed in the literature. Giesen et al. [8] derive a lower bound on the number of comparisons required to approximate an arbitrary ranking within a certain expected (Spearman's footrule) distance. In [6], the robustness of sorting and tournament algorithms against faulty comparisons is analyzed - asserting that in general, there exists a tradeoff between the number of comparisons and the accuracy of the result. The maximum likelihood estimation of total rank orders, given erroneous pairwise comparisons is tackled in [2]. Pelc [10] presents an overview of searching games with errors ("coping with liars"). General fault-tolerant computing is thematized in [7], where an approach is taken to design algorithms (with focus on computation trees) that work despite unreliable information.

2   Approximate Sorting

2.1   Problem Formulation

Let n be the number of items to be sorted. In mathematical terms, an ordering problem is solved by a permutation $\pi \in \mathbb{S}_n$ selected from the symmetric group $\mathbb{S}_n$. If we consider the ordering problem as a probabilistic inference problem due to noise in comparisons, then $\mathbb{S}_n$ denotes the hypothesis class of the inference problem.

The pairwise comparisons (the actual data) that a sorting algorithm has access to are provided in a pairwise comparison matrix $\mathbf{X} = (x_{ij}) \in \{0,1\}^{n \times n}$, $1 \leq i, j \leq n$[1]. A value of $x_{ij} = 1$ means that item i is larger than/preferred over item j.

The quality of a sorting is measured by a cost function $\mathcal{R}^{\text{Sort}}(\pi|\mathbf{X})$ that has to be optimized. Such a cost function also allows us to define the notion of *approximate sortings* as subsets of the symmetric group with near-optimal costs. A "natural" measure for the quality of a ranking π counts the number of disagreements between the *provided* pairwise comparisons $\mathbf{X} = (x_{ij})$ and the pairwise orderings $\mathbb{I}[\pi_i > \pi_j]$ induced by a proposal ranking $\pi \in \mathbb{S}_n$, i.e.,

$$\mathcal{R}^{\text{Sort}}(\pi|\mathbf{X}) = \sum_{i,j} x_{ij} \mathbb{I}[\pi_i > \pi_j] \tag{1}$$

$\mathbb{I}[\pi_i > \pi_j]$ indicates that the rank of item i (as induced by the ranking π) is higher than the rank of item j, meaning that item i is smaller/less preferred[2]. This cost function optimizes for a ranking that exhibits the least number of contradictions between the comparisons and the pairwise orderings.

---

[1] In order to stay within the standard conditions of sorting, it is assumed that multiple queries to the same pairwise comparison are not possible.

[2] I.e. please note that a ranking contains the ranks of items, not their order!

For inference, we will have to evaluate weighted sums (partition functions) over the hypothesis space $\mathbb{S}_n$ such as

$$Z_\beta^{\text{Sort}} = \sum_{\pi \in \mathbb{S}_n} \exp\left(-\beta \sum_{i,j} x_{ij} \mathbb{I}[\pi_i > \pi_j]\right), \tag{2}$$

The weighting factor β, often called an inverse computational temperature, defines a cost *scale*. Z_β^{Sort} is intractable for large n due to its exponential size ($Z_\beta^{\text{Sort}} \in \mathcal{O}(n!)$) and its non-factorial nature. The negative logarithm $-\ln Z/\beta =: \mathcal{F}$ is known as the free energy of a cost function. The maximum entropy distribution of the rankings π is defined as $\mathbf{P}^{\text{Sort}}(\pi|\mathbf{X}) = \exp\left(-\beta \mathcal{R}^{\text{Sort}}(\pi|\mathbf{X})\right)/Z_\beta^{\text{Sort}} = \exp(-\beta(\mathcal{R}^{\text{Sort}} - \mathcal{F}^{\text{Sort}}))$.

2.2   Mean-Field Equations for Sorting

The calculation of Z_β^{Sort} proves to be difficult due to the statistical coupling of object i to object j by the data x_{ij}. *Mean-field approximation*, a widely used approximation scheme for partition functions like Z_β^{Sort}, considers the assignments of items to ranks as a statistically independent random variable. Such a model might not yield an admissible ranking anymore since several objects might be assigned to the same rank. A cost function which describes this approach is defined by

$$\mathcal{R}^{\text{mf}}(\mathbf{M}|\mathcal{E}) = \sum_{i=1}^{n}\sum_{k=1}^{n} M_{ik}\mathcal{E}_{ik}, \quad M_{ik} := \mathbb{I}[\pi_i = k], \tag{3}$$

where the Boolean item-rank assignment M_{ik} encodes that item i has rank k. The average cost for this assignment is measured by the parameter (mean-field) $\mathcal{E}_{ik}$. The original sorting cost function (1) with the symmetric group as the hypothesis class is equivalent to $\mathcal{R}^{\text{Sort}}(\mathbf{M}|\mathbf{X}) = \sum_{i=1}^{n}\sum_{j=1}^{n}\sum_{k=1}^{n}\sum_{l=1}^{n} x_{ij}\mathbb{I}[k > l]M_{ik}M_{jl}$ with this new parametrization of the hypothesis class by a doubly stochastic rank assignment matrix $\mathbf{M}$. A unique assignment of an item to exactly one rank, i.e., $\mathbf{M} \in \mathcal{M} = \{M_{ik} : M_{ik} \in \{0,1\} \wedge \sum_{k=1}^{n} M_{ik} = 1 \; \forall i\}$ will be exactly enforced in inference (see also [11]). The second constraint that a particular rank k is only chosen for one object ($\sum_{i=1}^{n} M_{ik} = 1 \; \forall k$) is directly incorporated into the cost function as a soft constraint:

$$\mathcal{R}^{\text{mfs}}(\mathbf{M}|\mathcal{E}) = \sum_{i=1}^{n}\sum_{k=1}^{n} M_{ik}\mathcal{E}_{ik} + \sum_{k=1}^{n}\mu_k\left(\sum_{i=1}^{n} M_{ik} - 1\right) \tag{4}$$

The μ_k's effectively shift the mean-fields $\mathcal{E}_{ik} \rightarrow \mathcal{E}_{ik} + \mu_k$ such that the constraint $\sum_{i=1}^{n} M_{ik} = 1$ is fulfilled for all k. In the factorial model (4), partition functions can be calculated in a computationally efficient way

$$Z_\beta^{\text{mfs}} = \sum_{\mathbf{M} \in \mathcal{M}} \exp\left(-\beta \sum_{i=1}^{n}\sum_{k=1}^{n} M_{ik}(\mathcal{E}_{ik} + \mu_k)\right) = \prod_{i=1}^{n}\sum_{k=1}^{n} \exp\left(-\beta(\mathcal{E}_{ik} + \mu_k)\right). \tag{5}$$

The resulting maximum entropy probability distribution for these approximative item-rank assignments $\mathbf{M}$ is the Gibbs distribution $\mathbf{Q}(\mathbf{M}|\mathcal{E}, \boldsymbol{\mu}) = \exp(-\beta\mathcal{R}^{\mathrm{mfs}})/Z_\beta^{\mathrm{mfs}}$.

To determine the optimal mean-fields $\mathcal{E}_{ik}$ in Eq. (4), the Kullback-Leibler divergence between the approximative Gibbs distribution $\mathbf{Q}(\mathbf{M}|\mathcal{E}, \boldsymbol{\mu})$ and the intractable Gibbs distribution $\mathbf{P}^{\mathrm{Sort}}(\pi|\mathbf{X})$ is minimized w.r.t the mean-fields $\mathcal{E}_{ik}$

$$
\begin{aligned}
\mathcal{E}^{\mathrm{mfs}} &\in \arg\min_{\mathcal{E}} D_{\mathrm{KL}}\left(\mathbf{Q}(\mathbf{M}|\mathcal{E}, \boldsymbol{\mu}) \| \mathbf{P}^{\mathrm{Sort}}(\pi|\mathbf{X})\right) \\
&= \sum_{\mathbf{M}\in\mathcal{M}} \mathbf{Q}(\mathbf{M}|\mathcal{E}, \boldsymbol{\mu}) \log \frac{\mathbf{Q}(\mathbf{M}|\mathcal{E}, \boldsymbol{\mu})}{\exp(-\beta(\mathcal{R}^{\mathrm{Sort}} - \mathcal{F}^{\mathrm{Sort}}))} \\
&= \sum_{i=1}^{n}\sum_{k=1}^{n} q_{ik} \log q_{ik} + \beta\mathbb{E}_{\mathbf{Q}}\{\mathcal{R}^{\mathrm{Sort}}\} - \beta\mathcal{F}^{\mathrm{Sort}}.
\end{aligned} \tag{6}
$$

In this setting, $q_{ik} := \mathbb{E}_{\mathbf{Q}}\{\mathbb{I}[\pi_i = k]\}$ are *average* item-rank assignments, i.e. $\mathbf{Q}(\mathbf{M}|\mathcal{E}, \boldsymbol{\mu}) = \prod_{i=1}^{n}\sum_{k=1}^{n} M_{ik} q_{ik}$. Subject to the constraint of assigning item i to rank k, the expectation over all assignments is $\mathbb{E}_{\mathbf{Q}_{i\to k}}\{\mathcal{R}^{\mathrm{Sort}}\}$ with $\mathbf{Q}_{i\to k} = \mathbf{Q}(\mathbf{M}|\mathcal{E}, \boldsymbol{\mu}, M_{ik} = 1)$. The global minimum of bound (6) determines the mean-field assignments

$$
q_{ik} = \frac{\exp(-\beta(\mathcal{E}_{ik} + \mu_k))}{\sum_{k'} \exp(-\beta(\mathcal{E}_{ik'} + \mu_{k'}))}, \quad \text{with} \quad \mathcal{E}_{ik} = \mathbb{E}_{\mathbf{Q}_{i\to k}}\{\mathcal{R}^{\mathrm{Sort}}\}. \tag{7}
$$

To calculate the parameters $\mathcal{E}_{ik}, \mu_k$, the costs $\mathcal{R}^{\mathrm{Sort}}$ are decomposed into contributions which depend on item i and on the costs of all other items $j \neq i$. Each q_{ik} is influenced uniquely by the part which depends on the item i. For the sorting cost function Eq. (1) , meanfield approximation yields the parameters

$$
\mathcal{E}_{ik} = \sum_{j\neq i}\left((x_{ij}(\sum_{k'=1}^{k+1} q_{jk'})) + (x_{ji}(\sum_{k'=k+1}^{n} q_{jk'}))\right) + \text{const}. \tag{8}
$$

An iterative EM-like procedure computes the mean-fields $\mathcal{E}_{ik}$, the Lagrange variables μ_k and the probabilities q_{ik} by mutual conditioning. The tth iteration of the algorithm consists of two main steps. First, $q_{ik}^{(t)}$ is estimated as a function of $\mathcal{E}_{ik}^{(t-1)}, \mu_k^{(t-1)}$ (the q_{ik}'s can be used to determine the ranking by placing item i on rank $\arg\max_k q_{ik}$). Second, $\mathcal{E}_{ik}^{(t)}, \mu_k^{(t)}$ is calculated for given $q_{ik}^{(t)}$. For efficiency reasons, μ_k can be updated in an outer loop over index k, whereas $\mathcal{E}_{ik}, q_{ik}$ are updated in an inner loop over index i.

2.3 Approximation Set Coding for Sorting Problems

The sorting model is characterized by its cost function $\mathcal{R}^{\mathrm{Sort}}(\pi|\mathbf{X})$, where the solution $\pi^\star \in \arg\min_\pi \mathcal{R}^{\mathrm{Sort}}(\pi|\mathbf{X})$ captures the optimal order of the items. Let $\mathbf{X}^{(m)}, m \in \{1, 2\}$ be two datasets from the same total order, but with different noise instantiations in the empirically determined comparisons. In most cases, their total orders with minimal empirical costs are different due to different noise realizations. Hence, sorting the items by determining the empirically optimal total order lacks robustness. The Approximation Set Coding (ASC) framework [4] suggests to rank all sorting solutions by *approximation weights* $w(\pi, \mathbf{X})$. ASC uses the family of Boltzmann weights $w_\beta(\pi, \mathbf{X}) := \exp(-\beta \mathcal{R}^{\text{Sort}}(\pi|\mathbf{X}))$, parameterized by the inverse computational temperature β. Thereby two weight sums $(m \in \{1, 2\})$ are defined

$$Z_\beta^{(m)} := Z_\beta(\mathbf{X}^{(m)}) = \sum_{\pi \in \mathbb{S}_n} \exp\left(-\beta \mathcal{R}^{\text{Sort}}(\pi|\mathbf{X}^{(m)})\right), \tag{9}$$

and a joint weight sum is defined as

$$Z_\beta^{(12)} = \sum_{\pi \in \mathbb{S}_n} \exp\left(-\beta\left(\mathcal{R}^{\text{Sort}}(\pi|\mathbf{X}^{(1)}) + \mathcal{R}^{\text{Sort}}(\pi|\mathbf{X}^{(2)})\right)\right) \tag{10}$$

Essentially, $Z_\beta^{(m)}$ determines the resolution of the solution space. Very large β forces to select the empirical minimizer, which lacks robustness. Smaller β includes more solutions than just the minimizer in the approximation set, which yields a coarse resolution of the solution space, i.e. a stable solution set. Therefore, the key problem of learning is to find the optimal resolution, i.e. the optimal tradeoff between informativeness and stability. To answer this question, the ASC principle converts an optimization problem into a coding problem where a collection of randomly placed approximation sets [3] serves as a set of coding messages in the sense of Shannon's random coding theory. The asymptotically error free identifiability of these messages at a total communication rate[3] $\rho \log_2 |\mathbb{S}_n|$ yields a criterion $\mathbb{E}_{\mathbf{X}^{(1)}, \mathbf{X}^{(2)}} \hat{\mathcal{I}}_\beta(\mathbf{X}^{(1)}, \mathbf{X}^{(2)})$ to be optimized (detailed calculation in [3]), i.e.,

$$\mathbf{P}(\text{error}) \leq \exp\left(-\log |\mathbb{S}_n|\left(\mathbb{E}\hat{\mathcal{I}}_\beta - \rho\right)\right) \tag{11}$$

$$\hat{\mathcal{I}}_\beta(\mathbf{X}^{(1)}, \mathbf{X}^{(2)}) = \frac{1}{\log |\mathbb{S}_n|} \log \frac{|\mathbb{S}_n| \cdot Z_\beta^{12}(\mathbf{X}^{(1)}, \mathbf{X}^{(2)})}{Z_\beta^1(\mathbf{X}^{(1)}) \cdot Z_\beta^2(\mathbf{X}^{(2)})}. \tag{12}$$

The expectation in Eq. (11) is calculated for the random variables $\mathbf{X}^{(1)}, \mathbf{X}^{(2)}$ and the hat denotes an empirical variable. The rate parameter ρ should not exceed the function $\mathbb{E}_{\mathbf{X}^{(1)}, \mathbf{X}^{(2)}} \hat{\mathcal{I}}_\beta(\mathbf{X}^{(1)}, \mathbf{X}^{(2)})$ for asymptotically error free communication. Maximizing $\mathbb{E}\hat{\mathcal{I}}_\beta$ w.r.t. β, therefore, will yield the optimal rate and, equivalently the optimal resolution of the hypothesis class. $\mathbb{E}\hat{\mathcal{I}}_\beta$ can be interpreted as a mutual information [3] and its maximum defines the approximation capacity of cost function $\mathcal{R}^{\text{Sort}}(\pi|\mathbf{X})$. It determines the best tradeoff between stability and informativeness. $Z_\beta^{12}(\mathbf{X}^{(1)}, \mathbf{X}^{(2)})$ accounts for the overlap, how many ordering solutions of the first dataset are also in the approximation set of the

---

[3] The total rate scales as $\log_2(n!)$ for sorting instead of n in Shannon's case since the hypothesis class is the symmetric group and not the set of n-bit strings.

second dataset – at temperature β. For a fixed β, a large overlap means that the solution of the first dataset generalizes well to the second dataset, whereas a small or empty intersection indicates a lack of generalization.

2.4 Approximation Capacity of Sorting

Consider a sorting task of n given items to be solved by minimizing the costs (1). The potential $\mathcal{E}_{ik}$ (see 2.2) indicates the cost of placing item i on rank k. In our sorting problem, the potentials $\mathcal{E}_{ik}, 1 \leq i, k \leq n$ are provided from the mean-field together with the shift $\boldsymbol{\mu}$ for normalization. Given the potentials, approximation capacity is computed by (i.) calculating the weight sums $Z_\beta^{(m)}, m = 1, 2$, and the joint weight sum $Z_\beta^{(12)}$ and (ii.) maximizing $\hat{\mathcal{I}}_\beta$ (Eq. 12) with respect to β.

The weight sums are

$$Z_\beta^{(m)} = \prod_{i=1}^n \sum_{k=1}^n \exp\left(-\beta(\mathcal{E}_{ik}^{(m)} + \mu_k^{(m)})\right) \tag{13}$$

Similarly, the joint weight is calculated by

$$Z_\beta^{(12)} = \prod_{i=1}^n \sum_{k=1}^n \exp\left(-\beta(\mathcal{E}_{ik}^{(1)} + \mu_k^{(1)} + \mathcal{E}_{ik}^{(2)} + \mu_k^{(2)})\right) \tag{14}$$

Thus, the mutual information estimate $\hat{\mathcal{I}}_\beta$ yields

$$\hat{\mathcal{I}}_\beta = 1 + \frac{1}{\log_2 |\mathbb{S}_n|} \sum_{i=1}^n \log \sum_{k=1}^n \exp\left(-\beta(\mathcal{E}_{ik}^{(1)} + \mu_k^{(1)} + \mathcal{E}_{ik}^{(2)} + \mu_k^{(2)})\right)$$
$$- \frac{1}{\log_2 |\mathbb{S}_n|} \sum_{i=1}^n \log\left(\sum_{k=1}^n \exp(-\beta(\mathcal{E}_{ik}^{(1)} + \mu_k^{(1)})) \sum_{k'=1}^n \exp(-\beta(\mathcal{E}_{ik'}^{(2)} + \mu_{k'}^{(2)}))\right) \tag{15}$$

An empirical estimate of the approximation capacity is defined as the maximum of the mutual information $\hat{\mathcal{I}}_\beta$ over β, providing us with the corresponding $\beta^* := \arg\max_\beta \hat{\mathcal{I}}_\beta$. With this technology at hand, data drawn from a noisy pairwise comparison source can be sorted. The sorting results are sampled from the Gibbs distribution associated with the cost function given at the temperature $T^* = 1/\beta^*$). They optimally balance the tradeoff between extracting as much reliable order information as possible from the data, while at the same time being maximally robust against the noise type actually present in the data.

2.5 Experimental Study

Experimental results demonstrate that the new approximate sorting technique is capable of sensibly sorting noisy data. Experiments were performed for $n = 50$ items with varying noise levels. For generating the synthetic data, a simple noise model was assumed: the order between items which are close to each other is confused with the noise fraction specified in the experiment, whereas comparisons between distant items (e.g. between the first and the last item in the correct order) are corrupted with vanishing probability. Flip probabilities are interpolated between these extremes.

The inverse computational temperature β^* decreases with an increase in the noise level (see Fig. 2(a)). The more noise in the data, the higher the temperature must be at which we analyze the data (the less order information we can extract). With little noise, on contrary, one is able to extract a lot of structure. We then investigated the prediction performance of our approx-

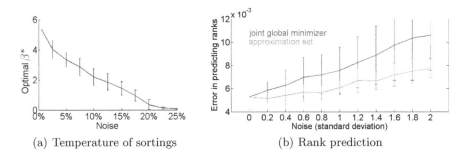

(a) Temperature of sortings   (b) Rank prediction

Fig. 2. Left: The resolution, at which we can look at orderings (as reflected in β), decreases with noise. Right: The error in predicting ranks versus noise present in the data. This result promises that predictions based on the approximation set outperform the global minimizer substantially! The superiority in particular is more pronounced when more noise is involved. In the noise free case, both cases fall together.

imation set in comparison with the global minimizer solution. To check the ability of recovering ranks, pairwise comparisons were impurified with noise by comparing two random draws from Normal distributions centered around the true ranks of the items under comparison (i.e. $\tilde{\pi}_i \sim \mathcal{N}(\mu = \pi_i, \sigma^2)$ and $\tilde{\pi}_j \sim \mathcal{N}(\mu = \pi_j, \sigma^2)$, $x_{ij} = \mathbb{I}[\tilde{\pi}_i < \tilde{\pi}_j]$. In Fig. 2(b), the standard deviation σ adjusting the noise was increased. For a fair comparison, the global minimizer was computed over both datasets $\mathbf{X}^{(1)}$ and $\mathbf{X}^{(2)}$, i.e. the ranking π which minimizes $\mathcal{R}^{\text{Sort}}(\pi|\mathbf{X}^{(1)}, \mathbf{X}^{(2)}) = \mathcal{R}^{\text{Sort}}(\pi|\mathbf{X}^{(1)}) + \mathcal{R}^{\text{Sort}}(\pi|\mathbf{X}^{(2)})$ was chosen for predicting ranks. The approximation set was fully automatically determined as proposed in this article. As we can see in Fig. 2(b), rank predictions based on approximate sorting are substantially better than considering only the global minimizer (which corresponds to cooling down to zero temperature). The proposed method is particularly helpful when there is a portion of noise in the data (as we can expect in many real-world situations, e.g. soccer matches). In the noise free case, both approaches naturally perform the same.

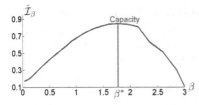

Method	Prediction error per rank		
	abs.	rel.	gain
Joint global minim.	0.29	14%	
Approximation set	0.14	6.8%	51%

(a) Sorting structure in chess data   (b) Prediction of chess league results

Fig. 3. Tournament data from the German chess league, years 2009 − 2011. Left: The approximate sorting technique is capable of finding the optimal amount of structure in the records of game wins and losses, thus discriminating signal and noise in an application- and context-sensitive way. Right: Numerical prediction results on chess data.

Real-World Data: Reliable Chess League Ranking. We analyzed tournaments from the German chess league competitions[4] ($n = 16$ teams are involved per league and season). The records of wins and losses in pairwise games constitute the data. The two instances $X^{(1)}$ and $X^{(2)}$ are drawn from two consecutive years, here from the seasons 2009 − 2010 and 2010 − 2011. In Fig. 3(b), the performance in predicting the final ranks of the teams at the end of the season is compared quantitatively. As a fair baseline, we again compared with the global minimizer that is optimized jointly over both instances as described in the previous paragraph. Approximate sorting solutions provide more predictive information for ranking the player teams (compared to the generalized global minimizer as baseline). For this real-world data, too, the ranks of approximation sets provide us with significantly improved estimates. Fig. 3(a) presents the information amount reliably extractable from the data (i.e. the signal part), dependent on the resolution parameter β. Our new method adjusts this tradeoff optimally.

Recovering University Scores from Rankings. We challenged the method with top-100 lists of universities (QS World University Rankings)[5], using the rankings from the years 2010 and 2011. Shown to the algorithm was only rank information, i.e. $X^{(1)}$ was prepared to hold the pairwise comparisons as induced by the 2010 ranking, and $X^{(2)}$ for 2011, respectively. Despite the fact that the method got access only to this relative *rank-order* information on pairs of universities, it

Method	Prediction error per rank		
	abs.	rel.	gain
Joint global minim.	1.68	29.9%	
Approximation set	1.32	23.5%	21%

(a) World University Rankings (QS).

Fig. 4. Approximate sorting improves university ranking data prediction

---

[4] Source: www.schachbundesliga.de
[5] Source: www.topuniversities.com/university-rankings/world-university-rankings

could reconstruct well the actual *numerical scores* that underly the ranking (see Fig. 4(a)). These scores were predicted using the Boltzmann-weighted ranks (Eq. 9) at the optimal temperature β^*. The relative improvement is smaller here compared to the chess data, since the problem is intrinsically harder as no individual pairwise comparisons like in the chess games scenario are available, but only one total order per instance. Nevertheless, the approximate sorting method can generate a substantial advantage over the baseline method.

3   Conclusion

This contribution considered the sorting problem under noisy conditions. We have derived an optimal sorting procedure based on information-theoretic model validation. Our approach also exemplifies how the Approximation Set Coding (ASC) principle [3,4] is employed to extract both informative and robust structure in a context-sensitive way.

Future work includes the design of new sorting algorithms that actively choose paired comparisons adaptively to the data with the goal of minimizing query costs while maximizing information content and robustness. Such studies will also shed new light on the relationship between computational complexity and statistical complexity, in particular since some sorting related problems like Minimum Feedback Arc Set are known to be NP-hard. The widely shared belief that robust and properly regularized optimization yields computationally tractable problems [1] can also be analyzed and tested for approximate sorting.

References

1. Bilu, Y., Linial, N.: Are stable instances easy? 1st Symp. Innovations in Computer Science, ICS (2010)
2. Braverman, M., Mossel, E.: Noisy sorting without resampling. SODA 2008 (2008)
3. Buhmann, J.M.: Information theoretic model validation for clustering. In: ISIT 2010. IEEE (2010)
4. Buhmann, J.M.: Context sensitive information: Model validation by information theory. In: Martínez-Trinidad, J.F., Carrasco-Ochoa, J.A., Ben-Youssef Brants, C., Hancock, E.R. (eds.) MCPR 2011. LNCS, vol. 6718, pp. 12–21. Springer, Heidelberg (2011)
5. Buhmann, J.M., Chehreghani, M.H., Streich, A.P., Frank, M.: Information theoretic model selection for pattern analysis. ICML Workshop on Unsupervised and Transfer Learning (2011)
6. Elmenreich, W., Ibounig, T., Fehervari, I.: Robustness versus performance in sorting and tournament algorithms. Acta Polytechnica Hungarica (2009)
7. Feige, U., Peleg, D., Raghavan, P., Upfal, E.: Computing with unreliable information. In: ACM Symposium on Theory of computing, STOC 1990 (1990)
8. Giesen, J., Schuberth, E., Stojaković, M.: Approximate sorting. In: Correa, J.R., Hevia, A., Kiwi, M. (eds.) LATIN 2006. LNCS, vol. 3887, pp. 524–531. Springer, Heidelberg (2006)

9. Knuth, D.E.: The art of computer programming, 2nd edn. sorting and searching, vol. 3. Addison-Wesley (1998)
10. Pelc, A.: Searching games with errors – fifty years of coping with liars. Journal Theoretical Computer Sciene 270 (2002)
11. Simic, P.: Statistical mechanics as the underlying theory of "elastic" and "neural" optimizations. Network 1, 89–103 (1990)

Sequential Gaussian Mixture Models for Two-Level Conditional Random Fields

Sergey Kosov, Franz Rottensteiner, and Christian Heipke

Institute of Photogrammetry and GeoInformation (IPI), Leibniz Universität Hanover

Abstract. Conditional Random Fields are among the most popular techniques for image labelling because of their flexibility in modelling dependencies between the labels and the image features. This paper addresses the problem of efficient classification of partially occluded objects. For this purpose we propose a novel Gaussian Mixture Model based on a sequential training procedure, in combination with multi-level CRF-framework. Our approach is evaluated on urban aerial images. It is shown to increase the classification accuracy in occluded areas by up to 14,4%.

1 Introduction

Labeling of image pixels is a classical problem in pattern recognition. Probabilistic models of context with the goal of achieving a smooth classification result have been increasingly used to model dependencies between neighbouring image sites. A recent comparison of smooth labelling techniques for remote sensing imagery has shown that this is essential, with Conditional Random Fields (CRF) [12] performing best among the compared techniqes [18].

CRF have been applied successfully to many labelling tasks in computer vision and remote sensing [12,18,19,22], but they have problems with proper labelling of partially occluded objects. Occlusion of roads by trees or cars has been known to be a major problem of road extraction from remote sensing imagery for a long time. Model-based techniques have tried to overcome this problem by treating such objects as context objects in an ad-hoc manner [8], but a sound statistical treatment of the problem is still missing.

Previous work on the recognition of partially occluded objects includes [13], where the objects in the scene are represented as an assembly of parts. The method is robust to the cases where some parts are occluded and, thus, can predict labels for occluded parts from neighbouring unoccluded sites. However, it can only handle small occlusions, and it does not consider the relations between the occluded and the occlusion objects. We handle this problem by using a two-layered CRF (*tCRF*) [10], which explicitly models *two* class labels for each image site, one for the occluded object and one for the occluding one. In this way, the 3D structure of the scene is explicitly considered in the structure of the CRF. Labelling is supported by depth information obtained from image matching.

There have been a few attempts to include multiple layers of class labels in CRFs [11,19,22,23]. However, these methods cannot be applied to our problem. Firstly, they use part-based models where the additional layer does not explicitly refer to occlusions, but encodes another label structure. Furthermore, many of

J. Weickert, M. Hein, and B. Schiele (Eds.): GCPR 2013, LNCS 8142, pp. 153–163, 2013.

them rely on object detectors. Thirdly, in vertical views (typical in remote sensing), models based on the absolute position or orientation in the image cannot be applied because there is no natural definition of a direction of reference such as the vertical in images of street scenes; applying such models would imply learning models of the distribution of features relative to the nadir point of an image or to the North direction. None of these publications use depth information as an additional cue to deal with occlusions.

tCRF does not need additional foreground object-detectors in order to separate the foreground from the background level. The information from neighbouring unoccluded objects as well as from the occluding layer will contribute to an improved labelling of occluded objects, assuming occluded objects show some spatial continuity. The interaction model between neighbouring image sites considers the relative frequency of class transitions, which is different from standard interaction terms such as the contrast-sensitive Potts-Model [2]. In this paper we also propose a new interaction model between two *tCRF* layers, wich is based on directed graph edges - *tCRFd*. For the data-dependent terms we use Gaussian Mixture Models (*GMM*) [16]. Training of *GMM* is frequently done by Expectation Maximization (*EM*), which, due to its iterative nature, is relatively slow and requires all the training data to be held in memory [14]. An alternative method for estimation *GMM* parameters could be the sequential Monte Carlo method, also known as Partcle Filters (*PF*) [7], which are usually used to estimate Bayesian models. Despite the fact that the *PF* have sequential nature, they are still based on the simulation model and therefore are very memory demanding. In order to reduce the memory consumption and to speed up training, we propose a new sequential learning scheme which is considerably faster than *EM*. Our method is demonstrated on the task of correctly labelling urban scenes containing crossroads, one of the major problems in road extraction [15], with the main goal of correctly predicting the class labels of image sites corresponding to the road surface.

2   Conditional Random Fields (CRF)

We assume an image $\mathbf{y}$ to consist of M image sites (pixels or segments) $i \in \mathbb{S}$ with observed data $\mathbf{y}_i$, i.e., $\mathbf{y} = (\mathbf{y}_1, \mathbf{y}_2, \ldots, \mathbf{y}_M)^T$, where $\mathbb{S}$ is the set of all sites. With each site i we associate a class label x_i from a given set of classes $\mathbb{C}$. Collecting the labels x_i in a vector $\mathbf{x} = (x_1, x_2, \ldots, x_M)^T$, we can formulate the classification problem as finding the label configuration $\hat{\mathbf{x}}$ that maximises the posterior probability of the labels given the observations, $p(\mathbf{x}|\mathbf{y})$. A CRF is a model of $p(\mathbf{x} \mid \mathbf{y})$ with an associated graph whose nodes are linked to the image sites and whose edges model interactions between neighbouring sites. Restricting ourselves to a pairwise interactions, $p(\mathbf{x}|\mathbf{y})$ can be modelled by [12]:

$$p(\mathbf{x} \mid \mathbf{y}) = \frac{1}{Z} \prod_{i \in \mathcal{S}} \varphi_i(x_i, \mathbf{y}) \prod_{j \in \mathcal{N}_i} \psi_{ij}(x_i, x_j, \mathbf{y}). \tag{1}$$

In Eq. 1, $\varphi_i(x_i, \mathbf{y})$ are the *association potentials* linking the observations to the class label at site i, $\psi_{ij}(x_i, x_j, \mathbf{y})$ are the *interaction potentials* modelling the dependencies between the class labels at two neighbouring sites i and j and the data $\mathbf{y}$, $\mathcal{N}_i$ is the set of neighbours of site i, and Z is a normalizing constant.

3   Two-Level Conditional Random Fields (tCRF)

In order to classify partially occluded regions we distinguish objects corresponding to the *base level*, i.e. the most distant objects that cannot occlude other objects but could be occluded, from objects corresponding to the *occlusion level*, i.e. all other objects. In a *two-level CRF*, two class labels $x_i^b \in \mathbb{C}^b$ and $x_i^o \in \mathbb{C}^o$ are determined for each image site i. They correspond to the base and occlusion levels, respectively; $\mathbb{C}^b$ and $\mathbb{C}^o$ are the corresponding sets of class labels with $\mathbb{C}^b \cap \mathbb{C}^o = \emptyset$. In general, one occlusion level is sufficient for remote sensing imagery. In our application, $\mathbb{C}^b$ consists of classes such as *road* or *building*, whereas $\mathbb{C}^o$ includes classes such as *car* and *tree*. $\mathbb{C}^o$ includes a special class *void* $\in \mathbb{C}^o$ to model situations where the base level is not occluded. We model the posterior probability $p(\mathbf{x}^b, \mathbf{x}^o | \mathbf{y})$ directly, expanding the model in Eq. 1:

$$p(\mathbf{x}^b, \mathbf{x}^o | \mathbf{y}) = \frac{1}{Z} \prod_{i \in \mathbb{S}} \xi_i(x_i^b, x_i^o) \prod_{l \in \{o,b\}} \varphi_i^l(x_i^l, \mathbf{y}) \prod_{j \in \mathcal{N}_i} \psi_{ij}^l(x_i^l, x_j^l, \mathbf{y}). \qquad (2)$$

The *association potentials* $\varphi_i^l, l \in \{o, b\}$ link the data $\mathbf{y}$ with the class labels x_i^l of image site i. They are related to the probability of a site i to take labels x_i^l given all image data $\mathbf{y}$ and ignoring the effects of other sites in the image. The *within-level interaction potentials* ψ_{ij}^l, model the dependencies between the data $\mathbf{y}$ and the labels at two neighbouring sites i and j at each level. They are related to the probability of how likely the two sites at level l are to take the labels x_i^l and x_j^l given the image data $\mathbf{y}$. Finally, an *inter-level interaction potential* $\xi(x_i^b, x_j^o)$ is defined to model the dependencies between labels from different levels, x_i^b and x_i^o. It expresses how likely an object from the base level with class label x_i^b could be occluded by an object from the occlusion level with class label x_i^o, ignoring the data $\mathbf{y}$. Fig. 1 shows the structure of our *tCRFd* model. Two levels are split mainly to increase the accuracy of the labelling of occluded regions, where the association potentials cannot provide the base level nodes with reliable information because the corresponding data are not observable.

Training the parameters of the potentials in Eq. 2 requires fully labelled training images. The classification of new images is carried out by maximizing the posterior probability in Eq. 2. Our definitions of the potentials and the techniques used for training and inference are described in the subsequent sections.

3.1   Potential Functions

Association Potential: Omitting the superscript indicating the level of the model, the association potentials $\varphi_i(x_i, \mathbf{y})$ are related to the probability of a label x_i taking a value c given the data $\mathbf{y}$ by $\varphi_i(x_i, \mathbf{y}) \propto p(x_i = c | \mathbf{f}_i(\mathbf{y}))$ [12], where the image data are represented by site-wise feature vectors $\mathbf{f}_i(\mathbf{y})$ that may

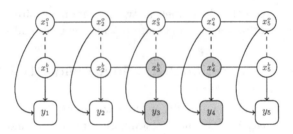

Fig. 1. Structure of the tCRF model. The second dimension and additional links between data and labels are omitted for simplicity. Squares: observations; circles: labels. The dark nodes correspond to a region with occlusion.

depend on all the data $\mathbf{y}$. The definition of $\mathbf{f}_i(\mathbf{y})$ may vary with the dataset. We use a *GMM* for $p(x_i = c \mid \mathbf{f}_i(\mathbf{y}))$ [16]:

$$p(x_i = c \mid \mathbf{f}_i(\mathbf{y})) = \sum_{k=1}^{N_c} \pi_{ck} \cdot \mathcal{N}(\mathbf{f}_i(\mathbf{y}), \mu_{ck}, \Sigma_{ck}). \tag{3}$$

In Eq. 3, $\mathcal{N}(\mathbf{f}_i(\mathbf{y}), \mu_{ck}, \Sigma_{ck})$ is the probability density function of a Gaussian with expectation μ_{ck} and covariance matrix Σ_{ck}, and π_{ck} are the mixture components measuring the contribution of cluster k to the joint probability density of class c. For each class c there are N_k sets of parameters $\pi_{ck}, \mu_{ck}, \Sigma_{ck}$. This applies to the models both for the base and for the occlusion levels, i.e. $\varphi_i^b(x_i^b, \mathbf{y})$ and $\varphi_i^o(x_i^o, \mathbf{y})$. The parameters for each class are determined from training data independently from each other, using a sequential learning approach explained in Section 3.3. In our experiments, we compare the *tCRF* model based on the GMM association potential with a model that uses a *naive Bayes* model with $p(x_i = c|\mathbf{f}_i(\mathbf{y})) = \prod_k p(f_i^k|x_i = c)$, where f_i^k is the kth element of $\mathbf{f}_i(\mathbf{y})$ and the probabilities $p(f_i^k|p(x_i = c)$ are derived from the histograms of the feature f_i^k [1].

Within-Level Interaction Potential: This potential describes how likely the pair of neighbouring sites i and j is to take the labels $(x_i, x_j) = (c, c')$ given the data: $\psi_{ij}(x_i, x_j, \mathbf{y}) \propto p(x_i = c, x_j = c'|\mathbf{y})$ [12]. We generate a 2D histogram $h'_\psi(x_i, x_j)$ of the co-occurrence of labels at neighbouring sites from the training data; $h'_\psi(x_i = c, x_j = c')$ is the number of occurrences of the classes (c, c') at neighbouring sites i and j. We scale the rows of $h'_\psi(x_i, x_j)$ so that the largest value in a row will be one to avoid a bias for classes covering a large area in the training data, which results in a matrix $h_\psi(x_i, x_j)$. We obtain $\psi_{ij}(x_i, x_j, \mathbf{y})$ by applying a penalization depending on the Euclidean distance $d_{ij} = \|\mathbf{f}_i(\mathbf{y}) - \mathbf{f}_j(\mathbf{y})\|$ of the feature vectors $\mathbf{f}_i$ and $\mathbf{f}_j$ to the diagonal of $h_\psi(x_i, x_j)$:

$$\psi_{ij}(x_i, x_j, \mathbf{y}) \equiv \psi_{ij}(x_i, x_j, d_{ij}) = \begin{cases} \frac{\lambda}{\sqrt{\lambda^2 + d_{ij}^2}} \cdot h_\psi(x_i, x_j) & \text{if } x_i = x_j \\ h_\psi(x_i, x_j) & \text{otherwise} \end{cases} \tag{4}$$

In Eq. 4, λ determines the relative weight of the within-level interaction potential compared to the association potential. As the largest entries of $h_\psi(x_i, x_j)$ are usually found in the diagonals, a model without the data-dependent term in Eq. 4 would favour identical class labels at neighbouring image sites and, thus, result in a smoothed label image. This will still be the case if the feature vectors $\mathbf{f}_i$ and $\mathbf{f}_j$ are identical. However, large differences between the features will reduce the impact of this smoothness assumption and make a class change between neighbouring image sites more likely. This model differs from the contrast-sensitive Potts model [2] by the use of the normalised histograms $h_\psi(x_i, x_j)$ in Eq. 4. As a consequence, the likelyhood of a class transition depends on the frequency with which it occurs in the training data. Again, the training of the models for the base and the occlusion levels, $\psi_{ij}^b(x_i^b, x_j^b, \mathbf{y})$ and $\psi_{ij}^o(x_i^o, x_j^o, \mathbf{y})$, respectively, are carried out independently from each other using fully labelled training data.

Inter-level Interaction Potential: This potential describes how likely x_i^b is to take the value $c \in \mathbb{C}^b$ given that the label x_i^o from the occlusion level takes the value $c' \in \mathbb{C}^o$: $\xi_i(x_i^b, x_i^o) = p(x_i^b = c | x_i^o = c')$. We generate a 2D histogram $h_\xi'(x_i^b, x_i^o)$ of the co-occurrence of labels at different layers and the same image site from the training data; $h_\xi'(c, c')$ is the number of image sites in the training data with $x_i^b = c$ and $x_i^o = c'$. The rows of $h_\xi'(x_i^b, x_i^o)$ are scaled so that the largest value in a row will be one, resulting in a matrix $h_\xi(x_i^b, x_i^o)$ that is the basis for the potential $\xi_i(x_i^b, x_i^o)$. Scaling is necessary to avoid a bias for classes covering a large area in the training data. In our experiments we will compare two different models for handling the inter-level interaction potential. Our model *tCRFd* corresponds to Fig. 1, where the edges connecting the two levels are directed, whereas in the state-of-the-art *tCRFu* model, the edges connecting the two levels are undirected. This difference only affects the inference (Section 3.2).

3.2 Training and Inference

Exact methods for training and inference of a CRF are computationally intractable [12,21]. Thus, approximate solutions have to be used. We determine the parameters of all potentials separately. The interaction potentials are derived from histograms of the co-occurrence of classes at neighbouring image sites in the way described in Section 3.1. The parameter λ in Eq. 4 is set to $\lambda = 4$, which was determined empirically; it could also be determined by a procedure such as cross validation [20]. The training of the GMM is described in Section 3.3. For inference we use Loopy Belief Propagation, a standard message passing technique for probability propagation in graphs with cycles [21]. In the model *tCRFu*, messages are sent from the base to the occlusion level and vice versa; in *tCRFd*, messages will only be sent from the occlusion level to the base level.

3.3 Sequential Gaussian Mixture Model Training

EM requires the simultaneous storage and processing of all the training samples and the prior definition of the number N_k of Gaussians in the mixture model [14]. In order to overcome these problems we propose a sequential training method for estimating the GMM parameters (cf. Algorithm 1). It requires two parameters, a threshold d_θ defining the minimum distance between Gaussians, and the maximum number $\mathbb{G}_{max}$ of Gaussians in the mixture model. We consider each training sample as an evidence for parameters μ_{ck} and Σ_{ck} of one of the Gaussians in Eq. 3. The samples are processed sequentially in the order in which they are collected. For each new sample we check whether it belongs to an existing Gaussian component k by evaluating the Euclidian distances d_k between the new sample and the centres μ_{ck} of the existing components. If the smallest distance d_{min} is shorter than d_θ, the sample is assigned to the component k_{min} corresponding to d_{min}, and the parameters of that component are updated. This will affect the centre μ_{ck} of that component, and consequently we check whether we can merge it with any of the others, this time by comparing the Euclidean distances of the class centres to the threshold d_θ. This is done to avoid having too many components. If the training sample does not fit to any existing component (which is, of course, the case for the first training sample to be processed), we generate a new Gaussian component and initialise its centre μ_{ck} by that sample. However, this is only done if the number of Gaussian components is lower than the limit $\mathbb{G}_{max}$, otherwise we discard the training sample. This method is fast because no iterations are required, and it does not require much memory due to its sequential nature. Moreover, we do not need to define the strict number of Gaussians in the GMM, but this number is adjusted to the training data.

Algorithm 1. Sequential GMM training

Data: distance threshold d_θ; max. number of Gaussians $\mathbb{G}_{max}$; *sample points*;
Result: *GaussianMixture*

```
1  while sample points do
2  │   p ← GetNextPoint();
3  │   if GaussianMixture.N = 0 then
4  │   │   N ← new Gaussian();
5  │   │   N.AddPoint(p);
6  │   │   GaussMixture.Append(N);
7  │   else
8  │   │   for N_k ∈ GaussianMixture do
9  │   │   │   d_k = distance(p, N_k.μ);
10 │   │   (d_min, k_min) ← MIN(d_k);
11 │   │   if (d_min > d_θ) AND (GaussianMixture.N < G_max) then
12 │   │   │   N ← new Gaussian();
13 │   │   │   N.AddPoint(p);
14 │   │   │   GaussMixture.Append(N);
15 │   │   else
16 │   │   │   N_{k_min}.AddPoint(p);
17 │   │   for N_k, N_m ∈ GaussianMixture, k ≠ m do
18 │   │   │   d = distance(N_k.μ, N_m.μ);
19 │   │   │   if d < d_θ then
20 │   │   │   │   N_k.MergeWith(N_m);
21 │   │   │   │   GaussianMixture.Erase(N_m);
```

---

4   Features

Our experiments are based on a *colour infrared* (CIR) image (orthophoto) and a *digital surface model* (DSM) image, where grayvalues represent the height of the earth's surface, including all objects on it. Having a DSM, it is possible to estimate the *digital terrain model* (DTM), which, in contrast to a DSM, represents the bare ground surface without any objects like plants and buildings. We do this estimation by applying to the DSM a morphological opening filter with a structural element size corresponding to the size of the largest off-terrain structure in the scene, followed by a median filter with the same kernel size. Both CIR and DSM images are defined on the same grid. From these input data, we derive the site-wise feature vectors $\mathbf{f}_i(\mathbf{y})$, consisting of 18 features. For numerical reasons, features are scaled and quantized by 8 bit. We use patches of 5×5 pixels as image sites for calculating $\mathbf{f}_i(\mathbf{y})$.

In this paper we use the following features: the *normalized difference vegetation index*, derived from the near infrared and the red band of the CIR image; the *saturation* component in LHS colour space; the *intensity*, calculated as the average of the blue and green channels. These 3 features are derived at 3 different scales: for the individual sites and as the average in a local neighbourhood of 10×10 and 100×100 pixels. Next we determine the *variances of intensity, saturation* and the *gradient* determined in a local neighbourhood of 13×13 pixels of each site. Road pixels are usually found in a certain distance either from road edges or road markings. The distance of an image site to its nearest edge pixel is used as the next feature. We also use *histograms of oriented gradients* (HOG) features [5], calculated for cells of 7×7 pixels and using blocks of 2×2 cells for normalization. Each histogram consists of 9 orientation bins. The gradient directions are determined relative to the main direction of the entire scene, supposed to correspond to the direction of one of the intersecting roads. We extract three features from the HOG descriptor, namely the value corresponding to the main direction and the values at its two neighbouring bins. Finally, we use the height difference between the DSM and the DTM as a feature, corresponding to the relative elevation of objects above ground. The last feature is the gradient strength of the DSM.

5   Evaluation

To evaluate our model we selected 90 crossroads from the Vaihingen data set[1]. For each crossroad, a CIR and a DSM were available, each covering an area of 80×80 m^2 with a ground sampling distance of 8 cm. The DSM and the orthophoto were generated from multiple aerial CIR images using semi-global matching [9]. Given our definition of the image sites, each graphical model consisted of 200×200 nodes. The neighbourhood $\mathcal{N}_i$ of an image site i is chosen to consist of the direct neighbours of i in the data grid. We defined 6 classes, namely *asphalt* (*asp.*), *building* (*bld.*), *tree*, *grass* (*gr.*), *agricultural* (*agr.*) and

---

[1] Provided by German Society for Photogrammetry, Rem. Sensing and Geoinf. [4].

car, so that $\mathbb{C}^b = \{asp., bld., gr., agr.\}$ and $\mathbb{C}^o = \{tree, car, void\}$. The two-level reference was generated by manually labeling the orthophotos using these classes and assumptions about the continuity of objects such as road edges in occluded areas to define the reference of the base level. Other existing benchmark datasets could not be used, because they are supplied with a one-layer reference only. For the evaluation we used cross validation. In each test run, 89 images were used for training, and the remaining one for testing. This was repeated so that each image was used as a test image once. The results were compared with the reference; we report the completeness / correctness of the results per class and the overall accuracy [17]. Our CRF-classification is based on the DGM C++ library [6].

We carried out 3 sets of experiments. In the 1st set, we used the *naive Bayes* model for the association potentials (*Bayes*), whereas in the 2nd set we used GMM training based on the OpenCV implementation of EM [3] (*emGMM*). Finally, in the 3rd set we evaluate our sequential GMM model (*seqGMM*). Each set included three experiments: in experiment *CRF*, each layer was processed independently, thus the inter-level interaction potentials were not considered; Experiments *tCRFu* and *tCRFd* used *tCRF* model with the inter-level interaction potentials represented by undirected and directed edges, respectively (cf. Section 3.1). The completeness and the correctness of the results achieved in these experiments are shown in Tab. 1. Fig. 2 shows the results for three crossroads.

Table 1. Completeness (*Cm.*), Correctness (*Cr.*), overall accuracy (*OA*) [%] and timings for Intel® Core™ i7 CPU 950 with 3.07 GHz required for training (t_t) and classification (t_c)

	Bayes						emGMM						seqGMM					
	CRF		tCRFu		tCRFd		CRF		tCRFu		tCRFd		CRF		tCRFu		tCRFd	
	Cm.	Cr.	Cm.	Cr.	Cm.	Cr.	Cm.	Cr.	Cm.	Cr.	Cm.	Cr.	Cm.	Cr.	Cm.	Cr.	Cm.	Cr.
asp.	83.7	77.1	85.7	73.9	82.8	81.2	93.8	58.0	86.6	81.6	83.3	86.6	93.7	58.2	86.5	81.7	83.8	86.5
bld.	65.7	92.2	63.8	93.3	75.4	88.3	72.2	92.0	73.6	91.6	81.0	86.7	72.0	92.2	73.6	91.7	81.0	86.8
gr.	51.6	75.9	88.9	77.2	88.3	81.5	58.5	81.0	91.2	78.8	90.1	83.4	58.6	81.0	91.5	78.7	90.2	83.9
agr.	36.2	96.9	38.4	95.8	68.3	81.5	47.5	97.4	47.9	96.9	81.0	88.5	47.5	97.9	47.8	97.2	80.9	88.5
OA_b	**69.1**		**81.5**		**82.3**		**71.0**		**82.3**		**85.7**		**71.2**		**82.4**		**85.6**	
void	85.8	94.3	88.3	93.5	85.8	94.3	90.2	91.9	90.7	91.1	90.0	92.5	90.4	92.0	90.6	91.2	90.4	92.0
tree	82.9	58.5	79.0	61.9	82.9	58.5	71.6	64.2	64,8	70.5	71.7	64.5	71.8	64.3	64,7	70.7	71.8	64.3
car	0.5	17.8	0.0	17.7	0.5	17.8	1.2	40.5	46.7	13.4	1.3	40.9	1.3	40.7	46.5	13.3	1.3	40.7
OA_o	**84.5**		**85.8**		**84.5**		**86.1**		**87.2**		**86.2**		**86.0**		**87.3**		**86.0**	
t_t	9.7 sec						546.0 sec						89.8 sec					
t_c	6.4 sec						64.0 sec						12.5 sec					
RAM	1.2 MB						2.44 GB						1.5 MB					

In the *seqGMM:CRF* experiment, the overall accuracy of the classification was 71.2% for the base level and 86.0% for the occlusion level. Considering the inter-level interactions in the *seqGMM:tCRFu* and *seqGMM:tCRFd* experiments increased the overall accuracy for the base level by 11% - 14%, with a slight advantage for the model based on directed edges (*seqGMM:tCRFd* with $OA_b=85.6\%$). This can be attributed by more accurate classification in the occlusion areas (cf. Fig. 2, particularly the areas where roads are partially occluded by trees). For the occlusion level, the overall accuracies of the *seqGMM:tCRFu* and *seqGMM:tCRFd* experiments were 87.3% and 86.0%, respectively; in this case, there is hardly any improvement over the variant not considering the inter-level interactions *seqGMM:CRF*, and the model *seqGMM:tCRFu* performed slightly better than the others. In all experiments, the results based on *seqGMM* are very similar to those achieved for the *emGMM* and in the same time are better than those achieved for the *Bayes* model, having similar behaviour. As far as completeness and correctness are concerned, the major improvement is an increased correctness for *asp.* and an improved completeness for *gr.*. The class *agr.*, corresponding to fields, has a rather low completeness in the model *tCRFu*, though a much better one in *tCRFd*. For the occlusion level, we observe the best performance when using *tCRFu*. As we can see from the Tab. 1, it achieved the best classification rate of the *car* class, though both the completeness and correctness of that class are still very low. This may be due to the fact that cars are small compared to the size of an image site (40 cm). Without base level support, they are smoothed out in the occlusion level (cf. Fig. 2).

The computation times for training the *tCRFd* model on 89 images were 9.7 sec and 89.8 sec for the *Bayes* and *seqGMM* models, respectively; the time for inference was 6.4 sec and 12.5 sec, respectively, per image. The memory consumption was slightly above 1 MB in both cases. For the *emGMM* experiments the computation times were 546.0 sec for training and 64.0 sec per image for inference, with a memory consumption of 2.44 GB. So *seqGMM* is much closer to the *Bayes* in terms of calculation time and memory requirements, while being close to *emGMM* in terms of classification accuracy.

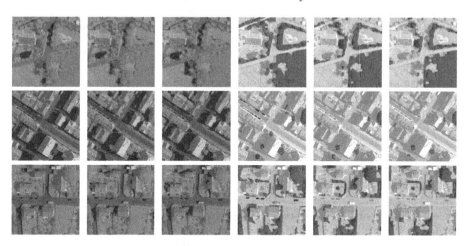

Fig. 2. Three example crossroads. 1st col.: reference; 2nd col.: CRF; 3rd col.: tCRFu. Occlusion level: 4th col.: reference; 5th col.: CRF; 6th col.: tCRFu.

6   Conclusion

We have presented a sequential approach for *GMM* training, which supports a *tCRF* model for considering occlusions in classification. Due to the two-level structure and incorporation of directed edges our model is capable of improving the accuracy of classification for partially occluded objects. Our sequential approach is more than 50 times faster and needs far less memory than classical EM. The method was evaluated on a set of airborne images and showed a considerable improvement of the overall accuracy in comparison to the CRF and $Bayes$ approaches. In the future we want to extend the model to an n-level architecture, which will require the removal of the restriction $\mathbb{C}^b \bigcap \mathbb{C}^o = \emptyset$.

References

1. Bishop, C.M.: Pattern Recognition and Machine Learning, 1st edn. Springer, New York (2006)
2. Boykov, Y., Jolly, M.: Interactive graph cuts for optimal boundary and region segmentation of objects in n-d images. In: Proc. ICCV., vol. I, pp. 105–112 (2001)
3. Bradski, G.: The OpenCV Library. Dr. Dobb's Journal of Software Tools (2000)
4. Cramer, M.: The DGPF test on digital aerial camera evaluation - overview and test design. Photogrammetrie-Fernerkundung-Geoinformation 2(2010), 73–82 (2010)
5. Dalal, N., Triggs, B.: Histograms of oriented gradients for human detection. In: Proc. CVPR, pp. 886–893 (2005)
6. DGM: Direct graphical models library (2013), http://research.project-10.de/dgm/
7. Fearnhead, P.: Particle filters for mixture models with an unknown number of components. Statistics and Computing 14(1), 11–21 (2004)
8. Hinz, S., Baumgartner, A.: Automatic extraction of urban road networks from multi-view aerial imagery. ISPRS J. Photogramm. & Rem. Sens. 58, 83–98 (2003)
9. Hirschmüller, H.: Stereo processing by semiglobal matching and mutual information. IEEE Trans. Pattern Anal. Mach. Intell. 30(2), 328–341 (2008)
10. Kosov, S., Kohli, P., Rottensteiner, F., Heipke, C.: A two-layer conditional random field for the classification of partially occluded objects arXiv:1307.3043 [cs.CV] (2013), http://arxiv.org/abs/1307.3043
11. Kumar, S., Hebert, M.: A hierarchical field framework for unified context-based classification. In: Proc. ICCV, pp. 1284–1291 (2005)
12. Kumar, S., Hebert, M.: Discriminative Random Fields. Int. J. Comput. Vis. 68(2), 179–201 (2006), http://www.springerlink.com/index/10.1007/s11263-006-7007-9
13. Leibe, B., Leonardis, A., Schiele, B.: Robust object detection with interleaved categorization and segmentation. Int. J. Comput. Vis. 77, 259–289 (2008)
14. McLachlan, G., Krishnan, T.: The EM algorithm and extensions, 2nd edn. Wiley series in probability and statistics. Wiley, Hoboken (2008)
15. Ravanbakhsh, M., Heipke, C., Pakzad, K.: Road junction extraction from high resolution aerial imagery. Photogrammetric Record 23, 405–423 (2008)
16. Reynolds, D.A.: Gaussian mixture models. In: Encyclopedia of Biometrics, pp. 659–663. Springer, US (2009)
17. Rutzinger, M., Rottensteiner, F., Pfeifer, N.: A comparison of evaluation techniques for building extraction from airborne laser scanning. JSTARS 2(1), 11–20 (2009)
18. Schindler, K.: An overview and comparison of smooth labeling methods for landcover classification. IEEE-TGARS 50, 4534–4545 (2012)
19. Schnitzspan, P., Fritz, M., Roth, S., Schiele, B.: Discriminative structure learning of hierarchical representations for object detection. In: CVPR, pp. 2238–2245 (2009)

20. Shotton, J., Winn, J., Rother, C., Criminisi, A.: Textonboost for image understanding: Multi-class object recognition and segmentation by jointly modeling texture, layout, and context. Int. J. Comput. Vis. 81, 2–23 (2009)
21. Vishwanathan, S.V.N., Schraudolph, N.N., Schmidt, M.W., Murphy, K.P.: Accelerated training of conditional random fields with stochastic gradient methods. In: Proc. 23rd ICML, pp. 969–976 (2006)
22. Winn, J., Shotton, J.: The layout consistent random field for recognizing and segmenting partially occluded objects. In: Proc. CVPR (2006)
23. Yang, Y., Hallman, S., Ramanan, D., Fowlkes, C.: Layered object detection for multi-class segmentation. In: CVPR (2010)

Synthesizing Real World Stereo Challenges

Ralf Haeusler[1] and Daniel Kondermann[2]

[1] Computer Science Department, The University of Auckland, New Zealand
[2] Heidelberg Collaboratory for Image Processing, Germany
http://hci.iwr.uni-heidelberg.de/

Abstract. Synthetic datasets for correspondence algorithm benchmarking recently gained more and more interest. The primary aim in its creation commonly has been to achieve highest possible realism for human observers which is regularly assumed to be the most important design target. But datasets must look realistic to the algorithm, not to the human observer. Therefore, we challenge the realism hypothesis in favor of posing specific, isolated and non-photorealistic problems to algorithms. There are three benefits: (i) Images can be created in large numbers at low cost. This addresses the currently largest problem in ground truth generation. (ii) We can combinatorially iterate through the design space to explore situations of highest relevance to the application. With increasing robustness of future stereo algorithms, datasets can be modified to increase matching challenges gradually. (iii) By isolating the core problems of stereo methods we can focus on each of them in turn. Our aim is not to produce a new dataset. Instead, we contribute with a new perspective on synthetic vision benchmark generation and show encouraging examples to validate our ideas. We believe that the potential of using synthetic data for evaluation in computer vision has not yet been fully utilized. Our first experiments demonstrate it is worthwhile to setup purpose designed datasets, as typical stereo failure can readily be reproduced, and thereby be better understood.

Datasets are made available online [1].

1 Introduction

Frequent discussions on performance benchmarking in computer vision [4,22,8] have not yet led to the field being brought much closer to good engineering practise. Algorithms are assumed to be of superior value, if performing with improved error metric on a small dataset with ground truth.

Little work has been done on defining criteria for datasets to be of significance in judging on capabilities of an algorithm to solve a specific task.

In particular, synthetic datasets, despite their well-known advantages, are little accepted in benchmarking for many classes of algorithms. We argue this is justified only if datasets are created with little thought in mind regarding what are specific problems of a computer vision algorithm.

In this paper, we refer to the stereo problem to illustrate our view that there is substantial potential in progressing methodology of benchmarking algorithms

J. Weickert, M. Hein, and B. Schiele (Eds.): GCPR 2013, LNCS 8142, pp. 164–173, 2013.

using appropriately designed datasets. This opens up the opportunity to increase matching challenges gradually with advances in robustness of stereo algorithms. Similar discussions are worthwhile for other ill-conditioned tasks such as optic flow, segmentation, feature matching and so forth, but beyond the scope of this paper.

Setup of recorded benchmarking stereo data with accurate ground truth is inherently difficult, increasingly so the more challenging (and therefore interesting) a dataset is. On the other hand, results of experiments of synthetic data with accurate ground truth are not accepted as a substitute of experiments on recorded data.

Results of top performing algorithms on widely used stereo benchmarks [20] do not predict robustness for applications with real world problems such as visual artifacts, specularities, poorly defined depth discontinuities, differences in image sensor characteristics across views and so forth.

In this paper, we present synthethic datasets modeling real-world issues that have not yet been subject to explicit evaluation to demonstrate that there are unused opportunities for learning more about behavior of stereo correspondence algorithms in challenging matching situations.

Section 2 discusses the value of established datasets for stereo benchmarking. Section 3 presents several challenges for stereo analysis observed on recorded data. Section 4 introduces synthetic datasets modeling challenges motivated by observations laid out in Section 3 and contains discussion about stereo matching results for a popular algorithm. Section 5 concludes and proposes future research directions.

2   Related Work

In this section, we review popular existing datasets for stereo benchmarking, first recorded data, then synthetic datasets. Finally we mention work combining recorded and synthetic data for algorithm evaluation purposes.

Ground Truth for Real World Recordings. A widely used recorded dataset of Middlebury College [21] has triggered substantial progress in stereo vision. Nowadays, these datasets are considered to be overused, as differences of error metrics amongst top performing algorithms are little significant. Depth from structured lighting for ground truth generation itself comes with limitations regarding potential complexity of datasets that can be created. Specular surfaces as well as intricate viewing occlusions cannot be tackled due to difficulties in reliably matching the projected pattern. The depth region of the images is restricted due to limited field of projector focus.

More challenging datasets of outdoor scenes with ground truth from high-end laser range finders [5] is not free of errors. Depth discontinuities are affected in particular. Ground truth does not cover image regions for which stereo is rather challenging. The accuracy of depth measurements is less than 3 pixels. For extremely challenging outdoor stereo data [14], laser range finding is not an option in generating dense accurate disparity maps due to technical limitations in sensing.

Synthetic Datasets. Early synthetic datasets for stereo testing, which also gained popularity in stereo benchmarking are random dot stereograms introduced by Julesz [12] in 1971. No object visible for human observers is present in these. Yet, random dot stereograms are useful, e.g., in testing the ability of stereo algorithms to accurately reconstruct depth discontinuities. For example, stereo block matching mehtods with adaptive window sizes were developed based on such datasets.

With the advent of photorealistic image generation [13,18], rendering of realistic images for vision benchmarking became increasingly popular. Proposed datasets frequently cover problem domain related scenes, such as corridors or road traffic surveillance scenarios. Newly introduced features of rendering engines were made use of quickly to achieve higher fidelity. For instance, Neilson *et al.* [16] used global illumination computed with sequential Monte Carlo methods to generate a large stereo benchmarking corpus.

Butler *et al.* created synthetic datasets for optical flow benchmarking [3]. These received considerable interest due to formerly unseen scene complexity. Data of 3D models and animations was drawn from an open source computer graphics repository and adapted to the requirements of flow benchmarking. Dataset modifications included corrections of flow ground truth maps and removal of semitransparent surfaces. Though appearently of increased benefit in comparison to overused data such as the 'Yosemite' sequence, it remained unclear which challenge for flow is actually present in specific frames of generated footage. Relevance for real-world applications was merely suggested by presenting look-alike images of recorded footage and comparison of first order statistics on image gradients and flow vector magnitudes. Similarity of first order flow statistics is no argument for increased challenge, as the statistics can be closely matched for any synthetic dataset, no matter how little challenging, by adjusting framerate. Observed similarity of first order statistics in image signals is an insufficient argument for realworld challenge being present, as these statistics can be altered arbitrarily using signal convolution with suitable parametrization.

To summarize, popular benchmarking datasets are characterized by a severe lack of systematic definition of specific matching problems and appropriate image data synthesis with well defined properties posing a specific challenge to vision algorithms.

Mixture of Recorded and Synthetic Datasets. For specific applications, recorded data was combined with synthetic elements, .e.g., to challenge object detection algorithms [17].

Little work has been done toward direct comparisons of real and synthetic data. Baker *et al.* [2] introduced a dataset for flow evaluation consisting of synthetic and engineered images. Correlation of different metrics applied to flow results were analyzed per dataset. Statistics describing the relation between results on synthetic vs. recorded data are not proposed in this work. Meister and

Kondermann [15] compared outcomes of optical flow analysis between real and rendered images of the same scene. The synthetic scene was created by modeling geometry and materials of the recorded scene accurately. Mean endpoint errors of resulting flow fields were found to be similar, however, not so the spatial distribution of errors.

3   Common Failure in Stereo Matching

To motivate the setup of specific synthetic datasets for stereo benchmarking we first outline a small set of common challenging situations encountered by stereo algorithms.

Low signal to noise ratios in image signals, or presence of textureless areas alike, is a major reason for mismatches. In global stereo methods, this issue is alleviated by enforcing smoothness contraints on the depth map. As the majority of stereo aggregation solutions do not explictly regularise for slanted surfaces, this generally results in a preference for fronto-parallel segments in reconstructed objects.

Decalibration of the stereo rig, whether affecting intrinsic parameters, extrinsic parameters, or both, lead to violation of standard epipolar geometry. In real world applications, it is often difficult to maintain calibration due to uncontrollable environmental influence [10].

Often, decalibration of intrinsics in a stereo rig due to environmental influence may be similar across views if cameras of same make and model are used. Regarding extrinsics, minute drift in relative orientation has a stronger impact than minute changes in relative position in narrow-baseline setups.

Whether good matches can be established depends not only on quality and magnitude of decalibration, but also on recorded image structure: While near vertical structure often does not incur gross matching error, near horizontal texture generally leads to multiplication of error [10].

Foreground fattening (also referred to as surface overextension or depth bleeding) is an inaccurate reconstruction of depth discontinuities and predominantly appears if background areas are poorly textured. Often, untextured backgrounds are missed out entirely by stereo matchers. In road traffic scenarios, this may be the case with untextured sky being entirely matched at same distance as the furthest visible adjacent object. Also, distinct objects (cars, pedestrians) may be merged due to background information of insufficient distinctiveness.

Visual artifacts are image signals with inconsistent structure across views, but this not being due to object occlusion. Such inconsistencies may be of small spatial extent, e.g., dead sensor pixels, or of large extent, e.g., lens flares. In a broader context, visual artifacts may include further inconsistencies across views, such as differences in noise levels or signal gains caused by differences in camera hardware, differences in aliasing or texturedness due to inconsistent focusing across views or deviations in locations of specularities on curved objects due to parallax.

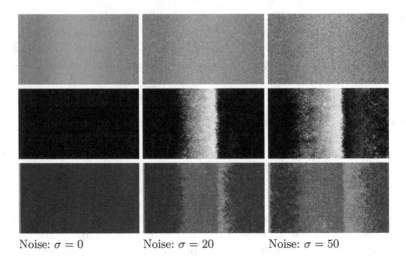

Noise: $\sigma = 0$ Noise: $\sigma = 20$ Noise: $\sigma = 50$

Fig. 1. Stereo on dataset 'Textureless area'. With equal arrangement in Figures 2, 3 and 4: Top to bottom: Synthetic image, error to ground truth for SGM stereo results (larger errors are displayed brighter), consistency map (detected mismatches in red, detected occlusions in green). Left to right: no noise (variance $\sigma = 0$), slight noise (variance $\sigma = 20$), strong noise(variance $\sigma = 50$).

4   Datasets and Experiments

We motivate the setup of datasets as simple as possible to experiment with stereo failure described in the previous section. Areas which are intended to facilitate safe correspondence are textured with image signals derived from Perlin noise [18] of suitable bandlimit in order to ensure presence of sufficient structure and avoid repetition or aliasing.

We discuss behavior of stereo analysis on these datasets, on the example of the popular semi global matching stereo [9] algorithm (*SGM*), using a robust census dataterm on a 7 by 7 matching window. Penalty parameters are set to $p_1 = 20$ and $p_2 = 100$ for smooth disparity changes and discontinuities respectively.

Low Signal to Noise Ratio

We render a slanted plane with an area in the center turning gradually less textured. As low signal to noise ratios result in unreliable dataterms, such datasets test the suitability of regularisers, consistency checks and interpolation methods to deal successfully with missing data. Experimenting with a slanted plane is motivated by the observation that many algorithms cope well with missing data in fronto parallel surfaces. Algorithms regularising for slanted planes need to be challenged with more intricate geometries.

SGM stereo can accomodate for textureless areas without problems, even on slanted surfaces, if no image noise is present. Disparity maps of left and right view are consistent throughout. Moderate noise causes mismatches on most textureless areas. However, the left right consistency check detects virtually all mismatches. A good interpolation method is needed for postprocessing, as there are extended areas with unknown disparities. Simple hole filling algorithms [9] would introduce streaking artifacts to textureless areas. Additional, more challenging geometries need to be created and tested, including non-planar surfaces.

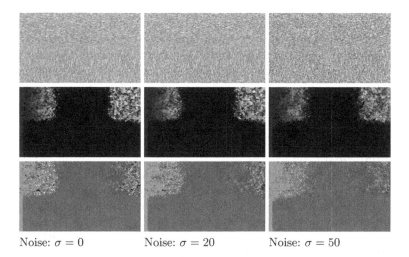

Noise: $\sigma = 0$ Noise: $\sigma = 20$ Noise: $\sigma = 50$

Fig. 2. Stereo on dataset 'Decalibrated'. The dataset consist of a texture with predominantly horizontal structures in the upper part and vertical structures in the lower image part with a smooth transition between both. The geometry is fronto-parallel, i.e. the simplest possible configuration for matchers. The right image is rotated slightly around the optical axis of the virtual camera, such that the result is a 2 px offset in the image corners. In areas with horizontal texture, stereo failure is more likely with smaller offsets in the presence of noise.

Decalibration

Decalibration in the dataset (see Fig. 2) is represented by rotating the right camera 0.12 degress with rotation axis coincident to the optical axis. At the choosen image resolution, this corresponds to a vertical scanline shift of at most two pixels, decreasing with proximity to the image center. We obtain a gradient of decalibration effects. Deviations in remaining camera parameters, intrinsic or extrinsic, equally lead to misalignment of scanlines. Essentially, spatial distributions of scanline misalignments in the image would change. The choosen case is amenable to study decalibration due to a smooth transition between well and poorly aligned scanlines.

Not only with SGM stereo, effects of decalibration vary significantly with underlying texture. Vertical texture can still be matched well. Note, however, that correct matches in case of decalibration cause slightly incorrect 3D measurements nevertheless. This is an issue in particular for distant objects, where resolution of depth measurements is low.

Texture containing unique horizontal components cause severe matching problems already at offsets of one pixel. At its current resolution, the image could caputure slightly higher frequencies without aliasing. In this case, offsets as low as 0.5 pixel may cause mismatches. Added image noise does have no major effects on mismatched areas.

Coverage of mismatch detections with left right consistency is far less accurate in affected areas in comparison to those on the textureless dataset. Added noise predominantly causes more incorrect mismatch detections in well matched areas.

Gross matching errors appear due to decalibrated cameras even on simple fronto-parallel geometry. For real-world applications, accurate detection of decalibration may increase quality of measurements based on stereo results significantly [7]. Accuracy of related algorithms to be developed can be tested best with synthetic datasets as proposed. These datasets should include a variety of scene configurations and textures.

Foreground Fattening

The dataset (see Fig. 3) facilitates to quantify the capability of stereo algorithms to correctly place disparity steps, if background objects bear less texture information than foreground objects. Wrong stereo estimation on large background areas happens as well. While correct solutions for such areas need strong priors (e.g. knowledge about background object shapes), good stereo algorithms should at least recognize matching problems and report low confidence.

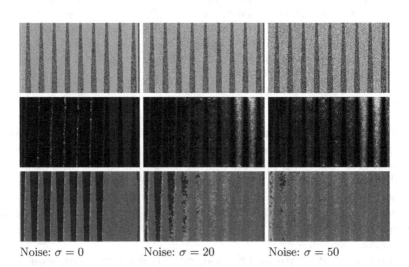

Noise: $\sigma = 0$ Noise: $\sigma = 20$ Noise: $\sigma = 50$

Fig. 3. Stereo on dataset 'Foreground fattening'. The dataset contains a group of thin, vertically oriented fronto-parallel foreground objects being of a size such that the ordering contraint is barely inviolated. The background contains a fronto parallel plane with gradient of decreasing texturedness from left to right. No background texture is present between the rightmost two foreground objects.

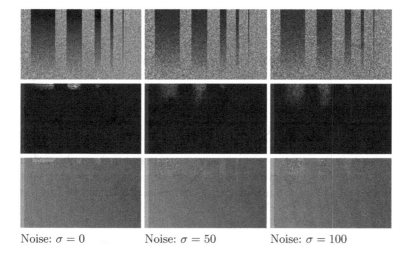

Noise: $\sigma = 0$ Noise: $\sigma = 50$ Noise: $\sigma = 100$

Fig. 4. Stereo on dataset 'Visual artifacts'. We model visual artifacts by introducing five differently sized, uniformly colored rectangular shapes of varying transparency. In opposition to the experiment with a textureless area (Fig. 1), these shapes are applied only to one view, and after rendering the 3D geometry (i.e. in a postprocessing step). The underlying geometry again is a slanted plane to challenge stereo analysis to some extent. Available texture can be matched easily. Note that stronger noise in comparison to remaining datasets is applied here.

On the noiseless dataset, SGM is missing out on two background areas between the three rightmost foreground objects. With increasing noise, background is matched with grossly wrong random values.

Left-right consistency cannot capture the absense of background areas in stereo results. In the noiseless image, detected areas of semi occlusion are well located. However, differentiation between detected occlusions and other mismatches is not entirely accurate.

With increasing presence of noise, more background areas are matched incorrectly. The consistency check fails to correctly identify a large amount of errors. This is not surprising, as fattening occurs likewise in both matching directions.

Visual Artifacts
We have set up a dataset (see Fig. 4) that facilitates to observe effects on stereo in the presence of view occlusions not caused by configuration of scene geometry. In practise, these may include, for instance, reflections caused by optical filters (particularly windscreens in driver assistance applications), lens flares, or opaque dirt in the optical path. To capture a broad set of potential effects, we vary introduced artifacts in size and transparency. For artifacts larger than matching window sizes, algorithms need to rely on regularization or interpolation. Semitransparent visual artifacts cause matching challenge in the presence of noise. Quantitative information thereon are of high value in deriving confidence information for disparity measurements. It is also of interest to experiment with artifacts bearing higher signal entropy.

Stereo mismatches are prominent whenever the size of the visual artifact exceeds the matching window size. In the noiseless image dataset, mismatches occur only at locations with completely intransparent artifacts. These mismatches are detected well by left-right consistency. Applied noise causes areas of mismatches to extend into semitransparent areas. The consistency check is increasingly missing out on bad pixels with increasing noise variance.

5   Conclusion and Future Work

We have generated synthetic stereo data presenting isolated matching challenges to stereo solvers, drawn from problems observed in stereo matching on unconstrained recorded data. In opposition to previous datasets, where image signals for algorithm testing are poorly motivated, we underpin the value of testing with suitable synthetic data.

Benchmarking results from synthetic data in general cannot predict quality of stereo outcomes on recorded data. However, following the proposed idea of designing purposive synthetic datasets, which we illustrated with a few examples, reduces these shortcomings of benchmarking with synthtetic data.

We currently design datasets containing further challenges, including specular materials and adverse lighting, repetitive signals and photometric effects due to imperfections in imaging such as dark response non uniformity and photo response non uniformity [14]. We integrate these into a system that allows for interactive combinatorial exploration (real-time stereo provided) of algorithm behavior on a superset of challenges described above, and develop an online service for generation of datasets with specified properties.

We work on improving justification for synthetic datasets by setting up related real world datasets and develop statistics that capture the similarity of a matching task in stereo vision.

To better understand spurious matching, stereo confidence measures [6,11,19] can be used. With synthetic datasets of well-defined matching challenges, these measures can undergo a principled evaluation regarding accuracy in detection of stereo mismatches. We expect this work to enable a more thourough theoretical understanding of stereo failure on challenging datasets.

References

1. Datasets and ground truth for experiments in this paper,
   http://hci.iwr.uni-heidelberg.de//Benchmarks/document/
   synthesizing_stereo_challenges/
2. Baker, S., Scharstein, D., Lewis, J.P., Roth, S., Black, M.J., Szeliski, R.: A database and evaluation methodology for optical flow. International Journal of Computer Vision 92(1), 1–31 (2011)
3. Butler, D.J., Wulff, J., Stanley, G.B., Black, M.J.: A naturalistic open source movie for optical flow evaluation. In: Fitzgibbon, A., Lazebnik, S., Perona, P., Sato, Y., Schmid, C. (eds.) ECCV 2012, Part VI. LNCS, vol. 7577, pp. 611–625. Springer, Heidelberg (2012)

4. Förstner, W.: 10 pros and cons against performance characterization of vision algorithms. In: Workshop on Performance Characterization of Vision Algorithms, pp. 13–29 (1996)
5. Geiger, A., Lenz, P., Urtasun, R.: Are we ready for autonomous driving? The KITTI vision benchmark suite. In: 2012 IEEE Conference on Computer Vision and Pattern Recognition (CVPR), pp. 3354–3361 (June 2012)
6. Haeusler, R., Nair, R., Kondermann, D.: Ensemble Learning for Confidence Measures in Stereo Vision. In: CVPR (to appear 2013)
7. Hansen, P., Alismail, H., Rander, P., Browning, B.: Online continuous stereo extrinsic parameter estimation. In: CVPR, pp. 1059–1066. IEEE (2012)
8. Haralick, R.M.: Performance characterization in computer vision. In: Chetverikov, D., Kropatsch, W.G. (eds.) CAIP 1993. LNCS, vol. 719, pp. 1–9. Springer, Heidelberg (1993)
9. Hirschmüller, H.: Stereo processing by semiglobal matching and mutual information. IEEE Trans. Pattern Anal. Mach. Intell. 30(2), 328–341 (2008)
10. Hirschmüller, H., Gehrig, S.K.: Stereo matching in the presence of sub-pixel calibration errors. In: CVPR, pp. 437–444 (2009)
11. Hu, X., Mordohai, P.: A quantitative evaluation of confidence measures for stereo vision. IEEE Trans. Pattern Anal. Mach. Intell. 34(11), 2121–2133 (2012)
12. Julesz, B., Papathomas, T.: Foundations of Cyclopean Perception. MIT Press (2006)
13. Kajiya, J.T.: The rendering equation. In: Evans, D.C., Athay, R.J. (eds.) SIGGRAPH, pp. 143–150. ACM (1986)
14. Meister, S., Jähne, B., Kondermann, D.: Outdoor stereo camera system for the generation of real-world benchmark data sets. Optical Engineering 51(02), 021107 (2012)
15. Meister, S., Kondermann, D.: Real versus realistically rendered scenes for optical flow evaluation. In: 2011 14th ITG Conference on Electronic Media Technology (CEMT), pp. 1–6. IEEE (2011)
16. Neilson, D., Yang, Y.H.: Evaluation of constructable match cost measures for stereo correspondence using cluster ranking. In: CVPR (2008)
17. Nilsson, J., Ödblom, A., Fredriksson, J., Zafar, A.: Using augmentation techniques for performance evaluation in automotive safety. In: Furht, B. (ed.) Handbook of Augmented Reality, pp. 631–649. Springer, New York (2011)
18. Perlin, K.: An image synthesizer. In: Proceedings of the 12th Annual Conference on Computer Graphics and Interactive Techniques, SIGGRAPH 1985, pp. 287–296. ACM, New York (1985), http://doi.acm.org/10.1145/325334.325247
19. Pfeiffer, D., Gehrig, S., Schneider, N.: Exploiting the Power of Stereo Confidences. In: CVPR (to appear 2013)
20. Scharstein, D., Szeliski, R.: A taxonomy and evaluation of dense two-frame stereo correspondence algorithms. International Journal of Computer Vision 47(1-3), 7–42 (2002)
21. Scharstein, D., Szeliski, R.: High-accuracy stereo depth maps using structured light. In: CVPR, vol. (1), pp. 195–202 (2003)
22. Thacker, N.A., Clark, A.F., Barron, J.L., Beveridge, J.R., Courtney, P., Crum, W.R., Ramesh, V., Clark, C.: Performance characterization in computer vision: A guide to best practices. Computer Vision and Image Understanding 109(3), 305–334 (2008)

Pedestrian Path Prediction with Recursive Bayesian Filters: A Comparative Study

Nicolas Schneider[1,2] and Dariu M. Gavrila[1,2]

[1] Environment Perception, Daimler R&D, Ulm, Germany
[2] Intelligent Systems Laboratory, Univ. of Amsterdam, The Netherlands

Abstract. In the context of intelligent vehicles, we perform a comparative study on recursive Bayesian filters for pedestrian path prediction at short time horizons ($< 2s$). We consider Extended Kalman Filters (EKF) based on single dynamical models and Interacting Multiple Models (IMM) combining several such basic models (constant velocity/acceleration/turn). These are applied to four typical pedestrian motion types (crossing, stopping, bending in, starting). Position measurements are provided by an external state-of-the-art stereo vision-based pedestrian detector. We investigate the accuracy of position estimation and path prediction, and the benefit of the IMMs vs. the simpler single dynamical models. Special care is given to the proper sensor modeling and parameter optimization. The dataset and evaluation framework are made public to facilitate benchmarking.

1 Introduction

Pedestrian path prediction is an important problem in several application contexts, such as architecture, social robotics and intelligent vehicles. Here we consider the intelligent vehicle context, in view of driver assistance and active pedestrian safety. Strong gains have been made over the years in improving computer vision-based pedestrian recognition performance. This has culminated in first active pedestrian safety systems reaching the market. For example, Mercedes-Benz introduces in its 2013 E- and S-Class models a novel stereo-vision based pedestrian system, which incorporates automatic full emergency braking.

A sophisticated situation assessment requires a precise estimation of the current and future position of the pedestrian with respect to the moving vehicle. A deviation of, say, 30 cm in the estimated lateral position of the pedestrian can make all the difference, as this might place the pedestrian just inside or outside the driving corridor. Current active pedestrian systems are typically designed conservatively in their warning and control strategy, emphasizing the current state rather than prediction, in order to avoid false system activations. Indeed, pedestrian path prediction is a challenging problem, due to the highly dynamic behavior of pedestrians. They can change their walking direction in an instance, or start/stop walking abruptly. As a consequence, sensible prediction horizons are typical short (we consider $< 2s$ in this paper).

J. Weickert, M. Hein, and B. Schiele (Eds.): GCPR 2013, LNCS 8142, pp. 174–183, 2013.

Fig. 1. Four typical pedestrian motion types: bending in (top left), stopping (top right), crossing (bottom left) and starting (bottom right) with detection bounding boxes

There has been surprisingly little analysis in previous work of the accuracy of pedestrian state estimation, let alone, that of prediction, in vehicle context. This paper addresses this by providing a quantitative comparative study of recursive Bayesian filters: we consider Extended Kalman Filters (EKF) based on single dynamical models and Interacting Multiple Models (IMM) combining several such basic models (constant velocity/acceleration/turn). These are applied to four typical pedestrian motion types (crossing, stopping, bending in, starting), see Fig. 1. Position measurements are provided by an external state-of-the-art stereo vision-based pedestrian detector. The rationale for focusing on recursive Bayesian filters in connection with modeling pedestrians as point targets is their relatively good performance and low computational cost (especially important in a vehicle context). We investigate the accuracy of position estimation and path prediction, and the benefit of the IMMs vs. the simpler single dynamical models. Special care is given to the proper sensor modeling and parameter optimization.

2   Previous Work

In this section, we focus on pedestrian state estimation based on parametric, recursive Bayesian filters. For an overview of vision-based pedestrian detection and tracking in more general context, see recent surveys (e.g. [7,8]).

A popular choice for target state estimation is the Kalman Filter (KF). Its applicability in real-time systems has been proven over many years for different sensors and application domains [1,3,4,18,21]. State parameters (e.g. position, velocity, acceleration) of the tracked target can be estimated with appropriate dynamical and measurement models. The KF can further be used for prediction by propagating the current state with the dynamical model without the inclusion of new measurements. Work by [3] on FIR-based pedestrian tracking uses a constant acceleration (CA) model in image space. Working in image space, however, makes it difficult to incorporate prior knowledge on the dynamics of pedestrian motion. Therefore, [2] track pedestrians on the ground plane using a KF in an indoor, static stereo camera setup. The use of a linear KF in the context of video-based pedestrian tracking in the world implies the use of 3D pseudo-measurements (i.e. back projection of 2D measurements); this does not account for the dependency of the longitudinal component of the noise on depth.

More accurate measurement models for the perspective projection of video sensors can be incorporated by means of non-linear Extended (EKF) or Unscented (UKF) Kalman filters. [15] use a UKF in a mono camera setup to track pedestrians on the ground plane (CV model). [19] apply the UKF to measurements from a stereo camera system comparing three different dynamical models (two CV and one constant position (CP) model) where two models have a state space in world coordinates and one in image coordinates.

KF-based approaches have also been used for pedestrian state estimation outside the video-only domain. [9] apply a CV model in a multi-sensor setup with an IR camera and laser scanner. In a previous paper [18], they used two different motion models (CA and CTRV), mentioning advantages of the latter model at near-zero pedestrian speeds. Work by [21] considers a setting where pedestrians wear electronic tags. It uses a KF with a turn motion model including orientation and velocity in polar coordinates (CTRV).

Maneuvering targets can be elegantly accounted for mathematically by means of the Interacting Multiple Model (IMM) framework [4,13]. [11] use an IMM (CP/CV) for analyzing walking vs. stopping pedestrian motion types from a stereo vision sensor on-board a vehicle. [5] use an IMM combining eight CV models with fixed velocities in eight directions. It further contains an online adaption algorithm for the IMM transition probability matrix.

Within the class of non-parametric methods for pedestrian path prediction and action classification, [11] proposes a probabilistic trajectory matching method to estimate whether a pedestrian walking towards the curbside intends to cross or not, when viewed from a stereo vision system on-board a vehicle. [12] considers the complementary case of whether a pedestrian standing will start to walk using a SVM-based classification approach, albeit from a static monocular camera.

Quantitative evaluations of pedestrian state (position) estimation have been few and limited. [3,5,9,15,18,21] do not include any such evaluation. [2] provides accuracy figures only related to its KF approach in indoor setting. [19] uses simulated data to compare CV and CP KFs. Our paper contribution is a broad quantitative study on pedestrian position estimation and path prediction using parametric Bayesian recursive filters in vehicle context. Compared to [11], we consider a wider range of pedestrian motion types. Whereas the IMM used by [11] uses 3D pseudo measurements and KFs, we use a more accurate stereo sensor modeling by EKFs.

3   Recursive Bayesian Filtering

3.1   Kalman Filter

The discrete-time KF estimates a state $\mathbf{x}(t)$ at time step t from measurement $\mathbf{z}(t)$ and previous state $\mathbf{x}(t-1)$ with the dynamical model

$$\mathbf{x}(t) = A\mathbf{x}(t-1) + Bu(t-1) + \boldsymbol{\omega}(t-1) \tag{1}$$

where the relation between measurement and state is given by

$$\mathbf{z}(t) = H\mathbf{x}(t) + \boldsymbol{\nu}(t). \tag{2}$$

A and B are transition matrices for the state $\mathbf{x}$ and the control input u, respectively, $\boldsymbol{\omega}(t-1)$ and $\boldsymbol{\nu}(t)$ are white, zero-mean, uncorrelated noise processes with covariances $\boldsymbol{\omega}(t) \sim (0, Q(t))$ and $\boldsymbol{\nu}(t) \sim (0, R(t))$. The filter process can be described as cycle of the two steps prediction (predicting the state $\mathbf{x}(t-1)$ to the next time step) and correction (updating the predicted state $\hat{\mathbf{x}}(t)$ with the current measurement) [20].

3.2   Interacting Multiple Model Kalman Filter

There are several KF extensions available to cover different motion types and maneuvers (see [13] for an overview), the most common is the Interacting Multiple Model KF (IMM). The IMM models that there is a probability of p_{ij} that the tracking target makes a transition from one type of motion (i) to another (j); these values are captured by the transition probability matrix (TPM). Each iteration of the IMM consists of the three steps: interaction, filtering and model probability update [4]. In the interaction step, the mixing probability $\mu_{ij}(t-1)$ (cond. probability that the target changed its type of motion) is calculated based on model probabilities and the TPM to produce mixed state estimates $\hat{\mathbf{x}}_j^0(t-1)$ and covariances $\hat{P}_j^0(t-1)$ for all models j. The mixed states are used as input in the filtering step where each model is predicted and updated with the standard KF equations. In the last step, the model probabilities are updated based on the measurement likelihood.

3.3   Measurement Model

Measurements come from a pedestrian detector applied on sequences recorded with a stereo camera system. A measurement vector (dropping time index t in the following) $\mathbf{z} = (u, d)$ is derived from the footpoint $p_f = (u, v)$ and the median disparity d of a pedestrian bounding box. The relation of a point in the image $p_i = (u, v)$ and its disparity d to a point $p_c = (x_c, y_c, z_c)$ in the camera coordinate system is given by the perspective camera model [1]:

$$\begin{pmatrix} u \\ v \\ d \end{pmatrix} = \begin{pmatrix} h_1(p_c) \\ h_2(p_c) \\ h_3(p_c) \end{pmatrix} = \begin{pmatrix} u_0 + \frac{f_u x_c}{z_c} \\ v_0 + \frac{-f_v y_c}{z_c} \\ \frac{f_u b}{z_c} \end{pmatrix} \tag{3}$$

where $f_u = \frac{f}{s_u}$ and $f_v = \frac{f}{s_v}$ with focal length f, baseline b, horizontal and vertical pixel width s_u and s_v, respectively. Eq. (3) leads to the nonlinear measurement function h. For a position $p_c^g = (x_c, z_c)$ on the groundplane h_2 can be ignored. To predict a measurement at time step t, the predicted state vector $\hat{\mathbf{x}}$ (camera coordinates) has to be projected into the measurement (image) space with $\hat{\mathbf{z}} = h(\hat{\mathbf{x}})$. For the EKF we further need to calculate the Jacobian $H = \frac{\partial h}{\partial \mathbf{x}}$.

Table 1. Mean sojourn times of different target dynamics in the training set (diagonals $P_{i,i}$ of the TPM based on a cycle time of $T \approx 60\,ms$). "Straight Walking" consists of the straight walking segments of starting, stopping and bending in sequences as well as complete crossing sequences. "Maneuver" relates to all other segments. "Turning", a subset of "Maneuver", relates to the turning segments within the bending in sequences.

Motion type	mean sojourn time τ_i (s)	$P_{ii}(T) = 1 - T/\tau_i$
Straight Walking	6.66	0.99
Maneuver	1.67	0.96
Turning	2.50	0.98

3.4 Dynamical Models

Several discretized continuous-time dynamical models are considered in this study: the popular constant velocity (white noise acceleration) model (CV), the constant acceleration (Wiener process acceleration) model (CA) and the constant turn model (CT) with Cartesian state vector. These characterized by their state vectors $\mathbf{x}$, transition matrices A and process noise matrices Q. The CV model state vector holds position and velocity ($\mathbf{x} = [x, z, v_x, v_z]$), the CA model further has acceleration ($\mathbf{x} = [x, z, v_x, v_z, a_x, a_z]$) and the CT model turn rate ($\mathbf{x} = [x, z, v_x, v_z, \omega]$) variables. For details, such as transition and process noise matrices, see [4,14].

Several approaches can be taken to specify the TPM. There is the ad-hoc approach to fill the diagonals with values close to one. [4,13] discuss the use of the mean sojourn time (the mean time a target stays in a motion type) for the TPM. Lastly, one could perform parameter optimization of the entries of the TPM directly. In preliminary experiments, we obtained similar best performance with the second and third approaches, thus we selected the sojourn time approach to specify the TPM, derived from a training set, see Section 4 and Table 1.

3.5 Ego Motion Compensation

At each time step, the filter state is projected from the previous camera coordinate system to the current one using the inertial motion matrix M_v (vehicle coordinates) based on velocity and yaw rate measured by on-board sensors. The inverse ego motion homography matrix is given by $M_c = D^{-1} M_v D$ (where D defines the relation between camera and vehicle coordinate system). Translational ego compensation is done using t_{M_c} as control vector u (Eq. (1) with $B = I_{2x2}$), the ego rotation is integrated into the transition matrix A_e (exemplary for the CV model) [16]:

$$A_e = \begin{bmatrix} R_{M_c} & 0_{2x2} \\ 0_{2x2} & R_{M_c} \end{bmatrix} A \qquad (4)$$

Table 2. Sequences in our dataset recorded with standing and moving vehicle

Sequences	veh. stand.	veh. mov.	total
Bending in	5	18	23
Stopping	5	13	18
Starting	0	9	9
Crossing	3	15	18

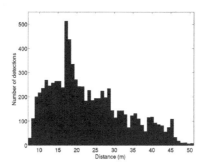

Fig. 2. Pedestrian distance distribution over entire dataset

4   Experiments[1]

Dataset. Image sequences were recorded with a stereo camera system (baseline $22\,cm$, $16\,fps$, 1176×640 pixels) mounted behind the windshield of a vehicle. They contain four typical pedestrian motion types: (walking laterally towards the street and) crossing, (walking laterally towards the street and) stopping, (standing at the curbside and) starting (to walk laterally) and (walking alongside the street,) bending in (and crossing). See Fig. 1. The dataset consists of 68 sequences of which 12485 images contain (single) pedestrians. 55 sequences were recorded at vehicle speeds of $20-30\,km/h$, the others involved a standing vehicle. See Table 2 and Figs. 2 and 6 (bottom left) for further data statistics. The dataset is splitted evenly in a training and test set. The latter was splitted 5-folds for evaluation in Fig.6 (bottom right); parameter optimization was quite time consuming, so we preferred not vary the training set as part of cross-validation.

Ground Truth (GT) is obtained by manual labeling of pedestrian bounding boxes and computating the median disparity over the rough upper pedestrian body area. The position of the pedestrian in the vehicle coordinate system is calculated with Eq. (3) and the camera-to-vehicle homography matrix. The transformed positions are fitted with a curvilinear model. The GT locations are obtained by longitudinal projections on the fitted curve. Sequences are further labeled with event tags and time-to-event (TTE in frames) values. For stopping

---

[1] The dataset and evaluation framework are made public for non-commercial research purposes. Follow the links from http://isla.science.uva.nl/ or contact the 2nd author.

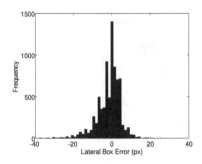 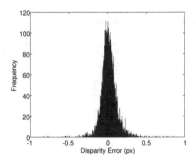

Fig. 3. Measurement error distribution: (left) lateral, u (right) longitudinal, d

Table 3. Optimized process noise parameters (σ_v, σ_a, $\{\sigma_v, \sigma_w\}$) for the different filters

Filter	EKF CV	EKF CA	EKF CT	IMM(CV,CA)	IMM(CV,CT*)
Process noise	0.77	0.44	$\{0.95, 0.90\}$	$(0.70, 0.80)$	$(0.75, \{0.40, 0.90\})$

pedestrians the last placement of the foot on the ground at the curbside is labeled as TTE = 0. For crossing pedestrians, the closest point to the curbside (before entering the roadway), for pedestrians bending in and starting to walk the first moment of visually recognizable body turning or leg movements are labeled with TTE = 0. All frames previous to an event have TTE values > 0, therefore all frames following the event have TTE values < 0.

A state-of-the-art HOG/linSVM pedestrian detector [6] provides measurements, given region-of-interests supplied by an obstacle detection component using dense stereo data [10]. The resulting bounding boxes are used to calculate a median disparity over the upper pedestrian body area based on the disparity maps. The measurement vector $\mathbf{z} = (u, d)$ is derived using the central lateral position of the bounding box and this median disparity value.

Evaluation Setup. Sequences have an average of 121 measurements (min. 39, max. 274), they start with a minimum of three consecutive measurements, and contain no missing detections longer than five consecutive frames. Evaluation is done with respect to the lateral localization error in TTE interval $[10, -50]$, corresponding to an evaluation interval from $0.60\,s$ before to $3.0\,s$ after the event. At each time step, predictions of up to 32 frames ($1.9\,s$) are made ahead. We use the predict and update functions of the EKF/UKF MATLAB toolbox [17].

Parameter Setting. The measurement noise ν (see Eq. (2)) has been derived statistically on the training set, in terms of lateral bounding box error σ_u and disparity error σ_d of the pedestrian detections w.r.t. the GT. See Fig. 3. The measurement noise matrix $R = diag(\sigma_u^2, \sigma_d^2)$ is thus set to $\sigma_u = 6.15$ and $\sigma_d = 0.32$.

Process noise ω is determined by $Q(t) = Q^0(t)q$, where $q \in \{\sigma_v^2, \sigma_a^2\}$ and for the CT model, $Q_{5,5}(t) = \dfrac{\sigma_\omega^2 Q_{5,5}^0(t)}{q}$ [4]. It has been optimized for each filter

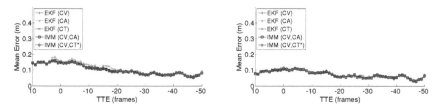

Fig. 4. Position error at current time $(t = 0)$ averaged over all sequences: lateral and longitudinal combined (left) and only lateral (right)

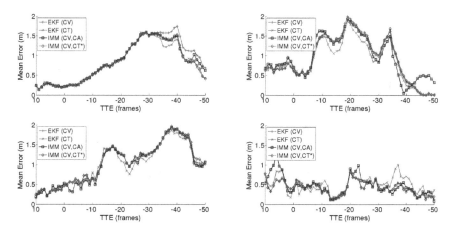

Fig. 5. Mean lateral position error when predicting 32 frames $(t = 1.9\,s)$ ahead

in terms of positions mean-squared-error (MSE) including all N position state estimates $\mathbf{x}_i(t = 0)$ $(i = 1, ..., N)$ and the corresponding P predictions $\mathbf{x}_i(t = 1, ..., P)$ $(P = 32)$ with the objective function:

$$\arg\min_{\sqrt{q}} \frac{1}{N} \sum_{i=1}^{N} \left(\sum_{t=0}^{P} \frac{MSE(\mathbf{x}_i(t))}{P+1} \right) \tag{5}$$

using a discrete parameter search on the training set. The outcome is shown in Table 3. Search space has been discretized using 60 steps for single models with one noise parameter (CV, CA) and 18 steps each for models with two noise parameters (CT, 324 parameter combinations). In a coarse-to-fine fashion discretization for the IMM(CV,CA) could be reduced based on single model results to 9 steps (81 parameter combinations). Including the TPM with a discretization of 12 values per diagonal in the optimization results in 11664 parameter combinations. Furthermore, the CT model has been optimized using only segments of bending in sequences around the labeled turn event (TTE $\in [10 - 50]$). The resulting "turn expert" filter will be termed CT* in the remainder.

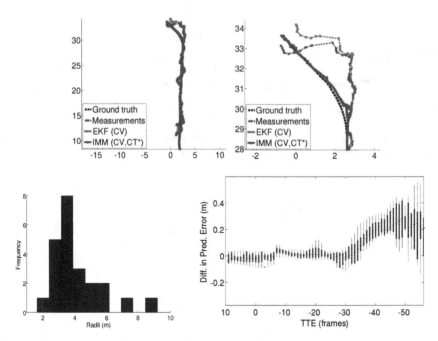

Fig. 6. Bending in: Bird's eye view of an example trajectory showing predictions (32 steps ahead) for various filters (top row, far view and close up, left and right). Turn radius distribution over the bending in sequences (bottom left). Distribution of the prediction error improvement by IMM(CV,CT*) vs. EKF(CV), based on cross-validation.

Results. Fig. 4 shows the position error at current time ($t = 0$), averaged over all sequences. One observes a similar performance for all filters. Performance differences become more evident when predicting 32 frames ($1.9\,s$) ahead, see Fig. 5 (the CA model was removed from the plots since its predictions were far off, i.e. velocities accumulate over the prediction horizon to implausible values). In terms of the single motion models (CV vs. CT), one observes benefits for the CV on the crossing sequences, and benefits for the CT on the others. For example, CT predictions during the turning of the bending in sequence are more accurate by up to $36\,cm$, compared to CV. The IMM(CV,CT*) combines the best of both worlds, it shows an improvement of up to $30\,cm$ vs. CV. One further observes that IMM(CV,CA) does not outperform CV and lags IMM(CV,CT*), overall. A more detailed analysis of the bending in case is given in Fig. 6.

5   Conclusions

In this paper, we studied several single dynamical models (CV, CA, CT) and IMMs combining such basic models for pedestrian position estimation and path prediction, in vehicle context. Results show no significant performance gain of the more sophisticated IMMs considered vs. the simpler CV, for current position estimation. We attribute this to the high sampling rate and the low measurement error for this application. For path prediction ($1.9\,s$ ahead), an IMM(CV,CT*) involving a constant velocity and a "turn expert" model, is shown to provide an improvement in the lateral position estimation of up to 30 *cm* during maneuvers. Future work involves extending the database, both in terms of motion types considered and in terms of their sample count.

References

1. Barth, A., Franke, U.: Estimating the driving state of oncoming vehicles from a moving platform using stereo vision. IEEE Trans. ITS 10(4), 560–571 (2009)
2. Bertozzi, M., et al.: Pedestrian localization and tracking system with Kalman filtering. In: IEEE Intell. Veh., pp. 584–589 (2004)
3. Binelli, E., et al.: A modular tracking system for far infrared pedestrian recognition. In: IEEE Intell. Veh., pp. 759–764 (2005)
4. Blackman, S., Popoli, R.: Design and Analysis of Modern Tracking Systems. Artech House Norwood, MA (1999)
5. Burlet, J., et al.: Pedestrian tracking in car parks: An adaptive Interacting Multiple Models based filtering method. In: Proc. of the IEEE ITSC, pp. 462–467 (2006)
6. Dalal, N., Triggs, B.: Histograms of oriented gradients for human detection. In: Proc. CVPR, vol. 1, pp. 886–893. IEEE (2005)
7. Dollár, P., et al.: Pedestrian detection: An evaluation of the state of the art. IEEE PAMI 34(4), 743–761 (2012)
8. Enzweiler, M., Gavrila, D.: Monocular pedestrian detection: Survey and experiments. IEEE PAMI 31(12), 2179–2195 (2009)
9. Fardi, B., Scheunert, U., Wanielik, G.: Shape and motion-based pedestrian detection in IR images: a multisensor approach. In: IEEE Intell. Veh., pp. 18–23 (2005)
10. Hirschmüller, H.: Stereo processing by semiglobal matching and mutual information. IEEE PAMI 30(2), 328–341 (2008)
11. Keller, C.G., Hermes, C., Gavrila, D.M.: Will the pedestrian cross? Probabilistic path prediction based on learned motion features. In: Mester, R., Felsberg, M. (eds.) DAGM 2011. LNCS, vol. 6835, pp. 386–395. Springer, Heidelberg (2011)
12. Köhler, S., et al.: Early detection of the pedestrians intention to cross the street. In: Proc. of the IEEE ITSC, pp. 1759–1764 (2012)
13. Li, X.R., Jilkov, V.P.: Survey of maneuvering target tracking. Part V. Multiple-model methods. IEEE Trans. Aerosp. Electron. Syst. 41(4), 1255–1321 (2005)
14. Li, X.R., Jilkov, V.: Survey of maneuvering target tracking. Part I. Dynamic models. IEEE Trans. Aerosp. Electron. Syst. 39(4), 1333–1364 (2003)
15. Meuter, M., et al.: Unscented Kalman filter for pedestrian tracking from a moving host. In: IEEE Intell. Veh., pp. 37–42 (2008)
16. Rabe, C.: Detection of Moving Objects by Spatio-Temporal Motion Analysis. Ph.D. thesis, University of Kiel, Kiel, Germany (2011)
17. Särkkä, S., Hartikainen, J., Solin, A.: EKF/UKF toolbox for Matlab v1.3 (2011), http://becs.aalto.fi/en/research/bayes/ekfukf/
18. Scheunert, U., et al.: Multi sensor based tracking of pedestrians: a survey of suitable movement models. In: IEEE Intell. Veh., pp. 774–778 (2004)
19. Tao, J., Klette, R.: Tracking of 2d or 3d irregular movement by a family of Unscented Kalman filters. JICCE 10(3), 307–314 (2012)
20. Welch, G., Bishop, G.: An introduction to the Kalman filter. In: Proc. of the ACM SIGGRAPH. ACM Press, Addison-Wesley, Los Angeles, CA (2001)
21. Westhofen, D., et al.: Transponder- and camera-based advanced driver assistance system. In: IEEE Intell. Veh., pp. 293–298 (2012)

An Improved Model
for Estimating the Meteorological Visibility
from a Road Surface Luminance Curve

Stephan Lenor[1,2], Bernd Jähne[1], Stefan Weber[2], and Ulrich Stopper[2]

[1] University of Heidelberg, Heidelberg Collaboratory for Image Processing,
Speyerer Straße 6, 69115 Heidelberg, Germany
{stephan.lenor,bernd.jaehne}@iwr.uni-heidelberg.de
[2] Robert Bosch GmbH, Daimlerstraße 6, 71229 Leonberg, Germany

Abstract. Hautière *et al.* [8] presented a model to describe the road surface luminance curve. Fitting this model to the reality allowed them to measure atmospheric parameters and, in turn, the meteorological visibility. We introduce a more complex and appropriate model based on the theory of radiative transfer. Through modeling the inscattered light by Koschmieder's Law and assuming a simple scene geometry we can find a correspondence between the extinction coefficient of the atmosphere and the inflection point of the luminance curve. Contrary to the work of Hautière *et al.*, this relation cannot be formulated explicitly. Nevertheless an approach based on look-up tables allows us to utilize the improved model for a low-cost algorithm.

1 Introduction

Light traveling from an object to an observer is heavily influenced by fog. Object light is absorbed and scattered away by each droplet; at the same time, surrounding light is scattered into the optical path in the observer's direction. As a consequence, under foggy conditions the contrast of objects is exponentially attenuated over distance. Especially in road traffic scenarios, fog can thus become dangerous, causing a significantly increased number of accidents.

Not only for road accident prevention purposes, measuring the atmospheric visibility conditions is an important challenge for visual environment perception. Video-based driver assistance systems could adapt sensor and algorithm parameters according to the current visibility conditions or inform the driver about the appropriate speed; furthermore, the speed and the lighting system (*e.g.* front and rear fog lamps, beam of headlamps) could be adapted automatically.

In addition, the measurement of the visibility conditions could also be interesting for static cameras, such as traffic surveillance cameras, in order to set the speed limit and inform drivers with variable-message signs.

In this work we will focus on the atmospheric parameter K called the *extinction coefficient,* which corresponds to the optical thickness of the atmospheric

J. Weickert, M. Hein, and B. Schiele (Eds.): GCPR 2013, LNCS 8142, pp. 184–193, 2013.

aerosol. It is directly related to the distance d_{met} where it is just possible to distinguish a dark object against the horizon:

$$d_{\mathrm{met}} := -\frac{\log(0.05)}{K};$$ (1)

we refer to this distance as *meteorological visibility* (cf. [12, Sec. 6.2.1], [5]).

1.1   Related Work

In the literature different approaches are described for estimating the reduced visibility range caused by adverse weather conditions using onboard cameras.

Pomerleau [14] was the first to estimate a visibility $\in [0, 1]$ using the attenuation of the contrast along similar road features such as road markings. Several years later Hautière *et al.* [8] were the first to measure the extinction coefficient by fitting a model on a road surface luminance curve in daytime fog; this algorithm is the initial point for our work (cf. Sec. 1.3). Similar to [8], Bronte *et al.* [3] presented an algorithm based on a road surface luminance curve. Contrary to Hautière *et al.*, this approach is based on a heuristic relation between the inflection point of the luminance curve and the visibility conditions only.

Another approach is based on a contrast-depth relation. Hautière *et al.* [7] used a stereo disparity map to combine it with the local contrast and estimated the mobilized visibility distance as the maximal distance where the apparent contrast lies above a given threshold. Some years later Boussard *et al.* [2] realised a similar algorithm based on structure from motion.

Pavlič *et al.* [13] demonstrated that the visibility range can roughly be obtained from SVM classification based on global frequency features.

Some other approaches relying on stationary cameras are interesting as well: Babari *et al.* [1]; Geng *et al.* [6]; Song *et al.* [15].

The only algorithm that is entirely based on an atmospheric model without using any heuristics is that of Hautière *et al.* [8]. Measuring the extinction coefficient K from the image requires several world and model assumptions, but it is worth developing it further.

1.2   Setting

As mentioned above we assume a scenario of homogenous fog in daytime. The monocular camera is situated at a certain height and angle above the ground pointing along the homogenous dark road. Moreover we rely on a linear camera model, *i.e.* $\exists \alpha_{\mathrm{I}}, \beta_{\mathrm{I}} \in \mathbb{R}$ s.t. an object of luminance L is represented by the image intensity $I = \alpha_{\mathrm{I}} L + \beta_{\mathrm{I}}$ apart from discretization, saturation, and spectral effects. The street is assumed to be an infinitely expanded plane.

The model and the resulting algorithm discussed in this work can be used in the context of both static and mobile cameras. In order to avoid cumbersome phrasing and the discussion of slight differences, this paper shall be limited to the case of video-based driver assistance systems.

1.3 Algorithm Based on Koschmieder's Law

In 1924 Koschmieder presented a theory on the apparent luminance of objects in horizontal vision (cf. [11]) resulting in *Koschmieder's Law*:

$$L = e^{-Kd}L_0 + \left(1 - e^{-Kd}\right)L_{\mathrm{air}}, \tag{2}$$

where L denotes the apparent luminance of an object with inherent luminance L_0 situated at distance d and assuming a homogeneous atmosphere with constant extinction coefficient K; L_{air} is an atmospheric parameter representing the ambient light scattered into the optical path between the object and the observer.

Based on Koschmieder's Law, Hautière *et al.* developed in [8] the first and only algorithm to estimate the extinction coefficient K for an onboard camera. Segmenting an image region containing part of the road and the sky, they extracted an intensity curve representing the line medians of the segmented region, which we refer to as the *road surface luminance curve* or simply the *luminance curve* (cf. Fig. 1).

Combining Koschmieder's Law with assumptions about the camera's and the world's geometry, Hautière *et al.* deduced a model for the luminance curve:

$$L^{\mathrm{Kos}}(v) := e^{-Kd(v)}L_0 + \left(1 - e^{-Kd(v)}\right)L_{\mathrm{air}} \tag{3}$$

with line dependent distance $d(v) = \lambda/(v - v_{\mathrm{h}})$ for $v > v_{\mathrm{h}}$ and $d(v) = \infty$ for $v \leq v_{\mathrm{h}}$, where λ represents a camera constant, which depends on the intrinsic camera parameters and the pitch angle of the camera relative to the road surface; the column u and the line v define the image coordinates $(u, v)^T$, where v_{h} represents the horizon line.

Fitting this model to the measured luminance curve allows the estimation of the atmospheric parameters. Hautière *et al.* determined that the model curve L^{Kos} has an inflection point at v_{i} which exactly corresponds to the parameters $(L_0, L_{\mathrm{air}}, K)$ in an explicit way (cf. [8, (16), (20), (21)]), more precisely

$$(L_0, L_{\mathrm{air}}, K) \quad \leftrightarrow \quad \left(v_{\mathrm{i}}, L^{\mathrm{Kos}}(v_{\mathrm{i}}), \partial_v L^{\mathrm{Kos}}(v_{\mathrm{i}})\right). \tag{4}$$

Fig. 1. The road surface luminance curve is extracted line by line from the segmented region in the middle of the camera frame.

Beyond this K corresponds directly to the value v_i in a simple way:

$$K = \frac{2(v_i - v_h)}{\lambda}. \tag{5}$$

This makes it possible to implement an efficient algorithm to estimate K and d_{met}, whose main costs involve extracting the luminance curve and its inflection point v_i.

2 Improved Model

The algorithm presented in Sec. 1.3 is a promising approach to estimate atmospheric parameters by using an onboard camera. However, a closer look at the class of luminance curves (3) reveals that the model is not capable of sufficiently describing the measured luminance curves (cf. Fig. 5(a)). In particular the fact that L^{Kos} remains constant above the horizon does not reflect reality.

The reason for this is that Koschmieder's Law assumes that the amount of ambient light scattered into the optical path is constant in direction and location. This is approximately true for horizontal vision, but changes with the angle of view.

2.1 Radiative Transfer Theory

Liquid droplets form the most important class of particles in fog that contribute to the reduction of the meteorological visibility. Thereby the size distribution and concentration of droplets determine the atmospheric extinction coefficient K, which represents the sum of the absorption and the scattering coefficient: $K = K_a + K_s$. For fog droplets, absorption effects can be disregarded (a more detailed discussion can be found in [12, Sec. 3.3.2]). We thus have $K \approx K_s$ and refer to this kind of atmosphere as a *scattering atmosphere*.

Chandrasekhar described in [4, Sec. I.7, I.8] that the transmission of light in direction $\sigma = (\sigma^x, \sigma^y, \sigma^z)^T \in \mathbb{S}^2 := \{x \in \mathbb{R}^3 : |x| = 1\}$ over a distance d to an observer $o \in \mathbb{R}^3$ through a scattering atmosphere can be expressed as

$$L(\sigma, d) = e^{-Kd} L_0 + \int_0^d K e^{-Ks} \int_{\mathbb{S}^2} L_{in}(\omega, s) \psi(\sigma, \omega) dS(\omega) ds. \tag{6}$$

Here the first term represents the exponentially attenuated inherent luminance L_0, and the second term represents the ambient light scattered into the optical path in the direction of the observer; it consists of a phase function ψ and an inscattering function L_{in}.

2.2 Inscattering Function

$L_{in}(\omega, s)$ denotes the inscattered light from direction $\omega = (\omega^x, \omega^y, \omega^z)^T \in \mathbb{S}^2$ at $o - s\sigma$, which is the point on the optical path that corresponds to the path

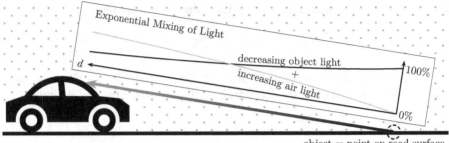

(a) Model based on Koschmieder's Law.

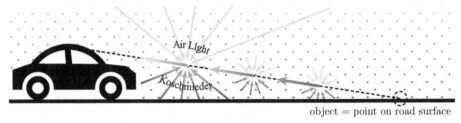

(b) Improved Model.

Fig. 2. The transmission of light through fog: While Koschmieder's Law explains it as an exponential mixing of light, the improved model considers the inscattered light to be dependent on location and direction on the optical path.

parameter $s \in [0, d]$. We model L_{in} by Koschmieder's Law (2) and the simple road geometry described in Sec. 1.2. This leads to (cf. Fig. 4)

$$L_{\text{in}}(\omega, s) = \begin{cases} L_{\text{air}} & , \quad \omega^z \geq 0 \\ e^{K\frac{h(s)}{\omega^z}} L_0 + \left(1 - e^{K\frac{h(s)}{\omega^z}}\right) L_{\text{air}} & , \quad \omega^z < 0 \end{cases}. \tag{7}$$

It is easy to see that the assumption that the amount of inscattered light L_{in} is constant in direction and location leads to the luminance curve model based on Koschmieder's Law. Thus the difference to the Koschmieder-based model exactly lies in taking the anisotropy and inhomogeneity of the inscattered light into account.

By introducing an $\mathbb{S}^2$ parameterization Φ, using the fact that the phase function is normalized (cf. Sec. 2.3), and applying basic integral calculus, the luminance model from (6) becomes

$$L(\sigma, d) = e^{-Kd} L_0 + \left(1 - e^{-Kd}\right) L_{\text{air}} + (L_0 - L_{\text{air}}) T(\sigma, d), \tag{8}$$

where

$$T(\sigma, d) := \int_0^d K e^{-Ks} \int_{\frac{\pi}{2}}^{\pi} \int_0^{2\pi} e^{K\frac{h(s)}{\cos(\theta)}} \psi(\sigma, \Phi(\varphi, \theta)) \sin(\theta) d\varphi d\theta ds. \tag{9}$$

The $\mathbb{S}^2$ parameterization $\Phi : (0, 2\pi) \times (0, \pi) \to \mathbb{S}^2$ is as usual given by $(\varphi, \theta) \mapsto (\sin(\theta)\sin(\varphi), \sin(\theta)\cos(\varphi), \cos(\theta))^T$.

2.3   Scattering Phase Function

The phase function $\psi : \mathbb{S}^2 \times \mathbb{S}^2 \to \mathbb{R}_{\geq 0}$ represents the directional scattering distribution. A phase function shall be integrable and for any $\omega \in \mathbb{S}^2$ satisfy $\int_{\mathbb{S}^2} \psi(\omega, \tilde{\omega}) dS(\tilde{\omega}) = 1$. As no world direction is preferred, ψ can usually be written in terms of $\langle \omega, \tilde{\omega} \rangle$; in particular we have $\psi(\omega, \tilde{\omega}) = \psi(\tilde{\omega}, \omega)$.

The shape of a phase function essentially depends on the particle's size in comparison to the wavelength of the electromagnetic wave scattered. In 1908, Mie presented a rigorous scattering theory for spherical particles (such as fog droplets) based on Maxwell's Equations; a full explanation can be found in [9, Sec. 9]. Due to versatile drop-size distributions, we have to choose the phase function as an average representation of scatterers. In the context of fog, the so called Henyey-Greenstein phase function is commonly used to describe this average scattering distribution (cf. [10])

$$\psi^{\mathrm{HG}}(\tilde{\omega}, \omega) := \frac{1}{4\pi} \frac{1 - q^2}{(1 + 2q\langle \tilde{\omega}, \omega \rangle + q^2)^{\frac{3}{2}}}, \tag{10}$$

where $q \in [0.8, 0.9]$ denotes the *forward-scattering parameter* and ω and $\tilde{\omega}$ are both directed outwards.

Note that the algorithm, which is based on the K-v_{i} relation, technically would work for any phase function.

2.4   Geometry

Let $(x, y, z)^T$ be the world coordinate system and $(u, v)^T$ the image coordinate system arranged according to Fig. 3. $(u_0, v_0)^T$ shall denote the principle point, v_{h} the line of horizon, f the focal length, H the camera height above ground and ξ the pitch angle of the camera relative to the road surface.

Straightforward calculations reveal that the horizon line can be written as $v_{\mathrm{h}} = v_0 - \tan(\xi)f$; the z-component (height) of $o - s\sigma$ is $h(s) = H - s\sigma^z$; the distance d to the road surface at the image coordinates $(u, v)^T$ is

$$d(u, v) = \begin{cases} \infty & , \quad v \leq v_h \\ H/\sigma^z(u, v) & , \quad v > v_{\mathrm{h}} \end{cases} ; \tag{11}$$

and the world coordinate direction σ at the image coordinates $(u, v)^T$ is

$$\sigma(u, v) = \frac{1}{\sqrt{f^2 + (u - u_0)^2 + (v - v_0)^2}} \begin{pmatrix} \sin(\xi)(v - v_0) - \cos(\xi)f \\ u - u_0 \\ \cos(\xi)(v - v_0) + \sin(\xi)f \end{pmatrix}. \tag{12}$$

Inserting $\sigma(u, v)$ and $d(u, v)$ in $L(\sigma, d)$ from (8) yields the improved luminance curve model:

$$L^{\mathrm{Im}}(u, v) := L(\sigma(u, v), d(u, v)). \tag{13}$$

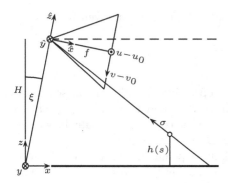

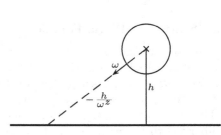

Fig. 3. Geometric quantities and coordinate systems.

Fig. 4. A droplet at height h above ground has distance $-h/\omega^z$ to the road surface in direction $\omega \in \mathbb{S}^2$.

2.5   Notes on Analysis and Numerics

The improved luminance curve model $v \mapsto L^{\mathrm{Im}}(u, v)$ introduced in (13) depends on several parameters: the *system parameters* H, ξ, f, u_0, v_0 and u, which are assumed as being given (*e.g.* from calibration and algorithms estimating the camera motion); and the *atmospheric parameters* K, L_0, L_{air} and q. Apart from u_0 and u, which are ignored by Hautière *et al.* for reasons of simplicity, the parameter q is the only new parameter appearing in the improved curve model.

Furthermore, like in the old model, linear changes in the new model exactly correspond to changes in the atmospheric parameters (L_0, L_{air}):

$$\forall \alpha, \beta \in \mathbb{R}: \quad \alpha L^{\mathrm{Im}}_{L_0, L_{\mathrm{air}}} + \beta \equiv L^{\mathrm{Im}}_{\alpha L_0 + \beta, \alpha L_{\mathrm{air}} + \beta}. \tag{14}$$

This leads to a useful relation between K and v_{i} which will help us to utilize the new model for a low-cost algorithm (cf. Sec. 3.1).

The main computational costs for calculating the improved luminance curve model lie in the triple integral in (9). Applying Fubini's Theorem and Lebesgue's Dominated Convergence Theorem to $\mathcal{T}(\sigma, d')$ for $d' \to d$ allows even for $d = \infty$ to replace the tripple integral with a numerically more cost-effective double integral:

$$\mathcal{T}(\sigma, d) = \int_{\frac{\pi}{2}}^{\pi} \int_0^d K e^{-Ks} e^{K \frac{h(s)}{\cos(\theta)}} ds \int_0^{2\pi} \psi(\sigma, \Phi(\varphi, \theta)) d\varphi \, \sin(\theta) d\theta. \tag{15}$$

To avoid numerical handling of infinity, we explicitly evaluate the first inner integral for $d = \infty$:

$$\int_0^\infty K e^{-Ks} e^{K \frac{h(s)}{\cos(\theta)}} ds = \frac{e^{K \frac{H}{\cos(\theta)}}}{1 + \frac{\sigma^z}{\cos(\theta)}}; \tag{16}$$

for $d < \infty$ this would require a numerically inefficient 0/0-handling.

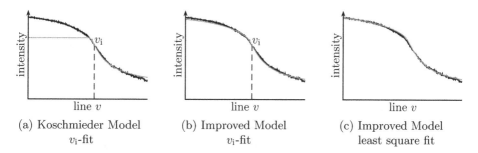

(a) Koschmieder Model v_i-fit

(b) Improved Model v_i-fit

(c) Improved Model least square fit

Fig. 5. In contrast to the improved model, the luminance curve model based on Koschmieder's Law is not capable of describing the measured road surface luminance curve sufficiently.

3 Low-Cost Algorithm and Experimental Results

The improved luminance curve model introduced in Sec. 2 is more complex than the Koschmieder-based model (3). Nevertheless the relation (14) allows us to ignore 2 of the 4 atmospheric parameters, fitting the model based on the inflection point (cf. Sec. 3.1). The forward-scattering parameter q can be hold constant without producing any significant error (cf. Sec. 3.2). If all other parameters are fixed, K and v_i remain in a bijective relation. That is why the complexity of the new model can be broken down to a precomputed look-up table (cf. Sec. 3.3).

3.1 Parameter Estimation

Although we investigated some numerical simplifications in Sec. 2.5, it remains computationally expensive to perform a full model fit in the 4 atmospheric parameters (cf. example Fig. 5(c)). Fortunately, due to (14), the inflection point is not affected by changes in the parameters L_0 and L_{air}. For given system parameters and fixed q, the extinction coefficient K and the inflection point v_i are directly related (cf. Fig. 6(a)). Beyond that, numerical experiments suggest that $K \mapsto v_i(K)$ is bijective so that K can be reobtained from v_i.

If necessary, we can additionally estimate the atmospheric parameters L_0 and L_{air} from $\left(v_i, L^{Im}(v_i), \partial_v L^{Im}(v_i)\right)$ (similar to (4)):

$$L_{air} = L^{Im}(v_i) - D\hat{L}^{Im}(v_i), \quad L_0 = D + L_{air}, \tag{17}$$

where $\hat{L}^{Im} := L^{Im}_{\hat{L}_0=1, \hat{L}_{air}=0}$ and $D := [\partial_v L^{Im}(v_i)]/[\partial_v \hat{L}^{Im}(v_i)]$. We refer to this as v_i-fit. When we fit the model to the measured data in this way, the improved model clearly outperforms the Koschmieder-based model (cf. Fig. 5(a,b)).

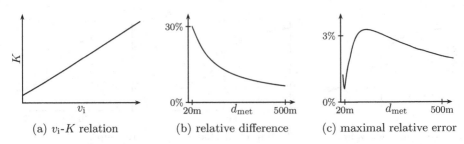

(a) v_i-K relation   (b) relative difference   (c) maximal relative error

Fig. 6. Numerical investigation for a typical automotive setting[2]: (a) The v_i-K relation seems to be almost linear for the improved model. (b) The difference between the old and the new d_{met} estimation is particularly high for small meteorological visibilities. (c) Fixing $q = 0.85$ corrupts the results only marginally.

3.2   Forward-Scattering Parameter

Without performing a full model fit we do not see any way to estimate the forward-scattering parameter q from the measured luminance curve. Fortunately fixing q as a specific value does not seem to cause any serious error; to evaluate this we set $q = 0.85$ and compute the maximal relative error over a typical automotive parameter setting[1]. This produces a maximal relative error in the meteorological visibility of about 3.3% (cf. Fig. 6(c)).

3.3   Look-Up Table

Using a predefined q, the mapping $v_i \mapsto K(v_i)$ can be precomputed for any setting of system parameters. Thus the improved model can be utilized for an algorithm that has basically the same computational costs as the algorithm based on Koschmieder's Law.

For the example setting from Sec. 3.2 this leads to a look-up table with $(51 \cdot 11 \cdot 21) \cdot 49 + 49 = 577318$ values. Using polynomial interpolation we are able to drastically reduce the number of values to 189. The worst-case error caused by this is 0.18% for our setting.

4   Conclusions

We have presented an improved model for road surface luminance curves and shown how to apply it for visibility measurements following the algorithm of Hautière *et al.* [8]. Its additional complexity makes it capable of sufficiently fitting real-world measurements, but also more difficult to handle for real-time

---

[1] $d_{met} \in \{20\,\text{m}, 30\,\text{m}, \ldots, 500\,\text{m}\}$, $\xi \in \{0°, 0.1°, \ldots, 5°\}$, $H \in \{1.250\,\text{m}, 1.255\,\text{m}, \ldots,$
   $1.300\,\text{m}\}$, $u \in \{u_0, u_0 \pm 10\text{px}, u_0 \pm 20\text{px}, \ldots, u_0 \pm 200\text{px}\}$, while the intrinsic camera
   parameters $f = 1200\text{px}$, $u_0 = 512\text{px}$, $v_0 = 256\text{px}$ do not change.
[2] Setting from Sec. 3.2; for Fig. 6(a,b) we selected $\xi = 0°$, $H = 1.25\,\text{m}$, $u = u_0$.

purposes. We have shown that the complexity can be broken down to highly compressible look-up tables.

The new model can be used to replace Koschmieder's Model in all algorithms that are based on road surface luminance curves, *e.g.* [8] and [15]. Especially in [15], where most geometric parameters are held constant, replacement by the improved model should be easy to realize.

Despite the highly improved model curves, future research needs to provide proof of the increased performance in the form of reference measurements. However, this work might call attention to inaccuracies arising from the assumption of isotropic homogeneous ambient light.

References

1. Babari, R., Hautière, N., Dumont, É., Brémond, R., Paparoditis, N.: A Model-Driven Approach to Estimate Atmospheric Visibility with Ordinary Cameras. Atmospheric Environment 45(30), 5316–5324 (2011)
2. Boussard, C., Hautière, N., d'Andréa Novel, B.: Visibility Distance Estimation based on Structure from Motion. In: 11th International Conference on Control Automation, Robotics and Vision, pp. 1416–1421. IEEE (December 2010)
3. Bronte, S., Bergasa, L., Alcantarilla, P.: Fog Detection System Based on Computer Vision Techniques. In: Proceedings of the 12th International Conference on Intelligent Transportation Systems, pp. 1–6. IEEE (October 2009)
4. Chandrasekhar, S.: Radiative Transfer. Dover Publications (1960)
5. CIE: Termlist (2012), http://eilv.cie.co.at/
6. Geng, W., Lu, X., Yang, L., Chen, W., Liu, Y.: Detection Algorithm of Video Image Distance based on Rectangular Pattern. In: 5th International Congress on Image and Signal Processing, pp. 856–860. IEEE (October 2012)
7. Hautière, N., Labayrade, R., Aubert, D.: Real-Time Disparity Contrast Combination for Onboard Estimation of the Visibility Distance. IEEE Transactions on Intelligent Transportation Systems 7(2), 201–212 (June 2006)
8. Hautière, N., Tarel, J.P., Lavenant, J., Aubert, D.: Automatic Fog Detection and Estimation of Visibility Distance through use of an Onboard Camera. Machine Vision and Applications 17(1), 8–20 (2006)
9. van de Hulst, H.C.: Light Scattering by Small Particles. Dover Publications (1957)
10. Ishimaru, A.: Wave Propagation and Scattering in Random Media, vol. 2. Academic Press, New York (1978)
11. Koschmieder, H.: Theorie der Horizontalen Sichtweite. Physik der Freien Atmosphäre 12, 33–55 (1924)
12. Middleton, W.E.K.: Vision Through the Atmosphere. University of Toronto Press (1952)
13. Pavlić, M., Belzner, H., Rigoll, G., Ilić, S.: Image based fog detection in vehicles. In: Proceedings of Intelligent Vehicles Symposium. pp. 1132–1137. IEEE (June 2012)
14. Pomerleau, D.: Visibility Estimation from a Moving Vehicle using the RALPH Vision System. In: Proceeding of the Conference on Intelligent Transportation System, pp. 906–911. IEEE (November 1997)
15. Song, H., Chen, Y., Gao, Y.: Homogenous Fog Condition Recognition based on Traffic Scene. In: Proceedings of the International Conference on Modelling, Identification and Control, pp. 612–617. IEEE (June 2012)

Performance Evaluation of Narrow Band Methods for Variational Stereo Reconstruction

Franz Stangl, Mohamed Souiai, and Daniel Cremers

TU Muenchen

Abstract. Convex relaxation techniques allow computing optimal or near-optimal solutions for a variety of multilabel problems in computer vision. Unfortunately, they are quite demanding in terms of memory and computation time making them unpractical for large-scale problems. In this paper, we systematically evaluate to what extent narrow band methods can be employed in order to improve the performance of variational multilabel optimization methods. We review variational methods, we present a narrow band formulation and demonstrate with a number of quantitative experiments that the narrow band formulation leads to a reduction in memory and computation time by orders of magnitude while preserving almost the same quality of results. In particular, we show that this formulation allows computing stereo depth maps for 6 Mpixels aerial image pairs on a single GPU in around one minute.

1 Introduction

1.1 Convex Multilabel Optimization and Narrow Band Methods

Most of the relevant algorithmic challenges in computer vision correspond to energy minimization problems with non-convex energies. While traditional approaches to segmentation [10], stereo [3] and optical flow [8] aimed at finding acceptable solutions by local minimization starting from an "appropriate" initialization, in the last few years researchers have proposed convex relaxation techniques which allow to compute optimal or near-optimal solutions [15,14,17,11,4,6]. The key idea in these algorithms which was inspired by Ishikawa's graph theoretic approach [9] is to increase the dimension of the optimization problem by enhancing the spatial dimensions with the label dimension. Specifically, it was shown in [15] that the non-convex stereo reconstruction problem in two spatial dimensions is equivalent to a convex optimization problem in three dimensions.

While bringing about a clear gain in optimality, this increased dimension comes with an important sacrifice in memory and computation since the size of these lifting methods increases linearly with the number of labels used for the reconstruction. As a consequence, these algorithms have limited practical use – even for smaller problems of around 640 × 480 pixel stereo reconstructions they can easily take a minute of computation time. Moreover, the direct application to large-scale aerial images of several megapixels is entirely infeasible due to memory limitations.

J. Weickert, M. Hein, and B. Schiele (Eds.): GCPR 2013, LNCS 8142, pp. 194–204, 2013.

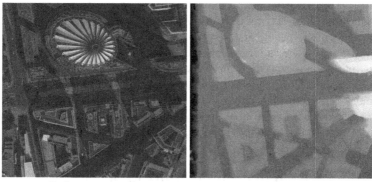

Left input image   Stereo reconstruction

Fig. 1. A large scale reconstruction (right) on two **2600 x 2400** aerial images[1] (left) with **300** disparity levels is performed on a NVIDIA GTX 680 GPU with 4 GB of memory. Memory demand for reconstruction is **2.6 GB** with a runtime of **77 seconds**.

A popular strategy to accelerate such algorithms and reduce their memory requirements is to apply coarse-to-fine narrow band methods [1,12,2]. Since in these algorithms the optimal stereo reconstruction is given by the isolevel of an embedding function defined on the 3D grid, one can compute the embedding function in a coarse to fine manner, considering on each scale of the hierarchy a narrow band of a few levels around the current solution. While this strategy does not preserve optimality for the finest scale – small unconnected fine-scale structures potentially being lost – it allows to drastically reduce memory and computation time.

1.2   Contribution

While there are local methods (e.g. [7]) which can handle large scale stereo reconstruction, we intend in this paper to systematically evaluate the tradeoff between the loss in accuracy and the increase in speed and memory brought about by narrow band methods for variational multilabel optimization. More specifically, we focus on the problem of stereo reconstruction using a variational approach with non-convex data term and convex total variation regularizer. In Section 2, we briefly review the variational approach of Pock et al. [15] for globally optimal stereo reconstruction. In Section 3, we will present a narrow band formulation of this approach. In Section 4, we will present a detailed quantitative analysis of the performance gain brought about by the narrow band formulation. We also study how the accuracy increases with the width of the narrow band. In particular, we will show that near-optimal solutions can be computed with drastically reduced memory and computation time. We can recover high-resolution stereo depth reconstruction from 6 megapixels images in around one minute on a

---

[1] Image courtesy of Heiko Hirschmüller, German Aerospace Center (DLR) Institute of Robotics and Mechatronics.

single end-user GPU. These experiments demonstrate that in combination with narrow band methods, convex relaxation techniques for multilabel optimization exhibit an enormous practical potential for highly accurate large-scale reconstruction. An example of a large scale reconstruction is given in Figure 1. While the input image pair exceeds 6 megapixels in resolution, we were able to perform the reconstruction using 300 depth labels on a consumer graphics card. The memory requirement is around 2.6 GB and is a drastic gain compared to a reconstruction with dense label space that would require 43 GB of memory which no commercially available graphics cards can offer.

2   A Convex Formulation of Multi Label Stereo

2.1   Continuous Setting

In this work we devote ourselves to the study of how to efficiently minimize the following variational problem:

$$\min_{u} \left\{ \int_{\Omega} |Du(x)| + \int_{\Omega} \varrho(u(x), x) dx \right\}, \tag{1}$$

where $\Omega \subset \mathbb{R}^2$ denotes a continuous image domain, and $u : \Omega \to \Gamma$ an unknown function which maps each point in Ω to a real valued range $\Gamma := [t_0, t_{end}]$. The second term in equation (1) assigns a point-wise cost for each pixel taking on a certain value from Γ. The data term in our application can be arbitrary and not necessarily convex as we will see in the convex relaxation Section 2.2. In order to impose a spatial regularity while preserving its discontinuity we make use of the total variation of function u given by the left term of equation (1). Note that Du is the gradient in the distributional sense since function u must not be differentiable as in the case of natural images. The energy given in (1) can be considered as the continuous counterpart of the discrete setting described by Ishikawa et al [9].

2.2   Convex Relaxation

Although the total variation regularizer in energy (1) is a convex functional, many interesting problems from vision are associated with a non-convex data term. This makes computing the global minimizer of the energy almost impossible and the straightforward minimization of the functional above is prone to getting stuck in local minimizers. We next describe an approach given in [15] which tackles the problems shown above.

The Functional Lifting Approach: The authors in [15] devise a level set formulation of energy (1):

$$\min_{v \in C} \left\{ \int_{\Omega \times \Gamma} |\nabla_x v(x, t)| + \varrho(x, t) |\nabla_t v(x, t)| \, dx dt \right\}, \tag{2}$$

where ∇_x and ∇_t denote the spatial gradient in Ω and respectively the gradient with respect to the label dimension Γ and where

$$C = \{v(x,t) : \Omega \times \Gamma \to \{0,1\}, v(\cdot,t_0) = 1, v(\cdot,t_{\text{end}}) = 0\}. \tag{3}$$

This new formulation is now a functional of the function v which is the indicator function of the subgraph of u hence

$$v(x,t) = \begin{cases} 1 & \text{if } t <= u(x) \\ 0 & \text{else.} \end{cases}$$

Energy (2) becomes convex if we relax the range of indicator function v to the unit interval $[0,1]$. Hence we constrain v by the relaxed constraint

$$\tilde{C} = \{v(x,t) : \Omega \times \Gamma \to [0,1], v(\cdot,t_0) = 1, v(\cdot,t_{\text{end}}) = 0\}. \tag{4}$$

The non-differentiability of the total variation is tackled by using its dual formulation which gives us overall the following saddle-point problem:

$$\min_{v \in \tilde{C}} \left\{ \sup_{\Phi \in \mathcal{K}} \int_{\Omega \times \Gamma} \Phi \cdot \nabla v \, dx dt \right\}, \tag{5}$$

with the dual variable $\Phi(x,t) = (\Phi^x(x,t), \Phi^t(x,t))^T$ constrained by the following convex set:

$$\mathcal{K} = \left\{ \Phi(x,t) : \Omega \times \Delta \to \mathbb{R}^3, |\Phi^x(x,t)| \le 1, |\Phi^t(x,t)| \le \varrho(x,t) \right\}.$$

Note that the saddle-point formulation (5) is linear in both its dual variable Φ and its primal variable v and is endowed with a convex constraint set. This renders our problem solvable using so called primal dual algorithms.

2.3   Convex Optimization

In order to solve problem (5) we make use of a first order primal-dual algorithm devised in [5] which essentially performs a gradient ascent in the dual variable and a gradient descent in the primal variable with subsequent orthogonals projection onto the respective convex sets. For more details see [5].

In the following, we detail solving the saddle-point problem using the primal dual scheme. We initialise $((\tilde{v})^0, (\varphi)^0) \in \tilde{C} \times \mathcal{K}$, let $(\hat{v})^0 = (\tilde{v})^0$ and choose the time-steps σ and τ according to a preconditioning scheme presented in [13]. Then the iterates of the primal dual algorithm can be written as follows:

$$\begin{cases} (\Phi)^{n+1} & = proj_\mathcal{K}((\Phi)^n + \sigma(\nabla \hat{v}^n)), \\ (\tilde{v})^{n+1} & = proj_{\tilde{C}}((\tilde{v})^n + \tau(\text{div } \Phi^{n+1})), \\ (\hat{v})^{n+1} & = 2(\tilde{v})^{n+1} - (\tilde{v})^n, \end{cases} \tag{6}$$

where the discretized divergence operator div is chosen to be adjoint to the discretisation of the gradient ∇. For the data term we choose a simple sum of

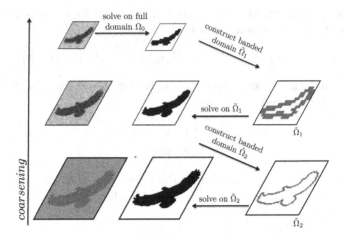

Fig. 2. An illustration of the narrow band method for 2 scales on a binary segmentation example. After coarsening the input image twice, a solution on the coarsest scale is computed. Using this solution the narrow band (red contour) of the next fine scale is computed and we perform the optimization solely on that region.

the channel-wise absolute differences between the rectified right and left image for every disparity level $t \in \Gamma$ i.e.

$$\varrho(x,t) = \frac{1}{3}\lambda \sum_{i\in\{r,g,b\}} \left| I_L^i(x) - I_R^i(x + (0,t)^T) \right|.$$

3   Narrow Band Formulation of Multilabel Optimization

While we are able to compute the global minimizer of energy (1), we pay the price of adding an additional dimension to the optimization problem. The increased amount of variables increases the runtime and the memory usage of our optimization algorithm tremendously. This makes the functional lifting approach scale bad with increasing resolution of the input images. Additionally, it becomes difficult computing depth maps of even moderate image sizes on consumer GPU's because of their limited memory. For example the dense reconstruction of a 6 megapixels image using 300 disparity levels, would require 43 GB of GPU memory which cannot be found on any graphics card on the market. In the following, we elaborate on the so called narrow band method which is a promising approach for leveraging these problems – see Figure 2.

3.1   The Narrow Band Idea

The basic idea of the narrow band method is to compute a solution on a coarse scale and use a narrow band around the 0-1 interface of its up-sampled version to construct a solution on the fine scale. This procedure can also be done for multiple scales where we propagate the computed solution via up sampling until we reach the original resolution. The coarsening process is done by resizing the two rectified images at each scale to half of their width and height. We use these down-sampled stereo pairs to compute the data term on each scale for the voxels that are represented by the NB and solve equation (1) by means of algorithm (6). Overall we perform the following steps for a NB method with K scales:

1. Construct an image pyramid of the input rectified image pairs and calculate a dense data term only for the lowest scale.
2. Compute solution v_0^* on the coarsest scale.
3. For $k : 1 \cdots K - 1$ do the following: Construct a banded domain $\hat{\Omega}_k$ using the neighbourhood of the 0-1 interface of the rounded solution v_{k-1}^* (for details see next section) and compute v_k^* on $\hat{\Omega}_k$.

An illustration of above algorithm can be found in Figure 2. Next section details the computation of the banded domain $\hat{\Omega}$.

3.2   Creating the Narrow Band

In the following we denote the discretisation of the domain by the superscript h. Creating an efficient representation for the narrow band in the domain $\Omega^h \times \Gamma^h$ is not straightforward. This is due to the loss of the natural grid indexing in the domain $\Omega^h \times \Gamma^h$ which requires a new strategy. We create the banded domain $\hat{\Omega}_{k+1}$ by the following 4 steps:

1. We transform the voxel $(k = 0)$ and respectively the narrow band $(k \geq 1)$ representation of the rounded solution v_k^* into a two dimensional array $I_k : \Omega_k^h \rightarrow \Gamma_k^h$ which holds for each pixel the individual label number.
2. Upsamling by factor of 2 from I_k to I_{k+1} by doubling the width and the height of the image domain as well as the label range.
3. Narrow Band creation: We implicitly represent the narrow band by creating an upper $U_{k+1} : \Omega_{k+1}^h \rightarrow \Gamma_{k+1}^h$ and lower bound $L_{k+1} : \Omega_{k+1}^h \rightarrow \Gamma_{k+1}^h$ on the voxel lying in the narrow band as follows:

$$L_{k+1}(x, y) = \min_{(v,w) \in B(x,y)} (I_k(v, w)) - \frac{NBT}{2} + 1$$

$$U_{k+1}(x, y) = \max_{(v,w) \in B(x,y)} (I_k(v, w)) + \frac{NBT}{2}$$

where $B(x, y)$ denotes a ball around pixel (x, y) and NBT is the chosen *Narrow Band Thickness*. We chose B to be an L^1 ball with the NBT as the diameter hence:

$$B(x, y) = \left\{ v, w \mid |v - x| + |w - y| \leq \frac{NBT}{2} \right\}.$$

We use $\min_{(v,w) \in B(x,y)}(I_k(v, w))$ and $\max_{(v,w) \in B(x,y)}(I_k(v, w))$ in order to account for the biggest jumps in the neighbourhood $B(x, y)$ and include these in the narrow band.

4. Now that we have located the banded domain $\hat{\Omega}_{k+1}$ by solely using the bounds L_{k+1} and U_{k+1}, we can store the narrow band efficiently without having to use the original domain. To this end we make use of a self referential array of the following structs:

struct   {float value; **int** vox_index, n1, n2, n3;} NB;

We calculate the indices of the local neighbourhood of each voxel according to the narrow band and store these in the variables n1, n2 and n3, which allows us to calculate the differential operators in algorithm 6. The variable vox_index stores the index that the struct element would have in the original voxel space. This is necessary for the transformation in step 1. In contrast to a linked list implementation the array implementation makes the approach easily parallelizable, since we can pass each NB **struct** element independently to different cores.

Fig. 3. Left input image[1] and solution for $NBT = 4$, with 500 iterations. Computation time is 31.7 s.

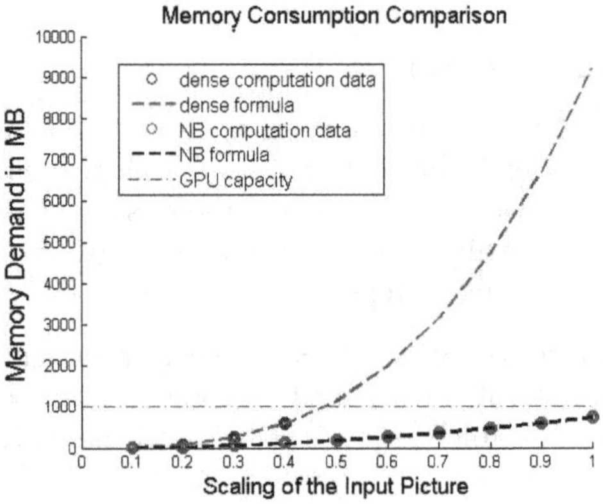

Fig. 4. The plot shows the memory consumption for different problem sizes. Scaling=0.1 stands for 152 x 132 pixels and 20 levels and scaling=1 corresponds to 1520 x 1320 x 200. Figure 3 shows the left input image and a solution example.

4   Experimental Evaluation

In this section we perform experimental evaluations of the narrow band method. To this end we will provide qualitative and quantitative results in order to empirically show that using a small bandwidth i.e. a fraction of the original domain we can approximate the true minimizer of the energy to an extent that most of the times is neither visible nor quantitative differences are to be seen . Addionally, we show that using merely a consumer low end card we are able to reconstruct depth information with a resolution that is not even possible on high end GPU's. The approach also scales well with recent graphics cards. Lastly we elaborate on the loss of fine details depending on the NBT. (c.f. Figure 1).

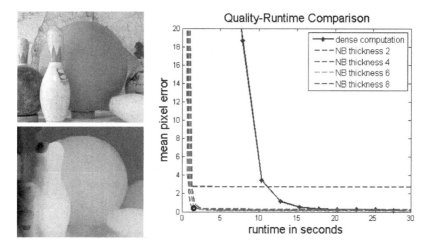

Fig. 5. The Solution corresponds to the black circle in Fig. 6

Fig. 6. Quality vs runtime plots for an 444 x 372 input image using 80 disparity levels, see Figure 5. The comparison is done by using pixel mean value error.

4.1 Setup

The hardware setting for our experiments is a Intel(R) Core(TM)2 Quad CPU Q8300 @ 2.50Ghz computer equipped with a low end graphics card of the type NVIDIA GeForce GTX 285 with 1 GB memory, which possesses 240 CUDA cores. The parallel implementation of the narrow band algorithm is based on NVIDIA's CUDA framework. We set the parameter for the dataterm to the value $\lambda = 50$ for all TV computations. All the results are based on a 2 scale NB method which works well for both small and large input stereo pairs. For the evaluation we used image pairs from the Middlebury datasets [16].

4.2 Memory Efficiency

Based on our implementation, we provide a memory demand estimator (MDE), for both the dense as well as the NB approach:

$$MDE_{dense} = \text{height} \cdot \text{width} \cdot (\text{levels} \cdot 24\text{byte} + 28\text{byte})$$
$$MDE_{NB} = \text{height} \cdot \text{width} \cdot (\bar{C} \cdot 56\text{byte} + 36\text{byte})$$

The factor $\bar{C}$ is the average number of voxels to be stored for each pixel in order to encode the narrow band around the graph of indicator variable u in our application. The graph is a manifold that describes the surface of the reconstructed 3D scenery which is bigger than the image size itself. Because of that $\bar{C}$ is at least as large as the chosen NBT. Experimentally $\bar{C}$ is in the order of the NBT. For example, the values for $\bar{C}$ in the experiments in Figure 4 are in the range 5.8 to 6.3 for an NBT of 4. Note that in the NB approach the third factor only depends on $\bar{C}$. Hence we practically obtain a complexity of a

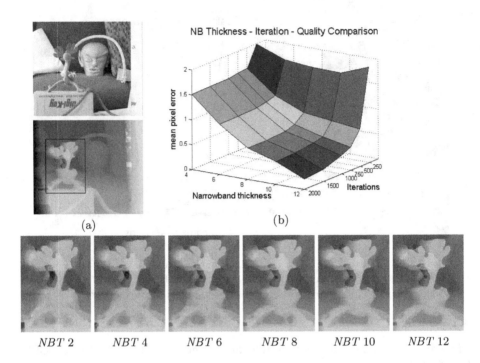

NBT 2   NBT 4   NBT 6   NBT 8   NBT 10   NBT 12

Fig. 7. (a) A 448 x 372 input image and the reconstruction on a dense 80 label space. (b) quality comparison for different NBT's. Below are 6 close up pictures of the reindeer for different NBT's.

variational problem in 2D. The above estimators are specific for our algorithmic approach, but the core idea that the complexity is independent of the number of levels is the same with any implementation.

4.3 Runtime Evaluation

For comparison we take a dense reconstruction (i.e. on the full domain) obtained after 15000 iterations as reference. We use 80 values for the discretization of the disparity space Γ. Figure 5 shows the left input image and a reconstruction example. To measure the quality of a solution we use the average pixel color difference between the reference result and the computed disparity. Figure 6 shows the runtime convergence comparison between the NB approach and the computation on a dense label space. We observe that the NB method outperforms the dense approach in terms of runtime.

4.4 Narrow Band Thickness and Fine Details

In this section we provide an empirical correlation between the NBT and the quality of the reconstruction. Figure 7 (b) shows the quality of reconstructions using NBT's between 4 and 12 depending on the number of iterations. The plot shows that the quality increases with the *NBT*. Problems arise for fine detail structures and a low *NBT* as can be seen in the close up pictures of the reindeer for different *NBT*'s in Figure 7. Only at a *NBT* of 10 the area around the legs of the reindeer is well represented. Therefore the approach introduces the drawbacks of classical coarse to fine schemes to multi-label optimization. This issue remains a challenging future work.

5   Conclusion

We provided a systematic experimental validation of narrow band methods for variational multilabel optimization. We revisited convex relaxation approaches to variational multilabel optimization, presented a coarse-to-fine narrow band formulation and experimentally evaluated the tradeoff between accuracy of recovered solutions on one hand and speed and memory requirements on the other. Considering the simplicity of our functional, our experiments demonstrate that the narrow band reformulation allows to reduce memory and computation time by orders of magnitude with moderate loss in accuracy. These experiments indicate that in conjunction with narrow band formulations, convex relaxation techniques for multilabel optimization exhibit the potential for solving large scale reconstruction problems.

References

1. Adalsteinsson, D., Sethian, J.A.: A fast level set method for propagating interfaces. Journal of Computational Physics 118, 269–277 (1994)
2. Baeza, A., Caselles, V., Gargallo, P., Papadakis, N.: A narrow band method for the convex formulation of discrete multilabel problems. Multiscale Modeling & Simulation 8(5), 2048–2078 (2010)
3. Barnard, S.: Stochastic stereo matching over scale. International Journal of Computer Vision 3(1), 17–32 (1989), http://dx.doi.org/10.1007/BF00054836
4. Chambolle, A., Cremers, D., Pock, T.: A convex approach to minimal partitions. J. Imaging Sci. 5(4), 1113–1158 (2012)
5. Chambolle, A., Pock, T.: A first-order primal-dual algorithm for convex problems with applications to imaging. Journal of Mathematical Imaging and Vision 40(1), 120–145 (2011)
6. Goldluecke, B., Strekalovskiy, E., Cremers, D.: Tight convex relaxations for vector-valued labeling. SIAM Journal on Imaging Sciences (to appear, 2013)
7. Hirschmuller, H.: Stereo processing by semiglobal matching and mutual information. IEEE Transactions on Pattern Analysis and Machine Intelligence 30(2), 328–341 (2008)
8. Horn, B., Schunck, B.: Determining optical flow. A.I. 17, 185–203 (1981)
9. Ishikawa, H.: Exact optimization for markov random fields with convex priors. IEEE Trans. Pattern Anal. Mach. Intell. 25(10), 1333–1336 (2003)
10. Kass, M., Witkin, A., Terzopoulos, D.: Snakes: Active contour models. International Journal of Computer Vision 1(4), 321–331 (1988)
11. Lellmann, J., Schnörr, C.: Continuous multiclass labeling approaches and algorithms. J. Imaging Sci. 4(4), 1049–1096 (2011)

12. Lombaert, H., Sun, Y., Grady, L., Xu, C.: A multilevel banded graph cuts method for fast image segmentation. In: Proceedings of the Tenth IEEE International Conference on Computer Vision (ICCV 2005), vol. 1, pp. 259–265. IEEE Computer Society, Washington, DC (2005)

13. Pock, T., Chambolle, A.: Diagonal preconditioning for first order primal-dual algorithms in convex optimization. In: ICCV (2011)

14. Pock, T., Cremers, D., Bischof, H., Chambolle, A.: Global solutions of variational models with convex regularization. SIAM J. Imaging Sciences 3(4), 1122–1145 (2010)

15. Pock, T., Schoenemann, T., Graber, G., Bischof, H., Cremers, D.: A convex formulation of continuous multi-label problems. In: Forsyth, D., Torr, P., Zisserman, A. (eds.) ECCV 2008, Part III. LNCS, vol. 5304, pp. 792–805. Springer, Heidelberg (2008)

16. Scharstein, D., Pal, C.: Learning conditional random fields for stereo. In: CVPR (2007)

17. Zach, C., Gallup, D., Frahm, J.M., Niethammer, M.: Fast global labeling for real-time stereo using multiple plane sweeps. In: Workshop on Vision, Modeling and Visualization (October 2008)

Discriminative Detection
and Alignment in Volumetric Data

Dominic Mai[1,2], Philipp Fischer[1], Thomas Blein[4], Jasmin Dürr[3],
Klaus Palme[2,3], Thomas Brox[1,2], and Olaf Ronneberger[1,2]

[1] Lehrstuhl für Mustererkennung und Bildverabeitung, Institut für Informatik
[2] BIOSS Centre of Biological Signalling Studies
[3] Institut für Biologie II, Albert-Ludwigs-Universität Freiburg
[4] INRA Versailles
maid@informatik.uni-freiburg.de

Abstract. In this paper, we aim for detection and segmentation of *Arabidopsis thaliana* cells in volumetric image data. To this end, we cluster the training samples by their size and aspect ratio and learn a detector and a shape model for each cluster. While the detector yields good cell hypotheses, additionally aligning the shape model to the image allows to better localize the detections and to reconstruct the cells in case of low quality input data. We show that due to the more accurate localization, the alignment also improves the detection performance.

1 Introduction

In biomedical image analysis, one is often interested in explaining and measuring observed image structures by fitting a model to the data. This enables a statistical analysis of imaged data, e.g., gene expression patterns. At the same time, it can be interesting to highlight deviations from the standard model, i.e., those patterns that are not explained by the fitted model.

In this paper, we focus on segmentation of specific cell types in volumetric data. A standard approach is to run a segmentation method, e.g. watershed segmentation, followed by a classification of the obtained regions [9]. This corresponds to approaches on object class segmentation that run classifiers on region hypotheses [3].

The opposite approach is to first run a discriminative detector of a trained model on the image data to obtain object class hypotheses, and then to obtain a refined segmentation by aligning the detected model to the image data [2].

In this paper, we focus on the latter approach and extend the idea to volumetric cell data. To this end, we set up a volumetric variant of HOG descriptors [5] inspired by [8] who construct a 3D HOG descriptor for 2D + time data for action recognition. We cluster the set of training samples and set up a cell model for each cluster. The model consists of a linear SVM for detection in a sliding window fashion, and a shape template for alignment. Compared to [2], we improve on the model template used for alignment. In particular, we learn a common mean

J. Weickert, M. Hein, and B. Schiele (Eds.): GCPR 2013, LNCS 8142, pp. 205–214, 2013.

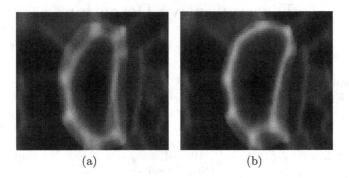

(a)   (b)

Fig. 1. The two images show a slice of the root in red. The green overlays show a detected cell without (a) and with alignment (b).

template from the training samples [13]. In this approach, a diffeomorphism is estimated between the initial template and all positive training samples, and the mean template is optimized with regard to the total deformation of all samples. For the alignment we use state-of-the-art elastic registration methods [1,11].

We quantitatively evaluate the approach by detecting and reconstructing cells of *Arabidopsis thaliana* in dense volumetric tissue. *Arabidopsis thaliana* is a model organism that is widely used in the research on plant development and genetics [7,10]. The structure of the root is visualized in Fig. 2(a). We demonstrate that the alignment improves the accuracy of the cell segmentation. Moreover, the alignment improves detection performance since the detections are better localized after alignment; see Fig. 1.

The detection based approach also allows to obtain good segmentations on lower quality data when a segmentation guided approach, such as in [9] yields unsatisfactory results.

2   Training the 3D Cell Detectors

In this section we will describe the training of the discriminative detection filters and the features that we use. The training input is a volumetric 3D image[1] $I : \Omega \to \mathbb{R}; \ \Omega \subset \mathbb{R}^3$ of the root, with segmentation masks $S_i : \Omega \to \{0,1\}$ for the cells that will be our positive examples.

In a classical detection framework all samples are assumed to have the same orientation, in our setting however, we have a rotational axis in the center of the root and the sliding window has to be rotated around this axis. Therefore, in this special case we determine a *root coordinate system* for rotation normalization. The fitting of a coordinate system to the root can be done automatically as shown in [12]. We will, however, use the simplified version illustrated in Fig. 2(b).

The outline of the training algorithm is as follows:

---

[1] In the biomedical field, the term "image" is used also for volumetric images.

1. Extract orientation normalized positive training images of cells by using the segmentation masks and the root coordinate system
2. Perform a k-means clustering using the bounding boxes of the shapes
3. Create an average segmentation mask for every cluster
4. Randomly sample orientation normalized negative images for every cluster
5. Train a linear SVM for every cluster using 3D HOG features

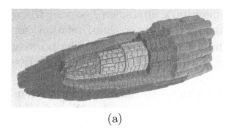

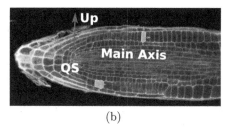

(a)   (b)

Fig. 2. In (a) the structure of the root can be clearly seen: It consists of cells of different shapes and sizes organized in concentric cylindrical layers. We use a cylindrical root coordinate system (b) to normalize the orientation of our training images. It is defined by the position of the *quiescent center* (QS), the translational direction along the main axis and a radial up-vector component pointing outwards from this axis.

2.1   Data Normalization and Clustering

The data that we are dealing with has rotational symmetry along one axis. The traditional sliding window approach does not deal with rotations. Therefore, we normalize them out for the training and the detection. This is similar to the different scales that one usually encounters in natural images. For the training they are normalized out and a filter is trained for one scale only. During test time, the filter is then applied to an image pyramid containing different scales.

The root coordinate system consists of the location and orientation of the main axis and an arbitrary but fixed component defining the "up" direction perpendicular to this axis. We use it to attach an orientation to every segmentation mask S_i and to compute a rigid transformation $\mathbf{H}_i : \mathbb{R}^3 \to \mathbb{R}^3$ that normalizes for location and rotation. The location normalization maps the center of mass of a cell to the coordinate origin. The resulting orientation normalized segmentation masks are then $\hat{S}_i = S_i \circ \mathbf{H}_i$, where $\circ$ denotes function composition, i.e. $(S_i \circ \mathbf{H}_i)(\mathbf{x}) = S_i(\mathbf{H}_i(\mathbf{x}))$

After normalization we perform a k-means clustering on the shape of the cuboidal bounding boxes of $\hat{S}_i$. They are defined as $\mathbf{s}_i = \mathbf{b}_{\text{high}}(\hat{S}_i) - \mathbf{b}_{\text{low}}(\hat{S}_i)$, with $\mathbf{b}_{\text{high}}, \mathbf{b}_{\text{low}}$ being functions that extract the tight bounding box, i.e. $\mathbf{b}_{\text{high}} : [\Omega \to \{0,1\}] \to \mathbb{R}^3$, and $\mathbf{b}_{\text{low}}$ accordingly. For each of the K clusters we define a set $\mathcal{C}_k = \{c_1, \dots, c_{N_k}\}$ containing the indices of the segmentation masks. We use the absolute bounding box sizes for clustering (instead of the common aspect ratios), because we know the scale of the microscopic images. In the experiments section, we evaluate the effect of the parameter K.

After the clustering, we determine the ranges $\mathbf{R}_{\text{high}}, \mathbf{R}_{\text{low}}$ of the filter box such that it can enclose all the shapes in a cluster.

$$\mathbf{R}_{\text{low}}^k = \mathbf{b}_{\text{low}}\left(\bigcup_{i \in C_k} \hat{S}_i\right) - \boldsymbol{\delta}, \quad \mathbf{R}_{\text{high}}^k = \mathbf{b}_{\text{high}}\left(\bigcup_{i \in C_k} \hat{S}_i\right) + \boldsymbol{\delta} \tag{1}$$

The parameter $\boldsymbol{\delta} \in \mathbb{R}^3$ specifies how much "context" we want to add to either side of the training images. As shown in [5], context improves the detector's performance significantly. The support domain of a filter then becomes $\Omega_k = \{\mathbf{x} \in \mathbb{R}^3 | \mathbf{R}_{\text{low}}^k \leq \mathbf{x} \leq \mathbf{R}_{\text{high}}^k\}$ where we define the "lesser than" relations for vectors, such that the relations for all components must be true. The positive training images X_i are obtained as $\hat{X}_i = I \circ \mathbf{H}_i$, defined on Ω_k for the respective cluster.

We create an average segmentation mask for the detection filter that gives us an estimate of the most likely location of a detected cell. Following [2] we do this by taking the 0.5 level set of the averaged normalized segmentation masks.

$$S^k(\mathbf{x}) = \begin{cases} 1, \text{ if } & \frac{1}{|C_k|} \sum_{i \in C_k} \hat{S}_i(\mathbf{x}) \geq 0.5 \\ 0, \text{ otherwise} \end{cases} \tag{2}$$

The negative examples are obtained by randomly sampling rotation normalized boxes from the training root. We make sure not to accidentally include positive training examples. In the next sections we will present the features that we use to represent our images.

2.2 Histograms of Oriented Gradients

The majority of information in an image lies in its edges and HOG has proven well for detection in 2D pictures. In our framework we build upon this idea and create a 3D detector in a similar manner.

We define a direction histogram binning function $b_i : \mathbb{R}^3 \to \mathbb{R}$, using N_d directions $\{\mathbf{d}_1, \ldots, \mathbf{d}_{N_d}\}$ with $\mathbf{d}_i \in \mathbb{R}^3$ and $\|\mathbf{d}_i\| = 1$ equally distributed on the unit sphere (here we use the vertices of a dodecahedron).

$$b_i(\mathbf{n}) = e^{-\frac{1}{2}\left(\frac{\mathbf{d}_i^\top \frac{\mathbf{n}}{\|\mathbf{n}\|} - 1}{\sigma}\right)^2} \tag{3}$$

where σ is selected such that the weight is approx. 0.5 at the middle between two bins, i.e. if $\mathbf{d}_j$ is a direct neighbor of $\mathbf{d}_i$, then $b_i((\mathbf{d}_i + \mathbf{d}_j)/2) \approx 0.5$. For easier notation, all binning functions are combined into one vector-valued binning function $\mathbf{b} : \mathbb{R}^3 \to \mathbb{R}^{N_d} \quad \mathbf{b}(\mathbf{n}) = [b_1(\mathbf{n}), \ldots, b_{N_d}(\mathbf{n})]^\top$.

Mapping an image $I : \Omega \to \mathbb{R}$ to and oriented gradient map $O : \Omega \to \mathbb{R}^{N_d}$ is then defined by the mapping $\mathbf{G} : [\Omega \to \mathbb{R}] \to [\Omega \to \mathbb{R}^{N_d}]$

$$\mathbf{G}(I)(\mathbf{x}) := \|\nabla I(\mathbf{x})\| \cdot \frac{\mathbf{b}(\nabla I(\mathbf{x}))}{\|\mathbf{b}(\nabla I(\mathbf{x}))\|} \tag{4}$$

2.3 Combining and Subsampling

To add robustness to small local deformations, in the 2D HOG framework, the gradients are accumulated in feature cells. We adopt this procedure and convolve the feature map $\mathbf{G}(I)$ with a triangular filter kernel $T : \mathbb{R}^3 \to \mathbb{R}$ with radius w,

$$T(\mathbf{x}) = \begin{cases} 1 - \frac{\|\mathbf{x}\|_{L_1}}{w} & , \text{ if } \|\mathbf{x}\|_{L_1} < w \\ 0 & \text{else} \end{cases} \tag{5}$$

This is equivalent to a soft binning in the standard setting. We normalize $\mathbf{G}(I)$ as $\tilde{\mathbf{G}}(I) = (T * \mathbf{G}(I))/(\|T * \mathbf{G}(I) + \epsilon\|)$ to have unit length at every position $\mathbf{x}$, while assuring not to include locations with too little structure by regularizing it with a suitable ϵ. To obtain the feature vector used for the SVM training we now discretize $\tilde{\mathbf{G}}(I)$ by sampling it at regular grid positions $\mathbf{g}_i \in \Omega$ for $i \in \{1, \ldots, N_g\}$ and concatenate the vectors to a single feature vector $\mathbf{F}(I) = \left[\tilde{\mathbf{G}}(I)(\mathbf{g}_1); \ldots; \tilde{\mathbf{G}}(I)(\mathbf{g}_{N_g})\right]$, where $\mathbf{F}(I) \in \mathbb{R}^{N_d \cdot N_g}$

2.4 SVM Training

We train a linear SVM [4] for every cluster $\mathcal{C}_k$. The amount of sampled negatives is five times the amount of positives for every cluster. As the dimensionality of our feature vector is orders of magnitude bigger than the number of examples per training (roughly $500.000 : 500$), we precompute the kernel matrix $\mathbf{X}^T\mathbf{X}$, where $\mathbf{X}$ contains the feature vectors of the positive and negative examples as column vectors.

3   Sharp Mean Image Generation

For a classical sliding window detector, the localization hypothesis for a detection is the bounding box of the filter. One can improve on this localization by incorporating the segmentation masks from the training. E.g. by using the average segmentation mask S_k (Eqn. 2). We propose to use elastic alignment of a *sharp mean image* to further improve the localization.

In this section we describe how we create a sharp mean image Z_k for each cluster $\mathcal{C}_k$. For an illustration see Fig. 3(b). For the generation we follow the ideas from [13], i.e. we want a sharp average image with respect to the intensities and deformations present in the cluster $\mathcal{C}_k$. To this end we need a reference image, to which we align all other images from the cluster. As reference image we take the image X_{r_k} with $r_k \in \mathcal{C}_k$, whose bounding box size has the minimal distance to the average bounding box. We use the publicly available diffeomorphic registration from the ANTS[1] toolkit to compute the transformations $\theta_{m,f} : \mathbb{R}^3 \to \mathbb{R}^3$ that maps the image I_m onto the image I_f. We use normalized cross correlation as data term with a diffeomorphic regularizer. For the computation of the sharp mean image $Z_k : \Omega \to \mathbb{R}$, we use the transformations θ_{j,r_k} to normalize the

(a)   (b)

Fig. 3. Volume rendering and slice view of an average cell formed from all positive examples of a cluster. In (a) the intensities of the rigidly aligned cells are averaged. The *sharp mean image* (b) resembles the structure much cleaner.

shape of every training image X_j in the cluster to the reference shape X_{r_k}. Then we average the intensities and use the average inverse transformation to compute the sharp mean image. Note that a relative deformation field can be computed from the absolute transformation by subtracting the identity.

$$Z_k = \underbrace{\left(\frac{1}{|\mathcal{C}_k|} \sum_{j \in \mathcal{C}_k} X_j \circ \boldsymbol{\theta}_{j,r_k} \right)}_{\text{average intensities}} \circ \underbrace{\left(\text{Id} + \frac{1}{|\mathcal{C}_k|} \sum_{j \in \mathcal{C}_k} \left(\boldsymbol{\theta}_{j,r_k}^{-1} - \text{Id} \right) \right)}_{\text{average deformation}} \quad (6)$$

For the generation of Z_k we dilate the segmentation masks S_i used to cut out the images X_i, as the segmentation only captures half of the cell wall and a little extra structure around the cell is needed for the elastic registration's data term to work properly. The "tight" sharp segmentation masks S_{Z_k} which will be used in the alignment, are computed by averaging the individual segmentation masks $\hat{S}_j$ after applying the same transformations as for the images.

4   Detection and Alignment

For the detection we apply a sliding window approach to the original data set and rotated versions of it, denoted as B_i. The rotations are sampled in 10 degree steps around the axis, defined by the root coordinate system, resulting in 36 data sets. For every B_i we compute the score maps for every detection filter at the grid positions. The necessary convolutions are computed efficiently in the Fourier domain. We ensure that within the volume of the average segmentation masks S^k (Eqn. 2), at most one local maximum appears. The lower scoring hypotheses are suppressed. Finally, we perform an upsampling by cubic interpolation of the score maps to obtain the detection locations with higher accuracy. As a last step we transform the detection locations back to the original root and assemble them in a greedy fashion, by starting with the highest scoring detection hypothesis.

4.1   Alignment

We perform an alignment for every detection. As initialization for the alignment we put the sharp mean image Z_k at the location where its tight segmenta-tion mask S_{Z_k} has the biggest overlap with the average segmentation mask S_k

from the detector (Fig. 1(a)). We use a fast combinatorial registration from the ViBE-Z [11] toolkit, where we replaced the data term (originally a locally normalized cross correlation) by a nonlinear gradient direction and gradient magnitude comparison, to obtain the same robustness properties as a HOG descriptor. The similarity of a local region Ω_i of the fixed image I and transformed moving image J is defined as

$$E_{\text{sim}}(I,J) = \frac{\int_{\Omega_i} \|\nabla I\| \cdot \|\nabla J\| \cdot \exp\left(-\frac{1}{2\sigma^2}\left(\cos^{-1}\left(\frac{(\nabla I)^{\top}\nabla J}{\|\nabla I\|\|\nabla J\|}\right)\right)^2\right) d\mathbf{x}}{\sqrt{\int_{\Omega_i} \|\nabla I\|^2 d\mathbf{x}} \cdot \sqrt{\int_{\Omega_i} \|\nabla J\|^2 d\mathbf{x}}} \tag{7}$$

We opted to choose this registration over the ANTS registration used in training as we do not need a diffeomorphic mapping and the runtime is faster by several orders of magnitude.

The ViBE-Z registration has several parameters that need to be adapted to the structures present in the data: The grid spacing α, the patch radius β, the label radius γ, and the Elasticity λ. We optimize these parameters automatically on the training set by maximizing the *intersection over union* (IOU) between the transformed sharp mean segmentation mask and the ground truth segmentation of a detection. For two volumes V and W the IOU is defined as

$$M_{iou}(V,W) = \frac{|V \cap W|}{|V \cup W|} \tag{8}$$

In the following section we provide quantitative evidence that it is crucial to work with the correct parameter settings.

5   Experiments

For the quantitative evaluation we had two roots with ground truth segmentations available. Ground truth segmentations are obtained by manually verifying a watershed segmentation computed on enhanced data [9]. This is very cumbersome work, as a root contains roughly 2.500 cells. During the verification, wrongly segmented cells are marked as invalid. In this study we concentrate on the about 250 cells of the cortex layer that have the most complex shape: The Green layer in Fig. 2(a).

We measure the quality of a detection hypothesis using the IOU (Eqn. 8) of its segmentation mask with the ground truth segmentation. For aligned detections, we take the aligned segmentation mask of the sharp mean image. For the precision-recall diagrams we apply the PASCAL VOC [6] criterion: A detection is accepted as a true positive iff $M_{\text{iou}} \geq 0.5$. All lower ranked detections in this location count as false positives. Note that in contrast to the PASCAL VOC challenge for natural images, we use the GT segmentations and not only the bounding boxes which makes the task more demanding. The average precision is computed as the area under the precision-recall curve.

Table 1. Effect of the number of clusteres K on the average precision (AP) with and without alignment

K	2	5	10	15	25
AP	0.45	0.58	0.63	**0.74**	0.72
AP-aligned	0.58	0.74	0.75	**0.88**	0.86

The test root that we used for evaluation has an image size of $944 \times 413 \times 360$ Voxel. We sampled $3 \times 36 = 108$ overlapping rotation normalized boxes of the size $301 \times 101 \times 131$ around the main axis of the root coordinate system. We found that it is sufficient to sample in $10°$ steps. On a six-core machine the detection for $K = 15$ takes about 1 hour while the majority of the time is spent on the computation of the HOG feature for each rotation normalized box. The remapping of the detections to the original space and the alignment takes another 30 minutes. Notice that the detection and alignment steps are nearly perfectly parallelizable – we noticed a quasi linear scaling of the processing time when we used more computers in parallel. For the alignment, we found that a parameter setting of $\alpha = 4, \beta = 7, \gamma = 10$, and $\lambda = 5$ gives best results on the training data. Table 1 and Fig. 4 summarize our findings: The choice of the right amount of clusters is crucial for the overall performance of our system. While a too small number of clusters cannot capture the variance present in the data, a too big number does not leave enough positive training examples for the SVM. The alignment of the sharp mean image boosts the AP by approximately $+14\%$, independent of

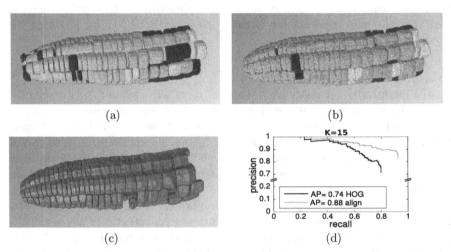

(a)   (b)

(c)   (d)

Fig. 4. Rendering of the best detection result ($K = 15$) before alignment (a) and after alignment (b). The ground truth is shown in (c). *Red* cells have an IOU below 0.5, *yellow* cells are detections at locations where GT segmentations are missing and *green* cells are correctly detected. In (d) you can see the corresponding *precision-recall* graphs. Notice how the alignment improves not only the AP but the overall quality of the reconstruction.

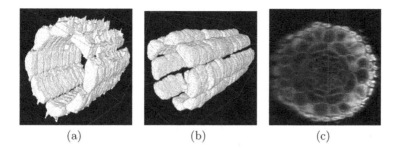

(a)   (b)   (c)

Fig. 5. Qualitative example on data of low recording quality. The watershed segmentation (a) leaks out at some cell-borders. Our approach (b) produces a more naturally looking result. A slice of the original raw data can be seen in (c).

the number of clusters. For the true positive detections, the average localization accuracy gets a boost from $\varnothing IOU = 0.66$ to $\varnothing IOU = 0.78$. When we use the average image instead of the sharp mean image(Fig. 3(a)), the AP gets reduced by about 2%. The alignment is also the reason for the gain in AP: Some of the detections that were poorly localized before the alignment get a boost in IOU big enough to make them count as true positive detections afterwards. Notice that we do not get any false positive detections outside the sought layer. False positive detections occur either when one GT cell is falsely explained by two detections or vice versa.

In Fig. 5 you can see a qualitative illustration of the ability of our approach to generalize to data of worse recording quality. While the watershed segmentation fails at many of the cell borders, we achieve a visually much more plausible result.

6   Conclusions

In this work we presented and evaluated how an elastic alignment can improve detection in volumetric data. With the *alignment* of a sharp mean image to the data we were able to improve the localization accuracy and average precision substantially. While the general idea of aligning some template to the data should also hold in 2D, the realization would be more difficult: One would have to deal with occlusions, viewpoint dependent distortions of the image and the articulated nature of some object classes, like e.g. humans.

However, we believe that this work is a significant step towards the goal to explain every voxel in a newly recorded data set based on learned Models.

Acknowledgements. This work was supported by the Excellence Initiative of the German Federal and State Governments: BIOSS Centre for Biological Signalling Studies (EXC 294) and the Bundesministerium für Bildung und Forschung (SYSTEC, 0101-31P5914). Philipp Fischer is supported by the Deutsche Telekom Stiftung.

References

1. Avants, B.B., Epstein, C.L., Grossman, M., Gee, J.C.: Symmetric diffeomorphic image registration with cross-correlation: Evaluating automated labeling of elderly and neurodegenerative brain. Medical Image Analysis 12(1), 26–41 (2008)
2. Brox, T., Bourdev, L., Maji, S., Malik, J.: Object segmentation by alignment of poselet activations to image contours. In: IEEE International Conference on Computer Vision and Pattern Recognition (CVPR) (2011)
3. Carreira, J., Sminchisescu, C.: CPMC: Automatic Object Segmentation Using Constrained Parametric Min-Cuts. IEEE Transactions on Pattern Analysis and Machine Intelligence (2012)
4. Chang, C.C., Lin, C.J.: LIBSVM: A library for support vector machines. ACM Transactions on Intelligent Systems and Technology 2, 27:1–27:27 (2011)
5. Dalal, N., Triggs, B.: Histograms of oriented gradients for human detection. In: Schmid, C., Soatto, S., Tomasi, C. (eds.) International Conference on Computer Vision & Pattern Recognition (2005)
6. Everingham, M., Van Gool, L., Williams, C.K.I., Winn, J., Zisserman, A.: The pascal visual object classes (voc) challenge. International Journal of Computer Vision 88(2), 303–338 (2010)
7. Fernandez, R., Das, P., Mirabet, V., Moscardi, E., Traas, J., Verdeil, J., Malandain, G., Godin, C.: Imaging plant growth in 4d: robust tissue reconstruction and lineaging at cell resolution. Nature Methods 7(7), 547–553 (2010)
8. Kläser, A., Marszalek, M., Schmid, C.: A spatio-temporal descriptor based on 3d-gradients. In: BMVC (2008)
9. Liu, K., Schmidt, T., Blein, T., Dürr, J., Palme, K., Ronneberger, O.: Joint 3d cell segmentation and classification in the arabidopsis root using energy minimization and shape priors. In: IEEE International Symposium on Biomedical Imaging (ISBI) (2013)
10. Marcuzzo, M., Quelhas, P., Campilho, A., Maria Mendonça, A., Campilho, A.: Automated arabidopsis plant root cell segmentation based on svm classification and region merging. Comput. Biol. Med. 39(9), 785–793 (2009)
11. Ronneberger, O., Liu, K., Rath, M., Ruess, D., Mueller, T., Skibbe, H., Drayer, B., Schmidt, T., Filippi, A., Nitschke, R., Brox, T., Burkhardt, H., Driever, W.: Vibe-z: A framework for 3d virtual colocalization analysis in zebrafish larval brains. Nature Methods 9(7), 735–742 (2012)
12. Schmidt, T., Keuper, M., Pasternak, T., Palme, K., Ronneberger, O.: Modeling of sparsely sampled tubular surfaces using coupled curves. In: Pinz, A., Pock, T., Bischof, H., Leberl, F. (eds.) DAGM and OAGM 2012. LNCS, vol. 7476, pp. 83–92. Springer, Heidelberg (2012)
13. Wu, G., Jia, H., Wang, Q., Shen, D.: Sharpmean: Groupwise registration guided by sharp mean image and tree-based registration. NeuroImage 56(4) (2011)

Distances Based on Non-rigid Alignment for Comparison of Different Object Instances

Benjamin Drayer and Thomas Brox

Department of Computer Science,
Centre of Biological Signalling Studies (BIOSS),
University of Freiburg, Germany
{drayer,brox}@cs.uni-freiburg.de

Abstract. Comparison of different object instances is hard due to the large intra-class variability. Part of this variability is due to viewpoint and pose, another due to subcategories and texture. The variability due to mild viewpoint changes, can be normalized out by aligning the samples. In contrast to the classical Procrustes distance, we propose distances based on non-rigid alignment and show that this increases performance in nearest neighbor tasks. We also investigate which matching costs and which optimization techniques are most appropriate in this context.

1 Introduction

A large part of the variability among images of an object class is due to viewpoint and pose. While large differences in viewpoint and pose render the images very different and leave little hope to compare them directly, object samples taken from approximately the same viewpoint share many common features. Descriptors that are invariant to small local deformations, such as HOG, have been the basis for establishing matches between such samples. But is the concept of grids of histograms sufficient?

In this paper, we show that a non-rigid alignment procedure on top of HOG improves the similarity of different object instances from the same class and seen in the same pose; see Fig. 1. This is particularly true if the deformation cost for the alignment is part of the distance.

Alignment procedures have been heavily used in the scope of matching faces. Since (frontal) faces are mostly planar, most face alignment methods focus on rigid or affine alignments, see for instance [7]. For general object classes with more variation, non-rigid alignment is more appropriate, as we show in this paper. Non-rigid alignment has been used also for face alignment [17] but required additional supervision by training fiducial detectors.

Unsupervised non-rigid alignment between object instances, as considered in this paper, is a hard problem, both with regard to the matching cost and with regard to the optimization. On the side of the matching cost, we build upon the idea of whitened HOG features as recently proposed in [6] in the scope of clustering and detection. Moreover, we find that a combination of the l_1 norm and the dot product behaves better than these norms alone.

J. Weickert, M. Hein, and B. Schiele (Eds.): GCPR 2013, LNCS 8142, pp. 215–224, 2013.
© Springer-Verlag Berlin Heidelberg 2013

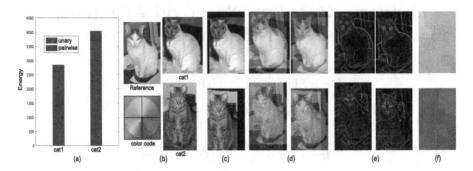

Fig. 1. Illustration and motivation of alignment based distances. (a) Optimum alignment energies. (b) Two cats with different poses to be aligned with the reference cat; color code for the deformation fields. (c) cat1 and cat2 after alignment with the reference. (d) Overlay of the images before and after alignment. (e) Overlay of the gradient images before and after alignment. (f) Estimated deformation fields. Samples that are similar enough to be aligned well yield low energies, whereas samples that cannot be aligned properly yield higher energies.

On the side of optimization, we investigate a set of efficient discrete optimization methods. Matching of different instances has been studied before, e.g., in Berg et al. [1], who solved the corresponding NP-hard optimization problem with a linear programming relaxation. Due to the computational complexity of this approximation, only correspondences of very sparse sets of feature points can be computed. In the context of label transfer between different scenes, SIFT flow [11] has been based on an optimization with belief propagation [15]. Apart from belief propagation, we investigate two other methods: fast primal-dual [8,9], and α-expansion with non-submodular binary cost functions, so-called fusion moves [10]. We compare the energies obtained with these three techniques, as well as the computation times.

We demonstrate the effect of non-rigid alignment on the distances between instances on four datasets, one on cars, two on cats and one on horses. We aim to find the visually most similar examples relative to a reference image. Each dataset consists of the references and the corresponding ground truth sets of the most similar nearest neighbors. We evaluate various distances with and without alignment. Furthermore, we compare against the scores obtained with an exemplar SVM [12] and with a rigid alignment. The results show that distances based on non-rigid alignment match the annotation much better than distances on raw HOG, whitened HOG features, rigid alignment, or a HOG based exemplar SVM.

2   Non-rigid Alignment

For each pair of examples we would like to compute the deformation field that optimally aligns one example with the other. This is much more difficult than,

e.g., optical flow estimation, since there is variation besides the sought deformation, and we do not yet know which features are reliable for matching. We build
upon the HOG [3] and the whitened HOG (WHO) descriptor [6]. The WHO descriptor is advantageous as it tends to give more weight to features that are most
relevant for the present object class. This feature weighting is potentially also
useful for alignment. Indeed, our experiments show an improved performance if
the alignment takes into account whitened HOG features.

Unfortunately, the whitening requires inversion of the covariance matrix. Only
feature vectors with less than 10000 dimensions can be handled in reasonable
time, which corresponds to HOG representations with 16×16 blocks. For finer
representations (using more but smaller cells), we must return to the classical HOG representation without whitening. As a consequence, we run a coarse
alignment on WHO features and use the resulting deformation field as a soft
constraint when optimizing the refined alignment based on HOG. The cost function consists of the matching costs E_D, which aim for maximum feature overlap,
and a regularization term E_P that penalizes strong deformations:

$$E(\mathbf{u}) = E_D(\mathbf{u}) + \lambda E_P(\mathbf{u}). \tag{1}$$

This cost function is minimized with respect of the deformation field $\mathbf{u}$. The
regularization parameter λ allows to emphasize either the deformation cost or
the matching cost. We empirically determined $\lambda = 1.0$ in case of WHO features
and $\lambda = 0.2$ for HOG features.

2.1   Matching Cost

As matching cost we use a combination of the l_1-norm and the dot product. The
advantage of the l_1-norm is its robustness, but at images where we have slightly
different features, it can prefer to match a weak feature to the background rather
than to the most similar feature; see Fig. 2. On the other hand, the dot product
tries to match as many features as possible, but it does not penalize unaligned
features. This leads to blurring effects. The combination prefers alignment of the
closest features while enforcing one-to-one assignments:

$$E_D(\mathbf{u}) = \sum_{\mathbf{x}} |F_2(\mathbf{x} + \mathbf{u}(\mathbf{x})) - F_1(\mathbf{x})|_1 - \langle F_2(\mathbf{x} + \mathbf{u}(\mathbf{x})), F_1(\mathbf{x}) \rangle \tag{2}$$

where $F(\mathbf{x})$ denotes the feature vector at position $\mathbf{x}$ (the respective cell of the
HOG descriptor).

2.2   Deformation Cost

For measuring the deformation cost, we use the total variation

$$E_P(\mathbf{u}) = \sum_{\mathbf{x}, \mathbf{y} \in \mathcal{N}(\mathbf{x})} |\mathbf{u}(\mathbf{x}) - \mathbf{u}(\mathbf{y})|_1, \tag{3}$$

where $\mathcal{N}(\mathbf{x})$ denotes the 4-connected neighborhood of $\mathbf{x}$. The total variation
regularization prefers piecewise constant deformation fields.

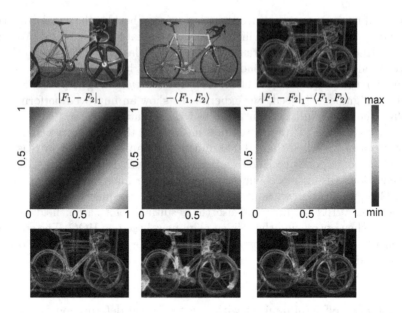

Fig. 2. Top row: Two bikes and the overlay of their gradients. **Center row:** Three different matching costs. **Bottom row:** Resulting alignments. **Left:** With the l1 norm, weak gradients are preferably matched to the background. **Middle:** With the dot product, smearing effects occur because matching to the background does not induce any cost. **Right:** The combination leads to the best alignment.

2.3 Refinement on a Finer Grid of HOG Cells

To exploit both the feature weighting of the WHO features and the higher accuracy of HOG with smaller cells, the initial alignment is obtained by minimizing Eq. 1 based on WHO features. The resulting deformation field $\mathbf{u}_{\text{WHO}}$ serves as a soft constraint in the successive dense alignment on a finer grid of HOG cells. At this fine level, we minimize:

$$E(\mathbf{u}) = \sum_{\mathbf{x}} \beta \, \delta(\mathbf{x}) \, |\mathbf{u}_{\text{WHO}} - \mathbf{u}|_1 + E_D(\mathbf{u}) + \lambda E_P(\mathbf{u})$$

$$\delta(\mathbf{x}) = \begin{cases} 1, & \text{If } \mathbf{u}_{\text{WHO}} \text{ defined at } \mathbf{x} \\ 0, & \text{otherwise} \end{cases} \tag{4}$$

The function $\delta(\mathbf{x})$ indicates the grid positions where the coarse deformation field $\mathbf{u}_{\text{WHO}}$ is available. The scaling factor $\beta = 0.03$ that regulates the influence of the initial alignment was determined empirically.

2.4 Energy Minimization

For the purpose of pairwise comparison, the optimization of the above energies must be fast on one hand, but also sufficiently reliable on the other hand. We

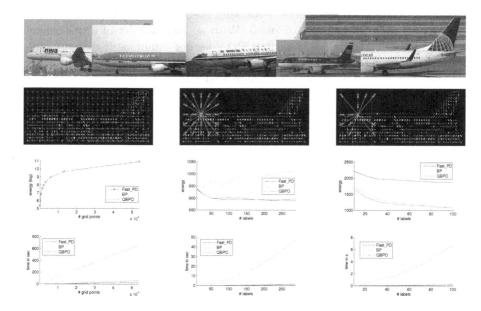

Fig. 3. Top row: Five images, for which we compare the energy minimization techniques. **Second row:** Images in HOG-feature space. In the left column we compare the behavior of the MRF-solvers when changing the number of nodes. In the middle we change the number of labels. The same set of labels is used everywhere, thus the binary subproblems are submodular. In the right column, the label set varies spatially based on the best k displacements. Thus the binary subproblems are no longer submodular. **Third row:** For submodular binary problems, Fast_PD and QPBO perform best. In the non-submodular case, BP and QPBO perform best. **Bottom row:** Run times of the different approaches depending on the number of grid points and labels. Fast_PD and QPBO are much faster than BP.

consider three multi-label MRF solvers: loopy belief propagation, Fast_PD [8,9] and α-expansion [2] with QPBO [13]. The Fast_PD algorithm solves a sequence of intermediate binary problems with min-cuts. The binary solution is only guaranteed to be optimal, if the binary problem is submodular. Also the α-expansion with QPBO solves a sequence of binary problems, which is done by so-called fusion moves [10]. In contrast to min-cuts, QPBO can solve a larger class of binary problems, the set of pseudo-boolean functions, which includes the submodular problems as a subset. Loopy belief propagation directly optimizes the multi-label problem, but there is neither any guarantee of optimality nor of convergence.

For the experiment in Fig. 3 we aligned five airplane images in HOG space and investigate the behavior of the three approximate optimization techniques, when changing the number of nodes, the number of labels and when we violate the submodularity property. If the labels correspond to the same displacement vectors everywhere, the binary subproblems are all submodular, because assigning the same label induces zero cost, while assigning another label induces higher cost. In this case, α-expansion with QPBO and Fast_PD minimize the energy equally well. Fast_PD scales a little better with the number of grid points, QPBO scales better with the number of labels. With an adaptive set of displacement vectors, submodularity is lost and Fast_PD does not minimize the energy anymore. Loopy belief propagation is unreliable, due to the missing convergence property, and very slow as the number of grid points or labels increases. The energies in Eq. 1 and 4 use a spatially fixed label set, but due to the better scaling with the number of labels, we used α-expansion with QPBO to compute the non-rigid alignment.

3   Distances Based on Alignment

A variety of distances can be defined based on the alignment of the previous section. As Fig. 1 indicates, the energy can be used directly as a distance measure. For this direct approach, there are three possibilities that we evaluated: the energy of Eq. 1 using HOG features (E_{HOG}) *or* WHO features (E_{WHO}), and the refinement based approach in Eq. 4 (E_{combi}) that uses both features.

Alternatively, distances can be defined based on the aligned features using the normalized dot product:

$$d(F_1, F_2) = \frac{\langle F_1, F_2 \rangle}{\|F_1\|_2 \cdot \|F_2\|_2},\tag{5}$$

F_1, F_2 are the HOG or WHO descriptors on the aligned images. The global normalization prevents images with rich gradients to be favored over those with less structure. To this distance we can add the deformation cost λE_P, which provides valuable information on how much the second image needed to be distorted to match the first one. Again, there are three possibilities how to compute the alignment (based on HOG, on WHO, or the combination of both). All these distances are evaluated in the next section.

4   Experiments

4.1   Dataset

We compared various distances between object instances in a simple experiment, where we find for a certain reference image the nearest neighbors according to this distance. To allow for a quantitative evaluation, we considered four datasets, 3D cars from [14], our own cat dataset, Pascal VOC cats [5] and Pascal VOC horses [4]. The 3D cars dataset consists of 10 different cars shown from 8 different viewing angles, and is typically used for viewpoint classification[1]. For each viewing angle we picked one car as a reference and used the other 9 as ground

---

[1] It is important to note that our experiment is *not* about viewpoint classification. We do not employ a training set to learn the best features to distinguish viewpoints. We are rather interested in an unsupervised definition of distances between examples that resemble human perception and test these distances in a nearest neighbor task.

Table 1. Comparison of various distances with and without non-rigid alignment in terms of average precision (AP). The distances in the left block use the energies directly, the two blocks in the middle use HOG and WHO features, before and after the alignment. Methods with $+\lambda E_P$ make use of the deformation cost computed during the alignment. In the last two blocks HOG and WHO were both used for alignment, which yields the best results.

	E_{HOG}	E_{WHO}	E_{combi}	HOG	HOG aligned	HOG $+\lambda E_P$	WHO	WHO aligned	WHO $+\lambda E_P$	HOG combi	WHO combi	HOG combi$+\lambda E_P$	WHO combi $+\lambda E_P$
Cars	30.39	30.4	31.74	30.79	44.94	43.57	28.09	30.05	30.45	39.42	30.05	**46.01**	33.8
Cats own	13.6	13.78	13.81	31.18	31.97	32.23	33.04	30.66	30.99	32.93	30.66	**33.41**	32.29
Cats Pascal	6.55	6.61	6.56	33.16	31.81	31.05	31.32	30.97	31.24	27.82	27.42	32.58	**33.17**
Horse Pascal	4.32	4.31	4.22	29.49	36.47	37.38	33.34	35.43	36.42	36.87	35.43	**38.83**	33.8
Mean	13.72	13.78	14.08	31.16	36.3	36.1	31.45	31.78	32.28	34.26	30.89	**37.71**	33.27

Table 2. Performance of ESVM [12], the rigid alignment and non-rigid aligned HOG-features. The non-rigid alignment consistently shows better AP.

	Cars	Cats own	Cats Pascal	Horse Pascal	Mean
ESVM [12]	24.07	16.83	10.68	19.08	17.67
rigid alignment	41.25	27.76	27.05	29.77	31.46
HOG aligned	44.94	31.97	31.81	36.47	**36.3**

truth set of nearest neighbors. Our cat dataset consists of 120 cats from Flickr provided by [16], we chose references representing the poses: portrait, walking left, walking front, sitting frontal, sitting left, sitting right and lying right. We manually defined a ground truth set of nearest neighbors for each of these poses. There are some images that do not fit to any of the references. In the same style we added annotation to the two Pascal VOC sets. The 200 cats from Pascal VOC 2006 show a great diversity, consequently we chose the three most frequent patterns (portrait, lying cat, sitting cat) as references together with their sets of nearest neighbors. Among the 724 horses from Pascal VOC 2007, the reference images represent horses from: front, left, right, left-front, right-front, jumping over the fence left and right, begging left and right. On the VOC images, we used the bounding box annotation to clip the image accordingly.

For the evaluation we compute precision and recall, where precision is the percentage of correct nearest neighbors and recall is the percentage of retrieved nearest neighbors. Comparison of samples to the reference based on the evaluated distance yields a ranked list, from which we computed a precision-recall curve. We report the average precision as the area under the precision-recall curve.

4.2   Results

In Table 1, we compare the different distances defined in Section 3. The raw energies do not perform well as they lack global normalization introduced in Eq. 5.

Fig. 4. Qualitative comparison between distance measures on non-aligned (HOG) and aligned (HOG combi+λE_P) images. The left column shows the reference image, the most similar images are ordered from left to right. For each reference image, we show the 9 most similar images with respect to non-aligned HOG features and aligned HOG features. The first example is from the car database [14], the second is from our own cat dataset, the third shows cats from Pascal VOC 2006 [5]. The remaining examples are from Pascal VOC 2007 [4]. In general, the samples found with the alignment based distance are more meaningful.

On average the alignment helps improve performance for the different features. It works best on cars and horses and does not improve on cats. This is because cats are particularly hard to align due to their large variability, e.g., various textures and large pose variation. The rigidness of the cars makes them the easiest case. Horses also come with non-rigid deformations, but their appearance is not as diverse as that of cats. Fig. 4 shows some qualitative results.

In Table 2 we verified if a simple rigid alignment can achieve a similar performance as a non-rigid alignment. Apart from the alignment model, the definition of the distances is equivalent. For simplicity, we evaluated only the HOG based alignment. The result confirms the need of a non-rigid alignment in case of non-planar objects (unlike faces). Even for cars, distances benefit from a non-rigid alignment.

Moreover, we compared to the score returned by the exemplar SVM (ESVM) [12]. In this approach one reference instance is taken as the only positive example and a linear SVM is trained to separate it from a large set of negative samples. This approach benefits from the SVM figuring out the relevant features that distinguish the positive sample from random samples. We used the reference images of the above datasets as exemplars and used the scores on the other images as similarity measure to pick the nearest neighbors. The result shows that the exemplar SVM is not useful for the purpose of distances. The linear decision function of the SVM lacks expressive power. It is interesting to note that a kernelized version of ESVM with an RBF kernel would be build upon a distance between the reference and negative samples, which takes us back to the definition of appropriate distances.

5   Conclusions

We have suggested distances between different object instances based on non-rigid alignment. We showed in a nearest neighbor experiment that distances based on non-rigid alignment perform better than distances based on an rigid alignment or no alignment at all. Moreover, thanks to an efficient optimization, non-rigid alignments can be computed also on larger datasets in reasonable time. Pairwise distances appear in many learning problems, such as clustering or kernel based classifiers. Hence, we believe that alignment based distances can have a positive effect in several applications.

Acknowledgements. This study was supported by the Excellence Initiative of the German Federal and State Governments (EXC 294) and by the ERC Starting Grant VIDEOLEARN.

References

1. Berg, A.C., Berg, T.L., Malik, J.: Shape matching and object recognition using low distortion correspondence. In: CVPR, pp. 26–33 (2005)
2. Boykov, Y., Veksler, O., Zabih, R.: Fast approximate energy minimization via graph cuts. IEEE Trans. Pattern Anal. Mach. Intell. 23(11), 1222–1239 (2001), http://dx.doi.org/10.1109/34.969114
3. Dalal, N., Triggs, B.: Histograms of oriented gradients for human detection. In: International Conference on Computer Vision & Pattern Recognition, vol. 2, pp. 886–893 (June 2005)

4. Everingham, M., Van Gool, L., Williams, C.K.I., Winn, J., Zisserman, A.: The PASCAL Visual Object Classes Challenge 2007 (VOC 2007) Results (2007), http://www.pascal-network.org/challenges/VOC/voc2007/workshop/index.html

5. Everingham, M., Zisserman, A., Williams, C.K.I., Van Gool, L.: The PASCAL Visual Object Classes Challenge 2006 (VOC 2006) Results (2006), http://www.pascal-network.org/challenges/VOC/voc2006/results.pdf

6. Hariharan, B., Malik, J., Ramanan, D.: Discriminative decorrelation for clustering and classification. In: Fitzgibbon, A., Lazebnik, S., Perona, P., Sato, Y., Schmid, C. (eds.) ECCV 2012, Part IV. LNCS, vol. 7575, pp. 459–472. Springer, Heidelberg (2012)

7. Huang, G.B., Mattar, M.A., Lee, H., Learned-Miller, E.G.: Learning to align from scratch. In: Bartlett, P.L., Pereira, F.C.N., Burges, C.J.C., Bottou, L., Weinberger, K.Q. (eds.) NIPS (2012)

8. Komodakis, N., Tziritas, G.: Approximate labeling via graph cuts based on linear programming. IEEE Trans. Pattern Anal. Mach. Intell. 29(8), 1436–1453 (2007)

9. Komodakis, N., Tziritas, G., Paragios, N.: Performance vs computational efficiency for optimizing single and dynamic mrfs: Setting the state of the art with primal-dual strategies. Comput. Vis. Image Underst. 112(1), 14–29 (2008), http://dx.doi.org/10.1016/j.cviu.2008.06.007

10. Lempitsky, V.S., Rother, C., Roth, S., Blake, A.: Fusion moves for markov random field optimization. IEEE Trans. Pattern Anal. Mach. Intell. 32(8), 1392–1405 (2010)

11. Liu, C., Yuen, J., Torralba, A., Sivic, J., Freeman, W.T.: SIFT flow: Dense correspondence across different scenes. In: Forsyth, D., Torr, P., Zisserman, A. (eds.) ECCV 2008, Part III. LNCS, vol. 5304, pp. 28–42. Springer, Heidelberg (2008)

12. Malisiewicz, T., Gupta, A., Efros, A.A.: Ensemble of exemplar-svms for object detection and beyond. In: ICCV (2011)

13. Rother, C., Kolmogorov, V., Lempitsky, V., Szummer, M.: Optimizing binary mrfs via extended roof duality. Tech. rep., In Proc. CVPR (2007)

14. Savarese, S., Fei-Fei, L.: 3d generic object categorization, localization and pose estimation. In: IEEE International Conference on Computer Vision, Rio de Janeiro, Brazil (October 2007)

15. Shekhovtsov, A., Kovtun, I., Hlaváč, V.: Efficient mrf deformation model for nonrigid image matching. In: IEEE Transactions on International Conference on Pattern Recognition (2007)

16. Zhang, W., Sun, J., Tang, X.: Cat head detection - how to effectively exploit shape and texture features. In: Forsyth, D., Torr, P., Zisserman, A. (eds.) ECCV 2008, Part IV. LNCS, vol. 5305, pp. 802–816. Springer, Heidelberg (2008)

17. Zhu, J., Gool, L.J.V., Hoi, S.C.H.: Unsupervised face alignment by robust nonrigid mapping. In: ICCV, pp. 1265–1272. IEEE (2009)

Stixel-Based Target Existence Estimation under Adverse Conditions

Timo Scharwächter

Daimler AG, Dept. Environment Perception

Abstract. Vision-based environment perception is particularly challenging in bad weather. Under such conditions, even most powerful stereo algorithms suffer from highly correlated, "blob"-like noise, that is hard to model. In this paper[1] we focus on extending an existing stereo-based scene representation – the Stixel World – to allow its application even under problematic conditions. To this end, we estimate the probability of existence for each detected obstacle. Results show that the amount of false detections can be reduced significantly by demanding temporal consistency of the representation and by analyzing cues that represent the geometry of typical obstacles.

1 Introduction

The importance of stereo image processing in the context of modern driver assistance increases steadily. Depth information is used to detect obstacles in the driving corridor [5] or to support pedestrian and vehicle classifiers by guiding the attention to relevant areas in the image [4].

There is no doubt, that for safety critical applications high accuracy and specificity of depth measurements is of utmost importance, as false detections can lead to unnecessary emergency maneuvers. At the same time, the range of stable system operation must be as wide as possible and should cover both well-conditioned input data and adverse conditions such as darkness, rain, reflections etc. Some of such typical scenarios a vision system is confronted with in real world applications are shown in Figure 1.

   (a) Mist   (b) Darkness   (c) Reflections   (d) Snow

Fig. 1. Input images under adverse conditions in the automotive context, that only show a few examples of the high variety of environmental effects

---

[1] Recommended for submission to YRF2012 by Dr. Uwe Franke, Daimler AG.

J. Weickert, M. Hein, and B. Schiele (Eds.): GCPR 2013, LNCS 8142, pp. 225–230, 2013.

To maintain a stable mode of operation as often as possible, it is necessary to explicitly address those situations. Therefore, this contribution focuses on the typical challenges of an automotive vision system under adverse conditions. To this end, the Stixel[2] representation proposed in [8] is extended to cope with adverse weather and input conditions by estimating the probability of existence for each Stixel. The estimation process is performed by analyzing the temporal and spatial behavior of the extracted Stixel representation.

2   System Overview

In this work, we rely on the semi-global matching (SGM) stereo algorithm introduced in [3]. SGM combines local pixel matching with approximated global smoothness. Steingrube et. al. [9] show that SGM outperforms other recent stereo algorithms in terms of detection performance (particularly in bad weather).

From the resulting disparity map, we extract the Stixel representation (see Figure 2), which provides a compact ($\sim$500 Stixels compared to $\sim$400.000 pixels) description of free space and obstacles by means of vertically stacked surfaces. For our purpose, the central objective of using this representation is that it performs a spatial regularization of the input data, which already reduces the impact of strong depth outliers. As a result, we obtain a compact and spatially smoothed representation of potential obstacles in the depicted scene.

However, at the time of this writing *temporal* coherence and *horizontal* (spatial) dependencies are not considered inherently in the Stixel representation. Under adverse conditions, this leads to so-called *phantom* Stixels that represent obstacles, although in fact no real obstacle is present. An analysis conducted prior to this work by Pfeiffer [6] shows that – under adverse conditions – such false Stixels pop up spontaneously from time to time (i.e. are temporally uncorrelated) and are spatially small. Some of those phantoms can be seen in the two example images in the middle of Figure 2, which depicts the general proceeding of the developed system.

To exploit these findings, we introduce a tracking scheme that allows to remove temporally uncorrelated Stixels and perform existence estimation based on cues that contain knowledge about the geometry of obstacles. In the following sections, Stixel tracking is discussed briefly and the existence estimation component is reviewed in more detail. Section 5 contains an evaluation of the developed framework and Section 6 ends with a conclusion.

3   Stixel Tracking

In dynamic environments temporal integration requires to track objects of interest to allow correct data association. The tracking component developed in the context of this work adopts the 6D-Vision principle presented in [2]. This allows to estimate the velocity and simultaneously improve the 3D world position of

---

[2] Derived from the two words *stick* and *pixel*.

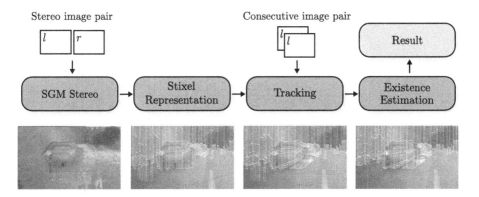

Fig. 2. General proceeding with result images for each respective component, applied to the first image of Figure 1 (best viewed in color)

Stixels (w.r.t. the observing camera) by means of Kalman filters. For our purpose, the filtered information provides a more robust basis for the subsequent cue computation.

Note that prior to this work, a different Stixel tracking approach has been presented [7] which also applies the 6D-Vision principle. However, the approach developed for our purpose allows to track several Stixels per column and retains the original grid the Stixel representation is given on. These are two properties required by subsequent analysis steps which are not fulfilled by the tracking presented in [7]. An example of the tracking result can be seen in Figure 2, indicated by the arrows at the bottom of Stixels covering the leading vehicle.

To exploit the large area of a Stixel, all optical flow measurements covered by a Stixel are used to calculate a single robust flow estimate. In our case, we apply a KLT-based tracking scheme and use the median to determine the flow result for a Stixel.

4   Existence Estimation

The existence of each Stixel is expressed as the posterior probability of a binary hypothesis, where $\exists :=$ "exists" and $\bar{\exists} :=$ "does *not* exist" and $P(\bar{\exists}_t \mid \mathbb{Z}^t) = 1 - P(\exists_t \mid \mathbb{Z}^t)$. The term $\mathbb{Z}^t = \{z_0, z_1, \ldots, z_{t-1}, z_t\}$ denotes the set of all framewise measurements (cues) z up to the current time step t. To separate real obstacles from phantoms, two cues are introduced later in Section 4.1.

To further take into account the temporal context obtained from the tracking component, the estimation problem is formulated time recursively according to a Bayes filter. This leads to the typical iteration between *prediction* (Equation 1) and *update* (Equation 2), where $P(\exists_t \mid \mathbb{Z}^t)$ is the sought quantity. The prediction is performed via a simple transition model, depicted in Figure 3.

$$P(\exists_t \mid \mathbb{Z}^{t-1}) = P(\exists_t \mid \exists_{t-1})\, P(\exists_{t-1} \mid \mathbb{Z}^{t-1}) +$$
$$P(\exists_t \mid \bar{\exists}_{t-1})\, [1 - P(\exists_{t-1} \mid \mathbb{Z}^{t-1})] \tag{1}$$

$$P(\exists_t \mid \mathbb{Z}^t) = \frac{P(z_t \mid \exists_t)\, P(\exists_k \mid \mathbb{Z}^{t-1})}{P(z_t \mid \exists_t)\, P(\exists_t \mid \mathbb{Z}^{t-1}) + P(z_t \mid \bar{\exists}_t)\, [1 - P(\exists_t \mid \mathbb{Z}^{t-1})]} \tag{2}$$

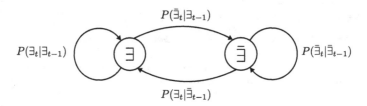

Fig. 3. Transition model to predict the current probability of existence before it is updated with new measurements

To avoid frequent label changes, the probability $P(\exists_t \mid \exists_{t-1})$ to remain in state $\exists$ is chosen relatively large while the probability $P(\exists_t \mid \bar{\exists}_{t-1})$ that a potential phantom changes to a real obstacle is rather small. However, it is still more likely than the change from a real obstacle to a phantom, which is a conservative and safe assumption. For our experiments we set $P(\exists_t \mid \exists_{t-1}) = 0.99$ and $P(\exists_t \mid \bar{\exists}_{t-1}) = 0.2$. A similar proceeding can also be found in [1], where a confidence measure for vehicle tracking is proposed.

4.1 Stixel-Wise Cues about Existence

In the following, two cues are introduced. From various cues tested, these two showed best performance for our purpose. The combination of cues is performed according to the naive Bayes approach, i.e. all N cues c_i are assumed independent, such that $P(z_t \mid x_t) = \prod_{i=1}^{N} P(c_{i,t} \mid x_t)$ with $x \in \{\exists, \bar{\exists}\}$. The two cues are:

Stixel Cluster Size Cue: The Stixel algorithm performs an optimal segmentation of the disparity data along the vertical image axis. As a consequence, horizontal smoothness is lost in favor of computational efficiency. To regain this lost information, we perform horizontal region growing on Stixel-level to cluster Stixels with similar depth and height[3]. The resulting cue value c_{CS} for each Stixel is the size of it's neighborhood region, such that $c_{CS} = w_{\text{cluster}} \times h_{\text{cluster}}\ [m^2]$. As the cluster size of phantom Stixels turns out to be rather small, the cue value is clipped to $1\ m^2$ if it exceeds this value.

---

[3] The stop criteria for region growing correspond to the geometry of typical obstacles.

Stixel Hypothesis Cue: The Stixel algorithm differentiates ground surface and obstacles by analyzing the progression of the disparity value along the vertical image axis. For the obstacle hypothesis, a constant disparity is assumed across the whole Stixel. The Stixel hypothesis cue evaluates the two likelihood functions (outcome of the Stixel optimization algorithm), that encode *how well* the disparity data matches both hypotheses. The final cue c_{SH} is chosen as the posterior probability of the object hypothesis, i.e. normalized to the range $[0, 1]$ by applying the law of total probability.

For both cue values it applies that a value close to one represents strong tendency towards a real obstacle while a cue value close to zero is more likely to belong to a phantom Stixel.

5   Evaluation

The detection performance of the proposed approach is presented by means of a receiver operator characteristic. To generate ground truth, we rely on an automated labeling strategy that we apply to 16 video sequences with 250 frames each, recorded under extremely bad conditions. Stixels falling into the unoccupied driving corridor are marked as negative examples (phantoms) and Stixels covering radar confirmed objects are marked as positive examples (real obstacles). This method of ground truth generation is also applied in [9]. In total we obtain roughly 12.000 negative and 55.000 positive examples which are split into a training and a test set.

The distributions of the introduced cues (see Figure 4 (a)) are learned from the training set and are then used on the test set to evaluate the existence probability and generate the ROC curve (see Figure 4 (b)).

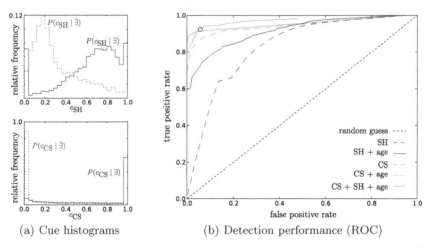

(a) Cue histograms   (b) Detection performance (ROC)

Fig. 4. Distribution of the three cue values for real obstacles and phantoms (a) and the resulting detection performance shown as ROC curve (b). The term "age" denotes temporal filtering here.

The results show, that both cues separate real obstacles from phantoms quite well. This also shows up in the final ROC result. It can be seen that temporally filtered cues (solid lines) always outperform the single-frame unfiltered cues (dashed lines) in terms of overall detection performance, which shows the effectiveness of the tracking component. Best performance with 93 % correctly classified Stixels is achieved with a combination of cluster size cue, hypothesis cue and temporal filtering (marked with a circle in Figure 4 (b)).

6   Conclusion

In this paper we showed a possibility to improve the bad weather performance of the Stixel representation by introducing existence estimation and temporal filtering for each Stixel. The evaluation shows a significant reduction of phantom Stixels while maintaining the majority of real obstacles. Furthermore, the introduced tracking scheme provides absolute velocity information for each Stixel that can be used for safety-relevant analysis, such as time-to-collision estimation.

References

1. Altendorfer, R., Matzka, S.: A confidence measure for vehicle tracking based on a generalization of Bayes estimation. In: Proceedings of the IEEE Intelligent Vehicles Symposium (IV), San Diego, CA (2010)
2. Franke, U., Rabe, C., Badino, H., Gehrig, S.K.: 6D-Vision: Fusion of Stereo and Motion for Robust Environment Perception. In: Kropatsch, W.G., Sablatnig, R., Hanbury, A. (eds.) DAGM 2005. LNCS, vol. 3663, pp. 216–223. Springer, Heidelberg (2005)
3. Hirschmüller, H.: Accurate and Efficient Stereo Processing by Semi-Global Matching and Mutual Information. In: Proceedings of the IEEE Conference on Computer Vision and Pattern Recognition (CVPR), pp. 807–814 (2005)
4. Keller, C., Enzweiler, M., Rohrbach, M., Llorca, D., Schnörr, C., Gavrila, D.: The benefits of dense stereo for pedestrian detection. IEEE Transactions on Intelligent Transportation Systems (99), 1–11 (2011)
5. Perrone, D., Iocchi, L., Antonello, P., Fiat, C.: Real-time Stereo Vision Obstacle Detection for Automotive Safety Application. Intelligent Autonomous Vehicles 7, 240–245 (2010)
6. Pfeiffer, D.: The Stixel World: A Compact Medium-level Representation for Efficiently Modeling Dynamic Three-dimensional Environments. Ph.D. thesis, Humboldt-Universität zu Berlin (2012)
7. Pfeiffer, D., Franke, U.: Efficient Representation of Traffic Scenes by Means of Dynamic Stixels. In: Proceedings of the IEEE Intelligent Vehicles Symposium (IV), San Diego, CA, pp. 217–224 (2010)
8. Pfeiffer, D., Franke, U.: Towards a Global Optimal Multi-Layer Stixel Representation of Dense 3D Data. In: British Machine Vision Conference (BMVC), Dundee, Scotland (2011)
9. Steingrube, P., Gehrig, S.K., Franke, U.: Performance evaluation of stereo algorithms for automotive applications. In: Fritz, M., Schiele, B., Piater, J.H. (eds.) ICVS 2009. LNCS, vol. 5815, pp. 285–294. Springer, Heidelberg (2009)

Three-Dimensional Data Compression
with Anisotropic Diffusion

Pascal Peter*

Mathematical Image Analysis Group, Faculty of Mathematics and Computer Science,
Campus E1.7, Saarland University, 66041 Saarbrücken, Germany
peter@mia.uni-saarland.de

Abstract. In 2-D image compression, recent approaches based on image inpainting with edge-enhancing anisotropic diffusion (EED) rival the transform-based quasi-standards JPEG and JPEG 2000 and are even able to surpass it. In this paper, we extend successful concepts from these 2-D methods to the 3-D setting, thereby establishing the first PDE-based 3-D image compression algorithm. This codec uses a cuboidal subdivision strategy to select and efficiently store a small set of sparse image data and reconstructs missing image parts with EED-based inpainting. An evaluation on real-world medical data substantiates the superior performance of this new algorithm in comparison to 2-D inpainting methods and the compression standard DICOM for medical data.

Keywords: 3-D image compression, edge-enhancing anisotropic diffusion, cuboidal subdivision, medical images.

1   Introduction

Even with today's advances in storage capacity and transfer bandwiths, image compression remains an important area of research. In addition to 2-D images, great amounts of volumetric 3-D data is produced from a wide variety of recording sources such as CT or MRI scans. With JPEG 2000 [9] and DICOM [7] for medical imaging, both the 2-D and 3-D setting are dominated by transform-based approaches. However, a new family of image compression algorithms based on partial differential equations (PDE) has recently emerged [1,6,8]. Those methods have successfully challenged and in some cases surpassed the quality of the established codecs. In this paper, we aim to achieve three goals: 1. Introduce the first PDE-based compression codec explicitly designed for 3-D data. 2. Assess its potential in relation to established codecs. 3. Analyse the influence of 3-D diffusion on compression quality.

Related Work. PDE-based approaches [1,6,8] rely on the common idea to store only a small, systematically chosen subset of the image efficiently and reconstruct the missing parts by PDE-based interpolation. Methods based on edge-enhancing diffusion (EED) [1,8] restrict the selection of known data for the sake of storage efficiency and compensate this with the powerful interpolation capacities of EED. Compression using edge information and homogeneous diffusion [6] is mostly efficient on cartoon-like images.

---

* Recommended for submission to YRF2012 by Prof. Joachim Weickert.

J. Weickert, M. Hein, and B. Schiele (Eds.): GCPR 2013, LNCS 8142, pp. 231–236, 2013.

Our 3-D compression algorithm is modelled after R-EED [8], an algorithm that chooses sparse data with a rectangular subdivision scheme and fills in missing image parts with EED-based interpolation. To our best knowledge, PDE-based codecs have not been used for spatial 3-D data before our approach. However, there are video codecs that rely on inpainting techniques [2,5,4,11]. In particular, PDE-based video compression approaches based on [1] were proposed in [2] and [4].

Our Contribution. We extend the *rectangular* 2-D subdivision scheme R-EED [8] to 3-D, thereby proposing the first PDE-based 3-D compression codec. We introduce *cuboidal* subdivision as a natural 3-D extension of R-EED's rectangular subdivision scheme in order to store a sparse subset of the 3-D data. The rest of the image is reconstructed using 3-D EED inpainting. Following R-EED's naming scheme, the new codec is called C-EED. Furthermore, we analyse the influence of the 3-D diffusion step on compression quality by identifying all sources for performance gains of C-EED in comparison to R-EED applied to a sequence of 2-D image slices. Finally, we compare the overall performance of C-EED, its predecessor R-EED and the DICOM standard [7] on medical data.

2   Three-Dimensional EED-Based Inpainting

PDE-based inpainting acts as the foundation of our compression algorithm. In general, inpainting denotes the reconstruction of missing image parts from known data. We exploit this concept for lossy compression by keeping only fractions of the original data and filling in the rest via inpainting. The following sections cover both a continuous model for inpainting as well as the discretisation that we apply in our method.

Continuous Inpainting Model. In the following, we consider 3-D grey value images as sufficiently smooth functions that map image coordinates from the cuboidal image domain $\Omega \subset \mathbb{R}^3$ to a continuous grey value range. The goal of the inpainting process is to use a set of known data, the so-called inpainting mask $M \subset \Omega$, to reconstruct the contents of the inpainting domain $\Omega \setminus M$. Based on its superior performance in 2-D [8] we choose edge-enhancing anisotropic diffusion (EED) [10] as the basis for the inpainting algorithm. EED inpainting is defined by a boundary value problem:

$$
\begin{aligned}
\partial_t u &= \mathrm{div}(\boldsymbol{D}\boldsymbol{\nabla}u) &&\text{on}\quad \Omega \setminus M \times (0,\infty),\\
u(\boldsymbol{x},t) &= f(\boldsymbol{x}) &&\text{on}\quad \partial M \times (0,\infty),\\
\langle \boldsymbol{D}\boldsymbol{\nabla}u, \boldsymbol{n}\rangle &= 0 &&\text{on}\quad \partial\Omega \times (0,\infty).
\end{aligned}
\tag{1}
$$

This system describes the evolution of the inpainted image u under EED with initial data f and mixed boundary conditions: on the image boundaries $\partial\Omega$, Neumann conditions are applied, while the boundary ∂M of the inpainting mask is treated with Dirichlet conditions. Here, $\boldsymbol{\nabla}u$ denotes the spatial gradient and div the spatial divergence operator.

The diffusion tensor $\boldsymbol{D} \in \mathbb{R}^{3\times3}$ defines the characteristic properties of EED: Diffusion is performed only along image edges, not across them. This behaviour is achieved by carefully designing $\boldsymbol{D}$ in terms of its eigenvectors $\boldsymbol{v}_1, \boldsymbol{v}_2, \boldsymbol{v}_3$ and eigenvalues μ_1, μ_2, μ_3. Each eigenvalue determines the amount of diffusion performed in the direction of the corresponding eigenvector. In 2-D, ∇u is perpendicular to the local edge direction. Thus, the relevant directions are defined parallel to ∇u (across the edge) and parallel to ∇u (edge direction). In 3-D, ∇u still defines the direction across the edge. However, diffusion along the edge is performed in the 2-D plane with normal vector ∇u.

$$v_1 \parallel \nabla u_\sigma \text{ with } \mu_1(\nabla u_\sigma) := \frac{1}{\sqrt{1 + \frac{|\nabla u_\sigma|^2}{\lambda^2}}} \tag{2}$$

$$v_2 \perp \nabla u_\sigma, v_3 \perp \nabla u_\sigma, v_2 \perp v_3 \text{ with } \mu_2 = \mu_3 := 1 \tag{3}$$

Equation (3) ensures unrestricted diffusion along the edges. As in [8], diffusion across edges is penalised proportional to the edge detector $|\nabla u_\sigma|^2$ by the Charbonnier diffusivity in Equation (2). The free parameter λ can be used to adjust the edge preservation of EED and thereby the contrast of the diffusion results. The presmoothing of the image u by convolution $u_\sigma := K_\sigma * u$ with a Gaussian kernel K_σ with standard deviation σ robustifies the edge detection.

Discretisation. We discretise the system (1) by a finite difference approximation on a spatiotemporal grid with grid sizes h_x, h_y, h_z and h_t. Solving the resulting equations for the evolved image after one discrete time step yields a so-called explicit scheme which allows to implement EED with a fast explicit diffusion approach [3]. In order to account for real-world images with nonuniform voxel size, we adapt the spatial grid sizes accordingly.

3   The C-EED Codec

Our C-EED algorithm is modeled after the 2-D codec R-EED [8]. Both methods share the common idea of reconstructing the image from a sparse subset of the image data. One of the most prominent changes is the 3-D inpainting described in the previous section. However, the inpainting process alone does not necessarily yield a good reconstruction. The choice of the inpainting mask M is an equally important problem.

Cuboidal Subdivision. Selecting the inpainting mask M is guided by three competing factors: 1. The choice of mask points influences the *quality* of the inpainting results. 2. *Storage efficiency* must be considered. This includes the storage of mask point locations and the influence on efficient grey value storage by entropy coding. 3. The *complexity* of finding the optimal mask for a given compression ratio is large. Paying tribute to all of these factors, the choice of mask points is restricted to an adaptive grid that allows to encode mask point locations in a binary tree. This tree is constructed by a threshold-based subdivision scheme. First, a static point pattern is chosen, in our case the corners and center of the cuboidal image domain. These points are added to the inpainting mask M and used to compute a preliminary reconstruction result. If the reconstruction error exceeds an error threshold E, the current image is split in the middle of its largest side into two cuboidal subimages of equal size. Mask points are added in these subimages according to the point pattern, and the splitting process is repeated for each subimage until all subimages respect the threshold E. Each split is represented by one node of the

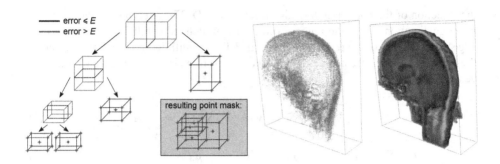

Fig. 1. Cuboidal Subdivision. The schematic representation on the left shows the construction of an inpainting mask with cuboidal subdivision. The two medical volume images are examples for an inpainting mask (middle) and a C-EED reconstruction (right).

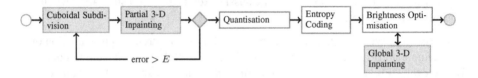

Fig. 2. Encoding with C-EED. The flow chart above describes the C-EED steps performed for image encoding. Highlighted steps mark prominent differences between C-EED and R-EED.

corresponding binary subdivision tree. The error threshold is adapted to the tree depth by the formula $E = a\ell^d$, where d is the tree depth and a and ℓ are free parameters. This subdivision scheme is illustrated by Fig. 1.

Encoding. The additional encoding steps that were not discussed in previous sections are natural extensions of the compressions steps of R-EED [8]. First, a *quantisation* of the grey value domain is performed in order to increase the efficiency of the final entropy coding step. Afterwards, the inpainting mask is computed by *cuboidal subdivision* with inpainting operations that are restricted to subimages. The inpainting quality can be increased further by *brightness optimisations*: grey values of the inpainting mask are modified in order to improve inpainting results. While this introduces an error to the mask points, the quality gain in the inpainting domain significantly outweighs this loss. Finally, the data is stored to the hard disk. The file header contains the image size and the compression parameters EED-contrast λ, number of quantised grey values q and swapping parameter s (see decoding step). Additionally the subdivision tree is saved in binary code. The grey value data is stored losslessly by *entropy-coding*. Note that the encoding procedure in Fig. 2 assumes that all free parameters are given. In practice, all parameters are optimised to achieve results of the highest quality possible.

Decoding. The compression parameters, subdivision tree and grey values are decoded. From these values, the inpainting mask is constructed and with a single inpainting step, the decompressed image is obtained. As a post processing step, an *interpolation swap* can be performed: the role of known and unknown data is inverted and thereby mask

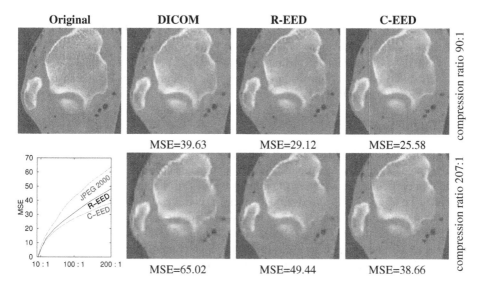

Fig. 3. Images obtained with DICOM, R-EED and C-EED with compression rates close to 90:1 (top) and 207:1 (bottom). The test image (size $256 \times 256 \times 64$) consists of the first 64 slices of a trabular bone CT provided by Wiro Niessen. The images above display the last 2-D slice of the test image. Smaller MSE values are better.

point degradation by quantisation and brightness optimisation can be attenuated. The new inpainting domain consists of spheres with radius s around all mask points.

4   Experiments

Experiment Design. Due to space constraints we present a small representative subset of our experiments with C-EED, R-EED and DICOM [7] on spatial 3-D data. Image quality is assessed with respect to the mean squared error (MSE). For compression with DICOM the most efficient method in the standard, JPEG 2000, is used. The application of 2-D codecs to 3-D data is usually achieved by separation of 3-D data into 2-D slices. On of our main goals is to assess the influence of 3-D EED-based inpainting in comparison to slice-wise inpainting with 2-D EED. In order to isolate the 3-D diffusion's contribution, further sources for efficiency improvements must be incorporated into R-EED: 1. *Header redundancies* appear due to duplicate header data in each compressed 2-D slice. 2. *Global entropy coding* is, in most cases, more efficient than individual coding for each slice. Therefore, all experiments were conducted with a modified version of R-EED that contains all improvements of C-EED except for 3-D EED.

Results. The results in Fig. 3 reveal that quality gaps between the different approaches in terms of the MSE are amplified for increasing compression rates. For medium to high compression rates the quality of DICOM degrades much faster than the PDE-based approaches. In the same range C-EED shows significant advantages over R-EED. Visually, DICOM suffers from heavy block artifacts, while R-EED and C-EED produce smooth results that only lose detail with increasing compression rate. Similar results were observed on all medical test data. On synthetic data with high redundancy in one dimension, C-EED yields improvements over R-EED of up to 50%.

Overall, the experiments demonstrate the application of 3-D inpainting in C-EED is very well suited for the compression of spatial 3-D data and offers significant advantages over R-EED and DICOM.

5   Conclusion

In this paper we introduced the first PDE-based 3-D image compression algorithm and demonstrated its superior performance on 3-D spatial data in comparison to DICOM and R-EED. In particular, we analysed the influence of 3-D diffusion on image quality and verified that it offers significant advantages over 3-D compression based on 2-D diffusion.

In future work, the potential of 3-D diffusion on other 3-D data should be closely investigated. In particular, C-EED should be well suited for seismic data sets with huge file sizes (1 TB and more) where the aim is very high compression rates. Furthermore, the potential of C-EED compression on spatiotemporal data should be investigated, since this could pave the way for competitive PDE-based video codecs.

References

1. Galić, I., Weickert, J., Welk, M., Bruhn, A., Belyaev, A., Seidel, H.P.: Image compression with anisotropic diffusion. Journal of Mathematical Imaging and Vision 31(2-3), 255–269 (2008)
2. Gao, Q.: Low bit rate video compression using inpainting PDEs and optic flow. Master's thesis, Dept. of Mathematics and Computer Science, Saarland University, Germany (2008)
3. Grewenig, S., Weickert, J., Bruhn, A.: From box filtering to fast explicit diffusion. In: Goesele, M., Roth, S., Kuijper, A., Schiele, B., Schindler, K. (eds.) DAGM 2010. LNCS, vol. 6376, pp. 533–542. Springer, Heidelberg (2010)
4. Köstler, H., Stürmer, M., Freundl, C., Rüde, U.: PDE based video compression in real time. Tech. Rep. 07-11, Lehrstuhl für Informatik 10, Univ. Erlangen–Nürnberg, Germany (2007)
5. Liu, D., Sun, X., Wu, F., Li, S., Zhang, Y.Q.: Image compression with edge-based inpainting. IEEE Transactions on Circuits, Systems and Video Technology 17(10), 1273–1286 (2007)
6. Mainberger, M., Weickert, J.: Edge-based image compression with homogeneous diffusion. In: Jiang, X., Petkov, N. (eds.) CAIP 2009. LNCS, vol. 5702, pp. 476–483. Springer, Heidelberg (2009)
7. National Electrical Manufacturers Association: Digital Imaging and Communications in Medicine (DICOM) – Part 5 Data Structures and Encoding. PS 3.5-2004 (2004)
8. Schmaltz, C., Weickert, J., Bruhn, A.: Beating the quality of JPEG 2000 with anisotropic diffusion. In: Denzler, J., Notni, G., Süße, H. (eds.) DAGM 2009. LNCS, vol. 5748, pp. 452–461. Springer, Heidelberg (2009)
9. Taubman, D.S., Marcellin, M.W. (eds.): JPEG 2000: Image Compression Fundamentals, Standards and Practice. Kluwer, Boston (2002)
10. Weickert, J.: Scale-space properties of nonlinear diffusion filtering with a diffusion tensor. Tech. Rep. 110, Laboratory of Technomathematics, University of Kaiserslautern, Germany (1994)
11. Zhu, C., Sun, X., Wu, F., Li, H.: Video coding with spatio-temporal texture synthesis and edge-based inpainting. In: Proc. 2008 IEEE International Conference on Multimedia and Expo, Hannover, Germany, pp. 813–816 (2008)

Automatic Level Set Based Cerebral Vessel Segmentation and Bone Removal in CT Angiography Data Sets

Stephanie Behrens

Department of Simulation and Graphics, University of Magdeburg, Germany

Abstract. Computed tomography angiography (CTA) data sets without hardware based bone subtraction have the disadvantage of containing the bone structures which particularly overlap with vessel intensities; therefore vessel segmentation is hampered. Segmentation methods developed for CTA without bones can not handle these data sets and manual cerebral vessel segmentation is not realizable in clinical routines. Therefore, an automatic intensity based cerebral bone removal with subsequent edge based level set vessel segmentation method is presented in this work. [1]

1 Introduction

A continuously increasing incidence of vascular diseases implies a rising quantity of angiographic data sets (MRA - magnetic resonance angiography, CTA) and therewith a time consuming evaluation for radiologists and medical scientists. Manual extraction of vessels in a 3d data set is an arduous and imprecise process. Therefore, an accurate and automated vessel segmentation method would be a considerable assistance for clinical diagnosis, quantitative analysis of vascular diseases and computer-assisted detection (CAD), but designing an automatic segmentation method for CTA data sets is still a challenging problem due to the complex structure of the vascular system, noise, gaps in object boundaries and an overlapping intensity distribution of vessels to other structures.

Using a simple threshold or region growing based technique results in good vessel segmentations in MRA data sets, though due to by contrast agent enhanced vessels an intensity overlap between small bones, cartilage and vessels occurs, whereby these techniques are inapplicable for CTA data sets. Therefore bone removal as preprocessing step is indispensable for an explicit background suppression.

Hardware based methods for bone removal like presented in [7] and their disadvantages are widely discussed in literature, though only a few approaches for software based bone masking were introduced [5],[6]. Kanitsar et al.[5] present a system for peripheral bone removal by dividing the data sets into "slabs" and filter them with three thresholds subsequent by a connectivity-analysis. In normal cases there are no intensities overlaps due to the bone thickness and

---

[1] Recommended for submission to YRF2012 by Klaus D. Tönnies.

J. Weickert, M. Hein, and B. Schiele (Eds.): GCPR 2013, LNCS 8142, pp. 237–242, 2013.

they vary only marginal in size, shape and thickness. Therefore, peripheral bone removal is simplified compared to intra cranial bone segmentation.

Another approach was presented by Kostopoulos et al. [6]. A two level decision tree was designed: first bones were distinguished from "vessel & parenchyma" followed by a differentiation between vasculature and parenchyma. The classification is based on a manually trained pixel-based classification algorithm. Training of a classifier algorithm is a tedious and protracted work and an adequate amount of samples is indispensable. Questionable is a successful training and classification for slices containing parts of the skull base, since the paper presents only a result for slices above the skull base.

Simple methods like thresholds, region growing or edge detection require homogeneous objects and closed object boundaries what is not given in CTA data sets. In contrast more complex methods like e.g. statistical models necessitate extensive apriori knowledge and user interaction. The software based approach presented in this paper will give reliable results for automatic bone removal in CTA data sets even in areas around the skull base. Due to the aforementioned properties of vasculature deformable models are the best choice for the use in vessel segmentation. Many approaches therefore can be found in literature like in [1]; [3], but level set based techniques ([8]) offer a multiplicity of advantages, the most important one being a topology-free representation. In Manniesing et al. [7] a level set algorithm is used for vessel segmentation with prior hardware based bone masking. Two intensity based speed functions were constructed for classifying edges to detect vessels. Using data sets with subtracted bones and by user placed seed points reduces the complexity for a vessel segmentation algorithm, in contrast in this work a solution for automatic software based bone removal subsequent by vessel segmentation is presented.

2 Method

The vessel segmentation method is divided into three steps: 1. bone removal, 2. initial model construction, 3. speed function calculation and level set vessel segmentation.

2.1 Bone Removal

The challenge in CTA bone removal is the intensity overlap of around 200 HU values of bony structures (200HU up to 4000HU) and contrast enhanced blood vessels (100-400HU). Especially the area around the skull base contains a multiplicity of small bones and cartilage where the intensity overlap reaches its maximum. Furthermore, vasculature can be located close to bones and be completely enclosed by them so that their rim potentially disappears. Reducing this behaviour is desirable and a requirement for the level set method. The preprocessing is organised in three sub steps: 1. edge enhancement, 2. bone segmentation and 3. bone masking.

In the first step we aim to enhance light edges for a simplification of the distinction between small bones and blood vessels. The edges are enhanced by morphological gradients which can be manipulated by a structural element (SE) [9]:

$$p_{n_{SE}}B = \delta_{n_{SE}}B - \omega_{n_{SE}}B \qquad (1)$$

the $\delta_{n_{SE}}B$ describing the dilation with a SE of size n and $\omega_{n_{SE}}B$ defines the erosion of size n. Afterwards, an area closing filter is applied to fill the areas inside the bones or vessels.

In the second step the bones are segmented on $p_{n_{SE}}B$. For bone segmentation a classification of three different intensity overlapping types of tissues is required: vessels, bones or cartilage and background. Using a simple threshold method results in under-/ or over segmentation due to the intensity overlap. This problem can be solved by the double threshold technique DBLT [9]. Four threshold values in two ranges are set: t_1 and t_4 as the wide range containing all intensities of the desired object and t_2 and t_3 forming the narrow range with the overlapping intensities:

$$DBLT_{[t_1 \leq t_2 \leq t_3 \leq t_4]}(f) = R^{\delta}_{T_{[t_1,t_4](f)}}[T_{[t_2,t_3]}(f)], \qquad (2)$$

with f as input and $R^{\delta}_T(f)$ as morphological reconstruction. Bone and rim of bone voxels can be thereby segmented without affecting the blood vessel voxels. In the last step, the input is masked with the segmented bones, so that vessels and background remains.

2.2   Vessel Segmentation

The initial model contains blood vessels and small parts of bony structures. Since no additionally manual placed seed points are used, it is important that the initial level set contains a rough segmentation of the cerebral vasculature to guarantee that the level set converges to a accurate solution.

The remaining non-vessel tissue features similar intensity values like the vessel voxels whereby an intensity based level set method is inapplicable and due to the created explicit object/background classification, an edge based level set approach was chosen. The level set vessel segmentation is divided in two steps: 1. edge preserving diffusion filtering for noise reduction; 2. Speed function construction and level set calculation.

The canny edge operator has been proven usefully to detect image edges, even light ones, independent from orientation or thickness. Small vessels and their rims can be therefore detected, whereby the canny filter the is best choice for this application and is applied to the diffusion filtered data set for speed function calculation. Speed functions are commonly build of three terms: the advection term to regulate the expansion in direction of extracted image features; the propagation term to control the expansion speed and the curvature term for a smooth solution. The used speed function was chosen in the following form:

$$I_{Canny(t)} = -\alpha(DT\nabla DT)\nabla I_{Canny} - \beta DT \, |\nabla I_{Canny}| + \epsilon \kappa_M \, |\nabla I_{Canny}|, \qquad (3)$$

whereby I_{Canny} represents the canny edge volume, t the time step, DT a distance transformation, κ_M a mean curvature and α, β, ϵ are weighting constants.

The DT inside the advection term regulates the distance between the actual level set and detected canny edges and represents a stopping criterion. For bridging gaps the DT is included into the propagation term as well. Starting from the initial level set the surface expands in the direction of the detected canny edges, whereupon the speed will be highly reduced at the edges. The propagation term prevents a leakage of the surface where no edges have been detected and is therefore, able to link associated vessels. Thus, the rough vessel segmentation can be optimised.

3   Parametrisation and Evaluation

The presented method was evaluated on 6 clinical CTA data sets. Comparison was restricted to the relevant parts and done on 20-40 slices containing parts of the jawbones and skull base (jb) and parts of the Circle of Willis (CoW). For evaluation 3 CTA sets were manually segmented by an experienced user and 3 data sets were registered to an MRA data set, that was manually segmented by thresholding. Ground truth is not available for clinical data, therefore manual segmentation was chosen, though the accuracy is strongly dependent on the user. In many cases the user segments over the viewable rim of vessels.

The method was implemented with ITK [4] functions and all data sets were tested with a set of default and optimised parameter values (for parameter details, see section 2). The optimised values were found within experimental tests. For preprocessing the size of the structural element (n_{SE}) and the size for the area closing filter λ have to be set. By default t_1, t_2, t_3 and t_4 were set to the average minimal values for bones ($t_1 = 250$), the average minimal values for bone boundaries ($t_2 = 350$), the average maximum bone boundary values ($t_3 = 800$) and the maximum intensity value of each data set ($t_4 = max(I)$). The speed

Table 1. Parameter range for preprocessing and level set segmentation on CTA data sets

Modality	Preprocessing					Canny detection		Level set function		
	n_{SE}	λ	t_1	t_2	t_3	σ^2	thr_c	α	β	Iso
CTA 1 (jb)	2	150-360	230-390	290-450	600-800	0.05-0.1	5-50	-3-(-8)	-7-(-15)	110-250
CTA 1 (CoW)	3	300-750	250-380	350-550	800-120	0.05-0.08	5-45	-4-(-8)	-8-(-15)	127-220

function calculation of the level set segmentation is based on the canny threshold value thr_c [2](controlling the length of the detected edges) and the variance σ^2 (size of smoothing filter). The values for $\sigma^2 = 0.05$ and $thr_c = 20$ were chosen to detect smaller vessels as well. According to a good initial model and a sensitive canny filter the constants α and β were set to -8 and -10. The level set

---

[2] Only the upper threshold has to be set, the lower threshold is automatically set $thr_L = thr_U/2$.

segmentation is controlled by the number of iterations $\#It = 100$ and in ITK an iso-surface Iso value has to be set which defines the relevant intensities. With a default value of 137 even small vessels will be considered. All parameter values are summarized in table 1.

The dice coefficient and the conformity score [2] were used as evaluation measures, whereby the conformity score measures the quantity of false segmented voxels at a fraction of correct segmented voxels. The results are given in table 2. Visual inspection showed that the majority of vessels were segmented correctly and only a small amount of bony structures were left (see 1(a) and 1(b)). The double threshold method worked well for data sets with vessel HU between 200 and 400, finding the suitable threshold values for higher intensities is challenging. Bones enclosing vessels can be segmented, if vessel and surrounding bone intensities differ less than 50 HU, vessels were segmented as well. Optimised parameter values gave in all cases better results due to a higher amount of segmented jawbones and remained vessels.

Table 2. Evaluation results for optimal parameter in %

	CTA 1		CTA 2		CTA 3		CTA 4		CTA 5		CTA 6		MRA 1	
	Jb	CoW	Jb	CoW	Jb	CoW	Jb	CoW	Jb	CoW	Jb	CoW	Jb	CoW
Dice	50	61	53	70	61	70	46	2,8	12	53	24	42	73	42
Conformity	-200	-123	-176	-84	-126	-83	-231	-6800	-1300	-171	-609	-270	-70	-179

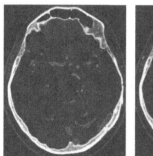
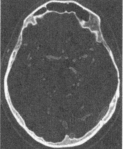
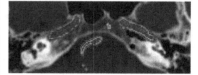

(a) Manual segmentation.   (b) Level set segmentation.   (c) Comparison of manual and level set segmentation.

Fig. 1. Comparison of level set and manual segmentation on CTA slices

The arduousness of manual segmentation reduced the evaluation results (see figure 1(c)). Some segmentation errors were induced by isolated thin bony structures, due to a high intensity overlap with vessel voxels and a missing connection to bones. Additionally, diffuse edges occurred in the registered data sets hampers the canny edge detection and the level set expansion. High vessel HU values caused by stenosis or stents increases the intensity overlap and complicates the initial model construction (like in CTA 6). The low concordance of CTA 5 is based on unusual low HU vessel values whereby the reference contains only an aneurysma.

4   Conclusion

The focus of this work was the development of a reliable bone removal technique for CTA data sets and a vessel segmentation. This was done by an intensity based preprocessing using the double threshold operator. The vessel segmentation is thereby simplified and an edge based level set vessel segmentation is used which produces good results. The presented method works automatically and by using the default parameter no user interaction is needed and parameter optimisation leads to slightly better results. The method can be used for MRA vessel segmentation as well. Automated parameter estimation would be desirable for the future. For the removal of isolated small-sized bony structures and the detection of pathological vessels apriori knowledge or user interaction would be a suitable method.

References

1. van Bemmel, C., Spreeuwers, L., Viergever, M., Niessen, W.: Level-set-based artery-vein separation in blood pool agent CE-MR angiograms. IEEE Transactions on Medical Imaging 22(10), 1224–1234 (2003)
2. Bogunovic, H., Pozo, J., Villa-Uriol, M., et al.: Automated segmentation of cerebral vasculature with aneurysms in 3dra and tof-mra using geodesic active regions: An evaluation study. Medical Physics-New York-Institute of Physics 38(1) (2011)
3. Deschamps, T., Schwartz, P., Trebotich, D., Colella, P., Saloner, D., Malladi, R.: Vessel segmentation and blood flow simulation using level-sets and embedded boundary methods. International Congress Series, vol. 1268, pp. 75–80. Elsevier (2004)
4. Ibanez, L., Schroeder, W., Ng, L., Cates, J., et al.: The itk software guide. Kitware Inc. (2005)
5. Kanitsar, A., Fleischmann, D., Wegenkittl, R., et al.: Computed tomography angiography: a case study of peripheral vessel investigation. In: Proceedings of the Conference on Visualization 2001, pp. 477–480. IEEE Computer Society (2001)
6. Kostopoulos, S., Glotsos, D., Kagadis, G., et al.: Development of a brain blood vessel segmentation method in ct-angiography (2005)
7. Manniesing, R., Velthuis, B., van Leeuwen, M., et al.: Level set based cerebral vasculature segmentation and diameter quantification in ct angiography. Medical Image Analysis 10(2), 200–214 (2006)
8. Osher, S., Sethian, J.: Fronts propagating with curvature-dependent speed: algorithms based on Hamilton-Jacobi formulations. Journal of Computational Physics 79(1), 12–49 (1988)
9. Soille, P.: Morphological image analysis: principles and applications. Springer-Verlag New York, Inc., Secaucus (2003)

Action Recognition with HOG-OF Features⋆

Florian Baumann

Institut für Informationsverarbeitung,
Leibniz Universität Hannover,
{last name}@tnt.uni-hannover.de

Abstract. In this paper a simple and efficient framework for single human action recognition is proposed. In two parallel processing streams, motion information and static object appearances are gathered by introducing a frame-by-frame learning approach. For each processing stream a Random Forest classifier is separately learned. The final decision is determined by combining both probability functions. The proposed recognition system is evaluated on the KTH data set for single human action recognition with original training/testing splits and a 5-fold cross validation. The results demonstrate state-of-the-art accuracies with an overall training time of 30 seconds on a standard workstation.

1 Introduction

Human action recognition is divided into human actions, human-human interactions, human-object interactions and group activities [1]. In this paper, we address the problem of recognizing actions performed by a single person like boxing, clapping, waving and walking, running, jogging. See Figure 1.
Aggarwal and Ryoo categorize the developed methods for human activity recognition into single-layered and hierarchical approaches. These approaches are further divided into several subcategories [1]. Poppe suggests to divide the methods in global and local approaches [12]. Global approaches construe the image as a whole leading to a sensitive representation to noise, occlusions or changes in viewpoint and background. Local approaches extract regional features, leading to a more accurate representation, invariant against viewpoint and background changes.

Contribution. In this paper, different feature types, such as HOG and optical flow features are used to separately learn two Random Forest classifiers which are then combined for final action recognition. HOGs are predestinated for gathering static information, since they are well-established at the task of human detection [4] while the optical flow is used for extracting motion information. Both features are local approaches, leading to an accurate representation, invariant against illumination, contrast and background changes.

Related Work. Earlier work was done by Mauthner et al. [10]. The authors use HOG-descriptors for appearance and motion detection. The feature vectors are represented by NMF coefficients and concatenated. An SVM is used to learn the classifier. Similar to this work, Seo and Milanfar [16] also use an one-shot learning method. Recent

---

⋆ This work has been partially funded by the ERC within the starting grant Dynamic MinVIP.

J. Weickert, M. Hein, and B. Schiele (Eds.): GCPR 2013, LNCS 8142, pp. 243–248, 2013.
© Springer-Verlag Berlin Heidelberg 2013

works that combine HOG- and HOF-features for single human action recognition were introduced by Wang et al. [19] and Laptev et al. [7]. Both use an SVM to recognize patterns. In contrast, we use HOG descriptors and OF trajectories to learn two independent Random Forest classifiers.

Fig. 1. Example images of KTH dataset [15]. The dataset contains six actions performed by 25 people under different conditions.

2   Approach

For human action recognition the use of static information as well as motion information is necessary to obtain robust classification results. In order to gather all information static-features from each frame and motion-features between frames are extracted. Two Random Forest classifiers are separately learned to find patterns.

2.1   Features

Frame-by-Frame Learning.   Static appearance information is extracted using histograms of oriented gradients. HOGs are well-established for human detection and mostly independent regarding illumination and contrast changes. First described in 2005 by Dalal und Triggs [4], HOGs became increasingly popular for different tasks of visual object detection. The computation proceeds as follows: to obtain a gradient image, a filter with [-1, 0, 1], without smoothing is applied to the image. For the computation of the HOG-Descriptor the gradient image is divided into 16x16 pixel non-overlapping blocks of four 8x8 pixel cells [4]. Next, the orientations of each cell are used for a weighted vote into 9 bins within a range of $0° - 180°$. Overlapping spatial blocks are contrast normalized and concatenated to build the final descriptor.

Motion Recognition. The optical flow is used to gather motion information. It bases on the assumption that points at the same location have constant intensities over a short duration [6]:

$$I(x, y, t) = I(x + \delta x, y + \delta y, t + \delta t), \tag{1}$$

where $I(x, y, t)$ is the image patch, displaced in time δt with distance $(\delta x, \delta y)$ in the x-/y-direction. The proposed framework comprises the method of Lucas Kanade optical flow [8] which bases on Equation 1 but additionally assumes that the intensities are constant in a small neighborhood. To compute the optical flow descriptor, strong corners in two consecutive frames at t and $t+1$ are detected with the Shi-Tomasi corner detector [17]. Next, tracking of these feature points is realized by a pyramidal Lucas Kanade tracker [2].

2.2   Random Forest by Leo Breiman [3]

A Random Forest consists of CART-like decision trees that are independently constructed on a bootstrap sample. Compared to other ensemble learning algorithms, i.e. boosting [5] that build a flat tree structure of decision stumps, a Random Forest uses an ensemble of decision trees and is multi-class capable. A completed classifier consists of several trees $1 \leq t \leq T$ in which the class probabilities, estimated by majority voting, are used to calculate the sample's label $y(x)$ with respect to a feature vector x:

$$y(x) = \operatorname*{argmax}_{c} \left(\frac{1}{T} \sum_{t=1}^{T} I_{h_t(x)=c} \right) \tag{2}$$

The decision function $h_t(x)$ provides the classification of one tree to a class c with the indicator function I:

$$I_{h_t(x)=c} = \begin{cases} 1, & h_t(x) = c, \\ 0, & \text{otherwise.} \end{cases} \tag{3}$$

Classification. A sample is classified by passing it down each tree until a leaf node is reached. A classification result is assigned to each leaf node and the final decision is determined by taking the class having the most votes, see Equation (2).

2.3   Combination

For each feature-type a Random Forest is separately learned to yield independent classifiers. The HOGs are used to learn a frame-by-frame classifier, so that a feature consists of a histogram obtained from each frame. A majority vote of all frames is leading to the sample's label while the class probabilities are averaged. Optical flow trajectories are calculated between two consecutive frames while a feature is constructed by concatenating the trajectories of all frames. Figure 2 shows an overview about the implemented framework. The final decision is determined by combining the class probabilities $\Pr(A_i)$ obtained by the HOG classifier and $\Pr(B_i)$ obtained by the optical flow classifier with the product law[1]: $\Pr(A_i \cap B_i) = \Pr(A_i) \Pr(B_i)$.

---

[1] With the assumption that events A_i and B_i are independent.

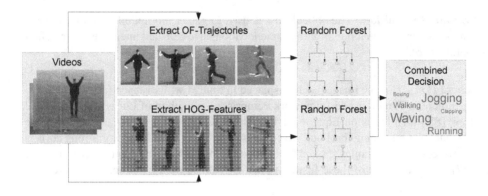

Fig. 2. Overview about the recognition system. In two parallel units static-features and motion-features are computed. For each feature-type a Random Forest classifier is separately learned. The final decision is determined by combining both classifiers using the product law.

3   Experimental Results

The proposed method is applied to the task of human action recognition. The goal is to recognize actions in several environments, under different illumination conditions and performed by different subjects. For the evaluation a well-established, publicly available dataset is used and the results are compared with several state-of-the-art methods.

3.1   KTH Action Dataset [15]

The KTH is a well-established, publicly available dataset for single human action recognition, consisting of 600 video files from 25 subjects performing six actions (walking, jogging, running, boxing, waving, clapping). Similar to [11], a fixed position bounding box with a temporal window of 32 frames is selected, based on annotations by Lui [9]. Presumably, a smaller number of frames is sufficient [14]. Furthermore, the original training/testing splits from [15] as well as a 5-fold cross validation strategy are used.

Jogging, running, walking, waving and clapping are perfectly learned but boxing and clapping/waving are confused. Table 1 compares the proposed framework with several state-of-the-art methods. Figure 3(a) shows the confusion matrix for 5-fold cross validation. The method achieves state-of-the-art results. Figure 3(b) shows the results for original training/testing splits. The proposed framework achieves competing results. Presumably due to the smaller training set the results are more worse than the 5-fold cross validation results. The overall training time is about 30 seconds, on a standard notebook with a single-threaded C++ implementation.

Table 1. Accuracies (%) in comparison of the proposed framework to state-of-the-art methods on the KTH dataset

Method	Validation	Accuracy (%)
Schindler and Gool [14]	5-fold	87,98
Zhang et al. [20]	5-fold	94,60
Proposed method	**5-fold**	**96,44**
Laptev et al. [15]	Original split	91,80
Zhang et al. [20]	Original split	94,00
Wang et al. [18]	Original split	94,20
Proposed method	**Original split**	**94,31**
O'Hara and Draper [11]	Original split	97,90
Sadanand and Corso [13]	Original split	98,20

(a)

	box	clap	wave	jog	run	walk
box	0.85	0.05	0.1	0	0	0
clap	0	1	0	0	0	0
wave	0	0	1	0	0	0
jog	0	0	0	1	0	0
run	0	0	0	0	1	0
walk	0	0	0	0	0	1

(b)

	box	clap	wave	jog	run	walk
box	1	0	0	0	0	0
clap	0.11	0.80	0.09	0	0	0
wave	0	0.12	0.88	0	0	0
jog	0	0	0	1	0	0
run	0	0	0	0	0.98	0.02
walk	0	0	0	0	0	1

Fig. 3. Confusion matrix for the KTH dataset. (a): 5-fold cross validation, (b) Original splits

4 Conclusion

In this paper a simple and efficient framework for single human action recognition is proposed. Optical flow features are used to gather motion information between frames while static object information is extracted by using histogram of oriented gradients. With a frame-by-frame learning approach two Random Forest classifiers are separately built and the final decision is determined by combining both class probabilities. The proposed framework is evaluated using two validation strategies on the well-known, publicly available KTH dataset for single human action recognition. The results demonstrate state-of-the-art accuracies while obtaining an overall training time of 30 seconds on a standard workstation.

References

1. Aggarwal, J., Ryoo, M.: Human activity analysis: A review. ACM Computing Surveys 43(3), 16:1–16:43 (2011)

2. Bouguet, J.Y.: Pyramidal implementation of the lucas kanade feature tracker. Intel Corporation (2000)
3. Breiman, L.: Random forests. In: Machine Learning, vol. 45, pp. 5–32 (2001)
4. Dalal, N., Triggs, B.: Histograms of oriented gradients for human detection. In: IEEE Conference on Computer Vision and Pattern Recognition (CVPR), vol. 1, pp. 886–893 (2005)
5. Freund, Y., Schapire, R.E.: Experiments with a new boosting algorithm. In: Proceedings of the Thirteenth International Conference on Machine Learning, pp. 148–156. IEEE (1996)
6. Horn, B.K., Schunck, B.G.: Determining optical flow. Artificial Intelligence 17 (1981)
7. Laptev, I., Marszalek, M., Schmid, C., Rozenfeld, B.: Learning realistic human actions from movies. In: IEEE Conference on Computer Vision and Pattern Recognition (CVPR) (2008)
8. Lucas, B.D., Kanade, T., et al.: An iterative image registration technique with an application to stereo vision. In: Proceedings of the 7th International Joint Conference on Artificial intelligence (1981)
9. Lui, Y.M., Beveridge, J., Kirby, M.: Action classification on product manifolds. In: IEEE Conference on Computer Vision and Pattern Recognition (CVPR), pp. 833–839 (2010)
10. Mauthner, T., Roth, P.M., Bischof, H.: Instant action recognition. In: Salberg, A.-B., Hardeberg, J.Y., Jenssen, R. (eds.) SCIA 2009. LNCS, vol. 5575, pp. 1–10. Springer, Heidelberg (2009)
11. O'Hara, S., Draper, B.: Scalable action recognition with a subspace forest. In: IEEE Conference on Computer Vision and Pattern Recognition (CVPR), pp. 1210–1217 (2012)
12. Poppe, R.: A survey on vision-based human action recognition. Image and Vision Computing 28(6), 976–990 (2010)
13. Sadanand, S., Corso, J.J.: Action bank: A high-level representation of activity in video. In: IEEE Conference on Computer Vision and Pattern Recognition (CVPR) (2012)
14. Schindler, K., Van Gool, L.: Action snippets: How many frames does human action recognition require? In: IEEE Conference on Computer Vision and Pattern Recognition (CVPR), pp. 1–8 (2008)
15. Schuldt, C., Laptev, I., Caputo, B.: Recognizing human actions: A local svm approach. In: Proceedings of the 17th International Conference on Pattern Recognition (ICPR), vol. 3, pp. 32–36 (2004)
16. Seo, H.J., Milanfar, P.: Action recognition from one example. IEEE Transactions on Pattern Analysis and Machine Intelligence 33(5), 867–882 (May)
17. Shi, J., Tomasi, C.: Good features to track. In: IEEE Conference on Computer Vision and Pattern Recognition (CVPR), pp. 593–600. IEEE (1994)
18. Wang, H., Klaser, A., Schmid, C., Liu, C.L.: Action recognition by dense trajectories. In: IEEE Conference on Computer Vision and Pattern Recognition (CVPR), pp. 3169–3176 (2011)
19. Wang, H., Ullah, M.M., Kläser, A., Laptev, I., Schmid, C.: Evaluation of local spatio-temporal features for action recognition. In: British Machine Vision Conference (BMVC) (2009)
20. Zhang, Y., Liu, X., Chang, M.-C., Ge, W., Chen, T.: Spatio-temporal phrases for activity recognition. In: Fitzgibbon, A., Lazebnik, S., Perona, P., Sato, Y., Schmid, C. (eds.) ECCV 2012, Part III. LNCS, vol. 7574, pp. 707–721. Springer, Heidelberg (2012)

Image Based 6-DOF Camera Pose Estimation with Weighted RANSAC 3D*

Johannes Wetzel

Fraunhofer Institute of Optronics, System Technologies and Image Exploitation
Fraunhoferstr. 1, 76131 Karlsruhe, Germany

Abstract. In this work an approach for image based 6-DOF pose estimation, with respect to a given 3D point cloud model, is presented. We use 3D annotated training views of the model from which we extract natural 2D features, which can be matched to the query image 2D features. In the next step typically the Perspective-N-Point Problem in combination with the popular RANSAC algorithm on the given 2D-3D point correspondences is used, to estimate the 6-D pose of the camera in respect to the model. We propose a novel extension of the RANSAC algorithm, named *w-RANSAC 3D*, which uses known 3D information to weight each match individually. The evaluation shows that w-RANSAC 3D leads to a more robust pose estimation while needing significantly less iterations.

Keywords: Camera Pose Estimation, Tracking, RANSAC, PnP.

1 Introduction

Determining accurate six degree-of-freedom (6-DOF) pose of a camera in respect to the environment is a vital task for many computer vision applications, such as Augmented Reality (AR). We focus on image based marker-less, inside-out-tracking approaches which are based on a point cloud as world model. Gordon and Lowe [5] use structure-from-motion techniques to build a world model and propose a marker-less pose estimation based on natural image features (SIFT [11]). Arth et al.[1] focus on pose estimation of smart phones in respect to huge urban areas. At run-time level a panorama image is stitched on the smart phone. Based on natural image features (SURF [2]) the panorama is matched to the world model. One disadvantage of this approach is that the observer can not change his position during the creation of the panorama image. Our approach is inspired by the work of Irschara et al. [7], who present a method for pose estimation in respect to a sparse structure-from-motion point cloud. Each point in the world model point cloud is associated to a set of 2D SIFT features. These 2D features are extracted from original images of the environment as well as from synthetic projections out of the world model. For final pose estimation the perspective-3-point problem [6] combined with RANSAC [3] is applied. In

---

* Recommended for submission to YRF2013 by Prof. Dr.-Ing. Astrid Laubenheimer.

J. Weickert, M. Hein, and B. Schiele (Eds.): GCPR 2013, LNCS 8142, pp. 249–254, 2013.

contrast to [7] we apply the perspective-n-point problem (PnP) as well as the P3P problem. There are several iterative approaches to solve the PnP like [10],[12] and problem independent meta-heuristics like the *Levenberg-Marquardt-Algorithm*. There are also closed-form solutions like [9],[14] for the PnP and [8],[4] for the P3P, which do not need an initial pose guess. For model estimation we propose an extension of the weighted RANSAC [15] method, named w-RANSAC 3D.

2   System Overview

In the following section we present our approach for the image based 6-DOF pose estimation. Initially the system gets trained with a given point cloud model $PC_M \subset \mathbb{R}^3$ of the environment. This point cloud may be obtained using sensors like the Kinect or stereo approaches. A set V_t of 3D annotated training views v_t is taken from the model by simply projecting the 3D points $\boldsymbol{P}_M \in PC_M$ to a virtual camera sensor. The virtual camera is rotated around the vertical axes with $30°$, since common feature descriptors like SIFT and SURF are robust against off-image plane rotations of approximately $30°$ [13]. For each pixel of the 3D annotated training views $v_t \in V_t$ the mapping $f(u, v) \mapsto \boldsymbol{P}_M(X, Y, Z)$ maps a pixel to its corresponding point $\boldsymbol{P}_M$ in the world. Furthermore a set F_t of training feature descriptors is extracted from all training views V_t. This means each feature descriptor $\boldsymbol{D}_t \in F_t$ can be clearly mapped to a world point $\boldsymbol{P}_M$.

To estimate the pose of the camera by a given query image v_q a set F_q of natural 2D feature descriptors is extracted from v_q. These query features are matched against the pre-build training features F_t to get 2D-3D point correspondences, which are used to solve the PnP problem. To get the 2D-3D point correspondences between a pixel $\boldsymbol{p}_q \in v_q$ from the query image and a world point $\boldsymbol{P}_M$, a brute-force approach finds for every query descriptor $\boldsymbol{D}_q \in F_q$ the best matching training descriptor $\boldsymbol{D}_t \in F_t$. The quality of a match $\boldsymbol{D}_q \leftrightarrow \boldsymbol{D}_t$ is determined by the euclidean norm $d = \|\boldsymbol{D}_q - \boldsymbol{D}_t\|$ of the descriptor vectors. Every correspondence $\boldsymbol{D}_q \leftrightarrow \boldsymbol{D}_t$ implies a correspondence $\boldsymbol{p}_q \leftrightarrow \boldsymbol{P}_M$ between a query image pixel and its corresponding point in world coordinates. To reduce computation time we take only the n best matches into account, given by

$$M_{2D-3D} = \{(\boldsymbol{p}_q, \boldsymbol{P}_M), \dots\} \text{ with } |M_{2D-3D}| = n. \tag{1}$$

To estimate the extrinsic parameters of the camera we solve the perspective-N-point problem in a two-phase approach:

(1) **Model estimation:** To be robust against outliers we use the model estimator RANSAC [3] in combination with the P3P implementation from Gao et al.[4] to estimate a consensus set M'_{2D-3D} of 2D-3D point correspondences and a first approximation of the extrinsic parameters $\boldsymbol{t}', \boldsymbol{r}'$.

(2) **Iterative optimization:** A Levenberg-Marquard-optimization is initialized with the given extrinsic parameter guess $\boldsymbol{t}', \boldsymbol{r}'$ and the set M'_{2D-3D} of consistent point correspondences to iteratively optimize the extrinsic parameters.

In the best case, all outliers have been removed in step (1) and step (2) estimates an accurate solution based on all $n = |M'_{2D-3D}|$ robust point correspondences.

3   w-RANSAC 3D

Since the set M_{2D-3D} in general contains a lot of outliers, estimating a good first pose guess can be a challenging task. Based on the weighted RANSAC (w-RANSAC) by Zhang et al.[15], we propose a novel extension of the RANSAC algorithm, named *w-RANSAC 3D*, which uses known 3D information to weight each match individually. Zhang et al. propose that in a w-RANSAC iteration a match $m \in M$ is chosen by the probability

$$P(m) = \frac{w(m)}{\sum_{x \in M} w(x)} \qquad (2)$$

while $w(m)$ is anti proportional to the distance d of two matching descriptors. The idea of our approach is to check for every match m if the pixel in the query view can be found on multiple overlapping training views, while referring to the same point in the world model. If this is true it is very likely that the match m fits well to the model. Thus this match gets a strong weight.

Based on this heuristic we propose a more advanced weight function $w(m) \mapsto \mathbb{R}^+$ (see Eq. 7) to determine how good a match fits to the world model. Therefore we first map a query descriptor not only to his best matching training descriptor, but to his k-best matching descriptors. A Match $m \in M$ is then defined as the (2k+2)-tuple

$$m = \left(\boldsymbol{D}_q, \boldsymbol{p}_q, \ \boldsymbol{D}_t^0, \dots, \boldsymbol{D}_t^{k-1}, \ \boldsymbol{P}_M^0, \dots, \boldsymbol{P}_M^{k-1} \right) \qquad (3)$$

while $\boldsymbol{D}_q$ and $\boldsymbol{p}_q$ are the descriptor and the corresponding pixel in the query image. Furthermore $\boldsymbol{D}_t^0, \dots, \boldsymbol{D}_t^{k-1} \in F_t$ are the training feature descriptors of the best k matches $\boldsymbol{D}_q \leftrightarrow \boldsymbol{D}_t^j$, while $\boldsymbol{D}_t^j$ refers to the j best matching descriptor. Respectively $\boldsymbol{P}_M^j \in \{\boldsymbol{P}_M^0, \dots, \boldsymbol{P}_M^{k-1}\}$ refers to corresponding world coordinates of the j-best matching feature descriptor. The mapping $v : F_t \mapsto V$ maps a training descriptor $\boldsymbol{D}_t \in F_t$ to the corresponding view $v_t \in V$, from which the descriptor is extracted. The so called *Lowe's Ratio* [11] is calculated for every j-best matching descriptor as $d_r^j = \frac{d^0}{d^j}$ where $d^j = \|\boldsymbol{D}_q - \boldsymbol{D}_t^j\|$ is the euclidean norm between a query descriptor and its j-best matching training descriptor. To get an absolute proportion of the quality of the 2D-2D matching we normalize the distance d_r^j to $d_N^j \in [0..1]$. To determine if two world points are close to each other in 3D space the euclidean norm $d_{3D}^j = \|\boldsymbol{P}_M^0 - \boldsymbol{P}_M^j\|$ is used.

Depending from which training view the training descriptors $\boldsymbol{D}_t^j$ are extracted, the weight function is divided into different parts which are represented by the characteristic variable $c_j \in \{0,1\}$. Let $j \in [0, \dots, k-1]$ then for the special case $j = 0$:

$$c_0 = \begin{cases} 1, & v(\boldsymbol{D}_t^0) = v(\boldsymbol{D}_t^1), \\ 0, & \text{else.} \end{cases} \qquad (4)$$

and for $j \in [1, \ldots, k-1]$:

$$V_j = \left\{ v(\boldsymbol{D}_t^0), \ldots, v(\boldsymbol{D}_t^j) \right\} \tag{5}$$

$$c_j = \begin{cases} 1, & |V_j| = j+1 \\ 0, & \text{else.} \end{cases} \tag{6}$$

Hence c_0 is true if the best and the second-best descriptor are extracted from the same view. The cases c_j for $j \in [1, \ldots, k-1]$ are true if the $j+1$ best matching descriptors are all extracted from disjoint views. According to these cases, the weight of a match m is defined as

$$w(m) = \left[c_0 \cdot \alpha \cdot g_3(d_r^1) + \prod_{j=1}^{k-1} \left(1 + c_j \cdot \beta_j \cdot g_1(d_{3D}^j) \cdot g_2(d_r^j) \right) \right] \cdot g_4(d_N^0) \tag{7}$$

To explain the weight function we distinguish between two exclusive cases depending on c_j:

Case 1 $(c_0 = 1)$ Here the weight is calculated based on the *Lowes' Ratio* d_r^1 of the best and second-best feature descriptors extracted from the same training view. The Gaussian function g_3 weights a match stronger if d_r^1 gets smaller.

Case 2 $(c_j = 1 \, , \, j \in [1, \ldots, k-1])$ The idea is to weight a match stronger if query pixel $\boldsymbol{p}_q$ matches good to similar world points $\boldsymbol{P}_M^0, \boldsymbol{P}_M^j$, each extracted from different training views. Thus the Gaussian functions g_1, g_2 increase the weight of a match if d_r^j approximates to 1 and d_{3D}^j approximates to 0.

Independent of c_j the weight of a match is influenced by the normalized ratio d_N^0 which represents the quality of the 2D-2D matching. If the descriptors match good $g_4(d_N^0)$ approximates to 1, for bad matches respectively to 0. The function g_4 is similar to the weight function used in w-RANSAC. The factors α, β_1, β_2 are parameters to control the influence on the summed weight.

4   Experiments

In the following, we present evaluation results illustrating the performance of our approach in comparison to RANSAC and w-RANSAC. We did experiments based on a set of 12 synthetic query images, reprojected from different poses around an indoor office scene with ground truth. To measure the quality of a pose estimate we apply the ground truth extrinsic parameters $\boldsymbol{t}, \boldsymbol{r}$ from the query image on every world point P_M which is visible on the current query view. As a result we get the point cloud P_g. Accordingly we apply the estimated extrinsic parameters to the same world points and get the corresponding set P_e. Hence we can define the point error as the mean euclidean norm between the corresponding points $\boldsymbol{p}_{gi} \in P_g, \boldsymbol{p}_{ei} \in P_e$. The point error is defined as $error = \frac{1}{n} \sum_{i=1}^{n} |\boldsymbol{p}_{gi} - \boldsymbol{p}_{ei}|$ with $n = |P_g| = |P_e|$. We present the mean point error of 100 iterations for every query view in meters.

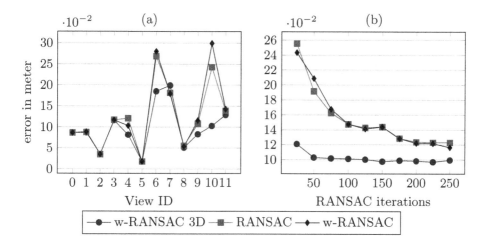

Fig. 1. Comparison of w-RANSAC, RANSAC and w-RANSAC 3D

In Fig. 1(a) the mean point error for every view of the test set is shown. It demonstrates that for the views 4,6,9,10 our approach leads to a more accurate pose estimation while for the other views the error is about the same for all three approaches. For view 7, w-RANSAC 3D performed slightly worse than RANSAC and w-RANSAC. This is due to misalignment of the view, meaning r, t are estimated more accurate but in this special case this leads to a higher point error. Fig. 1(b) shows the performance of the three approaches relative to the number of RANSAC iterations. Here the error is the mean over all test views. The figure illustrates that our approach approximates to its optimum in less than 50 iterations while RANSAC and w-RANSAC both need more than 200 iterations to reach their optimum.

Fig. 2 shows two example query images taken from a standard consumer camera and the reprojection of the estimated extrinsic parameters using w-RANSAC 3D.

Fig. 2. Real query images with corresponding reprojection from estimated extrinsic parameters. (a) is an example for an inaccurate pose estimation, (b) shows a quite accurate pose estimation.

5   Conclusion

In this work we presented w-RANSAC 3D, a novel extension of the RANSAC algorithm for image based 6-DOF pose estimation based on a reconstructed point cloud. In the evaluation we have shown that w-RANSAC 3D outperforms w-RANSAC and RANSAC in terms of robustness while needing significantly less iterations. For future work, we consider using the weights not only in the RANSAC algorithm, but also in the iterative PnP algorithm for a more robust and accurate solution. Furthermore there is the idea to improve the current weight function with additional heuristics like verifying if the geometric neighborhood suites to a match.

References

1. Arth, C., Klopschitz, M., Reitmayr, G., Schmalstieg, D.: Real-time self-localization from panoramic images on mobile devices. In: ISMAR, pp. 37–46 (2011)
2. Bay, H., Ess, A., Tuytelaars, T., Van Gool, L.: Speeded-up robust features (surf). Comput. Vis. Image Underst. 110(3), 346–359 (2008)
3. Fischler, M.A., Bolles, R.C.: Random sample consensus: A paradigm for model fitting with applications to image analysis and automated cartography. Commun. ACM 24(6), 381–395 (1981)
4. Gao, X.S., Hou, X.R., Tang, J., Cheng, H.F.: Complete solution classification for the perspective-three-point problem. TPAMI, 930–943 (2003)
5. Gordon, I., Lowe, D.G.: What and where: 3D object recognition with accurate pose. In: Ponce, J., Hebert, M., Schmid, C., Zisserman, A. (eds.) Toward Category-Level Object Recognition. LNCS, vol. 4170, pp. 67–82. Springer, Heidelberg (2006)
6. Haralick, R., Lee, D., Ottenburg, K., Nolle, M.: Analysis and solutions of the three point perspective pose estimation problem. In: CVPR, pp. 592–598 (1991)
7. Irschara, A., Zach, C., Frahm, J.M., Bischof, H.: From structure-from-motion point clouds to fast location recognition. In: CVPR, pp. 2599–2606 (2009)
8. Kneip, L., Scaramuzza, D., Siegwart, R.: A novel parametrization of the perspective-three-point problem for a direct computation of absolute camera position and orientation. In: CVPR, pp. 2969–2976 (2011)
9. Lepetit, V., Moreno-Noguer, F., Fua, P.: Epnp: An accurate o(n) solution to the pnp problem. IJCV 81(2), 155–166 (2009)
10. Lowe, D.G.: Fitting parameterized three-dimensional models to images. TPAMI 13, 441–450 (1991)
11. Lowe, D.G.: Distinctive image features from scale-invariant keypoints. IJCV 60, 91–110 (2004)
12. Lu, C.P., Hager, G., Mjolsness, E.: Fast and globally convergent pose estimation from video images. TPAMI 22(6), 610–622 (2000)
13. Mikolajczyk, K., Tuytelaars, T., Schmid, C., Zisserman, A., Matas, J., Schaffalitzky, F., Kadir, T., Gool, L.: A comparison of affine region detectors. IJCV 65(1), 43–72 (2005)
14. Quan, L., Lan, Z.: Linear n-point camera pose determination. TPAMI, 774 –780 (1999)
15. Zhang, D., Wang, W., Huang, Q., Jiang, S., Gao, W.: Matching images more efficiently with local descriptors. In: ICPR, pp. 1–4 (2008)

Symmetry-Based Detection and Diagnosis of DCIS in Breast MRI

Abhilash Srikantha

Fraunhofer MEVIS, Bremen and University of Bonn, Germany

Abstract. Detecting early stage breast cancers like Ductal Carcinoma In Situ (DCIS) is important, as it supports effective and minimally invasive treatments. Although Computer Aided Detection/Diagnosis (CADe/ CADx) systems have been successfully employed for highly malignant carcinomas, their performance on DCIS is inadequate. In this context, we propose a novel approach combining symmetry, kinetics and morphology that achieves superior performance. We base our work on contrast enhanced data of 18 pure DCIS cases with hand annotated lesions and 9 purely normal cases. The overall sensitivity and specificity of the system stood at 89% each[1].

1 Introduction

DCIS is an early stage cancer that propagates from milk ducts of breasts. Though such cancers are not life threatening, they can advance into variants that are. Therefore, diagnosing DCIS is desirable as it lends itself to early intervention. Although Dynamic Contrast Enhanced (DCE)-MRI is accepted as a reliable modality for diagnosis, its reading is among the most challenging tasks. Even for human observers, DCIS is not always easy to differentiate from patterns of active parenchymal enhancement or from benign alterations of breast tissue.

Several approaches have tried to devise computer aid for the detection and delineation of non-mass-like findings in breast MRI. These methods are based on the fact that cancerous lesions release angiogenic factors in that they trigger formation of new capillaries and vessels. These newly formed entities have relatively increased permeability resulting in increased perfusion of contrast agents into the surrounding hyperactive tissue. Therefore, malignancy of lesions is often described by characterizing both temporal (kinetic) and spatial (morphological) distributions of contrast agents. In terms of sensitivity and specificity, however, none achieve a performance matching CADe/CADx approaches for the detection and classification of solid masses [1–3].

In addition, two more clinical observations have facilitated further characterization of DCIS. Firstly, owing to weaker wash-out and enhancement characteristics, DCIS lesions manifest themselves as unilateral, segmental and weak enhancements [4] as opposed to benign lesions that manifest as segmental, weak

---

[1] The project was undertaken as a master thesis by Abhilash Srikantha and was supervised by Markus Harz: markus.harz@mevis.fraunhofer.de

J. Weickert, M. Hein, and B. Schiele (Eds.): GCPR 2013, LNCS 8142, pp. 255–260, 2013.
© Springer-Verlag Berlin Heidelberg 2013

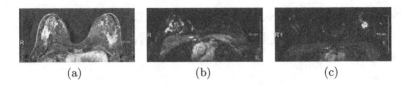

(a)   (b)   (c)

Fig. 1. Axial view of subtraction images (a) normal subject with high parenchymal enhancement in both breasts (b) segmental and linear DCIS enhancement in right breast (c) mass like invasive lesion in left breast

but bilateral enhancements and invasive lesions as mass-like, strong and unilateral enhancments. Secondly, due to ductal guidance, DCIS lesions are predominently directed towards the nipple against no directional preference exhibited by other lesion classes (see figure 1).

In this contribution, we show a novel approach to combine anatomical breast symmetry calculated on subtraction images of DCE-MRI, descriptive kinetic parameters, and lesion candidate morphology to achieve performances comparable to computer-aided methods used for masses. The development of the method is based on DCE-MRI data of 18 DCIS cases with hand-annotated lesions, complemented by DCE-MRI data of 9 normal cases. Our combined scheme then achieves a sensitivity and specificity of 89% each, matching CAD results for breast MRI on masses.

The paper is structured as follows: section 2 presents the data. Section 3 describes the system and its components. Section 4 presents results and conclusions are presented in section 5.

2   Methodology

2.1   Data

Subjects were scanned in prone position with breast suspended in a standard double breast coil [5]. Nine normal subjects' data was acquired from University of Medicine, Greifswald, Germany and eighteen DCIS subjects' data was acquired from Radboud Medical Center, Nijmegen, The Netherlands. Each data set was T1 weighted without fat suppression. After the acquisition of the pre-contrast series, Gadolinium-DTPA contrast agent was delivered intravenously followed by saline flush. Four post-contrast series were then acquired, the first after 89s and the rest after intervals of 69s.

2.2   Preprocessing

As the raw-input data is composed of several non-idealities, we first perform motion correction by a preimplemented intra-time point registration method to account for patient movements during data acquisition [6]. Next vessel segmentation based on tube filters [7] is applied on subtraction images. This step is

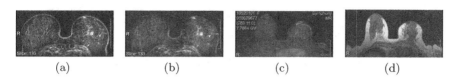

(a)	(b)	(c)	(d)

Fig. 2. Axial view of (a) original subtraction image (b) subtraction image after motion correction (c) vessel segmentation example (d) breast region segmentation example

important as vessel entities also manifest as enhancements that can be confused for DCIS lesions. Finally, an automatic breast region segmentation method is used to indicate those regions of the data that must be processed [8]. The result of various preprocessing modules are illustrated in figure 2.

2.3   Detection and Characterization of Non-mass Lesions

General Remarks. We will look at three feature classes in the subsequent sections: symmetry, morphological and kinetic features. In the classes of morphological and kinetic features, we assemble a set of multiple features and train random forests on them. Leave-one-out protocol is incorporated to be able to assess the classifier performance in all cases.

Symmetry. With the motivation of being capable of describing one breast w.r.t the other, we design the following methodology. We start with deriving probability mass functions (pmf) of both breasts on a slice-by-slice basis. Because we intend to model unilateral enhancements, such regions in the one breast can be modelled as low probability events w.r.t the pmf of other. These probability maps called suspicious maps where low probability regions indicate possible DCIS locations are binarized to yield binarized suspicious maps (see figure 3). For a given slice z in a given view, the symmetry measure $\mathcal{S}_{view}^z$ is then given by

$$\mathcal{S}_{view}^z = |H(\mathcal{M}_{thres}^{L_z}) - H(\mathcal{M}_{thres}^{R_z})| \qquad (1)$$

where $H(\cdot)$ calculates the binary entropy, $\mathcal{M}_{thres}^{L_z}$ is the binarized suspicious map of the left breast and $\mathcal{M}_{thres}^{L_z}$ is the binarized suspicious map of the right breast. The global symmetry measure in this view is given as

$$\mathcal{S}_{view} = \sum_{\forall z} w^z \mathcal{S}_{view}^z \qquad (2)$$

where w^z is the importance weight given to each slice and is proportional to the number of breast voxels it contains. This feature generated in both axial and coronal views to account for limited three-dimensional assessment, is used to fit the optimal decision boundary between DCIS and normal cases with a linear SVM and is smoothed by a sigmoid function. This step also yields connected components derived from binarized suspicious maps for further analysis. Owing to the comparitive approach, method is robust against non-idealities that affect both breasts similarly e.g. bias fields, scanner protocols, voxel sizes etc.

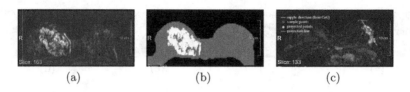

Fig. 3. **Fig. 3.** Illustrating binarized suspicious maps (a) subtraction image of DCIS subject (b) corresponding binarized suspicious map (c) illustrating morphological feature: Projected Variance

Morphology. The second classifier analyzes morphological features of each connected component. The features consist of shape (eigenvalues and ratios) and component directionality w.r.t. the nipple which is defined as the variance of points projected along the direction from the center of the connected component to the nipple (see figure 3). Exploiting this feature set, a DCIS vs. benign random forest of 100 trees is constructed [9]. Each tree uses two randomly picked features to grow to a maximum depth of four.

Kinetics. The third classsifier analyzes kinetic features derived from each connected component. The features consist of wash-in and wash-out slope, the integral under the enhancement curve, relative enhancement at the 120s time point and time to peak [10, 11]. For each lesion candidate, average of top three percentile most-malignant values are considered for classification. Exploiting this feature set, a DCIS vs. benign random forest of 100 trees is constructed. Each tree uses three randomly picked features to grow to a maximum depth of eight.

Combining Classifiers. The individual classifiers are linearly combined as a weighted sum into an overall risk score for each connected region, according to $\rho = (4\chi + 2\kappa + \mu)\cdot(1 - \nu)$, where $\chi \in [0,1]$ is the decision for the component from the symmetry classifier, κ, $\mu \in \{0,1\}$ are decisions from kinetic and morphological classifiers respectively and $\nu \in \{0,1\}$ is the vesselness score.

3   Results

The reference standard consists of manually annotated areas of DCIS. The DCIS regions were not segmented on a per-voxel basis, but fully covered in the breast MRI volume with one or more ellipsoids. By this method, large portions of healthy tissue are covered as well, thereby no studies of the kinetic/morphological feature robustness based on our DCIS detection versus the expert annotation was feasible.

Using only symmetry as a feature, 16/18 DCIS and 7/9 Normal cases were correctly classified resulting in a sensitivity of 89% and a specificity of 78%. This is in agreement with the observation that symmetry is a reliable feature for DCIS diagnosis. However, knowing atleast one breast is suspicious of being diseased is of limited clinical utility.

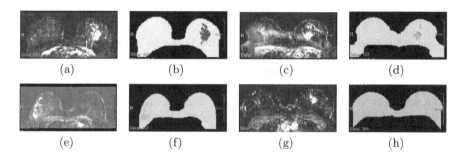

Fig. 4. DCIS cases and associated risk maps (a) DCIS subtraction image (b) DCIS confirmed by all three classifiers (c) DCIS subtraction image (d) DCIS confirmed by symmetry and kinetic classifiers only (d) DCIS subtraction image (e) DCIS confirmed by symmetry and morphological classifiers only (e) DCIS subtraction image (f) Failed case: confirmed only by kinetic classifier.

This shortcoming has been addressed by conjunction of additional classifiers that are capable of localizing DCIS lesions viz. morphological and kinetic classifiers that processed the candidate regions. The morphology based classifier performed with a sensitivity of 45% and a specificity of 96% and a kappa score of 0.44. The kinetics based classifier performed with a sensitivity of 88% and a specificity of 98% with a kappa score of 0.88. The classifiers that do not correlate with each other is pooled together by combining their individual results to form risk maps as shown in figure 4. In all, the sensitivity and specificity of 89% each was achieved in the combined system.

4   Conclusions and Future Work

Two relevant developments have been described in this work, namely (1) the implementation of a symmetry metric that is robust against influences in common clinical scenarios (bias field, changes of scanners or protocol, voxel sizes and isotropy, etc.) and does not require any parameter adjustments; and (2) a simple and efficient way to include the morphology of ductal enhancements with the metric dubbed projected variance. We found both developments to be robust and reliable, producing unprecedented sensitivity and specificity figures on our data. Lastly, we propose a risk map to be presented to radiologists, that can provide substantial aid to detect and characterize non-mass like enhancement patterns by providing a decision and a voxel-level segmentation.

We acknowledge one major limitation of our work: We can only consider our results preliminary, unless we can apply it to a larger data collection with normal and diseased cases; ultimately, we would like to apply the approach to a set of scans prospectively acquired from a high-risk MR screening site.

References

1. Orel, S.G., Schnall, M.D.: MR imaging of the breast for the detection, diagnosis, and staging of breast cancer. Radiology 220(1), 13–30 (2001)
2. Kuhl, C.K., et al.: MRI for diagnosis of pure ductal carcinoma in situ: A prospective observational study. Lancet 370, 485–492 (2007)
3. Jansen, S.A., et al.: The diverse pathology and kinetics of mass, nonmass, and focus enhancement on MR imaging of the breast. Journal of Magnetic Resonance Imaging: JMRI 33, 1382–1389 (2011)
4. Kuhl, C.K.: The current status of breast MR imaging. Part I. Choice of technique, image interpretation, diagnostic accuracy, and transfer to clinical practice. Radiology 244, 356–378 (2007)
5. Volzke, H., et al.: Cohort profile: The study of health in pomerania. International Journal of Epidemiology 40(2), 294–307 (2011)
6. Boehler, T., Wirtz, S., Peitgen, H.-O.: A combined algorithm for breast mri motion correction. In: Proceedings of the SPIE, vol. 6514, p. 6514R1 (2007)
7. Frangi, A.F., Niessen, W.J., Vincken, K.L., Viergever, M.A.: Multiscale vessel enhancement filtering. In: Wells, W.M., Colchester, A.C.F., Delp, S.L. (eds.) MICCAI 1998. LNCS, vol. 1496, pp. 130–137. Springer, Heidelberg (1998)
8. Wang, L., Filippatos, K., Friman, O., Hahn, H.: Fully automated segmentation of the pectoralis muscle boundary in breast MR images. In: SPIE Medical Imaging, Computer-Aided Diagnosis, vol. 7963 (2011)
9. Mark, H., et al.: The WEKA Data Mining Software: An Update. SIGKDD Explorations 11(1) (2009)
10. Jansen, S.A., et al.: Characterizing early contrast uptake of ductal carcinoma in situ with high temporal resolution dynamic contrast-enhanced MRI of the breast: A pilot study. Physics in Medicine and Biology 55, N473–N485 (2010)
11. Bhooshan, N., et al.: Cancerous breast lesions on dynamic contrast-enhanced MR images: Computerized characterization for image-based prognostic markers. Radiology 254, 680–690 (2010)

Ordinal Random Forests for Object Detection*

Samuel Schulter, Peter M. Roth, and Horst Bischof

Institute for Computer Graphics and Vision
Graz University of Technology, Austria
{schulter,pmroth,bischof}@icg.tugraz.at

Abstract. In this paper, we present a novel formulation of Random Forests, which introduces order statistics into the splitting functions of nodes. Order statistics, in general, neglect the absolute values of single feature dimensions and just consider the ordering of different feature dimensions. Recent works showed that such statistics have more discriminative power than just observing single feature dimensions. However, they were just used as a preprocessing step, transforming data into a higher dimensional feature space, or were limited to just consider two feature dimensions. In contrast, we integrate order statistics into the Random Forest framework, and thus avoid explicit mapping onto higher dimensional spaces. In this way, we can also exploit more than two feature dimensions, resulting in increased discriminative power. Moreover, we show that this idea can easily be extended for the popular Hough Forest framework. The experimental results demonstrate that using splitting functions building on order statistics can improve both, the performance for classification tasks (using Random Forests) and for object detection (using Hough Forests).

1 Introduction

Random Forests (RF), as introduced by Amit and Geman [1] and further developed by Breiman [6], became quite popular in recent years due to its simplicity and low computational costs. They find many applications in various sub-domains of computer vision, like object detection [10], tracking [11,12], and semantic image labeling [18]. Random Forests are ensembles of randomized decision trees, which separate the data via learned splitting functions and make predictions in the leaf nodes, *e.g.*, with estimated class-conditional probabilities for classification tasks. Random Forests are easy to implement and, due to the hierarchical tree structure, are very fast during both training and testing, making them a good choice for many computer vision applications.

In many of the aforementioned applications, Random Forests are adopted to suit the specific needs by changing the splitting functions. For instance, for fine-grained image categorization [21], max-margin classifiers are used to split the data in each node. Another example are Oblique Random Forests [14], which integrate random projections into the splitting functions. For object detection and

---

* The work was supported by the FFG projects Human Factors Technologies and Services (2371236) and Mobile Traffic Checker (8258408).

J. Weickert, M. Hein, and B. Schiele (Eds.): GCPR 2013, LNCS 8142, pp. 261–270, 2013.
© Springer-Verlag Berlin Heidelberg 2013

semantic image labeling, both Hough Forests [10] and Texton Forests [18] rely on splitting functions based on the difference of two randomly selected pixels on small image patches. The splitting functions used in the latter two approaches consider partial ordering statistics, *i.e.*, the ordering of different feature dimensions according to their feature values. However, both approaches rely on the differences between the pixel values and not directly on the ordering and are limited to two pixels only. Furthermore, they neither set their focus on these splitting functions nor explore their functionalities in more detail.

A totally different approach, which explicitly explores partial order statistics, is that of Yagnik *et al.* [19]. They propose a non-linear transformation that randomly selects a subset of the feature dimensions and encodes the index of the maximum value of this subset. This is repeated several times to build a feature vector. They use this new data representation for several vision tasks (*e.g.*, image classification) and show the discriminative power of this non-linear transformation. However, for good performance, they need to generate a huge number of completely random non-linear codes (*i.e.*, yielding a quite high dimensional feature vector). As not all codes are discriminative, this increases the computational costs.

In this work, we show how such non-linear and discriminative transformations can be seamlessly integrated into the splitting functions of Random Forests. We can thus avoid the explicit calculation of such high dimensional data as in [19], because each node in the RF only selects the most discriminative codes. This can be seen as a feature selection process that results in lower computational costs. Nevertheless, we still maintain the properties of the non-linear transformation in each tree, thus making the Random Forest more discriminative. Similar to [19], the novel splitting functions neglect absolute values of single features but rather observe their partial ordering. Such statistics are particularly interesting in computer vision as they are independent from the illumination. That is, our splitting functions for RFs depend on several feature dimensions simultaneously and exploit their ordering statistics to split the data (see Sec. 3), rather than considering only a single dimension as in standard RFs. In the sequel, we denote this RF formulation as *Ordinal Random Forest (ORF)*.

We also show how these splitting functions can be integrated into the Hough Forests [10] (see Sec. 4), which is a popular and widely applicable framework used for object detection [10], tracking [11,12], and action recognition [20]. This extension of Hough Forests, in the following denoted as *Ordinal Hough Forests (OHF)*, makes them more discriminative as we show in our experiments.

In Sec. 5, we evaluate our novel splitting functions on two different tasks: (i) image categorization and (ii) object detection. We first apply the *ORF* framework for image categorization on the popular *Caltech101* and *USPS* data sets. Then, in the second experiment, we show object detection results with the *OHF* framework on widely used data sets (*i.e.*, TUD pedestrian, TUD crossing, and TUD campus). Both experiments show relative improvements of *ORF* and *OHF* compared to standard Random Forest and Hough Forest, indicating the benefits of considering order statistics of several feature dimensions, rather than values of a single dimension.

2   Random Forests

Given labeled data $\{\mathbf{x}_i, y_i\}_{i=1}^N$, where $\mathbf{x}_i \in \mathbb{R}^D$ is a D-dimensional feature vector, $y_i \in 1, \ldots, C$ is the corresponding class label, and N is the number of training samples, the goal of a machine learning algorithm is to learn a mapping from a given test sample $\mathbf{x}$ to the correct class label y. For Random Forests [6] (RF), this is realized by building an ensemble of T randomized decision trees $\mathcal{T}_t$, $t = 1, \ldots, T$. The literal purpose of RFs was to solve a supervised classification problem, although this learning approach was already extended to other tasks like regression, semi-supervised learning or density estimation [7]. However, in this work we focus on the classification problem.

During training, the algorithm tries to split the given training data $\{\mathbf{x}_i, y_i\}_{i=1}^N$ in each node, such that samples from different classes are separated. This recursive algorithm continues to split the data until either the maximum depth of the tree is reached, the subset of the data in a node is pure, or the number of samples is below a threshold. If any of these conditions is met, a leaf node is created and the class probability $p(y|\mathbf{x})$ is estimated by simply counting the number of samples that fell into this leaf node for each class y, normalized such that $\sum_{y=1}^C p(y|\mathbf{x}) = 1$.

In order to split the data in a single splitting node, a pre-defined number Γ of splitting functions

$$\xi_{d,\tau}^j(\mathbf{x}) = \begin{cases} 0, & \text{if } x_d < \tau \\ 1, & \text{otherwise} \end{cases}, \tag{1}$$

is drawn randomly, where $j = 1, \ldots, \Gamma$, x_d denotes the d-th dimension (randomly drawn) in $\mathbf{x}$, and τ is a random threshold, which split the data to the left or right child node. The number Γ of randomly sampled splitting functions is a hyperparameter, pre-defined by the user. The current node selects the function $\xi_{d,\tau}^j$ that best splits the data according to

$$I = -\frac{|L|}{|L| + |R|} \cdot H(L) - \frac{|R|}{|L| + |R|} \cdot H(R), \tag{2}$$

where L and R are the left and right subsets of the data after splitting with $\xi_{d,\tau}^j$. In our implementation $H(\cdot) = -\sum_{y=1}^C p(y) \cdot (1 - p(y))$ is the Gini index, although the entropy can also be used; $p(y)$ is the class probability for class y. After having found the best splitting function $\xi_{d,\tau}^*$ among the Γ sampled ones, the data in that node is split and forwarded to the left and right child nodes, respectively, where the recursive algorithm continues.

During inference, a test sample $\mathbf{x}$ is traversed down all T trees and ends up in some leaf nodes. Each of these leaf nodes gives a prediction for a class label with its learned class probabilities $p(y|\mathbf{x})$. The prediction of the complete ensemble of trees is then given as the average of those class probability estimates:

$$y^* = \arg\max_{y \in 1,\ldots,C} \frac{1}{T} \sum_{t=1}^T p_t(y|\mathbf{x}). \tag{3}$$

One property of Random Forests is that the generalization error can be estimated as a function of the strength of the individual trees and the diversity among them [6]. The generalization error is given as

$$GE \leq \bar{\rho} \frac{1 - s^2}{s^2} , \qquad (4)$$

where $\bar{\rho}$ is the mean correlation between two pairs of trees and s is the strength of the trees in terms of prediction accuracy. Thus, strong but uncorrelated trees decrease the generalization error.

Random Forests have some desirable properties, especially for computer vision tasks. Due to their hierarchical structure, they are very fast during both training and testing. Furthermore, they can be easily parallelized (also on the GPU [17]) as the trees can be trained and tested independently from each other, making RFs even faster. RFs are inherently multi-class capable and do not rely on heuristic learning schemes like "one-vs.-all" or "one-vs.-one". Breiman [6] also states that RFs can handle significant amounts of noisy data. These reasons led to various applications for Random Forests [7], like semantic image labeling [18], object detection [10], object tracking [11,12], or image classification [4,15].

3   Ordinal Split Functions for Random Forests

In this section, we introduce our novel splitting function for Random Forests that is based on partial order statistics. We thus modify the splitting function in Eq. (1) with the goal to neglect absolute values of single dimensions in a feature vector $\mathbf{x}$ and observe order statistics between several features instead.

We define our novel splitting function as

$$\psi_{\mathbf{D},\delta}^j(\mathbf{x}) = \begin{cases} 0, & \text{if } \arg\max_{d \in \{0,\dots,K-1\}} x(\mathbf{D})_d = \delta \\ 1, & \text{otherwise} \end{cases}, \qquad (5)$$

where $\mathbf{D}$ is a vector of length K containing randomly sampled indices in the range $0, \dots, D-1$; $x(\mathbf{D})$ is the K-dimensional vector containing the feature dimension indexed by the vector $\mathbf{D}$; δ is an integer value in the range $[0, \dots, K-1]$. That is, to define such a splitting function, we have to construct the random vector $\mathbf{D}$ that selects K dimensions of the data sample $\mathbf{x}$, yielding the vector $x(\mathbf{D})$. Then, the response r of this data sample is defined as the index of the maximum element in $x(\mathbf{D})$, which is in the range $[0, \dots, K-1]$. If the response matches δ, the sample is forwarded to the left child node, otherwise to the right child node.

Let us now consider this splitting function in more detail. The standard splitting function given by Eq. (1) only considers a single feature dimension and thresholds the values of this dimension. Samples $\mathbf{x}$ having a higher/lower value in a single dimension x_d than a threshold τ are forwarded to the left/right child nodes. After having split the data, the only commonality of the samples in one of the child nodes is that the values in one dimension are above/below τ. On the other hand, considering our novel splitting functions $\psi_{\mathbf{D},\delta}^j$ in Eq. (5), the (enforced) commonality of split data is much higher, thus making the splitting functions stronger. Considering samples in the left child node after splitting, all samples within this node fulfill $K - 1$ inequalities. Namely, one of the randomly selected feature dimensions has a higher value than $K - 1$ other feature dimensions. Although samples in the right child node only fulfill a single constraint, namely that the selected feature dimension is not the maximum, the overall (enforced) commonality of split data is still higher than in standard RFs, thus yielding stronger decision trees.

However, making single trees in an ensemble method stronger can be harmful, as often the diversity is reduced. As mentioned above (see Eq. (4)), to reduce the generalization error, we have to increase the strength of single trees, while still keeping the diversity across the forest. The new splitting functions $\Psi_{\mathbf{D},\delta}^{j}$ make the trees stronger, but we keep the diversity as the functions are still drawn complete randomly. Additionally, the number of available ordinal splitting functions is now $\binom{D}{K}$, instead of only D in standard splitting functions. Thus, the number of available splitting functions increases with K, as long as $K \leq \frac{D}{2}$.

Finally, we have to note that such transformations [19] or splitting functions like in Eq. (5) are only meaningful if the distributions of data samples from different classes do not share the same covariance information. Otherwise, relations between feature dimensions are not discriminative at all. That is, pure machine learning or artificial data is often not suitable for such splitting functions, however, when working with vision data, partial order statistics make sense for most data representations (*e.g.*, consider simple pixel tests [10,18]).

4 Extension to Hough Forests

We now describe the extension of our splitting functions, introduced in Sec. 3, to the Hough Forests (HF) [10]. First, we briefly review HF and then integrate our novel splitting functions into the original formulation of [10].

Hough Forests work on small patches $\mathcal{P}_i$ extracted at random locations within a given bounding box from positive and negative training images of an object. Each patch is described with several features, termed channels. Positive samples additionally store an offset vector $\mathbf{o}_i$ pointing to the center of the bounding box. HFs then try to separate positive from negative patches and simultaneously cluster together similar positive patches according to their offset vectors $\mathbf{o}_i$.

The splitting functions in the HF framework are defined as follows:

$$\Omega(\mathcal{P}_i; a, p, q, r, s, \tau) = \begin{cases} 0, & \text{if } \mathcal{P}_i^a(p,q) < \mathcal{P}_i^a(r,s) + \tau \\ 1, & \text{otherwise} \end{cases}, \qquad (6)$$

where a indicates the feature channel, $\mathcal{P}_i^a$ is the calculated feature response of feature type a for patch $\mathcal{P}_i$, (p,q) and (r,s) define two pixel locations within $\mathcal{P}_i^a$ and τ is a threshold. That is, each node in the HF randomly selects a feature channel and two pixels within the patch $\mathcal{P}_i$ and calculates the difference of the feature values. This difference is then thresholded to determine which patches are forwarded to the left or the right child node. This is already quite similar to our previously defined splitting functions (Eq. (5)) based on partial order statistics, however, only two pixels are considered and a different thresholding is applied.

To integrate the ordinal splitting functions into the Hough Forest framework, we also build on only one feature channel but select $K \geq 2$ pixels. Then, we split the data in the same way as described in Sec. 3 by forwarding all patches $\mathcal{P}_i$ to the left child, if the maximum pixel index is equal to the "threshold" δ (an integer between 0 and $K-1$). Hence, we forward patches $\mathcal{P}_i$ to the left child node if all $K-1$ inequalities (*i.e.*, simple pixel tests) are fulfilled. All other patches are forwarded to the right child node. Then, the standard growing procedure of HFs continues by selecting the best randomly sampled splitting function according to the optimization objective (see [10] for more details).

In contrast to the works of Gall and Lempitsky [10] (and Shotton *et al.* [18]), we define splitting functions solely based on partial ordering of feature dimensions, not limited to two features (or pixels).

5   Experimental Evaluation

To demonstrate the benefits of our ordinal splitting functions, we perform two different experiments. First, image classification using Random Forests and, second, object detection using Hough Forests.

Table 1. Classification accuracy on the *Caltech101* data set, where the columns correspond to different forest sizes T. The rows show the evaluated methods, RF and ORF, where different values for the parameter K of ORF are tested. Best performing methods are marked **bold** for each forest size.

Method	$T = 1$	$T = 5$	$T = 10$	$T = 20$	$T = 50$	$T = 100$
RF	.161	.256	.347	.412	.461	.492
ORF, $K = 2$	.257	.363	.405	.445	.486	.496
ORF, $K = 3$	.262	.370	.402	.435	.483	.499
ORF, $K = 4$	.262	.372	.399	.443	.489	.508
ORF, $K = 5$	.266	.369	**.422**	**.460**	.488	.507
ORF, $K = 6$	**.273**	**.387**	.411	.455	.497	.511
ORF, $K = 7$	.269	.379	.421	.440	**.498**	**.520**

5.1   Image Classification

We first evaluate the novel ordinal splitting functions on two image classification tasks and compare it to the standard Random Forest framework [6]. We use the popular *Caltech101* object categorization data set [9] and the *USPS* digit categorization data set [13][1]. The *Caltech101* data set contains images from 101 categories (we leave out the additional background class), where we use 15 images per class for training and 10 images for testing. This results in a training set of 1515 images and a test set of 1010 images. As feature representation, we used *PHOW* features [5][2], for gray and color channels, each with a codebook size of 600 (computed with k-means), ending up in a 1200-dimensional feature vector.

---

[1] http://www.cs.nyu.edu/~roweis/data.html
[2] We use the publicly available toolbox from http://www.vlfeat.org/

The *USPS* data set consists of 7291 training samples and 2007 test samples from 10 different classes, *i.e.*, hand-written digits from 0 to 9. The 256 dimensions of the feature vectors in this data set contain the raw pixel values from a 16×16 gray scale image capturing the handwritten digits (the feature values are normalized in the range $[0, 1]$).

Table 2. Classification accuracy on the *USPS* data set, where the columns correspond to different forest sizes T. The rows show the evaluated methods, RF and ORF, where different values for the parameter K of ORF are tested. Best performing methods are marked **bold** for each forest size.

Method	$T = 1$	$T = 5$	$T = 10$	$T = 20$	$T = 50$	$T = 100$
RF	.820	.888	.917	.926	.936	.938
ORF, $K = 2$	**.851**	.924	**.939**	**.946**	.947	**.950**
ORF, $K = 3$	.841	**.926**	.936	.944	**.949**	.949
ORF, $K = 4$	.849	.917	.930	.941	.944	.949
ORF, $K = 5$	.834	.911	.929	.938	.945	.947
ORF, $K = 6$	.828	.904	.925	.938	.941	.943
ORF, $K = 7$	.816	.899	.927	.933	.939	.941

We compare our novel Ordinal Random Forest (ORF) framework with standard Random Forests[3]. We evaluate our approach for different numbers of trees in the forest and, for *ORF*, also for different values of the window size K. As suggested in [6], we set the number of randomly sampled splitting functions per node in the standard RF to $\sqrt{D}$, where D is the feature dimensionality. As already mentioned in Sec. 3 we have to increase the number of sampled splitting functions for our approach as the feature space is increasing when sampling more than one feature for a single splitting function. In fact, the number of possible combinations of K feature dimensions is $\binom{D}{K}$, resulting in $\sqrt{\binom{D}{K}}$ sampled splitting functions for *ORF*. However, to keep the computational effort on a reasonable level, we reduced the number of sample tests to 500, which has been shown to be enough for our purposes. We depict our results for both data sets in Tables 1 and 2, respectively. As can be seen from both tables, compared to the standard RF, *ORF* improves the classification scores for all sizes of the forest and different values of the parameter K. Furthermore, we note that best results are obtained with higher values of K on the *Caltech101* data set and with lower values on the *USPS* data set. A reason for this could be the large amount of classes in *Caltech101* in combination with the rather small amount of training data, thus requiring stronger splits.

5.2   Object Detection

In the second experiment, we evaluate our extension of HFs [10] with ordinal splitting functions (see Sec. 4) and compare it with the standard HF imple-

---

[3] We use public code from http://code.google.com/p/randomforest-matlab/

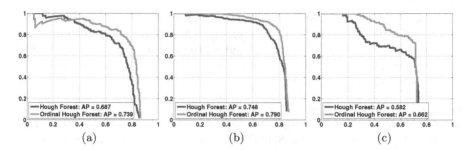

Fig. 1. (a-c) Precision-recall curves of OHF and HF on the three data sets, *i.e.*, *TUD-pedestrian*, *TUD-crossing*, and *TUD-campus*

mentation on three popular pedestrian detection benchmarks, namely the *TUD-pedestrian*, *TUD-crossing*, and *TUD-campus* data sets [2], which were often used for evaluating Hough Forest-based approaches [3,16].

The *TUD-pedestrian* data set contains 400 bounding-box annotated persons and 250 test images, capturing 311 pedestrians. The other data sets, *TUD-crossing* and *TUD-campus*, are smaller and contain only test sets with 201 and 71 images, respectively. We thus use the training images from the *TUD-pedestrian* data set as training data for all 3 test sets. For training, we uniformly extracted the patches from all training images, such that the total amount of positive training patches is around 10000; we use the same amount of negative patches, randomly cropped from the background.

For all our experiments we used 15 trees and a maximum depth of 15, similar to [10]. We use the publicly available implementation[4] for the Hough Forests, where we also build our extensions on. Due to computational reasons, we set the number of randomly sampled tests for both methods to 2000, although our splitting functions would theoretically require more, as soon as $K > 2$. Nevertheless, we also evaluate the influence of the number of randomly drawn splitting functions (see Table 3). For all other evaluations we set $K = 4$.

We depict our results as precision-recall curves in Figure 1 and also report the average precision values [8]. As can be seen from the figures, the novel splitting function can boost the performance on all three data sets. All results are averaged over 3 independent test runs to compensate for the randomness in the training procedure of the forests.

We also evaluate the influence of the parameter K and the number of sampled random tests per node, Γ, on the *Ordinal Hough Forest*. For comparison, we also added the performance of the standard Hough Forests (HF) for different values of Γ. Table 3 shows the results as average precision values. As can be seen from the table, *OHF* outperforms HF for all parameter settings. Furthermore, to get good performance, the number of randomly sampled splitting functions Γ has to be increased with K. This is somehow clear, as also the possible number of available splitting functions increases with K.

---

[4] http://www.vision.ee.ethz.ch/ gallju/projects/houghforest/houghforest.
html

Table 3. Average precision values on the *TUD-crossing* data set for different parameter values. The columns correspond to different numbers of randomly sampled splitting functions Γ. The rows show the evaluated methods, HF and *OHF* (with different values for K). Best performing methods are marked **bold** for each Γ.

Method	$\Gamma = 500$	$\Gamma = 1000$	$\Gamma = 2000$	$\Gamma = 3000$
HF	.757	.753	.761	.733
OHF, $K = 2$	.781	.776	.779	.767
OHF, $K = 3$	**.784**	**.782**	**.784**	.772
OHF, $K = 4$	.762	**.782**	.761	.769
OHF, $K = 5$	.771	.764	.769	.772
OHF, $K = 6$	.770	.763	.776	**.776**

6   Conclusion

Partial order statistics, which neglect absolute values of features and only consider relative differences and orderings, have recently shown good discriminative power; especially, when dealing with high dimensional data. In this work, we adopted these ideas and proposed a novel, more discriminative splitting function for Random Forests. We integrated this splitting function into both, the Random Forest and the Hough Forest frameworks. To demonstrate the benefits of the proposed approach, we applied it for two different tasks, *i.e.*, image categorization and object detection. In both cases the discriminative power can be increased, and we are able to show that using the new splitting function the standard implementations (*i.e.*, for Random Forests and Hough Forests) can be outperformed. Hence, the approach could also be used for other computer vision tasks. Furthermore, future work also includes the combination of both kinds of splitting functions (absolute feature values and order statistics), getting the best of both worlds.

References

1. Amit, Y., Geman, D.: Shape Quantization and Recognition with Randomized Trees 9(7), 1545–1588 (1997)
2. Andriluka, M., Roth, S., Schiele, B.: People-Tracking-by-Detection and People-Detection-by-Tracking. In: CVPR (2008)
3. Barinova, O., Lempitsky, V., Kohli, P.: On Detection of Multiple Object Instances using Hough Transforms. In: CVPR (2010)
4. Bosch, A., Zisserman, A., Munoz, X.: Image Classification using Random Forests and Ferns. In: ICCV (2007)
5. Bosch, A., Zisserman, A., Munoz, X.: Representing Shape with a Spatial Pyramid Kernel. In: CIVR (2007)
6. Breiman, L.: Random Forests. ML 45(1), 5–32 (2001)
7. Criminsi, A., Shotton, J.: Decision Forests for Computer Vision and Medical Image Analysis. Springer (2013)

8. Everingham, M., Van Gool, L., Williams, C.K.I., Winn, J., Zisserman, A.: The Pascal Visual Object Classes (VOC) Challenge. IJCV 88(2), 303–338 (2010)
9. Fei-Fei, L., Fergus, R., Perona, P.: One-Shot Learning of Object Categories. PAMI 28(4), 594–611 (2006)
10. Gall, J., Lempitsky, V.: Class-Specific Hough Forests for Object Detection. In: CVPR (2009)
11. Gall, J., Razavi, N., Van Gool, L.: On-line Adaption of Class-specific Codebooks for Instance Tracking. In: BMVC (2010)
12. Godec, M., Roth, P.M., Bischof, H.: Hough-based Tracking of Non-rigid Objects. In: ICCV (2011)
13. Hastie, T., Tibshirani, R., Friedman, J.H.: The Elements of Statistical Learning. Springer (2009)
14. Menze, B.H., Kelm, B.M., Splitthoff, D.N., Koethe, U., Hamprecht, F.A.: On Oblique Random Forests. In: Gunopulos, D., Hofmann, T., Malerba, D., Vazirgiannis, M. (eds.) ECML PKDD 2011, Part II. LNCS, vol. 6912, pp. 453–469. Springer, Heidelberg (2011)
15. Moosmann, F., Triggs, B., Jurie, F.: Fast discriminative visual codebooks using randomized clustering forests. In: NIPS (2006)
16. Razavi, N., Gall, J., Van Gool, L.: Backprojection Revisited: Scalable Multi-view Object Detection and Similarity Metrics for Detections. In: Daniilidis, K., Maragos, P., Paragios, N. (eds.) ECCV 2010, Part I. LNCS, vol. 6311, pp. 620–633. Springer, Heidelberg (2010)
17. Sharp, T.: Implementing Decision Trees and Forests on a GPU. In: Forsyth, D., Torr, P., Zisserman, A. (eds.) ECCV 2008, Part IV. LNCS, vol. 5305, pp. 595–608. Springer, Heidelberg (2008)
18. Shotton, J., Johnson, M., Cipolla, R.: Semantic texton forests for image categorization and segmentation. In: CVPR (2008)
19. Yagnik, J., Strelow, D., Ross, D.A., Lin, R.S.: The Power of Comparative Reasoning. In: ICCV (2011)
20. Yao, A., Gall, J., Van Gool, L.: A Hough transform-based voting framework for action recognition. In: CVPR (2010)
21. Yao, B., Aditya, K., Fei-Fei, L.: Combining Randomization and Discrimination for Fine-Grained Image Categorization. In: CVPR (2011)

Revisiting Loss-Specific Training of Filter-Based MRFs for Image Restoration

Yunjin Chen, Thomas Pock, René Ranftl, and Horst Bischof*

Institute for Computer Graphics and Vision, TU Graz

Abstract. It is now well known that Markov random fields (MRFs) are particularly effective for modeling image priors in low-level vision. Recent years have seen the emergence of two main approaches for learning the parameters in MRFs: (1) probabilistic learning using sampling-based algorithms and (2) loss-specific training based on MAP estimate. After investigating existing training approaches, it turns out that the performance of the loss-specific training has been significantly underestimated in existing work. In this paper, we revisit this approach and use techniques from bi-level optimization to solve it. We show that we can get a substantial gain in the final performance by solving the lower-level problem in the bi-level framework with high accuracy using our newly proposed algorithm. As a result, our trained model is on par with highly specialized image denoising algorithms and clearly outperforms probabilistically trained MRF models. Our findings suggest that for the loss-specific training scheme, solving the lower-level problem with higher accuracy is beneficial. Our trained model comes along with the additional advantage, that inference is extremely efficient. Our GPU-based implementation takes less than 1s to produce state-of-the-art performance.

1   Introduction and Previous Work

Nowadays the MRF prior is quite popular for solving various inverse problems in image processing in that it is a powerful tool for modeling the statistics of natural images. Image models based on MRFs, especially higher-order MRFs, have been extensively studied and applied to image processing tasks such as image denoising [14,16,15,7,19,18], deconvolution [17], inpainting [14,16,15], super-resolution [21], etc.

Due to its effectiveness, higher-order filter-based MRF models using the framework of the Field of Experts (FoE) [14], have gained the most attention. They are defined by a set of linear filters and the potential function. Based on the observation that responses of mean-zero linear filters typically exhibit heavy-tailed distributions [9] on natural images, three types of potential functions have been investigated, including the Student-t distribution (ST), generalized Laplace distribution (GLP) and Gaussian scale mixtures (GSMs) function.

---

* This work was supported by the Austrian Science Fund (project no. P22492) and the Austrian Research Promotion Agency (project no. 832366).

J. Weickert, M. Hein, and B. Schiele (Eds.): GCPR 2013, LNCS 8142, pp. 271–281, 2013.

Table 1. Summary of various typical MRF-based systems and the average denoising results on 68 test images [14] with $\sigma = 25$

model	potential	training	inference	PSNR
5 × 5 FoE	ST&Lap.	contrastive divergence	MAP, CG	27.77[14]
3 × 3 FoE	GSMs	contrastive divergence	Gibbs sampling	27.95[16]
5 × 5 FoE	GSMs	persistent contrastive divergence	Gibbs sampling	28.40[7]
5 × 5 FoE	ST	loss-specific(truncated optimization)	MAP, GD	28.24[2]
5 × 5 FoE	ST	loss-specific(truncated optimization)	MAP, lbfgs [11]	28.39[5]
5 × 5 FoE	ST	loss-specific(implicit differentiation)	MAP, CG	27.86[15]

In recent years several training approaches have emerged to learn the parameters of the MRF models [8,20,14,16,15,2,5,7]. Table 1 gives a summary of several typical methods and the corresponding average denoising PSNR results based on 68 test images from Berkeley database with $\sigma = 25$ Gaussian noise. Existing training approaches typically fall into two main types: (1) probabilistic training using (persistent) contrastive divergence ((P)CD); (2) loss-specific training. Roth and Black [14] first introduced the concept of FoE and proposed an approach to learn the parameters of FoE model which uses a sampling strategy and the idea of CD to estimate the expectation value over the model distribution. Schmidt *et al.* [16] improved the performance of their previous FoE model [14] by changing (1) the potential function to GSMs and (2) the inference method from MAP estimate to Bayesian minimum mean squared error estimate (MMSE). The same authors present their latest results in [7], where they achieve significant improvements by employing an improved learning scheme called PCD instead of previous CD.

Samuel and Tappen [15] present a novel loss-specific training approach to learn MRF parameters under the framework of bi-level optimization [3]. They use a plain gradient-descent technique to optimize the parameters, where the essence of this learning scheme - the gradients, are calculated by using implicit differentiation technique. Domke [5] and Barbu [2] propose two similar approaches for the training of MRF model parameters also under the framework of bi-level optimization. Their methods are some variants of standard bi-level optimization method [15]. In the modified setting, the MRF model is trained in terms of results after optimization is truncated to a fixed number of iterations, *i.e.*, they do not solve the energy minimization problem exactly; instead, they just run some specific optimization algorithm for a fixed number of steps.

In a recent work [10], the bi-level optimization technique is employed to train a non-parametric image restoration framework based on Regression Tree Fields (RTF), resulting a new state-of-the-art. This technique is also exploited for learning the so-called analysis sparsity priors [13], which is somewhat related to the FoE model.

2   Motivation and Contributions

Arguments: The loss-specific training criterion is formally expressed as the following bi-level optimization problem

$$\begin{cases} \arg\min_{\vartheta} L(x^*(\vartheta), g) \\ \text{subject to } x^*(\vartheta) = \arg\min_{x} E(x, f, \vartheta). \end{cases} \tag{1}$$

The goal of this model is to find the optimal parameters ϑ to minimize the loss function $L(x^*(\vartheta), g)$, which is called the upper-level problem in the bi-level framework. The MRF model is defined by the energy minimization problem $E(x, f, \vartheta)$, which is called the lower-level problem. The essential point for solving this bi-level optimization problem is to calculate the gradient of the loss function $L(x^*(\vartheta), g)$ with respect to the parameters ϑ. As aforementioned, [15] employs the implicit differentiation technique to calculate the gradients explicitly; in contrast, [5] and [2] make use of an approximation approach based on truncated optimization. All of them use the same ST-distribution as potential function; however, the latter two approaches surprisingly obtain much better performance than the former, as can be seen in Table 1.

In principle, Samuel and Tappen should achieve better (at least similar) results compared to the approximation approaches, because they use a "full" fitting training scheme, but actually they fail in practice. Therefore, we argue that there must exist something imperfect in their training scheme, and we believe that we will very likely achieve noticeable improvements by refining this "full" fitting training scheme.

Contributions: Motivated by the above investigation, we think it is necessary and worthwhile to restudy the loss-specific training scheme and we expect that we can achieve significant improvements. In this paper, we do not make any modifications to the training model used in [15] - we use exactly the same model capacity, potential function and training images. The only difference is the training algorithm. We exploit a refined training algorithm that we solve the lower-level problem in the loss-specific training with very high accuracy and make use of a more efficient quasi-Newton's method for model parameters optimization. We conduct a series of playback experiments and we show that the performance of loss-specific training is indeed underestimated in previous work [15]. We argue that the the critical reason is that they have not solved the lower-level problem to sufficient accuracy. We also demonstrate that solving the lower-level problem with higher accuracy is indeed beneficial. This argument about the loss-specific training scheme is the major contribution of our paper.

We further show that our trained model can obtain slight improvement by increasing the model size. It turns out that for image denoising task, our optimized MRF (opt-MRF) model of size 7×7 has achieved the best result among existing MRF-based systems and been on par with state-of-the-art methods. Due to the simplicity of our model, it is easy to implement the inference algorithm on parallel computation units, *e.g.*, GPU. Numerical results show that our GPU-based implementation can perform image denoising in near real-time with clear state-of-the-art performance.

3   Loss-Specific Training Scheme: Bi-level Optimization

In this section, we firstly present the loss-specific training model. Then we consider the optimization problem from a more general point of view. Our derivation shows that the implicit differentiation technique employed in previous work [15] is a special case of our general formulation.

3.1   The Basic Training Model

Our training model makes use of the bi-level optimization framework, and is conducted based on the image denoising task. For image denoising, the ST-distribution based MRF model is expressed as

$$\arg \min_x E(x) = \sum_{i=1}^{N_f} \alpha_i \sum_{p=1}^{N_p} \rho((K_i x)_p) + \frac{\lambda}{2} \|x - f\|_2^2. \qquad (2)$$

This is the lower-level problem in the bi-level framework. Wherein N_f is the number of filters, N_p is the number of pixels in image x, K_i is an $N_p \times N_p$ highly sparse matrix, which makes the convolution of the filter k_i with a two-dimensional image x equivalent to the product result of the matrix K_i with the vectorization form of x, i.e., $k_i * x \Leftrightarrow K_i x$. In our training model, we express the filter K_i as a linear combination of a set of basis filters $\{B_1, \cdots, B_{N_B}\}$, i.e., $K_i = \sum_{j=1}^{N_B} \beta_{ij} B_j$. Besides, $\alpha_i \geq 0$ is the parameters of ST-distribution for filter K_i, and λ defines the trade-off between the prior term and data fitting term. $\rho(\cdot)$ denotes the Lorentzian potential function $\rho(z) = \log(1 + z^2)$, which is derived from ST-distribution.

The loss function $L(x^*, g)$ (upper-level problem) is defined to measure the difference between the optimal solution of energy function and the ground-truth. In this paper, we make use of the same loss function as in [15], $L(x^*, g) = \frac{1}{2}\|x^* - g\|_2^2$, where g is the ground-truth image and x^* is the minimizer of (2).

Given the training samples $\{f_k, g_k\}_{k=1}^N$, where g_k and f_k are the kth clean image and the associated noisy version respectively, our aim is to learn an optimal MRF parameter $\vartheta = (\alpha, \beta)$ (we group the coefficients β_{ij} and weights α_i into a single vector ϑ), to minimize the overall loss function. Therefore, the learning model is formally formulated as the following bi-level optimization problem

$$\begin{cases} \min_{\alpha \geq 0, \beta} L(x^*(\alpha, \beta)) = \sum_{k=1}^{N} \frac{1}{2}\|x_k^*(\alpha, \beta) - g_k\|_2^2 \\ \text{where } x_k^*(\alpha, \beta) = \arg \min_x \sum_{i=1}^{N_f} \alpha_i \rho(K_i x) + \frac{1}{2}\|x - f_k\|_2^2, \end{cases} \qquad (3)$$

where $\rho(K_i x) = \sum_{p=1}^{N_p} \rho((K_i x)_p)$. We eliminate λ for simplicity, since it can be incorporated into weights α.

3.2   Solving the Bi-level Problem

In this paper, we consider the bi-level optimization problem from a general point of view. In the following derivation we only consider the case of a single training sample for convenience, and we show how to extend the framework to multiple training samples in the end.

According to the optimality condition, the solution of the lower-level problem in (3) is given by x^*, such that $\nabla_x E(x^*) = 0$. Therefore, we can rewrite problem (3) as following constrained optimization problem

$$\begin{cases} \min\limits_{\alpha \geq 0, \beta} L(x(\alpha, \beta)) = \frac{1}{2}\|x(\alpha, \beta) - g\|_2^2 \\ \text{subject to } \nabla_x E(x) = \sum_{i=1}^{N_f} \alpha_i K_i^T \rho'(K_i x) + x - f = 0, \end{cases} \quad (4)$$

where $\rho'(K_i x) = (\rho'((K_i x)_1), \cdots, \rho'((K_i x)_p))^T \in \mathbb{R}^{N_p}$. Now we can introduce Lagrange multipliers and study the Lagrange function

$$\mathcal{L}(x, \alpha, \beta, p, \mu) = \frac{1}{2}\|x - g\|_2^2 + \langle -\alpha, \mu \rangle + \langle \sum_{i=1}^{N_f} \alpha_i K_i^T \rho'(K_i x) + x - f, p \rangle, \quad (5)$$

where $\mu \in \mathbb{R}^{N_f}$ and $p \in \mathbb{R}^{N_p}$ are the Lagrange multipliers associated to the inequality constraint $\alpha \geq 0$ and the equality constraint in (4), respectively. Here $\langle \cdot, \cdot \rangle$ denotes the standard inner product. Taking into account the inequality constraint $\alpha \geq 0$, the first order necessary condition for optimality is given by

$$G(x, \alpha, \beta, p, \mu) = 0, \quad (6)$$

where

$$G(x, \alpha, \beta, p, \mu) = \begin{pmatrix} (\sum_{i=1}^{N_f} \alpha_i K_i^T \mathcal{D}_i K_i + \mathcal{I})p + x - g \\ (\langle K_i^T \rho'(K_i x), p \rangle)_{N_f \times 1} - \mu \\ (\langle B_j^T \rho'(K_i x) + K_i^T \mathcal{D}_i B_j x, p \rangle)_{n \times 1} \\ \sum_{i=1}^{N_f} \alpha_i K_i^T \rho'(K_i x) + x - f \\ \mu - \max(0, \mu - c\alpha) \end{pmatrix}.$$

Wherein $\mathcal{D}_i(K_i x) = \text{diag}(\rho''((K_i x)_1), \cdots, \rho''((K_i x)_p)) \in \mathbb{R}^{N_p \times N_p}$, $(\langle \cdot, p \rangle)_{N \times 1} = (\langle (\cdot)_1, p \rangle, \cdots, \langle (\cdot)_r, p \rangle)^T$, in the third formulation $n = N_f \times N_B$. Note that the last formulation is derived from the optimality condition for the inequality constraint $\alpha \geq 0$, which is expressed as $\alpha \geq 0, \mu \geq 0, \langle \alpha, \mu \rangle = 0$. It is easy to check that these three conditions are equivalent to $\mu - \max(0, \mu - c\alpha) = 0$ with c to be any positive scalar and max operates coordinate-wise.

Generally, we can continue to calculate the generalized Jacobian of G, *i.e.*, the Hessian matrix of Lagrange function, with which we can then employ a Newton's method to solve the necessary optimality system (6). However, for this problem calculating the Jacobian of G is computationally intensive; thus in this paper we do not consider it and only make use of the first derivatives.

Since what we are interested in is the MRF parameters $\vartheta = \{\alpha, \beta\}$, we can reduce unnecessary variables in (6). By solving for p and x in (6), and substituting them into the second and the third formulation, we arrive at the gradients of loss function with respect to parameters ϑ

$$\begin{cases} \nabla_{\beta_{ij}} L = -(B_j^T \rho'(K_i x) + K_i^T \mathcal{D}_i B_j x)^T (H_E(x))^{-1} (x - g) \\ \nabla_{\alpha_i} L = -(K_i^T \rho'(K_i x))^T (H_E(x))^{-1} (x - g) \\ \text{where } \nabla_x E(x) = \sum_{i=1}^{N_f} \alpha_i K_i^T \rho'(K_i x) + x - f = 0. \end{cases} \quad (7)$$

In (7), $H_E(x)$ denotes the Hessian matrix of $E(x)$,

$$H_E(x) = \sum_{i=1}^{N_f} \alpha_i K_i^T \mathcal{D}_i K_i + \mathcal{I}. \qquad (8)$$

In (7), we also eliminate the Lagrange multiplier μ associated to the inequality constraint $\alpha \geq 0$, as we utilize a quasi-Newton's method for optimization, which can easily handle this type of box constraints. We can see that (7) is equivalent to the results presented in previous work [15] using implicit differentiation.

Considering the case of N training samples, in fact it turns out that the derivatives of the overall loss function in (3) with respect to the parameters ϑ are just the sum of (7) over the training dataset.

As given by (7), we have collected all the necessary information to compute the required gradients, so we can now employ gradient descent based algorithms for optimization, e.g., steepest-descent algorithm. In this paper, we turn to a more efficient non-linear optimization method–the LBFGS quasi-Newton's method [11]. In our experiments, we will make use of the LBFGS implementation distributed by L. Stewart[1]. In our work, the third equation in (7) is completed the L-BFGS algorithm, since this problem is smooth, to which L-BFGS is perfectly applicable. The training algorithm is terminated when the relative change of the loss is less than a tolerance, e.g., $tol = 10^{-5}$ or a maximum number of iterations e.g., $maxiter = 500$ is reached or L-BFGS can not find a feasible step to decrease the loss.

4   Training Experiments

In order to demonstrate that the loss-specific training scheme was undervalued in previous work [15], we conducted a playback experiment using (1) the same 40 images for training and 68 images for testing; (2) the same model capacity– 24 filters of size 5×5; (3) the same basis –"inverse" whitened PCA [14], as in Samuel and Tappen's experiments. We randomly sampled four 51×51 patches from each training image, resulting in a total of 160 training samples. We then generated the noisy versions by adding Gaussian noise with standard deviation $\sigma = 25$.

The major difference between our training experiment and previous one is the training algorithm. In our refined training scheme, we employed (1) our proposed algorithm to solve the lower-level problem with very high accuracy, and (2) LBFGS to optimize the model parameters, but in contrast, Samuel and Tappen used non-linear conjugate gradient and plain gradient descent algorithm, respectively. In our refined training algorithm, we used the normalized norm of the gradient, i.e., $\frac{\|\nabla_x E(x^*)\|_2}{\sqrt{N}} \leq \varepsilon_l$ (N is the pixel number of the training patch) as the stopping criterion for solving the lower-level problem. In our training experiment, we set $\varepsilon_l = 10^{-5}$ (gray-value in range [0 255]), which implies a very accurate solution.

---

[1] http://www.cs.toronto.edu/~liam/software.shtml

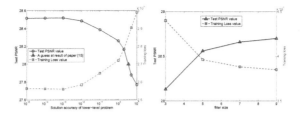

Fig. 1. Performance curves (test PSNR value and training loss value) *vs.*{the solution accuracy of the lower-level problem ε_l & the filter size}. It is clear that solving the lower-level problem with higher accuracy is beneficial and larger filter size can normally bring some improvement.

Based on this training configuration, we learned 24 filters of size 5×5, then we applied them to image denoising task to estimate the inference performance using the same 68 test images. Finally, we got an average PSNR value of 28.51dB for noise level $\sigma = 25$, which is significantly superior to previous result of 27.86dB in [15]. We argue that the major reason lies in our refined training algorithm that we solve the lower-level problem with very high accuracy.

To make this argument more clear, we need to eliminate the possibility of training dataset, because we did not exploit exactly the same training dataset as previous work (unfortunately we do not have their dataset in hand). Since the training patches were randomly selected, we could run the training experiment multiple times by using different training dataset. Finally, we found that the deviation of test PSNR values based on 68 test images is within 0.02dB, which is negligible. Therefore, it is clear that training dataset is not the reason for this improvement, and the only remaining reason is our refined training scheme.

The Influence of ε_l: To investigate the influence of the solution accuracy of the lower-level problem ε_l more detailedly, we conducted a series of training and testing experiments by setting ε_l to different magnitudes. Based on a fixed training dataset (160 patches of size 51×51) and 68 test images, we got the performance curves with respect to the solution accuracy ε_l, as shown in Figure 1 (left). From Figure 1 (left), we can clearly see that it is indeed the high solution accuracy that helps us to achieve the above siginificant improvement. This finding is the main contribution of our paper. We also make a guess how accurate Samuel and Tappen solve the lower-level problem according to their result and our performance curve, which is marked by a red triangle in Figure 1 (left). The argument that higher solution accuracy of the lower-level problem is helpful is explicable, the reason is described below.

As we know, the key aspect of our approach is to calculate the gradients of the loss function with respect to the parameters ϑ. According to (7), there is a precondition to obtain accurate gradients: both the lower-level problem and the inverse matrix of Hessian matrix H_E must be solved with high accuracy, *i.e.*, we need to calculate a x^* such that $\nabla_x E(x^*) = 0$ and compute $(H_E)^{-1}$ explicitly. Since the Hessian matrix H_E is highly sparse, we can solve the linear system $H_E x = b$ efficiently with very high accuracy (we use the "backslash" operator in

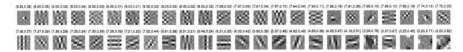

Fig. 2. 48 learned filters (7 × 7). The first number in the bracket is the weight α_i and the second one is the norm of the filter.

Matlab). However, for the lower-level problem, in practice we can only solve it to finite accuracy by using certain algorithms, *i.e.*, $\frac{\|\nabla_x E(x^*)\|_2}{\sqrt{N}} \leq \varepsilon_l$. If the lower-level problem is not solved to sufficient accuracy, the gradients $\nabla_\vartheta L$ are certainly inaccurate which will probably affect the training performance. This has been demonstrated in our experiments. Therefore, for the bi-level training framework, it is necessary to solve the lower-level problem as accurately as possible, *e.g.*, in our training we solved it to a very high accuracy with $\varepsilon_l = 10^{-5}$.

The Influence of Basis: In our playback experiments, we used the "inverse" whitened PCA basis to keep consistent with previous work. However, we argue that the DCT basis is a better choice, because meaningful filters should be mean-zero according to the findings in [9], which is guaranteed by DCT basis without the constant basis vector. Therefore, we will exploit the DCT filters excluding the filter with uniform entries from now on. Using this modified DCT basis, we retrained our model and we got a test PSNR result of 28.54dB.

The Influence of Training Dataset: To verify whether larger training dataset is beneficial, we retrained our model by using (1) 200 samples of size 64 × 64 and (2) 200 samples of size 100 × 100, which is about two times and four times larger than our previous dataset, respectively. Finally, we got a test PSNR result of 28.56dB for both cases. As shown before, the influence of training dataset is marginal.

The Influence of Model Capacity: In above experiments, we concentrated on the model of size 5 × 5 to keep consistent with previous work. We can also train models of different filter sizes, *e.g.*, 3 × 3, 7 × 7 or 9 × 9, to investigate the influence of model capacity. Based on the training dataset of 200 patches of size 64 × 64, we retrained our model with different filter size; the training results and testing performance are summarized in Figure 1 (right). We can see that normally increasing the filter size can bring some improvement. However, the improvement of filter size 9 × 9 is marginal compared to filter size 7 × 7, yet the former is much more time consuming. The training time for the model with 48 filters of size 7 × 7 was approximately 24 hours on a server (Intel X5675, 3.07GHz, 24 cores), but in contrast, the model of size 9 × 9 took about 20 days. More importantly, the inference time of the model of size 9 × 9 is certainly longer than the model of size 7 × 7, in that it involves more filters of larger size. Therefore, the model of size 7 × 7 offers the best trade-off between speed and quality, and we use it for the following applications. The learned 48 filters together with their associated weights and norms are presented in Figure 2.

Table 2. Summary of denoising experiments results (average PSNRs over 68 test images from the Berkeley database). We highlighted the state-of-the-art results.

σ	KSVD	FoE	BM3D	LSSC	EPLL	Ours
15	30.87	30.99	31.08	**31.27**	31.19	31.18
25	28.28	28.40	28.56	**28.70**	**28.68**	**28.66**
50	25.17	25.35	25.62	**25.72**	**25.67**	**25.70**

Table 3. Typical run time of the denoising methods for a 481×321 image ($\sigma = 25$) on a server (Intel X5675, 3.07GHz). The highlighted number is the run time of GPU implementation.

	KSVD	FoE	BM3D	LSSC	EPLL	Ours
T(s)	30	1600	4.3	700	99	12 (**0.3**)
psnr	28.28	28.40	28.56	28.70	28.68	28.66

5   Application Results

An important question for a learned prior model is how well it generalizes. To evaluate this, we directly applied the above 48 filters of size 7×7 trained based on image denoising task to various image restoration problems such as image deconvolution, inpainting and super-resolution, as well as denoising. Due to space limitation, here we only present denoising results and the comparison to state-of-the-arts. The other results will be shown in the final version [1].

We applied our opt-MRF model to image denoising problem and compared its performance with leading image denoising methods, including three state-of-the-art methods: (1) BM3D [4]; (2) LSSC [12]; (3) GMM-EPLL [22] along with two leading generic methods: (4) a MRF-based approach, FoE [7]; and (5) a synthesis sparse representation based method, KSVD [6] trained on natural image patches. All implementations were downloaded from the corresponding authors' homepages. We conducted denoising experiments over 68 test images with various noise levels $\sigma = \{15, 25, 50\}$. To make a fair comparison, we used exactly the same noisy version of each test image for different methods and different test images were added with distinct noise realizations. All results were computed per image and then averaged over the test dataset. We used L-BFGS to solve the MAP-based MRF model (2). When (2) is applied to various noise level σ, we need to tune the parameter λ (empirical choice $\lambda = 25/\sigma$).

Table 2 shows the summary of results. It is clear that our opt-MRF model outperforms two leading generic methods and has been on par with three state-of-the-art methods for any noise level. Comparing the result of our opt-MRF model with results presented in Table 1, our model has obviously achieved the best performance among all the MRF-based systems. To the best of our knowledge, this is the first time that a MRF model based on generic priors of natural images has achieved such clear state-of-the-art performance. We provide image denoising examples in the final version [1].

In additional, our opt-MRF model is well-suited to GPU parallel computation in that it only contains the operation of convolution. Our GPU implementation based on NVIDIA Geforce GTX 680 accelerates the inference procedure significantly; for a denoising task with $\sigma = 25$, typically it takes 0.42s for image size 512×512, 0.30s for 481×321 and 0.15s for 256×256. In Table 3, we show the average run time of the considered denoising methods on 481×321 images. Considering the speed and quality of our model, it is a perfect choice of the base methods in the image restoration framework recently proposed in [10], which leverages advantages of existing methods.

6 Conclusion

In this paper, we revisited the loss-specific training approach proposed by Samuel and Tappen in [15] by using a refined training algorithm. We have shown that the performance of the loss-specific training was indeed undervalued in previous work. We argued that the major reason lies in the solution accuracy of the lower-level problem in the bi-level framework, and we have demonstrated that solving the lower-level problem with higher accuracy is beneficial. We have shown that we can further improve the performance of the learned model a little bit by using larger filters. For image denoising task, our learned opt-MRF model of size 7×7 presented the best performance among existing MRF-based systems, and has already been on par with state-of-the-art denoising methods. The performance of our opt-MRF model proves two issues: (1) the loss-specific training scheme under the framework of bi-level optimization, which is convergence guaranteed, is highly effective for parameters learning; (2) MAP estimate should be still considered as one of the leading approaches in low-level vision.

References

1. http://gpu4vision.icg.tugraz.at/
2. Barbu, A.: Training an active random field for real-time image denoising. IEEE Trans. on Image Proc. 18(11), 2451–2462 (2009)
3. Colson, B., Marcotte, P., Savard, G.: An overview of bilevel optimization. Annals OR 153(1), 235–256 (2007)
4. Dabov, K., Foi, A., Katkovnik, V., Egiazarian, K.O.: Image denoising by sparse 3-d transform-domain collaborative filtering. IEEE Trans. on Image Proc. 16(8), 2080–2095 (2007)
5. Domke, J.: Generic methods for optimization-based modeling. Journal of Machine Learning Research - Proceedings Track 22, 318–326 (2012)
6. Elad, M., Aharon, M.: Image denoising via sparse and redundant representations over learned dictionaries. IEEE Trans. on Image Proc. 15(12), 3736–3745 (2006)
7. Gao, Q., Roth, S.: How well do filter-based MRFs model natural images? In: Pinz, A., Pock, T., Bischof, H., Leberl, F. (eds.) DAGM and OAGM 2012. LNCS, vol. 7476, pp. 62–72. Springer, Heidelberg (2012)
8. Hinton, G.E.: Training products of experts by minimizing contrastive divergence. Neural Computation 14(8), 1771–1800 (2002)

9. Huang, J., Mumford, D.: Statistics of natural images and models. In: CVPR, Fort Collins, CO, USA, pp. 541–547 (1999)
10. Jancsary, J., Nowozin, S., Rother, C.: Loss-specific training of non-parametric image restoration models: A new state of the art. In: Fitzgibbon, A., Lazebnik, S., Perona, P., Sato, Y., Schmid, C. (eds.) ECCV 2012, Part VII. LNCS, vol. 7578, pp. 112–125. Springer, Heidelberg (2012)
11. Liu, D.C., Nocedal, J.: On the limited memory BFGS method for large scale optimization. Mathematical Programming 45(1), 503–528 (1989)
12. Mairal, J., Bach, F., Ponce, J., Sapiro, G., Zisserman, A.: Non-local sparse models for image restoration. In: ICCV, pp. 2272–2279 (2009)
13. Peyré, G., Fadili, J.: Learning analysis sparsity priors. In: Proc. of Sampta 2011 (2011), http://hal.archives-ouvertes.fr/hal-00542016/
14. Roth, S., Black, M.J.: Fields of experts. International Journal of Computer Vision 82(2), 205–229 (2009)
15. Samuel, K.G.G., Tappen, M.: Learning optimized MAP estimates in continuously-valued MRF models. In: CVPR (2009)
16. Schmidt, U., Gao, Q., Roth, S.: A generative perspective on MRFs in low-level vision. In: CVPR, pp. 1751–1758 (2010)
17. Schmidt, U., Schelten, K., Roth, S.: Bayesian deblurring with integrated noise estimation. In: CVPR, pp. 2625–2632 (2011)
18. Tappen, M.F., Liu, C., Adelson, E.H., Freeman, W.T.: Learning gaussian conditional random fields for low-level vision. In: CVPR, pp. 1–8 (2007)
19. Tappen, M.F.: Utilizing variational optimization to learn markov random fields. In: CVPR, pp. 1–8 (2007)
20. Weiss, Y., Freeman, W.T.: What makes a good model of natural images? In: CVPR (2007)
21. Zhang, H., Zhang, Y., Li, H., Huang, T.S.: Generative bayesian image super resolution with natural image prior. IEEE Trans. on Image Proc. 21(9), 4054–4067 (2012)
22. Zoran, D., Weiss, Y.: From learning models of natural image patches to whole image restoration. In: ICCV, pp. 479–486 (2011)

Labeling Examples That Matter:
Relevance-Based Active Learning
with Gaussian Processes

Alexander Freytag[1], Erik Rodner[1,2], Paul Bodesheim[1], and Joachim Denzler[1]

[1] Computer Vision Group, Friedrich Schiller University Jena, Germany
http://www.inf-cv.uni-jena.de
[2] UC Berkeley ICSI & EECS, United States

Abstract. Active learning is an essential tool to reduce manual annotation costs in the presence of large amounts of unsupervised data. In this paper, we introduce new active learning methods based on measuring the impact of a new example on the current model. This is done by deriving model changes of Gaussian process models in closed form. Furthermore, we study typical pitfalls in active learning and show that our methods automatically balance between the exploitation and the exploration trade-off. Experiments are performed with established benchmark datasets for visual object recognition and show that our new active learning techniques are able to outperform state-of-the-art methods.

1 Introduction

The amount of visual data available on the Internet is tremendous and still rapidly increasing, for an example, around three million images are uploaded to Facebook every day. When annotated properly, such image collections are powerful sources for building and improving visual recognition algorithms that learn object and category models. The ImageNet project [6] for example used Internet search engines and manual filtering done by Amazon Mechanical Turk workers to provide labeled images for more than $10,000$ different classes and semantic concepts. However, the majority of available images on the net is biased towards very common and similar object instances (*e.g.*, standard white mugs in different resolutions). If we automatically select relevant sample images and manually ensure their correct labeling, we would generate annotated visual data more efficiently. Furthermore, for real-world robotics scenarios, limiting ourselves to a fixed number of classes beforehand is likely to fail due to the large variety of application-specific semantic concepts.

Due to these reasons, we consider active learning in this paper, which allows for actively obtaining labels from human annotators for samples that are likely to be important to improve the current classifier. In particular, given a set of unlabeled examples, an active learning algorithm has to pick a specific example, which is then labeled and added to the training set. The goal of active learning in this case is to save annotation budget and to allow for steeper learning curves that lead to higher recognition performances with fewer labeled training examples.

J. Weickert, M. Hein, and B. Schiele (Eds.): GCPR 2013, LNCS 8142, pp. 282–291, 2013.

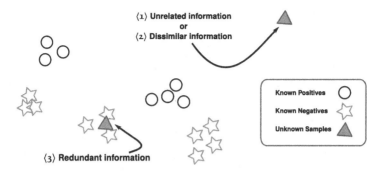

Fig. 1. Typical pitfalls in active learning scenarios: queried examples are either possible outliers (*unrelated* ⟨1⟩ or *dissimilar* ⟨2⟩ to the current distribution), or the samples will likely to be *redundant* ⟨3⟩. Our methods implicitly balance both extrema automatically by selecting samples that are useful (Given numbers reflect terms in Theorem 1).

The difficulty of active learning is the critical trade-off between exploration and exploitation, *i.e.*, is it beneficial to explore the feature space by selecting examples with a large distance to the current training set or should we select examples nearby with the risk that they are likely to be redundant (see Fig. 1)? Our approach directly tackles this trade-off by selecting examples that do have an impact on the classification model. For classification, we use Gaussian process (GP) models [13], which provide probabilistic non-linear classifiers and achieve comparable performance to SVM models. One of the advantages of the GP regression framework is that we can update the model in closed form for the case a new training example is added, which is derived in this paper. The update formulas allow us to measure the impact of an example on the model in various ways leading to new active learning methods. We also show the underlying relation to other approaches, like the one in [10], and compare our results to them in several experiments. The contributions of this paper are as follows:

1. **Model change for GP**: We derive update formulas for GP regression which give interesting insights into what is going on when new examples are added to the current model.
2. **Active learning strategies based on expected change**: We derive two strategies for binary scenarios based on the impact of a new example on the current classification model. Both strategies are shown to be suitable for active learning in several scenarios.
3. **Robustness with respect to initial set size**: In contrast to state-of-the-art query strategies, our methods are able to significantly reduce the labeling effort even in the presence of extremely few initially known samples.

We briefly review related approaches and active learning with Gaussian processes in Sect. 2 and 3. Closed-form model updates for GP regression are presented in detail and our active learning methods are derived in Sect. 4. Experimental results are given in Sect. 5 highlighting the benefits of our introduced methods in several active learning scenarios. A summary and outlook concludes the paper.

2   Related Work

Definition of Active Learning.   The pipeline in an active learning scenario is as follows: (1) collect a large number of unlabeled examples $\mathcal{U} = \{\widehat{\boldsymbol{x}}^{(1)}, \ldots, \widehat{\boldsymbol{x}}^{(m)}\}$, (2) hand them over to a query function $\mathcal{Q}$ to compute a score for every sample, and (3) choose a sample $\widehat{\boldsymbol{x}}^{(i)} \in \mathcal{U}$ with best score to label it and provide it as an additional training example for a classifier. State-of-the-art methods can be divided into those that directly aim at minimizing the expected future classification error of the classifier [8,14] or alternatively try to reduce the space of hypotheses consistent with the data known so far as fast as possible [4,15,16,17,10].

Combining Exploration and Exploitation.   In active learning scenarios, the decision has to be made whether to spend some (annotation) budget in exploring unseen regions of the feature space or whether to alternatively refine the current decision boundaries in order to improve separability of known classes. While the first aspect is denoted as *exploration*, the second one is usually referred to as *exploitation*. However, relying on a single active learning aspect is unfeasible for many if not all real-world applications [12,7]. Depending on the dataset as well as the actual problem and the currently known samples, both aspects need to be taken into account but are not equally important. Baram et al. [1] propose selecting the current criterion from a pool of query strategies using a multi-armed bandit. Osugi et al. [12] flip a biased coin to decide between pure exploration and pure exploitation. Furthermore, they update the probability depending on the change of the current model but without considering the actual success of the query. Ebert et al. [7] propose switching between different explorative and exploitative methods using a Markov decision process formulation and update the state transitions online as well. All of the previously presented approaches aim at explicitly selecting the currently most valuable query strategy. In contrast, our approach implicitly combines exploration and exploitation without the necessity of a selection step or a decision model.

Work Most Similar to Our Approach.   Cebron and Berthold [5] propose using a linear combination of an explorative and an exploitative strategy. However, the linear weighting has to be defined explicitly and in addition the exploration method is "out-of-the-box" without a clear relation to the classification model used. Kapoor et al. [10] propose combining expected mean and variance of a Gaussian process classifier by dividing both scores, which can only be justified heuristically. In contrast to both approaches, our techniques are derived from the underlying classification model without any parameters to tune. Similar in spirit is the approach of Vezhnevets et al. [18], where the expected change of a conditional random field after including a labeled example is taken as active learning score. To compute the expected change, assumptions and simplifications have to be made to handle computational costs. For Gaussian process models, Bodesheim et al. [3] introduced an approximation of the expected model change only based on the change of the model output for the new sample. In contrast to both techniques, our approach does not need any assumption or simplification to assess the change of the model.

3   Active Learning with Gaussian Processes

It has been shown that Gaussian process models are useful for active learning [16], especially in visual object categorization [10]. Using the Gaussian process regression framework, binary class labels $y_i \in \{1, -1\}$ of samples $\boldsymbol{x}^{(i)}$ are treated as continuous values which are assumed to be outputs of a latent function f. Following a Gaussian noise model, function values are assumed to be disturbed by white Gaussian noise $\epsilon \sim \mathcal{N}(0, \sigma_n^2)$ leading to $y_i = f(\boldsymbol{x}^{(i)}) + \epsilon$. Latent function values $\boldsymbol{f}$ for any finite set of samples $\mathbf{X} = \{\boldsymbol{x}^{(1)}, \ldots, \boldsymbol{x}^{(n)}\}$ are modeled to be jointly Gaussian with a zero mean function and a covariance function κ, i.e., $\boldsymbol{f} \sim \mathcal{GP}(\mathbf{0}, \kappa(\mathbf{X}, \mathbf{X}))$. Given a set of training samples, marginalization over latent function values leads to a Gaussian posterior distribution for the label of a test sample $\boldsymbol{x}^*$, where predictive mean and variance can be computed in closed form:

$$\mu_*(\boldsymbol{x}^*) = \boldsymbol{k}_*^{\mathrm{T}} \left(\mathbf{K} + \sigma_n^2 \mathbf{I}\right)^{-1} \boldsymbol{y} = \boldsymbol{k}_*^{\mathrm{T}} \boldsymbol{\alpha} \ , \tag{1}$$

$$\sigma_*^2(\boldsymbol{x}^*) = k_{**} + \sigma_n^2 - \boldsymbol{k}_*^{\mathrm{T}} \left(\mathbf{K} + \sigma_n^2 \mathbf{I}\right)^{-1} \boldsymbol{k}_* = \sigma_{f_*}^2 + \sigma_n^2 \ . \tag{2}$$

Here, we use $\mathbf{K}$, $\boldsymbol{k}_*$, and k_{**} to denote the kernel matrix containing covariances of training samples, the kernel vector containing covariances between the training samples and the test sample, and the covariance of the test sample to itself, respectively. The sign of the predictive mean is typically used for classification. Note that within this paper, we focus on binary classification as done by [10], which offers a large variety of scenarios to be tackled. Object detection methods for example rely on this setup and learn from positive samples of a specific object class and lots of negative data from arbitrary other classes and background textures. For multi-class settings, simple techniques like using the score difference between the best and the second best class usually work well.

As proposed in [10], samples from a huge pool of unlabeled data can be queried using one of the following three strategies. Selecting samples by minimum absolute predictive mean: $\mathcal{Q}_{\mu_*}(\mathcal{U}) = \mathrm{argmin}_{\widehat{\boldsymbol{x}}^{(i)} \in \mathcal{U}} |\mu_*(\widehat{\boldsymbol{x}}^{(i)})|$ is an exploitative strategy, since such samples are near the decision boundary of the classification model. Samples that are far from already known data can be selected via a large predictive variance: $\mathcal{Q}_{\sigma_*^2}(\mathcal{U}) = \mathrm{argmax}_{\widehat{\boldsymbol{x}}^{(i)} \in \mathcal{U}} \sigma_*^2(\widehat{\boldsymbol{x}}^{(i)})$ to explore the feature space. As a combination of exploitation and exploration it is suggested to query samples based on uncertainty defined by: $\mathcal{Q}_{\mathrm{unc}}(\mathcal{U}) = \mathrm{argmin}_{\widehat{\boldsymbol{x}}^{(i)} \in \mathcal{U}} \frac{|\mu_*(\widehat{\boldsymbol{x}}^{(i)})|}{\sqrt{\sigma_*^2(\widehat{\boldsymbol{x}}^{(i)})}}$.

However, rather than defining a combination of exploration and exploitation heuristically, we present strategies that are based on theoretical foundations of Gaussian process regression models and corresponding model changes. These strategies are derived in the next section.

4   Relevance-Based Active Learning

In an active learning setup, one seeks to query examples that are most valuable with respect to the given task. As presented in Sect. 2, several approaches exist to define what is *valuable*, e.g., examples that are maximally unknown or those leading to the largest estimated gain of recognition rates. However, when we pick a new example to be labeled, we should ensure that the labeling process will not be in vain, *i.e.*, that the chosen example will be taken into account when building the new model.

Due to the representer theorem, classification scores of many popular classification models can be computed as a weighted sum of similarities between test example x^* and all training data, *i.e.*, $s(x^*) = k_*^T \alpha$. Common examples are support vector machines (SVM) or Gaussian processes (GP), which have been briefly reviewed in the previous section. If an entry α_i is almost zero, the influence of the corresponding example vanishes. If we estimate or even predict the weight $\bar{\alpha}_{n+1}$ of the updated model parameters $\bar{\alpha}$ for a new example, we could only take examples into account for labeling, that have a large influence and are therefore worth being labeled.

4.1 Computing Impact Using Gaussian Processes

In contrast to SVMs, where $\bar{\alpha}$ is only available after convex optimization [19], we can indeed compute $\bar{\alpha}$ for GP in closed form. Let us have a closer look on the change of the weight vector when a new example x^* is added. The new kernel matrix $\bar{K}$ after selecting x^* with binary label y_* is given by:

$$\bar{K} = \begin{bmatrix} K + \sigma_n^2 \cdot I & k_* \\ k_*^T & \kappa(x^*, x^*) + \sigma_n^2 \end{bmatrix} . \tag{3}$$

Based on the following theorem[1] , we can compute new weights $\bar{\alpha}$ in closed form.

Theorem 1 (Closed form update of GP regression weights). *Let x^*, y_*, K, k_*, k_{**}, α, σ_n^2, and $\sigma_{f_*}^2$ be as previously defined. Then we can compute the weight vector $\bar{\alpha}$ after adding x^* to the training set as follows:*

$$\bar{\alpha} = \bar{K}^{-1} \begin{bmatrix} y \\ y_* \end{bmatrix} = \underbrace{\begin{bmatrix} \alpha \\ 0 \end{bmatrix}}_{\langle 1 \rangle} + \underbrace{\frac{1}{\sigma_{f_*}^2 + \sigma_n^2}}_{\langle 1 \rangle} \underbrace{\begin{bmatrix} \left(K + \sigma_n^2 \cdot I\right)^{-1} k_* \\ -1 \end{bmatrix}}_{\langle 2 \rangle} \underbrace{\left(k_*^T \alpha - y_*\right)}_{\langle 3 \rangle} . \tag{T1}$$

The three factors in Eq. (T1) can be nicely interpreted. The first term $\langle 1 \rangle$ states that if a new example is *unrelated* to the distribution of current training data, *i.e.*, the predictive variance is large indicating a possible outlier [11], the weight $\bar{\alpha}_{n+1}$ for the example as well as the overall model change $\triangle = ||\bar{\alpha} - (\alpha^T, 0)^T||$ will be small. Expression $\langle 2 \rangle$ can also be interpreted in a similar fashion as a weighted Parzen estimate and we observe that if a new example is again *dissimilar* with respect to currently known training examples, the overall model change $\triangle$ will again be small. Finally, in $\langle 3 \rangle$ we notice that if *redundant* information is to be added, *i.e.*, the new label can already be explained given the current model, the new weight $\bar{\alpha}_{n+1}$ as well as the overall model change $\triangle$ will be small as well. A visual explanation of this behavior is shown in Fig. 1.

---
[1] A complete proof based on block matrix inversion [2, p. 117] is given in the suppl. material.

4.2   Derived Active Learning Strategies

We derive two new GP query methods from the previous result. Whereas the first strategy only considers the resulting weight for a new example, the second takes the overall model change into account.

From Theorem 1 we know that the new entry of the updated alpha vector only depends on the first and third term. However, the ground-truth label y_* is not known before querying it, and we have to make assumptions based on the information currently available. In absence of further information, we choose the most pessimistic estimate of model change for a given example $\widehat{x}$:

$$Q_{\text{weight}}(\mathcal{U}) = \underset{\widehat{x}^{(i)} \in \mathcal{U}}{\arg\max} \; \underset{y^{(i)} \in \{-1,1\}}{\min} \frac{|\mu_*(\widehat{x}^{(i)}) - y^{(i)}|}{\sigma_f^2(\widehat{x}^{(i)}) + \sigma_n^2} \; . \tag{4}$$

This strategy can be interpreted as an implicit balancing between exploitative methods (enumerator) and explorative methods (denominator) [5,7].

As mentioned earlier, the second strategy will also take the overall model change into account. The underlying assumption is that a sample, which would heavily affect the current model even with the most plausible label, is worth being labeled. We make use of Theorem 1 and arrive at the following:

$$Q_{\text{impact}}(\mathcal{U}) = \underset{\widehat{x}^{(i)} \in \mathcal{U}}{\arg\max} \; \underset{y^{(i)} \in \{-1,1\}}{\min} \left\| \Delta \alpha^{(i)} \right\|_1 \tag{5}$$

$$= \underset{\widehat{x}^{(i)} \in \mathcal{U}}{\arg\max} \; \underset{y^{(i)} \in \{-1,1\}}{\min} \left\| \frac{|\mu_*(\widehat{x}^{(i)}) - y^{(i)}|}{\sigma_f^2(\widehat{x}^{(i)}) + \sigma_n^2} \cdot \begin{bmatrix} (\mathbf{K} + \sigma_n^2 \cdot \mathbf{I})^{-1} \, k_*^{(i)} \\ -1 \end{bmatrix} \right\|_1 \tag{6}$$

We see in the next section as well as in the experimental results (Sect. 5) that both methods implicitly adapt the amount of exploration and exploitation leading to superior learning rates compared to state-of-the-art techniques.

4.3   Trade-Off between Exploration and Exploitation

In the following, we analyze the behavior of the derived strategies on a synthetic 1D toy example. As visualized in Fig. 2, we only know two positive and a single negative example. Examples are represented based on a single 1D feature value, and similarity is measured using a standard RBF kernel. Both plots show the scores of the different GP based query strategies for a broad range of possible inputs. Note that we do not include Q_{unc} into the figure for the sake of simplicity. Apart from this, its behavior is pretty similar to Q_{μ_*}.

For computing the left plot, the bandwidth parameter of the RBF kernel σ_{RBF} was set to a rather small value of 0.15, which simulates a sparsely sampled feature space in the current region of investigation. Since there is almost no interaction between the different examples with respect to this modeling, exploration of almost every part of the space is important and will add valuable information. In contrast to this, the right plot was computed with $\sigma_{\text{RBF}} = 1.5$ which simulates a densely packed feature space. In this case, improving the actual discrimination

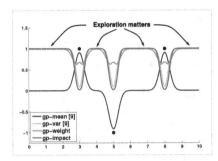 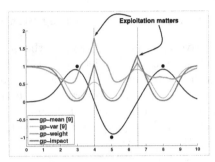

Fig. 2. A synthetic 1D example visualizing the different active learning strategies. In the left plot, known samples indicated by black dots are widely spread (a sparsely sampled feature space), *i.e.*, exploration matters, whereas in the right plot, known samples are close together (a densely packed space) where exploitation is more urgent.

ability of the model is more important and clarifying the actual class boundaries should be in the focus of actively selecting new samples. However, we note that both mean and variance favor samples maximally far away from the current distribution, which leads to outliers that are unrelated to the current problem. We see in the next section that these observations are confirmed in several visual recognition scenarios.

5   Experimental Evaluation

Active learning experiments are conducted on established image categorization datasets. Our findings can be summarized as follows:

1. For a **small number of initial training examples**, our new strategies perform significantly better than state-of-the-art strategies for GP due to a suitable trade-off between exploration and exploitation.
2. For **representative initial training sets**, our new strategies perform as good as established methods and lead to significant performance gains over random sampling.

Experimental Setup.   We conduct active learning experiments on popular image recognition datasets. For every dataset, we first randomly select 100 subsets consisting of a single positive and 9 negative classes, and average results over 10 random initializations per subset. In total, this results in 1,000 different active learning scenarios per dataset. Accuracies after every query are evaluated on disjoint test sets using the area under receiver operator curves (AUC). Final learning curves are computed by averaging AUC scores over all subsets and initializations. The noise parameter for model regularization was optimized by maximizing the marginal likelihood. Experiments were conducted in Matlab[2]. Runtimes are not visualized, since the majority of computational time is spent for updating classifier and kernel values. In addition, asymptotic runtimes

---

[2] Source code is available at www.inf-cv.uni-jena.de/active_learning

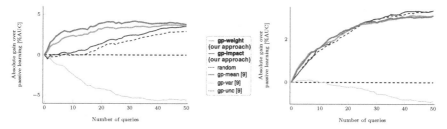

Fig. 3. Gain of active over passive learning on **Caltech-256**. Initial number of samples per class is 1 and 5, respectively.

for the introduced methods are in the same order of complexity as $\mathcal{Q}_{\sigma_*^2}$ and $\mathcal{Q}_{\mathrm{unc}}$. Results are presented for passive learning (random), three state-of-the-art strategies based on a GP model (gp-mean, gp-var, and gp-unc) as well as the two introduced strategies (gp-weight and gp-impact). **Note that absolute performance values are part of the supplementary material.**

Results on Caltech-256. A commonly used benchmark datasets for visual object recognition is Caltech-256, which consists of 256 object categories from different areas of real-world situations, *e.g.*, animals, vehicles, or persons. For the sake of simplicity and reproducibility, we represent images with L_1-normalized bag-of-visual-words histograms over densely sampled SIFT features[3].

In Fig. 3, experimental results averaged over $1,000$ binary settings are visualized[4]. First of all, we observe the prominent gain of active learning methods over passive learning except for variance-based queries. This clearly stresses the benefit of active learning in general. Apart from this, we note that the new strategies outperform existing methods in the presence of few labeled examples and lead to comparable results if more examples are already known. In both settings they outperform random querying by far.

Results on ImageNet. Within the last years, the ImageNet database became a standard benchmark for large-scale visual object classification. In total, $1,000$ different classes from a wide range of different synsets are provided. We again represent images with L_1-normalized bag-of-visual-words histograms over densely sampled SIFT features[5].

In Fig. 4, the experimental results are visualized[4]. If the number of initial samples is low, we again observe that state-of-the-art strategies cannot improve accuracies over passive learning, since the majority of unlabeled samples gives valuable information in this early stage. However, even for this setup our strategies are able to clearly improve results. Especially in medical applications, where obtaining even a handful of labeled samples is extremely expensive, choosing the informative ones is highly valuable. For larger initial sets, we notice that our new methods lead to results comparable to those of state-of-the-art strategies. Again, passive learning is significantly outperformed.

---

[3] http://homes.esat.kuleuven.be/~tuytelaa/unsup_features.html

[4] Further learning curves can be found in the supplementary material.

[5] http://www.image-net.org/download-features

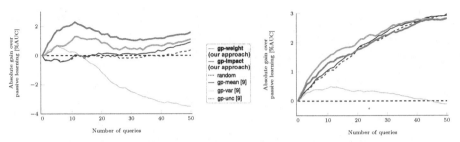

Fig. 4. Gain of active over passive learning on **ImageNet**. Initial number of samples per class is 1 and 5, respectively.

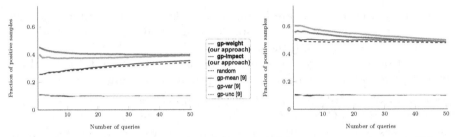

Fig. 5. Fraction of positive examples within queried images averaged over 1,000 experiments on ImageNet. Initial number of samples per class is 1 and 5, respectively.

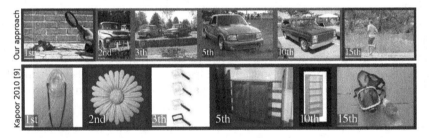

Fig. 6. Queried images using $\mathcal{Q}_{\mathrm{impact}}$ (*top*) and $\mathcal{Q}_{\sigma_*^2}$ (*bottom*) in a single run on ImageNet. Green and blue borders indicate images of positive and negative classes, respectively. Queries of the remaining strategies can be found in the supplementary material.

One reason for the superior behavior of our strategies can be derived from Fig. 5: both strategies $\mathcal{Q}_{\mathrm{weight}}$ and $\mathcal{Q}_{\mathrm{impact}}$ are able to balance the selection of positive and negative samples, which is essential for building a representative model. In contrast to that, established methods are more biased towards negative examples, which leads to models less useful for the binary classification task. A qualitative example is given in Fig. 6 which further highlights this observation.

6   Conclusion and Further Work

We presented new active learning methods that explicitly select non-redundant (relevant) unlabeled examples for annotation. Our methods are based on measuring the impact of an unlabeled example on a Gaussian process model in the case the example would be added as a new labeled training example. The resulting active learning approaches were able to outperform previous methods significantly on established benchmark datasets.

Future work will focus on combining active learning methods and learning optimal combinations from auxiliary data, *i.e.*, we would like to perform active learning in a transfer learning fashion, where we learn priors for suitable strategies from other (visual) classification tasks. Another topic is to combine our active learning methods with large-scale Gaussian process approaches [9].

References

1. Baram, Y., El-Yaniv, R., Luz, K.: Online choice of active learning algorithms. JMLR 5, 255–291 (2004)
2. Bernstein, D.S.: Matrix Mathematics, 2nd edn. Princeton University Press (2009)
3. Bodesheim, P., Rodner, E., Freytag, A., Denzler, J.: Divergence-based one-class classification using gaussian processes. In: BMVC, pp. 50.1–50.11 (2012)
4. Campbell, C., Cristianini, N., Smola, A.: Query learning with large margin classifiers. In: ICML (2000)
5. Cebron, N., Berthold, M.: Active learning for object classification: from exploration to exploitation. Data Mining and Knowledge Discovery 18, 283–299 (2009)
6. Deng, J., Dong, W., Socher, R., Li, L.J., Li, K., Fei-Fei, L.: Imagenet: A large-scale hierarchical image database. In: CVPR (2009)
7. Ebert, S., Fritz, M., Schiele, B.: Ralf: A reinforced active learning formulation for object class recognition. In: CVPR, pp. 3626–3633 (2012)
8. Freund, Y., Seung, H.S., Shamir, E., Tishby, N.: Selective sampling using the query by committee algorithm. Machine Learning 28, 133–168 (1997)
9. Freytag, A., Rodner, E., Bodesheim, P., Denzler, J.: Rapid uncertainty computation with gaussian processes and histogram intersection kernels. In: Lee, K.M., Matsushita, Y., Rehg, J.M., Hu, Z. (eds.) ACCV 2012, Part II. LNCS, vol. 7725, pp. 511–524. Springer, Heidelberg (2013)
10. Kapoor, A., Grauman, K., Urtasun, R., Darrell, T.: Gaussian processes for object categorization. IJCV 88, 169–188 (2010)
11. Kemmler, M., Rodner, E., Denzler, J.: One-class classification with gaussian processes. In: Kimmel, R., Klette, R., Sugimoto, A. (eds.) ACCV 2010, Part II. LNCS, vol. 6493, pp. 489–500. Springer, Heidelberg (2011)
12. Osugi, T., Kim, D., Scott, S.: Balancing exploration and exploitation: a new algorithm for active machine learning. In: ICDM, pp. 330–337 (2005)
13. Rasmussen, C.E., Williams, C.K.I.: Gaussian Processes for Machine Learning. Adaptive Computation and Machine Learning. The MIT Press (2006)
14. Roy, N., McCallum, A.: Toward optimal active learning through sampling estimation of error reduction. In: ICML, pp. 441–448 (2001)
15. Schohn, G., Cohn, D.: Less is more: Active learning with support vector machines. In: ICML, pp. 839–846 (2000)
16. Seo, S., Wallat, M., Graepel, T., Obermayer, K.: Gaussian process regression: Active data selection and test point rejection. In: IJCNN, pp. 241–246 (2010)
17. Tong, S., Koller, D.: Support vector machine active learning with applications to text classification. JMLR 2, 45–66 (2002)
18. Vezhnevets, A., Buhmann, J.M., Ferrari, V.: Active learning for semantic segmentation with expected change. In: CVPR, pp. 3162–3169 (2012)
19. Yeh, T., Darrell, T.: Dynamic visual category learning. In: CVPR, pp. 1–8 (2008)

Efficient Retrieval
for Large Scale Metric Learning

Martin Köstinger, Peter M. Roth, and Horst Bischof

Institute for Computer Graphics and Vision
Graz University of Technology, Austria
{koestinger,pmroth,bischof}@icg.tugraz.at

Abstract. In this paper, we address the problem of efficient k-NN classification. In particular, in the context of Mahalanobis metric learning. Mahalanobis metric learning recently demonstrated competitive results for a variety of tasks. However, such approaches have two main drawbacks. First, learning metrics requires often to solve complex and thus computationally very expensive optimization problems. Second, as the evaluation time linearly scales with the size of the data k-NN becomes cumbersome for large-scale problems or real-time applications with limited time budget. To overcome these problems, we propose a metric-based hashing strategy, allowing for both, efficient learning and evaluation. In particular, we adopt an efficient metric learning method for local sensitive hashing that recently demonstrated reasonable results for several large-scale benchmarks. In fact, if the intrinsic structure of the data is exploited by the metric in a meaningful way, using hashing we can compact the feature representation still obtaining competitive results. This leads to a drastically reduced evaluation effort. Results on a variety of challenging benchmarks with rather diverse nature demonstrate the power of our method. These include standard machine learning datasets as well as the challenging Public Figures Face Database. On the competitive machine learning benchmarks we obtain results comparable to the state-of-the-art Mahalanobis metric learning and hashing approaches. On the face benchmark we clearly outperform the state-of-the-art in Mahalanobis metric learning. In both cases, however, with drastically reduced evaluation effort.

1 Introduction

Among the various different classification schemes k-nearest neighbor (k-NN) based approaches using Mahalanobis metric learning have recently attracted a lot of interest in computer vision. Several powerful metric learning frameworks (*e.g.* [19,20], [4], or [7]) have been proposed that study different loss functions or regularizations. Conceptually, these methods take advantage of prior information in form of labels over simpler though more general similarity measures. Significant improvements have been observed for tracking [17], image retrieval [10], face identification [12], clustering [23], or person re-identification [9].

J. Weickert, M. Hein, and B. Schiele (Eds.): GCPR 2013, LNCS 8142, pp. 292–301, 2013.

The large-scale nature of computer vision applications poses several challenges and opportunities to the class of Mahalanobis metric learning algorithms. For instance we can learn a sophisticated distance metric that captures the structure of the dataset or learn multiple local metrics that better adapt to the intrinsic characteristics of the feature space. On larger datasets this usually leads to lower error rates [20]. In contrast, this is challenged by the computational burden in training and the needed label effort.

To reduce the required level of supervision, algorithms such as [4,11] have been introduced that are able to learn from pairwise labels. Others tackle the problem of time complexity in learning by special optimization techniques [4,20]. Nevertheless, one important aspect that is often neglected is the computational burden at test time as k-NN-search in high-dimensional spaces is cumbersome. For real-time applications with limited time budget this is even more critical; especially on larger datasets with tens of thousands of samples that have to be explored.

One strategy to alleviate this issue is to reduce the number of training samples and to introduce sparsity in the samples [3,24]. Ideally, one maintains only a relatively small set of representative prototypes which capture the discriminative essence of the dataset. This was also theoretically confirmed by Crammer *et al.* [3], who showed that prototype-based methods can be more accurate than nearest neighbor classification. Nevertheless, these methods require rather elaborate learning.

Another successful approach is to focus on sparsity in the variables and perform an efficient low dimensional embedding. For instance, one can accelerate nearest neighbor search by performing a binary Hamming embedding. This can be done by applying hashing functions directly [10] or on kernelized data [13]. In particular, hyperplanes or hyperspheres are used to partition the data. Data independent variants such as [6,2] ignore the structure of the data at all. Data dependent methods [22,8] consider the structure of the data, however these mostly build on an isotropic cluster assumption and thus do not exploit the general structure of the data.

In contrast, similar to [10] we want to exploit a general metric structure for hashing. Thus, the goal of this paper is to bridge efficient training and efficient evaluation in context of Mahalanobis metric learning. In particular, we build on an efficient metric learning approach, namely KISSME [11], which has shown competitive results on a range of benchmarks, and adopt it for two different hashing strategies. In addition, we introduce a metric-based re-ranking strategy, which further improves the classification results. The proposed approach finally enables us to drastically reduce the computational effort during training and evaluation while maintaining accuracy.

The rest of this paper is structured as follows. In Sec. 2 we first summarize the main ideas of the used metric learning approach and hashing in general and then show how both approaches can be integrated for efficient (image) retrieval. Succeeding, in Sec. 3 we show detailed experimental results on standard machine learning datasets and on the challenging PubFig [15] face recognition benchmark and also give a comparison to state-of-the-art hashing methods. Finally, in Sec. 4 we summarize and conclude the paper.

2   KISS HASH

In the following, we introduce our new metric-based k-NN classification scheme taking advantage of both, efficient learning and evaluation. The main idea is to efficiently learn a Mahalanobis metric, which better captures the intrinsic structure of the feature space, and to approximate it using hashing techniques.

The main goal of hashing is to reduce the classification effort by using a more compact representation. In particular, by mapping the features from a d-dimensional original space to a lower m-dimensional space, where $m \ll d$. A widely used approach is to apply a Hamming embedding, where the data is represented in form of binary strings. This allows for comparing the data via XOR operations, which can be computed efficiently by special purpose instructions on modern computer hardware. Given a sample $\mathbf{x}$, its binary hash-code $\mathbf{h}$ $(m \times 1)$ can be obtained via

$$\mathbf{h}(\mathbf{x}) = \mathrm{sign}\left(\mathbf{P}\mathbf{x} + \mathbf{t}\right) , \tag{1}$$

where $\mathbf{P}$ is a hashing matrix $(m \times d)$ and $\mathbf{t}$ $(m \times 1)$ is a threshold vector.

As minimization of the distances in Hamming space is related to the minimization of the distances in original space, in the following we derive two embedding strategies, exploiting the information captured by a Mahalanobis distance. The only requirement for this relation is that the hashing function sustains the locality sensitive hashing (LSH) requirement [6,2] that the probability of a collision in the hash table is related to the similarity in the original space. In the following, we first describe how to efficiently obtain a Mahalanobis metric in Sec. 2.1 and then derive two different metric-based hashing strategies: (a) via random hyperplane hashing (Sec. 2.2) and (b) via eigen-hashing (Sec. 2.3). In addition, in Sec. 2.4 we introduce a re-ranking scheme for hashing.

2.1   Efficient Mahalanobis Metric Learning

In general, the goal of Mahalanobis distance learning is to learn a distance function $d_{\mathbf{M}}^2$, which measures the squared distance between two data points $\mathbf{x}_i, \mathbf{x}_j \in \mathbb{R}^d$:

$$d_{\mathbf{M}}^2(\mathbf{x}_i, \mathbf{x}_j) = (\mathbf{x}_i - \mathbf{x}_j)^\top \mathbf{M}(\mathbf{x}_i - \mathbf{x}_j) , \tag{2}$$

where $\mathbf{M}$ induces a valid pseudo metric if it is a symmetric positive semi-definite matrix. Several different approaches (e.g., [20], [4], or [7]) have been proposed and are widely applied for various tasks. However, such approaches require complex iterative, computationally expensive optimization schemes, making them often infeasible for large-scale problems. To overcome these limitations, *KISS metric learning* (KISSME) [11] builds on a statistical motivated formulation that allows for learning just from equivalence constraints.

For the following discussion let $\mathbf{x}_i, \mathbf{x}_j \in \mathbb{R}^d$ be a pair of samples and $y_i, y_j \in \{1, 2, \ldots, c\}$ the labels. Further we define a set of similar pairs $\mathcal{S} = \{(i, j) \,|\, y_i = y_j\}$ and a set of dissimilar pairs $\mathcal{D} = \{(i, j) \,|\, y_i \neq y_j\}$. The goal of KISSME is to decide whether a pair (i, j) is similar or not. From a statistical inference point of view the optimal statistical decision can be obtained by a likelihood ratio test. Hereby, the hypothesis H_0 that the pair is dissimilar is tested against hypothesis H_1 that the pair is similar:

$$\delta(\mathbf{x}_{ij}) = \log\left(\frac{p(\mathbf{x}_{ij}|H_0)}{p(\mathbf{x}_{ij}|H_1)}\right) = \log\left(\frac{f(\mathbf{x}_{ij}|\theta_0)}{f(\mathbf{x}_{ij}|\theta_1)}\right) , \tag{3}$$

where δ is the log-likelihood ratio, $f(\mathbf{x}_{ij}|\theta)$ is a pdf with parameters θ and $\mathbf{x}_{ij} = \mathbf{x}_i - \mathbf{x}_j$.

Thus, KISSME casts the metric learning problem into the space of pairwise differences, as also the similarity Eq. (2) is defined via pairwise differences. This space has zero-mean and is invariant to the actual locality of the samples in the feature space. Assuming zero-mean Gaussian distributions within the difference space Eq. (3) can be re-written to

$$\delta(\mathbf{x}_{ij}) = \log\left(\frac{\frac{1}{\sqrt{2\pi|\Sigma_{\mathcal{D}}|}} \exp(-1/2\, \mathbf{x}_{ij}^T \Sigma_{\mathcal{D}}^{-1} \mathbf{x}_{ij})}{\frac{1}{\sqrt{2\pi|\Sigma_{\mathcal{S}}|}} \exp(-1/2\, \mathbf{x}_{ij}^T \Sigma_{\mathcal{S}}^{-1} \mathbf{x}_{ij})}\right) , \tag{4}$$

where $\Sigma_{\mathcal{S}}$ and $\Sigma_{\mathcal{D}}$ are the covariance matrices of $\mathcal{S}$ and $\mathcal{D}$, respectively.

The maximum likelihood estimate of the Gaussian is equivalent to minimize the distances from the mean in a least squares manner. This allows KISSME to find respective relevant directions for $\mathcal{S}$ and $\mathcal{D}$. By taking the log and discarding the constant terms we can simplify Eq. (4) to

$$\delta(\mathbf{x}_{ij}) = \mathbf{x}_{ij}^T \Sigma_{\mathcal{S}}^{-1} \mathbf{x}_{ij} - \mathbf{x}_{ij}^T \Sigma_{\mathcal{D}}^{-1} \mathbf{x}_{ij} = \mathbf{x}_{ij}^T(\Sigma_{\mathcal{S}}^{-1} - \Sigma_{\mathcal{D}}^{-1})\mathbf{x}_{ij} . \tag{5}$$

Finally, the Mahalanobis distance matrix $\mathbf{M}$ is obtained by

$$\mathbf{M} = \left(\Sigma_{\mathcal{S}}^{-1} - \Sigma_{\mathcal{D}}^{-1}\right) . \tag{6}$$

2.2   Hashing by Random Hyperplanes

As the metric matrix $\mathbf{M}$ is positive semi-definite (p.s.d.) we can decompose it as $\mathbf{M} = \mathbf{L}^\top \mathbf{L}$ by Cholesky factorization. The matrix $\mathbf{L}$ can be seen as linear transformation that scales and rotates the feature space according to $\mathbf{M}$. After applying the linear transformation one can perform standard locality sensitive hashing techniques as random hyperplane hashing.

Thus, to obtain the hash value for a single bit h_i the feature vector $\mathbf{x}$ is first transformed by $\mathbf{L}$ and then projected onto a random vector $\mathbf{r}_i$ that is drawn from a Gaussian distribution with zero mean and unit variance:

$$h_i(\mathbf{x}) = \begin{cases} 1 & \text{if } \mathbf{r}_i^\top \mathbf{L}\mathbf{x} \geq t_i \\ -1 & \text{otherwise .} \end{cases} \tag{7}$$

Let

$$\mathbf{R}_m = [\mathbf{r}_1 \ldots \mathbf{r}_m] \tag{8}$$

be a matrix composed of m random vectors, where m is the desired dimensionality. Then, according to Eq. (1) we can re-formulate Eq. (7) such that a hash code $\mathbf{h}(\mathbf{x})$ over all feature dimensions can be estimated:

$$\mathbf{h}(\mathbf{x}) = \text{sign}\left(\mathbf{R}_m^\top \mathbf{L}\mathbf{x} + \mathbf{t}\right) . \tag{9}$$

2.3 Hashing by Eigen-Decomposition

Since $\mathbf{M}$ is p.s.d. we can also perform an eigen-decomposition $\mathbf{M} = \mathbf{V}\mathbf{D}\mathbf{V}^\top$. This allows us to hash with eigenvectors $\mathbf{v}_i$ as follows:

$$h_i(\mathbf{x}) = \begin{cases} 1 & \text{if } \mathbf{v}_i^\top \mathbf{x}_i \geq t_i \\ -1 & \text{otherwise .} \end{cases} \tag{10}$$

Again, let

$$\mathbf{V}_m = [\mathbf{v}_1 \ldots \mathbf{v}_m] \tag{11}$$

be the matrix containing the eigenvectors associated with the largest eigenvalues, we can estimate an m-dimensional hash code for the the feature vector $\mathbf{x}$ by

$$\mathbf{h}(\mathbf{x}) = \text{sign}\left(\mathbf{V}_m^\top \mathbf{x} + \mathbf{t}\right) . \tag{12}$$

2.4 Retrieval of Hashed Examples

The Hamming embedding enables a very efficient search based on the compact binary representation. Further, on modern CPUs special purpose instructions exist that are even able to calculate the Hamming distance in a few clock-cycles. Also approximate search strategies exist that are tailored to the search in Hamming space (*e.g.*, [2] or [16]).

For the proposed method the focus is on short binary codes that can be efficiently matched followed by a re-ranking step. In particular, a short list of samples is generated by searching in Hamming space, which is then used for exact k-NN with the learned metric. To ensure efficiency compact codes are used in the first step and only a rather small subset of samples is re-ranked. In particular, we aim at re-ranking $\mathcal{O}(N^{\frac{1}{1+\epsilon}})$ samples, where N is the number of training samples in the respective dataset. For instance, if $\epsilon = 1$ only $\mathcal{O}(\sqrt{N})$ samples have to be checked. Thus, for higher values of ϵ less samples have to be re-ranked.

3   Experiments

To show the applicability of our method we conduct experiments on three standard benchmarks and on the Public Figures [15] face recognition benchmark. The goals of our experiments are twofold. First, we want to show that with a drastically reduced evaluation effort we are able to obtain similar results to KISSME and other metric learning baselines. Second, we want to prove that we are competitive to state-of-the-art hashing schemes, requiring less effort.

3.1   Machine Learning Databases

In the following, we benchmark our proposed method on MNIST [5], LETTER [5] and CHARS74k [1]. First, we give a brief overview of the databases. Second, we compare the performance related to the evaluation complexity between our method and other hashing approaches.

The MNIST database [5] of hand written digits contains in total 70,000 images in one train-test split. 60,000 samples are used for training and 10,000 for testing. The images have a resolution of 28×28 pixels and are in grayscale. In contrast, the LETTER [5] database contains a large number of synthesized images showing one of the 26 capital letters of the English alphabet. The images are represented as 16 dimensional feature vector which describes statistical moments and edge counts. Chars74K [1] contains a large mixed set of natural and synthesized characters. The images comprise one of the 26 capital or lowercase letters and digits, respectively. 7,705 characters are cropped of natural images, 3,410 are hand drawn and 62,992 are synthesized. Further, the database is split into one train/test set where 7400 samples are organized for testing and the rest for training.

In Figure 1 we compare our random hyperplane hashing method to its baseline on MNIST, LETTER, and CHARS74k. Therefore, we plot the 1-NN classification error in relation to the code length, where the maximum code length is restricted to 64 bits. In particular, we report the following results: (a) Standard KISSME without hashing, (b) nearest neighbor search in Hamming space, and (c) nearest neighbor search in Hamming space with short list re-ranking. For the re-ranking step we fix ϵ to 1, retrieving $\mathcal{O}(\sqrt{N})$ samples, which is roughly 1% of samples in these cases.

For the following discussion we focus on the results on MNIST of our random hyperplane based hashing method. The results for MNIST are visualized in Figure 1 (a), although the relative results are comparable on the different datasets. The direct nearest neighbor search in Hamming space performs initially significantly worse than the short list re-ranking method. By increasing the number of codes the performance gap gets smaller. However, ultimately for MNIST a performance gap of about 7.58% remains with a code length of 64 bits. This confirms the importance of the re-ranking step. If the short list is kept reasonable sized the computational effort is manageable. Comparing KISS-Hash with re-ranking to KISSME reveals that even with short codes comparable

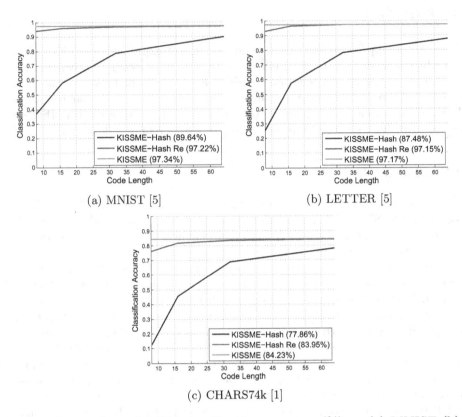

(a) MNIST [5]

(b) LETTER [5]

(c) CHARS74k [1]

Fig. 1. Comparison of 1-NN classification accuracy (%) on (a) MNIST (b) LETTER, and (c) CHARS74k for random hyperplane hashing. Numbers in parentheses denote the classification accuracy with 64 bits.

performance can be obtained. Starting from 16 bits nearly the same performance is reached at a much lower computational cost.

Next, in Table 1 we benchmark our method to various competing methods. In particular, we provide a closer look on different well-established Mahalanobis metric learning methods and hashing schemes. Comparing KISSME to other metric learning methods, *i.e.*, ITML, LDML, and LMNN, reveals that it is competitive in most cases, though requiring drastically less training time. Further, our random hyperplane hashing method as well as the eigenanalysis hashing have very similar performance to KISSME, though drastically reducing the evaluation time. Next, we compare the classification error between our methods and others and relate to their evaluation complexity. For the kernelized hashing approach of [13] the evaluation scales linearly with the number of kernel samples S times the kernel complexity K_c: $\mathcal{O}(SK_c)$. In most cases the kernel complexity is similar to a distance evaluation. KLSH requires many kernel samples to obtain similar results, we tested RBF and learned kernels (ITML). The locality-sensitive hashing approach of [10] scales with $\mathcal{O}(MD)$, where M is the length of the short list

Table 1. Comparison of classification error rates (%) on MNIST, LETTER and Chars74k. In particular we provide a closer look on different well-established Mahalanobis metric learning methods and further provide additional results for different locality-sensitive hashing methods.

Methods	MNIST	LETTER	Chars74K
Nearest Neighbors			
Nearest Neighbor (1-NN, 3-NN)	2.92 - 3.09	4.30 - 4.35	17.97 - 19.99
LMNN $_{\text{3-NN}}$ [19,20]	1.70	3.54	22.89
ITML $_{\text{1-NN}}$ [4]	2.17	4.75	17.00
ITML $_{\text{3-NN}}$ [4]	2.02	4.68	18.54
LDML $_{\text{1-NN}}$ [7]	4.04	11.25	18.62
LDML $_{\text{3-NN}}$ [7]	3.59	10.35	20.32
KISSME $_{\text{1-NN}}$ [11]	2.66	2.83	15.77
KISSME $_{\text{3-NN}}$ [11]	2.36	2.73	18.64
Locality-sensitive hashing			
KISS-HASH-RH $_{\text{1-NN}}$ (64 bit, $\epsilon = 1$)	2.78	2.85	16.05
KISS-HASH-EV $_{\text{1-NN}}$ (64 bit, $\epsilon = 1$)	2.77	3.25	15.68
KLSH [13,14] (10,000 kernel samples)	6.15	7.38	88.76
Image Search f. Learn. Metrics [10] ($\epsilon = 0.6$)	5.51	8.55	-
Spectral Hashing [22]	4.25	7.42	26.03
Multidimensional Spectral Hashing [21]	5.27	33.67	-
Spherical Hashing [8] (256 bit)	3.19	31.4	18.59

of samples generated by approximate search in Hamming space [2]. Even at a lower value of ϵ a performance gap remains. A lower value of ϵ means to retrieve more samples. Spherical hashing [8] scales with $\mathcal{O}(AD)$ where A is the number of anchor points (code length) where the hyper spheres are anchored. However, it does not match our performance using a comparable number of anchor points.

Recapitulating the different results and relating them to the evaluation complexity of related works reveals that we get competitive results and are more efficient. Moreover, we see that it is beneficial to integrate a metric and to be able to model different scalings and correlations of the feature space.

3.2 Public Figures Face Database

In the following, we demonstrate our method for face identification on the Public Figures Face Database (PubFig) [15]. PubFig is a large, real-world face dataset consisting of 58,797 images of 200 people. The evaluation set contains 42,461 images of 140 individuals. PubFig is considered as very challenging as it exhibits huge variations in pose, lighting, facial expression and general imaging and environmental conditions. To represent the faces we use the description of visual face traits [15]. They describe the presence or absence of 73 visual attributes, such as gender, race, hair color. Further, we apply a homogeneous χ^2 feature mapping

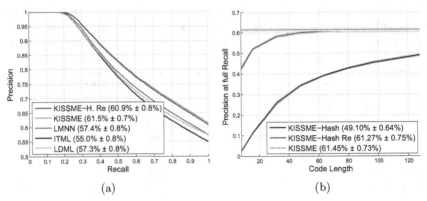

Fig. 2. Comparison of 1-NN classification accuracy (%) on Public Figures Face Database (PubFig). (a) recall / precision by ranking and thresholding classifier scores. Code length of 64 bits, $\epsilon = 1$. (b) Precision at full recall vs code length.

[18]. For the face identification benchmark we organize the data similar to the existing verification protocol in 10 folds for cross-validation. Therefore, we split the images of each individual into 10 disjoint sets.

In Figure 2 (a) we benchmark our random hyperplane hashing to recent Mahalanobis metric learning methods. The results for the eigenvalue hashing are similar. We report the face identification performance in a refusal to predict style. In that sense, recall means the percentage of samples which have a higher classifier score than the current threshold. Precision means the ratio of correctly labeled samples. We use a code length of 64 bits and $\epsilon = 1$. In Figure 2 (b) we report the precision at full recall compared to the code length. In particular, we show that our method generalizes better than LMNN [19], ITML [4] or LDML [7], which require more computational effort in evaluation. At full recall the performance difference to LMNN is 2.50%.

4 Conclusion

Mahalanobis metric learning methods have been recently successfully applied for a range of classification problems. However, such approaches have two main drawbacks: High computational effort during (a) training and (b) evaluation. In this paper, we proposed a metric-based hashing method that overcomes both problems. On the one hand side building on an efficient metric learning approach, we obtain competitive classification results on various challenging large-scale benchmarks. On the other hand side, exploiting the learned metric structure by hashing, finally leads to a drastically reduced effort at test time while maintaining the discriminative essence of the data.

Acknowledgments. The work was supported by the FFG projects Human Factors Technologies and Services (2371236) and Mobile Traffic Checker (8258408).

References

1. de Campo, T.E., Babu, B.R., Varma, M.: Character Recognition in Natural Images. In: Proc. VISAPP (2009)
2. Charikar, M.S.: Similarity estimation techniques from rounding algorithms. In: ACM Symposium on Theory of Computing (2002)
3. Crammer, K., Gilad-bachrach, R., Navot, A., Tishby, N.: Margin analysis of the LVQ algorithm. In: Advances NIPS (2002)
4. Davis, J.V., Kulis, B., Jain, P., Sra, S., Dhillon, I.S.: Information-theoretic metric learning. In: Proc. ICML (2007)
5. Frank, A., Asuncion, A.: UCI machine learning repository, university of California, Irvine, School of Information and Computer Sciences (2010), http://archive.ics.uci.edu/ml
6. Gionis, A., Indyk, P., Motwani, R.: Similarity search in high dimensions via hashing. In: Proc. Very Large Data Bases (1999)
7. Guillaumin, M., Verbeek, J., Schmid, C.: Is that you? Metric learning approaches for face identification. In: Proc. ICCV (2009)
8. Heo, J.P., Lee, Y., He, J., Chang, S.F., Yoon, S.E.: Spherical hashing. In: Proc. CVPR (2012)
9. Hirzer, M., Roth, P.M., Köstinger, M., Bischof, H.: Relaxed pairwise learned metric for person re-identification. In: Fitzgibbon, A., Lazebnik, S., Perona, P., Sato, Y., Schmid, C. (eds.) ECCV 2012, Part VI. LNCS, vol. 7577, pp. 780–793. Springer, Heidelberg (2012)
10. Jain, P., Kulis, B., Grauman, K.: Fast image search for learned metrics. In: Proc. CVPR (2008)
11. Köstinger, M., Hirzer, M., Wohlhart, P., Roth, P.M., Bischof, H.: Large scale metric learning from equivalence constraints. In: Proc. CVPR (2012)
12. Köstinger, M., Roth, P.M., Bischof, H.: Synergy-based learning of facial identity. In: Pinz, A., Pock, T., Bischof, H., Leberl, F. (eds.) DAGM and OAGM 2012. LNCS, vol. 7476, pp. 195–204. Springer, Heidelberg (2012)
13. Kulis, B., Grauman, K.: Kernelized locality-sensitive hashing. Trans. PAMI (2012)
14. Kulis, B., Grauman, K.: Kernelized locality-sensitive hashing for scalable image search. In: Proc. ICCV (2009)
15. Kumar, N., Berg, A.C., Belhumeur, P.N., Nayar, S.K.: Attribute and Simile Classifiers for Face Verification. In: Proc. ICCV (2009)
16. Norouzi, M., Punjani, A., Fleet, D.J.: Fast search in hamming space with multi-index hashing. In: Proc. CVPR (2012)
17. Shen, C.: Non-sparse linear representations for visual tracking with online reservoir metric learning. In: Proc. CVPR (2012)
18. Vedaldi, A., Zisserman, A.: Efficient additive kernels via explicit feature maps. Trans. PAMI 34(3) (2011)
19. Weinberger, K.Q., Blitzer, J., Saul, L.K.: Distance metric learning for large margin nearest neighbor classification. In: Advances NIPS (2006)
20. Weinberger, K.Q., Saul, L.K.: Fast solvers and efficient implementations for distance metric learning. In: Proc. ICML (2008)
21. Weiss, Y., Fergus, R., Torralba, A.: Multidimensional spectral hashing. In: Fitzgibbon, A., Lazebnik, S., Perona, P., Sato, Y., Schmid, C. (eds.) ECCV 2012, Part V. LNCS, vol. 7576, pp. 340–353. Springer, Heidelberg (2012)
22. Weiss, Y., Torralba, A., Fergus, R.: Spectral hashing. In: Advances NIPS (2008)
23. Ye, J., Zhao, Z., Liu, H.: Adaptive distance metric learning for clustering. In: Proc. CVPR (2007)
24. Zhang, Z., Sturgess, P., Sengupta, S., Crook, N., Torr, P.H.S.: Efficient discriminative learning of parametric nearest neighbor classifiers. In: Proc. CVPR (2012)

A Hierarchical Voxel Hash
for Fast 3D Nearest Neighbor Lookup

Bertram Drost[1] and Slobodan Ilic[2]

[1] MVTec Software GmbH
[2] Technische Universität München

Abstract. We propose a data structure for finding the exact nearest neighbors in 3D in approximately $O(\log(\log(N)))$ time. In contrast to standard approaches such as k-d-trees, the query time is independent of the location of the query point and the distribution of the data set. The method uses a hierarchical voxel approximation of the data point's Voronoi cells. This avoids backtracking during the query phase, which is a typical action for tree-based methods such as k-d-trees. In addition, voxels are stored in a hash table and a bisection on the voxel level is used to find the leaf voxel containing the query point. This is asymptotically faster than letting the query point fall down the tree. The experiments show the method's high performance compared to state-of-the-art approaches even for large point sets, independent of data and query set distributions, and illustrates its advantage in real-world applications.

1 Introduction

Quickly finding the closest point from a large set of data points in 3D is crucial for alignment algorithms, such as ICP, as well as industrial inspection and robotic navigation tasks. Most state-of-the-art methods for solving the nearest neighbor problem in 3D are based on recursive subdivisions of the underlying space to form a tree of volumes. The various subdivision strategies include uniform subdivisions, such as octrees [14], as well as non-uniform subdivisions, such as k-d-trees [2] and Delaunay or Voronoi based subdivisions.

Tree-based methods require two steps to find the exact nearest neighbor. First, the query point falls down the tree to find its corresponding leaf node. Since the query point might be closer to the boundary of the node's volume than to the data points contained in the leaf node, tree backtracking is required as a second step to search neighboring volumes for the closest data point. The proposed method improves the time for finding the leaf node and removes the need for potentially expensive backtracking by using voxels to recursively subdivide space. The leaf voxel that contains the query point is found by bisecting the voxel size. For trees of depth L, this approach requires only $O(\log(L))$ operations, instead of $O(L)$ operations when letting the query point fall down the tree. In addition, each voxel contains a list of all data points whose Voronoi cells intersect that voxel, such that no backtracking is necessary. By storing the voxels in a hash table and enforcing a limit on the number of Voronoi intersections per voxel, the total

J. Weickert, M. Hein, and B. Schiele (Eds.): GCPR 2013, LNCS 8142, pp. 302–312, 2013.

query time is independent of the position of the query point and the distribution of data points. The theoretical query time is of magnitude $O(\log(\log(N)))$, where N is the size of the target data point set.

The amount of backtracking that is required in tree-based methods depends on the position of the query point. Methods based on backtracking therefore have non-constant query times even when using the same dataset, making them difficult to use in real-time applications. Since the proposed method does not require backtracking, the query time becomes almost independent of the position of the query point. Further, the method is largely parameter free, does not require an a-priori definition of a maximum query range, and is straightforward and easy to implement.

We evaluate the proposed method on different synthetic datasets that show different distributions of the data and query point sets, and compare it to two state of the art methods: a self-implemented k-d-tree and the Approximate Nearest Neighbour (ANN) library [15], which, contrary to its name, allows also to search for exact nearest neighbors. The experiments show that the proposed method is significantly faster for larger data sets and shows an improved asymptotic behaviour. As a trade-off, the proposed method uses a more expensive preprocessing step. Finally, we demonstrate the performance of the proposed method within two applications on real-world datasets, pose refinement and surface inspection. The runtime of both applications is dominated by the nearest neighbor lookups, which is why both greatly benefit from the proposed method.

2   Related Work

An extensive overview over different nearest neighbor search strategies can be found in [17]. Nearest-neighbor search strategies can roughly be divided into tree-based and hash-based approaches. Concerning tree-based methods, variants of the k-d-tree [2] are state-of-the-art for applications such as ICP, navigation and surface inspection [8]. For high-dimensional datasets, such as images or iamge descriptors, embeddings into lower-dimensional spaces are sometimes used to reduce the complexity of the problem [13].

Many methods were proposed for improving the nearest neighbor query time by allowing small errors in the computed closest point, i.e., by solving the approximate nearest neighbor problem [1,11,6]. While faster, using approximations changes the nature of the lookup and is only applicable for methods such as ICP, where a small number of incorrect correspondences can be dealt with statistically. The iterative nature of ICP can be used to accelerate subsequent nearest neighbor lookups through caching [16,10]. Such approaches are, however, only usable for ICP and not for defect detection or other tasks.

Yan and Bowyer [18] proposed a regular 3D grid of voxels that allow constant-time lookup for a closest point, by storing a single closest point per voxel. However, such fixed-size voxel grids use excessive amounts of memory and require a tradeoff between memory consumption and lookup speed. The proposed multilevel adaptive voxel grid overcomes this problem, since more and smaller voxels are created only at the 'interesting' parts of the data point cloud, while the speed advantage of hashing is mostly preserved. Glassner [9] proposed to use a hash-table for accessing octrees, which is the basis for the proposed approach.

Using Voronoi cells is a natural way to approach the nearest neighbor problem, since a query point is always contained in the Voronoi cell of its nearest neighbor. Boada *et al.* [5] proposed an octree that approximates generalized Voronoi cells and that can be used to approximately solve the nearest neighbor problem [4]. Their work also gives insight into the construction costs of such an octree. Contrary to the proposed work, their work concentrates on the construction of the data structure and solves the nearest neighbor problem only approximately. Additionally, their proposed octree still requires $O(depth)$ operations for a query. However, their work indicates how the proposed method can be generalized to other metrics and to shapes other than points. Similar, [12] proposed an octree-like approximation of the Voronoi tesselation. Birn *et al.* [3] proposed a full hierarchy of Delaunay triangulations for 2D nearest neighbor lookups. However, the authors state that their approach is unlikely to work well in 3D and beyond.

3   Method

Notation and Overview. We denote points from the original data set as $\mathbf{x} \in D$ and points of the query set $\mathbf{q} \in Q$. Given a query point $\mathbf{q}$, the objective is to find the closest point $\mathrm{NN}(\mathbf{q}, D) = \mathrm{argmin}_{x \in D} |\mathbf{q} - \mathbf{x}|_2$. The individual Voronoi cells of the Voronoi diagram of D are denoted $voro(\mathbf{x})$, which we see as closed set.

The proposed method requires a pre-processing step where the voxel hash structure for the data set D is created. Once this data structure is precomputed, it remains unchanged and can be used for subsequent queries. The creation of the data structure is done in three steps: The computation of the Voronoi cells for the data set D, the creation of the octree and the transformation of the octree into a hash table.

Octree Creation. Using Voronoi cells is a natural way to approach the nearest neighbor problem. A query point $\mathbf{q}$ is always contained within the Voronoi cell of its closest point, i.e., $\mathbf{q} \in voro(\mathrm{NN}(\mathbf{q}, D))$. Thus, finding a Voronoi cell that contains $\mathbf{q}$ is equivalent to finding $\mathrm{NN}(\mathbf{q}, D)$. However, the irregular and data-dependent structure of the Voronoi tessellation does not allow a direct lookup. We thus use the octree to create a more regular structure on top of the Voronoi diagram, which allows to quickly find the corresponding Voronoi cell.

After computing the Voronoi cells for the data set D, an octree is created, whose root voxel contains the expected query range. Note that the root voxel can be several thousand times larger than the extend of the data set without significant performance implications.

Contrary to traditional octrees, where voxels are split based on the number of contained data points, we split each voxel based on the number of intersecting Voronoi cells: Each voxel that intersects more than M_{max} Voronoi cells is split

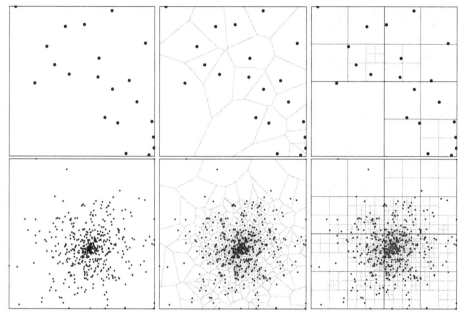

Fig. 1. Toy example in 2D of the creation of the hierarchical voxel structure. For the data point set (left), the Voronoi cells are computed (center). Starting with the root voxel that encloses all points, voxels are recursively split if the number of intersecting Voronoi cells exceeds M_{max}. In this example, the root voxel is split until each voxel intersects at most $M_{max} = 5$ Voronoi cells (right).

into eight sub-voxels, which are processed recursively. Fig. 1 shows a 2D example for this splitting. The set of data points whose Voronoi cells intersect a voxel v is denoted

$$L(D, v) = \{\mathbf{x} \in D : voro(\mathbf{x}) \cap v \neq \emptyset\}. \tag{1}$$

This splitting criterion allows a constant processing time during the query phase: For any query point $\mathbf{q}$ contained in a leaf voxel v_{leaf}, the Voronoi cell of the closest point $NN(\mathbf{q}, D)$ must intersect v_{leaf}. Therefore, once the leaf node voxel that contains $\mathbf{q}$ is found, at most M_{max} data points must be searched for the closest point. The given splitting criterion thus removes the requirement for backtracking.

The cost for this is a deeper tree, since a voxel typically intersects more Voronoi cells than it contains data points. The irregularity of the Voronoi tessellation and possible degenerated cases, as discussed below, make it difficult to give theoretical bounds on the depth of the octree. However, experimental validation shows that the number of created voxels scales linearly with the number of data points $|D|$ (see Fig. 4(a)).

Hash Table. The result of the recursive subdivision is an octree, as depicted in Fig. 1. To find the closest point of a given query point $\mathbf{q}$, two steps are required: Find the leaf voxel $v_{leaf}(\mathbf{q})$ which contains $\mathbf{q}$ and search all points in $L(D, v_{leaf}(q))$ for the closest point of q. The computation costs for finding the

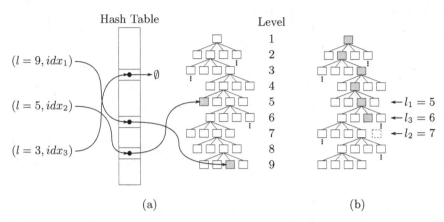

(a)   (b)

Fig. 2. (a) The hash table stores all voxels v, which are indexed through their level l and their index idx. The hash table allows to check for the existence of a voxel in constant time. (b) Toy example in 2D of how to find the leaf voxel by bisecting its level. Finding the leaf node by letting the query point fall down the tree would require $O(depth)$ operations on average (green path). Instead, the leaf node is found through bisection of its level. In each step, the hash table is used to check for the presence of the corresponding voxel. The search starts with the center level l_1 and, since the voxel exists, proceeds with l_2. Since the voxel at level l_2 does not exist, level l_3 is checked and the leaf node is found.

leaf node are on average $O(depth) \approx O(\log(|D|))$ when letting $\mathbf{q}$ fall down the tree. We propose to use the regularity of the octree to reduce those costs to $O(\log(depth)) \approx O(\log(\log(|D|)))$. For this, all voxels of the octree are stored in a hash table which is indexed by the voxel's level $l(v)$ and its index $idx(v) \in Z^d$ (Fig. 2(a)). $idx(v)$ is the integer-valued position of the voxel within the voxel grid of its level $l(v)$.

The leaf voxel $v_{leaf}(\mathbf{q})$ is then found through bisection of its level. The minimum and maximum voxel level is initialized as $l_{min} = 1$ and $l_{max} = depth$. The existence of the voxel with the 'center' level $l_c = \lfloor (l_{min} + l_{max})/2 \rfloor$ is tested using the hash table. If the voxel exists, the search proceeds with the interval $[l_c, l_{max}]$. Otherwise, it proceeds to search the interval $[l_{min}, l_c - 1]$. The search continues until the interval contains only one level, which is the level of the leaf voxel $v_{leaf}(\mathbf{q})$. Fig. 2 illustrates this bisection on a toy example.

Note that in our experiments, tree depths were in the order of 20-40 such that the expected speedup over the traditional method was around 5. Additionally, each voxel in the hash table contains the minimum and maximum depth of its subtree to speedup the bisection. Additionally, the lists $L(D, v)$ are stored only for the leaf nodes. The primary cost during the bisection are cache misses when accessing the hash table. Therefore, an inlined hash table is used to reduce the average amount of cache misses.

Degenerated Cases. For some degenerated cases, the proposed method for splitting voxels based on the number of intersecting Voronoi cells might not terminate. This happens when more than M_{max} Voronoi cells meet at a single

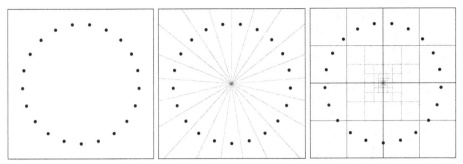

Fig. 3. Example of a degenerated point set (left) where many Voronoi cells meet at one point (center). In this case, the problem of finding the nearest neighbor is ill-posed for query points close to the center of the circle. To capture such degenerated cases, voxel splitting is stopped after L_{max} subdivisions (right). See the text for more comments on why such situations are not of practical interest.

Table 1. Performance in the real-world scenarios. $|D|$ is the number of data points, $|Q|$ the number of query points. The proposed voxel hash structure is up to one order of magnitude faster than k-d-trees, even for large values of M_{max}

			Voxel Hash, $M_{max} =$				
Dataset	$|D|$	$|Q|$	30	60	90	k-d-tree	ANN
ICP Matching	990,998	1,685,639	0.74 s	1.04 s	1.41 s	12.19 s	22.0 s
Comparison	990,998	2,633,591	0.85 s	1.29 s	1.87 s	10.62 s	232.1 s
ICP Room	260,595	916,873	0.26 s	0.37 s	0.41 s	0.97 s	2.5 s

point, as depicted in Fig. 3. To avoid infinite recursion, a limit L_{max} on the depth of the octree is enforced. In such cases, the query time for points that fall within such an unsplit leaf voxel is larger than for other query points. However, we found that in practice such cases appear only on synthetic datasets. Also, since the corresponding leaf voxels are very small, chances of a random query point to fall within the corresponding voxel are small. Additionally, note the problem of finding the closest point is ill-posed in situations where many Voronoi cells meet at a single point and the query point is close to that point: Small changes in the query point can lead to arbitrary changes of the nearest neighbor. The degradation in query time can be avoided by limiting the length of $L(D, v)$ of the corresponding leaf voxels. The maximum error made in this case is in bound by the diameter of the voxel of level L_{max}. For example, $L_{max} = 30$ reduces the error to 2^{-30} times the size of the root voxel, which is already smaller than the accuracy of single-precision floating point numbers. Summing up, the proposed method degrades only in artificial situations where the problem itself is ill-posed, but the method's performance guarantee can be restored at the cost of an arbitrary small error.

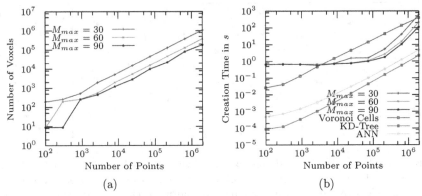

(a)   (b)

Fig. 4. Construction and memory costs of the proposed data structure for the CLUS-TER dataset. (a) The number of created voxels depends linearly on the size of the data cloud. As a rule of thumb, one voxel is created per data point. Note that in practice, each voxel requires around 16-24 bytes of memory. (b) The creation time of the voxel data structure. The creation of the Voronoi cells is independent of the value of M_{max} and its creation time is plotted separately. Though the creation of the voxel data structure is significantly slower than for the k-d-tree and the ANN library, the creation times are still reasonable for off-line processing. Note that the constant performance of the proposed method for less than 10^5 data points is based on our particular implementation, which is optimized for large data sets and requires constant time for the creation of several caches. Overall, larger values of M_{max} lead to faster and less memory consuming data structure creation, at the expense of matching time (see Fig. 6).

4   Results

Several experiments were conducted to evaluate the performance of the proposed method in different situations and to compare it to the k-d-tree and the ANN libary [15] as state-of-the-art methods. Both the k-d-tree and the voxel hash structure were implemented in C with similar optimization. The creation of the voxel data structure was parallelized, queries were not. Times were measured on an Intel Xenon E5-2665 with 2.4 GHz.

Data Structure Creation. Though the creation of the data structure is significantly more expensive than the creation of the k-d-tree and the ANN library, those costs are still within reasonable bounds. Fig. 4(b) compares the creation times for different values of M_{max}. The creation of the Voronoi cells is independent of the value of M_{max} and thus plotted separately. Fig. 4(a) shows the number of created voxels. They depend linearly on the number of data points, while the choice of M_{max} introduces an additional constant factor. Note that the constant performance of the proposed method for less than 10^5 data points is based on our particular implementation, which is optimized for large data sets and requires constant time for the creation of several caches.

Synthetic Datasets. We evaluate the performance on different datasets with different characteristics. Three synthetic datasets were used and are illustrated in

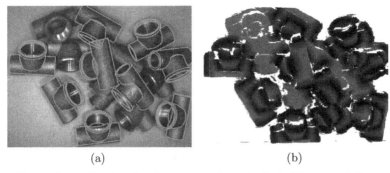

(a)   (b)

Fig. 5. Example application for the proposed method. A 3D scan of the scene was acquired using a multi-camera stereo setup and approximate poses of the pipe joint were found using the method of Drost *et al.* [7]. (a) The poses were refined using ICP. The corresponding nearest neighbor lookups were logged and used for the evaluation show in Table 1. (b) For each scene point close to one of the detected objects, the distance to the object is computed and visualized. This allows the detection of defects on the surface of the objects. The lookups were again logged and used for the performance evaluation in Table 1.

the top row of Fig. 6. For dataset RANDOM, the points are uniformly distributed in the unit cube $[0, 1]^3$. For CLUSTER, points are distributed using a Gaussian distribution. For SURFACE, points are taken from a 2D manifold and slightly disturbed. For each data set, two query sets with 1.000.000 points each were created. For the first set, points were distributed uniformly within the bounding cube surrounding the data point set. The corresponding times are shown in the center row of Fig. 6. The second query set has the same distribution as the data set, with the corresponding timings shown in the bottom row of Fig. 6.

The proposed data structure is significantly faster than the simple k-d-tree for all datasets with more than 10^5 points. The ANN library shows similar performance than the proposed method for $M_{max} = 30$ for the RANDOM and CLUSTER datasets. For the SURFACE dataset, our method clearly outperforms ANN even for smaller point clouds. Note that the SURFACE dataset represents a 2D manifold and thus shows the behaviour for ICP and other surface-based applications. Overall, the performance of the proposed method is less dependent on the distribution of data and query points. This advantage allows our method to be used in real-time environments.

Real-World Datasets. Finally, real-world examples were used for evaluating the proposed method's performance. First, several instances of an industrial object were detected in a scene acquired with a multi-camera stereo setup. The original scene and the matches are shown in Fig. 5. We found approximate positions of the target object using the method of Drost *et al.* [7] and subsequently used ICP for each match for a precise alignment. The nearest neighbor lookups during ICP were logged and later evaluated with the available methods. The sizes of the data clouds and the lookup times are shown in Table 1.

Afterwards, we used the proposed method to find surface defects of the detected objects. For this, the distances of the scene points to the closest found

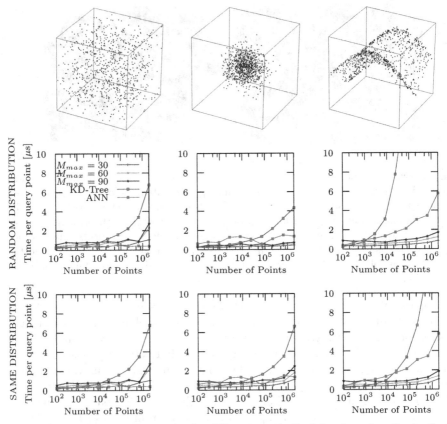

Fig. 6. Query time per query point for different synthetic datasets and methods. Each column represents a different dataset. From left to right: RANDOM, CLUSTER, and SURFACE dataset. The x-axis shows the number of data points, *i.e.*, $|D|$, the y-axis shows the average query time per query point. For the center row, query points were were randomly selected from the cuboid surrounding the data. For the bottom row, query points were taken from the same distribution as the data points. The query time for the proposed method is less dependent of the number of data points and almost independent of the distribution of the data and query points. It is especially of advantage for very large datasets, as well as for datasets representing 2D manifolds.

model were computed. The distances are visualized in Fig. 5(b) and show a systematic error in the modeling of the object. We are, however, only interested in the required inspection time, which is shown in Table 1.

Finally, we used a Kinect sensor to acquire two slightly rotated scans of an office room and aligned both scans using ICP. For all three datasets, the proposed method significantly outperforms both our k-d-tree implementation and the ANN library by up to one order of magnitude.

5   Conclusion

We proposed and evaluated a novel data structure for nearest-neighbor lookup in 3D, which can easily be extended to 2D. Compared to traditional tree-based methods, backtracking was made redundant by building an octree on top of the Voronoi diagram. In addition, a hash table was used, allowing a fast bisection search of the leaf voxel of a query point, which is faster than letting the query point fall down the tree. The proposed method combines the best of tree-based approaches and fixed voxel grids.

The evaluation on synthetic datasets shows that the proposed method is faster than traditional k-d-trees and the ANN library on larger datasets and has a query time which is almost independent of the data and query point distribution. Though the proposed structure takes significantly longer to be created, those times are still within reasonable bounds. The evaluation on real datasets shows that real-world scenarios such as ICP and surface defect detection greatly benefit from the performance of the method.

References

1. Arya, S., Mount, D.M., Netanyahu, N.S., Silverman, R., Wu, A.Y.: An optimal algorithm for approximate nearest neighbor searching fixed dimensions. JACM 45(6), 891–923 (1998)
2. Bentley, J.L.: Multidimensional binary search trees used for associative searching. Communications of the ACM 18(9), 509–517 (1975)
3. Birn, M., Holtgrewe, M., Sanders, P., Singler, J.: Simple and fast nearest neighbor search. In: 11th Workshop on Algorithm Engineering and Experiments (2010)
4. Boada, I., Coll, N., Madern, N., Sellares, J.A.: Approximations of 3D generalized voronoi diagrams. In: 21st Europ. Workshop on Comp. Geometry (2005)
5. Boada, I., Coll, N., Madern, N., Sellares, J.A.: Approximations of 2D and 3D generalized voronoi diagrams. Int. Journal of Computer Mathematics 85(7) (2008)
6. Choi, W.S., Oh, S.Y.: Fast nearest neighbor search using approximate cached kd tree. In: IROS (2012)
7. Drost, B., Ulrich, M., Navab, N., Ilic, S.: Model globally, match locally: Efficient and robust 3D object recognition. In: CVPR (2010)
8. Elseberg, J., Magnenat, S., Siegwart, R., Nuechter, A.: Comparison of nearest-neighbor-search strategies and implementations for efficient shape registration. Journal of Software Engineering for Robotics 3(1), 2–12 (2012)
9. Glassner, A.S.: Space subdivision for fast ray tracing. IEEE Computer Graphics and Applications 4(10), 15–24 (1984)
10. Greenspan, M., Godin, G.: A nearest neighbor method for efficient ICP. In: 3-D Digital Imaging and Modeling. IEEE (2001)
11. Greenspan, M., Yurick, M.: Approximate kd tree search for efficient ICP. In: 3DIM 2003. IEEE (2003)
12. Har-Peled, S.: A replacement for voronoi diagrams of near linear size. In: Proc. on Foundations of Computer Science, pp. 94–103 (2001)
13. Hwang, Y., Han, B., Ahn, H.K.: A fast nearest neighbor search algorithm by non-linear embedding. In: CVPR (2012)

14. Meagher, D.: Geometric modeling using octree encoding. Computer Graphics and Image Processing 19(2), 129–147 (1982)
15. Mount, D.M., Arya, S.: ANN: A library for approximate nearest neighbor searching, `http://www.cs.umd.edu/~mount/ANN/`
16. Nuchter, A., Lingemann, K., Hertzberg, J.: Cached kd tree search for ICP algorithms. In: 3DIM 2007. IEEE (2007)
17. Samet, H.: Foundations of Multidimensional And Metric Data Structures. Morgan Kaufmann (2006)
18. Yan, P., Bowyer, K.W.: A fast algorithm for ICP-based 3D shape biometrics. Computer Vision and Image Understanding 107(3) (2007)

Bone Age Assessment Using
the Classifying Generalized Hough Transform

Ferdinand Hahmann[1], Inga Berger[1], Heike Ruppertshofen[2],
Thomas Deserno[3], and Hauke Schramm[1]

[1] University of Applied Sciences Kiel
[2] Philips Technologie GmbH
[3] Department of Medical Informatics, RWTH Aachen University
`Ferdinand.Hahmann@fh-kiel.de`

Abstract. A theoretical description and experimental validation of the
Classifying Generalized Hough Transform (CGHT) is presented. This
general image classification technique is based on a discriminative training procedure that jointly estimates concurrent class-dependent shape
models for usage in a GHT voting procedure. The basic approach is extended by a coarse-to-fine classification strategy and a simple classifier
combination technique for a combined decision on several regions of interest in a given image. The framework is successfully applied to the task of
automatic bone age assessment and produces comparable results to other
state-of-the-art techniques on a public database. For the most difficult
age range of 9 to 16 years the automatic system achieves a mean error of
0.8 years compared to the average rating of two physicians. Unlike most
other image classification techniques, the trained CGHT models can be
visually interpreted, unveiling the most relevant anatomical structures
for class discrimination.

1 Introduction

Bone Age Assessment (BAA) based on left hand radiographs is a well-established
procedure for determining the skeletal maturity which is mainly applied for
diagnosing growth disorders or forensic age estimation. Manual BAA is usually
performed with one of two common methods: Greulich & Pyle (GP) [7] developed
an approach, in which the radiologist determines the bone age by comparing the
radiograph with a standard atlas. In contrast, Tanner & Whitehouse (TW) [17]
have proposed to consider only regions of interest (ROI) around the epiphyses
and the carpal bones. For each of these so-called eROIs a score based on the gap
and shape of the epiphysis is assigned. The sum of all scores determines the age.

Since the manual assessment is time consuming, subjective, and requires expert knowledge, an automatic method is desirable. In recent years, various automatic techniques have been proposed, which are usually based on some kind
of image feature extraction in combination with a standard classification technique. While some of these approaches employ heuristic features, like the length
and size of phalanges [6,9] or the distance between metaphysis and diaphysis

J. Weickert, M. Hein, and B. Schiele (Eds.): GCPR 2013, LNCS 8142, pp. 313–322, 2013.

[13], other methods directly utilize the TW rules, for example, by using a decision tree [1] or an artificial neural network [4]. The leading commercial product, BoneXpert, employs the rules from TW after applying an active shape model for the segmentation of 15 bones [18].

More general BAA approaches without any kind of heuristic feature selection are Kim & Kim [10] and Harmsen et al. [8]. Kim & Kim classify discrete cosine transform coefficients, computed from pixel intensity values in epiphyseal regions, with a linear discriminant analysis. Harmsen et al. analyze 14 epiphyseal regions of interest (eROIs) using the cross-correlation with 30 class-specific prototypes as features and employing a k-Nearest Neighbor algorithm (kNN) or a Support Vector Machine (SVM) for classification.

In this work, the Discriminative Generalized Hough Transform (DGHT) [14] is extended. The DGHT utilizes a discriminative training technique to estimate optimal shape models for usage in a standard Generalized Hough Transform (GHT) approach and achieves high localization rates for well-defined objects with medium shape variability. An unsupervised training method can be used to learn parallel variation-specific GHT models to deal with stronger variabilities [16] and returns the variation class together with the localization result. This approach can be modified towards a general image classification technique, called Classifying Generalized Hough Transform (CGHT) [15]. A first proof-of-concept has already been presented in [5], where CGHT-based models were successfully applied to the BAA task of separating the age classes 11-12 and 14-15 years. In this paper the method is theoretically described and comprehensively evaluated.

2   Method

2.1   Discriminative Generalized Hough Transform

The classification technique, presented in this paper, is based on the Generalized Hough Transform (GHT) [2] which is a general model-based localization method. For 2D images, a point model $M := \{\mathbf{m}\} \subset \mathbb{R}^2$ is used to represent the shape of the searched-for object in relation to a reference point, which is the target point for localization. Using this model, a voting procedure transforms a feature image X_n, usually a binary edge image, into a parameter space H, called Hough space. The Hough space is usually quantized and consists of so called Hough cells $\mathbf{c}$, which accumulate the votes in the respective region. The cells represent possible target point locations and, potentially, shape model transformations. The latter are not considered in this work, since moderate shape variations are learned into the shape model. Thus, the voting procedure may be simplified as follows:

$$H(\mathbf{x}) = \sum_{\forall \mathbf{e}_i \in X_n} \sum_{\forall \mathbf{m}_j \in M} \begin{cases} 1, & \text{if } \mathbf{x} = \mathbf{e}_i - \mathbf{m}_j \text{ and } |\varphi_i - \varphi_j| \leq \vartheta_\varphi \\ 0, & \text{otherwise.} \end{cases} \qquad (1)$$

Here, $\mathbf{e}_i$ represents the i-th feature point while $\mathbf{m}_j$ is the vector from the reference point to the j-th model point. A pair $(\mathbf{e}_i, \mathbf{m}_j)$ is allowed to vote if the difference of the gradient direction of $\mathbf{e}_i$ and the orientation of $\mathbf{m}_j$ is below the threshold ϑ_φ. The number of votes per accumulator cell $\mathbf{c}$ after the quantization reflects the degree of matching between the feature image X_n and the model M at this point. The best positioning of the model in the image is given by the Hough cell $\hat{\mathbf{c}} = \arg\max_{\mathbf{c}} H(\mathbf{c})$ with the highest degree of matching.

Since the accuracy of GHT localization highly depends on the quality of the shape model, the Discriminative Generalized Hough Transform (DGHT) additionally includes a machine learning approach for generating discriminative models. This procedure, which is described in detail in [14], assigns individual positive and negative weights to model points based on their importance for correct localizations on training images. The GHT-based classification technique, explained in the next section, is an extension of the DGHT which employs a number of competitively trained submodels.

2.2   Classifying Generalized Hough Transform

Given a classification task with K classes, the CGHT [15] combines a set of K competitive submodels M_k into a 3D GHT Model $M = \{M_k\}$, $k \in \{1, ..., K\}$. Each submodel in M represents one class and the whole set $\{M_k\}$ is jointly optimized with respect to a minimum classification error (Section 2.3). This competitive training procedure assigns large absolute weights to model points supporting the class discrimination while eliminating irrelevant model parts.

Applying the optimized 3D GHT model M on a 2D image results in a 3D Hough space $H(\mathbf{x}, k) = \{H_k(\mathbf{x})\}$, $k \in \{1, ..., K\}$ (Fig. 1), whereas the individual $H_k(\mathbf{x})$ have been obtained by applying the voting procedure in Equation 1 to the submodels M_k:

$$H_k(\mathbf{x}) = \sum_{\forall \mathbf{e}_i \in X_n} \sum_{\forall \mathbf{m}_j \in M_k} \begin{cases} 1, & \text{if } \mathbf{x} = \mathbf{e}_i - \mathbf{m}_j \text{ and } |\varphi_i - \varphi_j| \le \vartheta_\varphi \\ 0, & \text{otherwise.} \end{cases} \quad (2)$$

After the voting procedure has finished, the classification result $\hat{k}$ is given by the submodel with the highest degree of matching $\hat{k} = \arg\max_k[\max_{\mathbf{x}} H_k(\mathbf{x})]$.

Note that this procedure is flexible enough to compensate for a moderate variability of the object's position in the image. As long as the object to be classified is completely visible, localizing the peak in the Hough space does not effect the classification result.

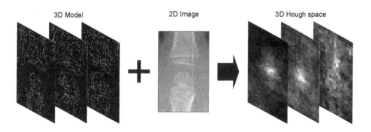

Fig. 1. Classification of an epiphyseal region of interest (eROI) using the Classifying Generalized Hough Transform

2.3   Training

The training procedure starts with an initial model $M = \{M_k\}$ composed of identical submodels $M_k \equiv M_{k'}$, $\forall (k', k)$, which is obtained by overlaying the features of several training images in a predefined region-of-interest around a manually annotated landmark. Other methods for obtaining an initial shape model are described in [14].

With this model the modified voting procedure in Equation (2) is applied producing a 3D Hough space $H(\mathbf{x}, k)$. Note that initially the $H_k(\mathbf{x})$ are identical for all K classes. To determine individual model point weights it is necessary to capture the influence of each single model point on the Hough space, which is achieved by the following feature function:

$$f_j^k(\mathbf{c}_i^k, X_n) = v_{i,j}^k. \tag{3}$$

For a given class k, this function denotes the number of votes $v_{i,j}^k$ from model point $\mathbf{m}_j^k$ in Hough cell $\mathbf{c}_i^k$. Considering the constraints of the GHT voting procedure for the entire model, the individual contributions of all model points have to be recombined into an overall distribution. To assure maximum objectivity, the maximum entropy distribution

$$p_{\Lambda_k}(\mathbf{c}_i^k | X_n) = \frac{\exp\left(\sum_j \lambda_j^k \cdot f_j^k(\mathbf{c}_i^k, X_n)\right)}{\sum_l \exp\left(\sum_j \lambda_j^k \cdot f_j^k(\mathbf{c}_l^k, X_n)\right)} \tag{4}$$

is used, which introduces class and model point specific weights $\Lambda_k = \{\lambda_1^k, ..., \lambda_{J_k}^k\}$. Note that this probabilistic representation of the Hough space is in line with the standard GHT theory, as the Hough space can be easily transferred into a probability distribution by using relative frequencies.

Since this work aims at a minimum classification error instead of a Hough space with maximized entropy, the λ_j^k are optimized using a Minimum Classification Error (MCE) training approach [3], which minimizes the smoothed error measure

$$E(\Lambda) = \sum_{n=1}^{N} \sum_{k=1}^{K} \sum_{i=1}^{I} \varepsilon(\mathbf{c}_i^k, \tilde{\mathbf{c}}_n^{k_n}) \cdot \frac{p_{\Lambda_k}(\mathbf{c}_i^k | X_n)^\eta}{\sum_l p_{\Lambda_k}(\mathbf{c}_l^k | X_n)^\eta}. \tag{5}$$

Here, the error is summed over the N images in the training corpus, the K classes and I Hough cells providing the votes $v_{i,j}^k$ in each class specific layer $H_k(\mathbf{x})$. For a given training image n, the error function $\varepsilon(\cdot)$ measures the distance of each Hough cell $\mathbf{c}_i^k$ to a given target cell $\tilde{\mathbf{c}}_n^{k_n}$, which might be the center of the object to be classified in the Hough space layer of the correct class k_n. While this function is realized as a Euclidean distance in the standard DGHT method, the CGHT may additionally employ a fixed inter-class penalty to enforce discrimination between the different class layers. However, since a focused peak in the layers $H_k(\mathbf{x})$ is not the target criterion, a simplified error measure has been applied finally which equally penalizes Hough cells of wrong classes:

$$\varepsilon(\mathbf{c}_i^k, \tilde{\mathbf{c}}_n^{k_n}) = \begin{cases} 0, & \text{if } k = k_n \\ 1, & \text{otherwise} \end{cases} \tag{6}$$

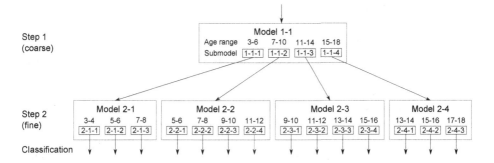

Fig. 2. Illustration of the used coarse-to-fine classification strategy

The second term in (5) is a sigmoidal smoothing function that controls the influence of the best hypotheses on the overall error measure with the parameter η. Consequently, the optimization procedure is adjusting the model weights particularly suppressing votes in the most likely cells of wrong classes.

For optimization of $E(\Lambda)$ over the model point weights $\Lambda = \{\Lambda_1, ..., \Lambda_K\}$, the method of steepest descent is used, which is not assuring a global minimum but has shown significant improvements compared to other weighting strategies in recent experiments [14].

The described optimization procedure assigns individual weights to each model point in M and allows for eliminating model parts with small absolute weights and therefore low influence on the overall classification result. The procedure can be repeated in an iterative manner [14] to gradually enhance the model with structures from training images not yet correctly classified. This has, however, not yet been studied.

3   Bone Age Classification

The proposed BAA procedure is solely based on analyzing eROIs, according to Tanner & Whitehouse [17]. The eROI extraction is done based on the given annotations from the corpus although it could be shown in [5] that a robust automatic localization of those regions can be done automatically by using the DGHT. Therefore, it is planned to combine the two techniques into a fully automated BAA system at a later time.

3.1   Coarse-to-Fine Classification Strategy

The BAA task is characterized by a large object variability in combination with a rather large number of classes. Therefore, it is necessary to restrict the inter-class confusion, which can be achieved by utilizing a coarse-to-fine classification strategy comprising of two levels (Fig. 2). The first level classifies a given image into one of four coarse age classes. The second level decides more precisely between age ranges of 2 years only. Due to the significant differences of the epi-physeal shapes between the coarse age ranges of the first level, the respective CGHT models may focus here on global characteristics, such as the size, while the models of the second level represent details to discriminate from neighboring classes of similar age.

It is apparent that in this scenario, misclassifications are more likely to occur at ages close to class boundaries. Therefore, the second level operates with over-lapping classes (Fig. 2). For the sake of clarification, let us consider a patient with a skeletal maturity of 12 years who should be assigned to class 11-14 years in the first level. Due to a misclassification during the first level it may occur that instead of the correct class, the class 7-10 years is selected which induces the utilization of Model 2-2 for the second level. This mistake may be corrected due to the incorporation of submodel 11-12 years in Model 2-2.

3.2   Combination of Classifiers

A combined decision based on several eROIs clearly improves the bone age clas-sification performance [8]. This idea has been tested in a first experiment to improve the Model 2-3, which corresponds to the age range 9 to 16 years. To this end, the three epiphyseal plates of the long finger have been analyzed with individually trained CGHT models producing four class-specific Hough spaces $H_k^a(\mathbf{x})$ per joint a for the submodels 2-3-1 to 2-3-4. Afterwards, a normalization step is applied, eliminating any bias from different model point numbers. Finally, the peaks in the normalized Hough spaces are linearly combined for the three joints and a decision is made for the class with the highest combined vote. As an alternative to this heuristic approach, a log linear combination of the classi-fiers [11] could be used in future attempts which, however, requires additional training data.

4   Data

Training as well as evaluation is performed on images of male patients in an overall age range between 3 and 18 years. The models are trained on non-public data from the University Hospital Aachen and the University Medical Center Schleswig-Holstein. To assure comparability with other studies, evaluation is performed on the public database from the University of Southern California (USC), where each image is assigned an individual age assessment from two radiologists. In order to eliminate debatable cases from our experiments, 156 images with an inter-observer variability of more than 1 year have been removed from the evaluation database as well as images with strong rotation (18 images), atypical positioning (2 images) or unsuitable spacing (5 images). In order to clarify the degree of deviation for these cases, some examples are provided in Figure 3. The remaining 481 images were annotated using the average of both expert readings.

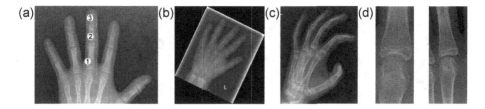

Fig. 3. Illustration of eROIs used in this paper. ① is used for single eROI classification, ② and ③ are additionally used for combined classification. (b-d) Examples of strong rotation (b), atypical positioning (c) and unsuitable spacing (d).

5 Experiments

In order to evaluate the GHT-based classification technique described above, two different experiments have been done. In the first investigation, described in Section 5.1, a single epiphysis has been analyzed to perform the age classification while the second experiment (Section 5.2) analyzes the combination of the classification results of three eROIs.

5.1 Single eROI Classification

In this experiment, the coarse-to-fine strategy (Section 3.1), has been applied to classify the metacarpophalangeal of the middle finger (① in Fig. 3). The training of each submodel in classification level 1, covering an age range of 4 years, could be performed using 84 images. Reducing the age range to 2 years, the amount of training data decreased to only 42 images per submodel. The trained models have been evaluated on 481 images and achieved a mean classification error of 1.11 years.

Figure 4 shows the resulting CGHT submodels of the first classification level. It can be seen that the training procedure has automatically learned reasonable representations of the 4 different age classes. The models have captured size and anatomical differences between the classes while at the same time preserving some level of intra-class shape variability. Studying the learned anatomical structures, it is interesting to note that the fusion of the epiphyseal cartilage can be observed in the submodels 11-14 and 15-18 years while the first two submodels 3-6 and 7-10 years are characterized by a clearly visible gap in this area, emphasized by highly weighted model points shown in red color.

Since a larger number of training images was available for the age range 9-16 years the training was repeated with an amount of 56, instead of 42, images per submodel in classification level 2. In this experiment a slight gain of the mean error to 1.15 years could be observed.

5.2 Combined Classification

The classifier combination described in Section 3.2 has been trained on 56 training images per class from the restricted age range 9 to 16 years and evaluated on

3 to 6 years	7 to 10 years	11 to 14 years	15 to 18 years

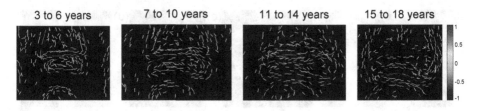

Fig. 4. CGHT submodels of classification level 1. The colors indicate positive and negative model point weighting.

253 test images. A combination of the metacarpophalangeal, proximal and distal interphalangeal of the middle finger (Fig. 3) led to a significant improvement of the mean error from 1.15 years, when using a single classifier, to 0.84 years.

Table 1 gives a comparison of the presented technique with other recently published methods which have been evaluated on the USC database. Note that these publications eliminate a similar amount of problematic images from the evaluation dataset and apply a scaling and orientation normalization prior to the actual classification. Note further, that the age range restriction in our experiments was only necessary due to the shortage of training data. The addressed age range for our combined classification experiments (9-16 years) is considered the most difficult [8] due to the fact that the growth differentials are significantly lower than in younger children.

Table 1. Comparison of BAA methods

Method	Database	Age range	#Images	Mean Error
BoneXpert[12]	Subset of USC[1]	2-17	1083	0.72
Harmsen[8] - six eROIs combined	Subset of USC[1]	0-18	1097	0.83
CGHT - single eROI	Subset of USC[1]	3-18 (male)	481	1.11
CGHT - single eROI	Subset of USC[1]	9-16 (male)	253	1.15
CGHT - three eROIs combined	Subset of USC[1]	9-16 (male)	253	0.84

6   Discussion

In the presented validation experiments, the proposed image classification method has shown good performance. A crucial aspect for the success of the proposed discriminative training technique is, however, the availability of sufficient training images since the data must reflect the large shape variability contained in clinical data. Apart from the general problem of finding comprehensive corpora with annotated hand radiographs three restricting factors have to be addressed when using the CGHT. First, all submodels M_k of a model M should be trained on the same number of images in order to prevent a preference for submodels

---

[1] Corpus from the University of South California: http://www.ipilab.org/BAAweb/

with a larger amount of training data. This is a direct consequence of using the smoothed error measure (Equation 5), which does not compensate for biased data. Therefore, the class with the smallest amount of available images determines the training amount for all classes of the same model. Second, working with the described coarse-to-fine strategy makes the training data situation worse since narrowing the age ranges in the second classification level reduces the available data per class. Due to the training data shortage the installation of a third classification level for an age range of 1 year is currently not feasible. The usage of age ranges of 2 years, however, already induces a best-case expected error of 0.5 years if the data is equally distributed with respect to the age. Third, the method is currently limited to images with restricted orientation and scaling variability, which required the omission of some strong outlier images as shown in Figure 3. A normalization step, based on the results of the prior epiphysis localization procedure, may allow for a better treatment of those cases and will probably additionally improve the classification rate by reducing the contained shape variability to mostly anatomical factors. As a consequence of the three mentioned aspects, it is expected that the observed results can be further improved by (1) increasing the amount of training data, (2) reducing the scaling and orientation variability by a prior normalization step, and (3) introducing further classification levels into the coarse-to-fine framework.

7   Conclusion

This contribution has, for the first time, presented a mathematical description and comprehensive experimental validation of the novel Classifying Generalized Hough Transform (CGHT). It could be shown that this general image classification method can be successfully applied to the task of automatic bone age assessment and achieves comparable results to other state-of-the-art techniques on a public database. In contrast to most other image classification methods, the learned models can be visually interpreted and unveil the most relevant anatomical structures for class discrimination. The basic approach has been extended by a coarse-to-fine classification strategy and a simple classifier combination framework for a combined decision based on several epiphyseal regions of interest. The latter method was shown to significantly improve the mean classification error which confirms the findings of other authors [8].

Since the success of the applied discriminative model training heavily depends upon the amount and quality of available training data, it is expected that further improvements can be achieved by using a larger amount of training images, providing high quality annotations and employing a normalization step prior to the actual classification. Besides these aspects, our future work will consider the combination of a larger number of eROIs, a more sophisticated, e.g. log-linear [11], classifier combination, and the integration of this classification approach with the automatic landmark detection technique based on the Discriminative Generalized Hough Transform (DGHT) [14].

Acknowledgement. The authors would like to thank the University Medical Center Schleswig-Holstein and the University of South California for providing the X-ray images used in this study. Additionally, the authors are grateful to the anonymous reviewers for their valuable comments.

References

1. Aja-Fernández, S., de Luis-García, R., Martın-Fernandez, M.A., Alberola-López, C.: A computational tw3 classifier for skeletal maturity assessment. A computing with words approach. Journal of Biomedical Informatics 37(2), 99–107 (2004)
2. Ballard, D.: Generalizing the Hough transform to detect arbitrary shapes. Pattern Recognition 13(2), 111–122 (1981)
3. Beyerlein, P.: Discriminative model combination. In: ICASSP, pp. 481–484 (1998)
4. Bocchi, L., Ferrara, F., Nicoletti, I., Valli, G.: An artificial neural network architecture for skeletal age assessment. In: ICIP, pp. 1077–1080 (2003)
5. Brunk, M., Ruppertshofen, H., Schmidt, S., Beyerlein, P., Schramm, H.: Bone age classification using the discriminative generalized hough transform. In: BVM, pp. 284–288 (2011)
6. Chang, C.H., Hsieh, C.W., Jong, T.L., Tiu, C.M.: A fully automatic computerized bone age assessment procedure based on phalange ossification analysis. In: IPPR, pp. 463–468 (2003)
7. Greulich, W.W., Pyle, S.I.: Radiographic atlas of skeletal development of the hand and wrist. The American Journal of the Medical Sciences 238(3), 393 (1959)
8. Harmsen, M., Fischer, B., Schramm, H., Seidl, T., Deserno, T.M.: Support vector machine classification based on correlation prototypes applied to bone age assessment. IEEE Transaction on Information Technology in Biomedicine (2012)
9. Hsieh, C., Jong, T., Chou, Y., Tiu, C.: Computerized geometric features of carpal bone for bone age estimation. Chinese Medical Journal 120(9), 767–770 (2007)
10. Kim, H.-J., Kim, W.-Y.: Computerized bone age assessment using DCT and LDA. In: Gagalowicz, A., Philips, W. (eds.) MIRAGE 2007. LNCS, vol. 4418, pp. 440–448. Springer, Heidelberg (2007)
11. Klakow, D.: Log-linear interpolation of language models. In: ICSLP (1998)
12. Martin, D.D., Deusch, D., Schweizer, R., Binder, G., Thodberg, H.H., Ranke, M.B.: Clinical application of automated greulich-pyle bone age determination in children with short stature. Pediatric Radiology 39(6), 598–607 (2009)
13. Pietka, E., Gertych, A., Pospiech, S., Cao, F., Huang, H., Gilsanz, V.: Computer-assisted bone age assessment: Image preprocessing and epiphyseal/metaphyseal roi extraction. IEEE Transactions on Medical Imaging 20(8), 715–729 (2001)
14. Ruppertshofen, H.: Automatic Modeling of Anatomical Variability for Object Localization in Medical Images. Ph.D. thesis, Otto-von-Guericke University Magdeburg (2013)
15. Ruppertshofen, H., Schramm, H.: The classifying generalized hough transform. German Patent Submission (2011)
16. Ruppertshofen, H., Bülow, T., von Berg, J., Schmidt, S., Beyerlein, P., Salah, Z., Rose, G., Schramm, H.: A multi-dimensional model for localization of highly variable objects. In: SPIE, vol. 8314, p. 88 (2012)
17. Tanner, J., Healy, M., Goldstein, H., Cameron, N.: Assessment of skeletal maturity and prediction of adult height (tw3). WB Saunders, London (2001)
18. Thodberg, H.H., Kreiborg, S., Juul, A., Pedersen, K.D.: The bonexpert method for automated determination of skeletal maturity. IEEE Transactions on Medical Imaging 28(1), 52–66 (2009)

Framework for Generation of Synthetic Ground Truth Data for Driver Assistance Applications

Vladimir Haltakov[1], Christian Unger[1,2], and Slobodan Ilic[2]

[1] BMW Group, Munich, Germany
{vladimir.haltakov,christian.unger}@bmw.de
[2] Technical University Munich, Germany
slobodan.ilic@in.tum.de

Abstract. High precision ground truth data is a very important factor for the development and evaluation of computer vision algorithms and especially for advanced driver assistance systems. Unfortunately, some types of data, like accurate optical flow and depth as well as pixel-wise semantic annotations are very difficult to obtain.

In order to address this problem, in this paper we present a new framework for the generation of high quality synthetic camera images, depth and optical flow maps and pixel-wise semantic annotations. The framework is based on a realistic driving simulator called VDrift [1], which allows us to create traffic scenarios very similar to those in real life.

We show how we can use the proposed framework to generate an extensive dataset for the task of multi-class image segmentation. We use the dataset to train a pairwise CRF model and to analyze the effects of using various combinations of features in different image modalities.

1 Introduction

The availability of high quality datasets is a crucial factor for the development of new computer vision algorithms. On one hand, learning-based methods need large amounts of ground truth data during their training phase and on the other hand, high quality data is crucial for a thorough and fair evaluation and comparison of different methods. Innovation in the computer vision and the machine learning fields has been largely driven by datasets and benchmark evaluations, which allow us to quantitatively measure the progress in the field.

Some types of data are relatively easy to obtain with high precision e.g. camera images or depth images in indoor scenarios. For such image modalities there are low-cost sensors available that can generate a lot of data very quickly. Other ground truth data, like object annotations or multi-class pixel-wise annotations of images, can be obtained by manual user annotation. Unfortunately, this is a very time consuming and expensive task. Other types of ground truth data, like depth images outdoors and optical flow, are also very difficult to obtain. Stereo cameras or laser scanners can deliver depth information, but suffer either in precision or deliver very sparse information. For optical flow there is no sensor that is able to measure it directly and manual annotation is practically impossible.

J. Weickert, M. Hein, and B. Schiele (Eds.): GCPR 2013, LNCS 8142, pp. 323–332, 2013.
© Springer-Verlag Berlin Heidelberg 2013

a) Camera image   b) Depth image   c) Optical flow   d) Segmentation

Fig. 1. Example images in 3 different modalities and the corresponding pixel-wise annotations generated with the proposed framework. In the flow image, pixels with flow of more than 10 px are shown in darker colors. More examples are available in the supplementary materials.

There are already several large-scale datasets for the evaluation of stereo [18,10], optical flow [2,7,26,10] and object detection [9,10]. However, for the task of outdoor multi-class image segmentation, there is still no extensive dataset that includes high quality video sequences of outdoor scenes, high precision dense depth maps and a large set of annotated images. Such datasets are particularly important in the field of advanced driver assistance systems (ADAS). While several datasets [4,8,16,15] provide some of this data, they either have only low quality images or very sparse or imprecise depth maps (see Section 2).

One way to easily obtain large amounts of high precision ground truth data is to generate it synthetically. While it is very difficult to claim that an algorithm that performs well on a synthetic dataset will also perform well on real images, synthetic images are often used during the development of new methods in order to better understand some of their properties. For example [14] use a synthetic rotating sphere for the evaluation of scene flow and [23,24] use synthetic traffic sequences rendered with POV-Ray to evaluate stereo and optical flow algorithms for driver assistance. Furthermore, benchmarks like the popular Middlebury dataset [2] or the recently introduced Syntel dataset [7,26] employ synthetic images for the evaluation of optical flow and [6] use synthetic scenes for the evaluation of background subtraction algorithms.

In this work we present a new open-source framework for generating synthetic data in multiple image modalities with corresponding pixel-wise semantic annotations with focus on driver assistance applications (see Fig. 1). The framework is based on the open-source driving simulator VDrift [1], which provides a very realistic rendering engine and physics simulation. Having full access to the source code and the 3D models of the simulator, we are able to modify it, so that we can generate not only camera images, but also high precision depth and optical flow maps, pixel-wise semantic annotations and to record the exact camera pose for every frame. The proposed framework also allows the user to define specific traffic scenarios that can be of particular interest for driver assistance applications. The framework is available at http://campar.in.tum.de/Main/VladimirHaltakov.

Using the proposed framework we show how to generate images in 3 different image modalities and train a pairwise conditional random field (CRF) model

Table 1. Summary of the most important properties of 12 publically available multi-class segmentation datasets and our proposal

Dataset	Image resolution	Video sequences	Depth data	Traffic scenes	Annotated images
Sowerby [12]	96 × 64	-	-	yes	104
Corel [12]	180 × 120	-	-	-	100
MSRC-21 [19]	320 × 213	-	-	-	591
Stanford Background [11]	320 × 240	-	only 3 classes	partially	715
CamVid [4], [5]	960 × 720	yes	motion stereo	yes	700
Dynamic scenes [25]	752 × 480	yes	-	yes	221
Leuven [15]	316 × 256	yes	partially	yes	70
City [8]	640 × 480	yes	stereo	yes	95
NYU Depth V1 [20]	640 × 480	yes	Kinect	-	2347
NYU Depth V2 [21]	640 × 480	yes	Kinect	-	1449
CMU RGB-D [16][1]	600 × 402	-	laser	yes	372
KITTI [10]	1384 × 1032	yes	stereo, laser	yes	-
Our framework	**2560 × 1600**	**yes**	**3D models**	**yes**	**7905[2]**

for multi-class image segmentation, similar to the one of [19]. We show how the multiple modalities allow us to explore the effects of different feature types.

2   Related Work

Since we are particularly interested in multi-class image segmentation of outdoor scenes (and especially in the context of ADAS), in this section we give an overview of some of the more important segmentation datasets. Table 1 gives a brief overview of the existing datasets and we discuss their advantages and disadvantages in detail below.

Most of the multi-class segmentation datasets, like *Sowerby* [12], *Corel* [12], *MSRC-21* [19] and the *Stanford Background dataset* [11], consist only of separate camera images with their corresponding semantic annotations. Therefore, they can only be used in segmentation methods that rely solely on texture information. Furthermore, all of the datasets mentioned above provide only relatively low resolution images (less than 320 × 240 pixels).

Some of the newer datasets, like *CamVid* [4,5] and the *Dynamic Scenes Dataset* of [25], include video sequences which can be used to compute optical flow or structure from motion point clouds. However, these methods do not deliver high quality depth information. This could be a problem for the evaluation, because it is difficult to tell which errors are caused by the input data and which by the model itself. Both datasets do not provide any other ground truth data apart from the pixel-wise annotations.

---

[1] Although the *CMU RGB-D* dataset contains images of resolution 3872 × 2592, the semantic annotations are created with a resolution of 600 × 402.

[2] More images can be easily generated with the provided framework.

The *Leuven* [15] dataset and the *City* [8] dataset provide not only video sequences of road scenes and semantic annotations but also stereo camera images. While the quality of the depth maps computed with stereo matching algorithms is in general better than with structure from motion methods, the depth data can still contain many errors around object boundaries or in the presence of reflections. Furthermore, the images provided by both datasets have a relatively small resolution and only less than 100 frames are annotated.

In order to deal with the problem of providing high quality 3D data, several works introduce datasets that use an additional high precision depth sensor along with the camera: the *NYU Depth V1* [20], the *NYU Depth V2* [21] and the *CMU Driving RGB-D* [16] datasets. The first two datasets use the Microsoft Kinect to record synchronized camera and range images in indoor environments. Additionally, many of the frames have pixel-wise annotations. However, outdoor scenarios pose significantly different challenges than indoor scenes and therefore those datasets cannot be used to develop or evaluate methods that are required to work in outdoor environments, like in the case of driver assistance systems. The *CMU RGB-D* driving dataset of [16] employs a laser scanner instead of the Kinect, which allows recording of outdoor scenes. However, the images provided in the dataset are recorded at a relatively low frame rate, which makes the computation of optical flow or the usage of temporal information almost impossible. Furthermore, the used laser scanner operates in push broom mode and therefore the depth maps are sparse and do not always overlap with the camera images.

The recent dataset *KITTI* [10] is also worth mentioning even though it does not provide pixel-wise semantic annotations. The dataset consists of a large amount of stereo camera video sequences of traffic scenes synchronized with the output of a 360 degree laser scanner providing precise, but sparse ground truth depth and flow data for the lower part of the camera's field of view. The authors also provide extensive benchmarks for the evaluation of stereo, optical flow, object detection and visual odometry methods. Unfortunately, the dataset contains only bounding box annotations for cars, pedestrians and cyclists and no pixel-wise semantic labels.

3 Framework

The ground truth data generation framework is based on the open source driving simulator VDrift [1]. We considered several driving games and simulators and we chose VDrift because it provides very realistic images, a sophisticated simulation engine and a lot of different track and car models. In addition, we have full access to the source code. As we show below, the last point is essential for the generation of some of the image modalities.

3.1 Image Modalities

Since our main goal is to generate data for different image modalities, we adapted the rendering pipeline of the simulator to suit our needs. We are able to control different rendering settings like lighting and shadow generation and we can access the 3D structure of the scenes. We are also able to control the camera pose relative to the car and in this way to simulate cameras mounted at different positions and orientations. We developed a set of OpenGL shaders that generate different image types efficiently and we are able to run the simulation in real time. The rest of the section describes in detail each of the image modalities that can be generated by our framework. One example frame can be seen on Fig. 1 and video sequences are provided in the supplementary material.

Camera Images. For the camera images we use the default rendering pipeline of the simulator, which is based on OpenGL. It employs several rendering techniques like anisotropic filtering, anti-aliasing, motion blur, ambient occlusion, shadows and reflections. The textures of the 3D models in the simulator are also of relatively high quality. This results in very realistic camera images with resolution of up to 2560×1600 pixels.

Depth Maps. From the 3D models of the scene, we are easily able to generate depth images by directly accessing the z coordinate (in the camera frame) of each pixel. Since our implementation is based on an OpenGL shader, we encode the depth information into all 3 color channels of the output image, which lieads to a precision of 24 bits per pixel. If the maximum distance is set to 1000 meters the resolution of the ground truth disparity map is 0.06 mm.

Optical Flow Maps. The generation of ground truth optical flow is more challenging than that of the depth maps, since the required information is not directly available. In OpenGL there are two matrices that have an effect on where a 3D point should be rendered in the image - the model matrix and the projection matrix. While the camera is moving around the scene, the model matrix of each object is updated in order to account for the camera motion, while the projection matrix is usually fixed.

At each frame we provide the optical flow shader with the current model matrix for each object and the model matrix from the previous frame. With this information we can compute the 3D movement vector of each point from the previous frame to the current one. By projecting this 3D vector onto the image plane of the camera, we get the corresponding optical flow for each 3D vertex, but we still have to compute the flow value for the points of each triangle defined by 3 vertices. Interpolating the flow between the vertices in 2D would lead to wrong flow values for the triangle's points. Instead, we interpolate the 3D position of each triangle point in the current and in the previous frame and then compute the correct flow value for each image point.

As for the depth maps, we encode the flow into the 3 color channels of the output image with a precision of 24 bits per pixel. The flow values in x and y direction are encoded into separate images, from which the original flow can be easily reconstructed. This means that in the case of sequences with a maximum flow value of 100 pixels, the resolutions of the ground truth data is 0.6×10^{-5} pixels.

Pixel-Wise Annotations. In the case of pixel-wise semantic annotations, each of the pixels in the image should be assigned a class from a set of predefined classes L that we are interested in. Here we define the set L that consists of 7 classes: SKY, TREE, GRASS, ROAD, MARKINGS, BUILDING and CAR. Unfortunately, VDrift does not support different semantic information for all of the object types listed above. For example, in the 3D model of the track, trees and buildings are indistinguishable, because they are simply modeled as 3D meshes. The road markings do not even have separate 3D structure at all. Therefore, the best way to distinguish the different object types is by their texture. We assigned a unique RGB color value to each of the classes above and modified the textures of several tracks by painting them uniformly with the corresponding colors. Rendering the scene with those textures results in a scene where each object is painted in the color specifying its class. In this case, it is very important to switch off all visual effects like lighting, shadows, reflections, anti-aliasing and mip-mapping in order to get the right color value for each pixel.

3.2   Scenario Generation

Since VDrift was originally created as a racing simulator, we modified the game engine in several ways in order to allow for the generation of scenarios that simulate real traffic conditions. Using the default AI settings, the cars would drive as fast as possible around the track. Therefore, we modified the replay system of the simulator so that we are able to manually record the movement of several cars separately and then combine all the replays into one. In this way we can create arbitrary scenarios of multiple cars driving like in normal traffic.

We also added the possibility to put stationary vehicles at arbitrary positions on the map. In this way we can simulate parked cars for more realistic scenes.

4   Evaluation

The ground truth data that we can generate using our framework gives us the possibility to explore the effects of using different image modalities for multi-class image segmentation based on a CRF. This is not possible with any of the existing datasets because they either do not include all 3 image modalities, the quality of the data is relatively poor or the amount of the training data is limited. For most of the existing segmentation datasets all of the above are true.

For the experiments we created 25 sequences on 5 different tracks simulating a car driving on country and city roads. Of those sequences, 12 were used for training and 13 for testing. The virtual camera was mounted behind the windshield of the car like a typical camera used for driver assistance systems in current vehicles. For each frame we generated images in all 3 possible modalities: camera images, depth maps and optical flow maps and the ground truth pixelwise semantic annotations. Running the simulation at 30 frames per second we generated 7905 images. However, since at this frame rate consecutive images are very similar, we took only each 5th image, which results in a training dataset of 669 images and an evaluation dataset of 912 images.

4.1   CRF Model

For the multi-class image segmentation task we use a pairwise CRF model very similar to the TextonBoost model of [19]. Each pixel of the image is first classified

Table 2. Pixel-wise accuracies from the evaluation of the CRF segmentation model trained on 7 different combinations of features

Model	Accuracy	Average	Road	Marking	Building	Grass	Tree	Car	Sky
T	89.0%	70.5%	79.5%	**20.0%**	61.9%	79.2%	73.6%	88.4%	**90.9%**
D	80.6%	58.8%	88.4%	0.0%	54.2%	68.0%	25.8%	92.3%	83.1%
F	75.0%	49.3%	82.3%	0.0%	52.8%	19.4%	16.7%	91.7%	82.5%
T+D	**91.2%**	**72.2%**	88.1%	10.0%	72.5%	82.0%	70.3%	92.5%	90.2%
D+F	79.8%	57.9%	84.5%	0.0%	55.3%	73.5%	15.1%	92.1%	84.6%
T+F	90.1%	70.9%	84.7%	10.4%	64.0%	79.4%	**74.3%**	93.1%	90.6%
T+D+F	91.0%	71.2%	**88.8%**	3.2%	**71.3%**	**82.7%**	68.2%	**93.2%**	90.9%

with a JointBoost classifier [22] based on various features extracted from the image and then inference is performed using the α-expansion algorithm [3] on the pairwise graph. Here, we do not use the color and location unary potentials of [19], but only the classifier based unary term, while the pairwise potentials have the form of the contrast sensitive Potts model as in [19]. We also use different features than the textons of [19] in order to incorporate the texture, depth and flow information and to evaluate the contribution of the different image modalities to the performance of the CRF model.

For the **texture features** we transform the image into *Lab* color space and for each color channel we compute the mean and the variance of the first 16 coefficients of the 2D Walsh-Hadamard transform [13] at several scales around each pixel as in [25]. For our experiments we used windows of 8, 16 and 32 pixels to compute the texture features. The **depth features** consist of the 3D coordinates of the corresponding 3D point, the coordinates of the surface normal at this point and the Fast Point Feature Histogram (FPFH) of [17]. For the **flow features**, we use the 2D vector of the flow directly. In order to incorporate context information, we also include the 2D coordinates of the pixel.

The segmentation is performed on cells of 8×8 pixels instead on each pixel, but the evaluation is done at the pixel level.

4.2 Results

We analyze the importance of different image modalities for the segmentation performance. We train and evaluate 7 variants of the CRF model described above by giving it access only to the features of different subsets of image modalities: texture (**T**), depth (**D**), flow (**F**), texture and depth (**T+D**), depth and flow (**D+F**), texture and flow (**T+F**) and all three together (**T+D+F**). The location features are used in every configuration. In Table 2 we report the percentage of correctly classified pixels over all evaluation images, for each class individually and the average precision over all classes. In Fig. 2 we show the segmentation computed by all 7 models on one frame of the evaluation dataset. More segmentation results are provided in the supplementary material.

Fig. 2. Input images in 3 different modalities, the ground truth annotation and the output segmentation of all 7 models for one frame from our evaluation dataset. More result images are provided as a video in the supplementary material.

Using only the texture features (**T**), the CRF model is already able to achieve very good results - 89.0% overall accuracy. However, for classes with big variations in appearance, like BUILDING or CAR (compared to the other configurations), the performance is not that good, which can also be seen on the result images. Using the depth (**D**) or the flow features (**F**) alone leads to relatively poor results - 80.6% and 75.0% respectively. While the numbers may not seem too bad, we can see from the resulting images that the segmentation is much worse than in case of using only the texture features. Traffic scenes often have similar structure - sky in the upper part of the image, road in the lower part and combination of buildings, trees and cars in the middle part. This allows the CRF model to achieve high accuracy rates relatively easy relying on the location features, but in order to evaluate the real quality of the segmentation, one should look into the details. For example, we can see both from the quantitative analysis and from the result images, that when using only depth or flow, the model has difficulties distinguishing between flat surfaces like ROAD and GRASS and the road markings cannot be detected at all. The average performance of those models over all classes is therefore also low.

It is not surprising to see that combining the texture features with either depth (**T+D**) or flow (**T+F**) features results in increased overall segmentation accuracy - 91.2% and 90.1% respectively. In most of the classes we see significant improvements, especially for ROAD, BUILDING and CAR. This is the case because those classes vary a lot in their appearance, but have well defined shapes, which can be better captured by the depth or flow features.

Combining all 3 feature types (**T+D+F**) gives overall accuracy of 91.0% that is only slightly worse (by 0.2%) than when using texture and depth features. This suggests that the information encoded by the depth and flow features is relatively similar. This is also confirmed by the model that uses them together (**D+F**). When combining those two modalities, no improvement is observed. However, in the case of more dynamic scenes this could change.

In conclusion we can say that it makes sense to use depth or flow features along with texture features extracted from the camera images, because they can improve the recognition of objects that have relatively well defined shapes like for example cars. When using relatively simple features for the depth and flow modalities, as in our case, it is not beneficial to include all three image modalities, but this may change if more sophisticated features are used.

5 Conclusion

In this paper we presented a new framework for the generation of ground truth data, which is based on the realistic driving simulator VDrift. The framework can be used to easily generate big amounts of high quality camera images, depth and optical flow maps and pixel-wise semantic annotations. Furthermore, the framework allows for the generation of specific driving scenarios that can be of particular interest for the development of advanced driver assistance systems.

We show how we can generate a dataset for the evaluation of multi-class segmentation algorithms that contains images in 3 different modalities and how we can use it to evaluate the performance of different feature types.

The proposed framework can also be used to generate ground truth data for other applications. One could easily generate images of two cameras and evaluate stereo matching algorithms given the ground truth depth data or one could use consecutive frames and the generated flow maps to evaluate optical flow and structure from motion methods. Other applications of the framework include the development and evaluation of visual odometry, scene flow and object detection methods.

References

1. http://www.vdrift.net
2. Baker, S., Scharstein, D., Lewis, J.P., Roth, S., Black, M.J., Szeliski, R.: A database and evaluation methodology for optical flow. In: IJCV (2011)
3. Boykov, Y., Veksler, O., Zabih, R.: Fast approximate energy minimization via graph cuts. PAMI (2001)
4. Brostow, G.J., Fauqueur, J., Cipolla, R.: Semantic object classes in video: A high-definition ground truth database. Pattern Recognition Letters (2008)
5. Brostow, G.J., Shotton, J., Fauqueur, J., Cipolla, R.: Segmentation and recognition using structure from motion point clouds. In: Forsyth, D., Torr, P., Zisserman, A. (eds.) ECCV 2008, Part I. LNCS, vol. 5302, pp. 44–57. Springer, Heidelberg (2008)
6. Brutzer, S., Höferlin, B., Heidemann, G.: Evaluation of background subtraction techniques for video surveillance. In: CVPR (2011)

7. Butler, D.J., Wulff, J., Stanley, G.B., Black, M.J.: A naturalistic open source movie for optical flow evaluation. In: Fitzgibbon, A., Lazebnik, S., Perona, P., Sato, Y., Schmid, C. (eds.) ECCV 2012, Part VI. LNCS, vol. 7577, pp. 611–625. Springer, Heidelberg (2012)

8. Ess, A., Mueller, T., Grabner, H., Gool, L.J.V.: Segmentation-based urban traffic scene understanding. In: BMVC (2009)

9. Everingham, M., Van Gool, L., Williams, C.K.I., Winn, J., Zisserman, A.: The pascal visual object classes (voc) challenge. IJCV (2010)

10. Geiger, A., Lenz, P., Urtasun, R.: Are we ready for autonomous driving? The KITTI vision benchmark suite. In: CVPR (2012)

11. Gould, S., Fulton, R., Koller, D.: Decomposing a scene into geometric and semantically consistent regions. In: ICCV (2009)

12. He, X., Zemel, R., Carreira-Perpin, M.: Multiscale conditional random fields for image labeling. In: CVPR (2004)

13. Hel-Or, Y., Hel-Or, H.: Real time pattern matching using projection kernels. In: ICCV (2003)

14. Huguet, F., Devernay, F.: A variational method for scene flow estimation from stereo sequences. In: ICCV (2007)

15. Ladický, L., Sturgess, P., Russell, C., Sengupta, S., Bastanlar, Y., Clocksin, W., Torr, P.H.: Joint optimisation for object class segmentation and dense stereo reconstruction. In: BMVC (2010)

16. Munoz, D., Bagnell, J.A., Hebert, M.: Co-inference for multi-modal scene analysis. In: Fitzgibbon, A., Lazebnik, S., Perona, P., Sato, Y., Schmid, C. (eds.) ECCV 2012, Part VI. LNCS, vol. 7577, pp. 668–681. Springer, Heidelberg (2012)

17. Rusu, R., Blodow, N., Beetz, M.: Fast point feature histograms (fpfh) for 3d registration. In: ICRA (2009)

18. Scharstein, D., Szeliski, R.: A taxonomy and evaluation of dense two-frame stereo correspondence algorithms. In: IJCV (2002)

19. Shotton, J., Winn, J., Rother, C., Criminisi, A.: *TextonBoost*: Joint appearance, shape and context modeling for multi-class object recognition and segmentation. In: Leonardis, A., Bischof, H., Pinz, A. (eds.) ECCV 2006, Part I. LNCS, vol. 3951, pp. 1–15. Springer, Heidelberg (2006)

20. Silberman, N., Fergus, R.: Indoor scene segmentation using a structured light sensor. In: ICCV - Workshop on 3D Representation and Recognition (2011)

21. Silberman, N., Hoiem, D., Kohli, P., Fergus, R.: Indoor segmentation and support inference from RGBD images. In: Fitzgibbon, A., Lazebnik, S., Perona, P., Sato, Y., Schmid, C. (eds.) ECCV 2012, Part V. LNCS, vol. 7576, pp. 746–760. Springer, Heidelberg (2012)

22. Torralba, A., Murphy, K.P., Freeman, W.T.: Sharing visual features for multiclass and multiview object detection. PAMI (2007)

23. Vaudrey, T., Rabe, C., Klette, R., Milburn, J.: Differences between stereo and motion behaviour on synthetic and real-world stereo sequences. In: IVCNZ (2008)

24. Wedel, A., Brox, T., Vaudrey, T., Rabe, C., Franke, U., Cremers, D.: Stereoscopic scene flow computation for 3d motion understanding. IJCV (2011)

25. Wojek, C., Schiele, B.: A dynamic conditional random field model for joint labeling of object and scene classes. In: Forsyth, D., Torr, P., Zisserman, A. (eds.) ECCV 2008, Part IV. LNCS, vol. 5305, pp. 733–747. Springer, Heidelberg (2008)

26. Wulff, J., Butler, D.J., Stanley, G.B., Black, M.J.: Lessons and insights from creating a synthetic optical flow benchmark. In: Fusiello, A., Murino, V., Cucchiara, R. (eds.) ECCV 2012 Ws/Demos, Part II. LNCS, vol. 7584, pp. 168–177. Springer, Heidelberg (2012)

Refractive Plane Sweep for Underwater Images

Anne Jordt-Sedlazeck*, Daniel Jung, and Reinhard Koch

Institute of Computer Science, Kiel University, 24118 Kiel, Germany
{as,djung,rk}@mip.informatik.uni-kiel.de

Abstract. In underwater imaging, refraction changes the geometry of image formation, causing the perspective camera model to be invalid. Hence, a systematic model error occurs when computing 3D models using the perspective camera model. This paper deals with the problem of computing dense depth maps of underwater scenes with explicit incorporation of refraction of light at the underwater housing. It is assumed that extrinsic, intrinsic, and housing parameters have been calibrated for all cameras. Due to the refractive camera's characteristics it is not possible to directly apply epipolar geometry or rectification to images because the single-view-point model and, consequently, homographies are invalid. Additionally, the projection of 3D points into the camera cannot be computed efficiently, but requires solving a 12th degree polynomial. Therefore, the method proposed is an adapted plane sweep algorithm that is based on the idea of back-projecting rays for each pixel and view onto the 3D-hypothesis planes using the GPU. This allows to efficiently warp all images onto the plane, where they can be compared. Consequently, projections of 3D points and homographies are not utilized.

1 Introduction

During the last decade, a lot of applications arose, where images captured below water examine underwater scenes, for example off shore wind and oil production, ship hull or cable inspection, or scientific surveys, in the area of geology, where seafloor structures are examined, but also in the areas of biology or archeology. In most of these applications, images can be utilized to retrieve geometry information about the scene for simple measurements, but also for 3D reconstruction and/or navigation. However, in order to capture underwater images, the camera is confined in an underwater housing, viewing the scene through a piece of glass, often a flat port. Sometimes, cameras need to capture images at great water depths, consequently, the glass of the underwater housing can be several centimeters thick. The inside of the housing is filled with air, causing a light ray entering the housing from the water to cross two interfaces, first, the water-glass interface, then the glass-air interface. Therefore, it is refracted twice, hence changing its direction depending on the incidence angle. This refraction

---

* This work has been supported by the German Science Foundation (DFG), KO 2044/6-1/2: 3D Modeling of Seafloor Structures from ROV-based Video Sequences.

J. Weickert, M. Hein, and B. Schiele (Eds.): GCPR 2013, LNCS 8142, pp. 333–342, 2013.

changes the imaging geometry and causes the commonly used perspective camera model to become invalid because the light rays do not intersect in the center of projection anymore (non-Single-View-Point (nSVP) model, Fig. 1). In spite of this, in the literature, mostly the perspective camera model has been used on underwater images by allowing focal length and radial distortion to approximate the bulk of the refractive effect [6]. Using this approximation, methods like stereo-measurement, mosaicing, and Structure-from-motion, originally designed for above water applications, have been applied to underwater images (refer to [4,5,11] respectively), causing systematic measurement errors.

However, it is also possible to explicitly model refraction in computer vision applications. In order to design adapted, refractive methods for SfM or mosaicing, the camera housing needs to be parametrized and calibrated. Treibitz et al. [20] introduce a method for measuring the deviation from the perspective camera model by caustics and show a method for calibrating a camera with very thin glass and parallelism between imaging sensor and glass. [1] showed that the nSVP camera is in fact an axial camera, i.e. all rays intersect a common axis, and introduced a calibration method based on that insight. Additionally, they showed that in order to project a 3D point into a refractive camera, a 12th degree polynomial needs to be solved, hence, projections of 3D points are far less efficient than in a classic perspective camera. [12] build upon [1] as an initialization and proposed an analysis-by-synthesis optimization. Once the camera intrinsics and housing parameters are calibrated, applications like SfM can be used to determine camera movement. [3] derive a complete framework for refractive SfM, but no results are presented. [2] introduce a system for refractive SfM, but assume the camera to view the scene through the water surface with known camera yaw and pitch. Most recently, [13] introduced a method on how to compute 3D models from two views. Maas et al. [14] showed that in presence of refraction, an epipolar line is really an epipolar curve in the second image. Hence, it is impossible to rectify flat port underwater images and all methods for dense depth estimation based on rectified images, e.g. [10], cannot be adapted to refraction easily. Additionally, homographies are invalid, due to the single-view-point model being invalid, hence preventing a straight-forward adaptation of classic plane sweep methods like [8]. [13] showed that with known 3D point cloud and extrinsics from two views, PMVS, a method for computing dense models out of sparse point clouds, originally proposed by Furukawa and Ponce [7], can be adapted to explicitly model refraction. However, due to the need of costly 3D projections and not being able to use epipolar lines for guiding correspondence search, the run-time of a refractive adaptation of PMVS becomes infeasible for more than a few images.

Our Contribution: in this paper, we propose a new refractive plane sweep method that back-projects 2D image points onto the 3D hypothesis planes of the plane sweep, which can be computed efficiently for all pixels in all images, hence allowing to warp complete images onto the hypothesis planes, where image patches can be compared in order to determine correct depth. It builds on the ability of GPU shaders to automatically interpolate between vertices, and relies

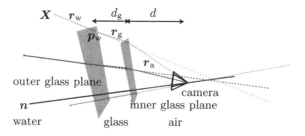

Fig. 1. Refractive camera with inner and outer glass plane. The blue line depicts the interface normal intersecting the camera's center of projection. In cyan, red, and green are 3 exemplary rays that are refracted by the interface. The dashed lines show that the rays in water r_w do not intersect in one common center of projection anymore, but in the blue line.

only on efficient forward-mapping of image pixels onto the sweep planes, never on expensive refractive projection.

In the following, the refractive camera is introduced followed by a description of the proposed method. Experiments show the performance of the proposed method compared to perspective plane sweep on underwater images and compared to the refractive adaptation of PMVS.

2 Refractive Underwater Camera Model

The camera model used throughout this work is made of a perspective camera with radial and tangential distortion (e.g. [19]), for which a glass interface is parametrized by the distance d between the camera center and the glass, the glass thickness d_g, and the interface normal n. For a pixel in the image, a ray in air r_a can be back-projected using the intrinsic parameters of the perspective camera model. Using Snell's law and the indexes of refraction for air n_a, glass n_g, and water n_w, the ray in glass r_g can be computed from r_a:

$$r_\mathrm{g} = \frac{n_\mathrm{a}}{n_\mathrm{g}} r_\mathrm{a} + \left(-\frac{n_\mathrm{a}}{n_\mathrm{g}} r_\mathrm{a}^\mathrm{T} n + \sqrt{1 - \frac{n_\mathrm{a}}{n_\mathrm{g}} (1 - (r_\mathrm{a}^\mathrm{T} n)^2)} \right) n . \qquad (1)$$

Likewise, the ray in water r_w can be computed from the ray in glass r_g. So for each pixel in the image, the ray in water and a starting point $p_\mathrm{w} = \frac{d}{r_\mathrm{a}^\mathrm{T} n} r_\mathrm{a} + \frac{d_\mathrm{g}}{r_\mathrm{g}^\mathrm{T} n} r_\mathrm{g}$ on the outer glass interface can be computed (Fig. 1). Note, that projecting 3D points into a refractive camera is much more involved. [1] showed that a 12th-degree polynomial needs to be solved for each projection and this insight was a huge improvement compared to the optimization using the back-projection that has been used before that. Note, that the interface distance d can be negative in case the center of projection is located in front of the entrance pupil [20].

2.1   Effects on Color

In addition to the above described effects on imaging geometry, the water also affects image color, observable in the typical green or blue hue of underwater images. Effects on color are wavelength dependent and caused by attenuation and back-scattering of light while traveling through the water body. Light coming from an underwater object is attenuated on its way to the camera, depending on the distance traveled. In addition, back-scatter is added to the light reaching the camera stemming from multiple scattering events, thus creating the so-called veiling light, which increases with increasing camera object distance [16]:

$$L_\lambda = \underbrace{I_\lambda e^{-\eta_\lambda z}}_{\text{attenuation}} + \underbrace{B_{\infty_\lambda}(1 - e^{-\eta_\lambda z})}_{\text{back-scatter}}, \tag{2}$$

where λ is the wavelength, I_λ the original color of the object immersed in water, η_λ the attenuation coefficient, B_{∞_λ} the veiling light color, and z the distance between object and camera. L_λ is then the color recorded by the camera. If the characteristics of the local water body are known, i.e. η_λ and B_{∞_λ} have been calibrated for the three color channels [17], it is possible to correct image color for known depths, thus making dense depth algorithms more robust. This idea has already been presented in [15], however, the method did not consider refraction.

In summary, a refractive dense depth method cannot make use of rectified images, homographies, or repetitive projections of image points on whole images. However, the model on light attenuation and scattering can be used to improve block-matching. These constraints led to the design of the following algorithm.

3   Dense Depth Estimation

The key idea to satisfying all of the above constraints is simple: we make use of the plane sweep algorithm. However, instead of using a homography to warp entire images into the reference view, all image pixels are back-projected onto the 3D hypothesis planes of the sweep planes and compared there. This eliminates the need of using projections of 3D points and does not require a valid homography. Since this is a forward mapping of the image onto the hypothesis planes, naturally, the resulting plane images are incomplete, i.e. contain holes. However, by using *OpenGL* for the GPU implementation, those holes are automatically filled with interpolated color values during rasterization. In general, the plane sweep algorithm is particularly suitable for implementation on the graphics hardware due to efficient computation of perspective projections, fast texture look-up, and efficient texture filtering.

3.1   Refractive GPU-Based Plane Sweep

As an initial step, a mapping from the pixel of the input images to the corresponding light rays at the outer surface of the underwater housing is precomputed according to the underwater camera model (see Sec. 2, Eq. 1), consisting

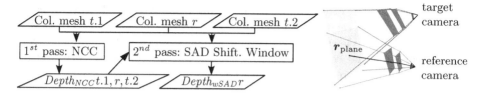

Fig. 2. Computation of the final depth map for the reference view (left) and plane sweep (right). The green plane is the image that is being drawn via forward mapping from both cameras. In case the viewing area overlaps, matching costs can be computed.

of the position of the light ray on the underwater housing p_w and its normal in local camera coordinates r_w. The mapping is computed in a vertex shader, allowing for a discrete sub-sampling via the number of vertices that are used to span the mesh that covers the viewport. The position and normal of the light rays are bilinearly interpolated during rasterization between the vertices, yielding a ray for every pixel of the input image, stored in a texture on the graphics hardware for fast access during plane sweep. Note that, assuming the image sequence is recorded from a single moving camera, the mapping between pixel and light rays has to be computed only once. The proposed refractive plane sweep is not limited to the underwater case, but can handle almost arbitrary camera models like the raxel model proposed by Grossberg and Nayar [9] or the even more general model introduced by Sturm et al. [18]. Especially the perspective camera model can be used to determine a ray for each pixel. Thus, an equivalent implementation of a perspective plane sweep is used in the experiments. A consequence of this approach is that the mapping of pixel to ray contains all refractive geometry, and no refractive projections need to be carried out, which significantly accelerates the sweep.

The view for which the depth map is computed will be called *reference view* and the view(s) against which the reference view is matched will be called *target view(s)* in the remainder. The left side of Figure 2 shows an overview of the proposed algorithm. The first sweep matches the reference view (r) against two target views ($t.1$ and $t.2$) using the normalized cross correlation (NCC) as measurement costs. After the depth maps for all input views are computed ($t.1, r, t.2$), a second plane sweep is executed for the reference view (r), against the two target views ($t.1$ and $t.2$) using the sum of absolute differences (SAD) with a shiftable window. The SAD costs of the second plane sweep are reduced when the depth hypothesis of the second sweep matches the NCC depth map of the first plane sweep and if the NCC matching costs are below a given threshold.

A sweep for the reference view is performed by placing a plane in space for every depth hypothesis. The plane is defined via the normal of the light ray belonging to the principal point of the reference view and placed at the distance of the current depth hypothesis (black ray in Fig. 2, right). The area of interest on the plane is computed by intersecting the corners of the reference view with the plane (green rays in Fig. 2, right). The key idea is to use a dense mesh for every view that should be matched, texture it with the input image, calculate the position of each vertex on the plane by intersecting the light rays of each pixel with the plane, render the area of interest for every view, and finally match the rendered target views against the reference view. In case the parameters for color attenuation and scattering (Eq. 2) are known, the colors are corrected in accordance to the current depth hypothesis.

4 Experiments

In order to evaluate the proposed method, both refractive and perspective camera models are used in equivalent implementations. For the perspective model to approximate the refractive effect as closely as possible, checkerboard images are used to calibrate the perspective camera allowing the parameters to absorb refraction. In general, all intrinsic parameters, housing parameters, and camera poses are assumed to be known prior to applying the proposed method. In the following, first results on synthetic images are presented, showing the accuracy in comparison to ground truth. Then, both refractive and perspective implementations are applied to real images.

4.1 Synthetic Images

For comparing the perspective plane sweep with the proposed method, images with different housing configurations were rendered. The interface distance was $d \in \{-5\,\text{mm}, 0\,\text{mm}, 5\,\text{mm}, 10\,\text{mm}, 20\,\text{mm}, 50\,\text{mm}, 100\,\text{mm}\}$ and the interface tilt was chosen from $\theta \in \{0°, 0.5°, 1°, 3°\}$, leading to 28 different configurations. The camera inside the housing had a focal length of 800 px for an image size of 800×600 px. The principal point was located in the middle of the image and no radial distortion was added. For each housing configuration, the same trajectory of 10 images was rendered and then used for plane sweep computation. Fig. 3 shows the resulting average error over the whole depth map across all images for each housing configuration. Clearly, the proposed refractive method outperforms the perspective camera model, for which the error increases with increasing interface distance and tilt. The accuracy of the approximation of the perspective camera model to refraction is depending on the imaging distance. Therefore, a second set of images was rendered with a different camera trajectory and greater imaging distance for all 28 housing configurations, this time further away from the camera. Again, the proposed refractive method was more accurate than the perspective model on underwater images (Fig. 4). As can be seen by this experiment, a systematic error is introduced in the perspective model, depending on the parameters of the camera housing. The refractive model is invariant to these changes, hence, no systematic error occurs. Figure 5 shows the resulting depth maps for both models and negated difference images to ground truth depth for an exemplary image from the second scene. Note the systematic error on the back plane in the difference image of the perspective model. Here, the error was around 200 mm, increasing toward the right part of the image, while the error of the refractive model stayed below or close to the sweeping distance of 10 mm.

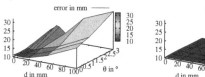
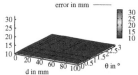

Fig. 3. Results of plane sweep for all 28 housing configurations. The distance between scene and camera was between 1500 mm and 4000 mm. Left: error for perspective plane sweep on underwater images. Right: error for proposed refractive plane sweep on underwater images.

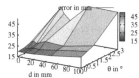
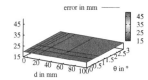

Fig. 4. Results for scene with imaging distance between 4000 mm and 9000 mm. Left: error for perspective model on underwater images. Right: error for refractive model on underwater images.

In Table 1 run-time of the proposed method was compared to a prototype implementation on the CPU. The CPU implementation can only compare two images using SAD, therefore, GPU+SAD shows results for a comparable configuration. In summary, the CPU implementation requires over 550 ms for each plane on an 800x600 px image, while the comparable simplified version of the proposed method on the GPU requires only about 5 ms for each plane. The proposed method running on 3 views and combining SAD and NCC takes about 43 ms for each plane. It is difficult to compare run-times of PMVS, but a run with 5 images took approximately 10 minutes. With 6 images run-time increases to over an hour using all eight available processor cores.

4.2   Real Images

The proposed method was tested on real images captured in a lab fish tank (1000 mm × 500 mm × 500 mm). The camera was placed outside the tank in four different camera-glass configurations. For each configuration, checkerboard images were used to calibrate the perspective camera model and the glass of the refractive camera model. Since the camera with respect to the glass was not allowed to move after calibration, a model of the entrance to the Abu Simbel temple in Egypt of the size 380 mm × 280 mm × 180 mm was placed inside the water and moved around at object-camera distances between 300 mm and 700 mm.

Fig. 5. Exemplary result for interface distance $d = 100\,\mathrm{mm}$ and interface tilt $\theta = 3°$. Left: input image and ground truth depth map. Center: depth errors and result depth map for perspective camera model on underwater images. Right: depth errors and result depth map for refractive camera model on underwater images.

Table 1. Run-time in ms for one plane. Top row: GPU implementation as described. Below: GPU with SAD on 2 views in comparison with a prototype CPU implementation with SAD on 2 views.

Method	plane dist. [mm]	# planes	Shader [ms]	CPU [ms]	total [ms]	Method	total [ms]	Speed-up
GPU	10	491	29.68	13.40	43.08	n.a.	n.a.	n.a.
GPU+SAD	10	491	3.43	1.69	5.12		554.0	108
	50	99	3.40	1.72	5.12	CPU	532.3	104
	100	50	3.40	1.80	5.20		537.8	103

Therefore, the background and mirrored parts of the model in the glass violate the rigid scene assumption, which is why in all input images and output depth maps the model foreground is segmented. Note that in case of real images, the camera poses are unknown. Hence, they were computed using refractive and perspective SfM respectively. Consequently, any comparison between perspective and refractive results combines errors introduced during SfM as well as errors introduced during dense depth estimation. However, in order to minimize erroneous influences from SfM, only the dense depth results from the first two images will be compared, where the resulting camera poses for refractive and perspective runs were almost identical. Figure 6 shows results for 2 different glass configurations, with very plausible looking dense depth maps for both, perspective and refractive camera models. However, the differences between perspective and refractive results are up to 33 mm measured only for pixels depicting the actual model, not the background. This is a significant difference for an imaging distance between 300 mm and 700 mm. In accordance to the results on synthetic

Fig. 6. Depth estimation results for Abu Simbel model. Top: results for sequence 1. Botton: results for sequence 2. From left to right: input image, resulting perspective depth map, resulting refractive depth map, negated difference between perspective and refractive depth maps with differences between 25 mm - 33 mm for the first sequence and differences on the model between 15 mm - 27 mm for the second sequence.

images, it can be observed that the difference between the perspective and refractive plane sweep increases with an increasing object-camera distance.

5 Conclusion and Future Work

We proposed a new method that allows to compute dense depth for underwater images using the plane sweep algorithm for the refractive camera model, thus allowing to create accurate and dense 3D models for underwater images. Experiments prove that it can estimate dense depth in presence of refraction accurately, being invariant to changes in underwater housing configurations. An equivalent implementation utilizing the perspective camera model suffers from a systematic model error that increases with increasing interface distance and tilt. The proposed method cannot only deal with refractive underwater camera models, but also compute dense depth for arbitrary camera models as long as a ray defined by starting point and direction can be specified for each pixel.

References

1. Agrawal, A., Ramalingam, S., Taguchi, Y., Chari, V.: A theory of multi-layer flat refractive geometry. In: CVPR (2012)
2. Chang, Y.J., Chen, T.: Multi-view 3d reconstruction for scenes under the refractive plane with known vertical direction. In: IEEE International Conference on Computer Vision (ICCV) (2011)
3. Chari, V., Sturm, P.: Multiple-view geometry of the refractive plane. In: Proceedings of the 20th British Machine Vision Conference, London, UK (September 2009)
4. Costa, C., Loy, A., Cataudella, S., Davis, D., Scardi, M.: Extracting fish size using dual underwater cameras. Aquacultural Engineering 35(3), 218–227 (2006)

5. Eustice, R., Singh, H., Howland, J.: Image registration underwater for fluid flow measurements and mosaicking. In: OCEANS 2000 MTS/IEEE Conference and Exhibition, vol. 3, pp. 1529–1534 (2000)
6. Fryer, J.G., Fraser, C.S.: On the calibration of underwater cameras. The Photogrammetric Record 12, 73–85 (1986)
7. Furukawa, Y., Ponce, J.: Accurate, dense, and robust multi-view stereopsis. IEEE Trans. on Pattern Analysis and Machine Intelligence 32(8), 1362–1376 (2010)
8. Gallup, D., Frahm, J.M., Mordohai, P., Yang, Q., Pollefeys, M.: Real-time plane-sweeping stereo with multiple sweeping directions. In: IEEE Conference on Computer Vision and Pattern Recognition, CVPR 2007, pp. 1–8 (2007)
9. Grossberg, M.D., Nayar, S.K.: The raxel imaging model and ray-based calibration. International Journal of Computer Vision 61(2), 119–137 (2005)
10. Hirschmueller, H.: Improvements in real-time correlation-based stereo vision. In: Proc. of IEEE Workshop on Stereo and Multi-Baseline Vision, Kauai, Hawaii (2001)
11. Johnson-Roberson, M., Pizarro, O., Williams, S., Mahon, I.: Generation and visualization of large-scale three-dimensional reconstructions from underwater robotic surveys. Journal of Field Robotics 27 (2010)
12. Jordt-Sedlazeck, A., Koch, R.: Refractive calibration of underwater cameras. In: Fitzgibbon, A., Lazebnik, S., Perona, P., Sato, Y., Schmid, C. (eds.) ECCV 2012, Part V. LNCS, vol. 7576, pp. 846–859. Springer, Heidelberg (2012)
13. Kang, L., Wu, L., Yang, Y.H.: Two-view underwater structure and motion for cameras under flat refractive interfaces. In: Fitzgibbon, A., Lazebnik, S., Perona, P., Sato, Y., Schmid, C. (eds.) ECCV 2012, Part IV. LNCS, vol. 7575, pp. 303–316. Springer, Heidelberg (2012)
14. Maas, H.G.: New developments in multimedia photogrammetry. In: Optical 3-D Measurement Techniques III. Wichmann Verlag, Karlsruhe (1995)
15. do Nascimento, E.R., Campos, M.F.M., de Barros, W.F.: Stereo based structure recovery of underwater scenes from automatically restored images. In: Proceedings SIBGRAPI 2009 (Brazilian Symposium on Computer Graphics and Image Processing), October 11-14 (2009)
16. Schechner, Y.Y., Karpel, N.: Clear underwater vision. In: Proc. IEEE Computer Society Conference on Computer Vision and Pattern Recognition, CVPR 2004, vol. 1, pp. I-536–I-543 (2004)
17. Sedlazeck, A., Koser, K., Koch, R.: 3d reconstruction based on underwater video from rov kiel 6000 considering underwater imaging conditions. In: Proc. OCEANS 2009, OCEANS 2009-EUROPE, pp. 1–10 (2009)
18. Sturm, P., Ramalingam, S., Lodha, S.: On calibration, structure from motion and multi-view geometry for generic camera models. In: Daniilidis, K., Klette, R. (eds.) Imaging Beyond the Pinhole Camera, Computational Imaging and Vision, vol. 33. Springer (2006)
19. Szeliski, R.: Computer Vision Algorithms and Applications. Springer (2011)
20. Treibitz, T., Schechner, Y., Singh, H.: Flat refractive geometry. In: Proc. IEEE Conference on Computer Vision and Pattern Recognition, CVPR 2008, pp. 1–8 (2008)

An Evaluation of Data Costs for Optical Flow

Christoph Vogel[1], Stefan Roth[2], and Konrad Schindler[1]

[1] Photogrammetry and Remote Sensing, ETH Zurich, Switzerland
[2] Department of Computer Science, TU Darmstadt, Germany

Abstract. Motion estimation in realistic outdoor settings is significantly challenged by cast shadows, reflections, glare, saturation, automatic gain control, *etc.* To allow robust optical flow estimation in these cases, it is important to choose appropriate data cost functions for matching. Recent years have seen a growing trend toward patch-based data costs, as they are already common in stereo. Systematic evaluations of different costs in the context of optical flow have been limited to certain cost types, and carried out on data without challenging appearance. In this paper, we contribute a systematic evaluation of various pixel- and patch-based data costs using a state-of-the-art algorithmic testbed and the realistic KITTI dataset as basis. Akin to previous findings in stereo, we find the Census transformation to be particularly suitable for challenging real-world scenes.

1 Introduction and Related Work

Optical flow estimation has come far since the pioneering works of Lucas/Kanade [16] and Horn/Schunck [14]. Modern optical flow algorithms are reaching a point where they become suitable for deployment in real-world vision systems, *e.g.* [17]. Still, most state-of-the-art methods continue to be variants of the continuous energy minimization framework of [14], *i.e.* they formulate an energy that aggregates data and smoothness costs over the image as a function of the flow field, and then seek to minimize it.

Aside from the enormous growth in compute power, various factors have driven the progress of optical flow methods: *(i)* Every optical flow approach needs to incorporate prior assumptions due to the ill-posedness of estimating 2D motion vectors from changes in image brightness (the so-called aperture problem). Robust [3,6] and non-local regularizers [24,27] have greatly improved the ability to estimate flow in areas where the observed image data is weak or ambiguous. *(ii)* Also the data costs (respectively likelihoods) have evolved to better deal with noise, lighting changes, *etc.* While optical flow methods were originally based on the brightness constancy assumption [14], and later robust versions of it [3], there has been a recent trend towards more expressive, usually patch-based cost functions [17,23], as is already common in stereo matching [13]. *(iii)* Sophisticated optimization schemes [7,8,29] have made flow estimation much more efficient. Moreover, other algorithmic advances, such as pre-filtering or outlier removal [26], have further increased the robustness of the estimate.

Designing robust optical flow approaches that work well in realistic settings, such as challenging outdoor scenes with cast shadows, reflections, glare, saturation, automatic gain control, *etc.*, requires carefully choosing all components of the approach. Not only for this reason, benchmarking has a long tradition in optical flow research [1,2]. Yet, the

J. Weickert, M. Hein, and B. Schiele (Eds.): GCPR 2013, LNCS 8142, pp. 343–353, 2013.
© Springer-Verlag Berlin Heidelberg 2013

focus of quantitative evaluations typically lies on showing the relative performance of entire methods, which differ from one another in terms of the regularizer, the mathematical and algorithmic framework, and sometimes also the data cost. Systematic studies of the benefit of the individual components are scarce, and have been largely limited to choices related to the prior and algorithmic aspects [24]. Systematic evaluations of data costs, especially patch-based ones, are rare and limited to a few metrics [23]. We address this by evaluating different cost functions for optical flow estimation in a consistent framework, in order to isolate the contribution of the data cost.

We focus on global optical flow methods and use standard total variation [29] and more powerful total generalized variation [5] regularizers as testbed, along with primal-dual optimization [8]. Our evaluation relies on two suitable benchmark datasets, the now classic *Middlebury* benchmark [1], and the more recent *KITTI* dataset [9]. Our testbed matches the performance of other implementations on Middlebury, thus suggesting that it is representative of the current state-of-the-art. We make the following contributions: *(i)* We conduct an evaluation and comparison of several data terms – brightness constancy with and without prefiltering [26], normalized cross correlation [27], mutual information [18], and the census transform [17] – in a consistent framework; *(ii)* we introduce a variant of the census transform that allows it to be embedded in gradient-based inference schemes; *(iii)* in the course of the evaluation, we achieve some of the most accurate results reported to date on the challenging *KITTI* dataset.

2   Optical Flow Testbed

Given two subsequent images from a video sequence $I_0, I_1 : \Omega \to \mathbb{R}^+$, defined over an image domain Ω, we aim to estimate the optical flow $\mathbf{v} : \Omega \to \mathbb{R}^2$ composed of a horizontal and vertical component, $\mathbf{v} = (u, v)$. More precisely, we aim to compute the 2D motion field, such that the image points $I_0(\mathbf{p})$ and $I_1(\mathbf{p}+\mathbf{v_p})$ are observations of the same physical scene point. To assess how well a given motion field explains the image data, a similarity measure $E_D(I_0, I_1, \mathbf{v})$ over matching pixels, termed "data cost", is defined. The simplest one is the pixelwise brightness constancy assumption (BCA).

Only demanding data fidelity leaves optical flow estimation ill-posed. This is resolved by imposing prior assumptions, such as the smoothness of the motion field, through a regularizer $E_S(\mathbf{v})$. Most modern optical flow algorithms minimize a global cost function consisting of a weighted combination of both energies:

$$\lambda E_D(I_0, I_1, \mathbf{v}) + E_S(\mathbf{v}) \quad \to \min_{\mathbf{v}} \tag{1}$$

Since the data cost is not convex due to the inherent ambiguity in matching, optimization typically proceeds in a coarse-to-fine manner to cope with large displacements [6].

A popular choice for $E_S(\mathbf{v})$ is the Total Variation [21,29] regularizer defined as $\mathrm{TV}(\mathbf{v}) = \mathrm{TV}(u) + \mathrm{TV}(v) = \int_\Omega |\nabla u| + |\nabla v| \, \mathrm{dp}$. Later, [5] generalized TV to Total Generalized Variation (TGV). While TV favors piecewise constant flow, TGV allows for solutions of a higher polynomial degree: a regularizer TGV_α^k of order k assigns zero energy to polynomials of order $k - 1$. In its primal form, TGV_α^2 can be written as

$$\mathrm{TGV}_\alpha^2(u) = \min_w \left(\alpha_1 \int_\Omega |\nabla u - w| \, \mathrm{d}\mathbf{p} + \alpha_0 \int_\Omega |\nabla w| \, \mathrm{d}\mathbf{p} \right). \tag{2}$$

As for TV, we define $\mathrm{TGV}_\alpha^2(\mathbf{v}) = \mathrm{TGV}_\alpha^2(u) + \mathrm{TGV}_\alpha^2(v)$. For Middlebury, which has largely fronto-parallel scenes, we found TV to work better, and consequently use it in our evaluation. On the contrary, the geometric layout of street scenes causes approximately piecewise linear flow fields when viewed by a forward-moving observer. For KITTI we thus use TGV_α^2, which we found to clearly outperform TV on that dataset.

Estimation Algorithm. To minimize TV and TGV we follow [8], which proposes an efficient primal-dual solver for problems of the type

$$\min_{\mathbf{v}} F(D\mathbf{v}) + G(\mathbf{v}). \tag{3}$$

Here, it is assumed that the optimization (*i.e.* the flow field $\mathbf{v}$) is discretized to a regular $M \times N$ pixel grid. To see how this applies to optical flow, we consider the case of TV, to simplify notation. The derivation for TGV is similar.

We define $D : V \rightarrow Y$ to be a linear operator that for a (vectorized) flow field $\mathbf{v} \in V = \mathbb{R}^{2NM}$ yields the horizontal and vertical flow derivatives, approximated by finite differences, and concatenated into a vector in $Y = \mathbb{R}^{4NM}$. We can now estimate optical flow according to Eq. (1) by setting $G = \lambda E_D$ and $F(D\mathbf{v}) = \sum_{\mathbf{p}} ||(D\mathbf{v})_{\mathbf{p}}|| = \sum_{\mathbf{p}} \sqrt{\nabla u_{\mathbf{p}}^t \nabla u_{\mathbf{p}} + \nabla v_{\mathbf{p}}^t \nabla v_{\mathbf{p}}}$. If both F and G are convex mappings, the primal formulation can be recast as a saddle point problem, via the Legendre-Fenchel transform:

$$\min_{\mathbf{v} \in V} \max_{\mathbf{y} \in Y} \langle D\mathbf{v}, \mathbf{y} \rangle - F^*(\mathbf{y}) + G(\mathbf{v}), \tag{4}$$

where $F^*(\mathbf{y}) = \sup_{\mathbf{z} \in Y} \langle \mathbf{z}, \mathbf{y} \rangle - F(\mathbf{z})$ is the conjugate function of F. Starting from $\mathbf{v}_0 \in V, \mathbf{y}_0 \in Y$, Eq. (4) can now be minimized efficiently [8] by iterating over k and updating $(\mathbf{v}_k, \mathbf{y}_k)$ according to

$$\mathbf{v}^{k+1} = (I + \tau \partial G)^{-1} (\mathbf{v}^k - \tau D^T \mathbf{y}^k) \tag{5a}$$

$$\mathbf{y}^{k+1} = (I + \sigma \partial F^*)^{-1} (\mathbf{y}^k + \sigma D(2\mathbf{v}^{k+1} - \mathbf{v}^k)), \tag{5b}$$

with $\sigma^{-1} \cdot \tau^{-1} \leq ||D||^2 = 8$ to ensure convergence (in practice normally $\sigma = \tau = 1/\sqrt{8}$). The proximal operator $(I + \tau \partial G)^{-1}(\hat{\mathbf{v}})$, needed to solve Eq. (5a), is then given as

$$(I + \tau \partial G)^{-1}(\hat{\mathbf{v}}) := \arg \min_{\mathbf{v}} \frac{1}{2\tau} ||\mathbf{v} - \hat{\mathbf{v}}||^2 + G(\mathbf{v}). \tag{6}$$

The proximal operator for F^* is defined similarly and given by a pixelwise projection

$$\left((I + \sigma \partial F^*)^{-1}(\mathbf{y})\right)_{\mathbf{p}} = \frac{\mathbf{y}_{\mathbf{p}}}{\max(1, ||\mathbf{y}_{\mathbf{p}}||)}, \tag{7}$$

onto the unit ball. The algorithm for TGV_α^2 proceeds in the same way, using a different linear operator, see *e.g.* [20]. Note that in this case the update step width can be set individually per pixel $(\tau_{\mathbf{p}}, \sigma_{\mathbf{p}})$, following [19].

Datasets. The *Middlebury* dataset [1] has been the standard optical flow benchmark for several years. It is widely used (90 entries as of July 2013) and has very precise, dense ground truth. Its main limitations are the somewhat artificial scenes, with strong contrasts, well-saturated colors, and little deviation from diffuse surface shading. Also, the scenes have a bias towards piecewise planarity and fronto-parallel depth layers.

The more recent *KITTI* dataset [9] is recorded outdoors from a moving vehicle. The images exhibit more realistic imaging conditions, with cast shadows, glare, specular reflections, changes in camera gain, *etc.*, complicating flow estimation. Weaknesses include the ground truth from a laser scanner, which is only available at a sparse set of points. These points are irregularly distributed with a noticeable "near-field bias": Surfaces closer to the camera have many more ground truth points (thus influence on the error); also the maximum depth in the field of view regularly exceeds the scanner's depth range, and the scenes are almost completely static except for the ego-motion.[1]

3   Evaluated Data Costs

We first introduce the different data terms independent of a particular optimization framework, and defer details on how to embed them in the specific algorithm used here (*i.e.* how to efficiently solve the corresponding proximal maps). Note that for all patch-based data terms we warp I_1 based on the current motion field, and evaluate the similarity w.r.t. the warped image. This is in contrast to approaches that assume fronto-parallel patch motion, *cf.* also [4]. Even though interesting, we do not consider explicit models of brightness changes, *e.g.* [11], in this necessarily limited study.

BCA. Probably the simplest and most common data cost embodies the brightness constancy assumption (BCA), *i.e.* penalizing grayvalue changes of a moving surface point:

$$\mathrm{BCA}(\mathbf{v}) = \int_\Omega |I_0(\mathbf{p}) - I_1(\mathbf{p} + \mathbf{v})| \, \mathrm{d}\mathbf{p}. \tag{8}$$

It is common to linearize the BCA (*cf.* Sec. 3.1) and employ a robust penalizer, *e.g.* L_1 (Eq. 8) or a differentiable approximation. In real scenes the BCA is often violated due to non-Lambertian reflectance, varying illumination, *etc.* To mitigate the impact of brightness changes, one can apply structure-texture (TV-L_2) decomposition (STT, [21]) as a preprocessing step, *cf.* [26]. The images are separated into a piecewise constant "structure" part and a high-frequency "texture" part, from which the flow is estimated.

NCC. Another popular data cost is the normalized cross correlation (NCC, [23,27]). For a single pixel location $\mathbf{p}$, the NCC is defined as the integral over a small neighborhood $\mathcal{N}(\mathbf{p})$, specified with a box filter B,

$$\mathrm{NCC}(\mathbf{p}, \mathbf{v}) = \int_\Omega \frac{\left(I_0(\mathbf{y}) - \mu_0(\mathbf{p})\right)\left(I_1(\mathbf{y} + \mathbf{v_y}) - \mu_1(\mathbf{p} + \mathbf{v_p})\right)}{\sigma_0(\mathbf{p})\sigma_1(\mathbf{p} + \mathbf{v_p})} B_\mathcal{N}(\mathbf{p} - \mathbf{y}) \, \mathrm{d}\mathbf{y}, \tag{9}$$

with the mean μ and variance σ calculated over the same neighborhood $\mathcal{N}(\mathbf{p})$. The NCC is by construction invariant to linear brightness changes (offset and contrast scaling). In practice, it can be computed efficiently after discretization to the pixel raster, with the help of discrete box filters and integral images. Moreover, truncating the NCC ignores negative correlations [27]: $\mathrm{TNCC}(\mathbf{p}, \mathbf{v}) := \min(1, 1 - \mathrm{NCC}(\mathbf{p}, \mathbf{v}))$. The full data cost is then simply the integral over the image domain: $\mathrm{TNCC}(\mathbf{v}) = \int_\Omega \mathrm{TNCC}(\mathbf{p}, \mathbf{v}) \, \mathrm{d}\mathbf{p}$.

---

[1] Some methods thus explicitly enforce the epipolar constraint ("motion stereo"). We refrain from this, as we consider it an instance of stereo matching rather than optical flow estimation.

Mutual Information. The mutual information (MI) is a data cost from the alignment literature [25], with even stronger invariance properties. It is popular in stereo matching [13] and has been integrated into optical flow [18]. MI expresses the statistical dependence between two random variables, here image intensities:

$$\mathrm{MI}(I_0, I_1(\mathbf{v})) = \mathrm{H}(I_1(\mathbf{v})) - \mathrm{H}(I_1(\mathbf{v})|I_0) = \mathrm{H}(I_0) + \mathrm{H}(I_1(\mathbf{v})) - \mathrm{H}(I_1(\mathbf{v}), I_0), \quad (10)$$

where $\mathrm{H}(I_1(\mathbf{v}), I_0)$ is the the joint entropy. Mutual information is high if the intensity I_1 can be predicted well from the corresponding I_0; accordingly the negative MI serves as data cost. In practice, intensity statistics are approximated with histograms over pixel values, usually smoothed with an isotropic Gaussian K_ω with kernel size ω.

Census Transform. The original Census transform [28] and its ternary variant [22] have recently found more widespread use, particularly addressing challenging outdoor lighting conditions [17]. This includes methods ranking high in the KITTI benchmark [12,20]. The (ternary) Census data term at location $\mathbf{p}$ is defined as

$$\mathrm{Cen}(\mathbf{p}, \mathbf{v}) = \int_\Omega \mathbb{1}_{c_\epsilon(I_0,\mathbf{p},\mathbf{y}) \neq c_\epsilon(I_1,\mathbf{p}+\mathbf{v},\mathbf{y}+\mathbf{v})} B_\mathcal{N}(\mathbf{p} - \mathbf{y}) \, \mathrm{d}\mathbf{y} \quad (11)$$

$$\text{with} \quad c_\epsilon(I, \mathbf{p}, \mathbf{q}) = \mathrm{sgn}(I(\mathbf{p}) - I(\mathbf{q})) \mathbb{1}_{|I(\mathbf{p}) - I(\mathbf{q})| > \epsilon}, \quad (12)$$

where $\mathbb{1}$ is the indicator function, B is again a box-filter, and $\mathcal{N}(\mathbf{p})$ denotes the corresponding neighborhood. The full Census data cost for a flow field $\mathbf{v}$ is again obtained by integrating over the image domain, $\mathrm{Cen}(\mathbf{v}) = \int_\Omega \mathrm{Cen}(\mathbf{p}, \mathbf{v}) \, \mathrm{d}\mathbf{p}$. Although Census has been incorporated in continuous optimization approaches to optical flow, we are not aware of any work that explains how this is done in detail. The Census cost is a piecewise constant function that is neither locally convex nor continuous. Its gradient is 0 or ∞ everywhere, thus there is no obvious linearization (Fig. 1).

To facilitate optimization, we here propose a convex approximation of Eq. (11):

$$\mathrm{CSAD}(\mathbf{p}, \mathbf{v}) = \int_\Omega |I_0(\mathbf{p}) - I_0(\mathbf{y}) - (I_1(\mathbf{p} + \mathbf{v}) - I_1(\mathbf{y} + \mathbf{v}))| B_\mathcal{N}(\mathbf{p} - \mathbf{y}) \, \mathrm{d}\mathbf{y}, \quad (13)$$

where the "soft" L_1-norm serves as a proxy for the hard thresholding step. We denote the new data term by CSAD, as it is formally a sum of centralized absolute differences. Note that by using absolute differences one foregoes some of the robustness of the ternary census, but gains tractability. As before the full data cost is given by integration over the image domain, *i.e.* $\mathrm{CSAD}(\mathbf{v}) = \int_\Omega \mathrm{CSAD}(\mathbf{p}, \mathbf{v}) \, \mathrm{d}\mathbf{p}$. Note also that CSAD bears connections to the widely used gradient constancy assumption (GCA, [6]). Very recently, [10] showed that a continous variant of Census is a generalization of GCA; the discretization bears some resemblance to Eq. 13 and aggregates derivatives of pixel differences.

3.1 Data Costs in the Primal-Dual Framework

Several modern optical flow estimation techniques [8,29], including the primal-dual scheme used here, decouple the optimization of prior and data term, hereby allowing to optimize the data cost independently per pixel. We now describe the update steps (*i.e.*, the proximal operator $(I + \tau \partial G)^{-1}$) for the different data terms, restricted to a single pixel for readability. We first recall the following soft thresholding scheme [15]:

Soft Thresholding. The solution $\bar{x}$ to the optimization problem:

$$\arg\min_{x\in\mathbb{R}} \sum_{i=1}^{n} w_i|x - b_i| + F(x) \tag{14}$$

with $b_i \leq b_{i+1}, \forall i$ and $W_i = -\sum_{j=1}^{i} w_j + \sum_{j=i+1}^{n} w_j, \forall i$, and F being strictly convex and differentiable with a bijective derivative F', can be computed via a median

$$\bar{x} = \text{median}(b_1, \ldots, b_n, a_0, \ldots a_n), \tag{15}$$

where $a_i = (F')^{-1}(W_i)$. If a data term G can be written as a component-wise weighted sum of L_1-norms as in Eq. (14), one can set $F(x) = x^2/(2\tau)$ and directly solve the proximal map pointwise, through Eq. (15).

BCA. In order to employ Eqs. (4,5), we require a convex data cost G. To that end, we rely on the usual first order Taylor expansion of the brightness of the warped image around an initial solution for the flow field, $\mathbf{v}_0$: $I_1(\mathbf{p}+\mathbf{v}) \approx I_1(\mathbf{p}+\mathbf{v}_0)+(\mathbf{v}-\mathbf{v}_0)^T\nabla I_1$. Our convexified data cost becomes $G_{\text{BCA}}(\mathbf{v}) = \lambda|I_1(\mathbf{p}+\mathbf{v}_0)+(\mathbf{v}-\mathbf{v}_0)^T\nabla I_1 - I_0(\mathbf{p})|$. With that we can write the proximal map for the BCA data cost at pixel $\mathbf{p}$ as

$$(I+\tau\partial G)^{-1}(\hat{\mathbf{v}}) = \arg\min_{\mathbf{v}} \frac{1}{2\tau}(\hat{\mathbf{v}}-\mathbf{v})^2+\lambda|I_1(\mathbf{p}+\mathbf{v}_0)+(\mathbf{v}-\mathbf{v}_0)^T\nabla I_1-I_0(\mathbf{p})|. \tag{16}$$

One important observation here is that due to the isotropy of the quadratic term in the proximal map, Eq. (16) can be reduced to a one dimensional problem. In particular, setting $\mathbf{v} = \hat{\mathbf{v}} + \delta\nabla I_1/|\nabla I_1| + \delta^+\nabla^+ I_1/|\nabla^+ I_1|$ the proximal map reduces to:

$$\arg\min_{\delta} \frac{1}{2\tau}\delta^2 + \lambda|\nabla I_1|\underbrace{\left|\frac{I_1(\mathbf{p} + \mathbf{v}_0) + (\hat{\mathbf{v}} - \mathbf{v}_0)^T\nabla I_1 - I_0(\mathbf{p})}{|\nabla I_1|} + \delta\right|}_{=:\hat{G}(\hat{\mathbf{v}})}, \tag{17}$$

hence $\delta^+ = 0$. Here ∇^+ is a vector orthogonal to the gradient. This can also be generalized to different data terms by using brightness linearization of the warped image. Applying Eq. (15) we can solve for the optimal δ and derive a soft-thresholding scheme: $(I + \tau\partial G)^{-1}(\hat{\mathbf{v}}) := \hat{\mathbf{v}} + \nabla I_1/|\nabla I_1| \cdot \text{median}\{-\hat{G}(\hat{\mathbf{v}}), \pm\lambda\tau|\nabla I_1|\}$.

NCC. The (T)NCC cost function is not convex, and a closed form solution for the proximal map does not exist. Following [27], a second order Taylor expansion can be used to build a convex approximation; off-diagonal entries of the Hessian are dropped to make it positive definite. At pixel $\mathbf{p}$ the convexified data term G_{TNCC} becomes

$$G_{\text{TNCC}}(\mathbf{v})=\lambda\big(\text{TNCC}(\mathbf{p}, \mathbf{v}_0)+(\mathbf{v}-\mathbf{v}_0)^T\nabla_{\text{TNCC}}+\frac{1}{2}(\mathbf{v}-\mathbf{v}_0)^T\nabla^2_{+,\text{TNCC}}(\mathbf{v}-\mathbf{v}_0)\big), \tag{18}$$

where the Taylor expansion was developed at $\mathbf{v}_0 = (u_0, v_0)$, and the modified Hessian is given by $\nabla^2_{+,\text{TNCC}} = \text{diag}(\max(0, \partial^2\text{TNCC}/\partial^2 u), \max(0, \partial^2\text{TNCC}/\partial^2 v))$.

Mutual Information. The local convexification of the MI data cost from [18] is similar to the second order approximation introduced in Eq. (18), but here applied to the MI data cost $G_{\text{MI}} = -\lambda\text{MI}$. We again modify the second order term to ensure positive definiteness, and reduce the problem to 1D (Eq. 17). For details please refer to [18].

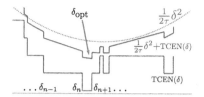

Fig. 1. Optimization of the ternary census data cost: The proximal map is the sum of the piecewise constant census score and a quadratic.

CSAD. Similar to the BCA, we linearize the intensity around the center pixel, which allows reducing the problem to 1D (Eq. 17). The proximal map at $\mathbf{p}$ again takes the form of Eq. (14), which can be solved using the soft-thresholding scheme. Due to the constant weights, the solution to the proximal map reduces to an efficient median search. In preliminary experiments we also considered the generalization of GCA described in [10], by introducing appropriate spatial weights. The weighting did not improve the results, thus we did not pursue it further. Moreover, we note that we find CSAD to work best with larger windows (see below), suggesting a benefit over GCA.

Census. Rather than use the CSAD approximation to the ternary census, we now show how to solve the proximal map directly for the census data cost. We start by linearizing the brightness in Eq. (11) (at the patch center). Following the same reasoning as for BCA (*cf.* Eq. 17), the optimal displacement must be in the direction of the image gradient. Hence, we again need to solve a one-dimensional optimization problem and use $I_1(\mathbf{p}+\mathbf{v}_0)+\delta\nabla I_1/|\nabla I_1|$ as replacement for the intensity at the center pixel in Eq. (11); the intensity is now a function of δ. By inspection of that function (Fig. 1), we can identify discontinuities, *i.e.* locations where one summand of the census cost changes (or can change). The trick is to precompute these at most $2|\mathcal{N}(\mathbf{p})|$ locations $\{\delta_n\}$, which we sort in increasing order. At each δ_n we determine whether the cost increases or decreases by 1, or stays constant. We can then determine the value of the census cost using a cumulative sum of the cost changes. This allows us to efficiently find the minimum of the proximal map by considering the identified candidate locations, and taking into account the quadratic penalty $\frac{1}{2\tau}\delta^2$. The data cost changes depend only on I_0 and can be computed once per pyramid level of the coarse-to-fine scheme; the respective $\{\delta_n\}$ need to be computed and sorted only once per warp.

4   Evaluation

We evaluate the different data costs on two datasets, the well established Middlebury data set [1], containing 8 test images with ground truth, and the more recent KITTI dataset [9] with 194 scenes. See Sec. 2 for a discussion. Parameters have been determined empirically, for best performance on the KITTI training set. In all experiments we apply coarse-to-fine estimation with a pyramid scale factor of 0.9, 40 warps and 5 inner iterations per pyramid level, and outlier removal through median filtering after each pyramid level [26]. Derivatives are computed with bicubic interpolation [24]. For our evaluation on KITTI we use TGV^2_α regularization with $\alpha_0 = 5, \alpha_1 = 1$. In case of Middlebury, we use TV instead. The weight for the data cost is set to: $\lambda = 8/9$ for TNCC, $\lambda = 80/|\mathcal{N}-1|$ for CSAD and Census, and to $\lambda = 25$ for BCA. The threshold for Census is set to $\epsilon = 0.005$. For MI we use a 15×15 Gaussian filter with $\omega = 3$.

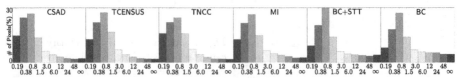

Fig. 2. Histograms of endpoint errors for different data costs, on complete KITTI training set. Methods are ordered w.r.t. the number of pixels with endpoint error < 1.5px. See text for details.

Table 1. Average endpoint error [px] on *Middlebury* training dataset

data cost	win.size	Dimetrodon	Grove2	Grove3	Hydrangea	Rubberwhale	Urban2	Urban3	Venus
BC	—	0.19	0.21	0.64	0.21	0.15	0.35	0.69	0.34
BC+STT	—	0.22	0.22	0.67	0.21	0.15	0.39	0.85	0.39
MI	—	**0.17**	0.21	0.65	0.20	**0.12**	0.35	0.73	0.33
	3 × 3	0.24	0.25	0.66	**0.18**	0.14	0.37	0.79	0.34
CSAD	5 × 5	0.19	0.23	0.64	**0.18**	**0.12**	0.36	0.68	0.33
	7 × 7	0.18	0.23	**0.61**	**0.18**	**0.12**	0.36	0.63	**0.32**
	3 × 3	0.21	0.22	0.74	**0.18**	**0.12**	0.36	0.63	0.34
NCC	5 × 5	0.18	**0.20**	0.70	0.19	0.13	**0.34**	0.61	0.34
	7 × 7	**0.17**	0.21	0.72	0.20	0.15	0.35	0.69	0.34
	3 × 3	0.31	0.24	0.72	0.22	0.17	0.45	0.74	0.40
Census	5 × 5	0.25	0.22	0.68	0.20	0.14	0.41	0.59	0.38
	7 × 7	0.24	0.21	0.66	0.19	0.14	0.39	**0.56**	0.36

Middlebury. Table 1 reports the average endpoint error (AEP) for the Middlebury *training* set. The accuracy difference of the pixel-based data terms appears to be rather small: MI is on par with simple BCA; preprocessing with STT does not appear to help at all, performing worse than BCA in every case. Among the patch-based data terms CSAD achieved the best results. Compared to Census, soft rather than hard thresholding of brightness differences allows for a more fine-grained localization, see Fig. 2. Median filtering visibly increases the smoothness of the Census flow vectors especially for the smallest patch size. In general, larger patch sizes appear to perform better than smaller ones. The most important finding for Middlebury is that pixel-based data costs perform as well as patch-based ones.[2] We attribute this to the controlled lighting conditions. Difficulties lie rather in the non-rigid motion patterns, occlusions, or repetitive texture. Illumination invariant patch-based data costs cannot improve the results under these conditions. Importantly, however, the results do not deteriorate either.

KITTI. On the full KITTI training set in contrast (Tab. 2, left), we observe a clear performance improvement of the patch-based data costs over the pixel-based ones. Among the pixel-based ones, MI clearly outperforms BCA (with and without STT preprocessing). For the patch-based data terms, every measure is best for at least two settings, thus showing no clear winner. However, Census at the largest patch size can be identified as the overall winner. Interestingly, the performance of NCC peaks at small window sizes, while for CSAD and Census a larger patch size works best. However, the performance gain w.r.t. patch size saturates at 7×7 for all patch-based costs.

Fig. 2 shows the endpoint error distribution for all data costs, ordered by decreasing number of inliers (< 1.5px). CSAD and NCC show a higher fraction of flow vectors with low EPE (< 0.38), *i.e.* they offer a higher localization accuracy than the other

---

[2] We note that patch-based data costs are challenged by rotational motion, however these are not very prominent here (nor in many other application scenarios).

Table 2. *KITTI* metric (percentage of flow vectors above 2/3/4/5 pixels of endpoint error) and average endpoint error [px], for the complete *KITTI* training set, as well as for the illumination images selected for the GCPR special session.

	occluded pix.	2px	3px	4px	5px	2px	3px	4px	5px	×	✓	#44	#11	#15	#74	Av.	#44	#11	#15	#74	Av.
		× (KITTI)				✓ (KITTI)				AEP		✓ KITTI metric					✓ AEP				
BC	—	20.7	17.2	15.0	13.4	28.9	25.1	22.6	20.7	3.9	7.7	45.6	35.6	67.1	90.6	59.7	11.2	9.7	21.0	45.7	21.9
BC+STT	—	14.3	11.5	10.0	8.8	23.0	19.8	17.9	16.3	2.8	6.7	28.7	29.0	40.7	64.2	40.7	9.3	9.0	8.4	23.2	12.5
MI	—	12.2	9.4	7.9	6.9	20.9	17.5	15.5	13.8	2.5	5.3	22.5	33.8	19.9	62.0	34.6	6.3	10.2	5.7	**20.1**	10.6
CSAD	3×3	9.9	7.5	6.3	5.3	17.2	13.9	12.1	10.7	1.8	4.3	24.0	24.4	15.6	57.6	30.3	11.8	7.4	5.0	22.8	11.8
CSAD	5×5	**9.6**	7.2	6.0	5.1	17.0	13.8	11.9	10.6	1.7	4.2	22.1	**23.3**	16.4	59.8	30.4	10.2	6.6	**3.7**	23.3	10.9
CSAD	7×7	9.7	7.3	6.0	5.1	17.1	13.9	12.1	10.7	1.7	4.3	19.7	24.2	17.7	**58.6**	30.1	7.4	7.2	3.9	23.0	**10.4**
NCC	3×3	10.3	7.3	5.9	5.0	17.2	13.5	**11.4**	**10.0**	1.8	3.8	18.1	33.6	**14.2**	60.5	31.6	**6.1**	13.6	4.9	23.4	12.0
NCC	5×5	10.1	7.3	6.0	5.1	17.2	13.6	11.6	10.2	1.8	**3.7**	21.3	32.9	15.5	59.3	32.3	9.3	13.6	4.4	23.3	12.7
NCC	7×7	10.7	7.9	6.5	5.5	17.8	14.3	12.2	10.8	1.9	4.1	**17.9**	32.9	16.9	58.7	31.6	6.2	13.2	4.2	23.4	11.8
Census	3×3	10.4	7.7	6.4	5.5	17.7	14.2	12.3	10.9	2.0	4.5	19.2	27.8	18.6	59.9	31.4	6.4	9.0	6.6	23.9	11.5
Census	5×5	9.7	7.0	5.7	4.8	17.0	13.5	11.6	10.2	**1.7**	4.0	19.0	25.3	17.1	59.0	30.1	6.6	7.3	6.0	23.6	10.9
Census	7×7	**9.6**	**6.9**	**5.6**	**4.7**	**16.9**	**13.3**	**11.4**	**10.0**	1.7	**3.7**	18.7	24.4	15.9	59.5	**29.6**	6.3	**6.3**	5.0	23.7	**10.4**

data costs. We also evaluated one data cost (CSAD, 5×5) on the official test portion of the KITTI benchmark, where our method ("Data-Flow") is ranked 6th at the time of publication, which shows that our testbed is state-of-the-art. We observe 8.2% outliers excluding and 15.8% outliers including occluded regions.

Illumination Changes. We also report results for particularly challenging test images as part of the *Robust Optical Flow Challenge* (Tab. 2, right). We did not adapt the parameters in any way. While the outlier percentages are generally high, owing to the difficulty of the challenge, the patch-based data costs allow the approach to significantly outperform the official baseline techniques. On average 7×7 Census and 7×7 CSAD perform slightly better than the remaining patch-based data costs. The gap to the pixel-based error metrics is again large, with the exception of MI, which produces only 5% more outliers than the best patch-based measure. On the selected subset our TNCC implementation has about 20% fewer outliers than [27], which uses the same data term, but TV regularization. This might be an indication that the data term alone cannot compensate for using a prior that is not suitable for the scenario.

5 Conclusion

Based on a state-of-the-art testbed and challenging image data, we provided an evaluation of several pixel-based and patch-based data costs. While on the standard Middlebury dataset, patch-based measures cannot provide a clear benefit, they show significant gains on the more challenging KITTI dataset. Overall, the Census transform and the proposed CSAD variant, which is well-suited for standard continuous optimization, show a slight overall performance lead. By avoiding thresholding, CSAD showed to be particularly well suited for accurate flow localization.

References

1. Baker, S., Scharstein, D., Lewis, J.P., Roth, S., Black, M.J., Szeliski, R.: A database and evaluation methodology for optical flow. In: ICCV (2007)
2. Barron, J., Fleet, D., Beauchemin, S.: Performance of optical flow techniques. IJCV (1994)
3. Black, M.J., Anandan, P.: A framework for the robust estimation of optical flow. In: ICCV (1993)
4. Bleyer, M., Rhemann, C., Rother, C.: PatchMatch Stereo – Stereo matching with slanted support windows. In: BMVC (2011)
5. Bredies, K., Kunisch, K., Pock, T.: Total generalized variation. SIAM J. Imaging Sciences 3(3), 492–526 (2010)
6. Brox, T., Bruhn, A., Papenberg, N., Weickert, J.: High accuracy optical flow estimation based on a theory for warping. In: Pajdla, T., Matas, J(G.) (eds.) ECCV 2004. LNCS, vol. 3024, pp. 25–36. Springer, Heidelberg (2004)
7. Bruhn, A., Weickert, J., Kohlberger, T., Schnörr, C.: A multigrid platform for real-time motion computation with discontinuity-preserving variational methods. IJCV 70(3) (2006)
8. Chambolle, A., Pock, T.: A first-order primal-dual algorithm for convex problems with applications to imaging. JMIV 40(1), 120–145 (2011)
9. Geiger, A., Lenz, P., Urtasun, R.: Are we ready for autonomous driving? The KITTI vision benchmark suite. In: CVPR (2012)
10. Hafner, D., Demetz, O., Weickert, J.: Why is the census transform good for robust optic flow computation? In: Kuijper, A., Bredies, K., Pock, T., Bischof, H. (eds.) SSVM 2013. LNCS, vol. 7893, pp. 210–221. Springer, Heidelberg (2013)
11. Haussecker, H.W., Fleet, D.J.: Computing optical flow with physical models of brightness variation. In: CVPR, vol. 2 (2000)
12. Hermann, S., Klette, R.: Hierarchical scan-line dynamic programming for optical flow using semi-global matching. In: Park, J.-I., Kim, J. (eds.) ACCV Workshops 2012, Part II. LNCS, vol. 7729, pp. 556–567. Springer, Heidelberg (2013)
13. Hirschmüller, H., Scharstein, D.: Evaluation of cost functions for stereo matching. In: CVPR (2007)
14. Horn, B.K.P., Schunck, B.G.: Determining optical flow. Artif. Intell. 17(1-3) (1981)
15. Li, Y., Osher, S.: A new median formula with applications to PDE based denoising. Commun. Math. Sci. 7(3), 741–753 (2009)
16. Lucas, B.D., Kanade, T.: An iterative image registration technique with an application to stereo vision. In: IJCAI (1981)
17. Müller, T., Rabe, C., Rannacher, J., Franke, U., Mester, R.: Illumination-robust dense optical flow using census signatures. In: Mester, R., Felsberg, M. (eds.) DAGM 2011. LNCS, vol. 6835, pp. 236–245. Springer, Heidelberg (2011)
18. Panin, G.: Mutual information for multi-modal, discontinuity-preserving image registration. In: Bebis, G., Boyle, R., Parvin, B., Koracin, D., Fowlkes, C., Wang, S., Choi, M.-H., Mantler, S., Schulze, J., Acevedo, D., Mueller, K., Papka, M. (eds.) ISVC 2012, Part II. LNCS, vol. 7432, pp. 70–81. Springer, Heidelberg (2012)
19. Pock, T., Chambolle, A.: Diagonal preconditioning for first order primal-dual algorithms in convex optimization. In: ICCV (2011)
20. Ranftl, R., Gehrig, S., Pock, T., Bischof, H.: Pushing the limits of stereo using variational stereo estimation. In: Intelligent Vehicle Symposium (2012)
21. Rudin, L.I., Osher, S., Fatemi, E.: Nonlinear total variation based noise removal algorithms. Physica D: Nonlinear Phenomena 60(1-4), 259–268 (1992)
22. Stein, F.: Efficient computation of optical flow using the census transform. In: Rasmussen, C.E., Bülthoff, H.H., Schölkopf, B., Giese, M.A. (eds.) DAGM 2004. LNCS, vol. 3175, pp. 79–86. Springer, Heidelberg (2004)

23. Steinbrücker, F., Pock, T., Cremers, D.: Advanced data terms for variational optic flow estimation. In: VMV (2009)
24. Sun, D., Roth, S., Black, M.J.: Secrets of optical flow estimation and their principles. In: CVPR (2010)
25. Viola, P., Wells III, W.: Alignment by maximization of mutual information. In: ICCV (1995)
26. Wedel, A., Pock, T., Zach, C., Bischof, H., Cremers, D.: An improved algorithm for TV-L1 optical flow. In: Cremers, D., Rosenhahn, B., Yuille, A.L., Schmidt, F.R. (eds.) Statistical and Geometrical Approaches to Visual Motion Analysis. LNCS, vol. 5604, pp. 23–45. Springer, Heidelberg (2009)
27. Werlberger, M., Pock, T., Bischof, H.: Motion estimation with non-local total variation regularization. In: CVPR (2010)
28. Zabih, R., Woodfill, J.: Non-parametric local transforms for computing visual correspondence. In: Eklundh, J.-O. (ed.) ECCV 1994. LNCS, vol. 801, pp. 151–158. Springer, Heidelberg (1994)
29. Zach, C., Pock, T., Bischof, H.: A duality based approach for realtime TV-L1 optical flow. In: Hamprecht, F.A., Schnörr, C., Jähne, B. (eds.) DAGM 2007. LNCS, vol. 4713, pp. 214–223. Springer, Heidelberg (2007)

Illumination Robust Optical Flow Model Based on Histogram of Oriented Gradients

Hatem A. Rashwan[1], Mahmoud A. Mohamed[2], Miguel Angel García[3],
Bärbel Mertsching[2], and Domenec Puig[1]

[1] Rovira i Virgili University
{hatem.abdellatif,domenec.puig}@urv.cat
[2] Get Lab. Paderborn University
{mahmoud,mertsching}@get.upb.de
[3] Autonomous University of Madrid
miguelangel.garcia@uam.es

Abstract. The brightness constancy assumption has widely been used in variational optical flow approaches as their basic foundation. Unfortunately, this assumption does not hold when illumination changes or for objects that move into a part of the scene with different brightness conditions. This paper proposes a variation of the L1-norm dual total variational (TV-L1) optical flow model with a new illumination-robust data term defined from the histogram of oriented gradients computed from two consecutive frames. In addition, a weighted non-local term is utilized for denoising the resulting flow field. Experiments with complex textured images belonging to different scenarios show results comparable to state-of-the-art optical flow models, although being significantly more robust to illumination changes.

1 Introduction

Optical flow estimation is already a mature field. A wide variety of approaches have been proposed during the last years achieving outstanding levels of accuracy[1]. Among them, variational approaches are considered to provide the best results due to their ability to fill gaps where motion information is not available. However, most of these techniques are based on two main assumptions: brightness and gradient constancy. Both constancy assumptions respectively depend on the brightness and the derivative of the brightness of the pixels contained in a given pair of images. However, the brightness of a point on an object can dramatically change if the object moves to another part of the scene with different illumination or after global or local illumination changes [6].

In order to reduce this dependency on brightness, classical approaches apply a structure-texture decompensation of the input images, such as ROF[12], as a preprocessing stage to reduce the effect of illumination changes. In addition, [8] has suggested a more realistic model by assuming that the brightness at

---

[1] Middlebury datasets, http://vision.middlebury.edu/flow/data/

J. Weickert, M. Hein, and B. Schiele (Eds.): GCPR 2013, LNCS 8142, pp. 354–363, 2013.
© Springer-Verlag Berlin Heidelberg 2013

time $t + dt$ is related to the brightness at time t through a set of parameters that can be estimated from the image sequence. However, [8] fails at motion discontinuities. In turn, [6] has solved this problem through an approach that simultaneously deals with motion discontinuities and large illumination variations in an integrated framework by taking into account multiplicative and additive illumination factors. Notwithstanding, the accuracy of the estimated optical flow field can be affected by the coupling between the two factors and the corresponding components of the flow field, in addition, the optimization problem becomes much more complex.

Furthermore, [9] has proposed both a non-linear scheme and a linearized scheme for a variational optical flow model based on the normalized cross-correlation. In addition, [15] has incorporated a low-level image segmentation process by considering an illumination-robust data term based on the normalized cross correlation, as well as a non-local term in order to tackle the problems of poorly textured regions, occlusions and small scale image structure. In turn, [17] has presented an advanced data term that is robust to outliers and varying illumination conditions by using constraint normalization, as well as an HSV color representation with high-order constancy (gradient constancy) assumptions to cope with illumination changes. However, the gradient constancy is affected by large illumination changes and it is very sensitive to noise.

Moreover, [10] has proposed the census transform descriptor in order to implement a texture constancy assumption by replacing the classical data term by the Hamming distance between two census transform signatures. Unfortunately, the census transform is not accurate enough and has various shortcomings, such as the inability to discriminate between dark and bright regions in a neighborhood, as well as being very sensitive to noise.

In addition, [7] has proposed a method based on the SIFT descriptor to compute a dense correspondence field between two images through a discrete optimization based on a belief propagation approach. While, the SIFT flow algorithm proposed in [7] is based on matching or visual features and yields pixel accuracy, the optical flow model proposed in the present work is based on the classical motion estimation and yields sub-pixel accuracy. In turn, [2] integrates a discrete pixel matching term based on a HOG/SIFT-like descriptor into the continuous variational energy function in order to cope with large displacements while preserving the classical data term based on the brightness and high-order constancy assumptions.

This work proposes the replacement of the classical brightness constancy assumption of the TV-L1 optical flow model [11] by a local texture descriptor that is highly invariant to illumination changes. In particular, the Histogram of Oriented Gradients (HOG) is proposed as a texture descriptor in order to extract texture features from two consecutive images [4]. These features are then utilized in order to implement a texture constancy assumption for the data term of the TV-L1 model. In addition, the loss of accuracy of the estimated flow field due to the use of an isotropic regularization term is compensated for with an additional weighted non-local term similar to the one proposed in [14].

The rest of this paper is organized as follows. Section 2 summarizes the proposed variational optical flow model, which consists of a data term, a regularization term and a weighted non-local term. The HOG descriptor and its benefits are discussed in section 3. Experimental results are shown and discussed in section 4, including a comparison with state-of-the-art optical flow methods. Finally, conclusions and future work are given in section 5.

2 Optical Flow Model

Optical flow is defined as the apparent motion of pixels between a frame $I_1(x, y)$ at time t and a frame $I_2(x + u, y + v)$ at time $t + 1$. The duality of the TV-L1 optical flow model [11] is used to compute the vector flow field $w = (u, v)$ associated with every pixel $p = (x, y)$ belonging to the image domain Ω:

$$E(x, y, w) = \int_\Omega (\lambda E_D(w) + E_s(w)) \ d\Omega, \tag{1}$$

where E_D is a data term, E_s a regularization term (a total variational term [11]) and λ is the weight of the data term. The energy functional is divided into two parts that are solved iteratively:

$$E_{data}(x, y, w) = \int_\Omega (\lambda E_D(w) + E_c(w, \hat{w})) \ d\Omega, \tag{2}$$

$$E_{smooth}(x, y, \hat{w}) = \int_\Omega (E_c(w, \hat{w}) + E_s(\hat{w})) \ d\Omega, \tag{3}$$

where E_c is a coupling term and $\hat{w}$ an auxiliary vector flow field.

2.1 Data and Regularization Terms

In the proposed technique, the data term includes the residual of two texture features extracted from the input images in order to ensure texture constancy:

$$E_{data}(x, y, w) = \int_\Omega \left(\lambda \psi(S(x, y, w)) + \frac{1}{2\theta}(w - \hat{w})^2 \right) \ d\Omega, \tag{4}$$

where $\frac{1}{2\theta}$ is the weight of the coupling term. $S(x, y, w)$ can be formulated as:

$$S(x, y, w) = S_2(x + u, y + v) - S_1(x, y) = 0, \tag{5}$$

such that $S_1(x, y)$ and $S_2(x + u, y + v)$ are the texture features extracted from two consecutive images $I_1(x, y)$ and $I_2(x + u, y + v)$, respectively. In turn, $\psi(x)$ is a convex penalization function. Thus, (5) implements a texture constancy assumption that assumes that texture features do not change when objects move.

The residual S can be linearized around the starting value w as:

$$S(x, y, w) \approx \tilde{S}(x, y, w) = (S_2(x, y) - S_1(x, y)) + \nabla^T S(x, y, \hat{w})(w - \hat{w}),$$

$$= S_t + \nabla^T S(x, y, \hat{w})(w - \hat{w}), \tag{6}$$

where $\nabla^T S(x, y, \hat{w}) = [\frac{\partial S}{\partial x} = S_x, \frac{\partial S}{\partial y} = S_y]$. Now, (4) can be solved for $w = (u, v)$ by doing:

$$\frac{\partial}{\partial u}(\lambda \psi(\tilde{S}(x, y, w))) + \frac{1}{2\theta}(u - \hat{u})^2) = 0,$$

$$\frac{\partial}{\partial v}(\lambda \psi(\tilde{S}(x, y, w))) + \frac{1}{2\theta}(v - \hat{v})^2) = 0. \tag{7}$$

Both equations with a quadratic penalization can be expressed in vector form as:

$$2\lambda \tilde{S}(x, y, w)\nabla S(x, y, \hat{w}) + \frac{1}{\theta}(w - \hat{w}) = 0. \tag{8}$$

Since (8) is linear in (u, v), it can be solved as a linear system, $Aw = b$. In addition, the final data term can be extended in order to be applicable to a multi-channel descriptor:

$$\arg min_{(w)} \int_\Omega \left(\lambda \sum_{i=1}^n (\tilde{S}_i(x, y, w))^2 + \frac{1}{2\theta}(w - \hat{w})^2 \right) d\Omega, \tag{9}$$

where n is the number of channels of the texture descriptor used in the data term. Hence, A and b can be written as:

$$A = \begin{pmatrix} \frac{1}{\theta} + 2\lambda \sum_{i=1}^n S_{i_x}^2 & 2\lambda \sum_{i=1}^n S_{i_x} S_{i_y} \\ 2\lambda \sum_{i=1}^n S_{i_x} S_{i_y} & \frac{1}{\theta} + 2\lambda \sum_{i=1}^n S_{i_y}^2 \end{pmatrix}, \tag{10}$$

and:

$$b = \frac{1}{\theta}\begin{pmatrix} \hat{u} \\ \hat{v} \end{pmatrix} - 2\lambda \begin{pmatrix} \sum_{i=1}^n S_{i_x} \\ \sum_{i=1}^n S_{i_y} \end{pmatrix} \left(\sum_{i=1}^n S_{i_t} - \left(\sum_{i=1}^n S_{i_x}\hat{u} + \sum_{i=1}^n S_{i_y}\hat{v} \right) \right). \tag{11}$$

Similarly, the smoothness term represents the isotropic total variation [11]. As a result, (3) can be decomposed into two equations: E_u and E_v. The fixed-point iterative scheme has been used to solve E_u and E_v, as illustrated in [11].

Furthermore, a multi-scale, coarse-to-fine scheme is used for solving the energy functional (1) in order to allow for both small and large displacements and to improve the accuracy of the estimated flow fields. In each pyramid level, the scaled images are warped representations of the input images based on the flow estimated at every preceding scale [1].

2.2   Anisotropic Filtering Based on a Weighted Non-local Term

The smoothing term utilized in the energy functional (1) described above is isotropic and propagates the flow field in all directions. Thus, flow vectors near motion discontinuities are usually inaccurate due to occlusions and over-smoothing. In order to tackle this problem, the resulting flow fields at every pyramid level require a stage that preserves edge and object boundaries and details. Therefore, the estimated flow fields are improved by detecting motion boundaries through the Sobel operator, and then by dilating the detected regions through a 5×5 mask in order to obtain flow boundary regions. For each pixel $p = (x, y)$ in these regions, a robust weighted median filter proposed in [14] is applied:

$$E_{wnl} = \sum_{\Omega} \sum_{(\acute{x},\acute{y}) \in N_{x,y}} \varpi_{p,\acute{p}}(|\hat{u}_{x,y} - \hat{u}_{\acute{x},\acute{y}}| + |\hat{v}_{x,y} - \hat{v}_{\acute{x},\acute{y}}|), \qquad (12)$$

where $(\acute{x}, \acute{y})$ is the spatial position of every pixel $\acute{p}$ belonging to a neighborhood of p in a possibly large region $N_{x,y}$, and $\varpi_{p,\acute{p}}$ is a weighting function that takes into account the occlusion state of pixels as proposed in [13], as well as the intensity difference and the spatial distance. Thus, the weighting function $\varpi_{p,\acute{p}}$ is formulated as:

$$\varpi_{p,\acute{p}} \propto exp\left(-\frac{(p - \acute{p})^2}{2\sigma_s^2} - \frac{(I(p) - I(\acute{p}))^2}{2\sigma_r^2}\right)\frac{O(\acute{p})}{O(p)}, \qquad (13)$$

where $I(p)$ and $I(\acute{p})$ are the intensity values of pixels p and $\acute{p}$, respectively, and σ_s and σ_r are standard deviations experimentally set to 7.0 and 0.1, respectively. In addition, $O(p)$ is the occlusion state of pixels.

3 Histogram of Oriented Gradients

Histograms of oriented gradients [4] are a robust visual descriptor that allows the discrimination of the objects present in a scene, since the local appearance and shape of objects can be characterized to a large extent by the local distribution of intensity gradients, which, in addition, is largely invariant to shadows and illumination changes.

The HOG descriptor proposed in [4] is based on dominant edge orientations. The gradient operator has been applied by computing local image gradients, d_x and d_y, within a local window (3×3 or 5×5) using a centered derivative mask. The magnitudes and orientations of the resulting derivatives for every window are computed. In addition, the orientations are divided into n localized bins. In practice, the angles between 0 and 2π are divided into a number of bins (experimentally set to 8 in this work). The value of each bin is obtained by summing the magnitudes of the gradients whose orientations are mapped to that bin. The obtained histogram is normalized using $L2 - norm$, $L1 - norm$ or $L2 - sqrt$ [4].

The pair of images $I_1(x, y)$ and $I_2(x+u, y+v)$ used to estimate the optical flow field yield multi-channel images $S_1(x, y)$ and $S_2(x+u, y+v)$, respectively. $S_1(x, y)$ consists of n channels, such that each channel contains the values corresponding to an orientation bin of the resulting normalized histogram for every pixel.

In order to illustrate the advantages of the HOG descriptor with respect to the census transform, Figure 1 shows the features extracted with the census transform, as well as the HOG signatures for two windows that contain both a bright and a dark region. In particular, Figure 1 shows the gray values within a 3×3 window with a central pixel equal to 110, for the first and the second window. The census transform has been computed for the two windows yielding the 8-bit string 11111111, since all neighbors are larger than the value of the central pixel. On the other hand, the features with the HOG descriptor have been computed after calculating the 8 bin histogram of the resulting orientations of the input windows. For simplicity, a centered mask has been used for computing the gradients and each bin has been obtained by counting the number of orientations associated with that bin. The HOG descriptors obtained for the input windows are 01131111 and 03210210, respectively. Clearly, the census transform produces the same code for different textures and is not able to cope with image blocks with a saturated center pixel, whereas HOG can detect changes in the intensity regions by yielding a different descriptor.

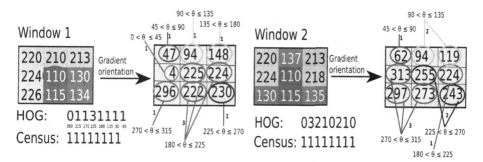

Fig. 1. Comparison of a 3×3 HOG descriptor and a 3×3 census descriptor

4   Experiments

The variational optical flow model described in section 2 has been tested with different features descriptors by using sequence GROVE2 from the Middlebury datasets with ground-truth by changing the illumination of the second frame as:

$$I_o = uint8 \left(255 \left(\frac{mI_i}{255} \right)^{\gamma} \right), \tag{14}$$

where I_i and I_o are the input and output frames, respectively, $m > 0$ is a multiplicative factor, and $\gamma > 0$ is the gamma correction. The experiments are conducted in Matlab and the function $uint8$ is used for quantizing the values to 8-bit unsigned integer format. Figure 2 shows a qualitative comparison of the average end-point error (AEE) and the average angular error (AAE) between the flow fields obtained with HOG, the census transform, both determined in a 3×3 neighborhood, as well as the gradient constancy. The effects of different values of m and γ have individually been assessed by varying γ while keeping $m = 1$, and by changing m with $\gamma = 1$.

As shown in Figure 2, the gradient constancy is robust against small changes of both γ and m. In turn, HOG shows a higher robustness against both small and large changes of γ and m. In addition, the census transform yields adequate values for both AEE and AAE.

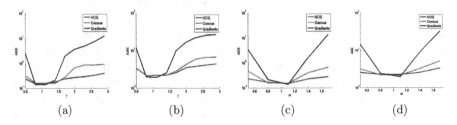

(a)   (b)   (c)   (d)

Fig. 2. AEE and AAE for HOG, census transform and gradient constancy. (a-b) change of γ and, (c-d) change of m.

At the time of submission (April 2013), the results of the proposed model with HOG (TVL1-HOG) have been evaluated with the KITTI Vision Benchmark, which contains 195 testing image sequences with ground truths, and it has been ranked in the seven position against current state-of-the-art optical flow algorithms [2]. The KITTI benchmark considers the bad flow vectors at all pixels that are above a spatial distance of 3 pixels from the ground truth. (TVL1-HOG) has average of 8.31% bad pixels, in turn the baseline methods [16] and [14] have 30.75% and 24.64%, respectively.

Furthermore, the proposed variational optical flow method based on the HOG descriptor is evaluated with eight real image sequences that include illumination changes and large displacements, as well as low-textured areas, reflections and specularities. Table 1 shows the AEE and bad pixels corresponding to four sequences with illumination changes and large displacements calculated for the methods proposed in [17], [14], [3], [5], and [15], in addition to the proposed method based on HOG, the census transform and the gradient constancy.

In another experiment, the estimated flow fields with HOG (3×3 and 5×5) have visually been compared with the proposed optical flow method by using the data term based on the brightness constancy assumption, as well as the one based on the census transform. Figure 3 shows the estimated flow field for sequence 15, which includes illumination changes, as well as the error images and the error histograms. In addition, Figure 4 shows the same information for sequence 181, which includes large displacements[3].

Among the evaluated approaches, the optical flow model based on HOG yields the most accurate flow fields with respect to the state-of-the-art methods for real images of KITTI datasets that include both illumination changes and large displacements.

---

[2] http://www.cvlibs.net/datasets/kitti
[3] More details and results with high resolutions images can be found at: http://getwww.upb.de/research/staff_research/optical_flow/TVL1_HOG/index_html

Table 1. Percentage of bad pixels and AEE for the state-of-the-art methods and the proposed method with four sequences of KITTI datasets: sequences 15 and 74, which include illumination changes, and sequences 144 and 181, which include large displacements.

Method	Seq 15	Seq 74	Seq 144	Seq 181
HOG(3 × 3)	**22.30% (6.48)**	53.79% (20.03)	36.64% (14.40)	55.58% (42.97)
HOG(5 × 5)	24.90% (7.64)	**52.74% (19.79)**	**31.64 % (12.86)**	**44.89 % (33.72)**
Census(3 × 3)	33.74% (9.11)	57.43%(20.53)	48.97% (16.83)	73.63% (58.58)
Census(5 × 5)	29.04% (8.70)	57.57% (20.80)	47.68% (16.75)	73.85% (58.59)
Gradients	26.41% (8.47)	59.20% (23.07)	44.51%(18.67)	67.63%(58.40)
OFH 2011 [17]	32.20% (9.06)	62.90% (24.00)	42.04% (15.01)	63.86% (50.52)
SRB 2010 [14]	32.85% (9.72)	62.94% (24.27)	50.67% (19.03)	67.11% (47.70)
SRBF 2010[14]	35.13% (12.17)	64.89% (24.64)	50.66% (19.34)	68.41% (48.81)
BW 2005 [3]	47.70% (12.40)	71.44% (25.15)	46.98% (16.85)	69.04% (45.27)
HS 1981 [5]	58.08% (12.89)	82.14% (28.75)	51.89% (14.81)	74.11% (49.28)
WPB 2010 [15]	67.28% (28.36)	88.67% (30.68)	52.25% (17.94)	76.00% (50.18)

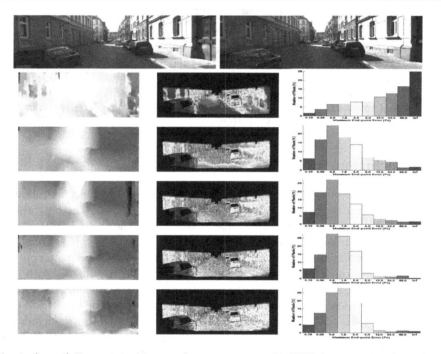

Fig. 3. (row 1) Two original images for sequence 15 of KITTI datasets. Resulting flow field, error image and error histogram for the proposed optical flow model with: (row 2) brightness constancy, (row 3) 3 × 3 census transform, (row 4) 5 × 5 census transform, (row 5) 3 × 3 HOG, and (row 6) 5 × 5 HOG.

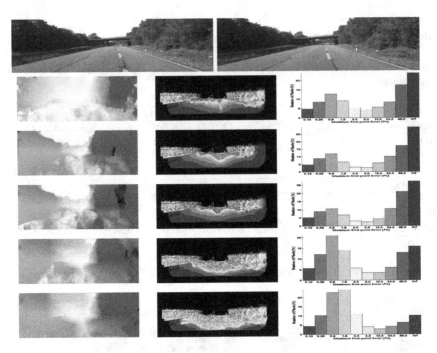

Fig. 4. Row 1: Two original images for sequence 181 of KITTI datasets. Resulting flow field, error image and error histogram for the proposed optical flow model with: (row 2) brightness constancy, (row 3) 3×3 census transform, (row 4) 5×5 census transform, (row 5) 3×3 HOG, and (row 6) 5×5 HOG.

5   Conclusion

This paper presents an approach which is very robust concerning illumination changes based on the histogram of oriented gradients (HOG). The optical flow model estimates dense flow fields using a duality of the TV-L1 optical flow model with a non-local term. The HOG descriptor, which is robust to illumination changes, has been used in order to define an alterative data term. The proposed approach yields the most accurate flow fields for real images with both illumination changes and large displacements. On-going work aims at merging different feature descriptors into the same data term to have the benefits of each descriptor in order to develop a variational optical flow model invariant not only to illumination, but also to other environmental factors such as noise. In turn, future work aims at applying the proposed optical flow model to mobile robotics and real surveillance systems for tracking and gait recognition applications.

References

1. Brox, T., Bruhn, A., Papenberg, N., Weickert, J.: High accuracy optical flow estimation based on a theory for warping. In: Pajdla, T., Matas, J. (eds.) ECCV 2004. LNCS, vol. 3024, pp. 25–36. Springer, Heidelberg (2004)

2. Brox, T., Malik, J.: Large displacement optical flow: Descriptor matching in variational motion estimation. IEEE Transactions on Pattern Analysis and Machine Intelligence 33(3), 500–513 (2011)
3. Bruhn, A., Weickert, J.: Towards ultimate motion estimation: Combining highest accuracy with real-time performance. In: ICCV, pp. 749–755. IEEE Computer Society (2005)
4. Dalal, N., Triggs, B.: Histograms of oriented gradients for human detection. In: CVPR (1), pp. 886–893. IEEE Computer Society (2005)
5. Horn, B.K.P., Schunck, B.G.: Determining optical flow. Artifical Intelligence 17(1-3), 185–203 (1981)
6. Kim, Y.H., Martínez, A.M., Kak, A.C.: Robust motion estimation under varying illumination. Image Vision Comput. 23(4), 365–375 (2005)
7. Liu, C., Yuen, J., Torralba, A.: Sift flow: Dense correspondence across scenes and its applications. IEEE Transactions on Pattern Analysis and Machine Intelligence 33(5), 978–994 (2011)
8. Mattavelli, M., Nicoulin, A.N.: Motion estimation relaxing the constancy brightness constraint. In: ICIP, pp. 770–774. IEEE (1994)
9. Molnar, J., Chetverikov, D., Fazekas, S.: Illumination-robust variational optical flow using cross-correlation. Computer Vision and Image Understanding 114(10), 1104–1114 (2010)
10. Müller, T., Rabe, C., Rannacher, J., Franke, U., Mester, R.: Illumination-robust dense optical flow using census signatures. In: Mester, R., Felsberg, M. (eds.) DAGM 2011. LNCS, vol. 6835, pp. 236–245. Springer, Heidelberg (2011)
11. Pock, T., Urschler, M., Zach, C., Beichel, R., Bischof, H.: A duality based algorithm for TV-L^1-optical-flow image registration. In: Ayache, N., Ourselin, S., Maeder, A. (eds.) MICCAI 2007, Part II. LNCS, vol. 4792, pp. 511–518. Springer, Heidelberg (2007)
12. Rudin, L.I., Osher, S.J., Fatemi, E.: Nonlinear total variation based noise removal algorithms 60, 259–268 (1992),
http://dx.doi.org/10.1016/0167-2789(92)90242-F
13. Sand, P., Teller, S.J.: Particle video: Long-range motion estimation using point trajectories. International Journal of Computer Vision 80(1), 72–91 (2008)
14. Sun, D., Roth, S., Black, M.J.: Secrets of optical flow estimation and their principles. In: CVPR, pp. 2432–2439. IEEE (2010)
15. Werlberger, M., Pock, T., Bischof, H.: Motion estimation with non-local total variation regularization. In: CVPR, pp. 2464–2471. IEEE (2010)
16. Zach, C., Pock, T., Bischof, H.: A duality based approach for realtime tv- l1 optical flow. In: Hamprecht, F.A., Schnörr, C., Jähne, B. (eds.) DAGM 2007. LNCS, vol. 4713, pp. 214–223. Springer, Heidelberg (2007)
17. Zimmer, H., Bruhn, A., Weickert, J.: Optic flow in harmony. International Journal of Computer Vision 93(3), 368–388 (2011)

Spatial Pattern Templates for Recognition of Objects with Regular Structure

Radim Tyleček and Radim Šára

Center for Machine Perception
Czech Technical University in Prague

Abstract. We propose a method for semantic parsing of images with regular structure. The structured objects are modeled in a densely connected CRF. The paper describes how to embody specific spatial relations in a representation called *Spatial Pattern Templates* (SPT), which allows us to capture regularity constraints of alignment and equal spacing in pairwise and ternary potentials.

Assuming the input image is pre-segmented to salient regions the SPT describe which segments could interact in the structured graphical model. The model parameters are learnt to describe the formal language of semantic labelings. Given an input image, a consistent labeling over its segments linked in the CRF is recognized as a word from this language.

The CRF framework allows us to apply efficient algorithms for both recognition and learning. We demonstrate the approach on the problem of facade image parsing and show that results comparable with state of the art methods are achieved without introducing additional manually designed detectors for specific terminal objects.

1 Introduction

The recent development in the areas of object detection and image segmentation is centered around the incorporation of contextual cues. Published results confirm the hypothesis that modeling relations between neighboring pixels or segments (superpixels) can significantly improve recognition accuracy for structured data. The first choice one has to make here is to choose the neighbor relation, or in other words, which primitive elements participate in constraints on labels. The constraints are usually specified with a formal language of spatial arrangements. A common choice for the relation is the adjacency of element pairs in the image plane, such as 4 or 8-neighborhood of pixels in a grid, which supports the language model [1]. This can be extended in various directions: In 'depth' when we have more concurrent segmentations, or in cardinality when we connect more elements together. Generally speaking, in this paper we will take a closer look on this design process and introduce a concept called *Spatial Pattern Templates* (SPT).

A convenient framework to embed such patterns into are probabilistic graphical models, where image elements correspond to nodes and edges (or higher-order cliques) to the relations among them. In such a graph, our pattern templates

J. Weickert, M. Hein, and B. Schiele (Eds.): GCPR 2013, LNCS 8142, pp. 364–374, 2013.

correspond to cliques or factors, as they describe how a given joint probability factorizes. We choose Conditional Random Fields (CRF [9]) as a suitable model, which allows us to concentrate on the element relations and not to care much about how the data are generated. Specifically, we propose pattern templates to deal with regular segmentations and call them *Aligned Pairs (AP)* and *Regular Triplets (RT)*.

We identify regular segmentations as those where object geometry, shape or appearance exhibit symmetry, particularly translational, which manifests in alignment and similarity. Such principles often apply to images with man-made objects, even though such phenomena are also common in the nature. Urban scenes have some of the most regular yet variable segmentations and their semantic analysis is receiving more attention nowadays, as it can aid other computer vision tasks such as image-based urban reconstruction. We design our method with this application in mind, specifically targeting parsing of facade images (a multi-class labeling problem).

In this task, we exploit the properties of largely orthogonal facade images. We start by training a classifier to recognize the patches given by unsupervised segmentation. Based on the initial segments we build a CRF with binary relative location potentials on *AP* and ternary label consistency potentials on *RT*. For intuition, this can be seen as a process where all segments jointly vote for terminal labels of the other segments, with voting scheme following the chosen spatial patterns. The concept of template design, its embedding in the CRF and implementation for regular objects with *Regular Triplets* and *Aligned Pairs* are the contributions of this paper.

2   Related Work

Contextual models. Relative location prior on label pairs is used in [4] for multi-class segmentation. Every segment votes for the label of all other segments based on their relative location and classifier output. Ideally, such interactions should be modeled with a complete graph CRF, where an edge expresses the joint probability of the two labels given their relative location, but this would soon make the inference intractable with the growing number of segments. Instead Gould et al. [4] resort to a voting scheme and use CRF with pairwise terms for directly adjacent segments only. In our approach, we include the discretized relative location prior in a CRF but limit the number of interactions by choosing a suitable pattern template.

CRFs are popular for high-level vision tasks also thanks to the number of algorithms available for inference and learning [11]. However, useful exact algorithms are known only for a specific class of potential functions (obeying *submodularity*). Kohli et al. [5] fit in this limitation with a robust version of a generalized Potts model, which softly enforces label consistency among any number of elements in a high order clique (pixels in segments). We can use this model for *RT*, but because the pairwise relative location potentials may have arbitrary form, we cannot apply the efficient α-expansion optimization used in [5].

Structure learning. A number of methods for learning general structures on graphs have been recently developed [3,12,13]. They learn edge-specific weights in a fully connected graph, which is directly tractable only when the number of nodes n is small (10 segments and 4 spatial relations in [3]) due to edge number growing with $\mathcal{O}(n^2)$. Scalability of the approach has been extended by Schmidt et al. by block-wise regularization for sparsity [12] (16 segments) and subsequently also for higher-order potentials with a hierarchical constraint [13] (30 segments). Since we deal with ~ 500 segments, this approach cannot be directly applied and, as suggested in [12], a restriction on the edge set has to be considered. The SPT can be here seen as a principled implementation of this restriction to keep the problem tractable.

Facade parsing. There are two major approaches to the facade parsing problem. Top-down approach relies on the construction of a generative rule set, usually a grammar, and the result is obtained stochastically as a word in the language best matching the input image [14]. So far there are no methods for automatic construction of the grammars and they do not generalize well outside of the style they were designed for. Learning is possible for very simple grammars (e.g. grid [17]) but it cannot express other structural relations.

Bottom-up approaches instead combine weak general principles, which are more flexible and their parameters can be learned. Regularity of spacing, shape similarity and alignment is used in [18] to find weakly regular structures, but the model cannot be simply extended for more classes than one (*window*). The hierarchical CRF [8], which aggregates information from multiple segmentations at different scales, has been applied to facades in [19], where binary potentials model consistency of adjacent labels within as well as across segmentations. Here neighboring segments with similar appearance are more likely to have the same label (contrast-sensitive Potts model). The recent three-staged method [10] combines local and object detectors with a binary Potts CRF on pixels. The result is further sequentially processed to adjust the labels according to the alignment, similarity, symmetry and co-occurence principles, each of them applied with a rather heuristic procedure. Additional principles are designed for a specific dataset and in fact resemble grammatical rules. In contrast, our method accommodates the general assumption of regularity in a principled and general way as a part of the model, which is based on the CRF and can benefit from the joint learning and inference.

3   Spatial Pattern Template Model

Initially we obtain a set of segments S in the input image with a generic method such as [2], tuned to produce over-segmentation of the ground truth objects. The image parsing task is to assign labels $L = \{l_i \in C\}_{i=1}^N$ of known classes $C = \{c_j\}_{j=1}^K$ to given segments $S = \{s_i \subset \operatorname{dom} I\}_{i=1}^N$ in an image I. Let $X = \{x_i \subset I\}_{i=1}^N$ be the image data of segments S. With segments corresponding to nodes in a graph and labels L being the node variables, we construct a CRF with potentials taking the general form of

$$p(L|X,S) = \frac{1}{Z(X,S)} \prod_{q \in \mathcal{Q}} e^{-\sum_{j \in \phi(q)} \theta_j \varphi_j(\mathbf{l}_q | \mathbf{x}_q, \mathbf{s}_q)}, \tag{1}$$

where $\mathcal{Q}$ is the set of cliques, φ_j are potential functions from a predefined set $\phi(q)$ defined for a clique q. The φ_j is a function of all node variables in collections $\mathbf{l}_q, \mathbf{x}_q, \mathbf{s}_q$, their weights are θ_j and $Z(X,S)$ is the normalizing partition function. The design of a specific CRF model now lies in the choice of cliques $\mathcal{Q}$ defining **topology** on top of the segments and their potential functions φ_j, which act on all node variables in the clique and set up the **probabilistic model**.

3.1   Spatial Templates for Data-Dependent Topology

As a generalization of the *adjacency*, used i.e. in [19], we can think of other choices for the graph topology that may suit our domain by including inter-actions between distant image elements, which are 'close' to each other in a different sense. As mentioned in Sec. 2, the scale of the problem does not allow us to reach complete connectivity. To allow dense connectivity while keeping the problem tractable, we need to restrict the number of cliques (edges). We describe this restriction with a *template* and, with the geometrical context in mind, we limit ourselves to *spatial* templates, which assign segments to cliques based on their geometrical attributes (shape, location). In principle other attributes (appearance) could be used in the template too. The meaning of this representation is to provide a systematic procedure for automatic learning of which interactions are the most efficient ones for the recognition task at hand.

In order to describe the process of designing a complex data dependent topology for a CRF, we first have to decompose the process behind clique template design into individual steps:

1. The first step is the specification of **core attribute relation functions** $\delta_i : A^n \to \mathbb{R}$ based on the domain knowledge. The relations act on easily measurable attributes A of n-tuples of segments. *Example: Positions of two points in a plane as attributes $A_x, A_y \in \mathbb{R}^2$ and their signed distances in directions x and y as the relations δ_x, δ_y.*
2. The ranges of relations δ_i are **discretized** to ordered sets Δ_i and $d_i : A^n \to \Delta_i$ becomes the discrete counterpart of function δ_i. *Example: The signed distance is divided into three intervals, $\Delta_x = \{\text{left}, \text{equal}, \text{right}\}$, $\Delta_y = \{\text{below}, \text{equal}, \text{above}\}$.*
3. In the next step the Cartesian product of m relation ranges Δ_i gives domain $D = \Delta_1 \times \cdots \times \Delta_m$, where subsets define logical **meta relations** (*and, or, equal*). *Example: Three intervals on two axes give 3^2 combinations in $D_{xy} = \Delta_x \times \Delta_y$.*
4. The **spatial template** is a subset $\Omega \subset D$ representing a concrete relation. The template is specified by an indicator function $\omega : D \to \{0,1\}$ representing the allowed combinations. *Example: For alignment in one direction we set $\omega_{xy} = 1$ when $d_x = $ equal or $d_y = $ equal, otherwise $\omega_{xy} = 0$.*

The template design may be viewed as a kind of declarative programming framework for model design, a representation that can incorporate the specific knowledge in a generic way with combinations of core relations δ_i. Each spatial template is related to one potential function φ_j in (1).

In summary, the result of this process describes which subsets of segments S labeled L should be jointly modeled in a graphical model; which of these are effective is subject to learning. Figure 2 shows how the segments correspond to nodes and their subsets define factors in $p(L|X, S)$. In this work we introduce two templates suitable for regular segmentations.

Aligned Pairs (AP). Out of all pairs of segments u, v we choose those which are aligned either vertically or horizontally. It is useful to connect segments not directly adjacent when the labels in such pairs follow some pattern, i.e. windows are aligned with some free space in between.

The specification follows the spatial template design steps: 1) Based on the position attribute we choose horizontal and vertical **alignment** δ_h, δ_v with $\delta_h :$ $(s_u, s_v) \rightarrow \mathbb{R}$ and $\delta_h = 0$ when the segments are exactly aligned, otherwise according to Fig. 1 (analogically δ_v for vertical). 2) Quantized d_h, d_v take values from Δ_a according to Fig. 3 evaluated on segment bounding boxes. 3) Combinations of horizontal and vertical alignment are then represented by joining d_h, d_v in a discrete domain $D_{AP} = \Delta_a^2$ limited by maximum distance. 4) Finally we specify the AP template with $\omega_{AP} = 1$ in the blue region in Fig. 1.

Note that *adjacency* (4-neighborhood) is a special case of AP when we specify $\omega_{AP} = 1$ only for four specific values in D_{AP} (directly above/under/left/right, red squares in Fig. 1). Similarly values of $|d_h| \leq 5$ together with $|d_v| \leq 5$ correspond to *overlap* or *nesting* of segments.

Regular Triplets (RT). Here we combine two *Aligned Pairs* in a triplet u, v, w with regular spacing, in which the v is the shared segment. Including triplets allows to express a basis for repetitive structures (rows, columns) of primitive objects of the same label (*window, balcony*).

1) In addition to position alignment δ_h, δ_v we introduce ternary relation functions for **size similarity** $\delta_s : (s_u, s_v, s_w) \rightarrow \mathbb{R}$ (relative difference in size of segments) and **regular spacing** $\delta_r : (s_u, s_v, s_w) \rightarrow \mathbb{R}$ (relative difference in free space between segments). 2) Based on them we define binary function $d_s : (s_u, s_v, s_w) \rightarrow \{0, 1\}$ to be 1 when $|\delta_s| < 0.1$ and similarly $d_r : (s_u, s_v, s_w) \rightarrow$ $\{0, 1\}$ to be 1 when $|\delta_r| < 0.1$. 3) All functions $d_h(s_u, s_v), d_v(s_u, s_v), d_h(s_v, s_w)$, $d_v(s_v, s_w), d_s(s_u, s_v, s_w)$ and $d_r(s_u, s_v, s_w)$ are then joined in a six-dimensional domain $D_{RT} = \Delta_a^4 \times \{0, 1\}^2$. 4) Finally we specify $\omega_{RT} = 1$ in the subspace of D_{RT} where $d_s = 1, d_r = 1$ and values of d_h, d_v indicate that the three segments are pair-wise aligned in the same direction (horizontal or vertical).

3.2   Probabilistic Model for Label Patterns

Given the fixed set of segments S, we will now make use of the SPT topology to model regular contextual information with a CRF for the graphical model.

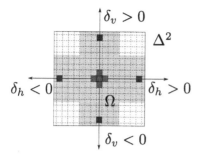

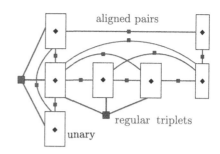

Fig. 1. Spatial template Ω is a subspace in the domain D_{AP} given by relation functions δ_h, δ_v. The center corresponds to the exact alignment in both axes. If segment u (green) is located in the center, other squares (red for *adjacency*, blue belong to *Aligned Pairs*) correspond to discrete relative positions of segment v.

Fig. 2. Factor graph for regular SPT. Segments S are shown as blue rectangles s_i (i.e. corresponding to *window* frames), factors are solid squares. *Aligned Pairs* connect only segments in mutual relative position specified by the template in Fig. 1. *Regular Triplets* then combine two aligned and equally spaced pairs together.

For clarity we rewrite (1) in a convenient form

$$p(L|X, S) \propto \prod_{u \in S} e^{\varphi_1(\nu_u)} \times \prod_{(uv) \in AP} e^{\varphi_2(\nu_u, \nu_v)} \times \prod_{(uvw) \in RT} e^{\varphi_3(\nu_u, \nu_v, \nu_w)}, \quad (2)$$

where $\nu_i = (l_i | s_i, x_i)$ are variables related to node i and $\varphi_1, \varphi_2, \varphi_3$ are unary, pair-wise (AP) and ternary (RT) potential functions (factors) respectively. We will now discuss features used in these factors.

The unary potentials $\varphi_1(\nu_i) = \log p(l_i | s_i, x_i)$ are outputs of a multi-class classifier evaluated on the features for an image patch x_i of the segment s_i. The feature vector $f(x_i)$ is extracted from the image data by appending histogram of gradients (HoG), color (HSV), relative size, position, aspect ratio and 2D auto-correlation function.

Pairwise potentials for AP are restrictions on the template learned for concrete label pairs. They are based on a discretized version of the relative location distribution [4], similar form is used in [15] for *adjacency*. It is the statistical function

$$\varphi_2(\nu_u, \nu_v) = \theta_{2, d_h, d_v} \log p(l_u, l_v \mid d_h, d_v), \quad (3)$$

where d_h are the values of horizontal alignment $d_h(s_{u1}, s_{v1})$ specified in Fig. 3, analogically d_v for vertical. The **pattern** of labels l_u, l_v is the empirical distribution in the given relative locations d_h, d_v computed as the second order co-occurrence statistics of the labels for pairs of segments observed in a training set. The co-occurrence frequencies are obtained from a training set for each pair of class labels and are accumulated for all values in the spatial template domain Ω_{AP}. Figure 4 shows the resulting histograms of AP in Fig. 1.

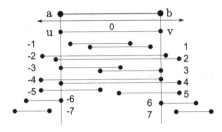

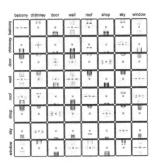

Fig. 3. Given interval (a, b) the figure shows the values Δ_a of alignment relation function d_a for a set of intervals (u, v), ranging from 0 (aligned) to ± 7 (no overlap). More free space between intervals corresponds to higher absolute values $(8, 9, 10, \dots)$ in Δ. Positions are considered equal within 10% tolerance of the interval length

Fig. 4. Discrete relative co-occurrence location histogram $p(l_u, l_v, d_h, d_v)$ for label pairs in the *ECP-Monge* dataset. It holds information such as 'sky is usually above windows' or 'balconies are aligned vertically with windows'. Dark colors correspond to high frequency, blue cross marks $d = 0$ (equality).

Ternary potentials models regularity by encouraging some labels in RT to have the same value (i.e. *window*) in

$$\varphi_3(\nu_u, \nu_v, \nu_w) = \begin{cases} \theta_{3,c} & \text{if } l_u = l_v = l_w = c, \\ \theta_{3,0} & \text{otherwise,} \end{cases} \qquad (4)$$

which is a generalized Potts model [5] and $\theta_{3,c}$ is a learned class-specific parameter. We do not use the complex ternary co-occurrence statistic with this potential because there is not enough data for its training. To facilitate efficient learning, we convert ternary potentials into pairwise by adding a hidden variable for each ternary factor φ_3.

Piece-wise parameter learning. The unary potential classifiers are trained independently to reduce the number of free parameters in the joint CRF learning process. For binary potentials (including the reduced ternary potentials) we use pseudo-likelihood learning procedure to obtain values of the potential weights θ. This process corresponds to structure learning within the domain Ω_{AP} limited by the SPT topology, resulting in $\theta_2 \to 0$ where the relation does not contribute to the discriminative power of the CRF. In practice this amounts to learning ~ 200 parameters based on likelihood in 50 sampled images, each of them with approximately 500 label variables, 3000 pair and 100 triplet factors. The training process takes several hours to complete (8 cores, 2 GHz) using Mark Schmidt's UGM library (www.di.ens.fr/~mschmidt/Software/UGM.html).

Inference. Because some of our potentials have a general form, exact inference is not possible and we use an approximate algorithm [6] to compute the marginal distributions of the labels, with run time around 30 s per image.

Table 1. Pixel-wise accuracy comparison on facade datasets (number of classes in brackets). *Abbreviations*: *SGT*=Segments with Ground Truth labels, *NC*=No Context, *AP*=Aligned Pairs, *RT*=Regular Triplets, *Cooc*=Coocurence, *BSG*=Binary Split Grammar, *HAdj*=Hieararchical Adjacency, *RNN*=Recursive Neural Network, *RF*=Randomized Forest, *SG*=Shape Grammar, *HCRF*=Hierarchical CRF.

Method	SGT	SPT (proposed)			Three Layers [10]		SG [14]	HCRF [19]
Classifier	*SGT*	SVM			RNN		RF	RDF
Spatial pattern		NC	AP	**APRT**	NC	Adjacency	BSG	HAdj
Prob. model		-	Cooc	**Cooc**	-	Potts	SG	CS-Potts
ECP-Monge (8)	88.5	59.6	79.0	**84.2**	82.6	85.1	74.7	-
eTrims (8)	93.7	56.7	77.4	**82.1**	81.1	81.9	-	65.8
CMP Facade (12)	84.8	33.2	54.3	**60.3**	-	-	-	-

4 Experimental Results

We have validated our method on two public datasets annotated into 8 classes (like *wall, window, balcony* etc.). In addition in this paper we introduce a new large facade dataset.

The public *ECP-Monge* dataset is available from [14] (we use corrected ground truth labellings from [10]). It contains 104 rectified facade images from Paris, all in uniform Hausmannian style. Next, the public *eTrims* database [7] contains 60 images of buildings and facades in various architectural styles (neoclassical, modern and other). We rectified them using vanishing points.

We have compiled a new publicly available larger *CMP Facade* database [16] with ∼ 400 images of greater diversity of styles and 12 object classes.

Figure 5 shows parsing results for different contextual models, additional results can be found in the report [16]. Table 1 provides their pixel-wise accuracy and comparison with other methods based on 5-fold cross validation. We have used method [2] to extract averagely 500 segments (independently on the image resolution) and show it under *SGT*, where ground truth labels of pixels within each segment have been collected and the most frequent label among them selected for the entire segment. The result is the maximum achievable accuracy with this segmentation, inaccurate localization of the segment borders is currently the main limiting factor (we are 4.3% below the limit on *ECP-Monge*).

The main observation is that contextual information improves the accuracy averagely by 20% when statistics on *AP* is used, and by further 4% when *RT* are included. The *RT* help mostly with window and balcony identification, thanks to the statistics of these labels following regular pattern in the dataset. The qualitative improvement is noticeable, even when their effect on the total pixel-wise accuracy is small, which is a sign it is not a very suitable measure. A more sophisticated local classifier could make the structural part of the model almost unnecessary, as observed in [10], but such model may be overly reliant on a good training set and perhaps prone to overfitting.

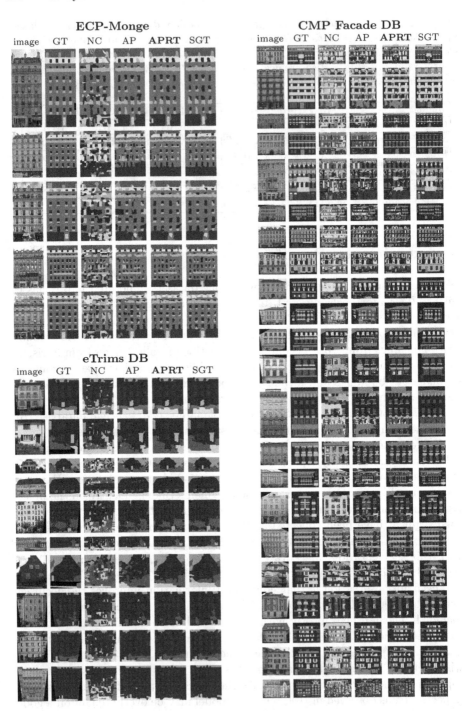

Fig. 5. Selected visual results on facade dataset, our result with full model is under *APRT*, (note it cannot be better than *SGT*). See legend in Tab. 1 for abbreviations.

5 Conclusion

We have introduced the concept of *Spatial Pattern Templates* for contextual models. The proposed *Aligned Pairs* and *Regular Triplets* templates have been found useful for segmentation of regular scenes by increasing accuracy of facade image parsing. Our next interest is to improve the quality of the segment extraction to increase accuracy of their borders.

Acknowledgement. This work was supported by the Czech Science Foundation under Project P103/12/1578.

References

1. Čech, J., Šára, R.: Languages for constrained binary segmentation based on maximum a posteriori probability labeling. IJIST 19(2), 69–79 (2009)
2. Felzenszwalb, P.F., Huttenlocher, D.P.: Efficient graph-based image segmentation. IJCV 59(2), 167–181 (2004)
3. Galleguillos, C., Rabinovich, A., Belongie, S.: Object categorization using co-occurrence, location and appearance. In: Proc. CVPR (2008)
4. Gould, S., Rodgers, J., Cohen, D., Elidan, G., Koller, D.: Multi-class segmentation with relative location prior. IJCV 80(3), 300–316 (2008)
5. Kohli, P., Ladicky, L., Torr, P.: Robust higher order potentials for enforcing label consistency. IJCV 82(3), 302–324 (2009)
6. Kolmogorov, V.: Convergent tree-reweighted message passing for energy minimization. Trans. PAMI 28(10), 1568–1583 (2006)
7. Korč, F., Förstner, W.: eTRIMS image database for interpreting images of man-made scenes. Tech. Rep. TR-IGG-P-2009-01 (2009)
8. Ladicky, L., Russell, C., Kohli, P., Torr, P.: Associative hierarchical CRFs for object class image segmentation. In: Proc. ICCV, pp. 739–746 (2009)
9. Lafferty, J., McCallum, A., Pereira, F.: Conditional random fields: Probabilistic models for segmenting and labeling sequence data. In: Proc. ICML (2001)
10. Martinović, A., Mathias, M., Weissenberg, J., Van Gool, L.: A three-layered approach to facade parsing. In: Fitzgibbon, A., Lazebnik, S., Perona, P., Sato, Y., Schmid, C. (eds.) ECCV 2012, Part VII. LNCS, vol. 7578, pp. 416–429. Springer, Heidelberg (2012)
11. Nowozin, S., Gehler, P.V., Lampert, C.H.: On parameter learning in CRF-based approaches to object class image segmentation. In: Daniilidis, K., Maragos, P., Paragios, N. (eds.) ECCV 2010, Part VI. LNCS, vol. 6316, pp. 98–111. Springer, Heidelberg (2010)
12. Schmidt, M., Murphy, K., Fung, G., Rosales, R.: Structure learning in random fields for heart motion abnormality detection. In: Proc. CVPR (2008)
13. Schmidt, M., Murphy, K.: Convex structure learning in log-linear models: Beyond pairwise potentials. In: Proc. AISTATS (2010)
14. Simon, L., Teboul, O., Koutsourakis, P., Paragios, N.: Random exploration of the procedural space for single-view 3D modeling of buildings. IJCV 93(2) (2011)
15. Tighe, J., Lazebnik, S.: Understanding scenes on many levels. In: Proc. ICCV, pp. 335–342 (2011)

16. Tyleček, R.: The CMP facade database. Research Report CTU–CMP–2012–24. Czech Technical University (2012), http://cmp.felk.cvut.cz/~tylecr1/facade
17. Tyleček, R., Šára, R.: Modeling symmetries for stochastic structural recognition. In: Proc. ICCV Workshops, pp. 632–639 (2011)
18. Tyleček, R., Šára, R.: Stochastic recognition of regular structures in facade images. IPSJ Trans. Computer Vision and Applications 4, 12–21 (2012)
19. Yang, M., Förstner, W.: A hierarchical conditional random field model for labeling and classifying images of man-made scenes. In: Proc. ICCV Workshops (2011)

K-Smallest Spanning Tree Segmentations

Christoph Straehle, Sven Peter, Ullrich Köthe, and Fred A. Hamprecht

HCI, University of Heidelberg

Abstract. Real-world images often admit many different segmentations
that have nearly the same quality according to the underlying energy
function. The diversity of these solutions may be a powerful uncertainty
indicator. We provide the crucial prerequisite in the context of seeded
segmentation with minimum spanning trees (i.e. edge-weighted watersheds). Specifically, we show how to efficiently enumerate the k smallest
spanning trees that result in *different* segmentations; and we prove that
solutions are indeed found in the correct order. Experiments show that
about half of the trees considered by our algorithm represent unique segmentations. This redundancy is orders of magnitude lower than can be
achieved by just enumerating the k-smallest MSTs, making the algorithm
viable in practice.

1 Introduction

The most popular algorithms for interactive segmentation are Ising type Markov
random fields (MRFs) [3], the random walker [11] and the seeded watershed
[13]. Their smoothness terms penalize label changes with the L_1,L_2 and L_∞
norms respectively [6]. However, in the process of finding the single lowest energy
solution to the graph partitioning problem a lot of information is lost and other
modes of the solution space which may convey important aspects of the problem
are ignored. An enumeration of more than one low energy solution allows to
obtain a more robust segmentation, and can help defining an uncertainty of
the resulting segmentation which may be used in downstream processing. Thus,
recent work on these algorithms has focused on finding the M lowest energy
solutions [9,14,20], ideally subject to a diversity constraint [1]. These references
solve the problem for Ising-type MRFs. However, systematic empirical studies
[17] show that the seeded watershed outperforms MRFs in certain datasets and
offers computational advantages. The near linear runtime of a seeded watershed
stems from its connection to the minimum spanning tree (MST) of the image
graph [12,7]. The present work presents the first viable algorithm that provides
analogous M-best results for the seeded watershed cut. We build on the seminal
work of Gabow [10] to enumerate only those spanning trees (ST) in an edge-
weighted graph that lead to a change in the resulting segmentation. Furthermore
we give a modification of Gabow's algorithm that allows to enumerate the M-best
diverse solutions similar to [1], by enforcing a user specified distance between
some of the generated segmentations. Such a diverse set of solutions can in turn
be combined into a final segmentation [4].

J. Weickert, M. Hein, and B. Schiele (Eds.): GCPR 2013, LNCS 8142, pp. 375–384, 2013.

2   Related Work

The M-best solutions problem has been studied in the context of discrete graphical models [2] where it is known as the M-best MAP problem. Several types
of algorithms have been proposed for the M-Best MAP problem: junction tree
based exact algorithms [14,16], dynamic programming based algorithms [15] and
max marginal based algorithms [20]. An interesting extension of the M-best MAP
problem was proposed and studied in [1]. Here, the authors give an algorithm
to enumerate a *diverse* set of solutions. This is an attractive approach since the
M-best solutions tend to be very similar to the MAP solution for a low M and
thus important aspects of the solution space cannot be found. Generating such
a set of diverse solutions was shown in [1] to remedy the problem of M-best
solutions: when the initial M-best solutions are too close, important aspects of
the solution space may only be found by enforcing a certain amount of diversity.
The authors show that this diverse set of solutions which differ in a user specified
amount from the MAP solution do not exhibit this problem.

The seeded watershed algorithm [13,19] which we adapt enjoys great popularity in applications where large amounts of data have to be processed, including
medical and biological 3D image analysis [17], and where the shrinking bias
typical of MRFs is detrimental.

We rely on the equivalence of the edge weighted seeded watershed and the
minimum spanning tree (MST) algorithm [12,7,8] and draw on the seminal work
of Gabow [10] who solved the k-smallest minimum spanning trees problem.

3   Image Segmentation with Minimum Spanning Trees

We formulate the interactive image segmentation problem as a graph partitioning
problem on the pixel neighborhood graph $G(E, V)$. All neighboring pixels $v \in V$
are connected with edges $(i, j) \in E$. All edges have an associated edge weight
$w_{ij} \in \mathbb{R}$ which expresses the dissimilarity between the neighboring pixels. The
edge weights w_{ij} can be computed for example from the color gradient or another
suitable boundary indicator. It is well known [12,7] that the seeded watershed
cut on a graph G is equivalent to a minimum spanning tree computation on a
suitably augmented graph $G'(V', E')$ that contains a supernode v_0 connected to
seed nodes v_{-l} for each label class $l \in L$. These seed nodes are connected to
the root node v_0 with zero weight edges. All labeled nodes (i.e. all supervoxels
holding a user seed) are also connected to these seed nodes with zero-weight
edges $w_{i,-l} = 0$, which are guaranteed to remain in the MST. Once the MST
with root node v_0 has been constructed, subtrees originating from seed nodes v_{-l}
form segments of the final segmentation. This graph construction is illustrated
in Figure 1.

4   Gabow's Algorithm for the k Smallest Spanning Trees

The MST segmentation algorithm outlined in the previous section finds the
single smallest spanning tree of the augmented graph. In the next section, we will

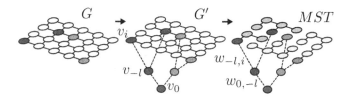

Fig. 1. Seeded image segmentation using minimum spanning trees. The image nodes which the user has seeded (blue, green) are connected to virtual seed nodes v_{-l} which in turn are connected to a virtual root node v_0. The associated edge weights are set to 0 which ensures that the edges belong to the minimum spanning tree of the augmented graph G'. The final label of an image node depends on the subtree to which the node is assigned in the resulting minimum spanning tree.

propose to generalize the algorithm by Gabow [10] to enumerate spanning trees that result in *different* segmentations. To lay the foundation for our extension, we start with a description of Gabow's original algorithm.

Gabow's algorithm starts with a minimum spanning tree for the graph generated by e.g. Kruskal's algorithm. This MST constitutes the first solution. The algorithm then enumerates different spanning trees in the order of increasing weight by swapping out an edge e belonging to the current spanning tree, and replacing it by another edge f which is currently not in the tree.

To obtain the smallest spanning tree under such a so-called e, f-exchange, it finds the pair e, f that gives the smallest weight increase $w(f) - w(e)$.

The main idea of the algorithm is to maintain a set of branchings and two lists associated with each branch, called IN and OUT, which prevent the algorithm from enumerating a spanning tree twice. All edges contained in the IN list have to stay in the spanning tree and all edges contained in the OUT list cannot enter the spanning tree.

To enumerate all spanning trees in order, the algorithm finds the smallest weight e, f-exchange which is feasible according to the IN and OUT lists of the current state and branches on this exchange. Branching is done by considering two different cases: one branch is constructed by adding the f edge to the OUT list, the other branch is established by adding f to the IN list. Any further branching which is executed in the two cases inherits the respective IN and OUT lists from its parent state. Thus, any spanning tree constructed in the first branch excludes edge f and any spanning tree constructed in the second branch includes edge f. By visiting all branchings strictly in the order of increasing tree weight, the first k minimum spanning trees are constructed in the correct order. This process is illustrated in Figure 2.

5   Enumerating Changing Segmentations

While Gabow's algorithm finds the k smallest spanning trees of a given graph, it cannot be used to find the different modes of a segmentation: a grid graph

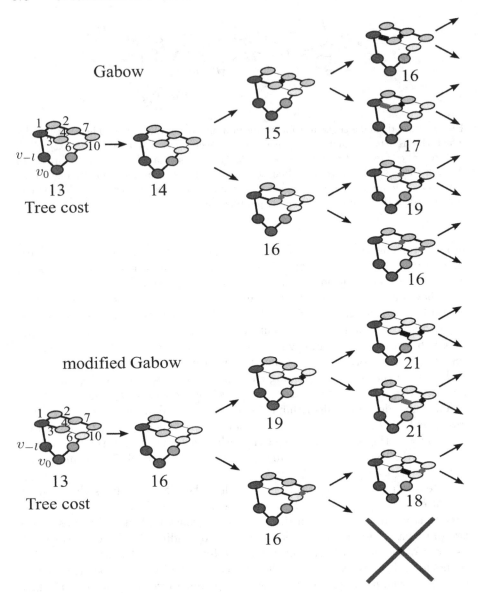

Fig. 2. Illustration of Gabow's algorithm and our modification (best viewed in color). The algorithm of Gabow branches after each e, f-exchange into an upper case where the edge f (indicated by thick black stroke) must stay in the tree and a lower case where the edge f (thick red stroke) must stay out of the tree. Our modified algorithm works in the same way, but only considers edges $f \in C(ST)$ which are part of the cut set for the current spanning tree. By definition, this induces a changed segmentation in each step. In contrast, in the original Gabow algorithm the segmentation often stays unchanged. Some of the k smallest spanning trees have a cut set fully contained in the OUT list and hence do not allow further branching: the set of viable edges for an exchange has been depleted (crossed out state).

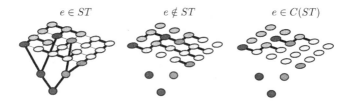

Fig. 3. Illustration of cut edges. On the left, all edges of a spanning tree (ST) are shown in bold. In the middle all edges not belonging to the spanning tree a shown. The subset of the middle edges which belong to the seeded watershed cut – i.e. the edges which connect the different segments – are shown on the right. We modify Gabow's algorithm by only considering these cut edges in any e, f-exchange. This enforces a changing segmentation between any two STs in the hierarchy of Figure 2, but does not guarantee that all resulting segmentations are unique.

has exponentially many spanning trees (10^{40} for a 4-connected grid graph of size 10×10, [18]). In typical images, exceedingly many spanning trees lead to the same segmentation. This effect is visible in the illustration of Gabow's algorithm in Figure 2: while the algorithm always produces a new spanning tree, the associated segmentation does not necessarily change. This is especially true when there are large basins, or areas with low edge weights, as are typical for graphs constructed from natural images.

Thus, when generating the k smallest spanning trees, many if not all (when k is small) of the trees correspond to the same segmentation result. Luckily we can identify the sufficient and necessary condition that leads to a different segmentation result (compared to the previous state) in an e, f-exchange in Gabow's algorithm.

In the case of a spanning tree segmentation, the assigned label (color) of a node depends on the subtree to which the node is connected in the spanning tree: the node is assigned the label of the virtual seed node v_{-l} of which it is a child in the spanning tree (see Figure 1). All edges in the spanning tree connect nodes of the *same* color. An edge connecting two nodes of *different* color cannot be part of the spanning tree segmentation.

Now, if an e, f-exchange removes an edge e from the tree and replaces it with an edge f that connects two nodes of the same color it is clear that the segmentation cannot change: the resulting spanning tree is merely a different way to express the same segmentation.

We now come to the core idea: to enforce a different segmentation, the edge f that is swapped in has to connect two nodes of *different* colors. After swapping in the edge f, both nodes belong to the same subtree and thus one of the two nodes changes its color. The resulting segmentation is different.

We call these edges f that connect nodes of different color in a ST segmentation "cut edges" $f \in C(ST)$. See Figure 3 for an illustration.

At this point, we are able to modify Gabow's algorithm to not only enumerate different spanning trees in order of increasing weight, but to enumerate *changing* segmentations in the order of increasing weight.

A small change is sufficient to reach the desired behavior: by adding all edges f which are not part of the cut set to a list OUTC $= \{f : f \notin C(ST)\}$, Gabow's algorithm can only consider edges $f \in C(ST)$ for any e, f-exchange since all edges in the OUT and OUTC list are not eligible. Thus the segmentation of any spanning tree that is generated differs from the previous segmentation. The OUTC list is always updated once a new spanning tree has been generated and ensures the desired behavior.

Our modification of Gabow's algorithm does not change its computational complexity, the scanning of the edges and the calculation of the OUTC list take time proportional to the number of edges in the graph which is of the same order as the normal Gabow algorithm takes in each iteration.

5.1   Algorithm Correctness

Our algorithm may enumerate a segmentation (though not a spanning tree) more than one time and in that sense is an approximation. However, our modification of Gabow's algorithm generates all possible segmentations in their order of increasing weight and finds the lowest cost spanning tree that represents each segmentation. We first show that any spanning tree of minimum weight that represents a segmenation is found by our algorithm.

Definition: *A minimum spanning tree S of a given segmentation* can be found by computing the cut edges $C(S)$ of the desired segmentation: it contains all edges $c = (i, j), x_i \neq x_j$ that connect nodes of different color $x_i \neq x_j$. The minimum spanning tree S of this segmentation can then be found by removing these edges from the graph (or adding them to the OUT list) and computing the minimum spanning tree of the modified graph.

A set of constraints IN_S, OUT_S that induce the minimum spanning tree S for a given segmentation can be found easily: the largest such set is $IN_S = \{e : e \in S\}$, $OUT_S = \{e : e \notin S\}$. Computing a spanning tree obeying these constraints will produce S. This shows the existence of at least one such set of constraints.

Theorem 1: Let T be a minimum spanning tree of graph G and let S be the minimum weight spanning tree that induces a given segmentation. Let IN_S, OUT_S be a set of constraints that induce spanning tree S. Then there exists a series of branchings that leads to IN_S, OUT_S.

Proof. Let $C(T)$ be the cut edges of spanning tree T. Then any edge $f \in C(T)$ which is eligible for an e, f-exchange in our algorithm is either (a) $\notin S$ or (b) $\in S$. The algorithm now picks the $f \in C(T)$ that has the smallest exchange weight $w(f) - w(e)$ using their best respective exchange partner e. In case (a) if $f \notin S$ we follow the branch where f is added to the OUT list. This leads to a new state that has the same induced segmentation (and cut set) but a modified OUT list. In the new state the next best exchange pair e', f' with $f' \in C(T)$ will be considered and the same case consideration applies. In case (b) when $f \in S$ we follow the other branch by adding f to the IN list. This leads to a new state with a new segmentation (and new cut set), but starting from this new state the same consideration applies. Both cases (a) and (b) lead to a state which is closer to a set of constraints IN_S, OUT_S. After a finite number of branchings we end up with a set of constraints IN_S, OUT_S that define the minimum cost spanning tree that induces a given segmentation.

The proof shows that all segmentations that are representable by a spanning tree will be found by our algorithm, forbidden branchings as in Figure 2 do not pose a problem: they occur when the OUT list contains all edges in the current cut set. By construction of the proof, for all edges $f \in OUT$ we know $f \notin S$. Since the current cut set is fully contained in the OUT list no edge in the current cut set can be part of the segmentation inducing spanning tree S. But if no edge of the current cut set is $\in S$ then the current state already defines the correct segmentation.

Definition [10]: T-exchange. Let T be a spanning tree of graph G. A T-exchange is a pair of edges e, f where $e \in T$, $f \notin T$, and $T - e \cup f$ is a spanning tree.

Lemma 1 [10]: A spanning tree T has minimum weight if and only if no T-exchange has negative weight.

Theorem 2: Let T be a minimum spanning tree of graph G and let f be an edge not in T. Let e, f be a T-exchange having the smallest weight of all exchanges e', f. Then $T - e \cup f$ is a minimum weight spanning tree of graph G under the constraint that f is in this tree.

Proof. Let $S = T - e \cup f$. Suppose S does not have minimum weight. By Lemma 1, there is a S-exchange g, h having negative weight. We derive a contradiction below. Let $T - e$ consist of the two trees U, V. Edge e joins U and V. Edge f must also join U and V since e, f is a T-exchange. Edge h also joins U and V. For if not, assume without loss of generality that h joins two vertices in U. Since g, h is an S-exchange g is also in subtree U and thus g, h is also a T-exchange. Thus, by Lemma 1 it has positive weight which violates our assumption, thus h must join U and V. Edge $g \neq f$ is in $U \cup V$ since exchange g, h cannot remove edge f from S due to the constraint. Assume without loss of generality that $g \in U$. Now let $U - g$ consist of the two trees W, X. Edge e is incident to one of those trees, say W. Since $T - e - g \cup f \cup h$ is a spanning tree, either f or h is incident to X. If h is incident to X then g, h is also a T-exchange which would violate Lemma 1 and leads to a contradiction. If f is incident to X then g, f is also a T-exchange, but since $w(g) \leq w(e)$ this would imply the T-exchange e, h being negative since $w(h) \leq w(g) \leq w(e)$: also a contradiction.

Induction and Theorem 2 gives us the property that our algorithm always produces spanning trees of increasing weight. No permitted e, f-exchange is of negative weight.

From Theorem 1 and Theorem 2 we have that our algorithm produces all possible segmentations in the order of increasing weight.

6   Enumerating Diverse Segmentations

When enumerating the M-best solutions and choosing a sensible M, say 50, there is a certain danger that the returned solution set is very similar and only differs marginally from the lowest energy solution. To remedy this problem in the M-best MAP setting the authors in [1] propose to enumerate diverse solutions S that obey a given minimum distance $\Delta(MAP, S)$ to the MAP solution. We now show that a similar constraint can be incorporated into our algorithm without increasing computational complexity. We will modify our algorithm that enumerates changing segmentations in such a way that it returns a changing segmentation which differs in at least Δ nodes from the previous segmentation.

The core part of our modified Gabow algorithm from the previous section is the e, f-exchange with a restriction that only allows edges f from the current cut set to be moved into the tree. This restriction of f enforces that at least one node changes its color because it is attached (via edge f) to a differently colored subtree. The exact number of nodes that change their color depends on the edge e which is removed from the tree: all nodes and edges below edge e are reconnected by edge f to another subtree with different color. Thus, by also restricting the edges e for an e, f-exchange we can control how many nodes will change their color in that exchange.

The exact implementation is straightforward: in each step of our modified algorithm, we compute for each edge e the number of nodes $\#(e)$ below this edge. This can be done in time linear in the number of edges. Then, we add all edges e which do not fullfill the user specified diversity requirement Δ to an IND list: IND $= \{e : \#(e) < \Delta\}$. The algorithm is adapted to use both lists, IN and IND. Thus, the IND edges are not considered for an e, f-exchange in the current iteration since they must stay in the tree and any eligible e, f-exchange must change the color of at least Δ nodes. The IND list is updated in each iteration of the algorithm.

7   Experiments

The proposed algorithm is a heuristic because it may produce multiple spanning trees that induce the same segmentation, see section 5.1. To study how many unique segmentations are generated, we choose a segmentation task that is suitable for a minimum spanning tree segmentation [17]: the segmentation of single cells in neural tissue. We ran Gabow's original algorithm and our modified version and compared the induced segmentation of each generated spanning tree to all previous generated segmentations to see how many unique segmentations each of the algorithm generates. As can be seen in Figure 5, Gabow's original algorithm fails to generate even two unique segmentations in $k' = 300$ iterations. Each generated spanning tree differs, but all spanning trees induce an equivalent segmentation. The same effect can be observed in the toy example in Figure 2. Our modification ensures that each generated spanning tree induces a different segmentation compared to the previous state. It works well in practice: more than half of the generated MST's induce a unique segmentation.

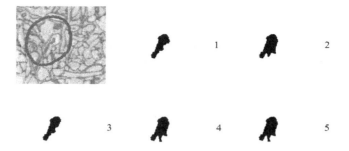

Fig. 4. Modified Gabow example. The top-left image shows an electron micropscopy image of cells in neural tissue [5] and user given seeds (red,green). The $k = 1, 2, 3, 4, 5$ first segmentations generated by our modified Gabow algorithm are shown in black and white. The algorithm successfully finds different modes of the segmentation.

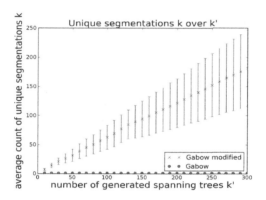

Fig. 5. This plot shows how many unique segmentations are generated when varying the parameter k' that determines how many spanning trees are generated. Shown are the results for Gabow's original algorithm and for our modified version. Gabow's original algorithm fails to generate different segmentations: the spanning trees differ, but the induced segmentation is always the same. In contrast, in the proposed algorithm, more than half of the generated spanning trees induce a unique segmentation.

8   Conclusion

Recently a way to enumerate the diverse M-best solutions for Markov random fields has been proposed in [1]. We present an algorithm that allows to enumerate locally changing segmentations in order of increasing spanning tree weight. We prove that the algorithm finds the smallest weight spanning tree that represents a given segmentation. We experimentally validate the algorithm and show that it can be used to effectively enumerate different smallest spanning tree segmentations. Furthermore we show how a diversity constraint can be incorporated into the algorithm that allows to enumerate segmentations which differ in a user specified number of nodes.

We expect the proposed algorithm to be of value in the pursuit of meaningful uncertainty measures as well as user guidance in a 3D segmentation setting. We also trust that more robust segmentations can be obtained by taking into account the information contained in a diverse set of solutions.

References

1. Batra, D., Yadollahpour, P., Guzman-Rivera, A., Shakhnarovich, G.: Diverse M-best solutions in markov random fields. In: Fitzgibbon, A., Lazebnik, S., Perona, P., Sato, Y., Schmid, C. (eds.) ECCV 2012, Part V. LNCS, vol. 7576, pp. 1–16. Springer, Heidelberg (2012)
2. Blake, A., Kohli, P., Rother, C.: Markov random fields for vision and image processing. MIT Press (2011)
3. Boykov, Y., Jolly, M.: Interactive graph cuts for optimal boundary and region segmentation of objects in ND images. In: ICCV (2001)
4. Brendel, W., Todorovic, S.: Segmentation as maximumweight independent set. In: NIPS, vol. 4 (2010)
5. Briggman, K.L., Denk, W., et al.: Towards neural circuit reconstruction with volume electron microscopy techniques. Current Opinion in Neurobiology (2006)
6. Couprie, C., Grady, L., Najman, L., Talbot, H.: Power watershed: A unifying graph-based optimization framework. IEEE PAMI (2010)
7. Cousty, J., Bertrand, G., Najman, L., Couprie, M.: Watershed cuts: Minimum spanning forests and the drop of water principle. IEEE PAMI, 1362–1374 (2009)
8. Falcão, A.X., Stolfi, J., Lotufo, R.A.: The image foresting transform: Theory, algorithms, and applications. IEEE PAMI 26 (2004)
9. Fromer, M., Globerson, A.: An LP view of the M-best MAP problem. NIPS (2009)
10. Gabow, H.: Two algorithms for generating weighted spanning trees in order. SIAM Journal on Computing (1977)
11. Grady, L.: Random walks for image segmentation. IEEE PAMI 28 (2006)
12. Meyer, F.: Minimum spanning forests for morphological segmentation. In: Mathematical Morphology and its Applications to Image Processing, pp. 77–84. Springer (1994)
13. Meyer, F., Beucher, S.: Morphological segmentation. Journal of Visual Communication and Image Representation 1(1), 21–46 (1990)
14. Nilsson, D.: An efficient algorithm for finding the M most probable configurations in probabilistic expert systems. Statistics and Computing 8(2), 159–173 (1998)
15. Rollon, N.E., Dechter, R.: Inference schemes for M-best solutions for soft CSPs. In: Proceedings of Workshop on Preferences and Soft Constraints, vol. 2 (2011)
16. Seroussi, B., Golmard, J.: An algorithm directly finding the K most probable configurations in bayesian networks. International Journal of Approximate Reasoning 11(3), 205–233 (1994)
17. Straehle, C.N., Köthe, U., Knott, G., Hamprecht, F.A.: Carving: Scalable interactive segmentation of neural volume electron microscopy images. In: Fichtinger, G., Martel, A., Peters, T. (eds.) MICCAI 2011, Part I. LNCS, vol. 6891, pp. 653–660. Springer, Heidelberg (2011)
18. Tzeng, W.J., Wu, F.: Spanning trees on hypercubic lattices and nonorientable surfaces. Applied Mathematics Letters 13 (2000)
19. Vincent, L., Soille, P.: Watersheds in digital spaces: an efficient algorithm based on immersion simulations. IEEE PAMI (1991)
20. Yanover, C., Weiss, Y.: Finding the AI most probable configurations using loopy belief propagation. In: NIPS (2004)

Discriminable Points That Stick Out of Their Environment

Dominik Alexander Klein and Armin Bernd Cremers

Intelligent Vision Systems Group, Institute of Computer Science III,
University of Bonn, Germany

Abstract. In this paper, we introduce BoSP (Bonn Salient Points), a method comprising a pair of a keypoint detector and descriptor in image data that are deeply geared to one another. Our detector identifies points of interest to be local maxima of appearance contrast to their surroundings in a statistical manner. This criterion admits a selection of particularly repeatable, but diverse looking keypoints. Besides, those textural statistics collected around a keypoint location directly serve as its descriptor. An important component in this framework is how to gather and represent local statistics. Regarding this, we further improved the efficient ML-estimation procedure for multivariate normal distributions previously introduced by Klein and Frintrop [6]. This Gaussian representation of feature statistics enables a quickly computable, closed-form solution of the $\mathcal{W}_2$-distance, which we utilize as a measure of appearance contrast. Evaluations were conducted comparing several recent detector/descriptor pairs on a well-recognized, publicly available dataset.

1 Introduction and Related Work

Interest point detection and matching is an important basis for many algorithms in applied computer vision, since it establishes correspondences between images. Such tasks include image and object representation and recognition, 3D-reconstruction, visual odometry, and simultaneous localization and mapping (SLAM). According to Tuytelaars and Mikolajczyk [14], good keypoints have a high *repeatability* as well as *distinctiveness*, and they are accurately locatable. Further criteria might comprise computational efficiency and keypoint density. Nevertheless, one could not specify a single detector/descriptor pair to be an optimal choice in general, but has to consider special requirements of different use cases. Thus, many different approaches evolved and became popular in the recent past, among them convolution based ones as SIFT [8], Harris-Laplace [9] or SURF [1], and binary test based such as FAST+ORB [11,12] and BRISK [7].

Certainly, the interplay of a detector and a descriptor affects the quality of a keypoint. However, these two problems are often solved separately: e.g. a difference of Gaussian detector picks blob-like structures which are subsequently described by histograms of gradients (SIFT [8]). Although many such approaches had been developed during the last decades, they raise two issues: first, is the descriptor able to capture the proper information that is not predictably common among all keypoints extracted by a certain detector? E.g., what is the

J. Weickert, M. Hein, and B. Schiele (Eds.): GCPR 2013, LNCS 8142, pp. 385–394, 2013.

Fig. 1. Left: Saliency function (Eq. (6)) computed on the finest scale of the image in the center. Center/Right: 786 BoSP keypoint pairs assumed to be correctly matched by simple two-way nearest-neighbor check of descriptor distances due to subsequent robust epipolar constraint verification. Note the variety of underlying image patterns at which keypoints are found (best viewed when zoomed in).

distinct difference between thousands of corners? Second, is it efficient to compute the detector/descriptor individually or could one share results/optimize them together? We answer both of this questions introducing a joint interest point detection and description algorithm. In a coherent approach it computes the feature statistics in the image, detects discriminative ones, and uses them as descriptor to represent the local environment of each keypoint.

The core of our novel keypoints algorithm is the concept of visual saliency [4]. A salient region sticks out from its local surrounding in some aspect. For example, a yellow buoy on the blue sea is very salient. This property makes our keypoints stably locatable and discriminative by definition. Furthermore, we show that our saliency measure is suitable to sort and select keypoints for high reproducibility. This is especially useful in SLAM approaches, when sparse feature maps are advantageous to become aware of loop closures [15]. While most classic approaches on computational visual attention estimate saliency directly from the feature difference of a center location to its average surround, recently, Klein and Frintrop proposed an alternative that instead uses continuous distributions that are represented by multivariate normals in feature space [6]. Here, we improve on the saliency framework from [6] and build up a coherent approach for salient keypoint detection and description. Figure 1 shows an example for wide baseline stereo matching.

2   Salient Keypoints Detector

From basic feature vectors, that could e.g. consist of intensity, colors, gradients, or them altogether, local maximum-likelihood estimations of (multivariate) normal distributions are performed to describe the textural appearance. With this, local maxima of center-surround contrast are detected, utilizing a sophisticated distance measure between distributions. Calculation of the saliency function whose peaks define locations of our keypoints part-way follows the conspicuity computations in [6]. Finally, positions of keypoints are refined and their orientation is determined by the direction of minimal texture similarity.

2.1 Fast Local Feature Distribution Estimation

Arbitrary attributes of image pixels or their combinations can serve as basic features. Thus, we use the term *pixel* synonymously for a feature vector $\boldsymbol{f} = (f_1, \ldots, f_n)$. Accordingly, an image $I(x, y)$ is a 2d-map of such feature vectors. For example, the framework could be applied to grayscale (1D), gradients (2D), or CIELAB (3D) features.

From the feature image $I(x, y)$, we construct a scale space pyramid $I(x, y; \sigma_t)$. After each smoothing of the image by one octave (doubling σ_t of the smoothing kernel), its spatial resolution is halved. Each octave is subdivided to intermediate scale steps at exponentially regular intervals plus the upper and lower adjacent scales that are needed for scale space extrema detection. Here, one must take care of proper scale space normalization factors when dealing with derivative features. Next, each pixel at each scale of the pyramid is supplemented with all possible two-valued multiplicative feature combinations, becoming the extended, $\frac{n^2+3n}{2}$-dimensional feature vector

$$\boldsymbol{f}_+ = (f_1, \ldots, f_n, \quad f_1^2, \ldots, f_i f_j, \ldots, f_n^2) \quad | \; 1 \leq i \leq j \leq n. \tag{1}$$

By convolution with a weighted integration window in image space, feature vectors are locally averaged, denoted $\overline{\boldsymbol{f}_+}$. This enables fast ML-estimation of normal distributions at each pixel: For some neighborhood $\boldsymbol{f}_1, \ldots, \boldsymbol{f}_N$ and integration weights $w_1, \ldots, w_N$ summing up to 1 their mean in feature dimension j respectively sample covariance between dimensions j and k result in

$$\hat{\mu}_j = \sum_{i=1}^{N} w_i f_{j,i} = \overline{f_j} \quad \text{and} \quad \hat{\Sigma}_{j,k} = \sum_{i=1}^{N} w_i (f_{j,i} - \overline{f_j})(f_{k,i} - \overline{f_k}) = \overline{f_j f_k} - \overline{f_j}\,\overline{f_k}. \tag{2}$$

2.2 Keypoints That Stick Out of Their Surroundings

In order to measure local contrasts of textural appearance, for each pixel and scale we estimate center distributions of features using a narrow Gaussian integration window $g_\bullet$, as well as surround distributions applying a wider integration window $g_\odot$ and removing the center influence. These center ($\bullet$) and wider ($\odot$) statistics can be gathered efficiently applying stepwise Gaussian smoothing, since

$$I_{\odot,+} = g_\odot * I_+ = g_{\odot-\bullet} * \overbrace{g_\bullet * I_+}^{=I_{\bullet,+}}. \tag{3}$$

Further optimizations include separation of the Gaussian filter into horizontal and vertical components, as well as approximations of those by repeated box-filtering. Finally, the surround ($\odot$) statistics are computed as

$$I_{\odot,+} = \frac{1}{1-\alpha} \left(I_{\odot,+} - \alpha\, I_{\bullet,+} \right), \; \text{with } \alpha = \frac{\sigma_\bullet^2}{\sigma_\odot^2} \tag{4}$$

for the purpose of removing the center influence from the wider statistics. This requires only two vector scalings and one subtraction per pixel. Please note

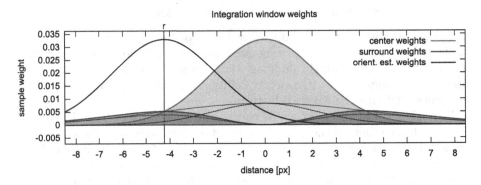

Fig. 2. Center and surround weights of pixel samples dependent on the distance to the analyzed location. Integration scales jointly increase with the pyramid scale of basic features. Curves implied with dots and dashes additionally show the wider surround $g_{\odot}$, the α-rescaled center and their difference before normalization to a sum of 1. r depicts the radius at which the surround influence is highest. Please note that a cross section through the center of the symmetric 2D Gaussians is shown.

that a simple difference of Gaussians filtering without smart rescaling would not suffice, since for distribution estimation, sample integration weights must be positive and sum up to one. Figure 2 visualizes those steps conducted in equation (4).

The Wasserstein distance on Euclidean norm for arbitrary probability measures χ and υ in $\mathbb{R}^n$ is defined as

$$W_2(\chi, \upsilon) = \left[\inf_{\gamma \in \Gamma(\chi, \upsilon)} \int_{\mathbb{R}^n \times \mathbb{R}^n} \|X - Y\|^2 \, \mathrm{d}\gamma(X, Y) \right]^{\frac{1}{2}} \tag{5}$$

with $\Gamma(\chi, \upsilon)$ denoting the set of all their possible couplings. For discrete densities (histograms), it is also known as Earth Mover's distance due to the pictured representation that it measures the amount of "dirt" (probability mass) times the distance it has to be moved to transform a "pile" χ into a second one υ. This integral term was solved algebraically by Dowson and Landau [2] for multivariate normals, resulting in the closed form expression

$$W_2(\mathcal{N}_\bullet, \mathcal{N}_\odot) = \left[\|\mu_\bullet - \mu_\odot\|_2^2 + \mathrm{tr}\left(\Sigma_\bullet\right) + \mathrm{tr}\left(\Sigma_\odot\right) - 2\,\mathrm{tr}\left(\sqrt{\Sigma_\bullet \Sigma_\odot}\right) \right]^{\frac{1}{2}} \tag{6}$$

when applied to measure the contrast between center and surround distributions of basic feature vectors.

After we obtained a pyramid of center-surround contrasts of textural appearances this way, keypoints are selected to be local maxima with respect to their 26-pixel direct neighborhood. Then, positions are refined computing the location between pixels from the maximum of the quadratic Taylor-polynomial in x, y, and scale direction [8]. Same principal curvature criterion as in [8] is applied to filter out keypoint candidates on very elongated ridges in the contrast maps, looking at the ratio of eigenvalues of the Hessian matrix.

2.3 Rotational Invariance via Minimal Similarity

The extracted keypoints are maximally dissimilar with respect to their surroundings. However, we would like to know in which direction the textural appearance changes most in order to assign a stable orientation to each keypoint. The function of weights for the surround integration window is crater-shaped (cf. Fig. 2, red curve). This function attains its maxima at the distance radius

$$r = \sigma_{\bullet} \sqrt{\frac{-2 \ln \alpha}{1 - \alpha}} \tag{7}$$

with α as in Eq. (4). Here, the influence of the surroundings is highest. Thus, we compare distributions integrated at same scale $\sigma_{\bullet}$, but regularly sampled in steps of $10°$ at an offset r around the keypoint against the center distribution (see Fig. 2 and 3, blue against green) using $\mathcal{W}_2$. Next, we smooth these distances with a Gaussian of $\sigma = 12°$ to eliminate noisy and low contrast directions. The main orientation of the keypoint is the direction $\hat{\theta}$ of minimal similarity (maximum $\mathcal{W}_2$-distance), denoted $d_{\hat{\theta}}$. There could occur additional sub-orientations $\theta_1, \ldots, \theta_m$ of only locally maximal distances $d_{\theta_1}, \ldots, d_{\theta_m}$. We store accordingly oriented copies of the keypoint, but with a saliency response (cf. Eq. (6)) appropriately reduced by a factor of $d_{\theta_i}/d_{\hat{\theta}}$. All orientations are refined by Lagrange-interpolation of a parabola through the neighboring samples and estimating the peak direction.

3 Seamless Salient Descriptors

A main difference of our approach to many previous ones is that the detector maximizes the difference in textural appearance on the same basic feature distributions that are reused for the descriptor. As a result, regions around extracted interest points are more likely to produce distinguishable descriptors. Second, the extraction of descriptors comes at almost no additional costs. Furthermore, from the saliency (center-surround contrast) of a keypoint one could draw inferences about detector repeatability as well as descriptor matching performance, in other words one could choose subsets of good keypoints.

3.1 Descriptor Aggregation

Our descriptor is composed of the normal distributions $\mathcal{N}_{\bullet}$ and $\mathcal{N}_{\odot}$ of features integrated at that scale the keypoint was localized, plus optionally some circumjacent distributions of scale $\sigma_{\bullet}$ aligned with the keypoint orientation θ. We suggest using patterns with six or 18 circumjacent distributions, derived from *optimal circle packing* [3], a well known problem in computational geometry. Figure 4 shows this descriptor aggregation-patterns. It would also be possible to extract a pattern similar to DAISY [13] from our pyramid of continuous distributions. However, it is sensible to make use of those distributions optimized for dissimilarity by the detector. All information required for the descriptors had been computed already during the keypoint detection step. There is only an interpolation step left per distribution, since keypoints are located with sub-pixel

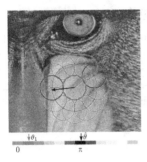

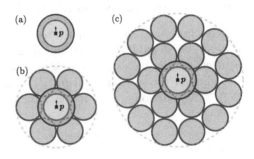

Fig. 3. Keypoint orientation assignment from minimal textural similarity in a distance r (cf. Eq. (7))

Fig. 4. Descriptor aggregation-patterns with center and surround, plus varying number of circumjacent distributions of features around keypoint p. Circles are proportional to σ-integration scales.

and -scale precision. Each keypoint is inside a cube of eight enclosing neighbors with known distributions. Since neighboring pixels represent the texture of almost the same integration area, we assume them to be dependent on each other. Thus, interpolation is performed as a simple, trilinearly weighted average.

Orientation Normalization. In case the basic features are oriented themselves, e.g. gradients, and had been calculated with respect to the image axis, one needs to align the feature normal distributions with respect to the keypoint orientation θ by rotating into the opposite direction: $\boldsymbol{\mu}_\theta = \mathrm{R}_{-\theta}\,\boldsymbol{\mu}$ and $\Sigma_\theta = \mathrm{R}_{-\theta}\,\Sigma\,\mathrm{R}_{-\theta}^{\mathsf{T}}$.

Brightness Normalization. In most applications, a descriptor should be invariant against changes in lighting conditions. If the input feature vector $\boldsymbol{f}$ contains intensity, one has to locally normalize this dimension to achieve invariance. For this, we shift each center ($\mu_{\bullet,\mathrm{Int}}$) and surround ($\mu_{\odot,\mathrm{Int}}$) distribution means in the intensity dimension by the locally averaged intensity $\mu_{\odot,\mathrm{Int}}$. Thus, the intensity dimension of the feature distributions still quantifies the center-surround contrasts, but not the absolute intensity. This normalization does not affect the keypoint response (cf. Eq. (6)).

Taken together, we obtain an expressive, scale, intensity and rotation invariant descriptor χ_p of the textural appearance around the keypoint location at very low additional costs. This representation is very compact, using k circumjacent distributions the dimensionality of this descriptor is only $d = (k+2)\frac{n^2+3n}{2}$. For example the complex pattern in Figure 4.c ($k = 18$) applied to gradient features ($n = 2$) would result in an 100-dimensional descriptor.

3.2 Descriptor Distance Measure

Our descriptor is a combination of several multivariate normal distributions of locally sampled features, hence to compare them we apply the same $\mathcal{W}_2$ distribution distance between the corresponding parts:

$$\mathcal{D}(\chi_a, \chi_b) = \sum_{i=1}^{k+2} \lambda_i \, \mathcal{W}_2 \left(\mathcal{N}_{a,i}, \mathcal{N}_{b,i} \right).$$

(8)

The factor λ_i is Gaussian weighted on the distance in the aggregation pattern between the ith distribution and the keypoint location.

4 Evaluation

The evaluation is twofold and based on the popular keypoints article of Mikolaj-czyk et al. [10]: in a first step, we examine the *repeatability* of our new detector under different photometric variations. In a second step, we evaluate the entire detector/descriptor combination looking at the *nearest neighbor matching score*. We compare results against a number of state-of-the-art keypoint detector/descriptor pairs provided by OpenCV-library[1], namely SIFT [8], SURF [1], FAST+ORB [11,12] and BRISK [7].

The benchmark datasets are publicly available for download[2]. We made use of the *bark*, *bikes*, *boat*, *graf*, *leuven*, *trees*, and *wall* sequences, but not the *ubc*, since the rather extreme JPEG-compression artifacts tested there can usually be avoided in real applications.

4.1 Input Feature Space

While the input images are RGB encoded, at first we transform them into a different color space. The target space combines intensity and pure opponent-colors,

$$\boldsymbol{f} = \begin{pmatrix} \text{Int} \\ \text{Opp}_a \\ \text{Opp}_b \end{pmatrix} = \begin{pmatrix} {}^{R+G+B}/_3 \\ {}^{R-G}/_{R+G+B} \\ {}^{B-0.5(R+G)}/_{R+G+B} \end{pmatrix},$$

(9)

thus only the first dimension needs to get brightness normalized (cf. Sec. 3.1). Furthermore, this input space is psychologically motivated following the opponent-process theory [5], leading to keypoints that are more salient in a human-comprehensible way.

4.2 Detector Repeatability

As in [10], we compute the repeatability of regions as quality measure. The repeatability of keypoints in the common parts of two images, denoted I_j and I_k, is defined as the ratio between the number of correspondences in these common image parts and the smaller of the number of detected regions:

$$\text{repeatability}(I_j, I_k) = \frac{\# \, \text{keypoints in } I_j \text{ with correspondence in } I_k}{\min(\# \, \text{keypoints in } I_j, \# \, \text{keypoints in } I_k)}.$$

---

[1] Version 2.4.4, http://www.opencv.org
[2] http://www.featurespace.org

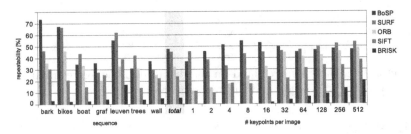

Fig. 5. The average (arithmetic mean of corresponding results) repeatability of each detector, in total, and itemized by sequence as well as number of keypoints per image

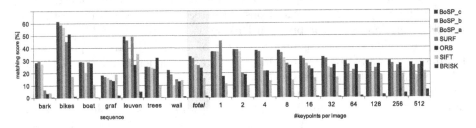

Fig. 6. The average matching score of each detector/descriptor combination, in total, and itemized by sequence as well as number of keypoints per image. The three variants of BoSP correspond to the patterns shown in Fig. 4a, b, and c.

A keypoint in I_j has a corresponding partner in I_k, if its projection based on the known homography between I_j, I_k has a region overlap error of at most 40% to that partner. In our experiments, we fixed the number of keypoints extracted per image by each detector to $2^i, i \in \{0, \ldots, 9\}$. This is done by selecting the s keypoints of highest *response*. In case of BoSP this stands for center-surround appearance contrasts (cf. Eq. (6)), for SIFT it means the DoG-function value, SURF utilizes the approximated determinant of the Hessian matrix, ORB computes the Harris-Score (windowed SSD), while BRISK employs the FAST-score. This procedure has two main advantages against the original evaluation protocol: first, it compensates the effect of keypoint density on repeatability. Second, one can assess how suited the several response functions are for selecting a subset of strong keypoints.

Figure 5 gives an overview on our results. Every sequence consists of 6 images, where each first image is tested against the five others. We run the experiments with 10 different number of keypoints extracted per image, thus evaluated $7 \times 5 \times 10 = 350$ image pairs in total. On average BoSP achieves the best repeatability (47.9%), while SURF is close behind (45.5%). On third place follows ORB (32.2%) ahead of SIFT (23.9%) and BRISK (5.4%). Those excellent average results of BoSP and SURF can be explained when looking at the capability to order and select keypoints by responses: BoSP attains high repeatability already with very few keypoints per image, and SURF is also doing well. The others exhibit a tendency to perform the better the more keypoints are extracted.

Especially BRISK seems incapable to pick keypoints by response. Subsequent to scale space smoothing, our BoSP algorithm further integrates pixel neighborhoods for distribution estimation. Hence BoSP keypoints are larger than others on average and at the same time the number of strong points per image is smaller. This is why repeatability of BoSP cannot gain as much from a fixed high number of keypoints. Analyzed by sequence, BoSP is able to cope with scale changes plus in-plane rotations (*bark*, *boat*), increasing blur (*bikes*, *trees*), decreasing light (*leuven*), as well as viewpoint changes (*graf*, *wall*), often performing best, sometimes second best. Please note that with the *boat* sequence, for BoSP we solely used one-dimensional intensity distributions, since these images are black-and-white.

4.3   Matching Score / System Comparison

A high repeatability is certainly the most important aspect of a keypoint detector. However, in most applications one additionally has to identify the detected among many previously seen keypoints, thus needs a descriptor to compare them. The *matching score* measures performance of the whole system. It considers the interplay of a detector and a descriptor. In this experiments, a keypoint is correctly matched, if its nearest neighbor in descriptor space (most similar keypoint) in the second image further fulfills the criterion of at most 40% region overlap error. The examined descriptors differ in what kind of metric spaces they utilize. Our descriptor works on a vector space of multivariate normal distributions where the metric is given in Equation (8). SIFT is based on histograms of gradient directions, while SURF combines oriented Haar wavelet responses. They both use the Euclidean metric. ORB and BRISK both define a set of binary tests on the local intensity pattern. The metric applied to vectors of binary test results is the Hamming distance.

The average results are shown in Figure 6. Once more, we broke down the overall average matching score into matching scores per sequence and matching scores per number of extracted keypoints per image. Since correct matching introduces an additional requirement, this scores are usually lower than corresponding repeatabilities. We investigated the influence of the aggregation pattern (cf. Fig. 4) on the performance of BoSP. Unsurprisingly, the more complex patterns yield the clearly better results (33.3% resp. 31.9%). Nonetheless, even the rudimentary BoSP pattern of just the center and surround distributions achieves on average a slightly better matching score (26.7%) than SURF (26.1%), ORB (24%), SIFT (15.7%), and BRISK (1.4%). Our descriptor likewise proved to be invariant against all photometric changes occurring in these sequences. When solely using intensity variations (*boat*), the descriptor performed just as well and correctly assigned most of those keypoint pairs detected in both images (repeatability 34.7% vs. matching score 28.8%).

We recorded runtimes of the detector/descriptor pairs on a PC with a core i7-3770 CPU. The methods were applied on a 640×480 pixels image containing much structure. BoSP took 153ms with a 1D input feature, 343ms in 2D mode, and 577ms in case of 3D to compute all keypoints and descriptors. The same task requiered 573ms using SURF and 339ms with SIFT. The algorithms based on binary tests needed only 26ms (ORB) and 21ms (BRISK).

5 Conclusions and Future Work

In this work we introduced a novel keypoint detector/descriptor framework that is tightly build around the basis of fast estimation of local, multivariate normal distributions of input features. While the detector optimizes a center-surround appearance contrast, the descriptor makes use of those same, diverse-looking textures. We have experimentally shown that our detector competes very well against state-of-the-art approaches, and paired with our seamless descriptor even outperforms them. It is especially appropriate to choose a subset of strong keypoints by saliency response. In future work we will investigate advantages of different input features in various settings and tasks. Furthermore, we plan to optimize computational efficiency for higher dimensional input features by means of parallelization as well as analytically.

References

1. Bay, H., Tuytelaars, T., Van Gool, L.: SURF: Speeded up robust features. In: Leonardis, A., Bischof, H., Pinz, A. (eds.) ECCV 2006, Part I. LNCS, vol. 3951, pp. 404–417. Springer, Heidelberg (2006)
2. Dowson, D.C., Landau, B.V.: The Fréchet distance between multivariate normal distributions. J. of Multivariate Analysis 12(3) (March 1982)
3. Fodor, F.: The densest packing of 19 congruent circles in a circle. Geometriae Dedicata 74(2) (1999)
4. Frintrop, S., Rome, E., Christensen, H.I.: Computational visual attention systems and their cognitive foundation: A survey. Trans. on Applied Perception 7(1) (2010)
5. Hurvich, L., Jameson, D.: An opponent-process theory of color vision. Psychological Review 64(6) (1957)
6. Klein, D.A., Frintrop, S.: Salient Pattern Detection using W_2 on Multivariate Normal Distributions. In: Pinz, A., Pock, T., Bischof, H., Leberl, F. (eds.) DAGM and OAGM 2012. LNCS, vol. 7476, pp. 246–255. Springer, Heidelberg (2012)
7. Leutenegger, S., Chli, M., Siegwart, R.Y.: BRISK: Binary robust invariant scalable keypoints. In: Proc. of Int. Conf. on Computer Vision (ICCV) (2011)
8. Lowe, D.G.: Distinctive image features from scale-invariant keypoints. Int'l J. of Computer Vision (IJCV) 60(2), 91–110 (2004)
9. Mikolajczyk, K., Schmid, C.: Scale & affine invariant interest point detectors. Int'l J. of Computer Vision (IJCV) (2004)
10. Mikolajczyk, K., Tuytelaars, T., Schmid, C., Zissermann, A., Matas, J., van Gool, L.: A comparison of affine region detectors. Int'l J. of CV 65(1-2), 43–72 (2005)
11. Rosten, E., Porter, R., Drummond, T.: FASTER and better: A machine learning approach to corner detection. Trans. on PAMI 32, 105–119 (2010)
12. Rublee, E., Rabaud, V., Konolige, K., Bradski, G.: ORB: An efficient alternative to SIFT or SURF. In: Proc. of Int. Conf. on Computer Vision (ICCV) (2011)
13. Tola, E., Lepetit, V., Fua, P.: DAISY: An efficient dense descriptor applied to wide-baseline stereo. Trans. on PAMI 32(5) (May 2010)
14. Tuytelaars, T., Mikolajczyk, K.: Local invariant feature detectors: A survey. Foundations and Trends in Computer Graphics and Vision 3(3), 177–280 (2007)
15. Zhang, H.: BoRF: Loop-closure detection with scale invariant visual features. In: Proc. of Int. Conf. on Robotics and Automation (ICRA) (2011)

Representation Learning for Cloud Classification

David Bernecker, Christian Riess, Vincent Christlein,
Elli Angelopoulou, and Joachim Hornegger

Pattern Recognition Lab, Department of Computer Science,
Friedrich-Alexander-Universität Erlangen-Nürnberg, Erlangen, Germany
{david.bernecker,christian.riess,vincent.christlein,
elli.angelopoulou,joachim.hornegger}@cs.fau.de

Abstract. Proper cloud segmentation can serve as an important precursor to predicting the output of solar power plants. However, due to the high variability of cloud appearance, and the high dynamic range between different sky regions, cloud segmentation is a surprisingly difficult task.

In this paper, we present an approach to cloud segmentation and classification that is based on representation learning. Texture primitives of cloud regions are represented within a restricted Boltzmann Machine. Quantitative results are encouraging. Experimental results yield a relative improvement of the unweighted average (pixelwise) precision on a three-class problem by 11% to 94% in comparison to prior work.

1 Introduction

Solar power plants suffer from sudden, sharp drop-offs in the energy output when a single, thick cloud moves in front of the sun. This forces suppliers to combine each power plant with expensive batteries for backup. If it is possible to reliably predict such power drop-offs, slower backup systems can be set up, which lowers costs considerably. For predicting such sun occlusions, several groups investigate the exploitation of ground-based camera systems that observe the sky, e.g. [2, 4, 10]. Such systems aim to track the overall cloud motion in the sky.

However, to assess the impact of an occluding cloud on the generated power profile, it is very reasonable to setup predictors that incorporate the consistency and exact shape of the cloud. Towards this goal, we present a vision-based method that distinguishes sky, thin clouds and dense clouds.

Cloud segmentation is a challenging problem. Its main difficulty lies in the varying appearance and non-rigidity of clouds, as well as the high brightness close to the sun. Explicit feature design is difficult: structural features face the fact that there is barely any distinct "cloud structure". Using color also yields severe ambiguities due to the color similarity of denser clouds with non-cloud regions [11]: no sunlight passes through dense clouds, and these clouds are only illuminated by the light reflected from the earth's surface. This leads to a bluish-grey color that is hard to distinguish from the color of the sky. The opposite situation, blue sky with the sun clearly visible, is also difficult to segment correctly. Around the sun lens

J. Weickert, M. Hein, and B. Schiele (Eds.): GCPR 2013, LNCS 8142, pp. 395–404, 2013.

Fig. 1. Part of a sky image showing the difficulties when segmenting or classifying clouds. The dark parts of clouds (example region dashed) and sky have a similar color. For scale reference a patch of 40×40 pixels is marked.

flares occur, or a large glowing region is visible. Lastly, contextual information is difficult to incorporate correctly. For less overcast days, one may model dark clouds to be small dark-blue patches surrounded by white. However, with more clouds in the sky, the sky itself will only be visible as small dark-blue patches surrounded by white clouds. We are facing several such ambiguous situations.

We address these challenges by learning a representation of cloud structure from unlabeled data rather than designing features by hand. As training data, we use small image patches extracted from sky-images. The learning of the representation amounts to the training of a Restricted Boltzmann Machine (RBM) or Deep Belief Network (DBN). Since training is unsupervised, a large number of image patches can be used, as manual annotation is not required. To classify the clouds, the learned representation is treated as regular filters, i. e. sky-images are convolved with the learned 'filters' and classification is done pixel by pixel using the result of the convolution combined with the red/blue ratio as features.

The rest of the paper is organized as follows. Section 2 gives an overview over related work in cloud classification and representation learning. The concept of representation learning with Restricted Boltzmann Machines and Deep Belief Networks is introduced in Section 3. For comparison, a classical approach using handcrafted features is briefly illustrated in Section 4. The proposed use of a learned representation for cloud classification is evaluated in Section 5 and some examples of learned representations are shown and discussed in Section 5.1. This is followed by the evaluation of the actual cloud classification in Section 5.3. A short conclusion is given in Section 6.

2   Related Work

Recently, cloud segmentation or classification raised attention by meteorologists and researchers working on the integration of renewable energies into the existing power grid. The baseline method employs fixed thresholding on the ratio of the red and the blue color channel [12]. In a more recent work, Chow *et al.* [4] expand this approach by using a reference model trained on clear blue sky. Their model incorporates the effects of aerosols and airmass, which influence the perceived color of the sky near the horizon. Other approaches, e. g. the one by Richards *et al.* [11], investigate the use of texture as an additional feature. These texture features consist

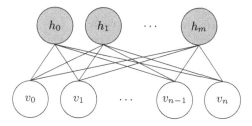

Fig. 2. Restricted Boltzmann Machine: a neural net consisting of n visible and m hidden units. Connections between nodes are undirected.

of combinations of the weighted average and basic spot and edge detectors over regions of the size of 3×3 pixels. In the same work, Richards *et al.* also extended the segmentation of the clouds to a classification into different cloud types. Unfortunately, the work does not provide a quantitative performance evaluation. We compare our results to the baseline method of color thresholding and a combination of color and texture features. Instead of the texture features used by Richards *et al.*, we are using the slightly more sophisticated Gabor filters.

Since Hinton *et al.* [6] presented an efficient approach for learning representations with Deep Belief Networks by pretraining each layer of the network individually, representation learning has become one of the most active research topics in image classification. For example, methods from representation learning have been used to improve the classification rates on several large-scale classification problems like MNIST [8]. For a recent survey article over various methods for representation learning and their applications one may refer to [1]. In our work, we focus on using Restricted Boltzmann Machines and Deep Belief Networks for learning representations. Note that Restricted Boltzmann Machines, which form a building block for DBNs, were originally invented under the name of "Harmonium" by Smolensky *et al.* [13] in 1986.

3   Representation Learning

Representation learning aims to learn a suitable representation from large amounts of unlabeled data. We present two variations of artificial neural networks, the Restricted Boltzmann Machine and the Deep Belief Network, and the fast training algorithm Contrastive Divergence introduced by Hinton *et al.* [6]. These are used to learn a representation of cloud structure. For a more extensive introduction to their principles and training, please refer to Hinton *et al.* [6,7].

3.1   Restricted Boltzmann Machines (RBM)

RBMs are neural networks, where the neurons form a bipartite graph (cf. Fig. 2) and connections between nodes are undirected. The two layers of the net are referred to as visible and hidden, their nodes are denoted as v_i and h_j, respectively.

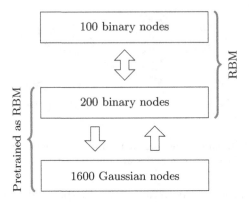

Fig. 3. Schematic of the DBN configuration that is used. The two lower levels are pretrained as an RBM. Afterwards the weights are fixed and the layers are treated as a regular neural net. The top two layers form an RBM with undirected connections.

The number of visible nodes is determined by the size of the input patch, while the number of hidden nodes can be chosen freely. We are choosing binary nodes in the hidden layer, and Gaussian nodes [15] for the visible layer.

The activation probability for the binary hidden nodes is given by:

$$P(h_j = 1|v) = \text{LS}\left(b_j + \sum_{i=1}^{n} w_{i,j} v_i\right) , \tag{1}$$

where $n = |v|$ is the number of visible nodes, LS denotes the logistic sigmoid function, b_j denotes the bias for the visible node h_j and $w_{i,j}$ are the individual weights.

In contrast, Gaussian nodes are linear nodes with an independent Gaussian noise. Thus, for input patches coming from natural images this type of nodes is more suitable. Besides the bias a_i, each node has a standard deviation σ_i associated with it. Instead of learning the standard deviation during training, it is easier to first normalize the training data to have zero mean and unit variance. Given the values of the hidden nodes, the value of a Gaussian visible node is then

$$v_i = a_i + \sum_{j=1}^{m} w_{i,j} h_j + \hat{n}_i \tag{2}$$

where m denotes the number of hidden nodes and $\hat{n}_i$ is Gaussian noise, i. e. $\hat{n} \sim N(0,1)$.

3.2   Contrastive Divergence (CD-k)

Hinton *et al.* [6] introduced *Contrastive Divergence* as an efficient learning algorithm for RBMs and DBNs. The general learning rule for RBMs is

$$\frac{\partial \log p(v)}{\partial w_{ij}} = \langle v_i h_j \rangle_{\text{data}} - \langle v_i h_j \rangle_{\text{model}} , \tag{3}$$

where for $\langle v_i h_j \rangle_{\text{data}}$ the values of the visible nodes are clamped to the current training data, and $\langle v_i h_j \rangle_{\text{model}}$ represents the current learned model of the data. To compute this value, in theory a Markov chain with the current training sample needs to be started and then Gibbs sampling (i. e. sampling the hidden nodes and then reconstructing the visible nodes) is performed until the chain has reached its equilibrium state. As this is not feasible for training, Hinton *et al.* [6] introduced Contrastive Divergence, where $\langle v_i h_j \rangle_{\text{model}}$ is replaced with $\langle v_i h_j \rangle_{\text{recon}}$. The latter is calculated by performing k steps of Gibbs sampling, starting from the current training sample. The calculated updates for the weight matrix are then multiplied by a factor $\epsilon \ll 1$, the learning rate.

We use a slight modification of this algorithm, where the Markov chain is persistent and is only restarted after each full iteration over all training samples. Furthermore, we use momentum to speed up the training and we encourage a sparse activation of the hidden nodes by introducing a penalty term if the average activation probability of a hidden node is above or below the target activation probability (sparsity target) of 10%. A comprehensive description of the variants of the Contrastive Divergence, and practical hints for training RBMs can be found in the work by Hinton [7].

3.3 Deep Belief Networks (DBN)

An extension of RBMs are DBNs, neural networks consisting of more than two layers. While the top two layers have undirected connections and can be interpreted as an RBM, the lower levels function as a regular neural network. Similar to the RBMs, our DBNs consist of a visible layer of Gaussian nodes, while all hidden layers use binary nodes. For training, the greedy, layer-wise strategy is used [6], where starting from the bottom, each pair of layers is seen as an RBM and is trained using Contrastive Divergence. After the training of such an RBM has finished, its weights are set fixed. Next, the activation probabilities for the current hidden nodes for all training samples are calculated and this is used for training the RBMs of the next two layers.

4 Handcrafted Features Using Gabor Filters

For comparison, we briefly describe an algorithm to cloud classification using handcrafted features. We follow the idea of Richards *et al.* [11], but use Gabor filters [5] to describe the cloud texture. With a total of 32 filters, this filter bank spans over different scales (σ_x, σ_y), frequencies (F) and orientations (θ).

$$G(x,y) = N \cdot \exp\left(\frac{x_r^2}{2\sigma_x^2} + \frac{y_r^2}{2\sigma_y^2} \right) \cdot \cos(2\pi F x_r) \tag{4}$$

where $x_r = x \sin\theta + y \cos\theta$ and $y_r = x \cos\theta - y \sin\theta$ denote rotated coordinates of x and y. Fig. 4 shows an example of different Gabor filters, generated by using different orientations and frequencies.

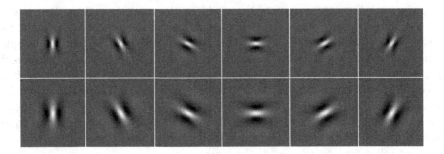

Fig. 4. Gabor Filters in different orientations and frequencies

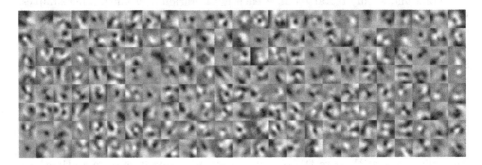

Fig. 5. Representation of cloud structure, obtained by training a RBM with 200 hidden nodes with CD-1

5   Evaluation

For representation learning, the usual pattern recognition pipeline of feature extraction, supervised training and subsequent testing of the classifier has to be slightly extended. First, the RBM or DBN is trained in an unsupervised manner (see Sec. 5.1). Then, the weight matrices of the RBM or DBN are interpreted as filters. The filter output is used as a feature vector within a classical pattern recognition pipeline. The evaluation protocol and error metrics are presented in Section 5.2, and quantitative results in Section 5.3.

5.1   Training of Learned Representations

We are considering two learned representations, RBM and DBN. The representations learned by an RBM with 200 hidden nodes is shown in Fig. 5. Fig. 6 depicts the learned representation using a three layer DBN that extends the RBM and has 100 hidden nodes in the top layer. The figures show that cloud structures are well represented and encourage to use these learned representations as discriminative features for cloud structures.

Fig. 6. Representation of cloud structure, obtained by training a three layer DBN. The RBM weights shown in Fig. 5 were used for the two lower levels, while the uppermost layer with 100 hidden nodes was trained with CD-1.

Training Data. For training the RBM or DBN, we use small patches of sky images of 40×40 pixels (cf. Fig. 1). These are extracted from 320 sky images that were captured over the course of one day. Out of these images, a total of about 160 000 non-overlapping patches are extracted and used for training.

Normalization. Two normalization steps are applied. Since our aim is to learn a representation of cloud structure, the absolute brightness is not important. Hence, we subtract from each patch its mean intensity. As a second step, pixel variation needs to be normalized. This comes from the fact that Gaussian visible nodes are required to model patches of natural images (cf. Section 3.1). To avoid learning the standard deviation of each node during training, each pixel of the patches is normalized over all training samples to have zero mean and unit variance.

RBM and DBN Parameters. The RBM is trained with 200 binary hidden nodes using the Contrastive Divergence algorithm with one step of Gibbs sampling (CD-1). The learning rate ϵ is set to 0.00001, momentum m to 0.9 and the sparsity target to 0.1 with a penalty factor of 1.0. Training consists of 750 epochs, and the weight updates are calculated for mini-batches of size 100.

This RBM is also used as the lowest layer of the three layer DBN. For training the latter, the following parameters are used: $\epsilon = 0.001$, $m = 0.9$, sparsity target 0.1 and sparsity penalty 0.01. Mini-batch size is 100, and the training algorithm runs for 500 epochs.

5.2 Evaluation Protocol and Error Metrics

We treat cloud classification as a three class problem, with the classes *sky*, *white cloud* and *thick cloud*. This classification task exhibits some particular characteristics. A large number of training samples is available when classifying each pixel of the data. However, the distribution of the label occurrences is strongly skewed among the large number of samples. The number of sky pixels is several orders of magnitude higher than the number of thick cloud pixels. For training, it is important that this spread between label occurrences is not too large, since our goal is a classifier that can safely distinguish between the individual classes. Thus, we set the maximum spread between the number of class occurrences for training to two, i. e. the number of samples in one class is at most by a factor two higher than the number of the other classes. For the classes with a higher number of occurrences, samples are randomly drawn from the total number of samples of the class.

Since we are interested in a performance measure that is independent of the imbalances in class occurrence, we are using the unweighted average recall (UAR) and unweighted average precision (UAP). These measures are commonly used in speech recognition [14]. UAR and UAP are simply the unweighted averages of the *recall* and *precision* values of all classes. Precision and recall are defined as:

$$PR = \frac{TP}{TP + FP}, \qquad RE = \frac{TP}{TP + FN}, \qquad (5)$$

where TP denotes the number of true positives, FP the number of false positives and FN the number of false negatives. Precision (PR) relates to the classifier's ability to identify positive results, while recall (RE) shows the probability that a class is identified correctly. Consequently, UAP and UAR are computed as

$$UAP = \frac{1}{K} \sum_{k=1}^{K} PR_k, \qquad UAR = \frac{1}{K} \sum_{k=1}^{K} RE_k, \qquad (6)$$

where K denotes the number of classes, i.e. in our case $K = 3$.

5.3   Results and Discussion

Overall, we compare four different types of features for cloud classification. As a baseline method we are using color information as a single feature. This color information is the ratio of the red and blue channel and widely used in cloud segmentation [4,12]. In this ratio, the distinction between white clouds and blue sky is the greatest. The second feature set is a combination of the color feature with Gabor filters. This set is closely related to the work of Richards *et al.* [11], who also use color and texture features. The third feature set contains the color feature and in addition the filters learned with an RBM that are shown in Fig. 5. The last feature set combines the color feature and filters learned with a three layer DBN.

For the classification a Random Forest[TM] [3] classifier is used. A total of about 500 000 samples are extracted from several sky images and labelled manually. 350 000 samples are used for training the Random Forest. During training cross-validation is used to find suitable parameters. The remaining 150 000 unseen samples are used for the evaluation. Particular care was taken that samples from one image were taken either for training, validation or testing, to avoid overfitting. A different set of sky images that was acquired at a different time and place, is used for learning the representation of cloud structures (i.e. training the RBM). That ensures that the learned representation is not directly fitted to the occurring clouds in the test set.

All classification results are summarized in Table 1. The upper part contains results on the features evaluated individually, the lower part on the combinations of features. We set color features as a baseline [12]. Gabor features, RBM and

Table 1. Overall classification results for the three class cloud classification problem using the unweighted average precision (UAP) and unweighted average recall (UAR) for the test set. The tables show the results using one single feature set (top) and the color ratio feature in combination with Gabor filters and the learned representations (bottom).

Single features	UAP	UAR
color (baseline)	0.85	0.83
Gabor	0.69	0.63
RBM	0.77	0.75
DBN	0.81	0.80

Feature combinations	UAP	UAR
color + Gabor	0.89	0.86
color + RBM	0.92	0.88
color + DBN	0.94	0.90

DBN in the top of Table 1 are computed on grayscale images. It turns out, that the baseline color features yield high UAP and UAR of 85% and 83%, resp., justifying its common use for cloud classification. Gabor filters perform worst, indicating that structural information alone does not solve this task well. RBM and DBN perform slightly better than Gabor. The slight increase between RBM and DBN meets the expectation that increasing the number of layers leads to a more descriptive learned representation.

In Table 1 (bottom) evaluation results are shown on combinations of color and texture (or structure) features. Interestingly, the combination of color and Gabor filters only slightly increases the performance over using solely color. This is in agreement with the texture classification work by Mäenpää et al. [9], who state that color and texture filters are not able to exploit their complementary information to full extend. Overall, the best result is obtained by combining the color feature and the representation learned with a three layer DBN. Both UAP and UAR are improved considerably. The relative improvement over the baseline is 11% and 8%, respectively.

6   Conclusion

For local, short-term predictions of solar power production, researchers investigate ground-based camera systems to monitor cloud movement in the sky. Cloud segmentation and thickness classification can act as important components in such monitoring systems.

We propose features from representation learning for a novel method for cloud segmentation and classification. In contrast to traditional, fixed texture filters, the proposed descriptors for cloud structure are learned from unlabeled sky images. We evaluate these learned features by posing the segmentation of clouds as a three-class classification problem. Quantitative results demonstrate that representation learning outperforms classical texture features like Gabor filters by a large margin. The best performance is achieved using a Deep Belief Network, which yields a relative improvement over the baseline by 11%.

References

1. Bengio, Y., Courville, A., Vincent, P.: Representation Learning: A Review and New Perspectives. ArXiv e-prints, arXiv:1206.5538 (June 2012)
2. Bernecker, D., Riess, C., Angelopoulou, E., Hornegger, J.: Towards Improving Solar Irradiance Forecasts with Methods from Computer Vision. In: Computer Vision in Applications Workshop (2012)
3. Breiman, L.: Random forests. Machine Learning 45, 5–32 (2001)
4. Chow, C.W., Urquhart, B., Lave, M., Dominguez, A., Kleissl, J., Shields, J., Washom, B.: Intra-hour forecasting with a total sky imager at the UC San Diego solar energy testbed. Solar Energy 85(11), 2881–2893 (2011)
5. Daugman, J.: Uncertainty relation for resolution in space, spatial frequency, and orientation optimized by two-dimensional visual cortical filters. Optical Society of America, Journal, A: Optics and Image Science 2(7), 1160–1169 (1985)
6. Hinton, G., Osindero, S., Teh, Y.: A fast learning algorithm for deep belief nets. Neural Computation 1554, 1527–1554 (2006)
7. Hinton, G.: A Practical Guide to Training Restricted Boltzmann Machines. Tech. rep., UTML TR 2010–003 (2010)
8. LeCun, Y., Bottou, L., Bengio, Y., Haffner, P.: Gradient-based learning applied to document recognition. Proceedings of the IEEE 86(11), 2278–2324 (1998)
9. Mäenpää, T., Pietikäinen, M.: Classification with color and texture: jointly or separately? Pattern Recognition 37(8), 1629–1640 (2004)
10. Marquez, R., Coimbra, C.F.: Intra-hour DNI forecasting based on cloud tracking image analysis. Solar Energy 91, 327–336 (2013)
11. Richards, K., Sullivan, G.: Estimation of cloud cover using colour and texture. In: British Machine Vision Conference (1992)
12. Shields, J.E., Karr, M.E., Burden, A.R., Johnson, R.W., Mikuls, V.W., Streeter, J.R., Hodgkiss, W.S.: Research toward Multi-Site Characterization of Sky Obscuration by Clouds, Final Report for Grant N00244-07-1-009, Marine Physical Laboratory, Scripps Institution of Oceanography, University of California San Diego. Tech. rep., Technical Note 274, DTIS (Stinet) File ADA126296 (2009)
13. Smolensky, P.: Information processing in dynamical systems: Foundations of harmony theory. In: Rumelhart, D., McClelland, J. (eds.) Parallel Distributed Processing: Explorations in the Microstructure of Cognition, vol. 1, pp. 194–281. MIT Press, Cambridge (1986)
14. Vinciarelli, A., Burkhardt, F., Son, R.V., Weninger, F., Eyben, F., Bocklet, T., Mohammadi, G., Weiss, B., Telekom, D., Laboratories, A.G.: The INTERSPEECH 2012 Speaker Trait Challenge. In: Proc. Interspeech (2012)
15. Welling, M., Rosen-Zvi, M., Hinton, G.: Exponential family harmoniums with an application to information retrieval. Advances in Neural Information Processing Systems 17, 1481–1488 (2005)

CopyMe3D:
Scanning and Printing Persons in 3D*

Jürgen Sturm[1], Erik Bylow[2], Fredrik Kahl[2], and Daniel Cremers[1]

[1] Computer Vision Group, Technical University of Munich, Germany
[2] Center for Mathematical Sciences, Lund University, Lund, Sweden

Abstract. In this paper, we describe a novel approach to create 3D miniatures of persons using a Kinect sensor and a 3D color printer. To achieve this, we acquire color and depth images while the person is rotating on a swivel chair. We represent the model with a signed distance function which is updated and visualized as the images are captured for immediate feedback. Our approach automatically fills small holes that stem from self-occlusions. To optimize the model for 3D printing, we extract a watertight but hollow shell to minimize the production costs. In extensive experiments, we evaluate the quality of the obtained models as a function of the rotation speed, the non-rigid deformations of a person during recording, the camera pose, and the resulting self-occlusions. Finally, we present a large number of reconstructions and fabricated figures to demonstrate the validity of our approach.

1 Introduction

The advancements in 3D printing technology have led to a significant break-through in rapid prototyping in recent years. Modern 3D printers are able to print colored 3D models at resolutions comparable to 2D paper printers. On the one hand, the creation of a detailed, printable 3D model is a cumbersome process and represents even for a skilled graphical designer a significant amount of effort. On the other hand, the advent of consumer depth sensors such as the Microsoft Kinect has led to novel approaches to 3D camera tracking and reconstruction [5,10,19]. Probably the most prominent approach is the KinectFusion algorithm [10] that demonstrated that dense 3D reconstructions can be acquired in real-time on a GPU.

However, the resulting models are not well suited for 3D printing as they are in general incomplete when acquired with a hand-held sensor, not watertight, unsegmented, and in many other respects not optimized for cost-effective fabrication. Therefore, the combination of both technologies into a general-purpose 3D copy machine is still an open research problem. It is clear that this application bears an enormous economical potential for the future.

In our endeavor towards this goal, we investigate in this paper how an accurate 3D model of a person can be acquired using an off-the-shelf Kinect camera

---

* This work has partially been supported by the DFG under contract number FO 180/17-1 in the Mapping on Demand (MOD) project.

J. Weickert, M. Hein, and B. Schiele (Eds.): GCPR 2013, LNCS 8142, pp. 405–414, 2013.

Fig. 1. We acquire the 3D model of a person sitting on a swivel chair. The acquisition process runs in real-time and displays a live view of the reconstruction model on the screen. Subsequently, the model can be printed in 3D.

and how the resulting model can be reproduced cost-effectively using a 3D color printer. Thus, our current solution corresponds to the 3D version of a classical photo booth. Our approach is based on the KinectFusion algorithm [10] for dense 3D reconstruction that we recently ameliorated for better speed and accuracy [1]. In this paper, we provide a detailed analysis of our approach, including a study of the influence of various parameters on the quality of the resulting models. Furthermore, we describe several extensions that facilitate the creation of a cost-effective, printable 3D model. Finally, we demonstrate the validity of our approach with a large number of fabricated figures.

2   Related Work

To acquire accurate 3D models of human bodies, various sensors and sensor setups have been proposed in the past [18,17]. Early 3D body scanners using multiple cameras in combination with line lasers or moiré patterns started to appear in the late 90s [7,6,20], and have many applications in medical analysis and apparel design. Camera domes consisting of up to hundreds of calibrated cameras can be used for accurate 3D reconstruction [14], but are in general not real-time capable, costly to acquire, and difficult to maintain.

Therefore, we focus in this paper on a setup that only relies on a single, hand-held sensor with which the user scans an otherwise static object. A pioneering approach was described in [13], where depth maps were computed from a combination of a structured light projector and a camera and fused into a single point cloud using ICP. More recent examples include [11,4,15] using monocular and stereo cameras, respectively. The advent of RGB-D cameras such as the Microsoft Kinect sensor further stimulated the development of approaches for live 3D reconstruction. While the first systems generated sparse representations (i.e., point clouds) of the environment [5,3], the seminal KinectFusion approach [10] used a truly dense representation of the environment based on signed distance functions [2]. Since then, several extensions of the original algorithm have appeared such as rolling reconstruction volumes [12,19] and the use of oct-trees [21]. Furthermore, the first commercial scanning solutions such as ReconstructMe, KScan, and Kinect@Home became available.

In contrast to all existing work, we propose in this paper a robust, flexible, and easy-to-use solution to acquire the 3D model of a person and a method to generate closed, watertight models suitable for 3D printing. Our work is based on our recent approach for dense reconstruction [1] that we extend here by the following components: We propose a novel weighting function to fill holes, a method for turn detection, model carving, and the automatic generation of a stand for the figure. We evaluate our approach on an extensive dataset partially acquired in a motion capture studio, and provide several examples of reconstructed and fabricated models.

3   CopyMe3D: Fast Unsupervised 3D Modeling of People

In this section, we explain how we acquire the 3D model of a person and how we prepare the model for 3D printing. Our experimental setup is as follows (see Fig. 1): The person to be scanned is sitting on a swivel chair in front of the Microsoft Kinect sensor. After the scanning software has been started, the person is rotated (by a second person) in front of the sensor. A live view of the colored 3D model is shown during scanning on the monitor to provide live feedback to the user. Scanning automatically terminates when a full turn is detected. Subsequently, a printable 3D model is generated and saved to disk. Typically, scanning takes around 10 seconds (300 frames) while the full process typically consumes less than one minute on a normal PC. In the following, we describe each of the processing steps in more detail.

3.1   Live Dense 3D Reconstruction

In this section, we briefly explain how we track the camera pose and generate the dense 3D model. We kept this section intentionally short and refer the interested reader to [10,1] for more details on signed distance functions, the KinectFusion algorithm, and our recent extensions.

Preliminaries. In each time step, we obtain a color image and a depth image from the Kinect sensor, i.e.,

$$I_{RGB} : \mathbb{R}^2 \to \mathbb{R}^3 \text{ and } I_Z : \mathbb{R}^2 \to \mathbb{R}. \tag{1}$$

We assume that the depth image is already registered on to the color image, so that pixels between both images correspond. Furthermore, we require a signed distance function (SDF), a weight function, and a color function that are defined for each 3D point $\mathbf{p} \in \mathbb{R}^3$ within the reconstruction volume:

$$D : \mathbb{R}^3 \to \mathbb{R}, W : \mathbb{R}^3 \to \mathbb{R}, \text{ and } C : \mathbb{R}^3 \to \mathbb{R}^3. \tag{2}$$

The SDF represents the distance of each point to the closest surface, i.e., $D(\mathbf{p}) = 0$ holds for all points $\mathbf{p}$ lying on surface, $D(\mathbf{p}) < 0$ for free space, and $D(\mathbf{p}) > 0$ for occupied space. In the following, we treat I_{RGB}, I_Z, D, W, and C as continuous functions, but we represent them internally as discrete pixel/voxel grids (of size 640×480 and 256×256×256, respectively). When access to a non-integer value is needed, we apply bi-/tri-linear interpolation between the neighboring values. We assume the pinhole camera model, which defines the relationship between a 3D point $\mathbf{p} = (x, y, z)^\top \in \mathbb{R}^3$ and a 2D pixel $\mathbf{x} = (i, j)^\top \in \mathbb{R}^2$ as follows,

$$(i, j)^\top = \pi(x, y, z) = \left(\frac{f_x x}{z} + c_x, \frac{f_y y}{z} + c_y \right)^\top. \tag{3}$$

Here, f_x, f_y, c_x, c_y refer to the focal length and the optical center of the camera, respectively. In reverse, given the depth $z = I_Z(i, j)$ of a pixel (i, j), we can reconstruct the corresponding 3D point using

$$\rho(i, j, z) = \left(\frac{(i - c_x)z}{f_x}, \frac{(j - c_y)z}{f_y}, z \right)^\top. \tag{4}$$

In each time step, we first estimate the current camera pose $\boldsymbol{\xi}$ given the current depth image I_Z and SDF D, and subsequently integrate the new data into the voxel grids. We represent the current camera pose using twist coordinates, i.e.,

$$\boldsymbol{\xi} = (\omega_1, \omega_2, \omega_3, v_1, v_2, v_3) \in \mathbb{R}^6. \tag{5}$$

These Lie algebra coordinates form a minimal representation and are well suited for numerical optimization. Twist coordinates can be easily converted to a rotation matrix $R \in \mathbb{R}^{3 \times 3}$ and translation vector $\mathbf{t} \in \mathbb{R}^3$ (and vice versa) when needed [9].

Finally, we assume that the noise of the Kinect sensor can be modeled with a Gaussian error function, i.e.,

$$p(z_{\mathrm{obs}} \mid z_{\mathrm{true}}) \propto \exp\left(-(z_{\mathrm{true}} - z_{\mathrm{obs}})^2 / \sigma^2 \right). \tag{6}$$

In principle, the noise of the Kinect (and any disparity-based distance sensor) is quadratically proportional to the distance, i.e., $\sigma \propto z_{\mathrm{true}}^2$. However, as our object of interest is located at a fixed distance to the sensor (typically 1.5m) and its depth variations are relatively small, we can assume σ to be constant over all pixels.

Camera Pose Estimation. Given a new depth image I_Z and our current estimate of the SDF D, our goal is to find the camera pose $\boldsymbol{\xi}$ that best aligns the depth image with the SDF, i.e., each pixel of the depth image should (ideally) map onto the zero crossing in the signed distance function. Due to noise and other inaccuracies, the depth image will of course never perfectly match the SDF (nor will our estimate of the SDF be perfect). Therefore, we seek the camera pose that maximizes the observation likelihood of all pixels in the depth image, i.e.,

$$p(I_Z \mid \boldsymbol{\xi}, D) \propto \prod_{i,j} \exp(-D(R\mathbf{x}_{ij} + \mathbf{t})^2 / \sigma^2), \tag{7}$$

	KinFu	Ours	Ratio
fr1/teddy	0.154m	0.089m	1.73
fr1/desk	0.057m	0.038m	1.50
fr1/desk2	0.420m	0.072m	5.83
fr1/360	0.913m	0.357m	2.56
fr1/room	0.313m	0.187m	1.67
fr1/plant	0.598m	0.050m	11.96
fr3/household	0.064m	0.039m	1.64

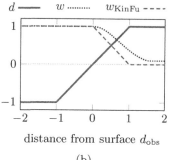

(a)   (b)

Fig. 2. (a) Our approach clearly outperforms KinFu on benchmark datasets in terms of the absolute trajectory error (RMSE). (b) We use a truncated signed distance function and a modified weighting function.

where $R = R(\xi)$ is a short hand for the current camera rotation, $\mathbf{t} = \mathbf{t}(\xi)$ for the camera translation, and $\mathbf{x}_{ij} = \rho(i, j, I_Z(i, j))$ for the reconstructed 3D point to keep our notation uncluttered. Note that a circular motion constraint is not imposed in the estimation process. By taking the negative logarithm, we obtain

$$L(\xi) \propto \sum_{i,j} D(R\mathbf{x}_{ij} + \mathbf{t})^2. \tag{8}$$

To find its minimum, we set the derivative to zero and apply the Gauss-Newton algorithm, i.e., we iteratively linearize $D(R\mathbf{x}_{ij} + \mathbf{t})$ with respect to the camera pose ξ at our current pose estimate and solve the linearized system.

Note that KinectFusion pursues a different (and less) effective approach to camera tracking, as it first extracts a second depth image from the SDF and then aligns the current depth image to the extracted depth image using the iteratively closest point algorithm (ICP). As this requires an intermediate data association step between both point clouds, this is computationally more involved. Furthermore, the projection of the SDF onto a depth image looses important information that cannot be used in the iterations of ICP. To evaluate the performance of both approaches, we recently compared [1] our approach with the free KinFu implementation in PCL [1] on publicly available datasets [16]. The results are presented in Fig. 2a and clearly show that our approach is significantly more accurate.

Updating the SDF. After the current camera pose has been estimated, we update the SDF D, the weights W, and the texture C similar to [2,1]. We transform the global 3D coordinates $\mathbf{p} = (x, y, z)^\top$ of the voxel cell into the local frame of the current camera $\mathbf{p}' = (x', y', z')^\top = R^\top(\mathbf{p} - \mathbf{t})$. Then we compare the depth of this voxel cell z' with the observed depth $I_Z(\pi(x', y', z'))$,

$$d_{\text{obs}} = z' - I_Z(\pi(x', y', z')). \tag{9}$$

---

[1] http://svn.pointclouds.org/pcl/trunk/

As d_{obs} is not the true distance but an approximation, d_{obs} gets increasingly inaccurate the further we are away from the surface. Furthermore, the projective distance is inaccurate when the viewing angle is far from 90° onto the surface as well as in the vicinity of object boundaries and discontinuities. Therefore, we follow the approach of [2] by truncating the distance function at a value of δ and defining a weighting function to express our confidence in this approximation:

$$d(d_{\text{obs}}) = \begin{cases} -\delta & \text{if} \quad d_{\text{obs}} < -\delta \\ d_{\text{obs}} & \text{if} \quad |d_{\text{obs}}| \leq \delta \\ \delta & \text{if} \quad d_{\text{obs}} > \delta \end{cases} , \tag{10}$$

$$w(d_{\text{obs}}) = \begin{cases} 1 & \text{if } d_{\text{obs}} \leq 0 \\ \max(w_{\min}, exp(-(d_{\text{obs}}/\sigma)^2)) & \text{if } d_{\text{obs}} > 0 \end{cases} . \tag{11}$$

Note that KinectFusion uses a linear weighting function w_{KinFu} that yields a weight of zero for $d > \delta$. In contrast, our weighting function w also decreases quickly, but assigns an update weight of at least $w_{\min}$. In this way, small holes that stem from occlusions are automatically filled. Yet, the small weight ensures that the values can be quickly overwritten when better observations becomes available. Experimentally, we determined $\delta = 0.02m$ and $w_{\min} = 0.01$ to work well for our application. A visualization of these functions is given in Fig. 2b. We update each voxel cell with (global) 3D coordinates $(x, y, z)^{\top}$ according to

$$D \leftarrow (WD + wd)/(W + w), \tag{12}$$
$$C \leftarrow (WC + wc)/(W + w), \tag{13}$$
$$W \leftarrow W + w, \tag{14}$$

where $c = I_{RGB}(\pi(x', y', z'))$ is the color from the RGB image.

Both steps (the estimation of the camera pose and updating the voxel grids) can be easily parallelized using CUDA. With our current implementation, the computation time per frame is approximately 27ms on a Nvidia GeForce GTX 560 with 384 cores, and runs thus easily in real-time with 30fps.

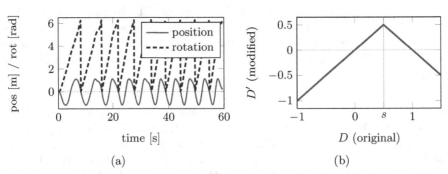

(a)   (b)

Fig. 3. (a) Analysis of our turn detection, 10 turns in a row. (b) Transfer function for the SDF to hollow out the model.

Live View and Turn Detection. With the algorithm described above, we obtain an estimate of the signed distance and color for every cell of the voxel grid. To display this model to the user, we copy the data every two seconds from the GPU to the CPU (which consumes 60ms) and run a threaded CPU implementation of the marching cubes algorithm [8]. The mesh generation takes around between 1000 and 1500ms on a single CPU core. The resulting triangle mesh typically consists of approximately 200.000–500.000 vertices (and faces), that we display together with the estimated camera trajectory to the user using OpenGL (see Fig. 1).

We implemented a simple strategy to detect when a full 360° turn is complete. To achieve this, we summarize the angular motion of the camera, i.e., we compute the motion between two consecutive frames and determine the rotation angle according to [9], i.e.,

$$\alpha_t = \cos^{-1}(\text{trace}(R_{t-1}^\top R_t) - 1). \tag{15}$$

We terminate data acquisition when $\sum_t \alpha_t > 2\pi$. Figure 3a compares the estimated rotation angle in comparison to the (absolute) position of the chair. We use this principle to automatically stop data acquisition after the person has performed a full turn.

3.2 Model Post-processing

While live feedback is important for the user (e.g., to find the right position for the chair), we found that further post-processing is required for 3D printing.

The first problem is that the triangle mesh is unclosed where objects stick out of the reconstruction volume. This is in particular the case at the bottom of the body, for which no triangles are generated. To remedy this problem, we augment the SDF by an additional layer from all sides with $D = -\delta$, which ensures that the triangle mesh is guaranteed to be closed and watertight and thus 3D printable (see Fig. 4a for a profile).

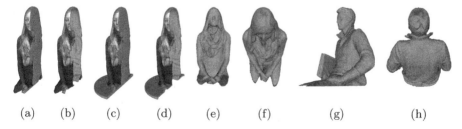

(a)   (b)   (c)   (d)   (e)   (f)   (g)   (h)

Fig. 4. Illustration of various parameters of the model acquisition process. (a) Profile of the solid model, (b) hollow model ($s=0.01$m), (c) automatically added solid stand, (d) hollow version. (e–g) Self-occlusions for a camera at eye height based on the accumulated weights W.

Depending on the body posture, the center of mass will not be above the footprint of the object, and thus the fabricated figure would fall over. To prevent this, we automatically add a small cylindrical stand to the model as shown in Fig. 4c+d. To this end, we first determine the center of mass x_m, y_m (by summing the positions of all voxel cells with $D > 0$) and the radius r of the model. Subsequently, we add a cylindrical disk below the model by updating each cell (x, y, z) of the SDF with $z < z_{base}$ according to

$$D = r - \sqrt{(x - x_m)^2 + (y - y_m)^2}.$$ (16)

Finally, we found that the printing costs prevailingly depend on the amount of the printed material, i.e., the printing costs can be reduced by a factor of five when the model is hollow. To achieve this, we transform the values in the SDF according to

$$D' = \begin{cases} s - D & \text{if } D > s/2 \\ D & \text{otherwise} \end{cases},$$ (17)

so that voxels that are located deeper than s within the object will be mapped to the outside afterwards. This transfer function is visualized in Fig. 3b. However, our estimate of the SDF is only a coarse approximation, so that the above transformation leads to strong artifacts and unconnected components. Therefore, we re-compute the SDF with the correct signed distance values by finding the nearest neighbor from the pre-computed triangulated mesh. To speed up this computation, we insert all vertices into an oct-tree structure and only update voxel cells within the object (i.e., cells with $D > 0$). Example profiles of the resulting models are given in Fig. 4b+d.

Fig. 5. More examples of 3D models acquired with our approach and the resulting printed figures

4 Results

Figures 1 and 5 show the acquired 3D models and printed figures of several persons. To obtain a high quality model, we observed that a raw beginner needs around two to three trials to reduce body motions and articulations during model acquisition. For example, a small head motion during recording can already lead to significant inaccuracies in the reconstructed model, such as a double nose.

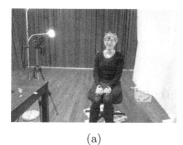

condition	rot. time [s]	deformation [mm]
external rotation	7.0 ($\pm$ 0.8)	22.3 ($\pm$ 21.7)
external, fast	2.7 ($\pm$ 0.3)	15.8 ($\pm$ 4.8)
self rotation	6.2 ($\pm$ 0.4)	46.2 ($\pm$ 15.3)
self, fast	2.6 ($\pm$ 0.8)	60.8 ($\pm$ 28.2)
mannequin	7.8 ($\pm$ 1.7)	8.9 ($\pm$ 4.8)
mannequin, fast	4.8 ($\pm$ 1.7)	11.4 ($\pm$ 1.3)

(a)   (b)

Fig. 6. Evaluation of non-rigidity due to body motions during model acquisition in a motion capture studio (see text). (a) Experimental setup. (b) Results.

To better understand the source and magnitude of body motions during recording, we tracked the positions of 15 distinct visual markers in a motion capture studio (see Fig. 6a). We tested four different conditions, i.e., external vs. self-propelled rotation, slow vs. fast rotation speed, and real persons vs. a shop-window mannequin. We averaged the results over five different persons with ten trials each. The results are given in Fig. 6b. We obtained the best results (least body motions) when the swivel chair was rotated quickly (3s) by a second person.

Furthermore, we analyzed the amount and locations of self-occlusions as a function of the camera configuration. We tried three different camera heights (at chest height, at eye height, above head) and inspected the resulting models. While all camera positions inevitably lead to some self-occlusions, we found that positioning the camera at eye height leads to the visually most pleasing result (see Fig. 4e–h for a visualization of the resulting self-occlusions).

Lastly, we evaluated how far we can lower the frame rate of the Kinect sensor before our reconstruction algorithm fails. Here, we found that our algorithm typically diverges for frame rates below 6 Hz for the slow and 15 Hz for the fast rotation speed. It should be noted that our algorithm never failed over ten trials on all subjects when operated at the full frame rate (30 Hz), neither for the slow, nor for the fast rotation speed. Therefore, we conclude that our approach is highly robust and still bears significant potential for further reduction of the computational requirements.

5 Conclusion

In this paper, we presented a novel approach to scan a person in 3D and reproduce the model using a color 3D printer. Our contributions on the scanning side include an efficient solution to camera tracking on SDFs, an improved weighting function that automatically closes holes, and a method for 3D texture estimation. To prepare the model for 3D printing, we described a technique to generate a closed, watertight model, to automatically add a stand, and to make it hollow. We evaluated the robustness of our algorithm with respect to the frame rate and rotation speed, and the severity of self-occlusions as a function of the camera pose. We presented a large number of 3D models from different persons and the corresponding printed figures. With this work, we hope to contribute to the development of a general, low-cost 3D copy machine.

References

1. Bylow, E., Sturm, J., Kerl, C., Kahl, F., Cremers, D.: Real-time camera tracking and 3D reconstruction using signed distance functions. In: RSS (2013)
2. Curless, B., Levoy, M.: A volumetric method for building complex models from range images. In: SIGGRAPH (1996)
3. Engelhard, N., Endres, F., Hess, J., Sturm, J., Burgard, W.: Real-time 3D visual SLAM with a hand-held camera. In: RGB-D Workshop at ERF (2011)
4. Fuhrmann, S., Goesele, M.: Fusion of depth maps with multiple scales. ACM Trans. Graph. 30(6), 148 (2011)
5. Henry, P., Krainin, M., Herbst, E., Ren, X., Fox, D.: RGB-D mapping: Using depth cameras for dense 3D modeling of indoor environments. In: ISER (2010)
6. Horiguchi, C.: BL (body line) scanner: The development of a new 3D measurement and reconstruction system. Photogrammetry and Remote Sensing 32 (1998)
7. Jones, R., Brooke-Wavell, K., West, G.: Format for human body modelling from 3D body scanning. International Journal on Clothing Science Technology (1995)
8. Lorensen, W.E., Cline, H.E.: Marching cubes: A high resolution 3D surface construction algorithm. Computer Graphics 21(4), 163–169 (1987)
9. Ma, Y., Soatto, S., Kosecka, J., Sastry, S.: An Invitation to 3D Vision: From Images to Geometric Models. Springer (2003)
10. Newcombe, R., Izadi, S., Hilliges, O., Molyneaux, D., Kim, D., Davison, A., Kohli, P., Shotton, J., Hodges, S., Fitzgibbon, A.: KinectFusion: Real-time dense surface mapping and tracking. In: ISMAR (2011)
11. Newcombe, R., Lovegrove, S., Davison, A.: DTAM: Dense tracking and mapping in real-time. In: ICCV (2011)
12. Roth, H., Vona, M.: Moving volume KinectFusion. In: BMVC (2012)
13. Rusinkiewicz, S., Hall-Holt, O., Levoy, M.: Real-time 3D model acquisition. In: SIGGRAPH (2002)
14. Seitz, S., Curless, B., Diebel, J., Scharstein, D., Szeliski, R.: A comparison and evaluation of multi-view stereo reconstruction algorithms. In: CVPR (2006)
15. Strobl, K., Mair, E., Bodenmüller, T., Kielhöfer, S., Sepp, W., Suppa, M., Burschka, D., Hirzinger, G.: The self-referenced DLR 3D-modeler. In: IROS (2009)
16. Sturm, J., Engelhard, N., Endres, F., Burgard, W., Cremers, D.: A benchmark for the evaluation of RGB-D SLAM systems. In: IROS (2012)
17. Weiss, A., Hirshberg, D., Black, M.: Home 3D body scans from noisy image and range data. In: ICCV (2011)
18. Werghi, N.: Segmentation and modelling of full human body shape from 3D scan data: A survey. In: VISAPP (2006)
19. Whelan, T., McDonald, J., Johannsson, H., Kaess, M., Leonard, J.: Robust tracking for dense RGB-D mapping with Kintinuous. In: ICRA (2013)
20. Winkelbach, S., Molkenstruck, S., Wahl, F.M.: Low-cost laser range scanner and fast surface registration approach. In: Franke, K., Müller, K.-R., Nickolay, B., Schäfer, R. (eds.) DAGM 2006. LNCS, vol. 4174, pp. 718–728. Springer, Heidelberg (2006)
21. Zeng, M., Zhao, F., Zheng, J., Liu, X.: Octree-based fusion for realtime 3D reconstruction. Graphical Models 75 (2012)

Monocular Pose Capture with a Depth Camera Using a Sums-of-Gaussians Body Model

Daniyar Kurmankhojayev, Nils Hasler, and Christian Theobalt

MPI Informatik

Abstract. We present a new markerless generative approach for Human Motion Tracking using a single depth camera. It is based on a Sums of Spatial Gaussians (SoGs) representation for modeling the scene. In contrast to existing systems our approach does not require a multi-view camera setup, exemplar database or training data. The proposed system is accurate, fast and capable of tracking complex motions including 360° turns and self-occlusion of limited duration. The motivation behind our approach is that representing the depth data and a given a priori human model by a SoGs, we can construct an efficient continuously differentiable similarity measure and estimate an optimal pose for each input frame using a local optimization algorithm (Modified Gradient Ascent Linear Search, MGALS).

1 Introduction

Human motion capture has a wide range of applications: from smart surveillance to animation. Various methods have been presented, among which marker-based systems are generally accurate and are widely commercially available. However, in addition to the high investment, they require a long markup process and a time-consuming post production phase.

As a consequence, marker-less camera-based motion capture systems have been researched intensively in the last decade [7].

The general availability of depth cameras has allowed researchers to decrease the number of cameras to one because, with these depth and scale information can be inferred from a single image, reducing pose ambiguities in the scene.

Here, we propose a new marker-less monocular Human Motion Tracking framework, which only requires a static depth camera, a static background. It is based on a SoG scene representation, which was presented for multi-view optical tracking before. Both the scene representation and the generative pose optimization scheme were adapted to handle depth images. In contrast to the methods in [1,4,12], our method requires neither a training dataset nor a pose database. Additionally, unlike the method in [13] it is invariant to texture variations and lighting conditions. Our method has a decent accuracy (average RMSE is 40 mm) and fast (2-10 FPS) for most types of motions and unlike the approaches in [1,4], it can handle 360° rotations and body poses with larger self-occlusions if they are of limited duration.

J. Weickert, M. Hein, and B. Schiele (Eds.): GCPR 2013, LNCS 8142, pp. 415–424, 2013.

The rest of the paper is structured as follows: first, related work is discussed in Section 2; then, the proposed solution is elaborated on in Section 3; after that, the performance of the framework is analyzed in Section 4; and finally, some conclusions and future work are presented in Section 5.

2   Related Work

The surveys [7,8,11] provide a thorough overview of the mature field. We now focus on monocular and selected multi-view methods inspiring our work. They can be classified in three main classes: model-free (discriminative) [12,10,15,5,14], model-based (generative) [2,6,9], and hybrid approaches [1,4].

Based on learning, a discriminative method in [10] detects body parts and their orientations. Shotton et al. [12] train randomized decision forest classifiers for pixel-wise labeling of body parts and predicting 3D positions of body joints from a single depth image. Further improvents are achieved by [5,14], where [5] increases the accuracy by detecting some occluded joints in non-frontal poses and [14] finds correspondences between body parts and a pose optimizing with respect to the pose and size parameters. However, in order to achieve a good level of accuracy the methods require an enormous amount of training data and computational resources. Additionally, the methods fail to find true poses of body parts that are invisible in the camera.

Generative approaches use an a priori model, which usually consists of a model of shape and a kinematic structure. They propose to fit the model to the depth data or a combination of depth and image features [2,6,9]. The generative method in [3] extends these methods with an ICP algorithm for a better fit.

Finally, there are hybrid approaches that combine generative and discriminative approaches, "correcting local optimization by discriminative component" [1]. [4] reconstructs human pose of an actor from depth image using local optimization with body part detection. The method in [1] outperforms the latter method in terms of accuracy and efficiency exploiting pre-recorded pose database and modified Dijkstra's algorithm for depth features selection. However, both methods fail when 360° rotations occur. Additionally, the models by [1,4] approximate the shape of the actor by meshes, which provides fine scale details of the actor. This makes working with the model computationally expensive, but the results are accurate. Nonetheless, for large scale motion tracking this is redundant.

As in [13], we represent the image data and human body by a SoGs, but using a monocular depth stream instead of a multi-view stream of color images. The reduction of the number of the cameras introduces self-occlusion problems, which is alleviated by the properties of the depth data. That allows us to efficiently track motions and overcome the problem of varying lighting conditions and similar textures in foreground and background. In contrast to the methods in [1,4] our approach does not require a training dataset or a shape database, and it is capable of handling 360° rotations.

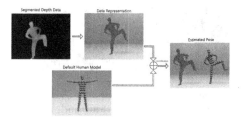

Fig. 1. Pipeline of the method: Initially a human model and a segmented depth image are given. The human model consists of a skeleton and a SoGs body model. From the image a SoGs image model is extracted by means of a quad tree algorithm. Then, the local optimization is applied on the both models, which gives a vector of parameters for the skeleton. Frames are optimized in a streaming fashion.

3 Motion Tracking with a Depth Camera

The current system is inspired by work presented by Stoll et al. [13]. We also model the shape of the actor by a SoG but since we only use a depth camera (e.g. Kinect or time of flight camera) storing a color for each Gaussian is unnecessary. Like Stoll et al. we do not address the problem of constructing a human model and its fitting to the tracked person. We assume a generic template human model is given. The model has a kinematic structure and Sum of Spatial Gaussians (SoGs) body model (Fig. 3). Similar to [13] the observed depth data is also converted into a SoGs representation as explained in Section 3.1. Further, in order to estimate the pose of the model a new efficient similarity measure is exploited (cf. Sec. 3.3). Additionally, we impose joint limit, self-collision, and silhouette constraints, which partially solve the problem of self-occlusion.

In the experimental part (Section 4) we provide a thorough quantitative and qualitative evaluation of the tracking performance as well as introduced parameters and their range of feasible values.

3.1 Data Acquisition and Representation

In the experiments the Kinect depth sensor is used. From the sensor we obtain a set of raw 2.5D depth images, which we can segment and convert into metric 3D point clouds. This can be done by approximating the real camera with the pinhole camera model using device specific camera calibration data.

Image Data Representation. Since working with all pixels of each frame is costly, we follow Stoll et al. and represent each depth image as a sum of spatial 3D Gaussians (SoG). The main advantage of this representation is that it will allow us to compute both the overlap and the corresponding derivative between depth image Gaussians and model Gaussians analytically and efficiently. The pipeline of the overall image data conversion procedure is shown in Figure 2.

Fig. 2. Image representation: each raw depth image is, first, segmented, then, divided onto a set of clusters using quad-tree algorithm; and, after that, given the camera intrinsic parameters a 3D Gaussian is assigned for each element of the set

First, each raw depth image is extended to a square and then segmented into foreground and background using the Kinect SDK. Next, the foreground region is segmented into regions of homogeneous depth using a quad tree clustering. The result of the clustering is the image data representation with equally sized square regions of homogeneous depth. After that, an isotropic Gaussian is fitted to each region: the center of the square becomes the mean value of the Gaussian, and the half-length of a side of the square becomes its standard deviation.

In order to control speed and accuracy of the system several parameters can be tweaked: depth deviation coefficient and scale level of the quad-tree, from which image gaussians are taken. The depth deviation coefficient helps to get rid of noise and boundary gaussians whereas scale level of the quad-tree implicitly controls the number of blobs.

Finally the set of filtered Gaussians is transformed into 3D space, given the camera intrinsic parameters and depth information. This gives an image model.

3.2   Human Model

The quality of the generated results depends on how accurately the human model represents the actual subject. We use an a priori model, which contains a skeleton and a SoGs attached to it (Figure 3). The shape of the model is scaled to the person in a preprocessing step, where the scale is defined by measuring the height of the subject in the first frame.

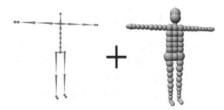

Fig. 3. The human model consists of a kinematic structure (left) and a Sum of 3D Spatial Gaussians (SoG) shape model [13]

The skeleton has a set of 61 joints with 43 DoFs. Each joint is defined by an offset to its parent joint and a rotation represented in an axis-angle form. We attach 63 Gaussians (proxies) to the set of joints, such that each proxy has a single parent joint [13].

3.3   Optimization and Objective Function

The objective function (1) consists of several parts: a similarity measure, silhouette constraints, self-collision constraints, and joint limit constraints. In order to balance the influence of these terms we have to choose the α values appropriately.

$$\mathcal{E}(\Theta) = \alpha_{sim}E_{sim} + \alpha_{silh}E_{silh} - \alpha_{selfcoll}E_{selfcoll} - \alpha_{lim}E_{lim} \tag{1}$$

where Θ is a vector of pose parameters.

Similarity Measure. Gaussians are continuous differentiable functions with infinite support, which allow analytical derivative computation. Based on the SoG model an efficient and robust similarity measure function can be defined.

$$E_{sim}(K_I, K_m) = \sum_{i \in K_I} min\left(\left(\sum_{j \in K_m} E_{ij}\right), \omega_{sim}E_{ii}\right) \tag{2}$$

where K_I is the image SoG model, K_m is the human SoG model, E_{ii} is the maximum energy of image blob i, ω_{sim} is a multiplicative constant (≥ 1), which increases the "relevance" of a Gaussian, and E_{ij} is the energy of the ith image blob and the jth proxy overlap, given by:

$$E_{ij} = \int_{R_3} B_i(x)B_j(x)dx = \left(2\pi \frac{\sigma_i^2\sigma_j^2}{\sigma_i^2 + \sigma_j^2}\right)^{\frac{3}{2}} exp\left(-\frac{\|\mu_i + d - \mu_j\|^2}{2(\sigma_i^2 + \sigma_j^2)}\right) \tag{3}$$

where μ_i and μ_j are the centers of Gaussians i and j (B_i and B_j), σ_i and σ_j are respective standard deviations, $d = (0, 0, \sigma_j - \sigma_i)^T$ is a shift in Z direction (depth in the input data) to make the proxies tangential to the observed surface.

Intuitively, the term says that if the centers of the Gaussians are close to each other then the resulting energy is large, otherwise it tends to zero with growing distance between the centers of the Gaussians. Therefore, E_{sim} tries to maximize the overlap regions of the two SoGs.

Each model proxy is "attracted" by all depth blobs, which can cause an "over-saturation" effect – all proxies are placed on top of each other. In order to prevent the over-saturation we clamp the energy, which a single image blob can contribute to the overall energy. It is clamped to the energy of the depth image blob overlap with itself times a multiplicative constant, which controls the amount of energy to contribute. When over-saturation occurs the corresponding image blob should not further affect the pose of the human model.

Silhouette Constraints. The second term of (1) is a silhouette constraint (4). It makes our objective functional symmetric (or two-sided). In spirit the term is close to E_{sim} (2). While the previous term makes sure that all image blobs are covered by proxies, the current one enforces that all proxies are covered by image blobs, which implicitly restricts the human model to lie inside the silhouette. However, instead of working in 3D it considers only a 2D projection of the data. Here the ω_{silh} has a similar function as ω_{sim}, controlling the amount of energy to be contributed.

$$E_{silh} = \sum_{i \in K_m} min\left(\sum_{j \in K_I} \left(\frac{2\pi\sigma_i^2\sigma_j^2}{\sigma_i^2 + \sigma_j^2} \right) exp\left(-\frac{\|\mu_i - \mu_j\|^2}{2(\sigma_i^2 + \sigma_j^2)} \right), \omega_{silh}\pi\sigma_i^2 \right) \quad (4)$$

Self-collision Constraints. $E_{selfcoll}$ penalizes intersection of body parts.

$$E_{selfcoll} = \sum_{i \in K_m} \sum_{j \in K_m, i \neq j} \omega_{ij} \left(\frac{2\pi\sigma_i^2\sigma_j^2}{\sigma_i^2 + \sigma_j^2} \right)^{\frac{3}{2}} exp\left(-\frac{\|\mu_i - \mu_j\|^2}{2(\sigma_i^2 + \sigma_j^2)} \right) \quad (5)$$

We use an adaptive weighting of proxies' intersection:

$$\omega_{ij} = \begin{cases} 0, & \text{if } \|\mu_i - \mu_j\|^2 - (\sigma_i^2 + \sigma_j^2) > 0 \\ 1, & \text{if } \|\mu_i - \mu_j\|^2 - (\sigma_i^2 + \sigma_j^2) \leq 0 \end{cases} \quad (6)$$

When the distance between proxy B_i and B_j is smaller than the sum of their standard deviations the weight is set to 1, otherwise to 0.

Joint Limit Constraints. The last term represents joint limit constraints (7), where $\Lambda = M\Theta$ is a linear mapping between parameters Θ and joint angles Λ. The matrix M is a $61 \times n_{DoF}$ matrix, which consists of influence weights of parameters on the joint angles. Here 61 is the number of joints. See [13] for more details.

$$E_{lim}(\Lambda) = \begin{cases} 0, & \text{if } l_l^{(l)} \leq \Lambda^{(l)} \leq l_h^{(l)} \\ \|l_l^{(l)} - \Lambda^{(l)}\|^2, & \text{if } \Lambda^{(l)} < l_l^{(l)} \\ \|\Lambda^{(l)} - l_h^{(l)}\|^2, & \text{if } \Lambda^{(l)} > l_h^{(l)} \end{cases} \quad (7)$$

The term keeps the pose of the model in the physiologically possible range for a real human. It is zero if the values of joint angles lie in the range of possible values, otherwise it is assigned a non-zero value.

Despite the high non-convexity of the objective function, we found that a local optimization strategy leads to good results and is significantly more efficient than global optimization. The probability of converging to non-optimal configurations is reduced by using a tracking approach. The temporal information is included in the prediction of the pose by linear extrapolation of the poses of previous time steps.

The prediction is used to initialize the numerical Modified Gradient Ascent Linear Search (MGALS) optimizer [13].

$$\Theta_{i+1}^t = \Theta_i^{t+1} + \nabla\mathcal{E}(\Theta_i^t) \circ \sigma_i \quad (8)$$

where $\nabla\mathcal{E}(\Theta_i^t)$ is a gradient of the objective function, $\circ$ is the component-wise Hadamard product of two vectors. MGALS uses conditioning vector σ_i, which prevents "zig-zaging between opposing walls of narrow landscape valleys of the energy function" [13]. It is updated after every iteration. See [13] for more details.

Fig. 4. Tracking results of the proposed method (red is a human model, greens are image models of different frames)

4   Experiments

The system's performance was tested on 7 sequences (200 frames long, sequences 2 and 4 show 360° rotations and occlusions) of different complexity, where the motions varied from simple fronto-parallel to 3D rotational. The resolution of the frames was set to 320×240. Figure 4 shows pose estimation results of our algorithm. The video in the supplementary material shows that our algorithm captures a variety of poses faithfully including poses with major occlusions of limited duration, which are very challenging for monocular methods.

Quantitative Evaluation. In order to estimate an error, which is independent of the optimization strategy, the two-sided Root-Mean-Squared-Error (RMSE) was adopted.

$$\xi_{avg} = \frac{1}{2T} \sum_{t=1}^{T} \left(\sqrt{\frac{\sum_{i=1}^{M^{(t)}} \|p_i^{(t)} - NN(K_I^{(t)})\|^2}{M^{(t)}}} + \sqrt{\frac{\sum_{i=1}^{I_i^{(t)}} \|q_i^{(t)} - NN(K_m^{(t)})\|^2}{I_i^{(t)}}} \right)$$
(9)

where T represents the number of frames, $p_i^{(t)}$ is a pixel of the human model $K_m^{(t)}$, and $M^{(t)}$ is the number of pixels of the human model. $q_i^{(t)}$ is a pixel of the depth image model $K_I^{(t)}$, $I^{(t)}$ is the total number of non-zero pixels of the segmented depth image, and $NN(.)$ is a nearest neighbor operator.

For each frame of a test sequence the mean distance between the points of the human model point cloud and their nearest neighbors from the depth image point cloud was computed (9). In order to make the RMSE function symmetric the same was done for all points of the image point cloud.

Constraint Weighting Parameters. In order to find the best combinations of constraint weighting parameters α_{sim}, α_{silh}, $\alpha_{selfcoll}$, and α_{lim} an exhaustive greedy search strategy was used.

The experiments showed that changing α_{sim} between values from 0.5×10^{-8} to 2.0×10^{-8} did not change the error much and the values larger than 2.0×10^{-8}

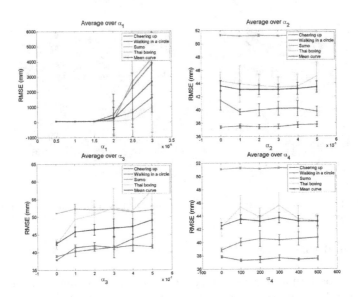

Fig. 5. Weighting parameters optimization: first, the range of feasible parameter values was identified, then, exhaustive greedy search was used to find a set of optimal values minimizing the error and the computational time by sequentially fixing one of the parameters at a time and averaging over all the others

increased it, because the incremental step size of the MGALS became too large placing the human model far away from the observed data. The silhouette term did not have a big impact on the error for the most part of the test sequences due to the nearly planar motions with minor rotation around the vertical axis $(<|\frac{\pi}{2}|)$. However, for the test sequences with a full turn (Fig. 4 bottom) it was found to be essential. None of the test sequences required the self-collision term and the joint limit term penalized physiologically impossible poses (back bending of elbows and knees) pushing the model to turn instead.

Therefore, we set the weights: $\alpha_{sim} = 1.5 \times 10^{-8}$, $\alpha_{silh} = 1 \times 10^{-5}$, $\alpha_{selfcoll} = 0 \times 10^{-7}$, and $\alpha_{lim} = 4 \times 10^{2}$.

Clustering Parameters. In addition to the evaluation function the generation of the image SoG model has, as described above, two parameters. Figure 6 visualizes the result of varying the deviation parameter d. It is easy to see that small values provided a too sparse image representation and large values result in noisy images.

The result of optimizing the second parameter is given in Table 1. The number of Gaussians varied from level to level by a factor of three. Consequently, the computational time also increased threefold.

Moreover, the difference in RMSE between the first and the second levels was relatively small (Table 2) but the difference in computational time is considerable. Optimal results were obtained when the quad-tree level was set to 2 and the deviation coefficient to 1000.

Fig. 6. Deviation coefficient: (left) $d = 100$; (middle) $d = 1000$; (right) $d = 10000$

Table 1. Influence of the quad tree level on computational time (s)

Level	Cheering up	Walking in a circle	Sumo	Thai boxing	# blobs
1	1.611915	1.133110	1.613120	2.786240	1700
2	0.292265	0.266060	0.327990	0.558560	400
3	0.078855	0.050700	0.065990	0.148435	156

Table 2. Influence of the quad tree level on RMSE (mm)

Level	Cheering up	Walking in a circle	Sumo	Thai boxing	# blobs
1	38.061848	38.606209	43.218719	45.428612	1700
2	38.774029	39.333969	43.279144	47.530163	400
3	51.341396	58.298346	55.391341	64.848015	156

Multiplicative Constants. The objective function has two terms, which required over-saturation control, namely the similarity measure and the silhouette constraints. By setting the ω_{sim} and ω_{silh} for these terms we can increase the influence of each image Gaussian on the overall energy without increasing the step size of the numerical optimization. It allowed to overcome the problem of sparse representation of the limbs and small size of the Gaussians. For almost all test sequences the most stable values for both constants varied from 1 to 3 – larger values "folded" the human model (put the proxies on top of each other). We used 2 and 2.5 respectively for all sequences.

Model Scaling. We also tested the influence of the scaling of the default model on the tracking results ("Cheering up" sequence, the other parameters were set as it was stated before). First, we intentionally decreased the scale of the default model by 10% and then increased it by the same amount. The first experiment took 0.59443 seconds per a frame and gave 43.6803 mm confidence measure. Visually the motion was tracked correctly, except the motion of ankles and wrists. The second experiment took 0.18585 seconds per frame and gave 45.8229 mm confidence measure. Inaccurate scaling caused head and ankle forward bending.

Therefore, the performance of the system highly depends on the accurate scaling estimation, which implicitly requires accurate depth image segmentation: because without background subtraction objects of the room are interpreted as part of depth image model and used for scale estimation.

Limitations. The system fails to track people wearing loose clothes because the shape model models the body's geometry and does not handle occlusions.

5   Conclusions

We have introduced a human motion tracking approach based on the method in [13]. Our main contribution is that the system setup is tremendously simplified with little effect on accuracy and speed of the tracking process. The system is capable of tracking fast motions, 360° turns and handles self-occlusion at approximately 2–10 frames per second. Moreover, the proposed approach can be easily extended further by using a multi-view depth camera setup, which further reduces the problem of occlusions, or by using a combination of depth and color cameras.Additionally, the system can be accelerated by moving the computations onto the GPU.

References

1. Baak, A.: Müller, M., Bharaj, G., Seidel, H.P., Theobalt, C.: A data-driven approach for real-time full body pose reconstruction from a depth camera. In: Proc. ICCV (2011)
2. Bleiweiss, A., Kutliroff, E., Eilat, G.: Markerless motion capture using a single depth sensor. In: SIGGRAPH ASIA, Sketches (2009)
3. Ganapathi, V., Plagemann, C., Koller, D., Thrun, S.: Real-time human pose tracking from range data. In: Fitzgibbon, A., Lazebnik, S., Perona, P., Sato, Y., Schmid, C. (eds.) ECCV 2012, Part VI. LNCS, vol. 7577, pp. 738–751. Springer, Heidelberg (2012)
4. Ganapathi, V., Plagemann, C., Koller, D., Thrun, S.: Real time motion capture using a single time-of-light camera. In: Proc. CVPR (2010)
5. Girshick, R., Shotton, J., P.K., Criminisi, A., Fitzgibbon, A.: Efficient regression of general-activity human poses from depth images. In ICCV pp. 415–422 (2011)
6. Knoop, S., Vacek, S., Dillmann, R.: Fusion of 2d and 3d sensor data for articulated body tracking. Robotics and Autonomous Systems 57(3), 321–329 (2009)
7. Moeslund, T., Granum, E.: A survey of computer vision-based human motion capture. Computer Vision and Image Understanding 81(3), 231–268 (2001)
8. Moeslund, T., Hilton, A.: Krüger, V.: A survey of advances in human motion capture and analysis. Computer Vision and Image Understanding 104(2) (2006)
9. Pekelny, Y., Gotsman, C.: Articulated object reconstruction and markerless motion capture from depth video. CGF 27(2), 399–408 (2008)
10. Plagemann, C., Ganapathi, V., Koller, D., Thrun, S.: Real-time identification and localization of body parts from depth images. In: ICRA, Anchorage, USA (2010)
11. Poppe, R.: Vision-based human motion analysis: An overview. CVIU 108 (2007)
12. Shotton, J., Fitzgibbon, A., Cook, M., Sharp, T., Finocchio, M., Moore, R., Kipman, A., Blake, A.: Real-time human pose recognition in parts from single depth images. In: Proc. CVPR Computer Vision and Image Understanding (2011)
13. Stoll, C., Hasler, N., Gall, J., Seidel, H.P., Theobalt, C.: Fast articulated motion tracking using a sums of gaussians body model. In: ICCV (2011)
14. Taylor, J., Shotton, J., Sharp, T., Fitzgibbon, A.: The vitruvian manifold: Inferring dense correspondences for one-shot human pose estimation. In: CVPR (2012)
15. Zhu, Y., Curless, B., Seitz, S.M.: Kinematic self retargeting: A framework for human pose estimation. CVIU 114(12), 1362–1375 (2010)

Robust Realtime Motion-Split-And-Merge for Motion Segmentation

Ralf Dragon[1], Jörn Ostermann[2], and Luc Van Gool[1]

[1] Computer Vision Lab. (CVL), ETH Zurich
{dragon,vangool}@vision.ee.ethz.ch
[2] Institut für Informationsverarbeitung (TNT), LUH Hannover
ostermann@tnt.uni-hannover.de

Abstract. In this paper, we analyze and modify the Motion-Split-and-Merge (MSAM) algorithm [3] for the motion segmentation of correspondences between two frames. Our goal is to make the algorithm suitable for practical use which means realtime processing speed at very low error rates. We compare our (robust realtime) RMSAM with J-Linkage [16] and Graph-Based Segmentation [5] and show that it is superior to both. Applying RMSAM in a multi-frame motion segmentation context to the Hopkins 155 benchmark, we show that compared to the original formulation, the error decreases from 2.05% to only 0.65% at a runtime reduced by 72%. The error is still higher than the best results reported so far, but RMSAM is dramatically faster and can handle outliers and missing data.

1 Introduction

In the past years, the motion segmentation of tracked features has been receiving increasing attention since it can be used as a strong prior in dense object segmentation [9], for the unsupervised learning of object detectors [11], or for tracking [14]. In order to track objects under occlusions, [3] proposed to apply motion segmentation on the basis of correspondences between independently detected SIFT keypoints instead of tracked features. In order to handle outliers and missing data, they carry out motion segmentation on the basis of multiple frame-to-frame motion segmentations, called multi-scale motion clustering (MSMC).

Fig. 1. Sequence *panning* from the Airport Dataset, segmented with our RMSAM & MSMC. The segmentation allows learning object keypoints from object motion.

J. Weickert, M. Hein, and B. Schiele (Eds.): GCPR 2013, LNCS 8142, pp. 425–434, 2013.

For the frame-to-frame core, they propose an adapted version of the classical split-and-merge for images, called motion-split-and-merge (MSAM). On one side MSMC allows the segmentation of trajectories with large amounts of unknown or erroneous data. On the other side, the MSAM core contains many parameters and is not stable and fast enough for real time applications.

In this paper, we thoroughly analyze the components of the MSAM algorithm and derive a robust realtime variant, coined RMSAM. Our contributions are the formulation of RMSAM, a detailed analysis of its parameters, and an extensive evaluation on the Hopkins 155 [18] benchmark and our new Airport Dataset[1]. This paper is organized as follows: In Sec. 2, we give an overview of related work. In Sec. 3, the original approach MSAM is explained, analyzed and modified towards realtime RMSAM. In Sec. 4, we provide experimental evaluations, and in Sec. 5, a summary and a short conclusion is given.

2   Related Work

2.1   Multi-frame Motion Segmentation

Existing approaches to multi-frame motion segmentation can be classified into *subspace-based* and *affinity-based*. In the first class, a measurement matrix $\mathbf{W}$ is constructed consisting of all points of all trajectories. Trajectories from different motions lie in different subspaces of $\mathbf{W}$, so the motion segmentation can be found by subspace assignment. This is algebraically elegant and allows very good results, as in agglomerative lossy clustering (ALC) [12] or sparse subspace clustering (SSC) [4]. However, these approaches require that tracked points only go missing (e.g. due to occlusions) in a certain way and up to a limited degree. For instance, ALC and SSC need at least one trajectory with complete data.

Affinity-based approaches do not come with such constraints since only the pairwise relationship between trajectories (affinity) is analyzed. Cheriyadat and Radke [2] decompose the trajectory features speed and direction using non-negative matrix factorization (NNMF). The resulting weights are used for an affinity measure. Fradet et al. [7] propose affine motion similarity as basis for affinities which are clustered by J-Linkage [16]. Brox and Malik [1] use spatial distance and similarity of translational motion to compute affinities which are then clustered with Spectral Clustering [8]. In order to render the motion similarity more precise, they propose to analyze triplets of trajectories [10] which allows them to add scale and rotation to the motion model. The MSMC approach [3] allows for arbitrary frame-to-frame motion models. First, correspondences between pairs of frames are motion-segmented at different time scales using MSAM. In a second step, ambiguities are resolved by observing common frame-to-frame motion during a longer time span.

---

[1] Available at http://www.vision.ee.ethz.ch/~dragonr/airport

2.2   Frame-to-Frame Motion Segmentation

In the MSMC-approach, the parametrization of motion plays an important role to resolve ambiguities. RANSAC [6] first tackles the parameter estimation of data from one underlying parametrization mixed with random data. Fischler and Bolles derived the number r of trials to find an inlier-only minimal sampling set (MSS) – the smallest set of inlier data points to estimate parameters:

$$r \geq \frac{\log(1-p)}{\log(1-w^L)},\tag{1}$$

where L is the cardinality of an MSS, w is the inlier ratio and p is the probability of finding an inlier-only MSS with r trials. In this paper we use $p = 0.95$. As it can be easily verified, L has a huge impact on r, especially if w is small.

Torr [17] extended RANSAC to the multi-model case by applying it sequentially on the remaining outliers. However, w is very small for the first motion since all other segments count as outliers. Additionally, sequential RANSAC is biased towards rendering small segments too small and big segments too big since it is too greedy [15]. A further problem pointed out by [19] is that sequential RANSAC detects *phantom motions* originating from the interaction of different moving objects. In the field of model selection, the problem is known as overfitting (too many degrees of freedom) vs. oversegmentation (too few degrees).

In order to tackle the multi-model problem, Schindler and Suter [13] proposed a sample-and-cluster paradigm. In the first step, N motion models are randomly sampled. In a model selection step, multiple models are selected such that a precise modeling is achieved at a low complexity. Similarly, in J-Linkage [16], an inlier matrix $\mathbf{I}$ is constructed. It specifies the inlier- and outlier relationship between all data points and N different motion parameters which are estimated from random local MSSs. The data is clustered bottom-up with agglomerative clustering. The affinity between segments is derived from common occurrences of inliers using the Jaccard distance.

A parameterless alternative is the graph-based image segmentation (GBS) [5]. Stalder et al. [14] adapted it to motion segmentation. In this approach, a graph between neighboring correspondences is established with difference in translational motion as weights. GBS finds segments such that intra-segment weights are low and inter-segment weights are high. In summary, in the MSMC context, the parametrization is essential to resolve ambiguities. We can use GBS as a strong parameterless baseline in frame-to-frame motion segmentation.

3   Robust Realtime Motion-Split-And-Merge (RMSAM)

Next, we derive the RMSAM algorithm. Its parameters are determined using ground-truth-labeled correspondences $\mathcal{Y}$ from our Airport Dataset. Given the ground truth object segments $\mathcal{V}_k$ as well as the best-matching permutation of the estimated segments $\mathcal{S}_k$, we compute the average object specific

$$\text{precision} = \frac{|\mathcal{S}_k \cap \mathcal{V}_k|}{|\mathcal{S}_k \cap \mathcal{V}_k| + |\mathcal{S}_k \cap (\mathcal{Y}\backslash\mathcal{V}_k)|}, \text{ recall} = \frac{|\mathcal{S}_k \cap \mathcal{V}_k|}{|\mathcal{S}_k \cap \mathcal{V}_k| + |(\mathcal{Y}\backslash\mathcal{S}_k) \cap \mathcal{V}_k|}\tag{2}$$

over all objects k and ground truth frames in a sequence. The results over all sequences are averaged. To show the variation over the sequences we additionally give 20% and 80% quantiles.

3.1   Enforcing Convergence

The original MSAM formulation consists of the following 4 steps which are carried out every iteration until all segments remain unchanged:

1. Split segments: Motion parameters p_k of each segment S_k are estimated using RANSAC, assuming an inlier ratio of $\tau(S_k \mid p_k) \geq \theta_s$ to determine the number of trials r according to (1). If this assumption holds, correspondences from S_k which are not inlier according to p_k are removed from S_k and added to the outlier segment S_O. Otherwise, the segment is split into two parts using an adapted version of J-Linkage, as further explained in Sec. 3.2.
2. Merge segments: Each pair of segments (S_k, S_l) is merged if the inlier ratio $\tau(S_l \mid p_k)$ of the smaller segment S_l according to parameters p_k is larger than a threshold θ_m.
3. Split outliers: Using the adapted J-Linkage, the outlier segment S_O is split into two like a regular segment in step 1. Resulting parts which are large enough are added as regular segments.
4. Merge outliers: Each correspondence from the outlier segment S_O is assigned to a segment S_k if it is inlier according to its parameters p_k.

Even if enforcing that merged segments cannot immediately be split again $(1 + \theta_m \geq 2\theta_s)$, it is easy to find an example in which a segment becomes cyclically split and merged. For instance, RANSAC might not find good parameters and the segment is accidentally split which is corrected by a merge in the following iteration, leading to the original state.

By discarding step 3 (Sec. 3.3) and imposing the following constraint, we enforce convergence: Once a valid parameter vector p_k with an inlier ratio $\tau(S_k \mid p_k) > \theta_s$ has been found in step 1, it is kept fixed for the segment. p_k is not recomputed if we merge a smaller segment (step 2) or outliers (step 4) to it. We call such a segment *consistent* since after the removal of outliers in step 1 of the following iteration, the inlier ratio is $\tau(S_k \mid p_k) = 1$. Besides enforced convergence, this measure allows speeding up step 2 by remembering a decision for further iterations. In RMSAM, we choose to split as early as possible, i.e. $\theta_s = 1/2 + \theta_m/2$. As Fig. 2a shows, the performance is not very dependent on the choice of θ_m. For highest precision, we use $\theta_m = 0.9$, thus $\theta_s = 0.95$.

Proof of Convergence: The approach finishes if no step is carried out. Equivalently, all segments S_k have an inlier ratio $\tau(S_k \mid p_k) = 1$, they cannot be merged and all correspondences from S_O cannot be merged into any segment. Since all steps necessarily lead to an increasing[2] $\tau(S_k \mid p_k)$, the algorithm has to converge.

---

[2] In the merge step 2 (including the successive outlier removal), the bigger segment has increasing τ and the smaller is dissolved. This ordering by size prevents cyclic growing and dissolving of a segment.

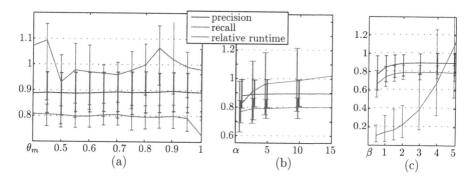

Fig. 2. (a) Analysis of the merging threshold θ_m, (b) the inlier sampling factor α and (c) the smallest detectable segment parameter β

3.2 Adaptive Fast Split into 2 Segments

In the original MSAM formulation, an adapted J-Linkage is proposed to split a segment S into two parts. It differs by the sampling strategy to construct the inlier matrix $\mathbf{I}$, and by the clustering method:

1. To raise the inlier ratio, a best-of-n strategy is applied which makes no assumption on the spatial distribution of the segments.
2. The segmentation is carried out with K-Means instead of agglomerative clustering since the number of clusters ($K = 2$) is known a-priori. The cluster vectors are the columns from an affinity matrix incorporating motion similarity through the Jaccard distance and spatial similarity through the Mahalanobis distance.

   In order to raise the probability of sampling an inlier-only MSS, we take into account the spatial distribution. However, in contrast to the J-Linkage approach, we choose the neighborhood size adaptive to the clustering problem. We propose adaptive localized sampling: The first point x_0 is drawn with uniform probability. All remaining points are drawn with

$$p(\boldsymbol{x}) \propto \exp\left(-\frac{M^2(\boldsymbol{x}, \boldsymbol{x}_0)}{2\sigma_s^2}\right), \tag{3}$$

where M is the Mahalanobis distance inside S, and σ_s, empirically set to 1, determines the neighborhood size. By this, enough inliers are found such that the best-of-n-sampling is not necessary. This leads to a significant runtime reduction to obtain the same amount of inliers, e.g., in the Airport Dataset by 84%.

   An open question is how many samples N should be used to construct $\mathbf{I}$. Too few samples lead to high uncertainty during the clustering, while too many lead to a long runtime. In MSAM, $N = 10$ was proposed while it is much higher in J-Linkage (usually 1000 or more). However, different split problems require a different amount of investigation. A heuristic that prevents using either too few or too many samples is to sample until more than $\alpha|S|$ inliers are found, where a reasonable choice is $\alpha = 10$ (Fig. 2b). With this, simple clustering problems are solved with a low N and complex ones with a high N to ensure a sufficiently detailed analysis of the data.

The sampling goal of finding $\alpha|\mathcal{S}|$ inliers might never be reached, e.g. when the segment completely consists of outliers. In order to limit the number of samples to an upper bound $N_{\max}$, we follow the idea of having a smallest detectable segment $\mathcal{S}_m$ in $\mathcal{S}$. Let $\beta = (|\mathcal{S}| - |\mathcal{S}_m|)/|\mathcal{S}_m|$ be its ratio of outliers to inliers. If $\mathcal{S}$ contains exactly one segment $\mathcal{S}'$ with $|\mathcal{S}'| \geq |\mathcal{S}_m|$, an inlier-only MSS is found with a probability p according to (1) in $r = N_{\max}$ trials:

$$N_{\max} = \frac{\log(1-p)}{\log\left(1 - \left(\frac{1}{\beta+1}\right)^L\right)}. \tag{4}$$

As shown in Fig. 2c, $\beta = 2$ is a reasonable trade-off between runtime and precision. This means that segments which are smaller that one third of the number of outliers are unlikely to be detected. In order to detect such segments, the best choice is to reduce the number of outliers by measures like stricter matching thresholds.

3.3 Re-Distilling

Step 3 from MSAM is necessary to find small segments which were accidentally added to the outlier segment. Apart from wanting to avoid the convergence problem (Sec. 3.1), it does not seem reasonable to carry it out during every iteration since $\mathcal{S}_O$ may remain unchanged. Especially if $\mathcal{S}_O$ is large or if many iterations are carried out, this has a huge impact on the runtime.

RMSAM handles this differently: Initially, all correspondences are put into one segment, which is iteratively processed with steps 1, 2 and 4. Upon convergence, the outlier segment $\mathcal{S}_O$ is treated as initial segment and iteratively processed with steps 1, 2 and 4 again – it is "distilled" a second time. All other consistent segments $\mathcal{S}_k$ stay the same during the re-distilling since all correspondences from $\mathcal{S}_O$ are not inliers to the parameters $\boldsymbol{p}_k$ and thus will never be merged into $\mathcal{S}_k$ in steps 2 or 4. Since the outlier segment may contain only true outliers, the re-distilling is only carried out a certain number of times ν_r. We choose $\nu_r = 3$ as this is the largest value that still yields a significant increase in precision (Fig. 3a).

4   Experiments

4.1   Model for Frame-to-Frame Motion

In this section, we compare the performance of the translational, affine, homographical and epipolar motion models[3]. If the model is too general, segments are

---

[3] Since epipolar motion only allows analyzing the model error in the direction orthogonal to the epipolar line, its inlier threshold ϵ is not comparable to the thresholds of the translational, affine and homographical motions. We empirically found the best results for an ϵ-threshold which is half that of the others.

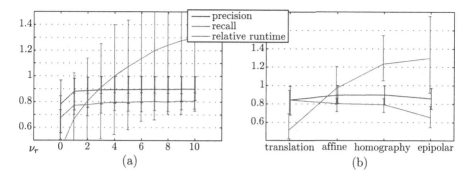

Fig. 3. (a) Analysis of the number ν_r of redistillation steps. (b) Comparison of translational, affine, perspective and epipolar motion models.

accidentally combined and precision and recall decrease (2). On the other hand if a motion model is too specific, the precision decreases and the recall increases due to oversegmentation.

The results are displayed in Fig. 3b. The ratios of runtimes are $0.53 : 1 : 1.27 : 1.3$, so the simple translational model is more than a factor of 2.5 faster than the epipolar model. Lower runtimes are not only related to lower computational complexities but also to smaller minimal sampling sets (MSS). The latter raises the probability of sampling an MSS from one underlying motion, thus allowing for a lower N during an adaptive split. The precision is the highest for the affine and homographical motion model with only very small differences between them. We use the first since it is significantly faster. The epipolar model performs worst in recall and runtime, so it can be discarded.

To conclude, the affine motion model is best suited for our motion segmentation. For fast segmentation, a translational motion model may be used at the cost of lower precision. We have to keep in mind that the choice of motion model is dependent on the observed scene and its motion, here the Airport Dataset. However, as we will show in Sec. 4.3, the affine motion model is also applicable in the Hopkins benchmark, so we are not overfitting to the training data.

4.2 RMSAM vs. GBS vs. JL

We now compare our RMSAM algorithm with J-Linkage (JL) and the graph-based segmentation (GBS) from [14]. For fair comparison, we treat segments with less than 8 correspondences as outlier segments. In GBS, the parameter k which describes the homogeneity of segments is empirically optimized as $k = 50$. JL is run with parameters which combine good performance and reasonable runtime: $N = 1000$ samples with a neighborhood of $\sigma = 1000$ pixel. The outlier threshold of RMSAM and JL is set to $\epsilon = 3$ pixel.

The results in terms of object precision, recall and runtime are given in Fig. 4. In Fig. 5, a qualitative comparison is given which allows to assess the different characteristics. Our RMSAM achieves the best average object precision and

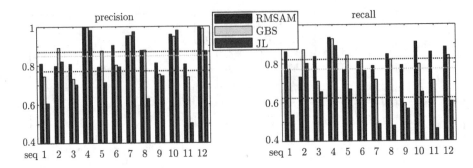

Fig. 4. Object precision and recall over the different sequences (bars) and their averages (dotted lines), using RMSAM, GBS and JL. The average runtimes per frame are 0.21 s, 0.20 s, and 4.90 s, respectively.

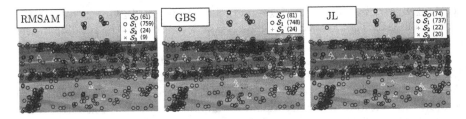

Fig. 5. Qualitative comparison of the segmentation of RMSAM, GBS and JL in the sequence 4 of the Airport Dataset. The numbers in parenthesis denote the number of correspondences inside a segment. JL tends towards oversegmentation, RMSAM towards combining outliers to ghost segments and GBS towards integrating outliers into regular clusters or vice-versa since it does not enforce a consistent parametrization along one segment.

recall at low processing times. Compared with JL, it performs better in almost all sequences at lower runtime. In sequences with slow motions, GBS, which does not use an outlier threshold, performs better than RMSAM. However, its results are much worse for sequences with large or non-translational motions since GBS' translational motion assumption is violated.

4.3   Hopkins 155 Benchmark

In order to evaluate the performance of RMSAM in a multi-frame motion segmentation context, we use it in combination with MSMC in the Hopkins 155 benchmark [18] consisting of the 3 categories Checkerboard, Traffic and Articulated. Since the Checkerboard sequences are mainly designed to verify analytic properties of subspace-based approaches and are not intuitive to cluster for humans, we skip these sequences, as [2,3,7] also do.

Table 1. Segmentation error rates and the recall in the Hopkins benchmark without missing data. The average CPU runtimes per sequence are collected from different papers with comparable systems (our system: 3.0 GHz quadcore standard desktop PC).

Approach	ALC [12]	SSC [4]	NNMF [2]	MSAM [3]	VLS [7]	**RMSAM**
Missing Data	constrained	constrained	yes	yes	yes	yes
Articulated, 2 motions, 11 sequences						
Error	10.70 %	0.62 %	10.00 %	6.03 %	5.38 %	2.38 %
Articulated, 3 motions, 2 sequences						
Error	21.08 %	1.42 %	15.00 %	8.27 %	20.41 %	1.91 %
Traffic, 2 motions, 31 sequences						
Error	1.75 %	0.02 %	0.10 %	0.66 %	1.92 %	0.06 %
Traffic, 3 motions, 7 sequences						
Error	8.86 %	0.58 %	0.10 %	0.17 %	4.89 %	0.16 %
All 51 sequences						
Runtime	261.3s	111.8s	3.0s	13.8s	5.7s	3.9s
Recall	1	1	1	0.977	1	0.978
Error	**5.41 %**	**0.28 %**	**2.82 %**	**2.05 %**	**3.80 %**	**0.65 %**

We compare our RMSAM & MSMC with results reported for subspace-based approaches (ALC [12] and SSC [4]) and for affinity-based approaches (NNMF [2], MSAM & MSMC [3], and VLS [7]). As MSMC may classify trajectories as outliers, we also report the recall according to [3, Eq. (15)]. To suppress randomness in RMSAM and K-Means, we average over 10 repetitions.

The results in terms of average error rate and recall are displayed in Table 1. Among all unconstrained approaches, we receive by far the best error rate at a recall very close to 1 and at a reasonable runtime. Compared to the very best result of SSC, we loose some accuracy, but 1) the speed goes up dramatically, and 2) the applicability is raised further by the fact that far fewer restrictions apply (like being able to handle any kind of missing data). It is also important to note that all other methods are optimized for the Hopkins benchmark, while we trained on the Airport Dataset, yet tested on the Hopkins benchmark. As has been shown in other comparisons like object class recognition, benchmarks tend to be biased and, as a result, training and then testing on different benchmarks may lead to rather serious losses in performance.

5   Summary and Conclusion

In this paper, we presented the robust realtime Motion-Split-and-Merge approach (RMSAM) for motion segmentation based on correspondences between two frames. We enforced convergence and introduced the adaptive fast split and re-distilling. Our experimental evaluation showed that RMSAM is superior to J-Linkage and has slightly better results than Graph-based Segmentation. However, because we parametrize motion, our approach can resolve ambiguities on a multi-frame level. Analyzing the performance of RMSAM on the Hopkins 155 benchmark, we showed that compared to the original formulation, the runtime is reduced by 72%, and the error from 2.05% to only 0.65%. The error is still higher than the best results reported so far, but RMSAM is dramatically faster, and it can handle outliers and unconstrained missing data.

Acknowledgment. This work was partially funded by ERC project VarCity, SNF project AerialCrowd and BMBF project ASEV.

References

1. Brox, T., Malik, J.: Object segmentation by long term analysis of point trajectories. In: Daniilidis, K., Maragos, P., Paragios, N. (eds.) ECCV 2010, Part V. LNCS, vol. 6315, pp. 282–295. Springer, Heidelberg (2010)
2. Cheriyadat, A.M., Radke, R.J.: Non-negative matrix factorization of partial track data for motion segmentation. In: ICCV, pp. 865–872 (October 2009)
3. Dragon, R., Rosenhahn, B., Ostermann, J.: Multi-scale clustering of frame-to-frame correspondences for motion segmentation. In: Fitzgibbon, A., Lazebnik, S., Perona, P., Sato, Y., Schmid, C. (eds.) ECCV 2012, Part II. LNCS, vol. 7573, pp. 445–458. Springer, Heidelberg (2012)
4. Elhamifar, E., Vidal, R.: Sparse subspace clustering. In: CVPR, pp. 2790–2797 (2009)
5. Felzenszwalb, P.F., Huttenlocher, D.P.: Efficient graph-based image segmentation. Intl. Journal of Computer Vision 59(2) (September 2004)
6. Fischler, M.A., Bolles, R.C.: Random sample consensus. Commun. ACM 24, 381–395 (1981)
7. Fradet, M., Robert, P., Perez, P.: Clustering point trajectories with various life-spans. In: CVMP, pp. 7–14 (2009)
8. Ng, A.Y., Jordan, M.I., Weiss, Y.: On spectral clustering: Analysis and an algorithm. In: NIPS, vol. 14, pp. 849–856 (2002)
9. Ochs, P., Brox, T.: Object segmentation in video: A hierarchical variational approach for turning point trajectories into dense regions. In: ICCV (2011)
10. Ochs, P., Brox, T.: Higher order models and spectral clustering. In: CVPR (2012)
11. Prest, A., Leistner, C., Civera, J., Schmid, C., Ferrari, V.: Learning object class detectors from weakly annotated video. In: CVPR (June 2012)
12. Rao, S., Tron, R., Vidal, R., Ma, Y.: Motion segmentation in the presence of outlying, incomplete, or corrupted trajectories. IEEE Trans. on Pattern Analysis and Machine Intelligence (TPAMI) 32, 1832–1845 (2010)
13. Schindler, K., Suter, D.: Two-view multibody structure-and-motion with outliers. In: CVPR (2005)
14. Stalder, S., Grabner, H., Van Gool, L.: Dynamic objectness for adaptive tracking. In: Lee, K.M., Matsushita, Y., Rehg, J.M., Hu, Z. (eds.) ACCV 2012, Part III. LNCS, vol. 7726, pp. 43–56. Springer, Heidelberg (2013)
15. Stewart, C.V.: Bias in robust estimation caused by discontinuities and multiple structures. IEEE Trans. on Pattern Analysis and Machine Intelligence (TPAMI) 19, 818–833 (1997)
16. Toldo, R., Fusiello, A.: Robust multiple structures estimation with J-linkage. In: Forsyth, D., Torr, P., Zisserman, A. (eds.) ECCV 2008, Part I. LNCS, vol. 5302, pp. 537–547. Springer, Heidelberg (2008)
17. Torr, P.H.S.: Geometric motion segmentation and model selection. Phil. Trans. Mathematical, Physical and Engineering Sciences 356(1740), 1321–1340 (1998)
18. Tron, R., Vidal, R.: A benchmark for the comparison of 3D motion segmentation algorithms. In: CVPR (2007)
19. Wills, J., Agarwal, S., Belongie, S.: A feature-based approach for dense segmentation and estimation of large disparity motion. Intl. Journal of Computer Vision 68(2), 125–143 (2006)

Efficient Multi-cue Scene Segmentation

Timo Scharwächter[1], Markus Enzweiler[1], Uwe Franke[1], and Stefan Roth[2]

[1] Environment Perception, Daimler R&D, Sindelfingen, Germany
firstname.lastname@daimler.com
[2] Department of Computer Science, TU Darmstadt, Darmstadt, Germany
sroth@cs.tu-darmstadt.de

Abstract. This paper presents a novel multi-cue framework for scene segmentation, involving a combination of appearance (grayscale images) and depth cues (dense stereo vision). An efficient 3D environment model is utilized to create a small set of meaningful free-form region hypotheses for object location and extent. Those regions are subsequently categorized into several object classes using an extended multi-cue bag-of-features pipeline. For that, we augment grayscale bag-of-features by *bag-of-depth-features* operating on dense disparity maps, as well as *height pooling* to incorporate a 3D geometric ordering into our region descriptor.

In experiments on a large real-world stereo vision data set, we obtain state-of-the-art segmentation results at significantly reduced computational costs. Our dataset is made public for benchmarking purposes.

1 Introduction

Image-based scene understanding is a key problem for many applications, such as intelligent vehicles or robotics. One foundational building block underlying such methods is the detection and classification of objects. Recent years have seen a steady progression from geometrically rigid (bounding box) classification methods, *e.g.* [5,6], through deformable part models, *e.g.* [9], towards the classification of free-form regions in the image, *e.g.* [4,11,16,22]. In this context, both dense features and orderless models (bag-of-features) have proven very effective [29], consisting of: local feature extraction within a free-form region, coding and spatial pooling of all features within the given region, and subsequent discriminative classification of the pooled feature vector.

Given the success of multi-cue methods for geometrically rigid object classification, *e.g.* [6], which combine grayscale imagery with other modalities, such as dense stereo or optical flow, little work has been done on transferring those ideas to bag-of-features methods. In this paper, we fill this gap and show various ways of exploiting dense stereo information in several processing stages of a bag-of-features pipeline in the context of scene segmentation: We create a set of free-form region hypotheses using the Stixel World [21] – a compact medium-level environment model computed from dense stereo data. Each region is encoded in terms of a spatially pooled multi-cue bag-of-features descriptor (grayscale and dense stereo), which additionally incorporates a stereo-based 3D variant of

J. Weickert, M. Hein, and B. Schiele (Eds.): GCPR 2013, LNCS 8142, pp. 435–445, 2013.

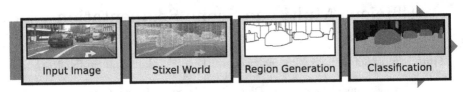

Fig. 1. System overview. Scene segmentation based on the classification of meaningful free-form regions acquired from the Stixel World [21].

the spatial-pyramid representation [17]. Finally, each region is classified using a multi-class discriminative model. The Stixel representation provides efficient access to the 3D scene geometry. This allows us to rapidly obtain meaningful image segments and dispense with costly spatial smoothing as a post-processing step, *e.g.* using conditional random fields [22]. See Fig. 1 for an overview.

2   Related Work

Semantic segmentation methods can roughly be separated into two classes: pixel-based approaches relying on local image cues, and region-based approaches that encode and pool local descriptors over larger image regions. Among a wealth of existing work, we focus on the most relevant aspects for our own: the use of multiple cues, as well as region-based classification and segmentation methods.

Sparse point clouds obtained from structure-from-motion (SfM) have been used for image segmentation both in isolation [3] and in combination with image-based cues, such as appearance and color [19,23]. The results indicate that the height of feature points relative to the camera is an informative cue. In [16], a joint formulation of semantic segmentation and dense stereo reconstruction within a pixel-wise conditional random field framework is proposed. Co-dependencies and interactions between segmentation and stereo reconstruction help boosting segmentation performance.

Region-based schemes have been applied in many approaches in order to obtain more discriminative features and to allow efficient inference. While fine-grained superpixels have been used as regions [11,19,28], recent work shows impressive performance using segmentation trees that contain larger region hypotheses [2,4]. In [10], stereo information is used to rectify image patches, resulting in viewpoint invariant patches (VIP) that are quantized together with SIFT [18]. Furthermore, features obtained from dense depth maps have also been quantized in the context of gesture recognition [14].

More recently, segmentation using RGB-D (color and depth) acquired from the Kinect sensor has become popular, *e.g.* [13,24]. Note that this depth data is only available in the near range up to $5m$ in indoor scenarios.

Our contributions are three-fold: (1) Following recent results that show how crucial meaningful initial regions are for segmentation performance, *e.g.* [2,4,26], we present an efficient method for obtaining relevant region hypotheses using dense stereo by means of the Stixel World [21].

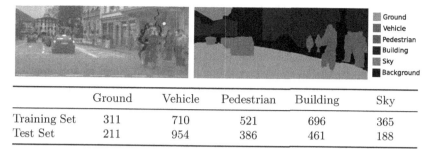

	Ground	Vehicle	Pedestrian	Building	Sky
Training Set	311	710	521	696	365
Test Set	211	954	386	461	188

Fig. 2. Excerpt of our dataset: Grayscale image with dense disparity overlaid (top left). Ground-truth annotation (top right). Number of annotated regions per class (bottom).

(2) We follow [3,10,19,23] and integrate depth and height cues into our region descriptor. In contrast to previous work, we directly exploit dense disparity images obtained from stereo vision in two ways: First, we introduce *bag-of-depth-features* - an extension of the popular SIFT-bag-of-features pipeline to dense stereo images. Second, we do not use height information directly as a cue, but propose *height pooling*, a 3D-variant of the spatial pyramid representation [17], where visual words are pooled into different height bins according to their height above ground to incorporate a geometric ordering into the descriptor.

(3) Given that most popular datasets for semantic segmentation do not provide stereo images (*e.g.*, PASCAL VOC [8], MSRC [22], or CamVid [3]), we present a challenging stereo vision dataset captured from a moving vehicle in complex urban traffic with manually labeled pixel-accurate ground-truth.

3   Benchmark Dataset

Our benchmark dataset[1] consists of 500 stereo image pairs and corresponding dense disparity images (obtained by semi-global matching stereo [15]) at a resolution of 1024×440 *px*. We provide pixel-accurate ground-truth segmentations for five object classes: Ground, Vehicle, Pedestrian, Building and Sky. The data is split into 300 training and 200 test images, where training and test data has been recorded at different locations to prevent overlap. See Fig. 2 for an overview.

To our knowledge, the only comparable urban segmentation dataset with stereo vision data has been proposed by [16], which our dataset exceeds in terms of size (500 *vs.* 70 annotated images) and image resolution (1024×440 *px vs.* 360×288 *px*), which is an essential factor for appearance-based segmentation.

4   Integrated Approach for Scene Segmentation

4.1   Region Generation

To generate hypotheses for object regions, we employ the multi-layered Stixel World [21], a medium-level representation of the local 3D environment, as an

---

[1] Available at http://www.6d-vision.com/aktuelle-forschung/scene-labeling/

initial segmentation result. The Stixel World defines a column-wise partition of the dense disparity map into ground surface and upright standing objects at different distances, see Fig. 1. As such, Stixels allow for an enormous reduction of the raw input data to a few hundred Stixels only. At the same time, Stixels give easy access to the most task-relevant information, such as free space and obstacles and thus bridge the gap between low-level (pixel-based) and high-level (object-based) vision.

To obtain larger regions R_i from the Stixel World we perform DBSCAN clustering [7], with the single parameter ϵ being the allowed depth difference between two Stixels. We define $\epsilon = \Delta z_{\max} + \sigma_z$ for Stixels that are spatially adjacent in the image and $\epsilon = \infty$ otherwise. The term σ_z is the noise of the stereo setup, which increases with distance and is used to avoid over-segmentation of objects far away. Fig. 1 and Fig. 6 show examples of our region hypotheses R_i.

4.2 Region Classification

Bag-of-Feature Classification. For each free-form region R_i, a set $\mathcal{D}_i$ of all SIFT descriptors d_j is collected, where the descriptor keypoint k_j lies within the region R_i, i.e. $\mathcal{D}_i = \{d_j \mid k_j \in R_i\}$. We then vector-encode each descriptor d_j to $e(d_j)$ and spatially pool all encoded descriptors $e(d_j)$ over R_i. As encoder, an extremely randomized clustering forest (ERC) is trained [20]. This method is adopted because several results indicate that random forests are superior over (hierarchical) k-Means for coding and segmentation [20,22]. We also observed this in preliminary experiments. The ERC forest is trained discriminatively using the SIFT descriptors and corresponding class labels of all annotated regions in the training set.

To build the final region descriptor, all SIFT descriptors $\mathcal{D}_i$ traverse each decision tree in the forest and a histogram over the occurring leaf node indices is accumulated per tree. The local histograms of all trees are then concatenated, so that for $\mathcal{T}$ trees and $\mathcal{L}$ leaf nodes per tree, the resulting bag-of-features histogram is of size $\mathcal{C}_{\text{ERC}} = \mathcal{T} \cdot \mathcal{L}$. This histogram is then passed to a multi-class histogram-intersection kernel SVM [27] classifier (one-vs-all model for each class).

In our experiments, we use the public VLFEAT library [25] to densely sample SIFT descriptors in combination with an ERC forest consisting of $\mathcal{T} = 5$ trees with $\mathcal{L} = 500$ leaves each. When operating on grayscale images only, this model represents one baseline (ERC$_\text{G}$) for our experimental evaluation, see Sec. 5.

Height Pooling. The spatial pyramid representation [17] is commonly used to overcome the prevalent loss of geometric ordering in a classical bag-of-features approach. Another solution (applied in [4]) is to use a rectangular bounding box around an object region and augment the SIFT descriptor with its location in relation to this bounding box. Our aim is to treat regions containing a single object instance similarly to regions containing several – possibly overlapping – objects of the same class (e.g., a single parked car vs. a row of parked cars). As such, the horizontal position of a descriptor relative to the region is subject to large variation, which makes the idea of [4] less suitable to our application setup.

Table 1. Overview of height bins

Bin	Height [m]
1	$-\infty$ – 0.0
2	0.0 – 0.5
3	0.5 – 1.0
4	1.0 – 1.5
5	1.5 – 2.0
6	2.0 – 4.0
7	4.0 – 10.0
8	10.0 – ∞

Fig. 3. Illustration of height pooling. Input images (top row), disparity image overlaid with the color coded height bins (bottom row) as given in Table 1. Each descriptor is pooled to one bin according to the height above ground of its keypoint.

However, we observe that the vertical position of descriptors (height above ground) is very consistent, under the assumption of ground-plane constraints and low (geometric) intra-class variance. This holds for our object classes of interest, *e.g.* pedestrians, vehicles and buildings have a typical geometric structure and well-defined orientation relative to the ground.

With depth information available at (almost) every descriptor keypoint, we perform *height pooling*, a pooling of descriptors into several discrete bins given by their height above ground. The histograms for all height bins are then concatenated to form the resulting region descriptor, effectively encoding the characteristic 3D height distribution of visual words within each object class. A key property is that the region descriptor remains invariant to scale changes and horizontal translation, which is convenient since objects, such as buildings, pedestrians and vehicles occur at various horizontal positions and distances, while their geometric structure remains very similar.

We assume a planar ground surface w.r.t. to the ego-vehicle coordinate system. To obtain the height value *independently* of the (known) position and orientation of the camera, each triangulated 3D point is transformed into the defined vehicle system. Note, that we do not estimate the ground plane explicitly.

In our experiments, we use a coarse binning into $\mathcal{H} = 8$ height regions, empirically set to obtain good coverage for the object classes at hand. More precisely, we pool encoded descriptors into the height bins given in Table 1. The new codevector after height pooling has $\mathcal{C}_{\mathrm{HP}} = \mathcal{H} \cdot \mathcal{C}_{\mathrm{ERC}}$ dimensions. Fig. 3 illustrates the idea of height pooling. Descriptors without valid disparity measurements are pooled into the last bin.

Bag-of-Depth-Features. The high density of the disparity maps allows us to extract complex features (such as SIFT) directly on the disparity image, similar to [6]. We apply the same bag-of-features pipeline as described above, simply replacing the grayscale image with the dense disparity image. The resulting bag-of-depth-features histogram then encodes the distribution of typical depth patterns present in a region. In our experiments, we compare the performance of each single modality individually (ERC$_{\mathrm{G}}$ – grayscale, ERC$_{\mathrm{D}}$ – depth) to a joint grayscale / disparity representation (ERC$_{GD}$), which is obtained by concatenating the individual bag-of-features-histograms before SVM classification.

5   Experimental Results

5.1   Classification Accuracy

In a first experiment on region classification, we assume ground-truth region segments to be given and show classification results by means of ROC curves.

We start by evaluating the impact of SIFT scales on the final region classification performance. Fig. 4 (left) shows results for the 'Vehicle' class when using only a single scale, where the cell size of SIFT is varied (the descriptor is built from 4×4 SIFT cells, as usual [18]). In Fig. 4 (right), the best performance with a fixed single scale (cell size 4 px) is compared against a multi-scale approach using the six best performing single scales (omitting cell sizes of 48 px and 64 px). Furthermore, we show the performance when using a single scale, where the cell size is adapted dynamically (using depth information) to cover a fixed width of 0.75 m in 3D space. We observe, that dynamic scale selection helps significantly when only a single scale is used. However, using features at multiple scales still yields better results. Therefore, despite the higher computational costs, we apply the multi-scale approach in our further experiments to retain best possible classification performance.

In a next experiment, we compare our proposed extensions (bag-of-depth-features and height pooling) against the baseline coding method ERC$_G$ and the state-of-the-art O$_2$P region descriptor from [4]. We adapted their publicly available code to our dataset and use their best performing single descriptor eMSIFT-F with log(2AvgP) pooling, omitting the dimensions for color. Results in Fig. 5 indicate that bag-of-depth-features (ERC$_D$) is outperformed by the grayscale method (ERC$_G$), while their joint combination (ERC$_{GD}$) is better on average. Furthermore, the application of height pooling (superscript HP) always results in a significant improvement. O$_2$P outperforms the ERC methods in this first experiment.

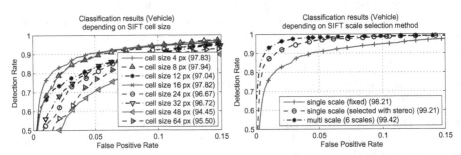

Fig. 4. Region classification performance of our base descriptor method ERC$_G$. Results when using a single SIFT scale with *fixed* cell size (left). Best result using a single fixed scale, a single scale selected with stereo and multi-scale using six scales (right). Additionally, the area under curve (AUC, in %) is given in the legend. Note, that (right) contains the boundary ROC over all single scales from (left), which explains the slightly increased AUC.

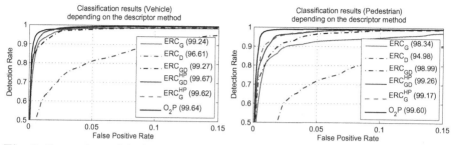

Fig. 5. Comparison of the baseline descriptor ERC$_\text{G}$ with our proposed extensions and the O$_2$P descriptor from [4], demonstrated using the 'Vehicle' and 'Pedestrian' classes. Again, we additionally show the area under curve (AUC, in %) in the legend.

In addition to ROC curves, we evaluate the classification accuracy using the PASCAL VOC intersection-over-union (IU) measure, which has become the standard method to assess segmentation performance [8], see Table 2. As in the previous experiment, ground-truth segments are used as region hypotheses, *i.e.* there is no actual online segmentation involved. In contrast to Fig. 5, the performance difference between all considered methods (in particular to ERC$_\text{D}$) is less pronounced. Unlike ROC, the IU measure explicitly takes the region size into account, given that it is a pixel-wise measure. As such, misclassifications of small objects have much less impact on absolute performance, which might affect ERC$_\text{D}$ to a much larger extent due to stereo reconstruction errors on far away objects (*cf.* Fig. 5 and Table 2). Note that we consistently outperform O$_2$P in all experiments that consider the IU measure.

5.2 Online Segmentation

In the following, we perform fully automated online segmentation. For our stereo-based region generation, we use $\Delta z_\text{max} = 2\ m$, resulting in an average of 44 regions per image. As grayscale-based reference for region generation, we further evaluate the performance using SLIC superpixels, parametrized to obtain approximately 150 regions per image. SLIC has recently been compared to various state-of-the-art superpixel methods and shows best boundary adherence with the least computational costs [1]. Table 3 shows the results for all combinations of region generation and descriptors.

We observe that our proposed stereo-based regions generally outperform SLIC region generation. The only exception from this trend is the 'Sky' class. This is an

Table 2. Classification performance on given ground-truth segments, evaluated using the PASCAL VOC (IU) measure. The average over all five classes is shown.

Regions				GT		
Descriptor	O$_2$P [4]	ERC$_\text{G}$	ERC$_\text{D}$	ERC$_\text{GD}$	ERC$_\text{G}^\text{HP}$	ERC$_\text{GD}^\text{HP}$
Average	93.7	92.6	90.7	**94.7**	93.3	93.9

artifact of stereo vision, since the disparity map is over-smoothed due to missing texture, resulting in erroneous regions. Hence, Table 3 (last line) additionally reports average performance for the most relevant object classes, *i.e.* vehicle, pedestrian, and building, where the difference between the proposed stereo and SLIC regions is more significant due to better stereo reconstruction.

Regarding bag-of-depth-features and height pooling, the multi-cue grayscale and depth descriptor (ERC_{GD}) outperforms the individual variants (ERC_G and ERC_D). Further, height pooling results in a significant performance gain (ERC_G^{HP} *vs.* ERC_G and ERC_{GD}^{HP} *vs.* ERC_{GD}). However, these observed improvements do not add-up. Integrating both multiple cues and height pooling in a single descriptor (ERC_{GD}^{HP}) does not improve over using height pooling (ERC_G^{HP}) alone.

Another insight is that ERC_G notably outperforms O_2P on SLIC segments even though O_2P was superior in our ROC evaluation on full ground-truth segments. This result might be explained by the often reported robustness of coding-based descriptors against large amounts of clutter and occlusion [12,20]. Note, that O_2P does not involve any descriptor coding at all [4]. We furthermore highlight that we treat O_2P as an appearance-only baseline and hence did not evaluate it on our stereo-based regions.

Finally, the results clearly support the statement that good initial image regions are crucial for the overall performance of the pipeline. Consequently, an integrated method for initial region generation using stereo (for close objects) and appearance (for far away objects) should further improve segmentation accuracy. Qualitative results of our approach are shown in Fig. 6.

5.3   Computational Efficiency

Using the best performing method from Table 3 (stereo regions and ERC_G^{HP} descriptor), we obtain average computation times of around 425 *ms* per image

Table 3. Results of the different descriptors during online segmentation, evaluated on SLIC segments and our stereo-based regions. ERC_G and O_2P evaluated on SLIC segments constitute two pure grayscale baseline methods. The best region-descriptor combination for each class is highlighted.

Regions	SLIC [1] / Stereo					
Descriptor	O_2P [4]	ERC_G	ERC_D	ERC_{GD}	ERC_G^{HP}	ERC_{GD}^{HP}
Ground	42.9/–	76.1/**82.4**	77.3/**82.8**	82.0/**82.8**	82.1/**82.8**	81.8/**82.8**
Vehicle	21.6/–	37.9/**64.8**	29.2/50.8	36.5/61.8	48.4/63.9	50.4/62.2
Pedestrian	25.3/–	29.7/41.9	23.3/42.9	33.6/51.9	39.9/53.6	42.8/**53.9**
Sky	52.9/–	51.1/30.9	17.7/ 6.8	21.5/30.4	**53.7**/29.0	32.8/28.3
Building	35.6/–	47.8/51.0	47.2/52.1	47.2/53.0	53.4/**53.8**	52.8/53.4
Average (all)	35.7/–	48.5/54.2	38.9/47.1	44.2/56.0	55.5/**56.6**	52.1/56.1
Average (objects)	27.5/–	38.5/52.6	33.2/48.6	39.1/55.6	47.2/**57.1**	48.7/56.5

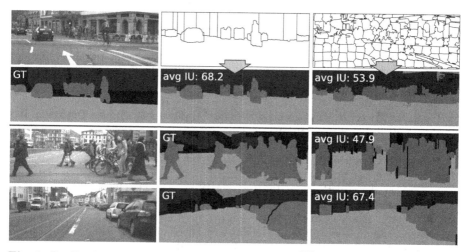

Fig. 6. Qualitative segmentation results using the ERC$_G^{HP}$ descriptor. The upper part shows a comparison between our stereo segments (top center) and SLIC segments (top right). In the lower part, two further results with stereo segments are shown. The average IU result over our three main classes vehicle, pedestrian and building is given.

on an Intel i7-3.33 GHz CPU with 6 cores. The largest part (65 %) is spent on the dense multi-scale extraction of SIFT descriptors, which could be reduced using our proposed stereo selected single-scale method. Encoding and pooling the roughly 100,000 SIFT descriptors per image with the ERC forest requires approximately 77 ms. Classifying all regions using the HIK-SVM adds another 40 ms. Given that dense stereo and Stixels are available in real-time [21], their computational costs can be neglected compared to the extraction and classification of all region descriptors. The proposed Stixel-based region generation only takes around 2 ms.

6   Conclusion

This paper proposed a multi-cue (grayscale and depth) bag-of-features pipeline for segmentation of highly cluttered urban traffic scenes, and introduced a novel height-based pooling approach. The pipeline's benefits include better segmentation performance and less computational cost. In the future, we plan to investigate more elaborate inference methods that include prior scene knowledge and spatio-temporal smoothing. With this paper and the provided stereo benchmark dataset, we hope to stimulate further research on this important problem.

References

1. Achanta, R., et al.: SLIC superpixels compared to state-of-the-art superpixel methods. IEEE Trans. PAMI 34(11), 2274–2282 (2012)
2. Arbeláez, P., Hariharan, B., Gu, C.: Semantic Segmentation using Regions and Parts. In: Proc. CVPR, pp. 3378–3385 (2012)

3. Brostow, G.J., Shotton, J., Fauqueur, J., Cipolla, R.: Segmentation and recognition using structure from motion point clouds. In: Forsyth, D., Torr, P., Zisserman, A. (eds.) ECCV 2008, Part I. LNCS, vol. 5302, pp. 44–57. Springer, Heidelberg (2008)

4. Carreira, J., Caseiro, R., Batista, J., Sminchisescu, C.: Semantic Segmentation with Second-Order Pooling. In: Fitzgibbon, A., Lazebnik, S., Perona, P., Sato, Y., Schmid, C. (eds.) ECCV 2012, Part VII. LNCS, vol. 7578, pp. 430–443. Springer, Heidelberg (2012)

5. Dalal, N., Triggs, B.: Histograms of Oriented Gradients for Human Detection. In: Proc. CVPR, vol. 1, pp. 886–893 (2005)

6. Enzweiler, M., Gavrila, D.: A Multi-Level Mixture-of-Experts Framework for Pedestrian Classification. IEEE Trans. IP 20(10), 2967–2979 (2011)

7. Ester, M., et al.: A Density-Based Algorithm for Discovering Clusters in Large Spatial Databases with Noise. In: Proc. KDD, pp. 226–231 (1996)

8. Everingham, M., et al.: The Pascal Visual Object Classes (VOC) Challenge. IJCV 88(2), 303–338 (2010)

9. Felzenszwalb, P., et al.: Object Detection with Discriminatively Trained Part Based Models. IEEE Trans. PAMI 32(9), 1627–1645 (2010)

10. Fraundorfer, F., et al.: Combining Monocular and Stereo Cues for Mobile Robot Localization Using Visual Words. In: Proc. ICPR, pp. 3927–3930 (2010)

11. Fulkerson, B., Vedaldi, A.: Class Segmentation and Object Localization with Superpixel Neighborhoods. In: Proc. ICCV, pp. 670–677 (2009)

12. Grauman, K., Darrell, T.: The Pyramid Match Kernel: Discriminative Classification with Sets of Image Features. In: Proc. ICCV, vol. 2, pp. 1458–1465 (2005)

13. Gupta, S., Arbeláez, P., Malik, J.: Perceptual Organization and Recognition of Indoor Scenes from RGB-D Images. In: Proc. CVPR (2013)

14. Hernández-Vela, A., et al.: BoVDW: Bag-of-Visual-and-Depth-Words for gesture recognition. In: Proc. ICPR, pp. 3–6 (2012)

15. Hirschmuller, H.: Stereo Processing by Semi-global Matching and Mutual Information. IEEE Trans. PAMI 30(2), 328–341 (2008)

16. Ladický, L., et al.: Joint Optimization for Object Class Segmentation and Dense Stereo Reconstruction. In: Proc. BMVC, pp. 1–11 (2010)

17. Lazebnik, S., et al.: Beyond Bags of Features: Spatial Pyramid Matching for Recognizing Natural Scene Categories. In: Proc. CVPR, pp. 2169–2178 (2006)

18. Lowe, D.: Distinctive Image Features from Scale-Invariant Keypoints. IJCV 60, 91–110 (2004)

19. Micusik, B.: Semantic Segmentation of Street Scenes by Superpixel Co-occurrence and 3D Geometry. In: Computer Vision Workshops (ICCV), pp. 625–632 (2009)

20. Moosmann, F., Triggs, B., Jurie, F.: Fast Discriminative Visual Codebooks using Randomized Clustering Forests. In: NIPS (2007)

21. Pfeiffer, D., Franke, U.: Towards a Global Optimal Multi-layer Stixel Representation of Dense 3D Data. In: BMVC, pp. 51.1–51.12 (2011)

22. Shotton, J., et al.: TextonBoost for Image Understanding: Multi-Class Object Recognition and Segmentation by Jointly Modeling Texture, Layout, and Context. IJCV 81(1), 2–23 (2009)

23. Sturgess, P., et al.: Combining Appearance and Structure from Motion Features for Road Scene Understanding. In: Proc. BMVC, pp. 62.1–62.11 (2009)

24. Tang, J., Miller, S.: A Textured Object Recognition Pipeline for Color and Depth Image Data. In: Proc. ICRA (2012)

25. Vedaldi, A., Fulkerson, B.: VLFeat: An Open and Portable Library of Computer Vision Algorithms (2008), http://www.vlfeat.org/

26. Vieux, R., et al.: Segmentation-based Multi-Class Semantic Object Detection. Multimedia Tools and Applications 60, 305–326 (2012)
27. Wu, J.: A Fast Dual Method for HIK SVM Learning. In: Daniilidis, K., Maragos, P., Paragios, N. (eds.) ECCV 2010, Part II. LNCS, vol. 6312, pp. 552–565. Springer, Heidelberg (2010)
28. Zhang, C., Wang, L., Yang, R.: Semantic Segmentation of Urban Scenes Using Dense Depth Maps. In: Daniilidis, K., Maragos, P., Paragios, N. (eds.) ECCV 2010, Part IV. LNCS, vol. 6314, pp. 708–721. Springer, Heidelberg (2010)
29. Zhang, J., et al.: Local Features and Kernels for Classification of Texture and Object Categories: A Comprehensive Study. IJCV 73(2), 213–238 (2006)

Author Index